THE KOVELS'
COMPLETE BOTTLE
PRICE LIST

BOOKS BY RALPH AND TERRY KOVEL

The Kovels' Complete Antiques Price List

Know Your Antiques

American Country Furniture 1780–1875

Dictionary of Marks—Pottery and Porcelain

The Kovels' Complete Bottle Price List

The Kovels' Collector's Guide to Limited Editions

The Kovels' Collector's Guide to American Art Pottery

A Directory of American Silver, Pewter, and Silver Plate

THE KOVELS' COMPLETE BOTTLE PRICE LIST

Fourth Edition

by Ralph M. and Terry H. Kovel

Illustrated

Crown Publishers, Inc., New York

Inquiries should be addressed to Crown Publishers, Inc.,
One Park Avenue, New York, N.Y. 10016.
Printed in the United States of America
Published simultaneously in Canada by General Publishing Company
Limited

Library of Congress Cataloging in Publication Data

Kovel, Ralph M
　　　The Kovels' complete bottle price list.

　　　First-2d ed. published under title: The official
bottle price list; 3d ed. published in 1975 under title:
The Kovels' official bottle price list.
　　　1. Bottles—United States—Catalogs.　I. Kovel,
Terry H., joint author.　II. Title.　III. Title:
Complete bottle price list.
NK5440.B6K6 1977　　　666'.19　　　77-4267
ISBN 0-517-53013-9

To President Jimmy Carter,
whose interest in our history
and heritage has made him
America's #1 bottle digger
and collector

AN IMPORTANT ANNOUNCEMENT TO COLLECTORS AND DEALERS

Every second year, *The Kovels' Complete Bottle Price List* is completely rewritten. Every entry and every picture is new because of the rapidly changing antiques market. The only way so complete a revision can be accomplished is by using a computer, making it possible to publish the bound book two months after the last price is received.

Yet many price changes occur between editions of *The Kovels' Complete Bottle Price List.* Important sales produce new record prices each day. Inflation, the changing price of silver and gold, and the international demand for some types of antiques influence sales in the United States.

The serious collector will want to keep up with developments from month to month rather than from year to year. Therefore, we call your attention to a new service to provide price information almost instantaneously: "Kovels on Antiques," a nationally distributed illustrated newsletter, published monthly.

This monthly newsletter reports the best places and ways to buy or sell, the current prices, collecting trends, landmark auction results, and tax, estate, security, and other pertinent news for collectors.

A complimentary copy and additional information about the newsletter are available from the authors at P.O. Box 22200, Beachwood, Ohio 44122

HOW TO USE THIS BOOK

Bottle collecting in America is a hobby that has gained stature, recognition, and high prices during 1975–1976. A record price of $26,000 was paid for a single bottle at a landmark auction that changed the pricing structure for the rare bottles and influenced the entire bottle-collecting field.

For five days in September and November, the Charles B. Gardner Collection of bottles was auctioned at the Robert Skinner Gallery in Massachusetts. Forty-six years of collecting had accumulated 3200 bottles. Rarities, unique examples, and bottles of rare colors or condition were in this exceptional collection. We attended the auction, met many of the most important bottles collectors in the country, and enjoyed the excitement of record-breaking prices.

Now, over a year later, it can be seen that the prices offered were not a one-time phenomenon. Many of the bottles have been resold at higher prices. Several other auctions have been held with individual bottles selling for over $10,000. This book includes most of the Gardner auction bottles. Each is indicated with an asterisk before the price. Some bottles are shown with the auction price and a second listing showing the price when the bottle was resold. The illustrated, priced catalog for the sale is still available from Robert Skinner, Route 117, Bolton, Massachusetts 01740 ($20.00).

Bottle clubs and bottle shows have set the rules for this *Complete Bottle Price List*. We have taken the terms from those in common usage and tried to organize the thousands of listings in easy-to-use form. Many abbreviations have been included that are part of the bottle collector's language. The Tibbits' abbreviations appear throughout the book.

ABM means automatic bottle machine.

BIMAL means blown in mold, applied lip.

BIMALOP means blown in mold, applied lip, open pontil.

FB means free blown.

SC means sun-colored.

SCA means sun-colored amethyst.

OP means open pontil.

To make the descriptions of the bottles as complete as possible, in some categories, an identification number has been added to the description. The serious collector knows the important books about his specialty and these books have numbered lists of styles of bottles. Included in this book are identification numbers for milk glass from Belknap, flasks from Van Rensselaer and McKearin, candy containers from Eikelberner, figurals from Umberger, bitters from Watson, and ink bottles from Covill. The full titles of the books used are included in the bibliography and listed in the introductory paragraph for each category.

Medicine bottles include all medicine or drugstore bottles, except those under the more specific headings of bitters or sarsaparilla. Modern liquor bottles are listed under the brand name if more than five of the bottles are in the collectible series. If you are not a regular at bottle shows, it may take a few tries to become accustomed to the method of listing. If you cannot find a bottle, try several related headings. For instance, hair dye is found under "household" bottles; many named bottles are found under "medicine," "food," "fruit jar," etc. If your fruit jar has several names, such as "Ball, Mason," look under "fruit jar, Ball," or "fruit jar, Mason."

Except for the specially marked Gardner auction pieces, the prices shown for old bottles are the actual prices asked for bottles during the past year. A few bottles have been included to complete a listing. When this has been done, the prices are estimates based on known prices of the past two years. The estimated prices appear only for modern bottles in a series. Pre-World War I bottles are all listed at actual sale price.

Prices may vary in different parts of the country, so a range is given. Because of the idiosyncrasies of the computer, it was impossible to place a range of prices on bottles that are illustrated. The price listed is an average.

Spelling is meant to help the collector. If the original bottle spelled the word "catsup" as "ketchup," that is the spelling that appears. If the period was omitted from "Dr." or the apostrophe from "Jones' sarsaparilla," that is the way it appears. A few bottles are included that had errors in the original spelling; these are listed under "error." "Whiskey" is used even if the bottle held Scotch or Canadian and should be spelled "whisky." Whiskey includes Kummel, Bourbon, Scotch, and some liqueurs.

Every bottle illustrated in black and white is indicated by the word "illus." in the text. Every bottle pictured in color is indicated by the word "color" in the listing.

There are a number of the color illustrated bottles shown without prices. These bottles have a price listing of XX.XX

We welcome any information about clubs, prices, or content for future books, but cannot give appraisals by mail. We have tried to be accurate, but we cannot be responsible for any errors in pricing.

Ralph and Terry Kovel, Senior Members
(American Society of Appraisers)

PICTURE ACKNOWLEDGMENTS

The color pictures of the old bottles used in this edition of *The Kovels' Complete Bottle Price List* were taken by a group of serious bottle collectors, members of the Federation of Historical Bottle Clubs. They include all types of bottles, rare and not so rare. They were chosen to interest the collector. Prices are not included if the bottle pictured had not been sold in 1976. To Jane Blancharski, Rev. Frank Dearing, Jim Evans, Larry and Kathy Fischer, Jerry Hostetler, Bill King, T. M. Schwartz, and Russell and Kitty Umbraco, the photographers and collectors of these bottles— thank you.

The Federation of Historical Bottle Clubs has also been of help. We suggest that any serious collector join the Federation or the local Federation bottle club to learn more about bottle collecting. The names are included in the club list.

To the following companies and collectors, our thanks for their help in obtaining pictures: Annette's Antiques; Vern and Sharon Atkins; James Beam Distilling Company; Joyce and Len Blake; Eugene and Betty Blasi; Bob and Peg's Bottles; Ezra Brooks Distilling Company; Fred and Sue Brown; Roy and Barbara Brown; Don Burkett; Jeff Burkhardt; Tom and Denna Caniff; Jim Coffman; Carl Conklin; Jack Daniel Distillery; J. W. Dant; Pete and Connie Dillman; Double Springs Distillers, Inc.; Roger Durflinger; Harry Frey; Charles and Jean Gaff; Bob and Sue Gilbert; Jim Hall; Randy and Jan Haviland; Leigh Heller; Holly City Bottle (Ed Johnson); Ann Johnson, George Judy; Gary Kilpatrick; Kontinental Spirits Kompanie; Lee's Antiques; Robert Lemos; Lionstone Distilleries, Ltd.; Jack Lyons; George and Janet Marie Loik; Mike and Barbara Matey; Bob and Beka Mebane; Jerry and Aryliss McCann; Pat and Pam Montgomery; Roger Moody; Doug Moore; Bob Morgan; Ruth Netherland; Bob Proskey; Jerry and Elaine Schmitt; Ed and Betty Schwennsen; Tony L. Shank; Doug Shutler; Paul Snyder (Donnelscreek Glass Co.); Kenneth Sosnowski; Ben Swanson; Sam and Eloise Taylor; John Tutton (Early America Workshop); Paul Van Vactor; Fred and Shirley Weck; L & E Wertheimer (Edward Wertheimer, III); Wheaton Commemoratives; Robert Wise; and Felix and Wanda Yor.

Special thanks to the Federation of Historical Bottle Clubs for permitting photographs to be taken at the 1976 National Antique Bottle-Jar Exposition; to Hal and Verna Wagner and Jerry Hostetler, in St. Louis, Missouri; and to the Midwest Antique Fruit Jar & Bottle Club show in Richmond, Indiana, and Ricky and Becky Norton.

BOTTLE CLUBS

There are hundreds of bottle clubs that welcome new members. This list is arranged by state and city so you can find the club nearest your home. If no club is listed nearby we suggest you contact the national organizations (see below). New clubs are formed each month. Members of the Federation of Historical Bottle Clubs are interested in old bottles. Modern bottles such as Avon, Ezra Brooks, and Beam have their own clubs in many areas.

Any active bottle club that is not listed and wishes to be included in future editions of *The Kovels' Complete Bottle Price List* should send the necessary information to the authors, c/o Crown Publishers, One Park Avenue, New York, New York 10016.

BOTTLE CLUBS

NATIONAL CLUBS

THE COLA CLAN
c/o Bob Buffaloe
3965 Pikes Peak
Memphis, Tennessee
38108

FEDERATION OF
HISTORICAL BOTTLE
CLUBS
c/o Bob Ferraro
515 Northridge Drive
Boulder City, Nevada
89005

INTERNATIONAL
ASSOCIATION OF JIM
BEAM BOTTLE &
SPECIALTIES CLUBS
1650 South Amphlett
Boulevard, No. 121
San Mateo, California
94402

LIONSTONE BOTTLE
COLLECTORS OF AMERICA
P.O. Box 75924
Los Angeles,
California 90075

MILKBOTTLES ONLY
ORGANIZATION (MOO)
P.O. Box 5456
Newport News,
Virginia 23605

NATIONAL ASSOCIATION
OF AVON CLUBS
Dale Robinson, National
Director
2823 E. 49th Street
Tulsa, Oklahoma 74105

NATIONAL ASSOCIATION
OF MINIATURE
ENTHUSIASTS (N.A.M.E.)
P.O. Box 2621
Brookhurst Center
Anaheim, California 92804

NATIONAL EZRA BROOKS
CLUBS
Gerald F. Marco,
Coordinator
645 N. Michigan Avenue
Chicago, Illinois 69611

THE NATIONAL GRENADIER
BOTTLE CLUB OF AMERICA
3155 Georgetown Road
Indianapolis, Indiana 46224

WESTERN WORLD AVON
CLUB
511 Harrison
San Francisco, California
94105

STATE CLUBS
Alabama

PIONEER BOTTLE CLUB OF
FAIRHOPE
P.O. Box 294
Battles Wharf,
Alabama 36533

ALABAMA BOTTLE
COLLECTORS' SOCIETY
1768 Hanover Circle
Birmingham,
Alabama 35205

NORTH ALABAMA BOTTLE
& GLASS CLUB
P.O. Box 109
Decatur, Alabama 35601

HUNTSVILLE HISTORICAL
BOTTLE CLUB
5605 Woodridge S.W.
Huntsville, Alabama 35802

MONTGOMERY, ALABAMA
BOTTLE CLUB
1940A Norman Bridge
Court
Montgomery, Alabama
36104

MOBILE BOTTLE
COLLECTORS CLUB
Rt. #4 Box 28
Theodore, Alabama 36582

TUSCALOOSA ANTIQUE
BOTTLE CLUB
1617 11th Street
Tuscaloosa,
Alabama 35401

Alaska

ALASKA BOTTLE CLUB
(formerly THE
ANCHORAGE BEAM CLUB)
8510 E. 10th
Anchorage, Alaska 99504

Arizona

WHITE MOUNTAIN
ANTIQUE BOTTLE
COLLECTORS
ASSOCIATION
P.O. Box 503
Eager, Arizona 85925

FORT SMITH AREA BOTTLE
COLLECTORS
ASSOCIATION
4618 So. "Q"
Fort Smith, Arizona 72901

AVON COLLECTORS CLUB
P.O. Box 1406
Mesa, Arizona 86201

KACHINA EZRA BROOKS
BOTTLE CLUB
3818 W. Cactus Wren Drive
Phoenix, Arizona 85021

PICK & SHOVEL ANTIQUES
BOTTLE CLUB OF ARIZONA
Box 7476
Phoenix, Arizona 85011

VALLEY OF THE SUN
BOTTLE & SPECIALTY
CLUB
212 East Minton
Tempe, Arizona 85281

ARIZONA TERRITORY
ANTIQUE BOTTLE CLUB
P.O. Box 6364
Speedway Station
Tucson, Arizona 85733

SOUTHERN ARIZONA
HISTORICAL COLLECTOR'S
ASSOCIATION, LTD.
6211 Piedra Seca
Tucson, Arizona 85718

Arkansas

SOUTHWEST ARKANSAS
BOTTLE CLUB
Star Route
Delight, Arkansas 71940

HEMPSTED COUNTY
BOTTLE CLUB
710 So. Hervey
Hope, Arkansas 71801

MADISON COUNTY BOTTLE
COLLECTORS CLUB
Rt. 2 Box 304
Huntsville, Arkansas 72740

LITTLE ROCK ANTIQUE
BOTTLE COLLECTORS
620 Carpenter Drive
Jacksonville, Arkansas
72076

California

GOLDEN GATE HISTORICAL
BOTTLE SOCIETY
P.O. Box 2129
Alameda, California 94501

CALIFORNIA SKI COUNTRY
BOTTLE CLUB
212 South El Molino Street
Alhambra, California 91801

QUEEN MARY BEAM &
SPECIALTY CLUB
P.O. Box 2054
Anaheim, California 92804

SHASTA ANTIQUE BOTTLE
COLLECTORS
ASSOCIATION
Route 1 Box 3147-A
Anderson, California 96007

KERN COUNTY ANTIQUE
BOTTLE CLUB
P.O. Box 6724
Bakersfield,
California 93306

PENINSULA BOTTLE CLUB
P.O. Box 886
Belmont, California 94002

JIM BEAM BOTTLE CLUB
139 Arlington
Berkeley, California 94707

BISHOP BELLES & BEAUX
BOTTLE CLUB
P.O. Box 1475
Bishop, California 93514

SAN BERNARDINO
HISTORICAL BOTTLE &
COLLECTIBLE CLUB
P.O. Box 127
Bloomington, California
92316

BIDWELL BOTTLE CLUB
Box 546
Chico, California 95926

MT. DIABLO BOTTLE
SOCIETY
1699 Laguna #110
Concord, California 94520

MT. BOTTLE CLUB
422 Orpheus
Encinitas, California 92024

HUMBOLDT ANTIQUE
BOTTLE CLUB
P.O. Box 6012
Eureka, California 95501

RELIC ACCUMULATORS
P.O. Box 3513
Eureka, California 95501

TEEN BOTTLE CLUB
Route 1 Box 60-TE
Eureka, California 95501

NORTHWESTERN BOTTLE
CLUB ASSOCIATION
10190 Martinelli Road
Forestville,
California 95436

MONTEREY BAY BEAM
BOTTLE & SPECIALTY
CLUB
P.O. Box 258
Freedom, California 95019

ANTIQUE BOTTLE CLUB
ASSOCIATION OF FRESNO
P.O. Box 1932
Fresno, California 93718

SAN JOAQUIN VALLEY JIM
BEAM BOTTLE &
SPECIALTIES CLUB
4085 North Wilson Avenue
Fresno, California 93704

HOLLYWOOD STARS-EZRA
BROOKS BOTTLE CLUB
2200 North Beachwood
Drive
Hollywood, California
90028

SAN FRANCISCO BAY AREA
MINIATURE BOTTLE CLUB
160 Lower Via Casitas #8
Kentfield, California 94904

SEQUOIA ANTIQUE BOTTLE
SOCIETY
1900 4th Avenue
Kingsburg, California
93631

LODI JIM BEAM BOTTLE
CLUB
429 E. Lodi Avenue
Lodi, California 95240

MT. WHITNEY BOTTLE
CLUB
P.O. Box 688
Lone Pine,
California 93545

AMETHYST BOTTLE CLUB
3245 Military Avenue
Los Angeles,
California 90034

JIM BEAM BOTTLE CLUB
OF SO. CALIF.
1114 Coronado Terrace
Los Angeles, California
90066

LOS ANGELES HISTORIC
BOTTLE CLUB
7631 Boeing Avenue
Los Angeles, California
90045

MISSION BELLS (BEAMS)
1114 Coronada Terrace
Los Angeles,
California 90026

ORIGINAL SIPPIN COUSINS
EZRA BROOKS
SPECIALTIES CLUB
12206 Malone Street
Los Angeles, California
90066

SOUTHERN CALIFORNIA
MINIATURE BOTTLE CLUB
5626 Corning Avenue
Los Angeles,
California 90056

SOUTH BAY ANTIQUE
BOTTLE CLUB
2589 1/2 Valley Drive
Manhattan Beach, California
90266

MODESTO OLD BOTTLE
CLUB (MOBC)
P.O. Box 1791
Modesto, California 95354

AVON BOTTLE &
SPECIALTIES COLLECTORS
Southern California Division
9233 Mills Avenue
Montclair, California 91763

NORTHERN CALIFORNIA
JIM BEAM BOTTLE &
SPECIALTY CLUB
P.O. Box 186
Montgomery Creek,
California 96065

CURIOSITY BOTTLE
ASSOCIATION
Box 103
Napa, California 94558

CAMELLIA CITY JIM BEAM
BOTTLE CLUB
3734 Lynhurst Way
North Highlands,
California 95660

JEWELS OF AVON
2297 Maple Avenue
Oroville, California 95965

SAN LUIS OBISPO BOTTLE
SOCIETY
124 21st Street
Paso Robles,
California 93446

NORTHWESTERN BOTTLE
COLLECTORS
ASSOCIATION
1 Keeler Street
Petaluma, California 94952

PETALUMA BOTTLE &
ANTIQUE CLUB
P.O. Box 1035
Petaluma, California 94952

MT. DIABLO BOTTLE CLUB
4166 Sandra Circle
Pittsburg, California 94565

TEHAMA COUNTY
ANTIQUE BOTTLE CLUB
P.O. Box 541
Red Bluff, California 96080

LIVERMORE AVON CLUB
6385 Claremont Avenue
Richmond,
California 94805

BEAM BOTTLE CLUB OF
SOUTHERN CALIFORNIA
3221 N. Jackson
Rosemead,
California 91770

SKI-COUNTRY BOTTLE
CLUB OF SOUTHERN
CALIFORNIA
3148 N. Walnut Grove
Rosemead,
California 91770

GOLDEN BEAR JIM BEAM
BOTTLE & SPECIALTY
CLUB
8808 Capricorn Way
San Diego, California
92126

GOLDEN BEAR EZRA
BROOKS BOTTLE CLUB
8808 Capricorn Way
San Diego, California
92126

SAN DIEGO ANTIQUE
BOTTLE CLUB
P.O. Box 536
San Diego,
California 92112

SAN DIEGO JIM BEAM
BOTTLE CLUB
2620 Mission Village Drive
San Diego, California
92123

GLASS BELLES OF SAN
GABRIEL
518 W. Neuby Avenue
San Gabriel,
California 91776

MISSION TRAILS EZRA
BROOKS BOTTLES &
SPECIALTIES CLUB, INC.
4923 Bel Canto Drive
San Jose, California 95124

SAN JOSE ANTIQUE
BOTTLE COLLECTORS
ASSOCIATION
P.O. Box 5432
San Jose, California 95150

SIERRA GOLD SKI
COUNTRY BOTTLE CLUB
5081 Rio Vista Avenue
San Jose, California 95129

ANTIQUE BOTTLE
COLLECTORS OF ORANGE
COUNTY
223 E. Ponona
Santa Ana,
California 92707

SANTA BARBARA BEAM
BOTTLE CLUB
5307 University Drive
Santa Barbara,
California 93111

NORTHWESTERN BOTTLE
COLLECTORS
ASSOCIATION
P.O. Box 1121
Santa Rosa,
California 95402

MISSION TRAIL
HISTORICAL BOTTLE CLUB
P.O. Box 721
Seaside, California 93940

HOFFMAN'S MR. LUCKY
BOTTLE CLUB
2104 Rhoda Street
Simi Valley,
California 93065

M. T. BOTTLE CLUB
P.O. Box 608
Solana Beach,
California 92075

STOCKTON HISTORIC
BOTTLE CLUB
Box 8584
Stockton, California 95204

CHIEF SOLANO BOTTLE
CLUB
4-D Boynton Avenue
Suisun, California 94585

SUNNYVALE ANTIQUE
BOTTLE COLLECTORS
ASSOCIATION
613 Torrington
Sunnyvale,
California 94087

TAFT ANTIQUE BOTTLE
CLUB
P.O. Box 334
Taft, California 93268

GLASSHOPPER FIGURAL
BOTTLE ASSOCIATION
P.O. Box 6642
Torrance, California 90504

LILLIPUTIAN BOTTLE CLUB
5119 Lee Street
Torrance, California 90503

GOLDEN GATE EZRA
BROOKS BOTTLE &
SPECIALTIES CLUB
715 Capra Drive
Vallejo, California 94590

NAPA-SOLANO BOTTLE
CLUB
1409 Delwood
Vallejo, California 94590

JUNIPER HILLS BOTTLE
CLUB
Rt. 1 Box 18
Valyerma, California 93563

CHERRY VALLEY BEAM
BOTTLE & SPECIALTY
CLUB
6851 Hood Drive
Westminster,
California 92683

FIRST DOUBLE SPRINGS
COLLECTORS CLUB
13311 Illinois Street
Westminster,
California 92683

Colorado

ALAMOSA BOTTLE
COLLECTORS
Route 2 Box 170
Alamosa, Colorado 81101

AVON CLUB OF COLORADO
SPRINGS, COLORADO
707 N. Farragut
Colorado Springs, Colorado
80909

LIONSTONE WESTERN
FIGURAL CLUB
P.O. Box 2275
Colorado Springs, Colorado
80901

PEAKS & PLAINS ANTIQUE
BOTTLE CLUB
P.O. Box 814
Colorado Springs, Colorado
80901

WESTERN FIGURAL & JIM
BEAM SPECIALTY CLUB
P.O. Box 4331
Colorado Springs,
Colorado 80930

FOUR CORNERS BOTTLE &
GLASS CLUB
P.O. Box 45
Cortez, Colorado 81321

ANTIQUE BOTTLE CLUB OF
COLORADO
P.O. Box 63
Denver, Colorado 80201

ROCKY MOUNTAIN JIM
BEAM BOTTLE &
SPECIALTY CLUB
Alcott Station
P.O. Box 12162
Denver, Colorado 80212

HORSETOOTH ANTIQUE
BOTTLE COLLECTORS
ASSOCIATION
P.O. Box 944
Fort Collins,
Colorado 80521

NORTHERN COLORADO
ANTIQUE BOTTLE CLUB
227 W. Beaver Avenue
Ft. Morgan,
Colorado 80701

WESTERN SLOPE BOTTLE
CLUB
607 Belford Avenue
Grand Junction, Colorado
81501

TELLURIDE ANTIQUE
BOTTLE COLLECTORS
P.O. Box 344
Telluride, Colorado 81435

COLORADO MILE-HIGH
EZRA BROOKS BOTTLE
CLUB
7401 Decatur Street
Westminster,
Colorado 80030

OLE FOXIE JIM BEAM CLUB
P.O. Box 560
Westminster,
Colorado 80020

Connecticut

GREENWICH ANTIQUE
BOTTLE COLLECTORS
CLUB
6 Relay Court
Cos Cob,
Connecticut 06807

HOUSATONIC ANTIQUE
BOTTLE ASSOCIATION
Falls Village,
Connecticut 06031

EAST COAST MINI BOTTLE
CLUB
156 Hillfield Road
Hamden, Connecticut

THE NUTMEG STATE EZRA
BROOKS BOTTLE CLUB
191 W. Main Street
Meriden, Connecticut
06450

SOUTHEASTERN NEW
ENGLAND ANTIQUE
BOTTLE CLUB
656 Noank Road
Mystic, Connecticut 06355

ANTIQUE BOTTLE CLUB OF
MIDDLETOWN
15 Elam Street, Apt. 10
New Britain, Connecticut
06053

SOUTHERN CONNECTICUT
ANTIQUE BOTTLE
COLLECTORS
ASSOCIATION, INC.
.P.O. Box 346
Seymour,
Connecticut 06483

SOMERS ANTIQUE BOTTLE
CLUB, INC.
Box 313
Somers, Connecticut 06071

CENTRAL CONNECTICUT
ANTIQUE BOTTLE
COLLECTORS
210 Rolling Hill Lane
Southington, Connecticut
06489

CONNECTICUT
SPECIALTIES BOTTLE CLUB
P.O. Box 624
Stratford,
Connecticut 06497

Delaware

MASON-DIXON BOTTLE
COLLECTORS
ASSOCIATION
P.O. Box 505
Lewes, Delaware 19958

TRI-STATE BOTTLE
COLLECTORS AND
DIGGERS CLUB
2807 Bexley Court
Wilmington, Delaware
19808

Florida

HALIFAX HISTORICAL
SOCIETY
224½ S. Beach Street
Daytona Beach, Florida
32018

M-T BOTTLE COLLECTORS
ASSOCIATION
P.O. Box 1581
Deland, Florida 32720

HARBOR CITY
1232 Causeway
Eau, Florida 32935

ANTIQUE BOTTLE
COLLECTORS OF FLORIDA,
INC.
2512 Davie Boulevard
Ft. Lauderdale, Florida
33312

ANTIQUE BOTTLE
COLLECTORS OF NORTH
FLORIDA
P.O. Box 4502
Jacksonville, Florida 32201

ORIGINAL FLORIDA KEYS
COLLECTORS CLUB
P.O. Box 212
Islamorada, Florida 33036

RIDGE AREA ANTIQUE
BOTTLE COLLECTORS
1219 Carlton
Lake Wales, Florida 33853

CROSSARMS COLLECTORS
CLUB
1756 N.W. 58th Avenue
Lauderhill, Florida 33313

LONGWOOD BOTTLE CLUB
Box 437
Longwood, Florida 32750

MID-STATE ANTIQUE
BOTTLE COLLECTORS INC.
88 Sweetbriar Branch
Longwood, Florida 32750

CENTRAL FLORIDA JIM
BEAM BOTTLE CLUB
5345 Lake Jessamine Drive
Orlando, Florida 32809

PENSACOLA BOTTLE &
RELIC COLLECTORS
ASSOCIATION
1004 Freemont Avenue
Pensacola, Florida 32505

NORTHWEST FLORIDA
REGIONAL BOTTLE CLUB
P.O. Box 282
Port St. Joe, Florida 32456

SUNCOAST ANTIQUE
BOTTLE CLUB
P.O. Box 12712
St. Petersburg,
Florida 33733

SANFORD ANTIQUE
BOTTLE COLLECTORS
CLUB
2656 Grandview Avenue
South
Sanford, Florida 32771

SUNCOAST JIM BEAM
BOTTLE & SPEC. CLUB
P.O. Box 5067
Sarasota, Florida 33579

WEST COAST FLORIDA
EZRA BROOKS BOTTLE
CLUB
1360 Harbor Drive
Sarasota, Florida 33579

TAMPA ANTIQUE BOTTLE
COLLECTORS
P.O. Box 4232
Tampa, Florida 33607

SOUTH FLORIDA JIM BEAM
BOTTLE & SPECIALTY
CLUB
7741 N.W. 35th Street
West Hollywood,
Florida 33024

GOLD COAST COLLECTORS
CLUB
Joseph I. Frakes
P.O. Box 10183
Wilton Manors, Florida
33305

Georgia

PEACHSTATE BOTTLE &
SPECIALTY CLUB
5040 Vallo Vista Court
Atlanta, Georgia 30342

BULLDOG DOUBLE
SPRINGS BOTTLE
COLLECTOR CLUB OF
AUGUSTA, GEORGIA
1916 Melrose Drive
Augusta, Georgia 30906

GEORGIA-CAROLINA
EMPTY BOTTLE CLUB
P.O. Box 1184
Augusta, Georgia 30903

FLINT ANTIQUE BOTTLE &
COIN CLUB
c/o Cordele-Crisp Co.
Recreation Department
204 2nd Street North
Cordele, Georgia 31015

GEORGIA BOTTLE CLUB
2996 Pangborn Road
Decatur, Georgia 30033

SOUTHEASTERN ANTIQUE
BOTTLE CLUB
Box 657
Decatur, Georgia 30033

MACON ANTIQUE BOTTLE
CLUB
P.O. Box 5395
Macon, Georgia 31208

THE MIDDLE GEORGIA
ANTIQUE BOTTLE CLUB
2746 Alden Street
Macon, Georgia 31206

COASTAL EMPIRE BOTTLE
CLUB
P.O. Box 3714 Station B
Savannah, Georgia 31404

Hawaii

HAWAII BOTTLE
COLLECTORS CLUB
5070 Paola Street
Honolulu, Hawaii 96821

HAUOLI BEAM BOTTLE
COLLECTORS CLUB OF
HAWAII
45-027 Ka-Hanahou Place
Kaneohe, Hawaii 96744

Idaho

GEM ANTIQUE BOTTLE
COLLECTORS
ASSOCIATION
1630 Londoner Avenue
Boise, Idaho 83706

BUHL ANTIQUE BOTTLE
CLUB
500 12th North
Buhl, Idaho 83316

ROCK & BOTTLE CLUB
Route 1
Fruitland, Idaho 83619

EM TEE BOTTLE CLUB
P.O. Box 62
Jerome, Idaho 83338

INLAND EMPIRE JIM BEAM
BOTTLE & COLLECTORS'
CLUB
1117 10th Street
Lewiston, Idaho 83501

FABULOUS VALLEY
ANTIQUE BOTTLE CLUB
P.O. Box 769
Osburn, Idaho 83849

IDAHO BOTTLE
COLLECTORS
ASSOCIATION
4530 South 5th Street
Pocatello, Idaho 83201

Illinois

ALTON AREA BOTTLE
CLUB
1110 Logan Street
Alton, Illinois 62002

ILLINI JIM BEAM BOTTLE &
SPECIALTY CLUB
P.O. Box 13
Champaign, Illinois 61820

CHICAGO EZRA BROOKS
BOTTLE & SPECIALTY
CLUB
3635 West 82nd Street
Chicago, Illinois 60652

FIRST CHICAGO BOTTLE
CLUB
P.O. Box A3382
Chicago, Illinois 60690

METRO EAST BOTTLE &
JAR ASSOCIATION
1702 North Keesler
Collinsville, Illinois 62234

LAND OF LINCOLN BOTTLE
CLUB
2515 Illinois Circle
Decatur, Illinois 62526

HEART OF ILLINOIS
ANTIQUE BOTTLE CLUB
2010 Bloomington Road
East Peoria, Illinois 61611

SWEET CORN CAPITOL
BOTTLE CLUB
1015 W. Orange
Hoopeston, Illinois 60942

ANTIQUE BOTTLE CLUB OF
NORTHERN ILLINOIS
P.O. Box 23
Ingleside, Illinois 60041

CHICAGO JIM BEAM
BOTTLE & SPECIALTY
CLUB
1305 W. Marion Street
Joliet, Illinois 60436

LOUIS JOLIET BOTTLE
CLUB
12 Kenmore
Joliet, Illinois 60433

NATIONAL EZRA BROOKS
BOTTLE & SPECIALTIES
CLUB
420 N. First Street
Kewanee, Illinois 61443

KELLY CLUB
147 North Brainard Avenue
La Grange, Illinois 60525

CENTRAL & MIDWESTERN
STATES BEAM &
SPECIALTIES CLUB
44 S. Westmore
Lombard, Illinois 60148

METRO EAST BOTTLE &
JAR ASSOCIATION
P.O. Box 185
Mascoutah, Illinois

PEKIN BOTTLE
COLLECTORS
ASSOCIATION
P.O. Box 372
Pekin, Illinois, 61554

BLACKHAWK JIM BEAM
BOTTLE & SPECIALTIES
CLUB
2003 Kishwaukee Street
Rockford, Illinois 61101

ILLINOIS BOTTLE CLUB
P.O. Box 181
Rushville, Illinois 62681

LEWIS & CLARK JIM BEAM
BOTTLE & SPECIALTY
CLUB
P.O. Box 451
Wood River, Illinois 62095

Indiana

THE OHIO VALLEY
ANTIQUE BOTTLE AND JAR
CLUB
214 John Street
Aurora, Indiana 47001

WE FOUND 'EM BOTTLE &
INSULATOR CLUB
P.O. Box 578
Bunker Hill, Indiana 46914

MIDWEST ANTIQUE FRUIT
JAR AND BOTTLE CLUB
Box 38
Flat Rock, Indiana 47234

FORT WAYNE HISTORICAL
BOTTLE CLUB
5124 Roberta Drive
Fort Wayne, Indiana 46805

HOOSIER JIM BEAM
BOTTLE & SPECIALTIES
CLUB
P.O. Box 24234
Indianapolis
Indiana 46224

INDIANA EZRA BROOKS
BOTTLE CLUB
P.O. Box 24344
Indianapolis,
Indiana 46224

MICHIANA JIM BEAM
BOTTLE & SPECIALTY
CLUB
58955 Locust Road
South Bend, Indiana 46614

STEEL CITY EZRA BROOKS
BOTTLE CLUB
R.R. #2 Box 32A
Valparaiso, Indiana 46383

Iowa

IOWA ANTIQUE
BOTTLERS
1506 Albia Road
Ottumwa, Iowa 52501

LARKIN BOTTLE CLUB
107 W. Grimes
Red Oak, Iowa 51566

Kansas

CHEROKEE STRIP EZRA
BROOKS BOTTLE &
SPECIALTY CLUB
P.O. Box 631
Arkansas City,
Kansas 67005

SOUTH EAST KANSAS
BOTTLE & RELIC CLUB
302 So. Western
Chanute, Kansas 66720

FLINT HILLS BEAM &
SPECIALTY CLUB
201 W. Pine
El Dorado, Kansas 67042

JAYHAWK BOTTLE CLUB
7919 Grant
Overland Park,
Kansas 66212

KANSAS CITY ANTIQUE
BOTTLE COLLECTORS
ASSOCIATION
5528 Aberdeen
Shawnee Mission, Kansas
66205

WICHITA EZRA BROOKS
BOTTLE & SPECIALTIES
CLUB
8045 Peachtree Street
Wichita, Kansas 67207

Kentucky

LOUISVILLE BOTTLE
COLLECTORS
11819 Garrs Avenue
Anchorage,
Kentucky 40223

KENTUCKY CARDINAL
BEAM BOTTLE CLUB
428 Templin
Bardstown,
Kentucky 41104

DERBY CITY JIM BEAM
BOTTLE CLUB
4105 Spring Hill Road
Louisville, Kentucky 40207

KENTUCKIANA ANTIQUE
BOTTLE SOCIETY
5801 River Knolls Drive
Louisville, Kentucky 40222

KENTUCKY BLUEGRASS
EZRA BROOKS BOTTLE
CLUB
6202 Tabor Drive
Louisville,
Kentucky 40218

Louisiana

"CAJUN COUNTRY
COUSINS" EZRA BROOKS
BOTTLE & SPECIALTIES
CLUB
1000 Chevis Street
Abbeville, Louisiana 70510

HISTORICAL BOTTLE
ASSOCIATION OF BATON
ROUGE
1843 Tudor Drive
Baton Rouge,
Louisiana 70815

CENLA BOTTLE & RELIC
CLUB
Route 1, Box 289
Dry Prong, Louisiana
71423

DIXIE DIGGERS BOTTLE
CLUB
P.O. Box 626
Empire, Louisiana 70050

NORTHEAST LOUISIANA
BOTTLE & INSULATOR
CLUB
P.O. Box 4192
Monroe, Louisiana 71201

BAYOU BOTTLE BUGS
216 Dahlia
New Iberia,
Louisiana 70560

NEW ORLEANS ANTIQUE
BOTTLE CLUB
1607 So. Salcedo Street
New Orleans, Louisiana
71025

NEW ALBANY GLASS
WORKS BOTTLE CLUB
732 N. Clark Boulevard
Parksville, Louisiana 47130

Maine

KENNEBEC VALLEY
BOTTLE CLUB
9 Glenwood Street
Augusta, Maine 04330

DIRIGO BOTTLE
COLLECTOR'S CLUB
59 Fruit Street
Bangor, Maine 04401

PAUL BUNYAN BOTTLE
CLUB
237 14th Street
Bangor, Maine 04401

WALDO COUNTY
BOTTLENECKS CLUB
Head-of-the-Tide
Belfast, Maine 04915

THE GLASS BUBBLE
BOTTLE CLUB
P.O. Box 91
Cape Neddick,
Maine 03902

TRI-COUNTY BOTTLE
COLLECTORS
ASSOCIATION
RFD 3
Dexter, Maine 04930

DOVER FOXCROFT BOTTLE
CLUB
50 Church Street
Dover Foxcroft,
Maine 04426

NEW ENGLAND BOTTLE
CLUB
45 Bolt Hill Road
Eliot, Maine 03903

JIM BEAM COLLECTORS
CLUB
10 Lunt Road
Falmouth, Maine 04105

PINE TREE ANTIQUE
BOTTLE CLUB
Buxton Road
Saco, Maine 04072

MID COAST BOTTLE CLUB
c/o Miriam Winchenbach
Waldoboro, Maine 04572

Maryland

MASON DIXON BOTTLE
COLLECTORS
ASSOCIATION
601 Market Street
Denton, Maryland 21629

BLUE & GRAY EZRA
BROOKS BOTTLE CLUB
2106 Sunnybrook Drive
Frederick, Maryland 21201

BALTIMORE ANTIQUE
BOTTLE HOUNDS
264 Mahothy Beh Road
Pasadena, Maryland 21122

SOUTH COUNTY BOTTLE
COLLECTOR'S CLUB
Bast Lane
Shady Side,
Maryland 20867

CATOCTIN BEAM BOTTLE
CLUB
P.O. Box 2126
Silver Spring, Maryland
20902

Massachusetts

MERRIMACK VALLEY
ANTIQUE BOTTLE CLUB
20 Prospect Street
Beverly, Massachusetts
01915

NEW ENGLAND BEAM &
SPECIALTY CLUB
1104 Northampton Street
Holyoke,
Massachusetts 01040

BERKSHIRE ANTIQUE
BOTTLE ASSOCIATION
Box 753
Lenox, Massachusetts
01240

SATUIT BOTTLE CLUB
54 Cedarwood Road
Scituate, Massachusetts
02066

THE BOTTLE
PROSPECTOR'S CLUB
143 Main Street
Yarmouth Port,
Massachusetts 02675

Michigan

TRAVERSE AREA BOTTLE &
INSULATOR CLUB
P.O. Box 205
Acme, Michigan 49610

GREAT LAKES MINIATURE
BOTTLE CLUB
P.O. Box 245
Fairhaven, Michigan 48023

FLINT ANTIQUE BOTTLE
COLLECTORS
ASSOCIATION
450 Leta Avenue
Flint, Michigan 48507

FLINT EAGLES EZRA
BROOKS CLUB
1117 W. Remington Avenue
Flint, Michigan 48507

MICHIGAN'S VEHICLE CITY
BEAM BOTTLES &
SPECIALTIES CLUB
907 Root Street
Flint, Michigan 48503

GRAND VALLEY BOTTLE
CLUB
31 Dickinson S.W.
Grand Rapids,
Michigan 49507

W.M.R.A.C.C.
331 Bellevue S.W.
Grand Rapids,
Michigan 49508

DICKINSON COUNTY
BOTTLE CLUB
717 Henford Avenue
Iron Mountain,
Michigan 49801

YE OLDE CORKERS
BOTTLE CLUB
Route 1
Iron River, Michigan 49935

MICHIGAN BOTTLE
COLLECTORS
ASSOCIATION
144 W. Clark Street
Jackson, Michigan 49203

MANISTEE COIN & BOTTLE
CLUB
207 E. Piney Road
Manistee, Michigan 49660

HURON VALLEY BOTTLE
CLUB
12475 Saline-Milan Road
Milan, Michigan 48160

METROPOLITAN DETROIT
ANTIQUE BOTTLE CLUB
40835 Moravian Drive
Mt. Clemens, Michigan
48043

WOLVERINE BEAM BOTTLE
& SPECIALTY CLUB OF
MICHIGAN
36009 Larchwood
Mt. Clemens,
Michigan 48043

NORTHERN MICHIGAN
BOTTLE CLUB
P.O. Box 421
Petoskey, Michigan 49770

CHIEF PONTIAC BOTTLE
CLUB
755 Scottwood
Pontiac, Michigan 48058

LIONSTONE COLLECTORS
BOTTLE & SPECIALTIES
CLUB OF MICHIGAN
3089 Grand Blanc Road
Swartz Creek,
Michigan 48473

WORLD WIDE AVON
BOTTLE COLLECTORS
CLUB
22708 Wick Road
Taylor, Michigan 48180

WEST MICHIGAN AVON
COLLECTORS
331 Bellevue S.W.
Wyoming, Michigan 49508

Minnesota

DUMP DIGGERS
P.O. Box 24
Dover, Minnesota 55929

LAKE SUPERIOR ANTIQUE
BOTTLE CLUB
P.O. Box 67
Knife River,
Minnesota 55609

MINNESOTA'S FIRST
ANTIQUE BOTTLE CLUB
5001 Queen Avenue North
Minneapolis,
Minnesota 55430

ARNFALT COLLECTORS
BEAM CLUB
New Richard
Minnesota 56072

NORTH STAR HISTORICAL
BOTTLE ASSOCIATION,
INC.
P.O. Box 30343
St. Paul, Minnesota 55175

Mississippi

MIDDLE MISSISSIPPI
ANTIQUE BOTTLE CLUB
P.O. Box 233
Jackson, Mississippi 39205

SOUTH MISSISSIPPI
ANTIQUE BOTTLE CLUB
203 S. 4th Avenue
Laurel, Mississippi 39440

OXFORD ANTIQUE
BOTTLERS
128 Vivian Street
Oxford, Mississippi 38633

Missouri

ANTIQUE BOTTLE & RELIC
CLUB OF CENTRAL
MISSOURI
c/o Ann Downing, Rt. 10
Columbia,
Missouri 65201

MID-WEST ANTIQUE
BOTTLE & HOBBY CLUB
122 Hightower Street
El Dorado Springs,
Missouri 64744

GREATER KANSAS CITY
JIM BEAM BOTTLE &
SPECIALTY CLUB
P.O. Box 6703
Kansas City,
Missouri 64123

KANSAS CITY ANTIQUE
BOTTLE COLLECTORS
ASSOCIATION
1131 East 77 Street
Kansas City,
Missouri 64131

MINERAL AREA BOTTLE
CLUB
Knob Lick, Missouri 63651

NORTHWEST MISSOURI
BOTTLE & RELIC CLUB
3006 S. 28th Street
St. Joseph, Missouri 64503

ST. LOUIS ANTIQUE
BOTTLE COLLECTORS
ASSOCIATION
506 N. Woodlawn
St. Louis, Missouri 63122

MOUND CITY JIM BEAM
DECANTER COLLECTORS
42 Webster Acres
Webster Groves,
Missouri 63119

ST. LOUIS EZRA BROOKS
CERAMICS CLUB
42 Webster Acres
Webster Groves,
Missouri 63119

Montana

HELLGATE ANTIQUE
BOTTLE CLUB
P.O. Box 411
Missoula, Montana 59801

Nebraska

MINI-SEEKERS
"A" Acres, Rt. 8
Lincoln, Nebraska 68506

NEBRASKA BIG RED
BOTTLE & SPECIALTY
CLUB
N. Street Drive-In
200 So. 18th Street
Lincoln, Nebraska 68508

NEBRASKA ANTIQUE
BOTTLE & COLLECTORS
CLUB
Box 37021
Omaha, Nebraska 68137

Nevada

MINERAL COUNTY
ANTIQUE BOTTLE CLUB
P.O. Box 349
Babbitt, Nevada 89415

VIRGINIA & TRUCKEE JIM
BEAM BOTTLE &
SPECIALTIES CLUB
P.O. Box 1596
Carson City, Nevada 89701

NEVADA BEAM CLUB
P.O. Box 426
Fallon, Nevada 89406

JIM BEAM BOTTLE CLUB
OF LAS VEGAS
212 N. Orland Street
Las Vegas, Nevada 89107

LAS VEGAS BOTTLE CLUB
884 Lulu Avenue
Las Vegas, Nevada 89119

SOUTHERN NEVADA
ANTIQUE BOTTLE CLUB
431 No. Spruce Street
Las Vegas, Nevada 89101

WEE BOTTLE CLUB
INTERNATIONAL
P.O. Box 1195
Las Vegas, Nevada 89101

LINCOLN COUNTY
ANTIQUE BOTTLE CLUB,
INC.
P.O. Box 371
Pioche, Nevada 89043

RENO-SPARKS ANTIQUE
BOTTLE COLLECTORS
ASSOCIATION
P.O. Box 6145
Reno, Nevada 89503

New Hampshire

GRANITE STATE BOTTLE
CLUB
R.F.D. #1
Belmont,
New Hampshire 03220

BOTTLEERS OF NEW
HAMPSHIRE
125A Central Street
Farmington,
New Hampshire 03835

YANKEE BOTTLE CLUB
P.O. Box 702
Keene,
New Hampshire 03431

New Jersey

ANTIQUE BOTTLE
COLLECTORS CLUB OF
BURLINGTON COUNTY
18 Willow Road
Bordentown, New Jersey
08505

NEW JERSEY EZRA
BROOKS BOTTLE CLUB
South Main Street
Cedarville,
New Jersey 08311

LAKELAND ANTIQUE
BOTTLE CLUB
18 Alan Lane
Mine Hill,
Dover, New Jersey 07801

TRENTON JIM BEAM
BOTTLE CLUB, INC.
17 Easy Street
Freehold,
New Jersey 07728

SOUTH JERSEY'S
HERITAGE BOTTLE &
GLASS CLUB
P.O. Box 122
Glassboro,
New Jersey 08028

WEST ESSEX BOTTLE CLUB
76 Beaufort Avenue
Livingston,
New Jersey 07039

THE JERSEY DEVIL BOTTLE
DIGGERS CLUB
14 Church Street
Mt. Holly, New Jersey
08060

SUSSEX COUNTY ANTIQUE
BOTTLE COLLECTORS
Division of Sussex County
Historical Society
82 Main Street
Newton, New Jersey 07860

TWIN BRIDGES BEAM
BOTTLE & SPECIALTY
CLUB
P.O. Box 347
Pennsville,
New Jersey 08070

LIONSTONE COLLECTORS
CLUB OF DELAWARE
VALLEY
R.D. #3 Box 93
Sewell, New Jersey 08080

THE JERSEY SHORE
BOTTLE CLUB
Box 995
Toms River,
New Jersey 08753

ARTIFACT HUNTERS
ASSOCIATION INC.
c/o 29 Lake Road
Wayne, New Jersey 07470

NORTH NEW JERSEY
ANTIQUE BOTTLE CLUB
ASSOCIATION
P.O. Box 617
Westwood,
New Jersey 07675

New Mexico

ROADRUNNER BOTTLE
CLUB OF NEW MEXICO
2341 Gay Road S.W.
Albuquerque,
New Mexico 87105

CAVE CITY ANTIQUE
BOTTLE CLUB
Route 1, Box 155
Carlsbad,
New Mexico 88220

New York

NORTHERN NEW YORK
BOTTLE CLUB
ASSOCIATION
P.O. Box 257
Adams Center,
New York 13606

NORTH COUNTRY BOTTLE
COLLECTORS
ASSOCIATION
Route 1
Canton, New York 13617

EMPIRE STATE JIM BEAM
BOTTLE CLUB
P.O. Box 561
Farmingdale Post Office,
Main Street
Farmingdale, New York
11735

EMPIRE STATE BOTTLE
COLLECTORS
ASSOCIATION
c/o Dr. L. Simpson, Rd #3
Fulton, New York 13069

FINGER LAKES BOTTLE
CLUB ASSOCIATION
P.O. Box 815
Ithaca, New York 14850

WESTERN NEW YORK
BOTTLE COLLECTORS
87 S. Bristol Avenue
Lockport, New York 14094

SUFFOLK COUNTY
ANTIQUE BOTTLE
ASSOCIATION OF LONG
ISLAND, INC.
P.O. Box 943
Melville, New York 11746

CATSKILL MOUNTAINS JIM
BEAM BOTTLE CLUB
Six Gardner Avenue
Middletown,
New York 10940

UPPER SUSQUEHANNA
BOTTLE CLUB
P.O. Box 183
Milford, New York 13807

HUDSON RIVER JIM BEAM
BOTTLE AND SPECIALTIES
CLUB
48 College Road
Monsey, New York 10952

HUDSON VALLEY BOTTLE
CLUB
255 Fostertown Road
Newburgh, New York
12550

SOUTHERN TIER BOTTLE &
INSULATOR COLLECTORS
ASSOCIATION
47 Dickinson Avenue
Port Dickinson,
New York 13901

GENESEE VALLEY BOTTLE
COLLECTORS
ASSOCIATION
P.O. Box 7528
West Ridge Station
Rochester, New York
14615

ROCHESTER NEW YORK
BOTTLE CLUB
7908 West Henrietta Road
Rush, New York 14543

CHAUTAUQUA COUNTY
BOTTLE COLLECTORS
CLUB
Morse Hotel
Main Street
Sherman, New York 14781

TRYON BOTTLE BADGERS
Box 146
Tribes Hill, New York
12177

RENSSELAER COUNTY
ANTIQUE BOTTLE CLUB
Box 792
Troy, New York 12180

AUBURN BOTTLE CLUB
27 Center Street, Box 138
Union Springs, New York
13160

WARWICK VALLEY BOTTLE
CLUB
Box 393
Warwick, New York 10990

EASTERN MONROE
COUNTY BOTTLE CLUB
c/o Bethlehem Lutheran
Church
1767 Plank Road
Webster, New York 14580

North Carolina

CAROLINA BOTTLE CLUB
c/o Industrial Piping Co.
Anonwood, Charlotte,
North Carolina 28210

BLUE RIDGE BOTTLE AND
JAR CLUB
Dogwood Lane
Black Mountain,
North Carolina
28711

CAROLINA JIM BEAM
BOTTLE CLUB
1014 N. Main Street
Burlington,
North Carolina 27215

YADKIN VALLEY BOTTLE
CLUB
General Delivery
Gold Hill, North Carolina
28071

GOLDSBORO BOTTLE CLUB
2406 E. Ash Street
Goldsboro, North Carolina
27530

GREATER GREENSBORO
MOOSE EZRA BROOKS
BOTTLE CLUB
217 S. Elm Street
Greensboro,
North Carolina 27401

KINSTON COLLECTORS
CLUB, INC.
325 E. Lenoir
Kinston,
North Carolina 28501

WILSON ANTIQUE BOTTLE
& ARTIFACT CLUB
Route 5 Box 414
Wilson, North Carolina
27893

Ohio

RUBBER CAPITOL JIM
BEAM CLUB
151 Stephens Road
Akron, Ohio 44312

OHIO BOTTLE CLUB
P.O. Box 585
Barberton, Ohio 44203

SARA LEE BOTTLE CLUB
27621 Chagrin Boulevard
Cleveland, Ohio 44122

BUCKEYE JIM BEAM
BOTTLE CLUB
1211 Ashland Avenue
Columbus, Ohio 43212

CENTRAL OHIO BOTTLE
CLUB
P.O. Box 19864
Columbus, Ohio 43219

DIAMOND PIN WINNERS
AVON CLUB
5281 Fredonia Avenue
Dayton, Ohio 45431

GEM CITY BEAM BOTTLE
CLUB
1463 E. Stroop Road
Dayton, Ohio 45429

TRI-STATE HISTORICAL
BOTTLE CLUB
P.O. Box 609
East Liverpool, Ohio 43920

THE BUCKEYE BOTTLE
CLUB
229 Oakwood Street
Elyria, Ohio 44035

OHIO EZRA BROOKS
BOTTLE CLUB
8741 Kirtland Chardon
Road
Kirtland Hills, Ohio 44094

FIRST CAPITAL BOTTLE
CLUB
Route 1, Box 94
Laurelville, Ohio 43135

NORTH EASTERN OHIO
BOTTLE CLUB
P.O. Box 57
Madison, Ohio 44057

NORTHWEST OHIO BOTTLE
CLUB
104 W. Main
Norwalk, Ohio 44857

BUCKEYE BOTTLE
DIGGERS
Route 1, Box 48
Thornville, Ohio 43076

JEFFERSON COUNTY
ANTIQUE BOTTLE CLUB
Fairview Heights
Toronto, Ohio 43964

SOUTHWESTERN OHIO
ANTIQUE BOTTLE & JAR
CLUB
393 Franklin Avenue
Xenia, Ohio 45385

Oklahoma

BAR-DEW ANTIQUE
BOTTLE CLUB
817 E. 7th Street
Dewey, Oklahoma 74029

LITTLE DIXIE ANTIQUE
BOTTLE CLUB
P.O. Box 741
Krebs, Oklahoma 74501

SOUTHWEST OKLAHOMA
ANTIQUE BOTTLE CLUB
35 S. 49th Street
Lawton, Oklahoma 73501

PONCA CITY OLD BOTTLE
CLUB
2408 Juanito
Ponca City,
Oklahoma 74601

McDONNELL DOUGLAS
ANTIQUE CLUB
5752 E. 25th Place
Tulsa, Oklahoma 74114

TULSA ANTIQUE BOTTLE &
RELIC CLUB
P.O. Box 4278
Tulsa, Oklahoma 74104

Oregon

EMERALD EMPIRE BOTTLE
CLUB
P.O. Box 292
Eugene, Oregon 97401

PIONEER FRUIT JAR
COLLECTORS
ASSOCIATION
P.O. Box 175
Grand Ronde,
Oregon 97347

CENTRAL SOUTH OREGON
ANTIQUE BOTTLE CLUB
708 South F. Street
Lakeview, Oregon 97630

GOLD DIGGERS ANTIQUE
BOTTLE CLUB
1958 S. Stage Road
Medford, Oregon 97501

SISKIYOU ANTIQUE
BOTTLE COLLECTORS
ASSOCIATION
Box 1335
Medford, Oregon 97501

OREGON ANTIQUE BOTTLE
CLUB
Route 3 Box 23
Molalla, Oregon 97038

MOLALLA BOTTLE CLUB
Route 1 Box 205
Mulino, Oregon 97042

FRONTIER COLLECTORS
504 N. W. Bailey
Pendleton, Oregon 97801

LEWIS & CLARK
HISTORICAL BOTTLE
SOCIETY
1711 N.E. Liberty
Portland, Oregon 97211

OREGON BOTTLE
COLLECTORS
ASSOCIATION
3661 S.E. Nehalem Street
Portland, Oregon 97202

CENTRAL OREGON BOTTLE
& RELIC CLUB
1545 Kalama Avenue
Redmond, Oregon 97756

THE OREGON BEAVER
BEAM BOTTLE &
SPECIALTIES
P.O. Box 7
Sheridan, Oregon 97378

Pennsylvania

EAST COAST DOUBLE
SPRINGS SPECIALTY
BOTTLE CLUB
P.O. Box 419
Carlisle,
Pennsylvania 17013

WASHINGTON COUNTY
BOTTLE & INSULATOR
CLUB
R.D. #1 Box 342
Carmichaels,
Pennsylvania 15320

FRIENDLY JIM'S BEAM
CLUB
508 Benjamin Franklin
H.W. East
Douglassville,
Pennsylvania 19518

FORKS OF THE DELAWARE
BOTTLE CLUB
P.O. Box 693
Easton, Pennsylvania
18042

PENNSYLVANIA DUTCH JIM
BEAM BOTTLE CLUB
812 Pointview Avenue
Ephrata,
Pennsylvania 17522

ERIE BOTTLE CLUB
P.O. Box 373
Erie, Pennsylvania 16512

ENDLESS MOUNTAIN
ANTIQUE BOTTLE CLUB
P.O. Box 75
Granville Summit,
Pennsylvania 16926

DELAWARE VALLEY
BOTTLE CLUB
12 Belmar Road
Hatboro, Pennsylvania
19040

INDIANA BOTTLE CLUB
240 Oak Street
Indiana,
Pennsylvania 15701

CAMOSET BOTTLE CLUB
Box 252
Johnstown, Pennsylvania
15901

FLOOD CITY JIM BEAM
BOTTLE CLUB
231 Market Street
Johnstown, Pennsylvania
15901

EAST COAST EZRA
BROOKS BOTTLE CLUB
2815 Fiddler Green
Lancaster,
Pennsylvania 17601

THE PENNSYLVANIA
BOTTLE COLLECTORS
ASSOCIATION
825 Robin Road
Lancaster, Pennsylvania
17601

BEAVER VALLEY JIM BEAM
CLUB
1335 Indiana Avenue
Monaca,
Pennsylvania 15061

ANTIQUE BOTTLE CLUB OF
BURLINGTON COUNTY
8445 Walker Street
Philadelphia, Pennsylvania
19136

PHILADELPHIA BOTTLE
CLUB
8203 Elberon Avenue
Philadelphia,
Pennsylvania 19111

TRI-COUNTY ANTIQUE
BOTTLE & TREASURE
CLUB
R.D. #2 Box 30
Reynoldsville,
Pennsylvania 15851

PITTSBURGH BOTTLE
CLUB
1528 Railroad Street
Sewickley, Pennsylvania
15143

DEL-VAL MINIATURE
BOTTLE CLUB
Cedarbrook Hill Apts.
B-PH-12
Wyncote, Pennsylvania
19095

Rhode Island

LITTLE RHODY BOTTLE
CLUB
3161 West Shore Road
Warwick, Rhode Island
02886

South Carolina

SOUTH CAROLINA BOTTLE
CLUB
1119 Greenridge Lane
Columbia,
South Carolina 29210

GREER BOTTLE
COLLECTORS CLUB
Box 142
Greer, South Carolina
29651

LEXINGTON COUNTY
ANTIQUE BOTTLE CLUB
201 Roberts Street
Lexington, South Carolina
29072

UNION BOTTLE CLUB
107 Pineneedle Road
Union,
South Carolina 29379

PIEDMONT BOTTLE
COLLECTORS
c/o R. W. Leizear
Route 3
Woodruff, South Carolina
29388

Tennessee

COTTON CARNIVAL BEAM
CLUB
P.O. Box 17951
Memphis, Tennessee
38117

MEMPHIS BOTTLE
COLLECTORS CLUB
232 Tilton Road
Memphis, Tennessee
38111

MIDDLE TENNESSEE
BOTTLE COLLECTORS
CLUB
6401 Jocelyn Hollow Road
Nashville, Tennessee
37205

Texas

AUSTIN BOTTLE
COLLECTORS
1614 Ashberry Drive
Austin, Texas 78723

GULF COAST BEAM CLUB
128 W. Bayshore Drive
Baytown, Texas 77520

FOARD C. HOBBY CLUB
P.O. Box 625
Crowell, Texas 79227

REPUBLIC OF TEXAS JIM
BEAM BOTTLE &
SPECIALTY CLUB
616 Donley Drive
Euless, Texas 76039

TEXAS LONGHORN BOTTLE
CLUB
P.O. Box 5346
Irving, Texas 75060

FOURSOME (Jim Beam)
1208 Azalea Drive
Longview, Texas 75601

GULF COAST BOTTLE &
JAR CLUB
P.O. Box 1754
Pasadena, Texas 77501

FORT CONCHO BOTTLE
CLUB
1703 West Avenue
N. San Angelo,
Texas 76901

ALAMO CHAPTER ANTIQUE
BOTTLE CLUB
ASSOCIATION
701 Castano Avenue
San Antonio, Texas 78209

SAN ANTONIO ANTIQUE
BOTTLE CLUB
c/o 3801 Broadway
Witte Museum-
Auditorium
San Antonio, Texas 78209

Utah

UTAH ANTIQUE BOTTLE
CLUB
P.O. Box 15
Ogden, Utah 84402

Virginia

YE OLD BOTTLE CLUB
General Delivery
Clarksville, Virginia 23927

DIXIE BEAM BOTTLE CLUB
Route 4, Box 94-A
Glen Allen, Virginia 23060

HISTORICAL BOTTLE
DIGGERS OF VIRGINIA
Route 3, Box 226
Harrisburg, Virginia 22801

BOTTLE CLUB OF THE
VIRGINIA PENINSULA
Box 5456
Newport News, Virginia
23605

TIDEWATER BEAM BOTTLE
& SPECIALTY CLUB
P.O. Box 14012
Norfolk, Virginia 23518

RICHMOND AREA ANTIQUE
BOTTLE COLLECTORS
ASSOCIATION
2203 McDonald Road
Richmond, Va. 23222 .

HAMPTON ROADS AREA
BOTTLE CLUB
1521 White Dogwood Trail
Suffolk, Virginia 23433

APPLE VALLEY BOTTLE
COLLECTORS CLUB, INC.
Route 1, Box 410
Winchester, Virginia 22601

POTOMAC BOTTLE
COLLECTORS
12717 Gordon Boulevard
Woodbridge, Virginia
22192

Washington

KLICKITAL BOTTLE CLUB
ASSOCIATION
Goldendale,
Washington 98620

THE CHINOOK EZRA
BROOKS BOTTLE CLUB
233 Kelso Drive
Kelso, Washington 98626

PACIFIC NORTHWEST
AVON BOTTLE CLUB
25425 68th South
Kent, Washington 98031

SOUTH WHEDLEY BOTTLE
CLUB
c/o Juanita Clyde
Langley, Washington 98260

MT. RAINIER EZRA
BROOKS BOTTLE CLUB
P.O. Box 1201
Lynwood, Washington
98178

SKAGIT BOTTLE & GLASS
COLLECTORS
1314 Virginia
Mt. Vernon,
Washington 98273

CAPITOL COLLECTORS
AND BOTTLE CLUB
P.O. Box 202
Olympia, Washington
98502

CASCADE TREASURE CLUB
254 N.E. 45th
Seattle, Washington 98105

EVERGREEN STATE BEAM
BOTTLE & SPECIALTY
CLUB
P.O. Box 99244
Seattle, Washington 98199

SEATTLE JIM BEAM
BOTTLE COLLECTORS
CLUB
8015 15th Avenue N.W.
Seattle, Washington 98107

WASHINGTON BOTTLE
COLLECTORS
ASSOCIATION
P.O. Box 80045
Seattle, Washington 98108

INLAND EMPIRE BOTTLE &
COLLECTORS CLUB
7703 E. Trent Avenue
Spokane, Washington
99206

NORTHWEST JIM BEAM
BOTTLE COLLECTORS
ASSOCIATION
P.O. Box 7401
Spokane,
Washington 99207

NORTHWEST TREASURE
HUNTER'S CLUB
East 107 Astor Drive
Spokane,
Washington 99208

West Virginia

WILD & WONDERFUL WEST
VIRGINIA EZRA BROOKS
BOTTLE & SPECIALTY
CLUB
1924 Pennsylvania Avenue
Weirton,
West Virginia 26062

Wisconsin

SOUTH CENTRAL
WISCONSIN BOTTLE CLUB
c/o Dr. T. M. Schwartz
Route 1
Arlington, Wisconsin 53911

CAMERON BOTTLE
DIGGERS
P.O. Box 276
314 South 1st Street
Cameron, Wisconsin 54822

BADGER BOTTLE DIGGERS
1420 McKinley Road
Eau Claire,
Wisconsin 54701

BADGER JIM BEAM CLUB
OF MADISON
P.O. Box 5612
Madison, Wisconsin 53705

MILWAUKEE ANTIQUE
BOTTLE CLUB
N 88 W 15211 Cleveland
Avenue
Menomonee Falls, Wisconsin
53051

MILWAUKEE JIM BEAM
BOTTLE AND SPECIALTIES
CLUB, LTD.
N. 95th St. W. 16548
Richmond Drive
Menomonee Falls, Wisconsin
53051

SHOT TOWER JIM BEAM
CLUB
818 Pleasant Street
Mineral Point, Wisconsin
53565

CENTRAL WISCONSIN
BOTTLE COLLECTORS
1608 Main Street
Stevens Point,
Wisconsin 54481

Wyoming

CHEYENNE ANTIQUE
BOTTLE CLUB
P.O. Box 1251
Cheyenne, Wyoming 82001

INSUBOTT BOTTLE CLUB
P.O. Box 34
Lander, Wyoming 82520

CANADIAN CLUBS
Alberta

FIRST CANADIAN BOTTLE
& SPECIALTY CLUB
P.O. Box 3232, Station B
Calgary 41, Alberta, Canada

WILD ROSE ANTIQUE
BOTTLE COLLECTORS
P.O. Box 1471, Main Post
Office
Edmonton, Alberta, Canada

RANGELAND BOTTLE AND
GLASS CLUB
P.O. Box 724
Lethbridge, Alberta, Canada

British Columbia

CAMPBELL RIVER ANTIQUE
BOTTLE & RELIC CLUB
#12 2705 (N Island) Hwy.
Campbell River,
British Columbia, Canada

DIGGERS CLUB
R.R. 2
Ladysmith, British
Columbia, Canada

NANAMINO OLD TIME
BOTTLE ASSOCIATION
Parkway Drive R.R. #1
Lantzville, British Columbia
VOR 2HO Canada

OLD TIME BOTTLE CLUB
OF BRITISH COLUMBIA
P.O. Box 77154
Postal Station 5
Vancouver/6,
British Columbia, Canada

VICTORIA GLASS &
BOTTLE COLLECTOR'S
SOCIETY
2349 Millstream Road
Victoria, British Columbia,
Canada

New Brunswick

SAINT JOHN ANTIQUE
BOTTLE CLUB
25 Orange Street
Saint John,
New Brunswick, Canada

Nova Scotia

ARCADIA BOTTLE CLUB
c/o 16 Quarry Road
Halifax, Nova Scotia,
Canada

PICTOU COUNTY
HISTORICAL BOTTLE CLUB
P. 09 Box 408
Westville, Nova Scotia,
Canada

Ontario

BYTOWN BOTTLE SEEKERS
Box 4099 Station E
Ottawa,
Ontario, Canada KIS 5B1

ESSEX COUNTY ANTIQUE
BOTTLE & INSULATOR
CLUB
1079 Tuscarora Street
Windsor, Ontario N9A 3N4,
Canada

Quebec

MONTREAL HISTORICAL
BOTTLE ASSOCIATION
P.O. Box 184
T.M.R. Montreal,
Quebec, Canada

Saskatchewan

BRIDGE CITY BOTTLE
CLUB
1314 Elevator Road
Saskatoon, Saskatchewan,
Canada

PARKLAND BOTTLE
COLLECTORS
Box 75
Spy Hill, Saskatchewan,
Canada

INTERNATIONAL CLUBS

Australia

AUSTRALIAN BOTTLE
COLLECTORS' CLUB
39 Ellington Street
Ekibin, Queensland, 4121,
Australia

Bahamas

NASSAU INTERNATIONAL
ANTIQUE BOTTLE CLUB
P.O. Box 6191
Nassau, New Providence
Island, Bahamas

Canal Zone

CANAL ZONE BOTTLE
CLUB ASSOCIATION
P.O. Box 2232
Balboa, Canal Zone

England

BRITISH BOTTLE
COLLECTORS' CLUB
49 Elizabeth Road
Brentwood, Essex, England

PUBLICATIONS OF INTEREST TO BOTTLE COLLECTORS

Many of the publications listed are regional in content. We suggest you see a copy before you subscribe. Some of these publications will send a sample copy on request.

NEWSPAPERS:

The American Collector
13920 Mt. McClelland Blvd.
Reno, Nevada 89506

Antique Monthly
P.O. Drawer 2
Tuscaloosa, Alabama 35401

Antiques News
P.O. Box B
Marietta, Pennsylvania 17547

Antique Trader Weekly
P.O. Box 1050
Dubuque, Iowa 52001

Chesapeake Antique Journal
P.O. Box 500
Warwick, Maryland 21912

Collector's News
P.O. Box 156
Grundy Center, Iowa 50638

The Collector
Drawer C
Kermit, Texas 79745

Maine Antique Digest
RFD 3 Box 76-A
Waldoboro, Maine 04572

Ohio Antique Review
72 E. North Street
Worthington, Ohio 43085

Southeast Trader
P.O. Box 1068
West Columbia, South Carolina
29169

Tri-State Trader
P.O. Box 90
Knightstown, Indiana 46148

NEWSLETTERS:

Kovels On Antiques
P.O. Box 22200
Beachwood, Ohio 44122

The Milking Parlor
MILKBOTTLES ONLY
ORGANIZATION (MOO)
P.O. Box 5456
Newport News, Virginia 23605

Miniature Bottle Mart
24 Gertrude Lane
West Haven, Connecticut 06516

*The Western World Avon
Quarterly*
511 Harrison Street
San Francisco, California 94105

MAGAZINES:

Antique Bottle World
5888 Executive Boulevard
Dayton, Ohio 45424

Antiques Journal
P.O. Box 1046
Dubuque, Iowa 52001

Bottle News
P.O. Box 1000
Kermit, Texas 79745

HOBBIES
Lightner Publishing Corporation
1006 South Michigan Avenue
Chicago, Illinois 60605

"the miniature bottle collector"
P.O. Box 2161
Palos Verdes Peninsula,
California 90274

Old Bottle Magazine
The Old Bottle Exchange
525 E. Revere
Bend, Oregon 97701

Ontario Bottle Magazine
6 Tasker Street
St. Catharines, Ontario
L2R 3Z9, Canada

Pictorial Bottle Review
Brisco Publications
P.O. Box 2161
Palos Verdes Peninsula,
California 90274

Relics
P.O. Box 3338
Austin, Texas 78764

Spinning Wheel
Everybody's Press
Fame Avenue
Hanover, Pennsylvania 17331

BIBLIOGRAPHY

Most of the books not published privately and listed in the bibliography can be obtained at local bookstores. Specialized shops that carry many books not normally stocked are:

Antique Publications
Emmitsburg, Maryland 21727

Collector Books
P.O. Box 3009
Paducah, Kentucky 42001

Hotchkiss House
18 Hearthstone
Pittsford, New York 14534

Old Bottle Magazine
Box 243
Bend, Oregon 97701

This list includes most of the books about bottles available in bookstores or through the mail. Out-of-print books or price books published before 1973 are not included unless of importance as research tools.

GENERAL:

Belknap, E. M. *Milk Glass*. New York: Crown Publishers, Inc., 1959. $6.00.

Freeman, Dr. Larry. *Grand Old American Bottles*. Watkins Glen, New York: Century House, 1964. $25.00.

Kendrick, Grace. *The Antique Bottle Collector, Including Latest Price Guide*. New York: Pyramid Books, 1971. $2.95.

————. *The Mouth-Blown Bottle*. Privately printed, 1968. $6.95.

Ketchum, William C., Jr. *A Treasury of American Bottles*. Indianapolis: The Bobbs-Merrill Company, 1975. $16.95.

Klamkin, Marian. *The Collector's Book of Bottles*. New York: Dodd, Mead & Company, 1971. $8.95.

Kovel, Ralph and Terry. **Know Your Antiques.** New York: Crown Publishers, Inc. 1973. $7.95.

————. **The Kovels' Complete Antiques Price List.** New York: Crown Publishers, Inc. $7.95.

McKearin, George L. and Helen. *Two Hundred Years of American Blown Glass*. New York: Crown Publishers, Inc., 1950. $15.00.

Munsey, Cecil. *The Illustrated Guide to Collecting Bottles*. New York: Hawthorn Books, Inc., 1970. $9.95.

Neal, Nelson and Marna. *Common Bottles for the Average Collector*. Wolfe City, Texas: The University Press, 1975. $4.95.

Ohio Bottle Club, The. *Ohio Bottles, Bicentennial Edition.* (Order from The Ohio Bottle Club, P.O. Box 585, Barberton, Ohio 44203).

Paul, John R., and Parmalee, Paul W. *Soft Drink Bottling, A History with Special Reference to Illinois.* Springfield, Illinois: Illinois State Museum Society, Illinois State Museum, 1973. $5.00.

Potomac Bottle Collectors. *Washington, D. C. Bottles.* 1976. (Order from Tom & Kaye Johnson, 7722 Woodstock St., Manassas, Virginia 22110, $2.00).

Rawlinson, Fred. *Old Bottles of the Virginia Peninsula, 1885–1941.* Privately printed, 1968. $4.30. (Order from FAR Publications, P.O. Box 5456, Newport News, Virginia 23605.)

Toulouse, Julian Harrison. *Bottle Makers and Their Marks.* Camden, New Jersey: Thomas Nelson, Inc., 1971. $15.00.

Unitt, Doris and Peter. *Bottles in Canada.* Peterborough, Ontario, Canada: Clock House Publications, 1972.

ENGLISH - GENERAL:

Beck, Doreen. *The Book of Bottle Collecting.* Feltham, Middlesex, England: The Hamlyn Publishing Group Limited, 1973.

Davis, Derek C. *English Bottles & Decanters 1650–1900.* New York: The World Publishing Company, 1972. $5.95.

Fletcher, Edward. *Bottle Collecting: Finding, Collecting and Displaying Antique Bottles.* London, England: Blandford Press Ltd., 1972.

MODERN:

Avon

Hastin, Bud. *Bud Hastin's Avon Bottle Encyclopedia.* 1976–77 ed. Privately printed, 1976. $12.95. (Order from author, Box 9868, Kansas City, Missouri 64134.)

Triangle Books. *Avon's Glass Figural Bottles.* 1975. $3.00. (Order from Triangle Books, P.O. Box 1406, Mesa, Arizona 85201.)

Underwood, Beatrice and Judith Ann. *Pacific Coast Avon Museum Catalogue, 1974 Edition.* 1974. $9.95. (Order from Pacific Coast Avon Museum, 137 Park Way South, Santa Cruz, California 95060.)

Western World. *Avon 4: Western World Handbook & Price Guide to Avon Bottles.* 1975. $12.95. (Order from Western World Publishers, 511 Harrison Street, San Francisco, California 94105.)

Beam

Cembura, Al, and Avery, Constance. *Jim Beam Bottles, Identification and Price Guide.* 1976 (8th) ed. Privately printed, 1976. $5.95. (Order from author, 139 Arlington Avenue, Berkeley, California 94707.)

Bischoff

Avery, Constance and Leslie, and Cembura, Al. *Bischoff Bottles. Identification and Price Guide.* Privately printed, 1969. $4.75. (Order from Al Cembura, 139 Arlington Avenue, Berkeley, California 94707.)

Ezra Brooks

Western Collector. *Western Collector's Handbook and Price Guide to Ezra Brooks Decanters.* San Francisco, California: Western World Publishers, 1970. $4.95. (Order from Western Collector Books, 511 Harrison Street, San Francisco, California 94105.)

Garnier

Avery, Constance, and Cembura, Al. *Garnier Bottles.* Privately printed, 1970. (Order from Al Cembura, 139 Arlington Avenue, Berkeley, California 94707.)

Schwartz, Jeri and Ed. *Just Figurals: A Guide to Garnier.* Privately printed, 1969. $4.25. (Order from author, North Broadway, Yonkers, New York 10701.)

Luxardo

Avery, Constance, and Cembura, Al. *Luxardo Bottles: Identification and Price Guide.* Privately printed, 1968. $4.75. (Order from Al Cembura, 139 Arlington Avenue, Berkeley, California 94707.)

BITTERS:

Watson, Richard. *Bitters Bottles.* Fort Davis, Texas: Bartholomew House, Publishers, 1970. $4.95.

————. *Supplement to Bitters Bottles.* Camden, New Jersey: Thomas Nelson & Sons, 1968. $6.50.

CANDY CONTAINERS:

Eikelberner, George, and Agadjanian, Serge. *American Glass Containers.* Privately printed, 1967. $7.50. (Order from Serge Agadjanian, River Road, Belle Mead, New Jersey 08502.)

————. *More American Glass Candy Containers.* Privately printed, 1970. $6.00.

COLA DRINKS:

Coca-Cola Company, The. *The Coca-Cola Company ... An Illustrated Profile.* Atlanta, Georgia: The Coca-Cola Company, 1974. $5.50 (Order from The Coca-Cola Company, P.O. Drawer 1734, Atlanta, Georgia 30301.)

Goldstein, Shelly and Helen. *Coca-Cola Collectibles with Current Prices and Photographs in Full Color.* Vols. 3 and 4. Privately printed, 1974 and 1975. Vol. 3, $10.95 and Vol. 4, $13.95. (Order from author, P.O. Box 301, Woodland Hills, California 91364.)

Munsey, Cecil. *The Illustrated Guide to the Collectibles of Coca-Cola.* New York: Hawthorn Books, Inc., 1972. $12.95.

Pitcock, Florene. *Soft Drink Bottle Guide.* Privately printed. (Order from author, 30 N. Powell Ave., Columbus, Ohio 43204.)

Rawlinson, Fred. *Brad's Drink, A Primer for Pepsi-Cola Collectors.* Privately printed, 1976. $5.50. (Order from FAR Publications, Box 5456, Newport News, Virginia 23605.)

Sidlow, Peter J. *The Real Thing Price Guide, Third Edition.* Privately printed, 1975. $1.75. (Order from The Real Thing, 11702 Ventura Boulevard, Studio City, California 91604.)

FIGURAL:

Revi, Albert Christian. *American Pressed Glass and Figure Bottles.* New York: Thomas Nelson & Sons, 1964. $15.00.

Umberger, Jewel and Arthur L. *Collectible Character Bottles.* Privately printed, 1969. $12.50. (Order from Corker Book Company, 819 West Wilson, Tyler, Texas.)

Wearin, Otha D. *Statues That Pour: The Story of Character Bottles.* Denver, Colorado: Sage Books, 2679 South York Street, 1965. $6.00.

FLASKS:

McKearin, George L. and Helen. *American Glass.* New York: Crown Publishers, Inc., 1959. $14.95.

Thomas, John L. *Picnics, Coffins, Shoo-Flies.* Privately printed, 1974. $8.25. (Order from author, P.O. Box 446, Weaverville, California 96093.)

Van Rensselaer, Stephen. *Early American Bottles & Flasks—Revised.* Privately printed, Stratford, Connecticut, 1969. $15.00 (Order from J. Edmund Edwards, 61 Winton Place, Stratford, Connecticut 06497.)

FRUIT JARS:

Brantley, William F. *A Collector's Guide to Ball Jars.* 1975. $6.95. (Order from Ball Corporation, Consumer Publications, Muncie, Indiana 47302.)

Creswick, Alice. *The Red Book of Fruit Jars No. 2.* Privately printed, 1973. $7.50. (Order from Alice M. Creswick, 0-8525 Kenowa SW, Grand Rapids, Michigan 49504.)

Milligan, Harry J. *Canning Jars of Canada. A "Colcasea's" Record Book and Price Guide.* Privately printed, 1975. $3.00. (Order from author, 121 Admiral Avenue, Sarnia, Ontario N7T 5L6, Canada.)

Toulouse, Julian Harrison. *Fruit Jars: A Collector's Manual.* Jointly published by Camden, New Jersey: Thomas Nelson & Sons, and Hanover, Pennsylvania: Everybody's Press, 1969. $15.00.

INKWELLS:

Covill, William E., Jr. *Ink Bottles and Inkwells.* Taunton, Massachusetts: William S. Sullwold, Publishing, 1971. $17.50.

MEDICINE:

Baldwin, Joseph K. *A Collector's Guide to Patent and Proprietary Medicine Bottles of the Nineteenth Century.* New York: Thomas Nelson, Inc., 1973. $15.00.

Blasi, Betty. *A Bit About Balsams. A Chapter in the History of Nineteenth Century Medicine.* Privately printed, 1974. $7.50. (Order from author, 5801 River Knolls Drive, Louisville, Kentucky 40222.)

MILK:

Rawlinson, Fred. *Make Mine Milk.* Privately printed, 1970. $3.85. (Order from FAR Publications Box 5456, Newport News, Virginia 23605.)

MINIATURES:

Cembura, Al, and Avery, Constance. *A Guide to Miniature Bottles.* Vol. 1–3. Privately printed, 1972 and 1973. Vol. 1, $3.95; Vols. 2 and 3, $2.95. (Order from authors, 139 Arlington Avenue, Berkeley, California 94708.)

POISON BOTTLES:

Durflinger, Roger L. *Poison Bottles Collectors Guide.* Vol. 1. Privately printed, 1972. $3.95. (Order from author, 132 W. Oak Street, Washington C. H., Ohio 43160.)

SARSAPARILLA:

Shimko, Phyllis. *Sarsaparilla Bottle Encyclopedia.* Privately printed, 1969. $6.50. (Order from author, Box 117, Aurora, Oregon 97002.)

SODA AND MINERAL WATER:

Herr, J. A. Breweries & Soda Works of St. Thomas, Ont., 1833–1933, An Illustrated History for Bottle Collectors. Vol. 1. Ontario Series. Privately printed, 1974. $2.95. (Order from Canada West Publishing Company, 175 Alma Street, St. Thomas, Ontario N5P 3B5, Canada.)

————. *The Ontario Soda Water Bottle Collector's Index and Price Guide.* Vol. 2. Ontario Series. Privately printed, 1975. $4.95. (Order from Canada West Publishing Company.)

————. *The Ontario Stone Ginger Beer Bottle Collector's Index and Price Guide.* Vol. 3. Ontario Series. Privately printed, 1975. (Order from Canada West Publishing Company.)

Markota, Peck and Audie. *Western Blob Top Soda and Mineral Water Bottles, Revised Edition.* Privately printed, 1972. (Order from authors, 8512 Pershing Avenue, Fair Oaks, California 95628.)

WHISKEY AND BEER:

Anderson, Sonja and Will. *Andersons' Turn-of-the-Century Brewery Dictionary.* Privately printed. $15.95. (Order from author, 1 Lindy Street, Carmel, New York 10512.)

Anderson, Will. *The Beer Book, An Illustrated Guide to American Breweriana.* Princeton, New Jersey: The Pyne Press, 1973. $17.50.

Martin, Byron and Vicky. *Here's to Beers, Blob Top Beer Bottles 1880–1910.* Privately printed, 1973. $5.00. (Order from The Achin Back Saloon, 8400 Darby Avenue, Northridge, California 91324.)

1976 DISCONTINUED AVONS LIST

The following decanters are no longer offered for sale. In keeping with Avon policy, should any of these decanters be reintroduced in the future, one of the following differentiations will occur: (1) In almost every case, the container or the closure (cap) will be different in color from the original issue; (2) In some cases, the decanter will appear identical to the original but will be identified with the letter "R" to mark it as a reissue. Please note that this policy applies to containers only. Product names may be reused in the future without notification.

YEAR OF
INTRODUCTION   PRODUCT

YEAR	PRODUCT	YEAR	PRODUCT
1969	A MAN'S WORLD AFTER SHAVE (globe)	1971	BATH URN (Foaming Bath Oil—5 oz. decanter)
1971	ABRAHAM LINCOLN DECANTER	1962	BAY RUM
1968	AFTER SHAVE CADDY	1965	BAY RUM GIFT DECANTER
1965	AFTER SHAVE LOTION STEIN (8 oz.—silvery)	1972	BIG WHISTLE, THE (After Shave)
1971	ALADDIN'S LAMP (Foaming Bath Oil)	1967	BIRDFEEDER
1966	ALPINE DECANTER (flask)	1970	BO-BO THE ELEPHANT
1971	AMERICAN EAGLE (After Shave—brown glass)	1973	BON BON (Cologne— black poodle)
1973	AMERICAN EAGLE (After Shave—black glass)	1971	BUCKING BRONCO (After Shave)
1970	ANGLER, THE	1968	BUD VASE COLOGNE
1971	ARISTOCRAT NON-TEAR SHAMPOO	1971	BUFFALO NICKEL DECANTER (After Shave)
1969	AVON CALLING FOR MEN (telephone)	1970	CANDLESTICK COLOGNE (red)
1966	AVON DEFENDER (cannon)	1970	CAPITOL DECANTER, THE (5 oz. After Shave)
1967	AVON GAVEL DECANTER	1964	CAPTAIN'S CHOICE
1971	AVON LEATHER (boot decanter—8 oz. Cologne—golden closure—no strap)	1970	CAPTAIN'S PRIDE (After Shave)
		1966	CASEY'S LANTERN
		1970	CHIEF SCRUBBEM (Liquid Soap)
1971	AVON PONY EXPRESS (After Shave)	1969	CHRISTMAS COLOGNE
1968	AVON PUMP DECANTER	1967	CHRISTMAS ORNAMENT
1965	AVON ROYAL ORB	1970	CHRISTMAS ORNAMENT BUBBLE BATH
1971	AVON SEA TREASURE FOAMING BATH OIL (conch shell)	1968	CHRISTMAS SPARKLER
		1968	CHRISTMAS TREE
1973	AVONSHIRE BLUE PERFUMED CANDLE HOLDER	1963	CLOSE HARMONY
		1971	CLUCK-A-DOO (Bubble Bath)
1971	BABY GRAND PERFUME GLACE	1971	COLLECTORS ORGANIZER (duck)
1967	BATH SEASONS	1973	COLLECTORS PIPE DECANTER (After Shave)
1968	BATH SEASONS		
1969	BATH SEASONS		
1963	BATH URN	1967	COLOGNE CLASSIC

1968	COLOGNE RIVIERA
1969	COLOGNE TRILOGY
1973	COUNTRY CHARM (Cologne—butter churn)
1971	COUNTRY GARDEN BEAUTY DUST
1973	COURTING CARRIAGE (Cologne)
1970	COVERED WAGON (After Shave)
1969	CRYSTAL CANDLELIER (fragranced candle chips)
1971	CRYSTALIQUE BEAUTY DUST
1970	CRYSTALLITE COLOGNE DECANTER (candlestick)
1970	DANISH MODERN CANDLE SET
1968	DAYLIGHT SHAVING TIME
1965	DECISIONS DECISIONS DECISIONS
1965	DECORATOR SOAP MINIATURES (apothecary jar)
1972	DELFT BLUE PITCHER & BOWL (SSS decanter)
1969	DEMI-CUP
1966	DOLLARS 'N SCENTS
1968	DOLPHIN DECANTER
1973	DOLPHIN MINIATURE (Cologne)
1972	DREAM GARDEN (Perfume Oil for Bath & Body)
1973	DUTCH GIRL FIGURINE COLOGNE
1971	DUTCH TREAT DEMI-CUP (Cream Lotion)
1971	DYNASTY PERFUMED CANDLE HOLDER
1968	EASTER DEC-A-DOO
1970	EIFFEL TOWER COLOGNE
1970	ELECTRIC CHARGER (After Shave—car)
1972	FASHION FIGURINE (Elizabethan)
1974	FASHION FIGURINE— GAY NINETIES (Cologne)
1971	FIELDER'S CHOICE (baseball mitt)
1970	FIRST DOWN DECANTER (football)
1971	FIRST VOLUNTEER (fire engine)
1971	FLAMINGO DECANTER
1971	FLORAL FRAGRANCE CANDLE
1972	FLOWER BASKET SOAP DISH & HOSTESS SOAPS
1968	FRAGRANCE BELL
1965	FRAGRANCE BELLE
1971	FRAGRANCE HOURS (Cologne)
1970	FREDDY THE FROG BUBBLE BATH MUG
1969	FUTURA
1970	GAYLORD GATOR NON-TEAR SHAMPOO MUG
1971	GENERAL, THE 4-4-0 (After Shave)
1968	GENTLEMEN'S COLLECTION
1974	GIFT COLOGNE FOR MEN
1962	GIFT FANCY (fan rocker bottle)
1968	GOLDEN ANGEL
1968	GOLDEN APPLE
1969	GOLDEN LEAF PIN (perfume glacé)
1971	GOLDEN MOMENTS PERFUME (watch)
1972	GOLDEN THIMBLE (Cologne)
1972	GRECIAN PITCHER (Skin-So-Soft Decanter)
1973	HEARTS AND FLOWERS FRAGRANCE CANDLE
1969	HER PRETTINESS ENCHANTED TREE COLOGNE MIST
1972	HUNTER'S STEIN
1970	INDIAN HEAD PENNY DECANTER (After Shave)
1969	INKWELL DECANTER
1964	JEWEL COLLECTION
1970	JUMPIN' JIMMINY BUBBLE BATH
1971	KANGA WINKS GAME BUBBLE BATH
1970	LADY SLIPPER (Perfumed Soap & Perfume)

1971	SIDE WHEELER DECANTER (After Shave)	1969	STRAIGHT EIGHT (After Shave—car)
1970	SILK & HONEY MILK BATH (milk can)	1971	STRAWBERRY BATH GELÉE
1970	SILVER DUESENBERG (After Shave)	1969	STRUCTURED FOR MAN (3 Colognes: Wood, Steel, Glass)
1971	SITTING PRETTY COLOGNE DECANTER	1971	SUPER CYCLE (green)
1966	SKIN-SO-SOFT DECANTER	1969	SURPRISE PACKAGE SNOOPY DECANTER
1964	SKIN-SO-SOFT DELUXE DECANTER (fluted)	1972	SWAN LAKE COLOGNE DECANTER
1965	SKIN-SO-SOFT URN	1973	TIFFANY LAMP COLOGNE
1962	SKIN-SO-SOFT VASE	1970	TOPSY-TURVY BUBBLE BATH
1972	SMALL WONDER (caterpillar perfume)	1968	TOUCH OF BEAUTY (soap dish and soaps)
1971	SMALL WORLD COLOGNE MIST	1968	TRIBUTE COLOGNE (frosted warrior)
1971	SMALL WORLD CREAM SACHET	1967	TRIBUTE DECANTER (blue & silver warrior —After Shave)
1971	SNOOPY'S BUBBLE TUB		
1972	SNOOPY'S SNOW FLYER (Bubble Bath)	1972	TURTLE CANDLE
1970	SOLID GOLD CADILLAC (After Shave)	1967	TWENTY PACES (duelling pistols)
1971	SONG BIRD COLOGNE	1972	VICTORIAN MANOR (Cologne)
1968	SPACE ACE (rocket)	1966	VIKING HORN
1970	SPIRIT OF ST. LOUIS	1973	VOLKSWAGEN (After Shave—blue bottle)
1970	SPLASH DOWN BUBBLE BATH	1972	WATER LILY FRAGRANCE CANDLE
1970	STAGECOACH DECANTER (5 oz. After Shave)	1968	WEATHER-OR-NOT DECANTER (After Shave)
1970	STAMP DECANTER		
1971	STATION WAGON (After Shave—car)	1967	WESTERN CHOICE (steer horns)
1968	STEIN (silver redesign— 6 oz.)	1971	WESTERN SADDLE (After Shave)
1968	STERLING SIX (After Shave)	1969	WISE CHOICE (owl)
		1968	WOLF, THE

THE KOVELS'
COMPLETE BOTTLE
PRICE LIST

Alpha Industries, Battle Of The Little Big Horn, Miniature, Set Of 5 .... 55.00
Apothecary, Amadou, Blue, 9 In. .... *Color* XXXX.XX
Apothecary, Benzina Rectific, Ground Pontil, 6 In. .... *Color* XXXX.XX
Apothecary, Blown, Pressed Stopper, Amethyst, 5 1/2 In. 40.00
Apothecary, C & C Co, Ground Stopper, BIMAL, Square, 3 1/2 In. 4.00
Apothecary, Chenopod Written On Front, Ground Stopper, 10 In. 20.00
Apothecary, Cobalt, 8 1/2 In., Pair 100.00
Apothecary, Collod. Officinale, Ground Pontil, 6 In. .... *Color* XXXX.XX
Apothecary, Deep Amber, 8 1/4 In. 12.00
Apothecary, E.S.Reed's Sons, Jersey Devil, Embossed, Milk Glass, 4 1/2 In. 20.00
Apothecary, Flint, Blown, 6 In. 12.00
Apothecary, Flint, Blown, 12 In. 16.00
Apothecary, Fluid Ext. Tongua Dipterix, Shaker, Blown, Aqua, 2 Quart 60.00
Apothecary, Free-Blown, Parcel Gilt Label, C.1850, Amethyst, 16 1/2 In. 70.00
Apothecary, Ground Stopper, Rounded Corners, Square, 3 1/2 In. 3.50
Apothecary, Melvin Badger In Circle, Stain, Square, Cobalt, 8 In. 15.00
Apothecary, Pairpoint Cut Glass, Knob Finial, Bull's-Eye & Diamond, 15 In. .... * 300.00
Apothecary, Parcel Gilt Label, Tole Cover, C.1850, 19 1/4 In., Pair 100.00
Apothecary, Pontil, Amethyst, 4 In. 40.00
Apothecary, Reproduction, Amethyst, 4 3/4 In. .... * 30.00
Apothecary, Tintura Kinae, Stenciled, Gallon 26.00
Apothecary, W.T.& Co., Ground Stopper, 3 Mold, 7 1/4 In. 7.50
Apothecary, Walton On Base, 1862, Glass Label, 9 3/4 In. 25.00
Atomizer, Cut Glass, Ruby To Clear, 5 In. 65.00
Atomizer, Galle, Ovoid, Red Poppies, Metal Mounts, Yellow, 8 3/4 In. 200.00
    Austin Nichols, see Wild Turkey
Austin Nichols, Wild Turkey, Turkey On Log, 1972 .... *Illus*   20.00
Austin Nichols, Wild Turkey, Turkey On The Wing, 1973 .... *Illus*   20.00
Austin Nichols, Wild Turkey, Tom Turkey In The Straw, 1971 .... *Illus*   22.00

Austin Nichols,   Austin Nichols, Wild Turkey,   Austin Nichols, Wild Turkey,
Wild Turkey, Tom Turkey   Turkey On The Wing, 1973   Turkey On Log, 1972
In The Straw, 1971

*Avon started in 1886 as the California Perfume Company. It was not
until 1929 that the name Avon was used. In 1939 it became the Avon
Products, Inc. Each year Avon sells many figural bottles filled with
cosmetic products. Ceramic, plastic, and glass bottles are made in limited
editions.*

Avon, A Winner Boxing Gloves, 1960, Full & Boxed .... 7.00 To 10.00
Avon, After Shave On Tap, 1974, Amber, Yellow Spigot, 3 In. 1.00
    Avon, Airplane, see Avon, Spirit of St.Louis
Avon, Aladdin's Lamp, 1971-72, Gold Cap, 7 1/2 In. 3.50

Avon, Amber, Cruet, 1975, Vertical Ribs, 7 In. 3.75
Avon, American Eagle, 1971-75, Gold Plastic Head, Black, 6 In. 3.00
Avon, American Schooner, 1972-73, Blue Plastic Cap, 7 1/2 In. 2.50
   Avon, Angel, see Avon, Golden Angel, Heavenly Angel
   Avon, Angler, see Avon, Gone Fishing
Avon, Angler, Fishing Reel, 1970, Silver Plastic Cap, Blue 3.00
Avon, At Point, 1973-74, Retriever, Brown Plastic Head, Amber, 7 In. 2.00
Avon, Athena Bath Urn, 1975, Ribbed, 8 In. 4.25
Avon, Atlantic 4-4-2, 1973-75, Train, Silver Plastic Parts, Silvered, 7 1/2 I 7.99
   Avon, Auto Horn, see Avon, Its A Blast
Avon, Auto Lantern, 1973-74, Gold Cap & Gilding, Amber Windows, 6 In. 6.00
Avon, Avon Calling, Man's Decanter, 1969, Full & Boxed 9.00
Avon, Avon Calling, 1973, Wall Telephone, Gold Plastic Bell, Amber, 6 In. 4.00
Avon, Avon Classic, 1969, White Glass Bottle, Gold Cap, 11 In. 7.00
Avon, Avon On The Air, Microphone, 1975, Silver Base, Black, 5 In. 3.99
Avon, Avon Open Golf Cart, 1972, Red Bag, Silver Clubs, Green, 5 1/2 In. 3.00
Avon, Avonshire Blue Decanter, 1973, Pitcher, Pressed Cameo Pattern, 6 In. 3.50
Avon, Baby Bear Tot 'n Tyke, Shampoo, 1966-67 .... 9.00
Avon, Barber Pole, 1974-75, Red, White, & Blue Stripes, 7 In. 2.99
   Avon, Barrel, see Avon After Shave On Tap
   Avon, Barometer, see Avon, Weather-Or-Not
   Avon, Baseball Mitt, see Avon, Fielder's Choice
Avon, Bath Urn, 1971-73, Milk Glass 4.00
Avon, Bay Rum Jug, 1962, White Enamel, Light Green Neck .... 7.00 To 9.00
Avon, Beautiful Awakening 1973, Bell Alarm Clock, Roman Numerals, 4 In. 6.00
   Avon Bell, see also Avon Bell Jar, Christmas Bells, Crystal
   Song, Fragrance Bell, Hobnail Bell, Liberty Bell
Avon, Benjamin Franklin Decanter, 1975, Plastic Head, White Enameled, 6 1/2 ...... 4.50
Avon, Big Game Rhino, 1972-73, Green Plastic Head, Green, 6 In. 2.50
Avon, Big Mack, 1973-75, Truck, Beige Plastic Trailer, Green, 7 In. 5.00
Avon, Big Whistle, 1972-73, Silver Plastic Cap, Blue, 5 1/2 In. 1.50
Avon, Bird Of Happiness Colgne, 1975, Blue, Gold Plastic Head, 3 In. 3.25
Avon, Blacksmith's Anvil, 1972-73, Black Glass, Silver Top, 3 1/2 In. 2.00
Avon, Blue Demicup, 1968-70 .... 3.00
Avon, Blue Eyes, Cat, 1975, White, 4 In. 3.99
Avon, Blue Royal Swan, 1974, Gold Crown Cap, Blue, 3 In. 3.00
Avon, Bon Bon Cologne, 1973, Poodle, Black, 5 In. 3.50
   Avon, Boot, see also Miss Lollypop CologneBoot, High Button
   Shoe, Fashion Boot Pincushion, Western Boot
Avon, Boot, 1965-66, Amber Silver Top 2.50
Avon, Boot, 1966-71, Amber Gold Top 2.50
Avon, Boots & Saddle, 1968, Boxed 15.00
Avon, Bottled By Avon, Seltzer Bottle, 1973, Silvered Dispenser Top, 8 In. 3.00
Avon, Brilliantine, 1936, Full 12.00
Avon, Bucking Bronco, Man's Decanter, 1971, Full & Boxed 6.00
Avon, Bucking Bronco, 1971-72, Cowboy, Plastic Hat, Dark Amber, 8 In. 3.00
   Avon, Bud Vase, see also Avon, Butterfly Garden, Cologne Elegante,
   Emerald, Empire Green, Floral, Garnet, Grape
Avon, Bud Vase Cologne, 1965, Full 6.00
Avon, Buffalo, 1975-76, Brown Plastic Head, Amber, 6 In. 5.99
Avon, Buffalo Nickel, 1971-72, Silver Cap, Silvered, 5 In. 1.50
Avon, Bulldog, 1972-73, Pipe, Black Plastic Stem, Beige Milk Glass, 6 In. 5.00
Avon, Butter Cup Candlestick, 1975, Yellow Flowers, Milk Glass, 8 In. 7.00
Avon, Butterfly Garden, Bud Vase, 1975, Square, Black Enameled, 8 In. 1.75
Avon, Butterfly, 1972-73, Gold Head Cap, 3 1/2 In. 3.00
Avon, Cable Car, 1974 .... 6.00
Avon, Cable Car, 1975-76, White Plastic Cap, Black, 7 In. 5.99
Avon, Calabash, 1975, Pipe, Black Plastic Stem, Yellow Enameled, 6 In. 5.99
Avon, Camper, 1972-74, Truck, Beige Plastic Top, Green, 7 1/2 In. 5.00
Avon, Canada Goose, 1973-74, Black Plastic Head, Amber, 6 1/2 In. 5.00
Avon, Candle, 1969, Gold & White, Boxed 8.00
   Avon, Candlestick, see also Avon, Buttercup Candlestick, Regency
   Candlestick
Avon, Candlestick Cologne, 1971, Gold Holder, Red, 5 1/2 In. 4.50
Avon, Candlestick Cologne, 1972-75, Silvered, 7 1/2 In. 6.00

Avon, Regency, Candlestick Cologne, 1973-74, 8 In. .... 3.50 To 7.00
Avon, Candlestick Cologne, 1975-76, Pressed Pattern, Cranberry, 8 1/2 In. 7.99
Avon, Candlestick, 1966, Silvered, Pair 10.00
Avon, Cannon see Defender Cannon, Revolutionary Cannon
Avon, Captain's Choice, 1964-65 .... 9.00
Avon, Captain's Lantern, 1864 Decanter, 1975-76, Black Base, 5 1/2 In. 5.00
Avon, Capitol, 1970-72, Gold Plastic Dome Cap, Light Amber 4.00
Avon, Car, Touring T Test, 1969, Amber 35.00
Avon, Car, 1968-70, Sterling Six, Black Plastic Tire Cap, Amber Shades 3.50
Avon, Car, 1969-70, Touring T, Black Plastic Top, Black Enameled, 7 In. 4.50
Avon, Car, 1969-71, Straight Eight, Black Plastic Cap, Dark Green 3.25
Avon, Car, 1969-73, Cadillac, Gold Plastic Cap, Gold Gilded 2.00
Avon, Car, 1970-72, Packard Roadster, Amber, 6 1/2 In. 4.00
Avon, Car, 1970-72, Silver Duesenberg, Silver Plastic Trunk, 7 1/2 In. 6.00
Avon, Car, 1970-72, Volkswagen, Black .... 2.50 To 5.00
Avon, Car, 1971-72, Electric Charger, Black Enameled, 6 In. 5.00
Avon, Car, 1971-72, Stanley Steamer, Cobalt, 6 In. 2.75
Avon, Car, 1970-72, Volkswagen, Black .... 2.50 To 5.00
Avon, Car, 1971-72, Volkswagen, Red Enameled, 6 In. .... 2.00 To 5.00
Avon, Car, 1971-73, Dune Buggy, Silver Plastic Engine Cap, Blue, 6 In. 3.00
Avon, Car, 1971-73, Station Wagon, Beige Plastic Top, Green, 7 In. 5.00
Avon, Car, 1972-73, Red Depot Wagon, Black Plastic Top, Amber, 5 In. 3.50
Avon, Car, 1972-74, Model A Ford, Yellow Enameled, 6 In. 4.00
Avon, Car, 1972-74, Sure Winner Race Car, Blue Plastic Cap, Blue 1.75
Avon, Car, 1972-74, 1923 Maxwell, Tan Plastic Top, Green 4.25
Avon, Car, 1972-75, Rolls Royce, Brown Plastic Hood, Beige Enameled, 8 In. 7.00
Avon, Car, 1973-74, Volkswagen, Blue 2.00
Avon, Car, 1973-74, 1902 Haynes Apperson, Plastic Grill, Green, 5 1/2 In. 3.00
Avon, Car, 1973, Jaguar, Green Plastic Trunk, Emerald Green, 7 In. 4.00
Avon, Car, 1973, Straight Eight, Black Plastic Trunk, Dark Green 1.50
Avon, Car, 1974-75, Army Jeep, Olive Enameled, 5 1/2 In. 3.99
Avon, Car, 1974-75, Bugatti'27, Silver Top & Trunk, Black, 9 1/2 In. 7.99
Avon, Car, 1974-75, 1936 M.G., White Plastic Top, Red Enameled, 7 In. 3.50
Avon, Car, 1974-76, Avon Triumph TR-3, 1956, Green, 5 In. 3.00
Avon, Car, 1974-76, Cord, 1937, Yellow Enameled, 8 1/2 In. 3.90
Avon, Car, 1974-76, Stock Car Racer, Red & Blue Plastic Trim, 6 1/2 In. 5.99
Avon, Car, 1974-76, Stutz Bearcat, 1914, Black Plastic Trunk, Red Enameled 4.00
Avon, Car, 1975-76, Corvette Stingray, 1965, Green, 5 In. 2.66
Avon, Car, 1975-76, Volkswagen Bus, Silver Motorcycle On Rear, Red, 6 In. 4.99
Avon, Car, 1975-76, 1951 Studebaker, Cobalt, 5 In. 2.50
Avon, Car, 1975-76, 1955 Chevy, White Plastic Top, Green Enameled, 7 In. 6.00
Avon, Car, 1975, Ferrari, 1953, Amber, 5 In. 2.75
Avon, Car, 1975, Pierce Arrow, 1933, White Plastic Trunk, Blue Enameled 5.96
Avon, Car, 1976, The Thomas Flyer, 1908, White Enameled, 7 1/2 In. 4.99
Avon, Casey's Lantern, 1966-67, Gold Caps & Enameling, Amber 10.00
Avon, Casey's Lantern, 1966-67, Gold Caps & Enameling, Green 10.00
Avon, Casey's Lantern, 1966-67, Gold Caps & Enameling, Red 6.00
Avon, Cat, see Blue Eyes, Kitten Little, Kitten Petite, Tabatha
Avon, Charisma Perfume, 1969, Boxed 10.00
Avon, Charmlight, 1975, Lamp, White Pleated Shade, Red, 4 1/2 In. 8.00
Avon, Chess Piece, 1971-75, Knight, Silver Plastic Head, Dark Amber 2.00
Avon, Chess Piece, 1972-75, King, Silver Plastic Head, Dark Amber, 5 1/2 In. 2.00
Avon, Chess Piece, 1974-75, Bishop, Silver Plastic Top, Dark Amber, 6 In. 2.99
Avon, Chess Piece, 1974-75, Pawn, Silver Top, Dark Amber 1.00
Avon, Chess Piece, 1974-75, Rook, Silver Plastic Top, Dark Amber, 5 1/2 In. 2.00
Avon, Chess Piece, 1975, Knight, Silver Base, Amber, 6 In. 2.99
Avon, Chess Piece, 1975, Queen, Silver Base, Amber, 6 In. 2.99
Avon, Chess Piece, 1975, Rook, Silver Base, Amber, 5 1/2 In. 2.99
Avon, Chess Piece, 1975-76, Pawn, Silver Base, Amber, 5 1/2 In. 2.50
Avon, Chimney Lamp, 1973-74, White Frosted Shade, Pressed Glass, 5 In. 4.00
Avon, Christmas Cologne, 1969-70, Faceted, Bronze With Yellow 1.50
Avon, Christmas Cologne, 1969-70, Faceted, Gold With Blue 1.50
Avon, Christmas Cologne, 1969-70, Faceted, Silver With Green 1.50
Avon, Christmas Cologne, 1969-70, Faceted, Silver With Pink 1.50
Avon, Christmas Ornament, 1967, Gold 2.00
Avon, Christmas Ornament, 1967, Green 4.00

Avon, Christmas Ornament, 1967, Red 3.25
Avon, Christmas Ornament, 1967, Silver .... 2.50 To 6.00
Avon, Christmas, Ornament, 1968-69, Faceted, Blue 3.00
Avon, Christmas Ornament, 1970-71, Plastic, Silver Cap, Green, 4 In. 1.00
Avon, Christmas Ornament, 1975, Elliptical, Green, 2 1/2 In. 2.99
Avon, Christmas Sparkler, 1968-69, Faceted, Gold 2.50
Avon, Christmas Sparkler, 1968-69, Faceted, Green 3.00
Avon, Christmas Sparkler, 1968-69, Faceted, Red 3.50
Avon, Christmas Sparkler, 1968, Faceted, Purple 12.00
Avon, Christmas Tree, 1968-70, Gold 3.75
Avon, Christmas Tree, 1968-70, Green 3.75
Avon, Christmas Tree, 1968-70, Red 3.75
Avon, Christmas Tree, 1968-70, Silver 3.75
Avon, Christmas Tree, 1974, Vertical Ribs, Green, 5 1/2 In. 3.25
Avon, Christmas Tree, 1975, Gold Star Top, 6 1/2 In. 4.99
Avon, Christmas Tree, 1975, Red Ball Top, Green, 4 In. 2.49
Avon, Classic Decanter, 1969, Goddess, White Glass, 11 In. .... 1.25 To 8.00
Avon, Classic Lion, 1973-75, Green Plastic Head, Green, 4 1/2 In. 2.00
    Avon, Clock, see Avon, Beautiful Awakening, Daylight Shaving Time,
    Enchanted Hours, Fragrance Hours Cologne Clock
Avon, Close Harmony, Barber Bottle, 1963 .... 20.00 To 22.00
    Avon, Coffee Mill, see Avon, Country Store Coffee Mill
Avon, Cologne Crystaleque, 1975, Full & Boxed 6.00
Avon, Cologne Elegante, 1971-72, Sculptured, Rose Stopper, 12 In. 2.00
Avon, Cologne Royale, 1972-74, Crown, Gold Cap, Pressed Glass, 2 1/2 In. 1.75
Avon, Cologne Trilogy, 1969, Full & Boxed 9.95
Avon, Colt Revolver, 1975-76, Silver Plastic Barrel, Amber, 11 In. 8.99
Avon, Commemorative, 1973 .... 35.00
Avon, Compote, 1972-75, Gold Cap, Milk Glass, 5 1/2 In. 3.99
Avon, Corncob Pipe, 1974-75, Light Amber, 7 In. 4.50
Avon, Cornucopia, 1971-75, Gold Cap, 5 1/2 In. .... 3.50 To 6.00
Avon, Cotillion Perfume, 1951, Full & Boxed 115.00
Avon, Cotillion Perfume, 1953, Full & Boxed 90.00
Avon, Country Charm, Butter Churn, 1973-74, Gold Cap, 6 In. 2.25
Avon, Country Kitchen, 1973-75, Rooster, Red Plastic Head, Milk Glass, 5 In. 3.50
Avon, Country Pump, 1975, Clear, 10 In. 1.75
Avon, Country Store Coffee Mill, 1972-75, Milk Glass, 6 In. 4.50
Avon, Country Style Coffeepot, 1975, White Plastic Top, 7 1/2 In 4.88
Avon, Country Vendor, Man's Decanter, 1973, Full & Boxed 8.00
Avon, Country Vendor, 1973, Truck, Brown Plastic Top, Amber, 7 In. 4.00
Avon, Courting Lamp, 1970-71, Milk Glass Shade, Blue 6.50
Avon, Courting Lamp, 1975, Milk Glass Shade, Pink, 4 1/2 In. 4.99
Avon, Courting Rose, 1974, Gold Cap & Stem, Red 5.00
Avon, Covered Wagon, 1970-71, Gold Cap, White Top, Amber, 4 1/2 In. 6.00
Avon, Cream Hair Lotion, 1948 .... 12.00
Avon, Creamy Decanter, Milk Can, 1973-75, Basket Of Flowers, 5 1/2 In. 5.00
Avon, Cruet Cologne Set, 1973 .... 20.00
Avon, Cruet, 1973-74, Pressed Glass, 8 1/2 In. 3.00
Avon, Crystal Glory, 1962 .... 12.00
Avon, Crystallite Cologne Candlestick, 1970, Full & Boxed 3.50
Avon, Dachshund, 1973-74, Cologne Decanter, Frosted, 5 1/2 In. 3.00
Avon, Daisies Won't Tell Set, 1957, Full & Boxed 39.50
Avon, Daylight Shaving Time, 1968-70, Pocket Watch, Gold Gilded 3.00
Avon, Dear Friends, 1974, Pink Plastic Top, Pink Enamel Skirt 4.00
Avon, Deep Woods, 1972, Log, Brown Simulated 1.00
Avon, Defender Cannon, 1966, Brown Plastic Stand, Amber, 9 1/2 In. 15.00
Avon, Delft Blue Pitcher & Bowl, 1972, Blue Delft Flowers, 6 In. 3.00
Avon, Delft Blue Pitcher, 1973, Blue Delft Flowers, 8 In. 4.50
    Avon, Dog, see Avon, At Point, Bon Bon Cologne, Dachshund, Lady
    Spaniel, Old Faithful, Queen Of Scots, Noble Prince, Snoopy
    Surprise, Suzette
Avon, Dollars & Scents, 1966-67, Green Dollar, Silver Cap, Milk Glass 10.00
Avon, Dolphin, 1968, Gold Plastic Tail Cap, Frosted, 9 In. .... 3.00 To 7.00
Avon, Dolphin, 1973-74, Gold Tail Cap, Frosted, 6 1/2 In. 3.00
Avon, Dovecote Cologne, 1974-75, Gold Plastic Top, White Doves, 4 In. 3.00

Avon, Dr. Hoot, 1975, Owl, Black Plastic Head, Milk Glass, 4 1/2 In.	4.99
Avon, Dream Garden, 1972-73, Watering Can, Gold Cap, Pink Frosted, 2 In.	2.00
Avon, Dueling Pistol 1760, 1973-75, Gold Plastic Cap, 11 1/2 In.	7.99
Avon, Dueling Pistol 1760, 1973-75, Silver Plastic Cap, 11 1/2 In.	7.99
Avon, Duesenberg, see Avon, Car, 1970-72, Silver Duesenberg	
Avon, Dutch Girl, 1973-74, Light Blue Top, Dark Blue Skirt, 7 In.	3.00
Avon, Dutch Pipe, 1973-74, Meerschaum, Blue Delft Scene, Milk Glass, 6 In.	5.50
Avon, Eiffel Tower, 1970, Pressed Glass, Gold Cap, 9 In.	1.50 To 3.00
Avon, Eight Ball, 1973, Billiard Ball, Black Glass, 3 In.	.75
Avon, Eighteenth Century Classic Figurine, Young Boy, 1975	5.99
Avon, Electric Charger, see Avon, Car, 1971-72, Electric Charger	
Avon, Electric Guitar, 1974-75, Silver Neck, Amber, 9 1/2 In.	3.50
Avon, Elizabethan, Fashion Figurine, 1972, Pink Skirt, 10 In.	5.00 To 8.00
Avon, Emerald, Bud Vase, 1972, Vertical Ribs & Flutes, Petal Stopper, 9 In.	2.00
Avon, Empire Green, Bud Vase, 1975-76, Tulip Stopper, Silvered Base, 9 In.	4.99
Avon, Enchanted Hours, 1973-74, Swiss Cuckoo Clock, Gold Top, 5 In.	4.00
Avon, Evening Glow, 1973-75, Lamp, Tulip Shade, Milk Glass, 3 In.	3.00 To 7.00
Avon, Excalibur Cologne, 1969	4.00
Avon, Fashion Boot Pincushion, 1972-76, 5 1/2 In.	2.99 To 3.75
Avon, Fielder's Choice, 1971, Full & Boxed	4.00
Avon, Fielder's Choice, 1971-72, Dark Amber, Black Plastic Cap, 5 In.	1.75
Avon, Fire Alarm Box, 1974-76, Black Plastic Top, Red, 5 In.	2.00
Avon, Fire Fighter, 1975, Red Enameled, 7 1/2 In.	5.99
Avon, First Class Male, 1970-71, Red Plastic Top, Blue, 4 1/2 In.	3.00
Avon, First CPC Club Bottle, 1972	70.00
Avon, First Down Football, 1970, Boxed	4.50
Avon, First Down, 1973, White Plastic Stand, Amber, 4 1/2 In.	3.00
Avon, First Edition Book, 1967	4.00
Avon, First Volunteer, 1971-72, Fire Truck, Gold Gilded	4.50
Avon, Fish, see Avon, Dolphin, Avon, Sea Spirit	
Avon, Flamingo, 1970, Full & Boxed	3.00
Avon, Flamingo, 1971-72, Gold Cap, 10 In.	1.75
Avon, Floral, Bud Vase, 1975, Milk Glass, 9 In.	3.80
Avon, Flower Maiden, 1973-75, Yellow Skirt, 5 1/2 In.	3.49 To 4.00
Avon, Flowers In The Wind Set, 1950, Full & Boxed	70.00
Avon, Flowertime Toilet Water, 1949, Full & Boxed	13.00
Avon, Fly-A-Balloon Boy, 1975, Holding Red Balloon, 8 1/2 In.	6.99
Avon, football, see Avon, First Down	
Avon, Football Helmet, see Avon, Opening Play	
Avon, Fragrance Bell, 1965	6.50
Avon, Fragrance Bell, 1968, Full & Boxed	3.00
Avon, Fragrance Bell Cologne, 1965, Full	10.00
Avon, Fragrance Bell Cologne, 1965-66, Clear Plastic Handle	2.25
Avon, Fragrance Hours Cologne Clock, 1970-72, Grandfather, 9 In.	2.50
Avon, Fragrance Ornament Set, 1965, Boxed	40.00
Avon, Fragrance Splendor, 1971, Full & Boxed	5.00
Avon, Fragrance Touch Hand Holding Bottle, 1969-70, White Stopper	1.25
Avon, French Telephone, 1971, Gold Cap & Receiver, Milk Glass, 5 In.	20.00
Avon, Futura, 1969	12.50
Avon, Garden Girl, 1975, Plastic Top, Yellow Skirt, 6 1/2 In.	3.99
Avon, Garnet, Bud Vase, 1973-74, Diamond Quilted, Garnet Red, 6 1/2 In.	3.00
Avon, Gavel, 1967-68, Brown Plastic Handle, Dark Amber, 8 In.	9.00 To 12.00
Avon, Gay 90's Figurine, see Avon, Victorian Lady	
Avon, Giraffe, 1975-76, Gold Plastic Head, 8 In.	3.00
Avon, Girl's Bust, 1975, Plastic Head, White Enameled	5.99
Avon, Gold Coast, 1974	50.00
Avon, Golden Angel, 1968	5.00
Avon, Golden Promise Cologne, 1947, Full	11.00
Avon, Golden Rocket, 0-2-2, 1971-75, Train, Gilded, 5 1/2 In.	5.99
Avon, Golden Thimble, 1972-74, Gold Cap, 3 1/2 In.	2.00
Avon, Golf, see Avon, Avon Open, Long Drive, Perfect Drive, Swinger, Tee Off	
Avon, Gone Fishing, 1973-74, Fisherman, Light Blue Boat, 8 1/2 In.	5.50
Avon, Good Luck Elephant, 1975-78, Gold Plastic Head, 3 1/2 In.	3.00
Avon, Grape, Bud Vase, 1973, Purple Grapes, 8 In.	2.75

Avon, Grecian, 1972-76, Pitcher, Milk Glass, 6 1/2 In. 4.00
Avon, Handy Frog, 1975, Red Top Hat, White, 5 1/2 In. .... 3.99 To 4.99
Avon, Harvester, 1973-75, Tractor, Brown Plastic Grill, Amber, 6 In. 5.00
Avon, Hearth Lamp, 1973-75, Yellow & White Shade, Black, 7 1/2 In. 7.00
Avon, Here's My Heart Cologne Mist, 1958 .... 5.00
Avon, High-Button Shoe, 1975-76, Gold Plastic Cap, 5 In. 2.99
Avon, Hobnail, Bud Vase, 1973-74, Milk Glass, 7 1/2 In. 2.25
Avon, Hobnail Decanter, 1972-74, Milk Glass, 5 1/2 In. 5.00
Avon, Homestead, 1973-74, Gray Plastic Chimney, Amber, 4 In. 3.00
Avon, Honey Bear, 1974, Bear Atop Beehive, Yellow Enameled 4.00
Avon, Hunter's Stein, 1972 .... 10.00
Avon, Icicle, 1967, Gold Top, Pressed Glass 10.00
Avon, Indian Chieftain, 1972-75, Gold Plastic Cap, Amber, 3 1/2 In. 1.00
Avon, Indian Head Penny, 1970-72, Bronze Plastic Cap, Bronzed, 4 In. 1.00
Avon, Indian Tepee, 1974-75, Gold Plastic Top, Dark Amber, 4 1/2 In. 2.99
Avon, Inkwell, 1969-70, Black Cap, Gold Pen, Amber 3.25
Avon, Inkwell, 1969-70, Black Cap, Silver Pen, Amber 3.25
Avon, Insect Repellent, 1959 .... 4.00
Avon, It's A Blast Horn, 1970-71, Black Rubber Bulb, Gold Gilded, 8 1/2 In. 3.50
Avon, Key Note, 1967, Key, Gold Plastic Cap 12.00
Avon, King Pin, 1969-70, Milk Glass, White Cap, 6 1/2 In. 1.25
Avon, Kitten Little, 1972, Kitten, Milk Glass 2.00
Avon, Kitten Little, 1975-76, Black Kitten, Plastic Head, Black, 3 1/2 In. 2.50
Avon, Kitten Petite, 1973-75, White Plastic Cap, Amber Ball, 2 1/2 In. 2.99
Avon, Kitten's Hideaway, 1974-76, White Plastic Cap, Dark Amber, 3 1/2 In. 2.25
Avon, La Belle Telephone, 1974-76, Gold Plastic Top & Receiver, 5 In. 4.44
Avon, Lady Spaniel, 1974-76, Plastic Head, Milk Glass, 4 In. 1.99
Avon, Ladybug, 1975-76, Gold Plastic Head, 2 In. 2.25
    Avon, Lamp, see Avon, Hurricane Lamp, Courting Lamp, Mansion Lamp,
    Ming Blue Lamp, Parlor Lamp, Tiffany Lamp
    Avon, Lantern, see Avon, Casey's Lantern
Avon, Lavender Toilet Water, 1938-43 .... 20.00
Avon, Leg Makeup, 1643, Full 12.00
Avon, Liberty Bell, 1975-76, Bronzed Glass, Plastic Cap, 5 1/2 In. 4.99
Avon, Liberty Bell, Man's Decanter, 1971-72, Full & Boxed 5.00
Avon, Liberty Dollar, 1970-72, Gold Gilded 25.00
Avon, Liberty Dollar, 1970-75, Silver Top, Silvered, 6 In. 4.44
Avon, Little Dutch Kettle, 1972-73, Dutch Kettle, Yellow Enameled 2.50
Avon, Little Dutch Kettle, 1972-75, Gold Cap, Orange Enameled, 3 In. 4.88
Avon, Little Girl Blue, 1972-73, Blue Plastic Top, Blue Enameled, 6 In. 2.00
Avon, Little Kate, 1973-74, Girl With Muff, Apricot Enameled, 5 1/2 In. 4.00
Avon, Liquid Deodorant For Men, 1962, 2 Ozs., Boxed 8.00
Avon, Liquid Milk Bath, Milk Bottle, 1974-75, Frosted, 6 In. 3.88
Avon, Long Drive Golf Club, 1973-74, Black Plastic Cap, Amber, 6 1/2 In. 3.50
Avon, Longhorn Steer, 1975, Brown Plastic Head, White Horns, Amber, 7 In. 6.99
Avon, Lotion Lovely, 1964 .... 4.00 To 8.00
Avon, Lovebird, 1969-70, Frosted, Silver Cap, 2 1/2 In. 3.50
Avon, Mallard, 1967-68, Silver Plastic Head, Green .... 7.50 To 10.00
Avon, Mallard, 1974-75, In Flight, Green Plastic Head, 6 1/2 In. 4.50
Avon, Man's World, 1969-70, World Globe, Brown Plastic Stand, Gold Gilded 4.00
Avon, Mansion Lamp, 1975-76, Ball Chimnney, Blue Pressed Glass, 10 In. 7.99
Avon, Marblesque Cologne Mist, 1974, Urn, Green Marbelized, 5 1/2 In. 2.50
Avon, Marine Binoculars, 1973-74, Black Enameled Glass Gold Cap, 6 In. 3.50
Avon, Men's After Shave, 1967, Boxed 15.00
Avon, Ming Blue Lamp, 1974-76, White Fluted Shade, Cobalt, 7 In. 4.00
Avon, Mini-Bike, 1972-73, Silver Handle Bars, Amber, 3 1/2 In. 5.00
Avon, Minuteman, 1975-76, White, 7 1/2 In. 6.99
Avon, Miss Lollypop Cologne Boot, 1967-69, Gold Cap, Red Tassel 2.00
Avon, Miss Lollypop Ice Cream Puff Perfume Talc, 1968 .... 3.00
Avon, Moonwind Cologne Mist, 1971 .... 2.00
Avon, Nearness Body Powder, 1956-58, Frosted Glass Bottle, Blue Cap 12.00
Avon, Nearness Gift Perfume, 1955, Satin Bag 100.00
Avon, Nile Blue Bath Urn, 1972, 9 In. 4.50
Avon, Nile Green Bath Urn, 1975, 9 In. 3.75
Avon, No Parking, 1975, Red, 6 1/2 In. 3.99

Avon, Noble Prince, 1975-76, German Shepherd, Amber, 6 1/2 In. 3.00
Avon, Occur Elegance Set, 1963, Full & Boxed 16.50
Avon, Occur Perfumed Talk, 1964-65 .... 4.00
Avon, Old Faithful, 1972-73, St.Bernard, Gold Keg, Amber, 4 1/2 In. 5.00
Avon, Old Faithful, 1972-73, St. Bernard, Silver, Keg, Amber, 4 Ozs. 10.00
Avon, Opening Play, 1968-69, Blue Stripe, 4 In. 6.50
Avon, Opening Play, 1968-69, Dull Gold, 4 In. 7.50
Avon, Opening Play, 1968-69, Shiny Gold, 4 In. 18.00
Avon, Opening Play, 1973-75, White Plastic Top, Blue, 9 1/2 In. 3.30
Avon, Orchard Blossoms Cologne, 1941 .... 60.00
Avon, Oriental Egg, 1975, Chinese Pheasant, Black Plastic Base, Opalescent 4.99
Avon, Oriental Egg, 1975, Delicate Blossoms, Plastic Base, Opalescent, 3 In. 4.99
Avon, Oriental Egg, 1975, Peach Orchard Decanter, Green Plastic Base 7.50
       Avon, Ornament, see Avon, Christmas Ornament, Christmas Sparkler
       Avon, Owl, see also Avon, Dr. Hoot, Precious Owl, Wise Choice
Avon, Paid Stamp, 1970-71, Black Cap, Dark Amber 4.00
Avon, Parlor Lamp, 1971, Gold Cap, Amber Shde, Yellow, 6 In. 6.00
Avon, Parlor Lamp, 1971-72, Amber Shade, Yellow Frosted 7.00
Avon, Partridge, 1973-75, Milk Glass, 4 In. 3.00
Avon, Parisian Garden Perfume Pitcher, 1974-75, Milk Glass, 2 1/2 In. 7.50
Avon, Pear Lumiere, 1975, Gold Leaf & Stem, Pressed Glass, 5 In. 3.85
Avon, Perfect Drive, Golfer, 1975, White Plastic Cap, Green, 9 In. 5.99
Avon, Perfection Furniture Polish, 1944, Full 30.00
Avon, Perfume Oil Petites, 1966, Full & Boxed 40.00
Avon, Perfume Oil Petites, 1966, Three Hearts On Pincushion 20.00
Avon, Perfume Petite Mouse, 1970, Gold Plastic Head, Gold Tail, Frosted 10.00
Avon, Perfume Pillowette Sachet, 1965, Boxed 20.00
Avon, Persian Pitcher, 1974-75, Blue, 8 In. 3.88
Avon, Pert Penguin, 1975-76, Gold Plastic Head, 4 In. 2.00
Avon, Petite Piglet, 1972, Pig, Gold Head, 2 In. 2.00
Avon, Petti Fleur, 1969-70, Gold Leaf Cap 2.50
Avon, Pheasant, 1972-74, Amber, Green Plastic Head, 5 1/2 In. 2.00
Avon, Piano, 1972, White Plastic Top, Amber, 4 In. 1.50
Avon, Picture Frame, 1970, Boxed 7.00
Avon, Picture Frame, 1970-71, Gold Plastic Frame & Cap, Gold Gilded, 4 In. 6.00
Avon, Pineapple Decanter, 1973-74, Green Plastic Leaves, 7 In. .... .50
Avon, Pineapple Petite Cologne, 1972-74, Gold Cap, Pressed Glass, 3 In. .... .50
Avon, Pipe Dream, 1967, Pipe, Black Plastic Stem, Dark Amber .... 10.00 To 15.00
Avon, Pipe Full Decanter, 1971-72, Black Plastic Stem, Amber 2.00
Avon, Pipe Full Decanter, 1972-74, Brown Plastic Stem, Light Green 2.00
       Avon, Pistols, see Avon, Twenty Paces
       Avon, Pipe, see also Pony Express Rider, Uncle Sam
       Avon, Pitcher, see Avon, Delft Blue, Parisian Garden, Victorian,
       Venetian
Avon, Pony Express Rider, , Pipe, 1975-76, Black Plastic Stem, 7 In. 4.00
Avon, Pony Express, 1971-72, Copper Plastic Figure, Amber, 6 In. .... 4.00 To 20.00
Avon, Pony Post, 1972-73, Bronze Plastic Cap & Ring, Bronzed, 8 In. 2.75
Avon, Pony Post, 1973-74, Gold Cap & Ring, Light Amber, 5 1/2 In. 3.00
Avon, Potbelly Stove, 1970-71, Black Plastic Top, Amber, 4 3/4 In. 2.00
Avon, Precious Owl, 1972 .... 3.00
Avon, Precious Owl, 1974-75, Gold Eyes, Milk Glass, 3 In. .... .50
Avon, Precious Slipper, 1972-73, Gold Rose Cap, Frosted, 2 1/2 In. 2.50
Avon, Precious Swan, 1974-76, Gold Plastic Head, 2 In. 2.29
Avon, Precious Turtle, 1975, Tortoiseshell Glass Top, Gold Gilded, 3 1/2 In. 3.99
Avon, President Lincoln, 1973, White Plastic Head, White Enameled 5.00
Avon, President Washington, 1974-76, Plastic Head, White Enameled, 6 1/2 In. 4.99
Avon, Pretty Girl Pink, 1975, Flower Girl, , Pink Plastic Top, 6 In. 3.33
       Avon, Pump, see Avon, Country Pump, Town Pump
Avon, Purse Petite Cologne, 1971, Gold Cap & Chain, Pressed Glass 1.00
Avon, Quail, 1973-75, Amber Gold Plastic Head, 6 In. 1.99
Avon, Quaintance Perfume, 1948, Dram, Boxed 65.00
Avon, Quaintance Perfume, 1950, Full & Boxed 115.00
Avon, Queen Of Scots, 1975-76, Scottie, Milk Glass, 3 1/2 In. 2.49
Avon, Radio, 1972-73, Gold Dial & Top, Amber, 5 In. .... 2.00 To 4.00
Avon, Rainbow Trout, 1973-74, Green Plastic Head, Green, 7 1/2 In. 3.50

Avon, Ram's Head, 1975-76, Black Plastic Base, Milk Glass, 4 In.	3.25
Avon, Regal Peacock, 1973-74, Blue, Gold Cap Head, 9 1/2 In.	5.50
Avon, Regence Cologne, 1969	2.00
Avon, Regence Perfume Oil, 1968-69	7.00
Avon, Regency, Decanter, 1975, Pressed Glass Diamond Quilted, 7 In.	4.00
Avon, Remember When School Desk, 1972-74, Red Apple Cap, Black, 3 1/2 In.	4.00
Avon, Revolutionary Cannon, 1975, Gold Gilded, 5 In.	3.99
Avon, Roadrunner, 1973-74, Motorcycle, Silver Handle Bars, Blue	3.00
Avon, Roaring Twenties Fashion Figurine, 1972-74, Purple Enameled, 6 In.	2.00
Avon, Robin Red-Breast, 1974-75, Silver Plastic Head, Red Frosted, 3 In.	3.33
Avon, Royal Apple, 1972-73, Red Frosted, Gold Leaf Cap, 3 1/2 In.	4.00
Avon, Royal Coach, 1972-73, Gold Crown Cap, Milk Glass, 4 1/2 In.	3.00
Avon, Royal Coach, 1973-74, Gold Cap, 3 In.	2.00
Avon, Royal Orb, 1965	12.00 To 22.00
Avon, Royal Pekingese, 1975, Plastic Head, Milk Glass, 3 1/2 In.	2.50
Avon, Scentiments Set, 1969, Full & Boxed	5.00 To 6.00
Avon, Scimitar, 1968-69, Gold Cap, Red Jewel Windows	7.50 To 15.00
Avon, Scottish Lass, 1975-76, Blue Plastic Top, Plaid Skirt, 6 In.	4.99
Avon, Sea Legend, 1974-75, Pearled Plastic Top, 5 In.	3.00 To 5.00
Avon, Sea Horse, 1970-72, Gold Head Cap, 9 In.	1.50 To 4.50
Avon, Sea Horse Miniature, 1973-75, 6 In.	2.00
Avon, Sea Maiden, 1971-72, Mermaid, Gold Cap, 10 In.	1.50
Avon, Sea Spirit, 1974-75, Carp, Green Milk Glass, 7 1/2 In.	4.00
Avon, Sea Treasure, 1971-72, Sea Shell, Gold Cap, 7 In.	5.00
Avon, Sea Trophy, 1972, Sword Fish, Blue Plastic Head, Light Blue, 10 In.	3.50
Avon, Seashell, see Avon, Sea Treasure	
Avon, Secret Tower, 1971, Red Plastic Roof, 4 1/2 In.	.50
Avon, Secretaire, 1972-75, Gold Plastic Top, Pink Milk Glass, 7 In.	3.88
Avon, Sewing Notions, 1975, Spool Of Thread, Thimble Top, Pink, 3 In.	2.00
Avon, Side Wheeler Steam Boat, 1971-72, Amber, Gold Plastic Cap, 6 In.	2.00
Avon, Sitting Pretty, 1971-73, Rocking Chair, Gold Plastic Cat Cap, 6 In.	2.25
Avon, Skin So Soft Decanter, 1965	4.00
Avon, Skin So Soft Decanter, 1966	6.00
Avon, Skip A Rope, 1975-76, Girl, Plastic Top, Yellow Enameled, 7 In.	5.99
Avon, Small Wonder Caterpillar, 1972, Gold Head, Frosted, 2 In.	3.50
Avon, Small Wonder, 1972, Full	5.00
Avon, Smart Move, see Avon, Chess Piece	
Avon, Smart Move, 1971, Chess Piece, Full & Boxed	5.00
Avon, Snail, 1973-75, Gold Head, 6 In.	4.25
Avon, Snoopy Surprise, 1969-71, Blue Plastic Hat, Milk Glass, 5 1/2 In.	3.00
Avon, Snow Bird, 1973-75, Milk Glass, Gold Beak & Eyes, 2 1/2	2.50
Avon, Snow Bunny, 1975-76, Rabbit, Gold Plastic Head, 4 In.	3.00
Avon, Snow Man, 1973-75, Gold Hat, Frosted, 2 In.	4.99
Avon, Snowmobile, 1974-75, Black & Yellow Plastic Parts, Blue, 8 In.	4.49
Avon, Solid Gold Cadillac, see Avon, Car	
Avon, Song Of The Sea, 1975, Fish, Blue Glass, 5 In.	8.50
Avon, Spanish Senorita, 1975, Pink Top, Red-Flowered Skirt, 6 In.	4.99
Avon, Sparkplug Decanter, 1975-76, White & Red, 5 In.	2.00
Avon, Special Award Christmas Ornament, 1964	25.00
Avon, Spirit Of St.Louis, 1970-72, Airplane, Silvered Glass, 7 1/2 In.	4.50
Avon, Splash & Spray Set, 1968	20.00
Avon, Sport Of Kings, 1975-76, Thoroughbred Horse, Amber, 6 In.	4.99
Avon, Stagecoach, 1970-71, Gold Cap, Dark Amber, 4 1/2 In.	2.00
Avon, Stein, 1965, Silvered Glass Holding Plastic Bottle, 8 Oz.	4.00 To 10.00
Avon, Stein, 1968, Silvered Glass Holding Plastic Bottle, 6 Oz.	5.00
Avon, Stein, 1972, Silvered Glass Holding Plastic Bottle, 8 Oz.	4.00
Avon, Sterling Six, 1968	17.00
Avon, Stockholder's Gift, 1972	16.00
Avon, Stop & Go Light, 1975, Green, 6 In.	2.66
Avon, Straight Eight, Car, see Avon, Car	
Avon, Strawberries & Cream, 1969	6.00
Avon, Strawberries & Cream, 1969, Boxed	7.00
Avon, Strawberry Fair Perfume, 1973, Full & Boxed	4.00
Avon, Strawberry Fair Perfume, 1974-75, Silver Leaf Cap, 2 In.	2.50 To 3.00
Avon, Super Cycle, 1971-72, Motorcycle, Silver Handle Bars, Gray, 7 In.	5.00

Avon, Super Shaver, 1973, Safety Razor, Gray Plastic Blade Top, Blue 1.75
Avon, Suzette, 1973-76, Decanter, Poodle, Beige Milk Glass 3.88
    Avon, Swan, see Avon, Blue Royal Swan, Precious Swan, Swan Lake
    Cologne
Avon, Swan Lake Cologne, 1972-76, Milk Glass, 8 In. 2.00
Avon, Swan Lake Set, 1947, 3 Pieces, Full & Boxed 90.00
Avon, Sweet Shoppe, Pincushion Cream Sachet Decanter, 1972-74, 5 In. 2.00
Avon, Sweet Treat Cupcake, 1972-75, Red Cherry Plastic Cap, 2 1/2 In. 2.50
Avon, Swinger Golf Bag, 1969, Black Plastic Top, Clubs, Black 1.75
Avon, Swiss Mouse, 1974, Plastic Mouse, Yellow Cheese, 4 In. 10.00
    Avon, sword, see Avon, Scimitar 500
Avon, Tabatha, Cat, 1975, Gold Collar, Black, 7 In. 4.99
Avon, Teatime Powder Sachet, 1975, Teapot, Floral, Frosted, 2 1/2 In. 3.99
Avon, Tee Off Golf Ball, 1973-75, Yellow Plastic Tee, Milk Glass, 4 In. 2.99
    Avon, Telephone, see Avon, Avon Calling, French Telephone,
    La Belle Telephone ....
Avon, Ten-Point Buck, 1973-74, Deer, Gold Antlers, Red Amber, 4 1/2 In. 5.00
Avon, Theodore Roosevelt, Decanter, 1975, Plastic Head, White Enameled, 7 In. 5.99
Avon, Tiffany Lamp, 1972-74, Pink Leaded Shade, Amber, 8 1/2 In. 8.50
Avon, To A Wild Rose Toilet Water, 1950, Full & Boxed 12.00
Avon, Totem Pole, 1975, Enamel Figures, Dark Amber, 9 1/2 In. 3.99
    Avon, Touring T Car, see Avon, Car
Avon, Town Pump, 1968-69, Gold Cap, Black, 8 In. 2.50
    Avon, Train, see Avon General 4-4-0
Avon, Treasure Turtle, 1971-73, Gold Head, Amber, 3 1/2 In. 3.50
Avon, Tribute Frosted, Warrior, 1968-71, Head, Silver Cap .... 2.00 To 4.00
Avon, Tribute Ribbed, Warrior, 1971-73, Silver Plastic Cap 1.00
Avon, Tribute Silver, Warrior, 1967, Head, Silver Cap, Blue & Silver Enamel 7.00
Avon, Triple Crown, 1975, Horseshoe, Red Plastic Top, Amber, 4 1/2 In. 1.00
    Avon, Turtle, see Avon, Precious Turtle, Treasure Turtle
Avon, Twenty Dollar Gold Piece, 1971-72, Gold Ball Cap, Gold Gilded, 6 In. 2.50
Avon, Twenty Paces, 1967, Red-Lined Box .... 20.00 To 35.00
Avon, Twenty Paces, 1967-69, Gold Gilded, Pair In Blue-Lined Box 50.00
Avon, Twenty Paces, 1967-69, Gold Gilded, 10 In., Pair In Black-Lined Box 25.00
Avon, Twenty Paces, 1967-69, 10 In., Pair In Red-Lined Box .... 12.00 To 35.00
Avon, Uncle Sam, Pipe, 1975, Black Stem, Milk Glass, 6 In. 4.99
Avon, Unicorn, 1974-75, Gold Plastic Cap, 5 1/2 In. 3.00
    Avon, Urn, see Avon, Bath Urn, Marblesque Cologne Mist, Athena
    Bath Urn
Avon, Venetian Pitcher, 1973-75, Silver Handle 3 Top, Black Plastic Coated 4.44
Avon, Vernafleur Bath Salts, 1936, Full 25.00
Avon, Victorian Fashion Figurine, 1973-74, Green Enameled, 6 In. 3.00
Avon, Victorian Lady, 1972-73, Plastic Top, Milk Glass, 9 In. .... 2.00 To 4.00
Avon, Victorian Manor, 1972-73, Pink Roof, White Enameled, 4 1/2 In. 5.00
Avon, Victorian Pitcher & Bowl, 1971-72, Pressed Rose, 5 In. 3.25
Avon, Victorian Sewing Basket, 1975, Lavender Top, Milk Glass, 4 In. 3.88
Avon, Victorian Washstand, 1975, White Top, Blue Cap, Buff, 4 In. 3.88
Avon, Viking Horn, 1966-67, Gold Plastic Cap, Dark Amber 17.00
    Avon, Warrior-see Avon, Tribute
Avon, Warrior, 1968 .... 4.00
Avon, Warrior, 1976, Head, Silver Cap, Blue 17.00
Avon, Washington, Man's Decanter, 1970, Full & Boxed 4.00
Avon, Weather Or Not, 1969 .... 5.00
Avon, Weather-Or-Not, 1969-71, Dark Amber, Gold Eagle Cap .... 3.25 To 5.00
Avon, Western Boot, 1973-75, Silver Plastic Top & Spurs, Amber, 6 In. 4.00
Avon, Western Choice, 1967, Steer Horns, Plastic Base, Red Center, Amber 12.00
Avon, Western Saddle, 1971-72, Brown Plastic Cap, Amber, 6 In. .... 3.00 To 10.00
Avon, Whale Oil Lantern, 1975, Silver Base & Handle, Green, 7 In. 6.50
Avon, Whale Organizer, 1973, Boxed .... 18.00 To 20.00
Avon, Whale Organizer, 1973, Full & Boxed 26.50
Avon, White Moire Cologne, 1945, White Cap 35.00
Avon, White Rose, 1915, Labels, C.P.C. 30.00
Avon, Wild Turkey, 1974-75, Silver Plastic Head, Light Amber, 8 In. 4.99
Avon, Windjammer Cologne, 1969-72 .... 1.50
Avon, Wise Choice, Owl, 1969-70, Silver Plastic Head, Amber 3.50

Avon, Wishing Toilet Water, 1947, 61st Anniversary, Gold, Boxed 20.00
Avon, World's Greatest Dad, 1971, Full & Boxed 3.00
✓ Avon, 1876 Cape Cod Collection Cruet, 1975-76, Pressed Glass, Ruby, 6 In. 7.99
Ballantine, Duck, Scotch Whiskey, 14 Years Old .... *Illus* 15.00
Ballantine, Fisherman, Blended Scotch Whiskey, 14 Years Old .... *Illus* 19.00
Ballantine, Golf Bag, Scotch Whiskey, 14 Years Old, 4/5 .... *Illus* 15.00

Ballantine, Duck, Scotch Whiskey, 14 Years Old

Ballantine, Fisherman,
Blended Scotch Whiskey,
14 Years Old

Barber, Bay Rum, 10 In.

Ballantine, Golf Bag,
Scotch Whiskey,
14 Years Old, 4/5

Ballantine, Mallard, see Ballantine, Duck
Ballantine, Scotch Whiskey, C.1930, Pottery Jug, 3 In. 8.00
Ballantine, Zebra .... 6.50 To 8.00
Bank, Bear, Snowcrest 5.00
Bank, Clown, Grapette 2.50
Bank, Elephant, Grapette .... 1.50 To 2.50
Bank, Lincoln .... 7.00 To 10.00
Bank, Lucky Joe, Donald Duck Face 1.50
Bar, Pressed Glass, Ashburton, Flint, Quart 40.00
Bar, Pressed Glass, Bellflower, Single Vine, Fine Rib, Applied Lip, Flint, Quart 95.00
Bar, Pressed Glass, Frosted Leaf, Pint 125.00
Bar, Pressed Glass, Pillar, 7 In. .... 23.00 To 26.00

*Barber bottles were used at either the barbershop or the home. They held
hair tonic. These special, fancy bottles were popular in the last half of
the nineteenth century.*
Bar, Pressed Glass, Pillar, 7 In. 26.00
Barber, Baked-On Floral Design, Pontil, 7 1/2 In. 58.00
Barber, Baked-On Floral, Pink Bottom Half, 7 1/4 In. 22.50
Barber, Bay Rum, 10 In. .... *Illus* 50.00

Barber, Blown, Enamel Decoration, Amethyst, 6 3/4 In.	45.00
Barber, Blown, Enamel Decoration, Sapphire Blue, 6 3/4 In.	45.00
Barber, Blue & White Opalescent, Stars & Stripes .... *Illus*	67.50
Barber, Bohemian Glass, 8 1/2 In.	55.00
Barber, Cut Glass, Pewter Shaker Top, Intaglio Floral & Leaf, 4 7/8 In.	25.00
Barber, Cut, Vaseline, 6 1/2 In.	47.50
Barber, Dorflinger, Blue & Opalescent Swirl, 9 1/2 In.	75.00
Barber, Enamel Floral, Pontil, Green, 6 1/2 In.	58.00
Barber, Free Blown, Corset Shape, Fiery Opalescent, 8 7/8 In.	* 35.00
Barber, Free Blown, Enamel, Pontil, Yellow Green, 8 In.	* 40.00
Barber, Gold Floral, Pontil, Milk Glass, 9 In.	39.00
Barber, Hobnail, Long Neck, Ground Base, Chips, Electric Blue, 7 3/4 In.	* 90.00
Barber, Hobnail, Tooled Mouth, Opalescent, 7 In.	20.00
Barber, Hobnail, Tooled Mouth, Polished Pontil, Cranberry, 7 In.	60.00
Barber, Hobnail, 4 Rows Of Hobs On Neck, Opalescent, 7 1/2 In.	35.00
Barber, Hunt Scene, Hand Decorated, Milk Glass .... *Illus*	65.00
Barber, Lady's Leg, Amber, 7 1/2 In.	25.00
Barber, Milk Glass, Baroque Shape, Enamel Floral, Blue, 10 In.	35.00
Barber, Pewter Stopper, Octagonal Neck, Clambroth, 7 In.	32.50
Barber, Pointed Hobnail, White & Clear, Opalescent .... *Illus*	60.00
Barber, Pointed Stopper, Floral Enamel, Silver Trim, Amethyst, 8 In.	47.00
Barber, Spanish Lace, Pewter Top, Cranberry, 8 1/2 In., Pair	150.00
Barber, 6 Flute, Tooled Mouth, Opalescent Overlay, 7 In.	10.00
Barber, 6 Flute, Tooled Mouth, Red & White Overlay, 7 In.	60.00
Barber, 6 Flute, Tooled Mouth, Smooth Base, Fiery Opalescent Overlay, 7 In.	35.00
Bardi, Elephant & Donkey, Pair	11.95
Bardi, Politicals, Pair	15.00
Barsottini, Clown	10.00
Barsottini, Elk's Head	16.95
Barsottini, Rabbit	12.95
Battery, Jar, Ground Mouth, Rectangular, Aqua, 10 1/4 X 7 1/4 X 3 3/4 In.	16.50

Barber, Blue & White Opalescent, Stars & Stripes

Barber, Hunt Scene, Hand Decorated, Milk Glass

Barber, Pointed Hobnail, White & Clear, Opalescent

Beam bottles are made as containers for the Kentucky Straight Bourbon made by the James Beam Distilling Company. The Beam ceramics were first made in 1953. Executive series bottles started in 1955. Regal china specialties were started in 1955 and political figures in 1956. Customer specialties were first made in 1956, trophy series in 1957, state series in 1958.

Beam, see also Beam, Bell's Scotch

Beam, Agnew Elephant, 1970	*Illus*	2400.00
Beam, Ahepa, 1972, Club		5.00
Beam, Ahepa, 1973		8.00 To 9.00
Beam, Alaska Purchase, 1966, Centennial		9.95 To 15.00
Beam, Amvets, 1970	*Illus*	7.00
Beam, Anaheim, 1972, 2nd Convention, Club		20.00
Beam, Antioch, 1967, Centennial		80.0
Beam, Antique Trader, 1968, 11th Anniversary	*Illus*	7.00
Beam, Armanetti Award Winner, 1969		4.50 To 8.00
Beam, Alaska Purchase, 1966, Centennial		9.95 To 15.00
Beam, Armanetti Fun Bottle, 1971		8.00

Beam, Agnew Elephant, 1970

Beam, Amvets, 1970

Beam, Antique Trader, 1968, 11th Anniversary

Beam, Armanetti Vase, 1968		9.00
Beam, Ashtray, Ivory, 1955		25.00
Beam, B.P.O. Does, 1971		7.00 To 9.00
Beam, Bartender's Association, 1973		6.50 To 10.00
Beam, Baseball Centennial, 1969		5.00 To 7.00
Beam, Bass, Small Mouth, 1973, Trophy		8.00 To 12.00
Beam, Bell's Scotch, 1970		6.50 To 8.00
Beam, Bell Ringer No 1, Plaid, 1970		6.50 To 8.00
Beam, Bell Ringer No.2, Coat Of Arms, 1970		15.00
Beam, Bicentennial, 1976, Norman Rockwell		6.50 To 7.00
Beam, Bing Crosby, 29th, Pro-Am, 1970	*Illus*	8.00
Beam, Bing Crosby, 30th Pro-Am, 1971		4.95 To 5.00
Beam, Bing Crosby, 31st Pro-Am, 1972		14.00 To 22.00
Beam, Bing Crosby, 32nd Pro-Am, 1973		14.00 To 18.00

Beam, Bing Crosby, 29th, Pro-Am, 1970
(See Page 12)

Beam, Blue Goose, 1971

Beam, Bing Crosby, 33rd Pro-Am, 1974	14.00 To 25.00
Beam, Bing Crosby, 34th Pro-Am, 1975	22.50 To 29.00
Beam, Binion's Horseshoe, 1970	12.00
Beam, Black Katz Cat, 1968	8.00 To 12.95
Beam, Blue Beauty, Zimmerman's, 1973	14.00 To 17.00
Beam, Blue Cherub, Executive, 1960	75.00 To 135.00
Beam, Blue Crystal, 1971	3.00 To 5.00
Beam, Blue Daisy, Zimmerman's, 1967	7.00
Beam, Blue Fox, 1967, Club	120.00 To 125.00
Beam, Blue Gill, 1974, Trophy	8.00
Beam, Blue Goose, 1971	*Illus* 8.00
Beam, Blue Jay, 1969, Trophy	8.00
Beam, Blue Sapphire	4.00 To 5.00
Beam, Blue Slot Machine, Harolds Club, 1967	10.00 To 12.00
Beam, Bob Hope Desert Classic, 1973	14.50 To 15.00
Beam, Bob Hope Desert Classic, 1974	9.50 To 12.00
Beam, Bohemian Girl, 1974	20.00
Beam, Bowling Proprietors Club, 1974	6.50 To 9.00
Beam, Boxer, Political Series, 1974	13.95
Beam, Boys Town Of Italy, 1973	8.00
Beam, Broadmoor Hotel, 1968	5.00
Beam, Bronze Shell, Florida, 1968, State	4.00 To 5.00
Beam, Buffalo Bill, 1974	5.00
Beam, Burmese Cat, 1967, Trophy	12.00
Beam, Burro Race, Beatty, 1973	14.00 To 16.00
Beam, C.P.O., Navy, 1974	10.00
Beam, C.R.L.D.A., Club, 1973	8.00 To 9.00
Beam, Cable Car, 1968, 1969	5.00
Beam, Cal-Neva, Customer Specialty	8.00
Beam, California Derby, 1971, Golden Gate Fields	18.00 To 21.00
Beam, California Mission Club, 1973	24.00
Beam, Cameo, 1956, Blue	4.00
Beam, Cannon, 1970	2.00 To 5.00
Beam, Cardinal, Female, 1973, Trophy	15.00 To 20.00
Beam, Cardinal, Male, 1968, Trophy	44.00
Beam, Cat, Burmese, 1967, Trophy	12.00
Beam, Cat, Siamese, 1967, Trophy	12.00
Beam, Cat, Tabby, 1967, Trophy	12.00
Beam, Cedars Of Lebanon, 1973	5.00
Beam, Centennial, 1960, Santa Fe	220.00 To 225.00
Beam, Centennial, 1961, Civil War, North	35.00 To 40.00

Beam, Centennial, 1961, Civil War, South 40.00
Beam, Centennial, 1964, St. Louis Arch .... 15.00 To 20.00
Beam, Centennial, 1966, Alaska Purchase .... 9.95 To 15.00
Beam, Centennial, 1967, Antioch 10.00
Beam, Centennial, 1967, Cheyenne .... *Illus* 8.00
Beam, Centennial, 1967, St. Louis Arch, Reissue 18.00
Beam, Centennial, 1968, Reno 5.00
Beam, Centennial, 1968, San Diego .... 4.95 To 5.00
Beam, Centennial, 1969, Baseball .... 4.95 To 5.00
Beam, Centennial, 1969, Laramie .... *Illus* 6.00
Beam, Centennial, 1969, Lombard Lilac .... 4.00 To 5.00
Beam, Centennial, 1970, Preakness .... 7.00 To 9.95
Beam, Centennial, 1971, Chicago Fire 8.00
Beam, Centennial, 1971, Indianapolis Sesquicentennial .... 4.95 To 8.00
Beam, Centennial, 1972, Colorado Springs .... 5.00 To 8.00
Beam, Centennial, 1972, Dodge City, Boothill .... 6.95 To 10.00
Beam, Centennial, 1973, Phi Sigma Kappa .... 5.95 To 10.00
Beam, Centennial, 1973, Reidsville, N.C. .... 14.00 To 16.00
Beam, Centennial, 1974, Churchill Downs, 100th 8.00
Beam, Centennial, 1975, Preakness, 100th 8.00
Beam, Charisma, Executive, 1970 .... 10.00 To 13.00
Beam, Cherry Hills Country Club, 1973, Reg. China 6.50
Beam, Cherub, Blue, Executive, 1960 .... 145.00 To 170.00
Beam, Cherub, Gray, Executive, 1958 .... 250.00 To 300.00
Beam, Cherub, Lavender, Zimmerman, 1968 .... 7.00
Beam, Cherub, Pink, Zimmerman, 1968 .... 7.00
Beam, Cheyenne, Centennial, 1967 .... 5.00 To 10.00
Beam, Chicago Art Institute, 1973 .... 15.00
Beam, Chicago Fire, Centennial, 1971 .... 8.00
Beam, Churchill Downs, 95th, Pink Roses, 1969, 1970 .... 3.95 To 5.95
Beam, Churchill Downs, 95th, Red Roses, 1969, 1970 .... 7.00 To 10.00
Beam, Churchill Downs, 96th, Red Roses, 1970 .... 4.50 To 7.95
Beam, Churchill Downs, 97th, Red Roses, 1971 .... 5.95 To 8.00
Beam, Churchill Downs, 98th, 1972 .... 7.00 To 12.95
Beam, Civil War, North, Centennial, 1961 .... 35.00 To 40.00
Beam, Civil War, South, Centennial, 1961 .... 40.00
Beam, Cleopatra, 1962, Rust 3.50
Beam, Cleopatra, 1962, Yellow 14.00
Beam, Clint Eastwood, 1973 .... 8.00
Beam, Coach Devaney, 1973, Regal China Specialty 6.50
Beam, Cocktail Shaker, 1953, Glass Specialty 6.50
Beam, Coffee Warmer, 1954, ... 11.00
Beam, Collector's Edition, On The Terrace, Vol.Ii, 1967 .... 6.00
Beam, Collector's Edition, Soldier & Girl, Vol.Ii, 1968 .... 4.50
Beam, Collector's Edition, Whistler's Mother, Vol.Iv, 1969 ..... 2.00 To 3.00
Beam, Colorado Springs, Centennial, 1972 .... 5.00 To 8.00
Beam, Convention, 1st, Denver, 1971 .... 12.00 To 14.00
Beam, Convention, 3rd, Detroit, 1973 .... 26.00
Beam, Convention, 4th, Lancaster, 1974 .... 22.00 To 24.00
Beam, Covered Wagon, Harolds Club, Blue, 1969 .... 4.00 To 7.00
Beam, Crystal, Blue, 1971, Glass Specialty 4.50
Beam, Crystal, Clear, Bourbon, 1967, Glass Specialty 4.00
Beam, Crystal, Clear, Scotch, 1966, Glass Specialty .... 4.00 To 8.00
Beam, Crystal, Clear, Vodka, 1967, Glass Specialty .... 4.00 To 6.00
Beam, Crystal, Emerald, 1968, Glass Specialty 4.50
Beam, Crystal, Marbelized, 1972, Glass Specialty 4.50
Beam, Covered Wagon, 1969, Green, Regal, China Specialty ... 3.00 To 5.00
Beam, Covered Wagon, 1974, Customer Specialty 17.00
Beam, Crystal, Opaline, 1969, Glass Specialty 4.50
Beam, Crystal, Ruby, 1967, Glass Specialty .... 5.00 To 8.00
Beam, Dancing Couple, 1964 .... 70.00 To 75.00
Beam, Dancing Scot, Short, 1963 .... 28.00
Beam, Dancing Scot, Tall, 1964 .... 8.95
Beam, Decanter, Pewter, 1975, Regal China Specialty * 6.50 To 5.00
Beam, Delft, Blue, 1963 .... 3.95 To 4.50

Beam, Denver Rocky Mountain, 1970	12.00
Beam, Doe, 1963, Trophy	27.00 To 35.00
Beam, Doe, 1967, Reissue	27.00 To 30.00
Beam, Doe, English Setter, 1959, Trophy	59.00 To 70.00
Beam, Duck, 1957, Trophy	32.00 To 35.00
Beam, Ducks & Geese, 1955, Glass Specialty	6.50
Beam, Ducks Unlimited, 1972	3.95 To 9.00
Beam, Eagle, New Hampshire, 1971	33.00 To 40.00
Beam, Eagle, 1966, Trophy	12.00
Beam, Emmett Kelly, 1973, Regal China Specialty	9.00

Beam, Centennial, 1967, Cheyenne
(See Page 14)

Beam, Centennial, 1969, Laramie
(See Page 14)

Beam, Executive, 1970, Charisma

Beam, Evergreen State, 1974	20.00 To 22.00
Beam, Executive, 1955, Royal Porcelain	180.00 To 265.00
Beam, Executive, 1956, Royal Gold	95.00 To 140.00
Beam, Executive, 1957, Royal Di Monte	65.00 To 84.00
Beam, Executive, 1958, Gray Cherub	250.00 To 310.00
Beam, Executive, 1959, Tavern Scene	65.00 To 76.00
Beam, Executive, 1960, Blue Cherub	145.00 To 175.00
Beam, Executive, 1961, Golden Chalice	69.95 To 75.00
Beam, Executive, 1962, Flower Basket	50.00 To 53.00
Beam, Executive, 1963, Royal Rose	45.00 To 60.00
Beam, Executive, 1964, Royal Gold Diamond	45.00 To 60.00
Beam, Executive, 1965, Marbled Fantasy	60.00 To 72.00
Beam, Executive, 1966, Majestic	32.00 To 35.00
Beam, Executive, 1967, Prestige	10.00 To 17.00
Beam, Executive, 1968, Presidential	5.95 To 9.00
Beam, Executive, 1969, Sovereign	6.95 To 10.00
Beam, Executive, 1970, Charisma	*Illus* 13.00
Beam, Executive, 1971, Fantasia	9.95 To 11.00
Beam, Executive, 1972, Regency	9.95 To 12.00
Beam, Executive, 1973, Phoenician	9.95 To 12.00
Beam, Executive, 1974, Twin Cherubs	14.00 To 15.00
Beam, Executive, 1974, Twin Cherubs, Case	12.00 To 18.50
Beam, Executive, 1975, Reflections In Gold	10.95
Beam, Executive, 1975, Reflections In Gold, Case	15.95 To 18.50
Beam, Executive, 1976	18.00 To 20.00
Beam, Executive, 1976, Reflections In Gold	18.00 To 20.00
Beam, Executive, 1976, Reflections In Gold, Case	16.50 To 22.00

Beam, Expo 74, Regal China Specialty .... 7.95 To 14.00
Beam, Expo 76, Regal China Specialty 14.00
Beam, Fantasia, Executive, 1971 .... 10.00 To 12.00
Beam, Fantasia, Executive, 1972 .... 10.00 To 12.00
Beam, Female Cardinal, 1973, Trophy 15.00
Beam, Fiesta Bowl Football, 1972, Regal China Specialty 12.00
Beam, Fiji Islands, Regal China Specialty, 1971 .... 5.00
Beam, First National Bank Of Chicago, Customer Specialty, 1964 .... 2800.00
Beam, Fish, 1957, Trophy .... 32.50 To 35.00
Beam, Flower Basket, Executive, 1962 .... 45.00 To 53.00
Beam, Football Hall Of Fame, Regal China Specialty 9.00
Beam, Ford Roadster, 1974 .... 20.00 To 24.50
Beam, Foremost Black & Gold, Customer Specialty, 1956 .... 200.00
Beam, Foremost Gray & Gold, Customer Specialty, 1956 .... 200.00
Beam, Foremost Pink Speckled, 1956, Customer Specialty 650.00
Beam, Fox, Gold, 1969, Club .... 65.00 To 75.00
Beam, Fox, Green, 1965, Trophy .... 29.95 To 35.00
Beam, Fox, Uncle Sam, 1971 .... 10.00 To 15.00
Beam, Fox, White, 1969, Club .... 32.00 To 36.00
Beam, Franklin Mint, 1970 .... Illus   7.00
Beam, Fun Bottle, Armanetti, 1971, Customer Specialty 8.00
Beam, General Stark, Centennial, 1972, Regal China 12.00
Beam, Genie, Smoked Crystal, 1964, Glass Specialty 8.00
Beam, Germany, Hansel & Gretel, 1971 .... 6.00 To 7.00
Beam, Germany, 1970, Regal China Specialty .... 5.00 To 7.00
Beam, Germany, 1973 .... 9.00 To 10.00
Beam, Golden Chalice, Executive, 1961 .... 65.00 To 75.00
Beam, Golden Gate Casino, 1973 .... Illus   12.00
Beam, Golden Gate Fields, 1971, California Derby .... 18.00 To 21.00
Beam, Golden Gate, 1969, Customer Specialty .... 44.50 To 50.00
Beam, Golden Nugget, 1969, Customer Specialty 50.00
Beam, Grand Canyon, 1969, Regal China Specialty 15.00
Beam, Gray Cherub, Executive, 1958 .... 150.00 To 170.00
Beam, Great Dane, 1976 .... 16.00 To 17.00
Beam, Grecian, 1956, Glass Specialty 3.95
Beam, Grecian, 1961, Glass Specialty .... 4.00 To 4.50
Beam, Green China Jug, 1965 .... 5.00 To 10.00
Beam, Grey Poodle, 1970, Trophy 7.00

Beam, Franklin Mint, 1970

Beam, Golden Gate Casino, 1973

Beam, Hannah Duston, 1973, Regal China Specialty 17.00
Beam, Hansel & Gretel, 1971, Fantasy Series 5.00
Beam, Harolds Club, Blue Slot Machine, 1967 $ 10.00 To 12.00
Beam, Harolds Club, Covered Wagon, 1969, Customer Specialty 5.00
Beam, Harolds Club, Gray Slot Machine, 1967 .... 4.00 To 9.00

Beam, Harolds Club, Gray Slot Machine, 1968 .... 5.00 To 9.00
Beam, Harolds Club, Man In Barrel, No.2, 1957, Customer Specialty 450.00
Beam, Harolds Club, Man In Barrel, No.2, 1958, Customer Specialty .... 250.00 To 285.00
Beam, Harolds Club, Nevada, Gray, 1963, Customer Specialty 200.00
Beam, Harolds Club, Nevada, Silver, 1964, Customer Specialty 200.00
Beam, Harolds Club, Pinwheel, 1965, Customer Specialty 70.00
Beam, Harolds Club, Silver, Opal, 1957 .... 20.00 To 22.00
Beam, Harolds Club, V.I.P., 1967, Customer Specialty .... 45.00 To 50.00
Beam, Harolds Club, V.I.P., 1968, Customer Specialty 50.00
Beam, Harolds Club, V.I.P., 1969, Customer Specialty .... 110.00 To 125.00
Beam, Harolds Club, V.I.P., 1970, Customer Specialty .... 55.00 To 65.00
Beam, Harolds Club, V.I.P., 1971, Customer Specialty .... 55.00 To 70.00
Beam, Harolds Club, V.I.P., 1972, Customer Specialty .... 35.00 To 45.00
Beam, Harolds Club, V.I.P., 1973, Customer Specialty .... 25.00 To 40.00
Beam, Harolds Club, V.I.P., 1974, Customer Specialty .... 25.00 To 30.00
Beam, Harrah's Nevada, Gray, 1963, Customer Specialty 700.00
Beam, Harrah's Nevada, Silver, 1963 .... 900.00
Beam, Harry Hoffman, 1969, Regal China 7.00
Beam, Harvey's Wagonwheel, 1969, Glass Specialty 6.00
Beam, Hatfield, 1973, Regal China Specialty 22.00
Beam, Hawaii Aloha, 1971, Regal China Specialty .... 6.00 To 7.00
Beam, Hawaii Club, 1971 .... 8.00 TO 10.00

Beam, Illinois, 1968, State
(See Page 18)

Beam, Kentucky Colonel, 1970
(See Page 18)

Beam, King Kamehameha, 1972
(See Page 18)

Beam, Hawaii Open Pro-Am, 1972, Pineapple, Regal China Specialty .... 4.95 To 8.00
Beam, Hawaii Open Pro-Am, 1973, Pineapple, Regal China Specialty .... 5.00 To 10.00
Beam, Hawaii Open Pro-Am, 1974 .... 8.00 To 9.00
Beam, Hawaii Open Pro-Am, 1974, Tiki God, Regal China Specialty .... 5.95 To 8.00
Beam, Hemisfair, 1968, Regal China Specialty .... 8.00 To 10.00
Beam, Hoffman, Harry, 1969 .... 7.00
Beam, Horse, Black, 1961, Trophy 20.00
Beam, Horse, Black, 1967, Reissue, Trophy .... 17.00 To 19.00
Beam, Horse, Brown, 1961, Trophy 20.00
Beam, Horse, Brown, 1967, Reissue, Trophy .... 15.00 To 18.00

Beam, Horse, White, 1961, Trophy 20.00
Beam, Horse, White, 1967, Reissue, Trophy 20.00
Beam, Horseshoe Club, 1969, Customer Specialty 8.00
Beam, Humboldt County Fair, 1970 .... 10.00
Beam, Hyatt House, 1971, Customer Specialty 12.00
Beam, Indianapolis Sesquicentennlal, 1971, Centonnial 4.95
Beam, Indianapolis 500, 1970, 54th Anniversary, Regal China 7.00
Beam, International Petroleum, 1971, Regal China 7.00
Beam, Illinois, 1968, State .... *Illus* 8.00
Beam, Ivory Ashtray, 1955 .... 18.00 To 25.00
Beam, Jackalope, 1971, Fantasy Series 11.00
Beam, Jackalope, 1972, Gold .... 22.00 To 30.00
Beam, Jade, 1956 .... 3.00 To 5.00
Beam, Jewel Tea Wagon, 1974, Customer Specialty 25.00
Beam, John Henry, 1972, Fantasy Series 65.00
Beam, Jug, Green, 1965, Regal China .... 5.00 To 10.00
Beam, Jug, Oatmeal, 1966 .... 35.00 To 42.00
Beam, Jug, Turquoise, 1966 .... 4.00 To 6.00
Beam, Jug, Two Handled, Zimmerman, 1965, Customer Specialty .... 100.00 To 125.00
Beam, Kaiser International, 1971, Regal China 5.00
Beam, Katz Cat, Black, 1967, Customer Specialty 25.00
Beam, Katz Cat, Black, 1968, Customer Specialty 10.00
Beam, Kentucky Colonel, 1970 .... *Illus* 6.00
Beam, Kentucky Derby, 95th, 1969, Pink Roses, Regal China .... 3.95 To 5.95
Beam, Kentucky Derby, 95th, 1969, Red Roses, Regal China 7.00
Beam, Kentucky Derby, 96th, 1970, Red Roses .... 6.00 To 7.00
Beam, Kentucky Derby, 97th, Churchill Downs, 1971, Regal China ...... 5.95 To 6.50
Beam, Kentucky Derby, 98th, 1972, Regal China .... 5.95 To 12.00
Beam, Key West, Florida, 1973, Centennial, Regal China ...... 6.00 To 9.00
Beam, King Kamehameha, 1972 .... *Illus* 8.95
Beam, Kiwi, 1973, Trophy 7.00
Beam, Kiwi, 1974, Backwards, Trophy 20.00
Beam, Koala Bear, 1973 .... 9.00 To 10.00
Beam, Laramie, Centennial, 1968 .... 4.00 To 6.00
Beam, Las Vegas Golden Gate, 1969, Customer Specialty ...... 40.00 To 52.00
Beam, Las Vegas Golden Nugget, 1969 .... 40.00 To 52.00
Beam, Las Vegas, 1969, Regal China 5.00
Beam, Lombard Lilac, Centennial, 1969 .... 4.00 To 5.00
Beam, London Bridge, 1971, Medallion, Regal China 25.00
Beam, London Bridge, 1971, Regal China 6.00
Beam, Man In Barrel No.1, Harolds Club, 1957, Customer Specialty 450.00
Beam, Man In Barrel No.2, Harolds Club, 1958, Customer Specialty 285.00
Beam, Marbled Fantasy, Executive, 1965 .... 64.50
Beam, Marina City, 1962, Customer Specialty 35.00
Beam, Mark Antony, 1962 .... 20.00 To 24.00
Beam, McCoy, 1973, Regal China 22.00
Beam, Michigan, 1972, State .... 9.00 To 12.00
Beam, Milwaukee Club Stein, 1972 .... 50.00
Beam, Minnesota Viking, 1973 .... 6.00 To 10.00
Beam, Mint 400, 1970 .... *Illus* 9.00
Beam, Mint 400, 1970, Ceramic Stopper, Regal China .... 12.00 To 14.00
Beam, Mint 400, 1970, Metal Stopper, Regal China .... 7.95 To 8.00
Beam, Mint 400, 1971, Motorcycle Stopper, Regal China .... 4.95 To 15.00
Beam, Mint 400, 1972, Helmet Stopper, Regal China .... 8.00 To 9.00
Beam, Mint 400, 1973, Desert Rallye .... 3.95 To 10.00
Beam, Mission Club, 1970, California .... 20.00 To 24.00
Beam, Model T Ford, Black, Regal China 25.00
Beam, Model T Ford, Green, Regal China 25.00
Beam, Moila Shrine, 1972, Club .... 21.00 To 26.00
Beam, Momence Flower Festival, 1974 .... 9.00 To 10.75
Beam, Musicians On Wine Cask, 1964, Regal China 12.00
Beam, Muskie, Wisconsin, 1971, Trophy .... 9.00 To 11.00
Beam, Muskie, Wisconsin, 1971, Gold .... 28.00 To 32.00
Beam, National Bank Of Chicago, 1964 .... 2250.00 To 3000.00
Beam, National Convention, 1st, 1971, Denver, Club .... 11.00 To 14.00

Beam, Mint 400, 1970
(See Page 18)

Beam, Nebraska, 1967, State

Beam, P.G.A., 1971

Beam, National Convention, 2nd, 1972	15.00 To 17.00
Beam, National Convention, 3rd, 1973, Detroit, Club	8.50 To 22.00
Beam, National Convention, 4th, 1974	20.00 To 24.50
Beam, National Convention, 5th, 1974, Sacramento, Club	15.00 To 22.00
Beam, National Tobacco, 1973	13.00 To 15.00
Beam, Navy, C.P.O., 1974	10.00 To 12.00
Beam, Nebraska, Coach Devaney, 1973	10.00 To 12.95
Beam, Nebraska, 1967, State	*Illus* 12.00
Beam, New Germany, 1973	9.00 To 10.00
Beam, New Hampshire, Eagle, 1971, Regal	40.00
Beam, New Mexico Vase, 1972	10.00 To 19.00
Beam, New York World's Fair, 1964, Regal China	15.00 To 22.00
Beam, Nixon Bottle & Plate Set	1700.00 To 1900.00
Beam, North Shore Club, Smith's, 1972	14.00 To 29.00
Beam, Oatmeal Jug, 1966	35.00 To 42.00
Beam, Odessa Texas Oil Show, 1972	7.00 To 11.00
Beam, Ohio Hall Of Fame, 1972	10.00 To 12.00
Beam, Ohio State Fair, 1973, Regal China	7.95 To 12.00
Beam, Oldsmobile, Curved Dash, 1972, Regal China	30.00
Beam, Olympia, 1971, Glass Specialty	3.50
Beam, Olympian, 1960, Glass Specialty	5.50 To 6.00
Beam, On The Terrace, 1966, Glass Specialty	6.00
Beam, Opaline Crystal, 1969	4.00 To 6.00
Beam, Oregon, 1959, State	30.00 To 40.00
Beam, Oriental Jade, 1956, Glass Specialty	3.95 To 4.00
Beam, Pearl Harbor, 1972, Club	13.00
Beam, Peddler, Zimmerman, 1971	14.00 To 17.00
Beam, Petroleum Man	5.00 To 6.00
Beam, P.G.A., 1971	5.00
Beam, P.G.A., 1971	*Illus* 8.00

Beam, Pheasant, 1960, Trophy .... 16.00 To 22.00
Beam, Pheasant, 1961, Trophy, Reissue .... 13.00 To 16.00
Beam, Pheasant, 1963, Trophy, Reissue .... 13.00 To 16.00
Beam, Pheasant, 1966, Trophy, Reissue .... 13.00 To 16.00
Beam, Pheasant, 1967, Trophy, Reissue .... 13.00 To 16.00
Beam, Pheasant, 1968, Trophy, Reissue .... 13.00 To 16.00
Beam, Phi Sigma Kappa, Centennial, 1973 .... 5.00 To 10.00
Beam, Pied Piper, 1974, Fantasy Series 7.00
Beam, Pin, Gold Top, 1949, Glass Specialty 7.00
Beam, Pin, Wood Top, Pint, 1952, Glass Specialty 8.00
Beam, Political, Agnew Elephant, 1970 .... Illus 2400.00
Beam, Political, Donkey, 1956, Ashtray 12.95
Beam, Political, Donkey, 1960, Campaigner .... 12.50 To 16.00
Beam, Political, Donkey, 1964, Boxer .... 13.95 To 16.00
Beam, Political, Donkey, 1968, Clown 3.95
Beam, Political, Donkey, 1972, Football .... 3.95 To 5.95
Beam, Political, Elephant, 1956, Ashtray 12.95
Beam, Political, Elephant, 1960, Campaigner .... 12.50 To 16.00
Beam, Political, Elephant, 1964, Boxer .... 13.95 To 16.00
Beam, Political, Elephant, 1968, Clown .... 3.95 To 6.95
Beam, Political, Elephant, 1972, Football .... 3.95 To 5.95
Beam, Ponderosa, 1969, Hat, Regal China .... 5.00 To 6.50
Beam, Ponderosa, 1972, Hat, Regal China 15.00
Beam, Pony Express, 1968, Regal China 5.00
Beam, Poodle, Gray, 1970, Trophy .... 5.00 To 8.00
Beam, Poodle, White, 1970, Trophy 8.00
Beam, Portland Roses, 1972, Regal China .... 8.00 To 15.00
Beam, Portola Trek, 1969, Glass Specialty 3.95
Beam, Powel Expedition, 1969, Glass Specialty 8.00
Beam, Presidential, Executive, 1968 .... 11.00
Beam, Prima Donna, 1969, Customer Specialty 8.00
Beam, Rabbit, Texas, 1971, Gold .... 28.00 To 32.00
Beam, Rabbit, Texas, 1971, Trophy .... 8.00 To 10.00
Beam, Ralph's Market, 1973, Customer Specialty 18.00
Beam, Ram, 1958, Trophy 155.00
Beam, Redfin Submarine, 1970, Regal China 5.00
Beam, Red Fox, Sales, 1974, Club 2000.00
Beam, Redwood, 1967 .... Illus 10.00
Beam, Redwood Map, 1967, Regal China 7.00
Beam, Regal, Customer Specialty, 1970 .... 8.00
Beam, Regency, Executive, 1972 .... 12.00 To 20.00
Beam, Reidsville, N.C., Centennial, 1973 .... 14.00 To 16.00
Beam, Rene, The Fox, 1974 .... 32.00
Beam, Rennie The Streaker, Club 10.00
Beam, Rennie The Surfin' Fox, 1975 .... 15.00
Beam, Reno, Centennial, 1968 .... 5.00 To 9.00
Beam, Richard's New Mexico, 1967, Customer Specialty 7.00
Beam, Rifle, Yuma, 1968 .... 20.00 To 30.00
Beam, Riverside, Centennial, 1970, Customer Specialty 7.00
Beam, Robin, 1969, Trophy 8.00
Beam, Rocky Marciano, 1973, Regal China 8.00
Beam, Rocky Mountain, 1970, Club 12.00
Beam, Royal Crystal, 1959, Glass Specialty .... 3.95 To 4.00
Beam, Royal Di Monte, Executive, 1957 .... 68.00 To 84.00
Beam, Royal Emperor, 1958, Glass Specialty 6.00
Beam, Royal Gold Diamond, Executive, 1964 .... 45.00 To 60.00
Beam, Royal Gold, Executive, 1956 $ 100.00 To 125.00
Beam, Royal Opal, 1957, Glass Specialty .... 8.00 To 9.95
Beam, Royal Porcelain, Executive, 1955 .... 180.00 To 265.00
Beam, Royal Reserve .... 4.00 To 5.00
Beam, Royal Rose, Executive, 1963 .... 45.00 To 60.00
Beam, Rubber Capitol, 1972, Akron, Club .... 28.00 To 29.00
Beam, Ruidoso, Downs, 1968, Regal China 5.00
Beam, Sahara Invitational, 1971, Regal China 5.00
Beam, Sailfish, 1957, Trophy .... ?/00 To 35.00
Beam, Salute To The Navy, 1973 .... 9.00 To 11.00

Beam, Samos, 1973, Regal China 10.00
Beam, San Diego, Centennial, 1968 .... 3.00 To 5.00
Beam, Santa Fe, Centennial, 1960 .... 175.00 To 225.00
Beam, Sapphire Teal Blue, 1973, Glass Sp. 4.50
Beam, Sea Fair, 1972, Regal China .... 5.95 To 9.50
Beam, Seattle Sea Fair, 1972 .... 7.00 To 11.00
Beam, Seattle World's Fair, 1962, Regal .... 12.95 To 22.00
Beam, Shriners, 1970, Blue .... 3.95 To 5.00
Beam, Smallmouth Bass, 1973, Trophy, Customer Specialty 10.00
Beam, Smith's North Shore Club, 1972 .... 15.00
Beam, South Carolina, 1970, State 8.50
Beam, South Dakota, Mt.Rushmore, 1969 .... Illus 7.00
Beam, Sovereign, Executive, 1969 .... 8.00 To 10.00
Beam, St.Louis Arch, Centennial, 1964 .... 20.00 To 21.00
Beam, St.Louis Arch, Centennial, 1967, Reissue 15.50
Beam, St.Louis Club, 1972 .... 24.00 To 35.00
Beam, State, Alaska, 1958 .... 70.00 To 80.00
Beam, State, Alaska, 1964, Reissue 75.00
Beam, State, Arizona, 1968, 1969 .... 5.00
Beam, State, Colorado, 1959 .... 40.00
Beam, State, Delaware, 1972 .... 9.00
Beam, State, Florida, Bronze Shell, 1968 .... 5.00
Beam, State, Florida, White Shell, 1968 .... 5.00
Beam, State, Hawaii, 1959 .... 50.00 To 55.00
Beam, State, Hawaii, 1967, Reissue .... 50.00 To 57.00
Beam, State, Idaho, 1963 .... 69.00
Beam, State, Illinois, 1968 .... 6.00
Beam, State, Kansas, 1960, 1961 .... 65.00
Beam, State, Kentucky, Black Head, 1967 .... 12.00
Beam, State, Kentucky, Brown Head, 1967 .... 20.00
Beam, State, Kentucky, White Head, 1967 .... 18.00

Beam, Redwood, 1967
(See Page 20)

Beam, South Dakota,
Mt.Rushmore, 1969

Beam, State, Maine, 1970 .... 5.00
Beam, State, Michigan, 1972 .... 9.00
Beam, State, Montana, 1963 .... 85.00
Beam, State, Nebraska, 1967 .... 8.00
Beam, State, Nevada, 1963, 1964 .... 50.00
Beam, State, New Hampshire, 1967 .... 9.00

Beam, State, New Jersey, Blue, 1963 .... 66.00 To 75.00
Beam, State, New Jersey, Gold, 1963 .... 57.00 To 65.00
Beam, State, New Jersey, Gray, 1963 .... 58.00
Beam, State, New Mexico, 1972 .... 10.00
Beam, State, North Dakota, 1964 .... 95.00
Beam, State, Ohio, 1966 .... 12.00
Beam, State, Oregon, 1959 .... 38.00
Beam, State, Pennsylvania, 1967 .... 8.00
Beam, State, South Carolina, 1970 .... 5.00
Beam, State, South Dakota, 1969, 1970 .... 5.00
Beam, State, West Virginia, 1963 .... 175.00
Beam, State, Wyoming, 1965 .... 65.00
Beam, Tavern Scene, Executive, 1959 .... 65.00 To 76.00
Beam, Texas Rabbit, 1971, Gold .... 28.00 To 32.00
Beam, Texas Rabbit, 1971, Trophy 9.00
Beam, Thailand, 1969, Regal China Specialty 6.00
Beam, Tiffiny, 1973, Club 11.00
Beam, Tobacco Festival, 1973, Regal China 10.00
Beam, Tombstone, 1973 .... 7.00
Beam, Travel Lodge, 1972, Regal China .... 6.00 To 9.00
Beam, Trophy, 1957, Duck .... 32.00 To 35.00
Beam, Trophy, 1957, Fish $ 32.50 To 35.00
Beam, Trophy, 1958, Ram 155.00
Beam, Trophy, 1959, Dog .... 5..00 To 70.00
Beam, Trophy, 1960, Pheasant .... 16.00 To 22.00
Beam, Trophy, 1961, Horse, Black .... 20.00 To 26.00
Beam, Trophy, 1961, Horse, Brown 20.00
Beam, Trophy, 1961, Horse, White 20.00
Beam, Trophy, 1961, Pheasant, Reissue .... 13.00 To 16.00
Beam, Trophy, 1963, Doe .... 2M.00 To 35.00
Beam, Trophy, 1963, Pheasant, Reissue .... 13.00 To 16.00
Beam, Trophy, 1965, Fox, Green .... 29.95 To 35.00
Beam, Trophy, 1966, Eagle 12.00
Beam, Trophy, 1966, Pheasant, Reissue .... 13.00 To 16.00
Beam, Trophy, 1967, Cat, Burmese 12.00
Beam, Trophy, 1967, Cat, Siamese 12.00
Beam, Trophy, 1967, Cat, Tabby 12.00
Beam, Trophy, 1967, Doe, Reissue .... 27.00 To 30.00
Beam, Trophy, 1967, Fox, Green, Reissue .... 35.00 To 38.00
Beam, Trophy, 1967, Horse, Black, Reissue 20.00
Beam, Trophy, 1967, Horse, Brown, Reissue 20.00
Beam, Trophy, 1967, Horse, White, Reissue 20.00
Beam, Trophy, 1967, Pheasant, Reissue .... 13.00 To 16.00
Beam, Trophy, 1968, Cardinal, Male 44.00
Beam, Trophy, 1968, Pheasant, Reissue .... 13.00 To 16.00
Beam, Trophy, 1969, Blue Jay 8.00
Beam, Trophy, 1969, Robin 8.00
Beam, Trophy, 1969, Woodpecker 8.00
Beam, Trophy, 1970, Poodle, Grey 7.00
Beam, Trophy, 1970, Poodle, White 7.00
Beam, Trophy, 1971, Texas Rabbit 9.00
Beam, Trophy, 1971, Wisconsin Muskie .... 9.00 To 11.00
Beam, Trophy, 1973, Cardinal, Female 15.00
Beam, Trophy, 1973, Koala Bear 9.00
Beam, Trophy, 1973, Smallmouth Bass 10.00
Beam, Trophy, 1973, Tiffiny 11.00
Beam, Trophy, 1974, Appaloosa 8.00
Beam, Trophy, 1974, Blue Gill 8.00
Beam, Trophy, 1974, Kiwi 7.00
Beam, Trophy, 1974, Kiwi, Backwards 20.00
Beam, Truth Or Consequences, 1973, Regal China 10.00
Beam, Turquoise China Jug, 1966 .... 4.00 To 6.00
Beam, Twin Bridges, 1971, Club 58.00
Beam, Two Handled Jug, Zimmerman, 1965 .... 100.00 To 125.00
Beam, U.S.Open, 1972 .... 12.00 To 18.00

Beam, Uncle Sam Fox, 1971, Club .... 10.00 To 15.00
Beam, V.F.W., 1971 .... 6.00
Beam, V.I.P., 1967, Harolds Club, Customer Specialty .... 45.00 To 50.00
Beam, V.I.P., 1968, Harolds Club, Customer Specialty .... 4.00 To 50.00
Beam, V.I.P., 1969, Harolds Club, Customer Specialty .... 110.00 To 125.00
Beam, V.I.P., 1970, Harolds Club, Customer Specialty .... 55.00 To 65.00
Beam, V.I.P., 1971, Harolds Club, Customer Specialty .... 55.00 To 70.00
Beam, V.I.P., 1972, Harolds Club, Customer Specialty .... 35.00 To 45.00
Beam, V.I.P., 1973, Harolds Club, Customer Specialty .... 25.00 To 40.00
Beam, Viking, 1973, Regal China 8.00
Beam, Volkswagen, Blue, 1973, Regal China 22.00
Beam, Volkswagen, Red, 1973, Regal China 22.00
Beam, W.G.A., 1971, Regal China 5.00
Beam, White Poodle, 1970, Trophy 7.00
Beam, Wisconsin Muskie, 1971, Trophy .... 9.00 To 11.00
Beam, Woodpecker, 1969, Redheaded, Trophy .... 8.00 To 9.00
Beam, Yellow Katz, 1967, Customer Specialty .... 18.00 To 22.00
Beam, Yellowstone, 1972, Regal China .... 5.00 To 12.00
Beam, Yosemite, 1967 .... *Illus*   6.00
Beam, Yuma Rifle Club, 1968, Club 30.00
Beam, Zimmerman Blue Beauty, 1973 .... *Illus*   17.00
Beam, Zimmerman Blue Daisy, 1967, Customer Specialty .... 4.00 To 8.00
Beam, Zimmerman Cherub, Lavender, 1968, Customer Specialty 7.00
Beam, Zimmerman Cherub, Salmon, 1969, Customer Specialty 7.00
Beam, Zimmerman Chicago Art Institute, 1972 .... 15.00
Beam, Zimmerman Glass, 1969 .... 4.00 To 6.00
Beam, Zimmerman Jug, Green, 1965 .... 4.00 To 6.00
Beam, Zimmerman Peddler, 1971 .... 12.00
Beam, Zimmerman Two Handled Jug, 1965 .... 100.00 To 125.00
Beam, Zimmerman Vase, Brown, 1972 .... 8.00
Beam, Zimmerman Vase, Green, 1972 .... 8.00
Beam, Zimmerman Z, 1970 .... 10.00

Beam, Yosemite, 1967   Beam, Zimmerman Blue Beauty, 1973

Beer was bottled in all parts of the United States by the time of the Civil War. Stoneware and the standard beer bottle shape of the 1870s are included in this category.

Beer, Ale, Black Amethyst, Quart 12.00
Beer, Bayview, Seattle, Whittled, Green, Quart 100.00
Beer, Beaver Dam, Wis., Paper Label, 12 Ozs. 1.00
Beer, Berkshire Ale, Painted, 8 Ozs. 3.00
Beer, Blob Top, Embossed, 1880, Amber, 12 In. 2.00
Beer, Bock, Goat With Glass Of Beer On Seal, Crockery, Quart 65.00
Beer, Born & Co., Columbus, O., Blob, Dug, Stain, Amber, 11 5/8 In. 4.50
Beer, Bosch Brewing Co., Lake Linden, Mich., Blob, Amber, Quart 5.00

Beer, **Bosch Lake,** Linden, Mich., Blob, Black Amber, Quart 5.00
Beer, **Buffalo Emblem,** California, Blob Top, Amber, Quart 12.00
Beer, **Buffalo,** Amber, Quart 10.00
Beer, **C.Conrad & Co.'s Original Budweiser,** C.1876, Aqua, Quart 25.00
Beer, **Calumet Brewing,** Blob Top, BIMAL, Amber, Quart 2.50
Beer, **Carnival Glass,** Pint 12.00
Beer, **Champagne Velvet,** Brown, 9 In. .... *Illus* 1.50
Beer, **Columbia Brewing Co.,** Logansport, Ind., Blob Top, Amber, Quart 7.50
Beer, **Coors,** 4 In. .... 5.00 To 7.00
Beer, **Denver Brand,** Pint 1.50
Beer, **Dick & Bros.,** K.C., Mo., Amber, Quart 60.00
Beer, **Dublin Extra Stout,** Guiness & Davres & Co., Olive Green, 9 3/4 In. 6.50
Beer, **Eastside,** Pabst Brewing Company, Foil Label, 4 1/4 In. .... 5.00 To 6.00
Beer, **Fauser,** San Francisco, Red Amber, Quart 65.00
Beer, **Fox Head,** 6 Ozs. 8.50
Beer, **Fredericksburg,** Amber, Quart 10.00
Beer, **Furniture City Brewing Co.,** Grand Rapids, Mich., Amber, 12 Ozs. 3.00
Beer, **Gambrinus,** San Francisco, Quart 16.00
Beer, **Golden Gate,** Bear, California, Blob Top, Amber, 1/2 Pint 35.00
Beer, **Grand Rapids Brewing Co.,** Mich., Crown Top, ABM, Amber, 12 Ozs. 3.00
Beer, **Grand Rapids Brewing Co.,** Mich., Crown Top, ABM, Aqua, 12 Ozs. 3.00
Beer, **Hartmann & Fehrebach Brewing Co.,** Flying Horse, Stain, Red Amber, Pint .... * 10.00
Beer, **Henry Dakenwodel,** Phila., Embossed, Flip Cap, 12 Ozs. 5.00
Beer, **Home Brew,** Amber, Quart 1.50
Beer, **Home Brew,** Light Green, Quart 1.50
Beer, **Houston Ice Brewing Co.,** Crown Top, Embossed Star & Floral, 6 Ozs. 5.00
Beer, **Indianapolis Brewing Co.,** Brown, 9 In. .... *Illus* 8.00
Beer, **Iron Range Brewing,** Tower, Minn., Bail & Stopper, Aqua, Quart 4.00
Beer, **John Repp,** Embossed, Stoneware, Black Blob, Stripes, Quart 30.00

Beer, Champagne Velvet,
Brown, 9 In.

Beer, Indianapolis Brewing
Co., Brown, 9 In.

Beer, **Johnny Pfeiffer,** Detroit, Mich., Red, White, & Blue, 6 In. .... 10.00 To 12.00
Beer, **Jung Brg.Co.,** Milwaukee, Blob, Amber, Quart 5.00
Beer, **L.Verner,** Washington Square, Worcester, Mass., Blob Top, 9 In. 5.75
Beer, **Los Angeles Brewing Co.,** Eagle On Union Crest, Bubbles, Amber, 11 In. 175.00
Beer, **Milk Glass,** Pint 9.50
Beer, **Miller Brewing Co.,** 1939, Brown, 12 Ozs. .... *Illus* 4.00
Beer, **Miller Brewing Co.,** 1936, 12 Ozs. .... *Illus* 5.00
Beer, **Miller,** Export, 1935, 12 Ozs. .... *Illus* 7.00
Beer, **Miller's Draught Picnic,** 1938, Brown, 1/2 Gallon .... *Illus* 7.00
Beer, **Miller's High Life,** 1935, 12 Ozs. .... *Illus* 5.00
Beer, **Miller's University Club Lager,** 1931, 12 Ozs. .... *Illus* 5.00
Beer, **Miller's University Club Lager,** 1935, 12 Ozs. .... *Illus* 5.00
Beer, **Miniature, see Miniature, Beer**
Beer, **National,** Eagle, A.D.B.Lang, California, Blob Top, Amber, Pint 20.00

Beer, Miller's University Club Lager,
1935, 12 Ozs.
Beer, Miller, Export, 1935, 12 Ozs.
Beer, Miller's High Life, 1935, 12 Ozs.
(See Page 24)

Beer, Miller's University Club Lager,
1931, 12 Ozs.
Beer, Miller's Draught Picnic, 1938, Brown, 1/2 Gallon
Beer, Miller Brewing Co., 1936, 12 Ozs.
Beer, Miller Brewing Co., 1939, Brown, 12 Ozs.
(See Page 24)

Beer, **National,** Eagle, A.D.B.Lang, California, Blob Top, Amber, Quart	30.00
Beer, **National,** 524 Fulton, Quart	28.00
Beer, **Oertel's Little Brown Jug Ale,** Chalkware, 3 In.	15.00 To 20.00
Beer, **Pabst Brewing Co.,** Milwaukee, Wis., Blob, Amber, Quart	5.00
Beer, **Pale Reserve,** Painted, 8 Ozs.	3.00
Beer, **Phil Scheuermann Brewery,** Hancock, Mich., Blob, Amber, Quart	5.00
Beer, **Porter,** C.1750, OP, Bubbles, Olive Green, 8 In.	65.00
Beer, **Ranier Bottling Works,** Reno, Nev., BIMAL, Amber, Quart	14.00
Beer, **Raspiller,** Eagle, California, Blob Top, Amber, Quart	45.00
Beer, **Reno,** Quart	8.00
Beer, **Reymann Brewing Co.,** Wheeling, W.Va., Blob Top, Amber, Quart	5.00
Beer, **Riverside Brewery,** Zanesville, Ohio, Blob Top, Quart	60.00 To 125.00
Beer, **Royal Bohemian,** Paper Label, 12 Ozs.	1.00
Beer, **Ruby Red,** Quart	10.00 To 25.00
Beer, **Sandkuhler's Weiss,** Baltimore, Crockery, 7 In.	15.00
Beer, **Schlitz,** C.1940, Anchor Glass, Royal Ruby, Quart	6.00
Beer, **Schlitz,** Crown Top, Embossed, Amber, Pint	10.00
Beer, **Schlitz,** Gold Globe	7.00 To 9.00
Beer, **Schlitz,** Ruby Red, Quart	6.00
Beer, **Schlitz,** Ruby Red, 7 Ozs.	15.00
Beer, **Sterling,** Paper Label, Quart	3.50
Beer, **Tennessee Brewing Co.,** Memphis, Paper Label, Squat, 12 Ozs.	7.50
Beer, **Tennessee Brewing Co.,** Memphis, Paper Label, 7 Ozs.	6.00
Beer, **Tennessee Brewing Co.,** Memphis, Paper Label, 12 Ozs.	5.00
Beer, **Tennessee Brewing Co.,** Memphis, Paper Label, 16 Ozs.	7.50
Beer, **Tivoli,** Pint	1.50
Beer, **Torch Lake Brewery,** Jos.Bosch & Co., Blob, Amber, Quart	5.00
Beer, **Uneeda Brewery,** Wheeling, W.Va., 1919, Quart	12.00
Beer, **Val Blatz,** Embossed, Aqua, 7 Ozs.	1.00
Beer, **Val Blatz,** Embossed, 7 1/2 Ozs.	1.00
Beer, **Van Merrit,** Burlington, Wis., Paper Label, 7 Ozs.	1.00
Beer, **Van Merrit,** Burlington, Wis., Paper Label, 12 Ozs.	1.00

Beer, W.H.Hennessey, Lynn, Mass., Crown Top, Paneled Base, Green, 9 1/2 In. 20.00
Beer, Walter Brewing Co., Pueblo, Colorado, Blop, Stain, Amber, Pint 12.00
Beer, William Simon Brewery, Buffalo, N.Y., 1934, Amber, 12 Ozs. 5.00
Beer, Ziegler Old Fashioned Lager, Paper Label, 8 Ozs. 1.00
Beer, 3 Mold, Blob Top With Skirt, Embossed Crown, Whittled, Black, 8 3/4 In. 12.00
Beer, 3 Mold, Collared Lip, Whittled, Retired Pontil, Black, 9 1/2 In. 12.00
Bininger & Co., Cannon Shape, Stain, Yellow Amber, 12 1/2 In. .... * 500.00
Bininger & Co., Jug, Applied Handle, Amber, 3/4 Quart .... * 210.00
Bininger & Co., Jug, Applied Handle, Golden Amber, 3/4 Quart .... * 340.00
Bininger & Co., Jug, Applied Handle, Olive Green, 3/4 Quart *1300.00
Bininger & Co., New York, Square, Amber, 3/4 Quart .... * 30.00
Bininger & Co., New York, Square, Apricot, 3/4 Quart .... * 210.00
Bininger & Co., 19 Broad St., Urn, Handle, Amber, 9 3/4 In. *1250.00
Bininger, Banana Juice, Collared Mouth, Olive Green, 3/4 Quart .... * 790.00
Bininger, Barrel, OP, Amber, Pint 150.00
Bininger, Barrel, OP, Amber, Quart 150.00
Bininger, Barrel, OP, Quart 165.00
Bininger, Cannon, 19 Broad St., Rough, Amber, 3/4 Quart .... Illus   300.00
Bininger, Clock, Regulator, No.19 Broad St., N.Y., OP, Dark Amber, 1/2 Pint 350.00
Bininger, Daydream, 19 Broad St., Applied Handle, Amber, 3/4 Quart *3200.00
Bininger, Dewitt Gin, N.Y., Tapered, Square, Olive Green, 3/4 Quart .... * 750.00
Bininger, Gin, N.Y., Applied Flared Mouth, Square, Green, 3/4 Quart 925.00
Bininger, Gin, Square Face, Collared Mouth, Green, 3/4 Quart *1400.00
Bininger, Golden Apple Cordial, 338 Broadway, Bruise, Olive, 3/4 Quart .... * 280.00
Bininger, Jug, Handle, Light Amber, 7 1/2 In. 225.00
Bininger, Knickerbocker, 19 Broad St., Handle, Crack, Amber, Pint .... * 900.00
Bininger, London Dock Gin, Amber, Pint 50.00
Bininger, London Dock Gin, Amber, Quart 50.00
Bininger, Night Cap, No.19 Broad St., Flask, Pontil, Amber, Pint .... * 270.00
Bininger, No.19 Broad St., Urn Shape, Yellow Amber, 9 3/4 In. .... * 950.00
Bininger, No.375 Broadway, N.Y., Square, Topaz, Quart .... * 45.00
Bininger, Old Dominion, Wheat Tonic, No.19, Amber, 3/4 Quart .... * 65.00
Bininger, Old Dominion, Wheat Tonic, Yellow Olive, 3/4 Quart .... * 70.00
Bininger, Old Kentuck Bourbon, 1848 .... Illus   90.00
Bininger, Old Kentucky Bourbon, 1849 Reserve, Handle, Yellow Amber .... * 110.00
Bininger, Old Kentucky Bourbon, 1849, Barrel, 14 Rings, Amber, 3/4 Quart .... * 150.00
Bininger, Old Kentucky Bourbon, 1849, Barrel, 16 Rings, Amber, Quart .... * 130.00
Bininger, Old Kentucky Bourbon, 1849, Barrel, 16 Rings, 3/4 Quart .... * 290.00
Bininger, Old Kentucky Bourbon, 1849, Yellow Green, 3/4 Quart .... * 100.00

Bininger, Cannon, 19 Broad Street,
Rough, Amber, 3/4 Quart

Bininger, Old Kentuck Bourbon, 1848

Bininger, Old London Dock Gin, No.17 Broad St., Blue Green, 3/4 Quart .... * 150.00
Bininger, Old London Dock Gin, No.17 Broad St., Yellow Olive, 3/4 Quart .... * 60.00
Bininger, Old London Dock Gin, No.19 Broad St., Amber, 8 In. 28.00
Bininger, Old London Dock Gin, No.19 Broad St., Golden Amber, 3/4 Quart .... * 50.00
Bininger, Old London Dock Gin, No.19 Broad St., Yellow Amber, 3/4 Quart .... * 40.00
Bininger, Old London Dock Gin, No.338 Broad St., Olive Green, 3/4 Quart .... * 35.00
Bininger, Old Times Family Rye, 1848, Yellow Green, Quart .... * 350.00
Bininger, Peep-O-Day, No.19 Broad St., Flask, Amber, Pint, Chip .... * 325.00
Bininger, Pioneer Bourbon, Applied Handle, Pontil, Amber, 3/4 Quart .... * 290.00
Bininger, Regulator Clock, Double Collared Mouth, Amber, Pint .... * 325.00
Bininger, Regulator, 19 Broad St., Chips, Amber, Pint .... * 300.00
Bininger, Regulator, 19 Broad St., Pontil, Aqua, Pint .... * 900.00
Bininger, Whiskey, Square, Quart 50.00

Bischoff Company has made fancy decanters since it was founded in 1777 in Trieste, Italy. The modern collectible Bischoff bottles have been imported to the United States since about 1950. Glass, porcelain, and stoneware decanters and figurals are made.
Bischoff, Doe 9.95

Bitters bottles held the famous 19th-century medicine called bitters. It was often of such a high alcohol content that the user felt healthier with each sip. The word bitters must be embossed on the glass or a paper label must be affixed for the collector to call the bottle a bitters bottle. Most date from 1840 to 1900. The numbers used in the entries in the form W-0 or W-L-0 refer to the books 'Bitters Bottles' and 'Supplement to Bitters Bottles' by Richard Watson.
Bitters, Abbott's, ABM, Pint 4.00
Bitters, African Stomach, Collared Mouth, Olive Yellow, 3/4 Quart, W-3 .... * 15.00
Bitters, African Stomach, Collared Mouth, Stain, Round, Amber, 3/4 Quart, W-3 .... * 20.00
Bitters, African Stomach, Spruance, Stanley & Co., Amber, 3/4 Quart, W-3 .... * 25.00
Bitters, Ageno, 9 1/2 In. .... *Illus* 35.00
Bitters, Alpine, Etched, Pour Spout & Stopper, Tooled, Stain, 3/4 Quart .... * 40.00
Bitters, Amer Picon, Philippeville, Embossed Hand, Green, 11 7/8 In. 8.50
Bitters, Angostura Bark, Eagle, Label, Contents, Amber, Miniature 150.00
Bitters, Angostura Bark, Eagle, Tooled Collared Mouth, Amber, 1/2 Pint, W-11 .... * 55.00
Bitters, Atwood's Jaundice, Georgetown, Mass., Aqua, 6 3/8 In. 2.00
Bitters, Atwood's Jaundice, Georgetown, Mass., 12 Sided, Aqua, 6 In. 4.95
Bitters, Atwood's Jaundice, 12 Sided, Free Sample, Aqua, 3 1/2 In. 10.00
Bitters, Atwood's Jaundice, 95 Percent Label, W-17f 8.00
Bitters, Atwood's Quinine Tonic, Stain, Rectangular, Aqua, 3/4 Quart, W-18 .... * 20.00
Bitters, Atwood's Quinine Tonic, W-18 .... 52.00
Bitters, Atwood's, Vegetable Dyspeptic, Pontil, Aqua, 1/2 Pint, W-19 .... * 100.00
Bitters, Atwood's Vegetable Jaundice, Georgetown, Aqua, 1/2 Pint, W-20 .... * 55.00
Bitters, Augauer, Chicago, Rectangular, Stain, Yellow Green, 3/4 Quart, W-21 .... * 50.00
Bitters, Augauer, Stain, Yellow Green, 3/4 Quart 75.00
Bitters, Austen's Oswego, Collared Mouth, Yellow Amber, 1/2 Pint, W-L13 .... * 30.00
Bitters, B.T. 1865 S.C.Smith's Druid, Barrel, 20 Rings, Dark Amber, W-308 .... * 525.00
Bitters, Baker's Orange Grove, Collared Mouth, Amber, 3/4 Quart, W-23 .... * 190.00
Bitters, Baker's Orange Grove, Red Amber, W-23 .... 150.00
Bitters, Baker's, Orange Grove, Roped Corners, Square, Amber, 3/4 Quart, W-23 .... 95.00
Bitters, Baker's Orange Grove, Roped Corners, Yellow Amber, 3/4 Quart, W-23 .... * 225.00
Bitters, Baker's Orange Grove, W-23 .... 145.00
Bitters, Bancroft's, Marshfield, Vt., Collared Mouth, Aqua, Pint, W-387 .... * 40.00
Bitters, Barber's Indian Vegetable Jaundice, 12 Sided, Aqua, 1/2 Pint, W-26 .... * 100.00
Bitters, Barrel, 10 Rings Above & Below Center Band, Blue, 3/4 Quart .... * 950.00
Bitters, Bavarian, Hoffheimer Brothers, Collared Mouth, Square, Amber, W-28 .... * 140.00
Bitters, Beck's Herb, York, Pa., Paneled, Applied Top, Square, Amber, 9 1/2 In. 90.00
Bitters, Beggs Dandelion, Amber, W-30 .... 45.00
Bitters, Beggs Dandelion, Flat, 7 In. 35.00
Bitters, Beggs Dandelion, Tooled Collared Mouth, Amber, 1/2 Pint, W-30 .... * 30.00
Bitters, Beggs Flask, W-30 .... 28.00
Bitters, Bell's Cocktail, N.Y., Lady's Leg, Mouth Ring, Amber, Pint, W-32 .... * 350.00
Bitters, Ben Franklin, Barrel, 20 Rings, Pontil, Crack, Amber, 3/4 Quart, W-L52 .... * 225.00
Bitters, Ben Franklin, Barrel, 20 Rings, Pontil, Olive Green, 3/4 Quart, W-L52 .... * 400.00

Bitters, Ageno, 9 1/2 In.
(See Page 27)

Bitters, Brown's Celebrated Indian
Herb, Amber, 3/4 Quart, W-57

Bitters, Brown's Celebrated Indian Herb,
Amber, W-57

Bitters, Ben-Hur, Amber, W-36	60.00
Bitters, Ben Hur, Tooled Collared Mouth, Square, Amber, 3/4 Quart, W-36	* 40.00
Bitters, Berkshire, Pig, Cincinnati, O., Collared Mouth, Amber, 3/4 Quart, W-38	*1100.00
Bitters, Berliner Magen, Tooled Collared Mouth, Amber, 3/4 Quart, W-39	* 25.00
Bitters, Best In America, Michigan, Cabin, Yellow Amber, 3/4 Quart, W-40	*1500.00
Bitters, Big Bill Best, Amber, W-41	95.00
Bitters, Big Bill Best, Tooled Collared Mouth, Square, Amber, 3/4 Quart, W-41	* 80.00
Bitters, Bitterquelle, 1/2 Pint	3.00
Bitters, Bitterquelle, Quart	3.00
Bitters, Boerhaves Holland, B.Page, Jr., & Co., Pa., Aqua, 1/2 Pint, W-48	* 50.00
Bitters, Boonekamp Type, Lady's Leg, Collared Mouth, Amber, Quart, W-L70	* 30.00
Bitters, Botanic Herzberg Bros., Amber, W-50	110.00
Bitters, Botanic, Herzberg Bros., N.Y., Stain, Yellow Amber, 3/4 Quart, W-50	* 150.00
Bitters, Bourbon Whiskey, Barrel, 20 Rings, Chip, Burnt Orange, W-52	* 200.00
Bitters, Bourbon Whiskey, Barrel, 20 Rings, Puce, W-52	* 250.00
Bitters, Bourbon Whiskey, Barrel, 20 Rings, Smooth Base, Gray Green, W-52	* 160.00
Bitters, Bouvier Buchu, Labels, Amber, W-394	110.00
Bitters, Boyer's Stomach, Cincinnati, Fluted Shoulder & Base, Stain, Quart	* 30.00
Bitters, Brady's, Olive Amber, W-54	85.00
Bitters, Brophy's, Light Green, 7 1/2 In., W-397	42.00
Bitters, Brophy's, Nokomis, Illinois, Stain, Aqua, 1/2 Pint, W-397	* 25.00
Bitters, Brown's Aromatic, Hannibal, Mo., Collared Mouth, Aqua, Pint, W-55	* 45.00
Bitters, Brown's Celebrated Indian Herb, Amber, W-57 ....Illus	330.00
Bitters, Brown's Celebrated Indian Herb, Amber, W-57 ....Color	XXXX.XX
Bitters, Brown's Celebrated Indian Herb, Amber, 3/4 Quart, W-57 ...Illus	400.00
Bitters, Brown's Celebrated Indian Herb, Dark Amber, W-57 ....Color	XXXX.XX
Bitters, Brown's Celebrated Indian Herb, Patent 1863, Bruise, Yellow, W-57	* 400.00
Bitters, Brown's Celebrated Indian Herb, Patent 1867, Amber, W-57	* 350.00
Bitters, Brown's Celebrated Indian Herb, Patent 1868, Crack, Amber, W-57	* 300.00
Bitters, Brown's Celebrated Indian Herb, Patent 1868, W-57a	*2000.00
Bitters, Buhrer's, Light Amber, W-402	95.00

Bitters, Suffolk, Pig, Amber, W-322

Bitters, Holtzerman's, Cabin, Honey Amber, W-172
Bitters, Holtzerman's, Cabin, Dark Amber, W-172

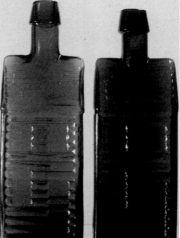

Bitters, Kelly's Old Cabin,   Bitters, Kelly's Old Cabin,
Citrine Green, W-199   Dark Green, W-199

Bitters, Simon's Centennial, Aqua, W-304

Bitters, McKeever's Army, Amber, W-228

Mineral Water, Congress, Amber, Pair

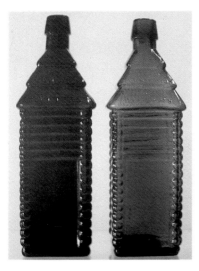

Bitters, Drake's Plantation, 6-Log,
Copper Puce, W-111

Bitters, Drake's Plantation, 6-Log,
Strawberry Puce, W-111

Bitters, National, Puce, W-236

Bitters, National, Aqua, W-236

Bitters, Brown's
Celebrated Indian Herb,
Dark Amber, W-57

Bitters, Brown's
Celebrated Indian
Herb, Amber, W-57

Bitters, Fish,
Light Green, W-125

Bitters, Fish, Clear,
W-125

Fruit Jar, Stoddard, C.1840, Olive, 12 In.

Flask, Pitkin, Green   Flask, Pitkin, American Eagle, Amber

Flask, Masonic, Olive Green

Flask, Success To The Railroad,
Olive Green

Whiskey, E.G.Booz,
Old Cabin, 1840, Amber

Ink, Hagan's Superior,
Philadelphia, Aqua

Ink, Carter's, Picture Label, Aqua

Ink, Express Company Marking,
Newark, N.J., Green

Ink, Davids Writing Fluid,
Paper Label, Cobalt

Ink, Thaddeus Davids Copying,
Paper Label, Green

Ink, Davids Writing Fluid,
Paper Label, Amber

Fruit Jar, Safety Valve, Ptd May 21, 1895

Bitters, Dr. Hostetter's, Standard
Size, Honey Amber

Drug, Parke Davis & Co., Det.
Palmer, Green, 7 1/2 In.

Whiskey, M. Salzman Co.,
Honey Amber, 12 In.

Whiskey, McLeod-Hatje Co.,
Honey Amber, 12 In.

Dresser, Gold Decoration,
Open Pontil, Cobalt, 6 1/4 In.

Pepper Sauce, Cathedral, Aqua,
Open Pontil, 8 3/4 In.

Whiskey, Victor Borothy,
Blob Top, 7 3/4 In.

Pickle, Cathedral,
Deep Aqua, 12 In.

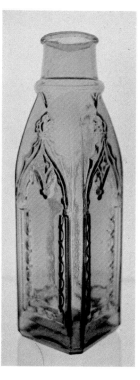

Perfume, Elysian, Detroit,
Emerald Green, 6 1/2 In.

Seal, P.Bastard, 1730,
Amber, 8 1/2 In.

Seal, P.Bastard, 1725,
Amber, 8 1/2 In.

Flask, Saddle, Persian, Aqua, 9 In.

Wine, English, C.1840,
Octagonal, Amber,
7 1/4 In.

Stiegel Type, Enamel
Decoration, C.1780, 6 In.

Wine, Dutch,
C.1740, Green,
10 In.

Wine, Dutch,
C.1740, Green,
8 1/4 In.

Flask, Bristol, C.1800,
Silver Mounts, Amethyst,
8 1/2 In.

Bitters, Burdock Blood, Foster Milburn & Co., Buffalo, Aqua, 8 1/2 In., W-60 .... 15.00
Bitters, Byrne Stomach, Great Universal Compound, Amber, 3/4 Quart, W-63 .... * 750.00
   Bitters, Byrne, see Bitters, Professor Byrne
Bitters, C.H.Swain's Bourbon, Stain, Amber, W-326 .... 125.00
Bitters, C.H.Swain's, Bourbon, Square, Stain, Olive Amber, W-326 .... * 65.00
   Bitters, C.W.Roback's, see also Bitters, Dr.C.W.Roback's
   Bitters, Cabin, see Bitters, Drake's Plantation, Bitters, Golden,
   Bitters, Kelly's Old Cabin, Bitters, Old Home, Bitters, Old
   Homestead Wild Cherry
Bitters, Cabin, Completely Logged On 3 Sides, 6 Logs On 4th Side, Amber .... * 250.00
Bitters, Caldwell's Herb, Great Tonic, Flake, Yellow Amber, 3/4 Quart, W-65b .... * 225.00
Bitters, Caldwell's Herb, Great Tonic, Triangular, Amber, 3/4 Quart, W-65 .... * 180.00
Bitters, California Fig & Herb, Chip, Square, Amber, 3/4 Quart, W-67 .... * 35.00
Bitters, California Fig, Square, Smooth Base, Amber, 3/4 Quart, W-66 .... * 35.00
Bitters, California Wine, M.Keller, Stain, Yellow Green, Quart, W-68 .... * 700.00
Bitters, Cannons, Tent, Flag, & Crossed Swords, Chip, Amber, 3/4 Quart .... * 525.00
Bitters, Canton Star, Lady's Leg, Applied Mouth Ring, Amber, 3/4 Quart, W-69 .... * 250.00
Bitters, Capuziner Stomach, Cabin, Tooled Mouth, Label, Amber .... * 260.00
Bitters, Carey's Grecian Bend, Roped Corners, Puce, 3/4 Quart, W-70 .... *3700.00
Bitters, Carmeliter Stomach, Square, Olive Green, 3/4 Quart, W-71a .... * 65.00
Bitters, Carmeliter, For Kidney & Liver, Flake, Amber, 3/4 Quart, W-71 .... * 15.00
Bitters, Carmeliter, Square, Amber, W-71 .... 35.00
Bitters, Caroni, Dug, Olive Green, 8 1/2 In., W-72 .... 20.00
Bitters, Caroni, Olive Green, 1/2 Pint, W-72b .... * 5.00
Bitters, Carpathian Herb, Amber, W-73 .... 48.00
Bitters, Carpathian Herb, Hollander Drug Co., Wear, Amber, 3/4 Quart, W-73 .... * 30.00
Bitters, Carter's Liver, C.M.Co., N.Y., Label, Golden Amber, W-75 .... * 65.00
Bitters, Catawba Wine, Wear, Square, Olive Yellow, 3/4 Quart, W-408 .... * 420.00
Bitters, Celebrated Crown, Chevalier, Amber, W-80 .... 125.00
Bitters, Chews Laxative, Barnegat, N.J., Rough, Amber, 1/2 Pint, W-410 .... * 85.00
Bitters, Clark's Giant, Phila., Collared Mouth, Aqua, 1/2 Pint, W-412 .... * 20.00
Bitters, Clark's Giant, Stain, Aqua, W-412 .... 12.50
Bitters, Clarke's Compound Mandrake, Collared Mouth, Oval, Aqua, Pint, W-85 .... * 5.00
Bitters, Clarke's Compound Mandrake, Aqua, Pint, W-85 .... 45.00
Bitters, Clarke's Sarsaparilla, Mass., Beveled, Aqua, Pint, W-86 .... * 260.00
Bitters, Clarke's Sherry Wine, Aqua, W-88 .... 20.00
Bitters, Clarke's Sherry Wine, Me., Crack, Rectangular, Aqua, 3/4 Quart, W-88 .... * 25.00
Bitters, Clarke's Sherry Wine, Rectangular, Aqua, Pint, W-88j .... * 50.00
Bitters, Clarke's Sherry Wine, Sharon, Mass., Aqua, 12 In., W-88 .... 99.00
Bitters, Clarke's Sherry Wine, Sharon, Mass., Pontil, Aqua, 3/4 Quart, W-88a .... * 85.00
Bitters, Clarke's Sherry Wine, 25 Cents, Stain, OP, Aqua, Pint, W-88b 650.00
Bitters, Clarke's Vegetable Sherry Wine, Mass., Aqua, 1/2 Gallon, W-88g 175.00
Bitters, Clarke's Vegetable Sherry Wine, Mass., Aqua, Gallon, W-88 .... * 95.00
Bitters, Clarke's Vegetable Sherry Wine, Mass., Stain, Aqua, 1/2 Gallon, W-88 .... * 35.00
Bitters, Clarke's Vegetable Sherry Wine, OP, Aqua, 1/2 Gallon, W-88 .... 100.00
Bitters, Climax, San Francisco, Square, Stain, Yellow Amber, 3/4 Quart, W-89 .... * 70.00
Bitters, Cocamoke, Hartford, Collared Mouth, Square, Amber, 3/4 Quart, W-90 .... * 65.00
Bitters, Cole Bros. Vegetable, N.Y., Amber, W-413 .... 58.00
Bitters, Cole Bros. Vegetable, N.Y., Aqua, W-413 .... 35.00
Bitters, Cole Bros. Vegetable, N.Y., Rectangular, Aqua, 1/2 Pint, W-413 .... * 10.00
Bitters, Colleton, Collared Mouth, Stain, Pontil, Aqua, 1/2 Pint, W-91 .... * 110.00
Bitters, Columbo Peptic, New Orleans, Square, Golden Amber, 3/4 Quart, W-93 .... * 30.00
Bitters, Columbo Peptic, Stain, Amber, 3/4 Quart, W-93 .... 20.00
Bitters, Compound Hepatica, H.F.Shaw, Me., Oval, Aqua, Pint, W-416 .... * 35.00
Bitters, Congress, Rectangular, Smooth Base, Aqua, Quart, W-94 .... * 80.00
Bitters, Constitution, Seward & Bentley, Buffalo, Puce, 9 1/4 In., W-95 .... 600.00
Bitters, Constitution, Seward & Bentley, Yellow Green, 3/4 Quart, W-95 .... * 650.00
Bitters, Curtis & Perkins Wild Cherry, Aqua, Pint, W-102 .... 38.00 To 70.00
Bitters, Curtis & Perkins Wild Cherry, Pontil, Aqua, Pint, W-102 .... * 150.00
Bitters, Curtis Cordial Calisaya, 1866 Ccc 1900, Amber, 3/4 Quart, W-101 .... * 575.00
Bitters, Damiana, Baja California, Lewis Hess, Aqua, 3/4 Quart, W-103 .... * 25.00
Bitters, Damiana, Baja California, Stain, Round, Aqua, 3/4 Quart, W-103 .... * 15.00
Bitters, Dandelion, XXX, Rectangular, Stain, Amber, 1/2 Pint, W-104 .... * 10.00
Bitters, Dandelion, XXX, Stain, Amber, W-104 .... 45.00
Bitters, Danziger Magenbitter, Gin Shape, Collared Mouth, Milk Glass, W-L39 .... * 100.00

Bitters, David Andrews Vegetable Jaundice, R.I., Collar, Aqua, Pint, W-10 .... * 350.00
Bitters, DeWitt's Stomach, Chicago, Rectangular, Amber, 7 3/4 In., W-107 .... 47.50
Bitters, DeWitt's Stomach, Collared Mouth, Rectangular, Amber, Pint, W-107 .... * 40.00
Bitters, DeWitt's Stomach, Square, Amber, W-426 .... 40.00
Bittore, Demuth's Stomach, Phila., Collared Mouth, Amber, 3/4 Quart, W-106 .... * 40.00
Bitters, Didier's, Tooled Mouth, Rectangular, Golden Amber, 1/2 Pint .... * 110.00
Bitters, Digestine, P.J.Bowlin & Son, St.Paul, Minn., 7 1/2 In. .... *Illus* 625.00
Bitters, Dimmit's, 50 Cents, St.Louis, Flask, Amber, 1/2 Pint, W-108 .... * 300.00
Bitters, Dingen's Napoleon, N.Y., Drum Shape, Smoky, Quart, W-109 .... *1650.00
Bitters, Doctor Fisch's, W.H.Ware Patent 1866, Fish, Collar, Amber, W-124 .... * 150.00
Bitters, Doyle's Hop, BIMAL, Stain, Amber, 9 1/2 In., W-110 .... 16.00
Bitters, Doyle's Hop, 1872, Amber, 9 1/2 In., W-110 .... 20.00
Bitters, Doyle's Hop, 1872, Cabin, Collar, Square, Amber, 3/4 Quart, W-110 .... 20.00
Bitters, Doyle's Hop, 1872, Deep Amber, 10 In., W-110 .... 35.00
Bitters, Doyle's Hop, 1872, Labels, Roofed Shoulders, Square, Amber, W-110 .... * 35.00
Bitters, Doyle's Hop, 1872, Roofed Shoulders, Square, Amber, W-110 .... * 25.00
Bitters, Doyle's Hop, 1872, Roofed Shoulders, Square, Golden Amber, W-110 .... * 20.00
Bitters, Doyle's Hop, 1872, Roofed Shoulders, Square, Yellow Amber, W-110 .... * 25.00
Bitters, Doyle's Hop, 1872, Stain, Flake, Golden Amber, W-110 .... * 20.00
Bitters, Dr.A.H.Smith's Old Style, O.S. 2781, Square, Amber, W-309 .... * 60.00
Bitters, Dr.A.S.Hopkins Union Stomach, Amber, 3/4 Quart, W-177a 45.00
Bitters, Dr.A.S.Hopkins Union Stomach, Machine Made, Amber, 10 In., W-177b 19.50
Bitters, Dr.A.S.Hopkins Union Stomach, Olive Yellow, W-177a .... * 45.00
Bitters, Dr.A.S.Hopkins Union Stomach, Square, Amber, 3/4 Quart, W-177b .... * 20.00

Bitters, Digestine, P.J.Bowlin & Son,
St.Paul, Minn., 7 1/2 In.

Bitters, Dr.John Bull's Compound,
Amber 10 In.
(See Page 31)

Bitters, Dr.Abell's Spice, Label, OP, Stain, Aqua, 7 In. 19.00
Bitters, Dr.Allen's Stomach, Bubbles, Refired Pontil, Aqua, W-381 .... 55.00
Bitters, Dr.Ball's Vegetable Stomachic, Pontil, Flake, Aqua, Pint, W-25 .... * 100.00
Bitters, Dr.Baxter's Mandrake, Lord Bros., Vt., 12 Sided, Aqua, 1/2 Pint, W-29 .... * 15.00
Bitters, Dr.Baxter's Mandrake, Lord Bros., Vt., 12 Sided, Aqua, 6 1/2 In. 12.00
Bitters, Dr.Beard's Alterative Tonic & Laxative, Chip, Oval, Aqua, Pint .... * 25.00
Bitters, Dr.Birmingham's Antibillious Blood, Yellow Green, Quart, W-42 .... * 500.00
Bitters, Dr.Bishops Wahoo, Conn., Collared Mouth, Yellow Amber, W-43 .... * 290.00
Bitters, Dr.Blake's, Aromatic, Pontil, Rectangular, Aqua, Pint, W-45 .... * 95.00
Bitters, Dr.Boyce's Tonic, Rolled Collared Mouth, 12 Sided, Aqua, Pint, W-53 .... * 10.00
Bitters, Dr.Boyce's Tonic, 12 Sided, Crack, Sample, Aqua, W-L20 .... * 20.00
Bitters, Dr.Bull's Superior Stomach, St.Louis, Stain, Amber, 3/4 Quart, W-403 .... * 25.00
Bitters, Dr.C.W.Roback's Stomach, Barrel, Amber, 10 1/4 In., W-280 .... 145.00
Bitters, Dr.C.W.Roback's Stomach, Barrel, Collared, Stain, Amber, 3/4 Quart 120.00
Bitters, Dr.C.W.Roback's Stomach, Barrel, 9 1/2 In., W-280 .... 90.00 To 180.00
Bitters, Dr.C.W.Roback's Stomach, Barrel, 20 Rings, Chip, Yellow, W-280a .... * 200.00

Bitters, Dr.C.W.Roback's Stomach, Barrel, 20 Rings, Crack, Green, W-280 * 850.00
Bitters, Dr.Caldwell's Herb, Great Tonic, Triangular, Amber, 3/4 Quart, W-65a .... * 100.00
Bitters, Dr.Carson's Stomach, Aqua, 1/2 Pint, W-74 .... 42.00
Bitters, Dr.C.W.Roback's Stomach, Barrel, 20 Rings, Golden Amber, W-280 .... * 325.00
Bitters, Dr.Carson's Stomach, Collared Mouth, Stain, Aqua, 1/2 Pint, W-74 .... * 10.00
Bitters, Dr.Chandler's Jamaica Ginger Root, Barrel, Amber, 3/4 Quart, W-82 .... *1950.00
Bitters, Dr.Charles Sweet's Celebrated Restorative Wine, Aqua, Pint, W-L127 .... * 10.00
Bitters, Dr.Copp's White Mountain, Rolled Collared Mouth, Aqua, Pint, W-98 .... 30.00
Bitters, Dr.E.P.Eastman's Yellow Dock, Lynn, Mass., Rectangular, Aqua, Q-112 .... * 130.00
Bitters, Dr.F.Woodbridge, Headache, Beveled Corners, Amber, 3/4 Quart, W-161 .... * 130.00
Bitters, Dr.F.Woodbridge, Headache, Recessed Panels, Amber, Quart, W-161 .... * 130.00
Bitters, Dr.Fleschhut's Celebrated Stomach, Square, Aqua, 3/4 Quart, W-431 .... * 70.00
Bitters, Dr.Flint's Quaker, R.I., Rectangular, Aqua, 3/4 Quart, W-126 .... * 50.00
Bitters, Dr.Flint's Quaker, R.I., Rectangular, Aqua, 3/4 Quart, W-126a .... * 50.00
Bitters, Dr.Flint's Quaker, Rectangular, Aqua, W-126 .... 25.00
Bitters, Dr.Flint's Quaker, Rectangular, Smooth Base, Aqua, W-126 .... * 25.00
Bitters, Dr.Flint's Quaker, Rectangular, Stain, Aqua, 3/4 Quart, W-126a .... * 25.00
Bitters, Dr.Geo. Pierce's Indian Restorative, Aqua, 3/4 Quart, W-258 .... * 15.00
Bitters, Dr.Geo. Pierce's Indian Restorative, Lowell, Mass., Aqua, 8 3/4 In. 25.00
Bitters, Dr.Geo. Pierce's Indian Restorative, Pontil, Aqua, Pint, W-258 .... * 55.00
Bitters, Dr.Gilbert's Rock & Rye Stomach, Square, Blue Green, Pint, W-132 .... * 190.00
Bitters, Dr.Goddin's Comp. Gentian, Roofed Shoulder, Aqua, 3/4 Quart, W-135 .... * 260.00
Bitters, Dr.Harter's Wild Cherry, Dayton, Ohio, 4 3/4 In., W-158d 23.00
Bitters, Dr.Harter's Wild Cherry, St.Louis, Mo., Oval, Aqua, Pint, W-157 .... * 310.00
Bitters, Dr.Harter's Wild Cherry, St.Louis, Amber, Sample, W-158b .... * 40.00
Bitters, Dr.Harter's Wild Cherry, St.Louis, Amber, 3 3/4 In. 24.00
Bitters, Dr.Harter's Wild Cherry, St.Louis, Cracked, Amber, 3/4 Quart, W-158 .... * 5.00
Bitters, Dr.Harter's Wild Cherry, St.Louis, Medium Amber, 4 1/2 In., W-158 .... 25.00
Bitters, Dr.Hartshorn's Family Medicines, Oval, Aqua, W-L59 .... 12.00
Bitters, Dr.Henley's Wild Grape Root IXL, Aqua, W-164 .... 48.00
Bitters, Dr.Henley's Wild Grape Root IXL, Light Green, Quart, W-164 .... * 80.00
Bitters, Dr.Henley's Wild Grape Root IXL, Smooth Base, Aqua, Quart, W-164 .... * 55.00
Bitters, Dr.Herbert John's Indian, Amber, 8 1/2 In., W-455 .... 145.00
Bitters, Dr.Hoofland's German, Aqua, 7 In., W-174 .... 28.00
Bitters, Dr.Hoofland's German, Aqua, 8 In., W-174 .... 24.00
Bitters, Dr.Hoofland's German, Dyspepsia & Liver, Aqua, Pint, W-174a .... * 45.00
Bitters, Dr.Hoofland's German, Liver Complaint, Pontil, Aqua, 1/2 Pint, W-174 .... * 55.00
    Bitters, Dr. Hostetter, see Bitters, Dr. J. Hostetter
Bitters, Dr.Huntington's Golden Tonic, Maine, Square, Amber, 3/4 Quart, W-182 .... * 80.00
Bitters, Dr.J.C.Chesley's Golden, 9 In. 95.00
Bitters, Dr.J.G.B.Siegert & Sons, Angostura On Base, Green, 1/2 Pint .... * 10.00
Bitters, Dr.J.Hostetter's Standard Size, Honey Amber, ...*Color* XXXX.XX
Bitters, Dr.J.Hostetter's Stomach, Amber, 8 3/4 In., W-179 .... 8.00
Bitters, Dr.J.Hostetter's Stomach, Dark Amber, 8 1/2 In., W-179 .... 5.00
Bitters, Dr.J.Hostetter's Stomach, H.V.S. Asparagus, Label, Amber, W-179 .... * 50.00
Bitters, Dr.J.Hostetter's Stomach, Square, Citron, W-179 .... * 50.00
Bitters, Dr.J.Hostetter's Stomach, Square, Olive Green, W-179a .... * 60.00
Bitters, Dr.J.Hostetter's Stomach, W-179 .... 4.50
Bitters, Dr.J.Sweet's, Strengthening, Square, Aqua, Pint, W-328 .... * 20.00
Bitters, Dr.J.Sweet's Strengthening, Square, Aqua, W-328 .... 65.00
Bitters, Dr.Jacob's, New Haven, Ct., S.A.Spencer, Aqua, Quart, W-190 .... * 110.00
Bitters, Dr.Jacob's, New Haven, S.A.Spencer, Pontil, Stain, Aqua, Pint, W-190 .... * 110.00
Bitters, Dr.John Bull's Compound, Amber 10 In. ....*Illus* 150.00
Bitters, Dr.L.G.Bertram's Long Life Aromatic, Stain, Amber, 3/4 Quart .... * 220.00
Bitters, Dr.Langleys Root & Herb, Label, Amber, 1/2 Pint, W-206 .... * 50.00
Bitters, Dr.Langleys Root & Herb, Light Apple Green, W-206 .... 25.00
Bitters, Dr.Langleys Root & Herb, 76 Union St., Blue Green, Pint, W-206a .... * 45.00
Bitters, Dr.Langleys Root & Herb, 76 Union St., Blue Green, W-206 .... * 30.00
Bitters, Dr.Langleys Root & Herb, 99 Union St., Chips, Aqua, Pint, W-206d .... * 20.00
Bitters, Dr.Langleys Root & Herb, 99 Union St., Green, 3/4 Quart, W-206b .... * 50.00
Bitters, Dr.Langleys, 99 Union St., Amber, 7 In.W-206b 45.00
Bitters, Dr.Langleys, 99 Union St., Amber, 8 1/2 In., W-206b 60.00
Bitters, Dr.Langleys, 99 Union St., Aqua, W-206 .... 28.00
Bitters, Dr.Loew's Celebrated Stomach, Emerald, 3/4 Quart, W-217 .... 195.00
Bitters, Dr.Loew's Celebrated Stomach, Yellow Green, 3/4 Quart, W-217 .... * 95.00

Bitters, Dr.Lovegood's Family, Cabin, Yellow Amber, Quart, W-220 .... *1250.00
Bitters, Dr.Lyford's, C.P.Herrick, Tilton, N.H., Chip, Oval, Aqua, Pint, W-222 .... * 20.00
Bitters, Dr.M.C.Ayer Restorative, Boston, Double Collar, Aqua, Pint, W-386 .... * 25.00
Bitters, Dr.M.M.Fenner's Capitol, Aqua, 10 1/2 In., W-122 .... 28.00
Bitters, Dr.M.M.Fenner's Capitol, Fredonia, N.Y., Rectangular, Aqua, W-122 .... * 30.00
Bitters, Dr.Mampe's Herb Stomach, Aqua, 7 In., W-225 .... 45.00
Bitters, Dr.Manly Hardy's Genuine Jaundice, Aqua, Pint, W-155 .... 28.00
Bitters, Dr.Manly Hardy's, Genuine, Jaundice, Pontil, Aqua, Pint, W-155 .... * 85.00
Bitters, Dr.Marcus, Universal, Philada., Pontil, Rectangular, Aqua, Pint, W-465 .... * 150.00
Bitters, Dr.Mowe's Vegetable, Lowell, Mass., Rectangular, Aqua, Quart, W-235 .... * 110.00
Bitters, Dr.Petzold's Genuine German, Incpt.1862, Amber, 1/2 Pint, W-256a .... * 100.00
Bitters, Dr.Petzold's Genuine German, Incpt.1862, Amber, 3/4 Quart, W-256 .... * 120.00
Bitters, Dr.Petzold's Genuine German, Incpt.1862, Dug, Amber, 10 1/2 In. 100.00
Bitters, Dr.Petzold's Genuine German, Incpt.1862, Haze, 6 In. 125.00
Bitters, Dr.Petzold's Genuine German, Incpt.1862, Stain, Amber, 7 In., W-256 .... 130.00
Bitters, Dr.Petzold's Genuine German, Incpt.1862, 9 1/2 In. ....*Illus* 150.00
Bitters, Dr.R.F.Hibbard's Wild Cherry, Crittenton, Aqua, 3/4 Quart, W-168 .... * 50.00
Bitters, Dr.Renz's Herb, Square, Amber, W-273 .... 65.00
Bitters, Dr.Rivenburgh's Indian, Vegetable, N.Y., Aqua, 3/4 Quart, W-279 .... * 700.00
Bitters, Dr.Sawen's Life Invigorating, Amber, W-295 .... 52.00
Bitters, Dr.Sawen's Life Invigorating, Square, Amber, 3/4 Quart, W-295-A .... * 40.00
Bitters, Dr.Sim's Anti-Constipation, Square, Smooth Base, Amber, W-305 .... * 45.00
Bitters, Dr.Skinner's, Celebrated 25 Cent, Mass., Stain, Aqua, Pint, W-306 .... * 55.00

Bitters, Dr.Petzold's Genuine German, Incpt. 1862, 9 1/2 In.

Bitters, Dr.Skinner's, Sherry Wine, Mass., Stain, Aqua, Pint, W-307 .... * 60.00
Bitters, Dr.Southworth's, Strap-Sided Flask, Amber, 7 1/2 In. 25.00
Bitters, Dr.Sperry's, Female Strengthening, Label, Rectangular, Aqua .... * 55.00
Bitters, Dr.Stanley's South American Indian, Square, Yellow Amber, W-314 .... * 35.00
Bitters, Dr.Stephen Jewett's, Celebrated, Olive Amber, Pint, W-193a .... * 425.00
Bitters, Dr.Stephen Jewett's, Celebrated, Pontil, Yellow Green, W-193 .... * 410.00
Bitters, Dr.Stephen Jewett's, Celebrated, Rough, Olive Amber, W-193 .... * 350.00
Bitters, Dr.Stewart's Tonic, Amber, W-500 .... 38.00
Bitters, Dr.Stoever's, Established 1837, Label, Square, Amber, W-320 .... * 55.00
Bitters, Dr.Thos. Hall's California Pepsin Wine, Amber, 9 In., W-153 .... 48.00
Bitters, Dr.Timpkin's Vegetable, Hole, Rectangular, Blue Green, W-504 .... * 65.00
Bitters, Dr.Van Dyke Holland, Embossed Panels, Trial, 5 1/4 In., W-L136 .... 8.50
Bitters, Dr.Von Hopf's Curacao, Chamberlain & Co., Amber, 1/2 Pint, W-344 .... * 130.00
Bitters, Dr.Von Hopf's Curacao, Chamberlain & Co., Amber, 9 1/4 In., W-344 .... 30.00
Bitters, Dr.Von Hopf's Curacao, Chamberlain & Co., Flask, W-343 .... 35.00
Bitters, Dr.W.L.Wilbur's, Aromatic, Fredonia, N.Y., Label, Square, Amber, W-365 ...... * 55.00
Bitters, Dr.Walkinshaw's, Curative, Batavia, N.Y., Square, Amber, Pint, W-352 .... * 145.00
Bitters, Dr.Warren's Bilious, Cloudy Flecks, Aqua, W-513 .... 43.00
Bitters, Dr.Warren's Bilious, John A.Perry, Oval, Aqua, 1/2 Pint, W-513 .... * 10.00
Bitters, Dr.Warren's Bilious, John A.Perry, Oval, Aqua, 1/2 Pint, W-513a .... * 25.00
Bitters, Dr.Wheeler's Tonic Sherry Wine, Label, Whittled, W-518 .... 300.00
Bitters, Dr.Wilsons Herbine, Brayley Drug Co., Chip, Aqua, 1/2 Pint, W-368 .... * 25.00
Bitters, Dr.Wilsons Herbine, J.W.Brayley, Montreal, Chip, W-368 .... * 10.00

Bitters, Dr.Wilson's Herbine, St.John, N.B., Oval, Aqua, 1/2 Pint, W-368 .... * 15.00
Bitters, Dr.Wilson's Herbine, St.John, N.B., Oval, Aqua, 1/2 Pint, W-368 .... 30.00
Bitters, Dr.Wood's, Sarsaparilla & Wild Cherry, Aqua, Pint, W-372 .... * 130.00
Bitters, Drake's Plantation, Patent 1862, 4 Log, Amber, W-111b .... * 160.00
Bitters, Drake's Plantation, Patent 1862, 6 Log, Puce, W-111b .... * 150.00
Bitters, Drake's Plantation, 4 Log .... 38.00 To 60.00
Bitters, Drake's Plantation, 4 Log, Amber, W-111b .... 50.00 To 90.00
Bitters, Drake's Plantation, 4 Log, Dark Amber, W-111b 60.00
Bitters, Drake's Plantation, 4 Log, Golden Amber, W-111b 75.00
Bitters, Drake's Plantation, 4 Log, Light Amber, W-111b .... 55.00 To 65.00
Bitters, Drake's Plantation, 4 Log, Light Honey Amber, W-111b 75.00
Bitters, Drake's Plantation, 4 Log, Light Yellow Amber .... 75.00 To 90.00
Bitters, Drake's Plantation, 4 Log, Medium Amber, W-111b 60.00
Bitters, Drake's Plantation, 4 Log, Medium To Light Amber 55.00
Bitters, Drake's Plantation, 4 Log, Whittled, Amber 62.00
Bitters, Drake's Plantation, 4 Log, Yellow, W-111b 125.00
Bitters, Drake's Plantation, 4 Log, Yellow Amber, W-111b .... 65.00 To 75.00
Bitters, Drake's Plantation, 5 Log, Amber, W-111d 175.00
Bitters, Drake's Plantation, 5 Log, Golden Citron, W-111d 250.00
Bitters, Drake's Plantation, 5 Log, Light Amber, W-111d 185.00
Bitters, Drake's Plantation, 5 Log, Light Orange Amber, W-111d 257.00
Bitters, Drake's Plantation, 5 Log, Medium Amber 200.00
Bitters, Drake's Plantation, 6 Log .... 50.00 To 62.00
Bitters, Drake's Plantation, 6 Log, Amber .... 45.00 To 75.00
Bitters, Drake's Plantation, 6 Log, Black Cherry Amber, W-111 .... 130.00
Bitters, Drake's Plantation, 6 Log, Burst Bubble, Claret, W-111 .... 125.00
Bitters, Drake's Plantation, 6 Log, Cherry Red, W-111 .... 95.00
Bitters, Drake's Plantation, 6 Log, Chocolate, W-111 .... 75.00
Bitters, Drake's Plantation, 6 Log, Claret .... 100.00 To 150.00
Bitters, Drake's Plantation, 6-Log, Copper Puce, W-111 ....Color XXXX.XX
Bitters, Drake's Plantation, 6 Log, Dark Amber, W-111 .... 43.00 To 85.00
Bitters, Drake's Plantation, 6 Log, Deep Red, W-111 .... 110.00
Bitters, Drake's Plantation, 6 Log, Dull Corner, Puce .... 85.00 To 100.00
Bitters, Drake's Plantation, 6 Log, Golden Amber, W-111 .... 75.00
Bitters, Drake's Plantation, 6 Log, Haze, Yellow Green, W-111 .... 85.00
Bitters, Drake's Plantation, 6 Log, Honey Amber .... 55.00 To 65.00
Bitters, Drake's Plantation, 6 Log, Light Amber 55.00
Bitters, Drake's Plantation, 6 Log, Light Golden Amber 65.00
Bitters, Drake's Plantation, 6 Log, Light Honey Amber 55.00
Bitters, Drake's Plantation, 6 Log, Light Lemon Amber 93.00
Bitters, Drake's Plantation, 6 Log, Light Pink, W-111 .... 150.00
Bitters, Drake's Plantation, 6 Log, Medium Amber .... 50.00 To 60.00
Bitters, Drake's Plantation, 6 Log, Medium Claret 100.00
Bitters, Drake's Plantation, 6 Log, Olive Yellow, W-111c 400.00
Bitters, Drake's Plantation, 6 Log, Persimmon 89.00
Bitters, Drake's Plantation, 6 Log, Puce, W-111 .... 100.00 To 125.00
Bitters, Drake's Plantation, 6 Log, Red Amber, W-111 .... 65.00
Bitters, Drake's Plantation, 6 Log, Red Puce, W-111 .... 135.00 To 140.00
Bitters, Drake's Plantation, 6 Log, Root Beer Color, W-111 .... 85.00
Bitters, Drake's Plantation, 6-Log, Strawberry Puce, W-111 ....Color XXXX.XX
Bitters, Drake's Plantation, 6 Log, Whittled, Golden Amber 75.00
Bitters, Drake's Plantation, 6 Log, Whittled, Honey Amber 48.00
Bitters, Drake's Plantation, 6 Log, Yellow, W-111 .... 85.00 To 100.00
Bitters, Drake's Plantation, 6 Log, Yellow Amber .... 65.00 To 125.00
Bitters, Drake's Plantation, 6 Log, Pink 150.00
Bitters, Drake's 1860 Plantation X, Patent 1862, Amber, 10 In. 45.00
Bitters, Drake's 1860 Plantation X, Patent 1862, Crack, Amber, W-111 .... * 50.00
Bitters, Drake's 1860 Plantation X, Patent 1862, Golden Amber, W-111 .... * 350.00
Bitters, Drake's 1860 Plantation X, Patent 1862, Light Amber, 10 In. 85.00
Bitters, Drake's 1860 Plantation X, Patent 1862, 4 Log, Amber, W-111 .... * 160.00
Bitters, Drake's 1860 Plantation X, Patent 1862, 4 Log, Green, W-111 .... *1200.00
Bitters, Drake's 1860 Plantation X, Patent 1862, 4 Log, Yellow Green, W-111 .... 90.00
Bitters, Drake's 1860 Plantation X, Patent 1862, 6 Log, Amber, W-111 .... 15.00
Bitters, Drake's 1860 Plantation X, Patent 1862, 6 Log, Crack, Puce, W-111 .... *1250.00
Bitters, Drake's 1860 Plantation X, Patent 1862, 6 Log, Puce, W-111 .... * 125.00

Bitters, Drake's 1860 Plantation X, Patent 1862, 6 Log, Topaz, W-111 .... * 900.00
Bitters, Drake's 1860 Plantation X, Patent 1862, 6 Log, Yellow Green, W-111 .... * 850.00
Bitters, Drake's 1860 Plantation X, 6 Log, Amber, 3/4 Quart, W-111 .... 50.00
Bitters, Drake's 1860 Plantation X, 6 Log, Olive Yellow, W-111 .... 350.00
Bitters, Drake's 1860 Plantation X, 6 Log, W-111 .... 55.00
Bitters, Drake's 1860 Plantation X, 6 Log, Yellow Olive, W-111 .... * 450.00
Bitters, Drake's 1860 Plantation, 4 Log, Amber 60.00
Bitters, Drake's 1860 Plantation, 6 Log, Amber 60.00
Bitters, E.Baker's Premium, Aqua, 6 1/2 In., W-24 .... 45.00
Bitters, E.J.Rose's Magador, Stomach, Kidney, & Liver, Square .... * 65.00
Bitters, Eagle Aromatic, Globular, Amber, 1/2 Pint .... * 50.00
    Bitters, Ear of Corn, see Bitters, National, Ear of Corn
Bitters, East India Root, Geo.P.Clapp, Boston, Square Gin, Amber, 3/4 Quart .... * 95.00
Bitters, Edw Wilder's Stomach, Louisville, Cabin, 5 Story, 3/4 Quart, W-366 .... * 130.00
Bitters, Edward's, Prepared By Stevens & Co., Pontil, Aqua, 3/4 Quart .... * 280.00
Bitters, Edward's, O.F.Nims Apothecary, Stain, Chip, Oval, Aqua, Pint .... * 25.00
Bitters, Electric Brand, H.E.Bucklen & Co., Chicago, Amber, 3/4 Quart, W-115 .... * 25.00
Bitters, Electric Brand, H.E.Bucklen & Co., Square, Amber, Pint, W-115 .... * 7.50
Bitters, Electric Brand, Square, Amber, 3/4 Quart, W-115a .... * 15.00
Bitters, Electric, H.E.Bucklen & Co., Amber, 8 1/2 In., W-114 .... 35.00
Bitters, Electric, H.E.Bucklen & Co., Chicago, Amber, Pint, W-114a 15.00
Bitters, Electric, H.E.Bucklen & Co., Chicago, Amber, Pint, W-114a .... * 10.00
Bitters, Electric, H.E.Bucklen & Co., Chicago, Square, Amber, Pint, W-114 .... * 15.00
Bitters, Electric, H.E.Bucklen & Co., 9 In., W-114 .... 17.00
Bitters, English Female, Dromgoole, Louisville, Rectangular, Pint, W-116 .... * 90.00
Bitters, Ernst L.Arp, Kiel, Whittled, Dark Aqua, 12 1/2 In. 10.50
Bitters, Excelsior Aromatic, 1800, Dr.D.S.Perry, Amber, 3/4 Quart, W-119 .... * 400.00
Bitters, Excelsior Herb, J.V.Mattison, N.J., Amber, 3/4 Quart, W-120 .... * 250.00
Bitters, F.Brown, Boston, Sarsaparilla & Tomato, Flake, Aqua, W-58 .... * 60.00
Bitters, F.Dittmar's Stomach, Chips, Square, Olive Green, 3/4 Quart .... * 180.00
Bitters, Faith Whitcomb's, Boston, Rectangular, Stain, Aqua, Pint, W-362 .... * 20.00
Bitters, Faith Whitcomb's, Boston, Rectangular, W-362 .... 35.00
Bitters, Favorite, Powell & Stutenroth, Barrel, Amber, Pint, W-121 .... *1000.00
Bitters, Fero-China Bisleri, Whittled, Olive Green, 10 3/4 In. 8.50
Bitters, Ferro Quina Stomach, Blood Maker, Square, Amber, 3/4 Quart, W-123 .... * 40.00
Bitters, Fish, Amber, 9 3/4 In. 7.00
Bitters, Fish, Clear, W-125 .... Color XXXX.XX
Bitters, Fish, Light Green, W-125 .... Color XXXX.XX
Bitters, Fish, W.H.Ware, Patent 1866, Amber, W-125 .... 95.00
Bitters, Fish, W.H.Ware, Patent 1866, Amber, 3/4 Quart, W-125 .... Illus 95.00
Bitters, Fish, W.H.Ware, Patent 1866, Amethystine, 3/4 Quart, W-125 .... * 800.00
Bitters, Fish, W.H.Ware, Patent 1866, Aqua .... Illus 350.00
Bitters, Fish, W.H.Ware, Patent 1866, Bruise, Yellow Green, 1/4 Pint, W-125 .... *1050.00
Bitters, Fish, W.H.Ware, Patent 1866, Label, Amber, 3/4 Quart, W-125 .... * 380.00
Bitters, Fish, W.H.Ware, Patent 1866, Lime Green, 3/4 Quart, W-125 .... *6300.00
Bitters, Fish, W.H.Ware, Patent 1866, Stain, Amber, 3/4 Quart, W-125 .... *2000.00
Bitters, Flint Diamond Thumbprint, Blob Top, 7 In. 95.00
Bitters, Gen'l Scotts, New York Artillery, Cannon, Amber, 13 In., W-298 .... *..11000.00
Bitters, Gentiana Root & Herb, Seth E.Clapp, Boston, Aqua, 3/4 Quart .... * 55.00
Bitters, Genuine Bull Wild Cherry, Collared Mouth, Rectangular, Quart, W-59 .... * 30.00
Bitters, German Balsam, W.M.Watson & Co., Milk Glass, 3/4 Quart, W-129 .... * 300.00
Bitters, German Hop, Dr.D.C.Warner, Stain, Yellow Amber, 3/4 Quart, W-130 .... * 140.00
Bitters, German Hop, 1872, Reading, Bruise, Square, Amber, 3/4 Quart, W-130 .... * 40.00
Bitters, Globe Tonic, Square, Amber, 3/4 Quart, W-134 .... * 30.00
Bitters, Globe, Byrne Bros. & Co., Neck Ring, Bruise, Amber, 3/4 Quart, W-133 .... * 300.00
Bitters, Goff's Herb, 95 Percent Label, W-137 .... 16.00
Bitters, Golden, Geo.C.Hubbel & Co., Rectangular, Aqua, 3/4 Quart, W-138 .... * 280.00
Bitters, Great Western Tonic, Patent Janny 21, 1868, Amber, 3/4 Quart, W-143 .... * 80.00
Bitters, Greeley's Bourbon Whiskey, Barrel, Stain, Aqua, W-145 .... *1000.00
Bitters, Greeley's Bourbon, Barrel, 20 Rings, Flake, Copper, W-145 .... * 190.00
Bitters, Greeley's Bourbon, Barrel, 20 Rings, Rough, Smoky Puce, W-144 .... * 250.00
Bitters, Greeley's Bourbon, Barrel, 20 Rings, Smoky Green Amber, W-144 .... * 310.00
Bitters, Greeley's Bourbon, Barrel, 20 Rings, Smoky Green, W-144 .... * 325.00
Bitters, Green Mountain Cider, Label, Crack, Aqua, 3/4 Quart, W-146 .... * 40.00
Bitters, Greer's Eclipse, Square, Amber, Pint, W-147 .... * 35.00

Bitters, Fish, W.H.Ware, Patent 1866,
Chip, Amber, 3/4 Quart
(See Page 34)

Bitters,
H.R.Wyenandts,
Green, 9 1/2 In.

Bitters, Fish, W.H.Ware, Patent 1866, Aqua
(See Page 34)

Bitters, H. P. Herb Wild Cherry, Cabin,
Amber, 3/4 Quart, W-148

Bitters, Griel's Herb, Aqua, 9 1/2 In., W-440	55.00
Bitters, H.P.Herb Wild Cherry, Cabin, Amber, 3/4 Quart, W-148 .... *Illus*	180.00
Bitters, H.P.Herb Wild Cherry, Cabin, Amber, 9 In.	250.00
Bitters, H.P.Herb Wild Cherry, Cabin, Amber, 10 1/4 In.	250.00
Bitters, H.P.Herb Wild Cherry, Cabin, Green, W-148a	*1000.00
Bitters, H.P.Herb Wild Cherry, Cabin, Paneled, Stain, Amber, 3/4 Quart, W-148	* 150.00
Bitters, H.R.Wyenandts, Green, 9 1/2 In. .... *Illus*	110.00
Bitters, Hagan's, Stain, Triangular, Amber, 3/4 Quart, W-149	* 110.00
Bitters, Hall's, Barrel, Flaw, Amber, 3/4 Quart, W-152	* 725.00
Bitters, Hall's, E.E.Hall, New Haven, 1842, Barrel, Yellow Amber, W-151	* 120.00
Bitters, Hansard's Trademark Genuine Hop, Pottery, Cream	* 100.00
Bitters, Hansard's Trademark Genuine Hop, Pottery, Yellow & Cream	* 130.00
Bitters, Hart's Star, Philadelphia, Fish, Stain, 3/4 Quart, W-156	* 250.00
Bitters, Hartwig Kantorowicz Posen, Hamburg, Germany, Milk Glass, 9 In.	50.00
Bitters, Hartwig Kantorowicz Posen, Milk Glass, 3/4 Quart, W-L84	* 100.00
Bitters, Hartwig Kantorowicz Posen, Milk Glass, 4 1/8 In.	275.00
Bitters, Harvey's Prairie, Series Of Barrels, Amber, 3/4 Quart, W-159	*1100.00
Bitters, Havis' Iron, Williamsburg Drug Co., Square, Amber, Pint, W-160	* 45.00
Bitters, Hentz's, Curative, Phila., Stain, Bruise, Square, 3/4 Quart, W-165	* 5.00
Bitters, Hentz's Curative, Sample, Square, Green, W-165	25.00
Bitters, Herkules, GA Monogram, Globular, Flat Panels, Green, Quart, W-166	*1050.00
Bitters, Hi Hi, Rock Island, Ill., Stain, Triangular, Amber, 3/4 Quart, W-167	* 60.00
Bitters, Hi Hi, Rock Island, Ill., Stain, Triangular, Amber, 9 5/8 In., W-4	65.00
Bitters, Hierapicra Botanical Society, Figs, Aqua, 3/4 Quart, W-168	* 85.00
Bitters, Highland & Scotch Tonic, Barrel, 20 Rings, Olive, 3/4 Quart, W-170	*1075.00
Bitters, Hill's Mountain, Indiana Drug, Rough, Amber, 1/2 Pint, W-L62	* 25.00
Bitters, Holtzermann's Patent Stomach, Cabin, Amber, 3/4 Quart, W-172a	* 550.00
Bitters, Holtzermanns Patent Stomach, Cabin, Amber, 9 7/8 In., W-172	140.00
Bitters, Holtzermann's Patent Stomach, Cabin, Label, Amber, 3/4 Quart, W-172 .... *Illus*	* 175.00
Bitters, Holtzermann's Patent, Cabin, Amber, 3/4 Quart, W-172	160.00
Bitters, Holtzermann's, Cabin, Dark Amber, W-172 .... *Color* XXXX.XX
Bitters, Holtzermann's Cabin, Honey Amber, W-172 .... *Color* XXXX.XX
Bitters, Holtzermann's, Cabin, 4-Sided Roof, W-172	95.00
Bitters, Home, Saint Louis, Mo., Square, Amber, 3/4 Quart, W-173	* 35.00
Bitters, Hop & Iron, Utica, N.Y., Label, Square, Amber, Pint, W-175	* 45.00
Bitters, Hops & Malt, Sheaf Of Wheat, Stain, Yellow Amber, 3/4 Quart, W-176	* 50.00
Bitters, Horseshoe Medicine Co., Horseshoe, Crack, Amber, 3/4 Quart, W-178	* 850.00
Bitters, **Hostetter's,** see Bitters, Dr. J. Hostetter	
Bitters, **Hubbel & Co.,** see Bitters, Golden	
Bitters, Hunkidori Stomach, H.B.Mathews, Stain, Amber, 3/4 Quart, W-181	* 60.00
Bitters, Hutching's, Dyspepsia, New York, Pontil, Bruise, Aqua, Pint, W-184	* 55.00

Bitters, Hygeia, Fox & Co., Square, Stain, Yellow Amber, 3/4 Quart, W-185 .... * 20.00
Bitters, Imperial, Russian, Tonic, Beaded Panels, Aqua, 3/4 Quart, W-450 .... * 525.00
    Bitters, Indian Restorative, see Bitters, Dr.George Pierce's
    Indian Restorative
Bitters, Indian Vegetable & Sarsaparilla, Pontil, Wear, Aqua, Pint, W-140 .... * 210.00
Bitters, Iron, Brown Chemical Co., Square, Amber, Pint, W-186 .... * 30.00
Bitters, Isaacson Seixas & Co., Wear, Yellow Amber, 3/4 Quart, W-187 .... * 475.00
Bitters, Ishams, Stomach, Burst Bubble, Square, Amber, 3/4 Quart, W-452 .... * 35.00
Bitters, J.C.& Co., Pineapple Shape, Double Collar, Pontil, Amber, 3/4 Quart .... * 700.00
Bitters, J.C.& Co., Pineapple Shape, Pontil, Deep Golden Amber .... * 700.00
Bitters, J.C.Segur's, Golden Seal, Springfield, Pontil, Aqua, Pint, W-300 .... * 80.00
Bitters, J.T.Higby Tonic, Milford, Ct., Square, Amber, W-331 .... 58.00
Bitters, J.T.Higby Tonic, Milford, Ct., Stain, Square, Amber, 3/4 Quart, W-331 .... * 35.00
Bitters, J.W.Colton's Nervine Strengthening, Chips, Amber, Pint, W-92 .... * 35.00
Bitters, J.Walker's Vinegar, Stain, W-L140 .... 7.50
Bitters, Jackson's Aromatic Life, Collared Mouth, Olive Green, W-188 .... * 325.00
Bitters, Jackson's Stonewall, Cabin, Yellow Amber, 3/4 Quart, W-189 .... *1400.00
Bitters, Jacob's Cabin Tonic, Aqua, 3/4 Quart, W-191 .... *4000.00
Bitters, Jacob's Cabin Tonic, Cabin, Pontil, Aqua, 3/4 Quart, W-191 .... *4000.00
Bitters, John Root's, 1834, Buffalo, N.Y., Rectangular, Amber, 3/4 Quart, W-284 .... * 175.00
Bitters, John W.Steele's Niagara, Star, Eagle, Flake, Square, Amber, W-316a .... * 150.00
Bitters, John W.Steele's Niagara, Star, Eagle, 1864 & 3 Stars, Amber, W-316a .... * 180.00
Bitters, John W.Steele's, Niagara, Star, Eagle, Square, Amber, W-316b .... * 160.00
Bitters, Johnson's Calisaya, Burlington, Vt., Square, Amber, 3/4 Quart, W-194 .... * 70.00
Bitters, Johnson's Calisaya, Burlington, Vt., W-194 .... 35.00 To 57.00
Bitters, Johnson's, Indian, Dyspeptic, Rectangular, Aqua, 1/2 Pint, W-195 .... * 120.00
Bitters, Jones' Indian Specific, Herb, 1868, Crack, Amber, 3/4 Quart, W-196 .... * 75.00
Bitters, Kaiser Wilhelm Co., Round, Stain, Amber, Quart, W-197 .... * 80.00
Bitters, Kelly's Old Cabin, Citrine Green, W-199 ....*Color* XXXX.XX
Bitters, Kelly's Old Cabin, Dark Green, W-199 ....*Color* XXXX.XX
Bitters, Kelly's Old Cabin, Patent 1863, Amber, W-199 .... 500.00

Bitters, Kelly's Old Cabin, Stain, Amber, 3/4 Quart, W-199

Bitters, Holtzermann's, Patent, Cabin,
Amber, 3/4 Quart, W-172
(See Page 35)

Bitters, Kelly's Old Cabin, Patent 1863, Cabin, Damage, Olive Amber, W-199 .... * 525.00
Bitters, Kelly's Old Cabin, Patent 1863, Cabin, Embossed, Olive Green, W-199 .... *1600.00
Bitters, Kelly's Old Cabin, Stain, Amber, 3/4 Quart, W-199 ....*Illus* 500.00
Bitters, Kennedy's East India, Iler & Co., Stain, Square, 3/4 Quart, W-200 .... * 15.00
Bitters, Kennedy's East India, Iler & Co., 9 In., W-200 .... 30.00
Bitters, Keystone, Barrel, Label, Amber, 3/4 Quart, W-201 .... * 350.00
Bitters, King Solomon's, Seattle, Wash., Rectangular, Amber, 7 1/4 In., W-457 .... 55.00
Bitters, King's, 25 Cents, Oval, Aqua, W-456 .... 48.00
Bitters, LaCour's Sarsapariphere, Crude Top, Green, W-204 .... 650.00
Bitters, LaCour's, Sarsapariphere, Pillar Shape, Stain, Chip, Amber, W-204 .... * 125.00
Bitters, Lady's Leg, Green, 12 1/2 In. 35.00
Bitters, Lady's Leg, Honey Amber, 12 1/2 In. 35.00

Bitters, Landsberg's Century, A.Heller & Bro., Chips, Square, Amber, W-205 .... * 125.00
Bitters, Landsberg's Century, Adler Co., St.Louis, Amber, 12 In. .... *Illus* 1200.00
Bitters, Langley's Root & Herb, BIMAL, Aqua, 5 1/2 In. 24.00
Bitters, Langley's, 99 Union Street, Pint 15.00
Bitters, Lash's Back Bar, Honey Amber, Quart, W-207 .... 85.00
Bitters, Lash's Kidney & Liver, Amber, W-208 .... 7.50 To 20.00
Bitters, Lash's, Natural Tonic Laxative, Square, Amber, Sample, W-207 .... * 50.00
Bitters, Lediard's, O.K. Plantation, 1840, Square, Stain, Amber, 3/4 Quart .... * 280.00
Bitters, Leipziger Burgunder Wein, Round, Yellow Green, Quart, W-212 .... * 60.00
Bitters, Lewis Red Jacket, New Haven, Conn., Amber, 3/4 Quart, W-213 .... 35.00
Bitters, Lewis Red Jacket, New Haven, Conn., Round, Amber, 3/4 Quart, W-213 .... * 30.00
Bitters, Life Of Man, C.Gates & Co., Aqua, W-214 .... 28.00
Bitters, Life Of Man, C.Gates & Co., Rectangular, Aqua, Pint, W-214 .... * 25.00

Bitters, Litthauer Stomach,
Invented 1864,
Milk Glass, 11 In.

Bitters, Landsbergs Century,
Adler Co., St.Louis,
Amber, 12 In.

Bitters, Lippman's Great German, New York & Savannah, Stain, Amber, W-215 .... * 60.00
Bitters, Lippman's Great German, Savannah, Square, Yellow Amber, W-215 .... * 170.00
    Bitters, Litthauer Stomach, see also Bitters, Hartwig Kantorowicz
    Posen
Bitters, Litthauer Stomach, Invented 1864, Gin Shape, 3/4 Quart, W-216 .... * 45.00
Bitters, Litthauer Stomach, Invented 1864, Milk Glass, 3/4 Quart, W-216 .... * 50.00
Bitters, Litthauer Stomach, Invented 1864, Milk Glass, 11 In. ....*Illus* 115.00
Bitters, Lohengrin, Adolph Marcus Von Buton, Milk Glass, 3/4 Quart, W-218 .... * 130.00
Bitters, Lorimer's, Juniper Tar, Elmira, N.Y., Square, Blue Green, W-219 .... * 325.00
Bitters, Lowell's, Invigorating, Boston, Mass., Square, Aqua, Pint, W-221 .... * 75.00
Bitters, Lyman's Dandelion, C.Sweet & Bro., Me., Aqua, 3/4 Quart 45.00
Bitters, Lyman's Dandelion, C.Sweet & Bro., Me., Aqua, 3/4 Quart, W-460 .... * 20.00
Bitters, M.G.Landsberg's, Stain, Flakes, Bruise, Amber, 3/4 Quart, W-205 .... * 70.00
Bitters, Malarion, Snyder Gue & Condell, Square, Amber, 3/4 Quart, W-223 .... * 25.00
Bitters, Malt Bitters Company, Boston, Yellow Green, Pint, W-224 .... * 20.00
Bitters, Malt Bitters Company, Boston, Yellow Green, 3/4 Quart, W-224 .... 20.00
Bitters, Malt, Company, Boston, Collared Mouth, Yellow Green, 3/4 Quart, W-224 .... 20.00
    Bitters, Mandrake, see Bitters, Dr.Baxter's Mandrake
Bitters, Marshall's, Best Laxative, Stain, Square, Amber, 3/4 Quart, W-227 .... * 30.00
Bitters, McKeever's Army, Amber, W-228 ....*Color* XXXX.XX
Bitters, McKeever's Army, Drum Shape, Amber, 3/4 Quart, W-228 .... 2300.00
Bitters, McKeevers Army, Drum Shape, Flakes, Amber, 3/4 Quart, W-228 .... *1500.00
Bitters, Mishler's Herb, Dr.S.B.Hartman & Co., Amber, 3/4 Quart, W-229 .... 35.00
Bitters, Mishler's Herb, Dr.S.B.Hartman & Co., Dark Amber, 3/4 Quart, W-229 .... * 40.00
Bitters, Mishler's Herb, Dr.S.B.Hartman & Co., Tablespoon, Citron, W-229a .... * 35.00
Bitters, Mishler's Herb, Stoeckels Grad Pat '66, Amber, 3/4 Quart, W-229b .... * 20.00
Bitters, Morning Star, Inceptum 5869, Triangular, Amber, 3/4 Quart, W-232 .... * 160.00
Bitters, Morning Star, IP, Amber, 3/4 Quart, W-232 .... 150.00 To 225.00
Bitters, Moultons Oloroso, Trademark, Stain, Aqua, 3/4 Quart, W-233 .... * 90.00
Bitters, N.K.Brown, Iron & Quinine, Rectangular, Chip, Aqua, 1/2 Pint .... * 45.00
Bitters, National, Ear Of Corn, Amber, 12 1/2 In. 190.00
Bitters, National, Ear Of Corn, Aqua, W-236 ....*Color* XXXX.XX

Bitters, National, Ear Of Corn, Aqua, W-236 .... *1600.00
Bitters, National, Ear Of Corn, Golden Amber, W-236 .... * 225.00
Bitters, National, Ear Of Corn, Label, Deep Puce, W-236 .... *1000.00
Bitters, National, Ear Of Corn, Puce, W-236 .... Color XXXX.XX
Bitters, National, Ear Of Corn, Stain, Aqua, 3/4 Quart, W-236 .... Illus 1050.00
Bitters, National, Ear Of Corn, Yellow, W-236 .... * 375.00
Bitters, New York Hop, Aqua, 9 3/4 In. 190.00
Bitters, New York Hop, Textured Glass, Aqua, W-472 .... 325.00
Bitters, Nightcap, Schmidlapp & Co., Cincinnati, Triangular, 3/4 Quart, W-238 .... * 100.00
Bitters, O.H.P.Rose's Great Peruvian King, Triangular, Amber, Quart, W-L110 .... * 60.00
Bitters, O.K.Plantation, 1840, Patent 1868, Gothic Windows, Triangular, Puce *1800.00
Bitters, O'Leary's 20th Century, Square, Amber, 3/4 Quart, W-245 .... * 45.00
Bitters, O'Leary's 20th Century, Square, Amber, 3/4 Quart, W-245 .... 75.00
Bitters, Old Cabin, Patent 1863, Cabin, Smooth Base, Amber, 3/4 Quart, W-239 .... * 900.00
Bitters, Old Continental, Rectangular, Smooth Base, Amber, W-240 .... * 150.00
Bitters, Old Dr.Goodhue's Root & Herb, J.H.Russell & Co., Aqua, Pint, W-437 .... * 25.00
Bitters, Old Dr.Goodhue's, Aqua, Pint, W-437 .... 58.00
Bitters, Old Dr.Solomon's, Great Indian, Rectangular, Stain, Aqua, Pint, W-311 .... * 55.00
Bitters, Old Dr.Solomon's, Indian Wine, Rectangular, Aqua, Pint, W-311 .... * 45.00
Bitters, Old Dr.Townsend's, Flattened Chestnut, Pontil, Amber, W-333 .... *3200.00
Bitters, Old Dr.Warren's, Quaker, Flint & Co., R.I., Aqua, 3/4 Quart, W-357 .... * 40.00
Bitters, Old Dr.Warren's, Quaker, Flint & Co., R.I., Rectangular, Aqua, W-357 .... * 40.00
Bitters, Old Home, Cabin, Square, Yellow Green, 14 In. 50.00
Bitters, Old Home, Laughlin Smith & Co., Wheeling, W.Va., Square, Amber, W-241 .... * 160.00
Bitters, Old Homestead Wild Cherry, Amber, 3/4 Quart, W-242 .... Illus 175.00
Bitters, Old Homestead Wild Cherry, Patent, Cabin, Amber, W-242 .... * 195.00
Bitters, Old Homestead Wild Cherry, Patent, Cabin, Flake, Yellow Green, W-242 .... * 550.00
Bitters, Old Homestead Wild Cherry, Patent, Cabin, Sapphire Blue, W-242 .... *16500.00
Bitters, Old Homestead Wild Cherry, Patent, Cabin, Smooth Base, Amber, W-242 .... * 250.00
Bitters, Old Jamaica Stomach, Applied Handle, Amber, 3/4 Quart, W-L72 .... * 50.00
Bitters, Old Sachem & Wigwam Tonic, Barrel, 20 Rings, Amber, 3/4 Quart, W-244 .... 165.00
Bitters, Old Sachem & Wigwam Tonic, Barrel, 20 Rings, Bruise, Yellow, W-244 .... * 375.00
Bitters, Old Sachem & Wigwam Tonic, Barrel, 20 Rings, Chip, Aqua, W-244a .... * 800.00
Bitters, Old Sachem & Wigwam Tonic, Barrel, 20 Rings, Chip, Yellow, W-244 .... * 175.00
Bitters, Old Sachem & Wigwam Tonic, Barrel, 20 Rings, Flakes, Puce, W-244 .... * 110.00
Bitters, Old Sachem & Wigwam Tonic, Barrel, 20 Rings, Smoky Olive, W-244 .... * 950.00
Bitters, Old Sachem & Wigwam Tonic, Burgundy, W-244 .... 225.00
Bitters, Only 25 Cents, Clarke's Sherry Wine, Pontil, Aqua, Pint, W-87 .... * 85.00
Bitters, Only 70 Cents, Clarke's Vegetable Sherry Wine, Bruise, Aqua, W-88i .... * 40.00
Bitters, Orange, Aqua, 12 In. 20.00
Bitters, Original Pocahontas, Y.Ferguson, Barrel, 20 Rings, Aqua, W-259 .... *1400.00
Bitters, Orruro, Round, Smooth Base, Green, 3/4 Quart, W-248 .... * 10.00
Bitters, Oswego, 25 Cents, Oval, Smooth Base, Amber, 1/2 Pint, W-477 .... * 75.00
Bitters, Oxygenated, Dyspepsia, Asthma, Aqua, 1/2 Pint, W-249b .... * 55.00
Bitters, Oxygenated, For Dyspepsia, Asthma, Pontil, Aqua, 1/2 Pint, W-249 .... * 40.00
Bitters, Parker's Celebrated Stomach, Amber, W-480 .... 75.00
Bitters, Parker's Celebrated Stomach, Square, Stain, Amber, W-480 .... * 20.00
Bitters, Pepsin Calisaya, Dr.Urssell Med. Co., Yellow Green, Pint, W-253 .... * 45.00

Bitters, Old Homestead Wild Cherry,
Amber, 3/4 Quart, W-242

Bitters, Peruvian Tonic, Bruise, Rectangular, Golden Amber, 3/4 Quart, W-255 .... * 60.00
Bitters, Peruvian, Flakes, Square, Amber, W-254 .... * 25.00
Bitters, Peruvian, Label, Square, Amber, W-254 .... * 25.00
Bitters, Phoenix, John Moffat, OP, Haze, Aqua, 5 1/2 In. 35.00
Bitters, Phoenix, Price 1 Dollar, Pontil, Crack, Olive Amber, 1/2 Pint, W-257b .... * 110.00
Bitters, Phoenix, Price 1 Dollar, Pontil, Golden Amber, W-257a .... * 275.00
Bitters, Phoenix, Price 1 Dollar, Pontil, Olive Amber, 1/2 Pint, W-257c .... * 140.00
Bitters, Phoenix, Price 1 Dollar, Pontil, Olive Green, 1/2 Pint, W-257 .... * 200.00
Bitters, Phoenix, Price 1 Dollar, Pontil, Rectangular, Aqua, 1/2 Pint, W-257a .... * 60.00
Bitters, Phoenix, Price 1 Dollar, Pontil, Rectangular, 1/2 Pint, W-257 .... * 180.00
   Bitters, Pig, see Bitters, Berkshire, Bitters, Suffolk
Bitters, Pine Tree Tar Cordial, L.Q.Wishart's Patent 1859, Green, 8 In. 40.00
Bitters, Pine Tree Tar Cordial, Phila., 1859, Green, 10 In. .... Illus 48.00
Bitters, Pineapple Shape, Pontil, Yellow Amber .... * 200.00
Bitters, Pineapple, Double Collared Mouth, Smooth Base, Amber, 3/4 Quart 100.00
Bitters, Pineapple, J.C.& Co., Amber, 3/4 Quart .... Illus 400.00
Bitters, Polo Club Stomach, Trade Mark, Square, Amber, W-260 .... * 30.00
Bitters, Polo Club, Square, Amber, W-260 .... 140.00
Bitters, Pond's Kidney & Liver, Square, Amber, W-487 .... 20.00
Bitters, Poor Man's Family, Label, Rectangular, Aqua, 1/2 Pint, W-262 .... * 30.00
Bitters, Poor Man's Family, Rectangular, Quart, 6 1/4 In., W-262 .... 22.00 To 30.00

Bitters, National, Ear of Corn, Stain, Aqua, 3/4 Quart, W-236
(See Page 38)

Bitters, Pine Tree Tar Cordial, Phila., 1859, Green, 10 In.

Bitters, Pineapple,
J.C. & Co., Amber,
3/4 Quart

Bitters, Prickly Ash, Label, Square, Amber, W-263a .... * 20.00
Bitters, Prickly Ash, Square, Amber, W-263 .... 20.00
Bitters, Professor Geo.J.Byrne, N.Y., Great Universal, 1870, 3/4 Quart, W-63 .... * 510.00
Bitters, Prune Stomach & Liver, Square, Amber, W-264 .... 65.00
   Bitters, Quaker, see Bitters, Dr.Flint's Quaker
Bitters, Ramsey's Trinidad, Stain, Round, Olive Amber, 1/2 Pint, W-268 .... * 25.00
Bitters, Red Jacket, Monheimer & Co., Square, Amber, 3/4 Quart, W-271 .... * 40.00
Bitters, Reed's, Lady's Leg, Stain, Amber, W-272 .... * 175.00
Bitters, Reed's, New London, Ct., Lady's Leg, Amber, 12 In. 85.00
Bitters, Renault, Label, ABM, Amber, Miniature 10.00
Bitters, Rex Kidney & Liver, Best Laxative & Blood Purifier, Amber, W-274a .... * 5.00
Bitters, Rex Kidney & Liver, Nothing Else, Square, Amber, W-274 .... * 30.00
Bitters, Rocky Mountain, Tonic, 1840 Try Me 1870, Burst Bubble, Amber, W-281 .... * 75.00
Bitters, Romaine's Crimean, Patent 1860, Stain, Amber, 3/4 Quart, W-282 .... * 140.00
Bitters, Romaine's Crimean, Patent 1863, Square, Amber, 3/4 Quart, W-282 .... * 160.00
Romaine's Crimean, Patent 1863, W-282a 175.00
Bitters, Rose Hill Stomach, H.M.Mosher & Co., Stain, Square, Citron .... * 120.00
Bitters, Royal Pepsin Stomach, L & A Scharff, Rectangular, Amber, Pint, W-287 .... 65.00
Bitters, Royal Pepsin Stomach, L & A Scharff, Rectangular, Amber, W-287 .... * 55.00

Bitters, Royce's Sherry Wine, Rectangular, Aqua, Pint, W-288 .... * 190.00
Bitters, Rush's, A.H.Flanders, M.D., N.Y., Square, W-289 .... 22.00
Bitters, Rush's, A.H.Flanders, M.D., N.Y., Square, Yellow Amber, W-289 .... * 20.00
Bitters, Russ St.Domingo, Bubbles, Citron, W-290 .... 140.00
Bitters, Russ St.Domingo, New York, Flake, Square, Amber, 3/4 Quart, W-290 .... * 15.00
Bitters, Russian, Woman Holding Tray With Bottle On Label, Aqua, 9 In. 150.00
Bitters, S.O.Dunbar, Taunton, Mass., Pontil, Stain, Aqua, Pint, W-L45 .... * 160.00
Bitters, S.O.Richardson's, BIMAL, Aqua, 7 In., W-275 .... 10.00 To 18.00
Bitters, S.O.Richardson's, Flared Lip, OP, W-275 .... 45.00
Bitters, S.O.Richardson's, South Reading, Pontil, Stain, Aqua, Pint, W-275 .... * 30.00
Bitters, S.Steinhardt Bros. & Co. On Base, Bruise, Amber, 1/2 Pint, W-373 .... * 25.00
    Bitters, S.T.Drake's, see Bitters, Drake's Plantation, Bitters,
    Drake's 1860 Plantation
Bitters, Saint Jacob's, Square, Stain, Amber, 3/4 Quart, W-453 .... * 20.00
Bitters, Salutaris, S.F., Byrne & Castree, Chip, Amber & Puce, W-292 .... * 410.00
Bitters, Sanitarium, Hi Hi Co., Ill., Stain, Yellow Green, 3/4 Quart, W-495 .... * 110.00
Bitters, Sarasina Stomach, Square, Amber, W-294 .... 35.00
Bitters, Sarasina Stomach, Square, Stain, Amber, W-294 .... * 25.00
Bitters, Sazarac Aromatic, Phd & Co., Lady's Leg, Cobalt, W-296 .... *7000.00
Bitters, Sazarac Aromatic, Phd & Co., Lady's Leg, Milk Glass, Pint, W-296a .... * 450.00
Bitters, Sazarac Aromatic, Phd & Co., Lady's Leg, Milk Glass, W-296 .... * 325.00
Bitters, Sazarac Aromatic, Phd & Co., Lady's Leg, Olive Amber, Pint, W-296a .... * 600.00
Bitters, Scandinavian Tonic, Label, Square, Golden Amber, W-L118 .... * 55.00
Bitters, Schroeder's, Louisville, Ky., Ky.G.W.Co., Lady's Leg, Amber, W-297 .... * 225.00
Bitters, Seaworth Co., Cape May, Lighthouse, Stain, Amber, 3/4 Quart, W-299 .... *2450.00
Bitters, Sharp's Mountain Herb, Square, Amber, W-301 .... * 40.00
Bitters, Sharp's Mountain Herb, Square, Amber, W-301 .... 125.00
Bitters, Shurtleff's Blood & Dyspepsia, Oval, W-303 .... 35.00
Bitters, Simon's Centennial, Aqua, W-304 .... Color XXXX.XX
Bitters, Simon's Centennial, Bust Of Washington, Amber, 3/4 Quart, W-304 .... *1200.00
Bitters, Simon's Centennial, Bust Of Washington, Aqua, W-304 .... * 650.00
Bitters, Simon's Centennial, Repro, Washington Bust, Amber, 3/4 Quart .... * 35.00
Bitters, Sol Franck's Panacea, Kayman & Rhine, Lighthouse, Amber, W-310 .... * 500.00
Bitters, Sonoma Wine, C.A.Richards & Co., Boston, Label, Square, Amber, W-L120 ..... * 15.00
Bitters, Spring, W.D.Shedd, Jamestown, N.Y., Label, Square, Amber .... * 50.00
Bitters, St.Goddard Herb, Mete & Kanne, St.Louis, Amber, 3/4 Quart, W-141 .... * 20.00
Bitters, St.Jacob's, Decanter, Crack, 3/4 Quart, W-453 .... * 50.00
Bitters, Steinfeld's French Cognac, 1867, Square, Yellow Amber, W-317 .... * 900.00
Bitters, Stekette's Blood Purifying, Chip, Square, Amber, 1/2 Pint, W-318 .... * 50.00
Bitters, Suffolk, Philbrook & Tucker, Pig, Yellow Amber, 3/4 Quart, W-322 .... * 525.00
Bitters, Suffolk, Pig, Amber, W-322 .... Color XXXX.XX
Bitters, Suffolk, Pig, Yellow Amber, 3/4 Quart, W-322 .... Illus 400.00
Bitters, Sunny Castle Stomach, Jos Dudenhoefer, Milwaukee, Amber, W-325 .... * 20.00
Bitters, Swiss Stomach, Zoeller Medical Co., 2 Grooves On Ends, Amber, W-329 .... * 70.00
Bitters, Tilton's Dandelion, Under Glass, Wicker Case, Amber, Quart, W-L131 .... * 275.00
Bitters, Tippecanoe, H.H.Warner & Co., Tree Bark, Bruises, Golden Amber .... * 50.00
Bitters, Tippecanoe, H.H.Warner & Co., Tree Bark, Bruises, Golden Amber .... * 100.00
Bitters, Tippecanoe, H.H.Warner & Co., Tree Bark, Golden Amber .... * 55.00
Bitters, Tippecanoe, H.H.Warner & Co., Tree Bark, Golden Amber .... * 70.00
Bitters, Tippecanoe, H.H.Warner & Co., Tree Bark, Label, Olive Amber .... * 130.00
Bitters, Tippecanoe, H.H.Warner & Co., Tree Bark, Olive Green .... * 800.00
Bitters, Tippecanoe, H.H.Warner, Patent Nov.20, '83, Tree Bark, Amber .... * 80.00
Bitters, Tippecanoe, H.H.Warner, Stomach Color .... XXXX.XX
Bitters, Toneco Stomach, Appetizer & Tonic, Dug, Square, 9 1/4 In., W-330 .... 22.50
Bitters, Traveler's, Figure Of Man, 1834 & 1870, Oval, Amber, 3/4 Quart, W-334 .... *2600.00
Bitters, Try Warner's Wild Cherry, Pontil, Restored, Amber, Quart, W-L230 .... * 40.00
Bitters, Tuft's Tonic, Label, Flecks, Cloudy, W-L133 .... 13.00
Bitters, Tyler's Standard American, Square, Golden Amber, W-337 .... * 75.00
Bitters, U.S.Gold, 20 Dollar Gold Piece, 1897, Square, Aqua, 3/4 Quart, W-340 .... * 325.00
Bitters, Udolpho Wolfe's Aromatic Schnapps, Schiedam, Olive Green, Quart 40.00
Bitters, Udolpho Wolfe's Aromatic Schnapps, Square, Yellow, 8 1/8 In. 58.00
Bitters, Udolpho Wolfe's Schiedam Aromatic Schnapps, Yellow Green, Pint 25.00
Bitters, Udolpho Wolfe's Schnapps, IP, Olive Green, Pint 19.00
Bitters, Udolpho Wolfe's Schnapps, Gloppy Lip, Olive Amber, Pint 26.00
Bitters, Udolpho Wolfe's Schnapps, Olive Green, 8 1/4 In. 15.00

Bitters, Udolpho Wolfe's Schnapps, Yellow, 9 1/2 In. 18.00
Bitters, Underberg, Lady's Leg, Stain, Red Amber, 12 1/2 In., W-L134 .... 25.00
Bitters, Von Humboldt's German, Liver Complaint, Aqua, 1/2 Pint, W-345 .... * 130.00
Bitters, W & Co., N.Y., Pineapple Shape, Applied Handle, Pontil, Amber *2100.00
Bitters, W & Co., N.Y., Pineapple Shape, Double Collar, IP, Olive Green *1000.00
Bitters, W & Co., N.Y., Pineapple Shape, Double Collar, Pontil, Amber .... * 250.00
Bitters, W & Co N.Y., Pineapple Shape, Pontil, Golden Amber *2100.00
Bitters, W.C., Brobst & Rentschler, Barrel, Amber, W-347 .... 510.00
Bitters, W.C., Brobst & Rentschler, Barrel, 3 Rings, Chip, Amber, W-347 .... * 375.00
Bitters, W.F.Servera, Stomach, Stain, Bruise, Square, Amber, W-321 .... * 10.00
Bitters, W.L.Richardson's, South Reading, Pontil, Aqua, W-276a .... * 220.00
Bitters, W.R.Tyree's, Chamomile, Square, Yellow Amber, Pint, W-338 .... * 120.00
Bitters, Wahoo & Calisaya, Jacob Pinkerton, Label, Square, Amber, W-349 .... * 170.00
Bitters, Wahoo & Calisaya, Jacob Pinkerton, Square, Amber, W-349 .... 125.00
Bitters, Wahoo, Loveridge, XXX, 1863, Crack, Square, Golden Amber, W-348 .... * 75.00
Bitters, Whaoo, Loveridge, XXX, 1863, Square, Amber, W-348 .... * 200.00
Bitters, Wait's Kidney & Liver, California's, Amber, 3/4 Quart, W-350 .... * 50.00
Bitters, Wakefield's Strengthening, Rectangular, Aqua, 1/2 Pint, W-510 .... * 15.00
Bitters, Walker's Cock-Tail, Lady's Leg, Similar To W-351, Amber .... * 225.00
Bitters, Walker's, V.B., Embossed Base, Round, Yellow Green, W-L140 .... * 20.00
Bitters, Wampoo, Blum Siegel & Bro., Stain, Yellow Amber, 3/4 Quart, W-354 .... * 45.00
Bitters, Wampoo, Siegel & Bro., N.Y., Square, Stain, Amber, 3/4 Quart, W-354a ...... * 50.00
Bitters, Warner's Safe Tonic, Rochester, N.Y., Label, Oval, Amber, W-L142 .... 200.00
Bitters, Warner's Safe, Amber, 7 1/2 In., W-356a 500.00
Bitters, Warner's Safe, Light Amber, 9 1/2 In., W-356 .... 500.00
Bitters, Warner's Safe, Rochester, N.Y.Oval, Amber, Pint, W-356 .... * 350.00

Bitters, Suffolk, Pig, Yellow Amber, 3/4 Quart, W-322
(See Page 40)

Bitters, Wishart's Pine Tree Tar Cordial, 1859, Aqua, 8 1/2 In.

Bitters, Washington Bust, Repro, Blue, 9 1/2 In. .... * 10.00
Bitters, Webb's Improved Stomach, C.E.Webb & Bro., Square, Amber, W-358 .... * 45.00
Bitters, Webb's Improved Stomach, C.E.Webb & Bro., Square, Amber, W-358 .... 75.00
Bitters, West India Stomach, St.Louis, Mo., Square, Label, Amber, W-359 .... * 30.00
Bitters, Wheat, Flakes, Bruise, Rectangular, Amber, W-360 .... * 45.00
Bitters, Wheeler's Berlin, Collared, Hexagonal, Olive Yellow, Quart, W-361 .... *4000.00
Bitters, Wheeler's Genuine, Oval, Aqua, W-517 .... 75.00
Bitters, Wheeler's Genuine, Smooth Base, Oval, Aqua, 3/4 Quart, W-517 .... * 45.00
Bitters, Whitwell's Temperance, Boston, Pontil, Rectangular, Aqua, Pint, W-364 ..... * 110.00
Bitters, Whitwell's Temperance, OP, Rectangular, Amber, W-364 .... 120.00
Bitters, Willard's Golden Seal, Oval, Aqua, Pint, W-367 .... * 30.00
Bitters, Willard's Golden Seal, Oval, Aqua, Pint, W-367 .... 35.00
Bitters, William Allen's Congress, Collar, Dark Puce, 3/4 Quart, W-5 .... * 325.00
Bitters, William Allen's Congress, Emerald Green, 3/4 Quart, W-4 .... * 250.00
Bitters, William Allen's Congress, Repro, Same As W-5, Amethyst, Pint .... * 60.00
Bitters, William Allen's Congress, Repro, Same As W-5, Amethyst, Pint .... * 250.00
Bitters, Wishart's Pine Tree Tar Cordial, 1859, Aqua, 8 1/2 In. .... *Illus* 50.00
Bitters, Wm.Rittmeier's California Wine, Yellow Amber, 3/4 Quart, W-492 .... * 50.00
Bitters, Woodbury's, Steinhardt Bros., N.Y., 16 Panels, Amber, Pint, W-373 .... * 40.00

Bitters, Woodcock Pepsin, John H.Schroeder, Stain, Amber, Pint, W-374 .... * 20.00
Bitters, Wonser's, U.S.A., Smooth Base, Square, Blue Green, W-519 .... * 80.00
Bitters, Yerba Buena, S.F., Cal., Crude Top, Light Amber, Pint, W-375 .... 85.00
Bitters, Yerba Buena, S.F., Cal., Flask, Amber, Pint, W-375 .... * 40.00
Bitters, Yerba Buena, S.F., Cal., Flask, Smooth Base, Amber, Quart, W-375a .... * 40.00
Bitters, Yerba Buena, S.F., Cal., Swirls Of Color, Pint, W-375 .... 60.00
Bitters, Yerba Buena, S.F., Cal., 2 On Shoulder, Flask, Bruise, Amber, W-375b .... * 35.00
Bitters, Yochim Bros. Celebrated Stomach, Labels, Square, Amber, W-376 .... * 35.00
Bitters, Yochim Bros. Celebrated Stomach, Square, Amber, W-376 .... 35.00
Bitters, Zingari, Dark Amber, 12 1/2 In. .... *Illus* 175.00
Bitters, Zingari, Lady's Leg, Flakes, Amber, W-377 .... * 140.00
Black & White, Scottie Dog 15.00
Black Amethyst, Weeks & Potter, Quart 25.00
  Blacking, see Shoe Polish
Blown, Applied Lip, Globular, Pale Green, 8 1/2 In. 65.00
Blown, Applied Top, Whittled, Deep Olive, Quart 15.00
Blown, Bar, Pittsburgh, Flint, Pillar Mold, Neck Ring, Ribbed, 14 1/4 In. 52.00
Blown, Beveled Corners, Pontil, White Specks, Rectangular, Amber, 8 In. .... * 290.00
Blown, Collared Mouth With Stopper, Globular, Crack, Olive Amber, 6 In. .... * 20.00
Blown, Collared Mouth With Stopper, Pontil, Square Gin Shape, 13 In. .... * 40.00
Blown, Collared Mouth, Globular, Pontil, Crack, Olive Amber, 3 1/4 In. .... * 45.00
Blown, Collared Mouth, Globular, Pontil, Dark Olive Amber, 7 1/4 In. .... * 85.00
Blown, Collared Mouth, Globular, Pontil, Light Amber, 3 In. .... * 80.00
Blown, Collared Mouth, Globular, Pontil, Light Yellow Green, 5 1/4 In. .... * 70.00
Blown, Collared Mouth, Globular, Pontil, Olive Amber, 2 1/4 In. .... * 200.00
Blown, Collared Mouth, Globular, Pontil, Olive Amber, 3 3/8 In. .... * 210.00
Blown, Collared Mouth, Globular, Pontil, Olive Amber, 3 5/8 In. .... * 160.00
Blown, Collared Mouth, Globular, Pontil, Olive Amber, 9 1/2 In. .... * 60.00
Blown, Collared Mouth, Globular, Pontil, Olive Green, 3 1/4 In. .... * 170.00
Blown, Collared Mouth, Globular, Pontil, Stain, Aqua, 8 1/8 In. .... * 30.00
Blown, Colored Spatter, 11 In. .... *Illus* 800.00
Blown, Cut Designs, Gilt Trim, Stopper, Pontil, 8 1/4 In. .... * 25.00
Blown, Diamond, 4 1/2 In. 7.50
Blown, Double Collared Mouth, Globular, Pontil, Olive Amber, 4 In. .... * 40.00
Blown, Expanded Flared Mouth, Pontil, Square Gin Shape, Amber, 11 In. .... * 450.00
Blown, Flared Mouth, Globular, Pontil, Amber, 5 1/8 In. .... * 100.00
Blown, Flared Mouth, Pontil, Flake, Flattened Sides, Green, 1 3/4 In. .... * 85.00
Blown, Flared Mouth, White Specks, Pontil, Ewer Shape, Olive Green, 9 In. .... * 310.00
Blown, Globular, Amber, 8 1/4 In. 175.00
Blown, High Kick-Up, Aqua, 6 1/2 In. 17.50
Blown, Jar, Applied Rings, Stopper, Pontil, 10 1/2 In. .... * 30.00
Blown, Jar, Beveled Corners, Pontil, Square, Olive Amber, 13 1/2 In. .... * 750.00
Blown, Jar, Collared Mouth, Pontil, Stain, 9 1/8 In. .... * 90.00
Blown, Jar, Flared Mouth, Painted Decoration, Pontil, Cobalt, 10 In. .... * 310.00
Blown, Jar, Flared Mouth, Pontil, Olive Amber, 7 1/2 In. .... * 120.00
Blown, Jar, Flared Mouth, Pontil, Olive Amber, 9 1/2 In. .... * 220.00
Blown, Jar, Flared Mouth, Pontil, Square, Aqua, 7 3/4 In. .... * 60.00
Blown, Jar, Lockport, N.Y., Flared Lip, Light Green, 13 1/2 In. 150.00
Blown, Jar, New England, Flared Lip, Olive Green, 12 1/2 In. 150.00
Blown, Jar, Olive Green, 12 1/2 In. 120.00
Blown, Jar, Olive Green, 13 3/8 In. 120.00
Blown, Jar, Olive Green, 14 1/4 In. 130.00
Blown, Jar, Pontil, Dark Olive Amber, 9 1/4 In. .... * 200.00
Blown, Jar, Pontil, Deep Olive Amber, 16 In. .... * 160.00
Blown, Jar, Pontil, Olive Amber, 8 In. .... * 250.00
Blown, Jar, Pontil, Olive Amber, 8 3/8 In. .... * 280.00
Blown, Jar, Pontil, Olive Amber, 15 1/4 In. .... * 325.00
Blown, Jar, Pontil, Olive Green, 9 3/8 In. .... * 170.00
Blown, Jar, Pontil, Square, Light Green, 8 1/8 In. .... * 85.00
Blown, Jar, Rolled Collared Mouth, Glass Lid, Pontil, Light Green, 9 In. .... * 75.00
Blown, Jar, Rolled Collared Mouth, Pontil, Light Green, 7 1/4 In. .... * 70.00
Blown, Jar, Rolled Collared Mouth, Pontil, Olive Green, 13 3/4 In. .... * 65.00
Blown, Jar, Salem Co., New Jersey, C.1840, 9 1/2 In. ....*Color* XXXX.XX
Blown, Jar, Sheared Mouth With Ring, Bulbous, Pontil, Olive Green, 9 3/4 In. .... * 700.00
Blown, Jar, Sheared Mouth With Ring, Crack, Olive Amber, 20 1/4 In. .... * 350.00

Bitters, Zingari, Dark Amber, 12 1/2 In.
(See Page 42)

Blown, Colored Spatter, 11 In.
(See Page 42)

Blown, Jar, Sheared Mouth With Ring, Pontil, Olive Amber, 13 In.	* 525.00
Blown, Jar, Sheared Mouth With Ring, Pontil, Olive Amber, 13 1/4 In.	* 450.00
Blown, Jar, Sheared Mouth With Ring, Pontil, Olive Amber, 16 3/4 In.	* 525.00
Blown, Jar, Sheared Mouth With Ring, Pontil, Squat, Olive Amber, 7 In.	* 425.00
Blown, Jar, Sheared Mouth With Ring, Pontil, 11 1/2 In.	* 25.00
Blown, Jar, Sheared Mouth, Pontil, Crack, Olive Amber, 6 3/4 In.	* 20.00
Blown, Jar, Sheared Mouth, Pontil, Crack, Olive Amber, 13 In.	100.00
Blown, Jar, Sheared Mouth, Pontil, Olive Amber, 10 In.	* 200.00
Blown, Jar, Sheared Mouth, Pontil, Olive Green, 9 3/4 In.	* 210.00
Blown, Jar, South Jersey, Covered, Applied Glass Bands, 10 In.	95.00
Blown, Jar, Tooled Collared Mouth, Pontil, Olive Green, 8 1/2 In.	* 230.00
Blown, Jar, Wide Mouth, Pontil, Yellow Green, 5 1/2 In.	* 100.00
Blown, Jug, Applied Handle, Collared Mouth, Pontil, Aqua, 13 In.	* 175.00
Blown, Medicine Type, Flared Mouth, Light Green, 5 3/8 In.	10.00
Blown, Midwestern, Ribbed, Globular, Pontil, Aqua, 11 3/4 In.	* 45.00
Blown, Midwestern, Ribs Swirled To Left, Globular, Amber, 7 3/4 In.	* 400.00
Blown, Midwestern, Ribs Swirled To Left, Globular, Amber, 8 1/4 In.	* 375.00
Blown, Midwestern, Ribs Swirled To Left, Globular, Amber, 8 1/2 In.	* 325.00
Blown, Midwestern, Ribs Swirled To Left, Globular, Amber, 8 7/8 In.	* 450.00
Blown, Midwestern, Ribs Swirled To Left, Globular, Aqua, 7 1/2 In.	* 100.00
Blown, Midwestern, Ribs Swirled To Left, Globular, Aqua, 10 1/2 In.	* 50.00
Blown, Midwestern, Ribs Swirled To Left, Globular, Pontil, Amber, 8 In.	* 75.00
Blown, Midwestern, Ribs Swirled To Left, Globular, Stain, Amber, 8 In.	* 350.00
Blown, Midwestern, Ribs Swirled To Left, Globular, Yellow Amber, 9 In.	* 450.00
Blown, Midwestern, Ribs Swirled To Left, Globular, Yellow Green, 8 In.	* 550.00
Blown, Midwestern, Ribs Swirled To Right, Globular, Amber, 7 3/4 In.	* 350.00
Blown, Midwestern, Ribs Swirled To Right, Globular, Amber, 8 1/4 In.	* 550.00
Blown, Midwestern, Ribs Swirled To Right, Globular, Aqua, 7 1/2 In.	* 130.00
Blown, Midwestern, Ribs Swirled To Right, Globular, Aqua, 7 3/4 In.	* 190.00
Blown, Midwestern, Ribs Swirled To Right, Globular, Aqua, 8 1/4 In.	* 100.00
Blown, Midwestern, Ribs Swirled To Right, Globular, Aqua, 8 3/4 In.	* 110.00
Blown, Midwestern, Ribs Swirled To Right, Globular, Pontil, Aqua	* 130.00
Blown, Midwestern, Ribs Swirled To Right, Globular, Pontil, Aqua, Quart	* 350.00
Blown, Midwestern, Ribs Swirled To Right, Globular, Wear, Amber, 10 In.	* 575.00
Blown, Midwestern, Ribs Swirled To Left, Globular, Pontil, Green, 7 In.	*1125.00
Blown, Midwestern, Vertical Ribs, Globular, Pontil, Wear, Aqua, 7 1/4 In.	* 50.00
Blown, Midwestern, 16 Ribs Swirled To Right, Globular, Aqua, 8 In.	* 40.00
Blown, Midwestern, 16 Swirled Ribs, Deep Amethyst, 5 1/4 In.	425.00
Blown, Midwestern, 20 Ribs, Globular, Flared Mouth, Pontil, Green, 6 In.	* 85.00
Blown, Midwestern, 24 Ribs Swirled To Left, Amber, 7 5/8 In.	500.00
Blown, Midwestern, 24 Ribs Swirled To Right, Globular, Amber, 7 3/4 In.	* 500.00

Blown, Midwestern, 24 Ribs, Globular, Pontil, Claret, 7 1/2 In. .... * 450.00
Blown, Olive Green, 9 1/2 In. 17.50
Blown, Pontil, Dark Olive Amber, 8 1/2 In. .... * 55.00
Blown, Pontil, Globular, Light Blue Green, 4 1/2 In. .... * 40.00
Blown, Pontil, Stain, Olive Green, 12 1/2 In. .... * 60.00
Blown, Ringed Neck & Body, Globular, Cobalt, Pint .... * 300.00
Blown, Rolled Collared Mouth, Globular, Pontil, Aqua, 3 3/8 In. .... * 95.00
Blown, Rolled Collared Mouth, Globular, Pontil, Aqua, 3 3/4 In. .... * 70.00
Blown, Rolled Collared Mouth, Globular, Pontil, Crack, Olive, 5 1/2 In. .... * 90.00
Blown, Rolled Collared Mouth, Pontil, Light Green, 4 In. .... * 20.00
Blown, Rolled Mouth, Globular, Pontil, Light Olive Amber, 3 In. .... * 350.00
Blown, Saddle, Sheared Mouth, Seedy Olive Amber, 8 In. .... * 50.00
Blown, Sheared Mouth With Ring, Flat Sides, Pontil, Olive Green, 4 1/4 In. .... * 75.00
Blown, Sheared Mouth With Ring, Globular, Bruise, Green, 3 1/2 In. .... * 190.00
Blown, Sheared Mouth With Ring, Globular, Pontil, Crack, Amber, 3 5/8 In. .... * 60.00
Blown, Sheared Mouth With Ring, Globular, Pontil, Green, 4 1/8 In. .... * 190.00
Blown, Sheared Mouth, Globular, Pontil, Chip, Dark Olive Amber, 4 1/4 In. .... * 210.00
Blown, Sheared Mouth, Pontil, Flask Shape, Olive Amber, 4 1/4 In. .... * 90.00
Blown, Square Gin Type, Pewter Top & Screw Cap, Stain, Olive Green, 12 In. .... * 270.00
Blown, Tapered Collar, Oval Shoulders, Misshapen, Aqua, 6 3/4 In. 12.00
Blown, Tooled Collared Mouth, Globular, Pontil, Olive Green, 3 7/8 In. .... * 210.00
Blown, Vial, Expanded Sheared Mouth, Pontil, Aqua, 10 1/8 In. .... * 25.00

Borghini ceramic containers are filled in Pisa, Italy. The more recent imports are stamped with the words "Borghini Collection Made in Italy, 1969."

Borghini, Horse's Head 8.00
Borghini, Lady 8.00
Borghini, Penguin .... 5.95 To 6.95
Brandy, Bulkley, Fiske & Co., Flat Chestnut, Aqua Handle, Yellow, 3/4 Quart *5600.00
Brandy, Clark's California Cherry Cordial, Quart 8.00
Brandy, Courvoisier, Display, 19 In. 20.00
Brandy, Good Samaritan, Gentry, Slote & Co., Chestnut, Bruises, Olive, Pint .... * 60.00
Brandy, Pond's Ginger, Quart 8.00
    Brooks, see Ezra Brooks
Burgie, Man, 1971 .... 8.95 To 19.95
Burgie, Salute To Los Angeles, 1973 .... 2.00
Buton, Amphora, Apricot Brandy, Silver Metal Trim, 5 In. 9.95
Buton, Amphora, Cherry Brandy, Silver Metal Trim, 5 In. 9.95
Buton, Stacked Dice .... 19.95 To 22.95
Buton, Stacked Dice, Milk Glass 49.95
    C.P.C., California Perfume Company, see Avon
    Cabin Still, see Old Fitzgerald
    Calabash, see Flask
Canadian Mist, Royal Canadian Mounted Policeman, Porcelain, 12 In. 10.00

Candy containers of glass were very popular after World War I. Small glass figural bottles held dime-store candy. Today many of the same shapes hold modern candy in plastic bottles.

Candy Container, Airplane, SOGW, 5 In. 25.00
Candy Container, Airplane, Army Bomber .... 5.95 To 15.00
Candy Container, Airplane, Spirit of Goodwill, Painted, 4 3/4 In. .... *Illus* 40.00
Candy Container, Airplane, Spirit Of Goodwill .... 35.00 To 65.00
Candy Container, Airplane, Tin Wings 22.50
Candy Container, Ambulance .... 15.00 To 18.00
Candy Container, Auto, Station Wagon, 1939 Style, Paneled Body, 5 In. 24.00
Candy Container, Auto, 1935 Style, Screw Opening In Rear, 4 In. 20.00
Candy Container, Auto, 1938 Style, Sloped Back, 4 5/8 In. 18.00
Candy Container, Auto, 4 Drive, Top Closure 30.00
Candy Container, Baby Grand Piano, Glass Top 12.00
Candy Container, Ball, Milk Glass 12.50
Candy Container, Barney Google, Black & Tan Paint, 3 3/4 In. .... *Illus* 120.00
Candy Container, Barney Google 68.00
Candy Container, Baseball .... 15.00 To 18.00
Candy Container, Basket .... 15.00 To 16.00

Candy Container, Airplane, Spirit of Goodwill,
Painted, 4 3/4 In.
(See Page 44)

Candy Container, Barney Google,
Black & Tan Painted, 3 3/4 In.
(See Page 44)

Candy Container, Binoculars, Milk Glass, 3 In.

Candy Container, Boat, 5 In.

Candy Container, Basket, Hanging	35.00
Candy Container, Battleship, 5 1/2 In.	21.00
Candy Container, Bear, Reading Book	35.00
Candy Container, Bear, Screw Top, 4 1/2 In.	2.00
Candy Container, Betty Boop	12.00
Candy Container, Billiken, Gold Paint	50.00
Candy Container, Binoculars, Milk Glass, 3 In. *Illus*	95.00
Candy Container, Black Bear	55.00
Candy Container, Boat, Cabin Cruiser, 5 In.	14.00
Candy Container, Boat, 5 In. *Illus*	3.00
Candy Container, Bond Mono Cell	20.00
Candy Container, Boot, Small Size	3.00 To 4.50
Candy Container, Boot, With Star	4.00
Candy Container, Bottle	8.50
Candy Container, Bottle, Nursing	5.00
Candy Container, Bottle, Nursing, Original Candy	2.50 To 7.00
Candy Container, Bottle, Nursing, Strough Label, Original Candy	7.00
Candy Container, Bowl	5.00
Candy Container, Bowl, Milk Glass	7.50
Candy Container, Boy On Drum, Painted, 4 1/2 In. *Illus*	95.00
Candy Container, Building, Milk Glass	45.00
Candy Container, Bulldog	6.00 To 25.00
Candy Container, Bulldog, Black	15.00
Candy Container, Bulldog, Painted	22.50
Candy Container, Bulldog, U.S.A., Brown, 4 In. *Illus*	25.00
Candy Container, Bulldog, Victory Glass, 1930	26.00

Candy Container, Boy On Drum, Painted, 4 1/2 In.
(See Page 45)

Candy Container, Bulldog, U.S.A.,
Brown, 4 In.
(See Page 45)

Candy Container, Bulldog, 1932	26.00
Candy Container, Bunker Hill Monument, 6 1/2 In.	12.00
Candy Container, Bus	35.00
Candy Container, Bus, San Francisco & New York, 4 1/4 In.	40.00
Candy Container, Bus, Victory Special, Painted	18.00
Candy Container, Camera On Tripod, Red & Black Painted, 5 In. ...... *Illus*	85.00
Candy Container, Candleholder	15.00
Candy Container, Car, Electric Coupe	40.00 To 50.00
Candy Container, Car, Sedan	18.00
Candy Container, Car, 1913 Sedan	55.00
Candy Container, Charlie Chaplin, Painted, 4 In. ...... *Illus*	45.00
Candy Container, Charlie Chaplin, Painted	45.00 To 65.00
Candy Container, Chicken	9.00 To 22.50
Candy Container, Chicken On Nest	8.50
Candy Container, Chicken On Nest, Millstein	22.00
Candy Container, Chicken On Nest, 1946	22.00
Candy Container, Chicken On Oblong Basket	23.00 To 55.00
Candy Container, Church, Tin Over Glass	27.00
Candy Container, Cigar, Amber	22.00
Candy Container, Clock, Mantel	45.00
Candy Container, Clock, Octagon	65.00
Candy Container, Clown Dog, Crossetti	3.00
Candy Container, Cruiser	3.00 To 12.50
Candy Container, Dirigible, Los Angeles	65.00
Candy Container, Dog, Sitting, 3 In.	6.50
Candy Container, Dog, Stripped Hat	20.00
Candy Container, Doll	17.50
Candy Container, Donkey Pulling Cart, 9 X 4 In.	26.00
Candy Container, Dresser, Compliments F.Roberts Furniture Store	125.00
Candy Container, Duck	16.50 To 22.50
Candy Container, Dutch Windmill	24.00
Candy Container, Elephant	18.00
Candy Container, Elephant, Frosted	18.00
Candy Container, Elephant, G.O.P., Gray	68.00 To 85.00
Candy Container, Engine	20.00
Candy Container, Fat Boy	22.00
Candy Container, Felix The Cat, Cork Closure, Germany	50.00
Candy Container, Fire Engine, Blue Tint	35.00
Candy Container, Fire Engine, Driver, C.1930, 5 In.	8.75

Candy Container, Fire Engine, Tin Wheels, 5 In. 40.00
Candy Container, Fire Engine, Victory Glass Co. 5.00
Candy Container, Fire Engine, 5 1/2 In. .... *Illus* 30.00
Candy Container, Fire Truck With Driver, Bell On Hood, 5 In. 24.00
Candy Container, Fire Truck With Driver, Steam Boiler On Back, 4 3/4 In. 25.00
Candy Container, Fire Truck With Driver, 5 In. .... 20.00 To 40.00
Candy Container, Fire Truck, Red Paint 8.50
Candy Container, Fish, Amber, 6 1/4 In. 8.00
Candy Container, Flatiron, 4 1/2 In. 15.00
Candy Container, George Washington 7.00
Candy Container, Girl With Muffle, 6 1/4 In. 25.00
Candy Container, Goose Girl 16.00
Candy Container, Gun, Blown 35.00
Candy Container, Gun, Original Candy 8.00
Candy Container, Gun, Screw Cap, 3 3/4 In. 4.50
Candy Container, Gun, Screw-On Cap, Cork Insert, 10 In. 15.00
Candy Container, Gun, Tin Closure 14.50
Candy Container, Gun, Yellow, Candy 23.00
Candy Container, Gun, 7 In. .... 10.00 To 12.50

Candy Container, Camera on Tripod,
Red & Black Painted, 5 In.
(See Page 46)

Candy Container, Charlie
Chaplin, Painted, 4 In.
(See Page 46)

Candy Container, Hand, 5 1/4 In. 20.00
Candy Container, Hat .... 17.50 To 25.00
Candy Container, Hat, Military Cap .... 7.50 To 20.00
Candy Container, Hat, Tin Brim 35.00
Candy Container, Hearse 75.00
Candy Container, Hearse With Tassel Window 50.00
Candy Container, Helicopter 25.00
Candy Container, Hen, Cardboard Closure 8.00
Candy Container, Hen, Sliding Tin Base 20.00
Candy Container, Horn, Original Candy 8.00
Candy Container, Horse, Spark Plug, Black & Orange Painted, 3 In. .... *Illus* 50.00
Candy Container, Horse & Wagon .... 7.00 To 12.00
Candy Container, Hound Dog 9.50
Candy Container, Hound Dog, Sitting, Screw Cap, 3 1/2 In. 4.00
Candy Container, Hound Pup With Soap 4.00
Candy Container, Hound Pup, Original Candy 6.00
Candy Container, House, Painted, Tin Slip Bottom, 3 In. 20.00
Candy Container, Independence Hall, 1876 .... 65.00
Candy Container, Iron 16.00
Candy Container, Iron, Tin Bottom 40.00

Candy Container, Fire Engine, 5 1/2 In.
(See Page 47)

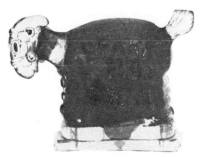

Candy Container, Horse, Spark Plug,
Black & Orange, Painted, 3 In.
(See Page 47)

Candy Container, **Jack-O'-Lantern**	55.00
Candy Container, **Jeep**	14.00
Candy Container, **Kettle,** Paper Bail	10.00
Candy Container, **Kewpie By Barrel**	27.00
Candy Container, **Kewpie,** Slotted Closure For Bank	50.00
Candy Container, **Kiddie Car,** Painted	75.00
Candy Container, **Lamp,** Original Candy	8.00
Candy Container, **Lamp,** Tin Top	12.50
Candy Container, **Lantern,** Barn	35.00
Candy Container, **Lantern,** Barn, Red	25.00 To 30.00
Candy Container, **Lantern,** Candy	5.00 To 10.00
Candy Container, **Lantern,** Dec.2, 1904	15.00
Candy Container, **Lantern,** Flint Globe	20.00
Candy Container, **Lantern,** Glass & Tin	9.00
Candy Container, **Lantern,** Glass & Tin, Metal Handle	15.00
Candy Container, **Lantern,** Metal Top & Bail	8.00
Candy Container, **Lantern,** Painted	22.50
Candy Container, **Lantern,** Tin Cover, 2 3/4 In.	8.00
Candy Container, **Lantern,** Tin Cover, 3 In.	8.00
Candy Container, **Lantern,** Tin Cover, 3 5/8 In.	4.50
Candy Container, **Lantern,** Tin Shade, Screw Cap, 3 In.	4.50
Candy Container, **Lantern,** Twins	8.00
Candy Container, **Lantern,** 2 1/4 In.	4.50
Candy Container, **Lantern,** 4 1/2 In. *Illus*	12.00
Candy Container, **Learned Fox**	32.50 To 45.00
Candy Container, **Liberty Bell**	35.00 To 76.50
Candy Container, **Liberty Bell,** Amber	18.00 To 30.00
Candy Container, **Liberty Bell,** Gold Paint, 4 In.	15.00
Candy Container, **Liberty Bell,** Wire Bail	22.00
Candy Container, **Liberty Bell,** 1776-1876, Cork Top	32.00
Candy Container, **Lighthouse**	25.00 To 26.00

Candy Container, Lincoln, Screw Top	6.00
Candy Container, Llama, Reclining, 7 In.	15.00
Candy Container, Locomotive	7.95 To 14.00
Candy Container, Locomotive 888	9.50
Candy Container, Locomotive, Switch Type, Lamp On Front Top, 4 1/4 In.	25.00
Candy Container, Madonna, Cobalt	22.00
Candy Container, Mickey Mouse, Japan, 3 In.	7.50
Candy Container, Midget Washer	12.50
Candy Container, Monkey, Screw Bottom, 5 In.	3.00
Candy Container, Moon Mullins	22.00 To 27.00
Candy Container, Moses, Ball Stopper, 10 In.	15.00
Candy Container, Motorboat	5.95
Candy Container, Mr.Pickwick	7.00
Candy Container, Mug	5.00 To 20.00
Candy Container, Mug, Drum	37.00
Candy Container, Naked Child	24.00 To 36.00
Candy Container, Oaken Bucket, Milk Glass	35.00 To 35.00
Candy Container, Opera Glasses	35.00
Candy Container, Opera Glasses, Milk Glass	65.00
Candy Container, Opera Glasses, Red, Plain Panels	45.00
Candy Container, Owl, 7 In.	18.00

Candy Container, Lantern, 4 1/2 In.
(See Page 48)

Candy Container, Rabbit,
Contents, 6 In.

Candy Container, Parrot, Milk Glass, 8 In.	18.00
Candy Container, Pencil	29.50 To 45.00
Candy Container, Perfume Girl	2.00
Candy Container, Peter Rabbit	9.00 To 12.50
Candy Container, Pig, Blown	7.00
Candy Container, Pig, Light Amber, 8 In.	18.00
Candy Container, Pig, Screw Top, 5 1/4 In.	2.00
Candy Container, Pipe	45.00
Candy Container, Pistol, Screw Cap, 7 In.	25.00
Candy Container, Pistol, 5 In.	15.00
Candy Container, Pistol, 7 1/2 In.	15.00
Candy Container, Pot	7.50
Candy Container, Powder Horn	25.00 To 32.50
Candy Container, Rabbit	8.50 To 22.00
Candy Container, Rabbit, Contents, 6 In.	Illus 13.50
Candy Container, Rabbit Eating Carrot	13.00
Candy Container, Rabbit In Cracked Egg	28.00
Candy Container, Rabbit In Cracked Egg, Gold	15.00 To 22.50
Candy Container, Rabbit, Metal Closure	22.00
Candy Container, Rabbit, Painted	28.00
Candy Container, Rabbit, Paws Next To Body, Painted	40.00
Candy Container, Rabbit, Sitting, Jeanette Glass Co., 6 1/2 In.	12.00
Candy Container, Rabbit, Sitting, 6 1/4 In.	18.00

Candy Container, **Rabbit,** Standing, Tin Screw Bottom	30.00
Candy Container, **Radio,** Tune-In	45.00
Candy Container, **Radio,** Tune-In, Horn, Jeanette, Pa., Paint	30.00
Candy Container, **Railroad Engine,** Covered, 6 In.	92.50
Candy Container, **Record Player,** Black Paint, 4 1/4 In. .... *Illus*	110.00
Candy Container, **Rolling Pin,** Glass Center, Wooden Handles, Tin Closure	25.00
Candy Container, **Rooster,** Crowing	50.00 To 70.00
Candy Container, **Russian Peasant**	70.00
Candy Container, **Safe,** Milk Glass	65.00 To 75.00
Candy Container, **Santa Claus,** Boot Section Holds Candy, Cardboard, Germany	8.00
Candy Container, **Santa Claus,** Celluloid Head	17.50 To 28.00
Candy Container, **Santa Claus,** Double Cuff	31.00
Candy Container, **Santa Claus,** German, 13 In.	22.50
Candy Container, **Santa Claus,** Holding Sack, Bisque, 4 In.	14.00
Candy Container, **Santa Claus,** Holding Sack, 3 In.	4.00
Candy Container, **Santa Claus,** Paneled Coat	45.00
Candy Container, **Santa Claus,** 5 In.	27.00
Candy Container, **Santa's Boot**	4.00
Candy Container, **Santa's Boot,** Paper Label	8.00

Candy Container, Record Player,
Black Paint, 4 1/4 In.

Candy Container, Scottie Dog

Candy Container, **Satchel**	18.50
Candy Container, **Satchel,** Handle, Tin Slide	22.00
Candy Container, **Scottie Dog** .... *Illus*	12.00
Candy Container, **Scottie Dog,** Standing	5.00
Candy Container, **Scottie Dog,** Tin Closure	12.00
Candy Container, **Seated Chinese Man,** Cork, 4 1/2 In.	30.00
Candy Container, **Ship**	20.00
Candy Container, **Shoe,** 3 1/2 In.	12.00
Candy Container, **Sitting Puppy**	3.95
Candy Container, **Skookum By Tree Stump**	125.00
Candy Container, **Soda Mug,** Design In Panels, 2 1/2 In.	10.00
Candy Container, **Spark Plug,** Closure	55.00 To 85.00
Candy Container, **Station Wagon,** 4 1/2 In. .... *Illus*	7.50
Candy Container, **Steamer Trunk,** Closure, Souvenir N.Y., Milk Glass	35.00
Candy Container, **Suitcase,** Milk Glass	30.00 To 35.00
Candy Container, **Suitcase,** Milk Glass, Decal Of Victorian Ladies	30.00
Candy Container, **Suitcase,** Tin Closure	15.00
Candy Container, **Suitcase,** Victorian Decal Scene, Tin Closure	28.00
Candy Container, **Suitcase,** 3 1/2 X 2 1/2 In.	25.00
Candy Container, **Tank**	9.00 To 18.00
Candy Container, **Tank,** Blown	18.00
Candy Container, **Tank,** World War I, Painted	50.00

Candy Container, Tank, 2 Cannons, U.S.A. & Star, 4 1/4 In. 25.00
Candy Container, Tank, 2 Cannons, Victory, U.S.A. & Star 28.00
Candy Container, Tank, 5 In. .... *Illus* 19.00
Candy Container, Telephone .... 9.00 To 25.00
Candy Container, Telephone, Dial 15.00
Candy Container, Telephone, Millstein's 20.00
Candy Container, Telephone, Original Candy, 5 In. 30.00
Candy Container, Telephone, Tot's 17.00
Candy Container, Telephone, Upright, 4 In. .... *Illus* 15.00
Candy Container, Toonerville Trolley, Painted, 3 1/2 In. .... *Illus* 310.00

Candy Container, Station Wagon, 4 1/2 In.
(See Page 50)

Candy Container, Tank, 5 In.

Candy Container,
Telephone, Upright, 4 In.

Candy Container, Toonerville Trolley,
Painted, 3 1/2 In.

Candy Container, Top 22.50
Candy Container, Top, Wooden Winder 25.00
Candy Container, Touring Car, Opaline 19.50
Candy Container, Train .... 15.00 To 49.50
Candy Container, Train, Musical, Candy 6.00
Candy Container, Trumpet, Milk Glass 60.00
Candy Container, Trunk 25.00
Candy Container, Trunk, Milk Glass 35.00
Candy Container, Trunk, Milk Glass, Butler Bros., C.1907 .... 60.00
Candy Container, Turkey Gobbler 35.00
Candy Container, Turkey, 2 Part, 7 In. 52.00
Candy Container, Twins 7.50
Candy Container, Uncle Sam 55.00
Candy Container, Violin, Applied Lip, 5 1/2 In. 35.00
Candy Container, Washboard 16.00
Candy Container, Wheelbarrow 30.00
Candy Container, Wheelbarrow, Red Closure & Wheel 32.50
Candy Container, Willys Jeep 6.00
Candy Container, Willys Jeep With Driver 18.00
Candy Container, Windmill .... 20.00 To 27.00
    Canning Jar, see Fruit Jar
Carboy, Tapered Collared Lip, Whittled Bottom, Aqua, 5 3/4 In. 9.00

Case bottles are those of the traditional shape known by this name. The bottles have flat sides and are almost square. Some taper and are narrower at the bottom. Case bottles can be of any age from the mid-1600s to the present day.

Case, Free Blown, Pontil, Rectangular, Olive Green, 8 1/4 In.	* 50.00
Case Gin, Applied Seal, Bubbles, Dark Olive, 8 1/2 In.	30.00
Case Gin, Applied Seal, Embossed, Olive, 10 3/4 In.	47.50
Case Gin, Applied Seal, 9 1/4 In.	17.50
Case Gin, Applied Seal, 10 1/4 In.	22.50
Case Gin, Applied Seal, 11 In.	25.00
Case Gin, Applied Top, Whittled, Air Bubbles, Olive Green, 10 1/2 In.	18.00
Case Gin, Avan Hoboken, Embossed Seal, Blob Top, 10 3/4 In.	37.50
Case Gin, Blown In Mold, Olive Green, 11 In.	22.00
Case Gin, Flared Lip, OP, Deep Olive Amber, 8 3/4 In.	45.00
Case Gin, Flared Lip, OP, 12 In Wooden Box	400.00
Case Gin, Inside Haze, Dark Olive Green, 10 7/8 In.	10.00
Case Gin, Olive Green, Quart	39.00
Case Gin, Olive Green, 5 1/2 In.	13.00
Case Gin, Olive, 10 1/4 In.	6.00
Case Gin, Olive, 11 In.	8.00
Case Gin, OP, Olive Amber, 10 In.	27.00
Case Gin, OP, Olive Green, 9 3/8 In.	35.00
Case Gin, OP, Olive Green, 10 In.	27.00
Case Gin, Palmboom, C.Meyer & Co., Schiedam, C.1860, Olive Green, 1/2 Gallon	75.00
Case Gin, Paper Label, 9 1/4 In.	17.50
Case Gin, Paper Label, 10 1/4 In.	22.50
Case Gin, Quart	2.00
Case Gin, 11 In.	8.00 To 25.00
Case, Amelung Type, Blown, Flint, Gilt Trim, Soda Lime, 7 1/4 In.	35.00
Case, Amelung Type, Blown, Flint, Rectangular, Soda Lime, 7 1/4 In.	35.00
Case, Amelung Type, Blown, Flint, Soda Lime, 5 1/4 In.	35.00
Case, Amelung Type, Blown, 5 1/4 In.	35.00
Case, Amelung Type, Blown, 7 1/4 In.	35.00
Case, Blown, Ball Stopper, Gilt Decoration, 8 1/2 In.	40.00
Case, Stiegel Type, Blown, Blob Type, Stopper, Gold Trim, C.1750, Pint	25.00
Case, Stiegel Type, Flint, Blown, Gilt Decoration, 8 1/2 In.	40.00
Case, Stiegel Type, Flint, Blown, Gilt Trim, 8 In.	35.00
Case, Stiegel Type, Flint, Blown, Gilt Trim, 8 1/2 In.	40.00
Case, Stiegel Type, Flint, Blown, 6 In.	35.00
Case, Stiegel Type, Half Post, Etched Shoulder, OP, 6 In.	19.00
Castor, McK G I-10, Blown, 3 Mold	24.00
Castor, McK G I-15, Blown, 3 Mold	22.00
Chemical, BIMAL, Short Applied Neck, Cobalt, 7 1/2 In.	3.25
Chemical, Eastman Kodak, BIMAL, Amber, 3 1/2 In.	3.00

Coca-Cola,
C.1900, 6 1/2 Ozs.
(See Page 53)

Coca-Cola, First Throwaway, 9 In.
(See Page 53)

Chemical, J.K.Palmer, Boston, Dug, 9 In. 20.00
Chemical, John Meyer, Mt.Clemens, Mich., Stain, Amber, 9 1/4 In. 7.00
Chemical, Maltine Mfg.Co., N.Y., Flat Oval Front, Amber, 7 1/2 In. 1.50
Chemical, Maltine Mfg.Co., N.Y., Oval, Amber, 7 1/2 In. 1.50
Chemical, Maltine Mfg.Co., N.Y., 3 Mold, Stain, Amber, 7 3/4 In. 7.25
Chemical, Oakland Comp'y, Flared Lip, Amber, 5 In. 3.25
Chemical, Oakland Comp'y, Skirted Collar, Stain, Amber, 5 In. 3.00
Chemical, Rumford Works, BIMAL, Teal, 5 1/2 In. 6.00
Chemical, Rumford Works, Green, 4 In. 12.00
Chemical, Rumford Works, Lockport, Teal, 6 In. 7.00
Chemical, Rumford Works, Lockport, Teal, 7 1/2 In. 12.00
Chemical, Rumford Works, Patent March 10, 1868, 8 Sided, Blue Green, 5 3/4 In 6.00
Chemical, Ruston Clark Co., New York, Aqua, 10 In. 45.00
Chemical, Undertaking Supply, Chicago, Ill., 8 In. 2.00
Chemical, United States Chemical, New York, Chicago, Blob Top, 1/2 Gallon 7.00
Chemical, W.C.Merchant, Chemist, Lockport, N.Y., Dark Green, 1/2 Pint, 4 In. 65.00
Chemical, Weeks & Potter, Boston, Mass.Paper Label, Lip Ring, Amber, 5 1/2 In 8.00
Clevenger Bros., Washington Co., Md., 1776-1976, Blue 9.00

Coca-Cola, Biedenharn Candy
Co., Vicksburg, Miss., C.1894

Coca-Cola, Registered, Biedenharn
Candy Co., Vicksburg, 8 In.

*Coca-Cola was first made in 1886. Since that time the drink has been
sold in all parts of the world in a variety of bottles. The "waisted" bottle
was first used in 1916.*

Coca-Cola, Biedenharn Candy Co., Vicksburg, Miss.C.1894 .... Illus   18.00
Coca-Cola, C.1900, 6 1/2 Ozs. .... Illus   25.00
Coca-Cola, Canadian, 6 Ozs. 2.00
Coca-Cola, Dec.25, 1923, Maui, T.H., 6 Ozs. 6.00
Coca-Cola, Christmas, Poughkeepsie, N.Y., 6 Ozs. .... 3.00 To 3.50
Coca-Cola, Dec.25, 1923, 20 In. 100.00
Coca-Cola, Donald Duck, Painted Pictures, 7 Ozs. .... 3.00 To 4.75
Coca-Cola, Embossed, Made In Taiwan, 2 1/2 In. .... .50
Coca-Cola, Embossed, 1975, Teal Green, 10 Ozs. 35.00
Coca-Cola, Embossed, 6 Ozs. 1.00
Coca-Cola, First Throwaway, 9 In. .... Illus   5.00
Coca-Cola, Hobble Skirt, Rejected, 64 Ozs. 7.50
Coca-Cola, Israel Exposition, 1975, 6 1/2 Ozs. 6.00
Coca-Cola, J.S.Francis, Avon Park, Fla., Patent 11-6-23, 6 Ozs. 5.00
Coca-Cola, Johnson & Johnson, Statesville, N.C., Olive Green, 6 1/2 Ozs. 5.00
Coca-Cola, Machined & Tooled Mouth, Amber, 1/2 Pint .... * 10.00
Coca-Cola, Registered, Biedenharn Candy Co., Vicksburg, 8 In. .... Illus   90.00

Coca-Cola, 1923, Display, 20 In. 95.00
Coca-Cola, 64 Ozs. 10.00
Collectors Art, Cardinal, Cologne, 7 In. .... *Illus* 12.50
Collectors Art, Hummingbird, Cologne, 7 In. .... *Illus* 12.50
Collectors Art, Parakeet, Cologne, 7 In. .... *Illus* 12.50
 Cologne, see also Perfume, Scent
Cologne, Alternating Vertical Diamond & Plain Panels, Blue, 5 5/8 In. .... * 85.00
Cologne, Aurene, Amphora Shape, Pedestal Base, Steeple Stopper, Blue, 7 In. 425.00
Cologne, Aurene, Amphora Shape, Pedestal, Peacock Blue Iridescent, 6 3/4 In. 385.00
Cologne, Barred, Ground Mouth, Pontil, Aqua, 2 7/8 In. .... * 15.00
Cologne, Basket Shape, Oval, Aqua, 3 In. .... * 35.00
Cologne, Beaded Rib, 8 In. 200.00
Cologne, Bell Shape, Flared Mouth With Stopper, Pontil, Cobalt, 5 In. .... * 65.00
Cologne, Bellows Shape, Flared Mouth, Pontil, 2 15/16 In. .... * 40.00
Cologne, Beveled Corners, Pontil, Rectangular, Aqua, 4 1/8 In. .... * 10.00
Cologne, Beveled Corners, Rectangular, Smooth Base, Cobalt, 4 7/8 In. .... * 95.00
Cologne, Blown, Flint, Arches, Basket Of Flowers, 5 Sided, 5 In. 35.00
Cologne, Blown, Pear Shape, Hollow Stopper, Ruby Stained, 9 1/2 In. 32.00
Cologne, Blown, Ruby Glass, 9 3/4 In. 28.00
Cologne, Bohemian Glass, Rococo Enameling, Pagoda Shape, Cranberry, 6 1/2 In 150.00
Cologne, Bristol Type, Corseted, Gold Decoration, Powder Blue, 5 3/8 In. .... * 60.00

Collectors Art, Cardinal, Collectors Art, Parakeet, Collectors Art,
Cologne, 7 In.   Cologne, 7 In.   Hummingbird,
               Cologne, 7 In.

Cologne, Bristol, Teardrop Stopper, White & Black Trim, Blue Frosted, 8 In. 50.00
Cologne, Building, Tooled Collared Mouth, Smooth Base, Milk Glass, 5 In. .... * 310.00
Cologne, Bulbous Jug, Applied Handle, Spout, Smooth Base, 3 1/2 In. .... * 7.50
Cologne, Bull's-Eye, Barrel, OP, Haze, Aqua, 3 In. 18.00
Cologne, Bunker Hill Monument, Figural, 6 1/2 In. 25.00
Cologne, Bunker Hill Monument, Figural, 11 3/4 In. 25.00
Cologne, Cathedral, OP, 5 3/4 In. .... *Illus* 100.00
Cologne, Charley Ross & Bust In Panel, Corset Shape, Smooth Base, 4 3/4 In. .... * 75.00
Cologne, Charley Ross & Bust In Panel, Corset Shape, Smooth Base, 5 1/2 In. .... * 170.00
Cologne, Charley Ross & Girl With Hoop, Corset Shape, 6 In. .... * 200.00
Cologne, Clamshell Design, Rolled Mouth, Stain, Oval, Aqua, 3 5/8 In. .... * 35.00
Cologne, Collared Mouth, Bulged Neck, Pontil, Rectangular, 5 1/4 In. .... * 20.00
Cologne, Corseted Near Base, Pontil, Aqua, 5 1/4 In. .... * 90.00
Cologne, Corseted, Flared Mouth, 12 Sided, Amethyst, 7 3/8 In. 210.00
Cologne, Corseted, Octagonal, Blue Opaque, 4 3/4 In. .... * 140.00
Cologne, Corseted, Painted Decoration, Opalescent, 5 In. .... * 35.00
Cologne, Corseted, Tooled Mouth, Octagonal, Blue, Opalescent, 4 3/4 In. .... * 450.00
Cologne, Cut Glass, American Strawberry Diamond & Floral, 6 1/2 In. 75.00

Cologne, Cut Glass, Engraved Lizzie, 1876, Paneled, Flared Base, 9 1/2 In. .... * 35.00
Cologne, Cut Glass, Faceted Stopper, Etched Bells & Ivy, Cane Base, 7 In. 35.00
Cologne, Cut Glass, Faceted Stopper, Harvard, 7 In., Pair 150.00
Cologne, Cut Glass, Faceted Stopper, Vertical Cuttings, 5 1/2 In. 35.00
Cologne, Cut Glass, Green To Clear, 5 1/2 In. 195.00
Cologne, Cut Glass, Hobstar, Fan, & Crosscut Diamond, 7 1/2 In. 80.00
Cologne, Cut Glass, Lapidary Stopper, Notched Prisms, Flute Neck, 6 In. 75.00
Cologne, Cut Glass, Leaves, Acid-Etched Blossoms, Black Enamel, 5 In. 20.00
Cologne, Cut Glass, Notched Prisms, 6 In., Pair 45.00
Cologne, Cut Glass, Red To Clear, 6 1/2 In. 225.00
Cologne, Cut Glass, Sterling Cap, Rectangular, Ruby, 3 3/8 In. 20.00
Cologne, Cut Glass, Victorian, Violets & Leaves, Sterling Cap, 5 1/2 In. 49.00
Cologne, Cut Glass, 5 X 3 1/2 In. 47.50
Cologne, Cylindrical, Tapering Neck, Amethyst, 9 3/8 In. 65.00
Cologne, Embossed, Milk Glass, 9 In., Pair 40.00
Cologne, Extrait Eau De, OP, 6 Sided, Aqua, 5 5/8 In. 12.00
Cologne, Fancy Corners, Tapered, Flared Mouth, Square, Aqua, 5 5/8 In. .... * 30.00

Cologne, Cathedral, OP, 5 3/4 In.
(See Page 54)

Cologne, Ground Stopper, Gold Trim, OP, Cobalt, 8 1/4 In.

Cologne, Fancy Corners, Tapering From Base To Neck, Square, 7 1/2 In. .... * 7.50
Cologne, Figural Shoe, Label, Tax Stamp, 5 3/4 In. 28.00
Cologne, Flared Mouth, Oval, Stain, Aqua, 6 In. .... * 45.00
Cologne, Flared Mouth, Partial Label, Pontil, Oval, 4 1/8 In. .... * 20.00
Cologne, Flared Mouth, Pontil, Oval, 4 In. .... * 20.00
Cologne, Flared Mouth, Pontil, Rectangular, Aqua, 5 5/8 In. .... * 55.00
Cologne, Flared Mouth, Pontil, Rectangular, 7 7/8 In. .... * 100.00
Cologne, Flared Mouth, Pontil, Stain, Rectangular, Aqua, 6 1/4 In. .... * 20.00
Cologne, Floradora, Footed, Cranberry, 9 In. 95.00
Cologne, Floral, Flattened Shape, Chip, Pontil, Aqua, 4 1/2 In. .... * 15.00
Cologne, Floral, Rolled Mouth, Pontil, Burst Bubble, Aqua, 5 7/8 In. .... * 35.00
Cologne, Floral, Rolled Mouth, Pontil, Rectangular, Aqua, 5 5/8 In. .... * 30.00
Cologne, Floral, Stain, Rectangular, 6 3/8 In. .... * 30.00
Cologne, Fluted Panel, Pontil, Stain, Aqua, 10 1/8 In. .... * 35.00
Cologne, Garfield, Bust Of Garfield Shape, Ground Mouth, Wood Base, 7 3/4 In .... * 200.00
Cologne, Gold On Stopper, Black Amethyst, 9 In. 36.00
Cologne, Grant Bust In Wreath, Oval, Smooth Base, 4 7/8 In. .... * 70.00
Cologne, Ground Stopper, Gold Trim, OP, Cobalt, 8 1/4 In. .... *Illus* 45.00
Cologne, H.W.& Co., Building, Pontil, Oval, Aqua, 4 In. .... * 45.00
Cologne, Hancock, Bust Of Hancock Shape, Label, 7 3/4 In. .... * 320.00
Cologne, Hawkes Glass, Sterling Silver Stopper, Venetian, 4 3/4 In., Pair 250.00
Cologne, Hire's, Philadelphia, 2 Panels, Sheared Top, Laydown, Aqua, 4 7/8 In. 6.50
Cologne, HL-176, Smooth Base, Lyre Shape, Oval, 2 7/8 In. .... * 96.00

Cologne, HL, Partial Label, Pontil, Oval, 3 15/16 In. .... * 30.00
Cologne, Hoyt's German, Lowell, Mass, Paper Label, 3 1/2 In. 5.50
Cologne, Indian, Cathedral, OP, Aqua, 4 In. 45.00
Cologne, Kaziun, Paperweight, Floral Stopper, Yellow Green Flower, 7 1/4 In. .... * 375.00
Cologne, L.Kossuth, Violin, Stain, Aqua, 5 3/4 In. .... * 300.00
Cologne, Label, Beveled Corners, Rectangular, Milk Glass, 3 3/4 In. .... * 75.00
Cologne, Label, Pontil, Hole, Oval, Aqua, 4 1/4 In. .... * 25.00
Cologne, Lion In Recessed Panel, Greek Key, Pontil, Cobalt, 4 7/8 In. *2600.00
Cologne, LM, Barrel, 4 In. .... * 60.00
Cologne, Madonna & Child, Cathedral, OP, Aqua, 5 3/4 In. 65.00
Cologne, Madonna & Child, Flared Collared Mouth, Pontil, Aqua, 5 1/2 In. .... * 50.00
Cologne, Man's Head & Urn, Flared Mouth, Pontil, Bruise, Aqua, 6 3/4 In. .... * 75.00
Cologne, Mary Gregory, Boy, Clear Stopper, Lavender, 7 1/2 In. 95.00
Cologne, Massachusetts, 5 In., Pair 50.00
Cologne, Molded, Pedestal Shape, 5 In. Stopper, Vaseline, 9 1/2 In. 46.00
Cologne, Monpelas, Sandwich, Cobalt, 9 1/2 In. ....*Illus* 70.00
Cologne, Monument, Chip, Square, Violet, 11 7/8 In. .... * 120.00
Cologne, Monument, Pontil, Chip, Square, Aqua, 4 1/2 In. .... * 20.00
Cologne, Monument, Sandwich Type, Chip, Square, 9 1/8 In. .... * 20.00
Cologne, Monument, Sandwich Type, Label & Stamp, Square, 6 1/2 In. .... * 25.00
Cologne, Monument, Sandwich Type, Rough, Square, 12 In. .... * 15.00
Cologne, Monument, Sandwich Type, Square, Amethyst, 6 1/2 In. .... * 250.00

Cologne, Monpelas, Sandwich, Cobalt, 9 1/2 In.

Cologne, Monument, Sandwich Type, Square, Cobalt, 7 7/8 In. .... * 110.00
Cologne, Monument, Sandwich Type, Square, Deep Amethyst, 11 3/4 In. .... * 280.00
Cologne, Monument, Sandwich Type, Square, Fiery Opalescent, 11 7/8 In. .... * 240.00
Cologne, Monument, Sandwich Type, Square, Lime Green, 9 1/8 In. .... * 180.00
Cologne, Monument, Sandwich Type, Square, Milk Glass, 6 1/2 In. .... * 80.00
Cologne, Monument, Sandwich Type, Square, Opalescent, 7 3/4 In. .... * 150.00
Cologne, Monument, Sandwich Type, Square, Smooth Base, 6 1/2 In. .... * 10.00
Cologne, Monument, Sandwich Type, Square, Smooth Base, 8 In. .... * 25.00
Cologne, Monument, Sandwich Type, Square, Teal Blue, 8 1/4 In. .... * 200.00
Cologne, Monument, Sandwich Type, Square, Teal Green, 6 1/2 In. .... * 210.00
Cologne, Monument, Square, Green, 11 7/8 In. .... * 220.00
Cologne, Monument, Square, Smooth Base, Fiery Opalescent, 8 In. .... * 75.00
Cologne, Monument, Square, Smooth Base, Square, 9 5/8 In. .... * 20.00
Cologne, Monument, Square, 9 5/8 In. 40.00
Cologne, Moses In The Bulrushes Figural, 5 In. 35.00
Cologne, NSP, Floral, Pontil, Rectangular, 5 1/2 In. .... * 75.00
Cologne, Pressed Glass, Daisy & Button, Square, Rounded Corners, 8 In., Pair 37.50
Cologne, Ribbed & Plain Panels, Bruise, 12 Sided, Smoky Amethyst, 5 5/8 In. .... * 150.00
Cologne, Ribs Swirled To Left, Cobalt, 5 3/8 In. .... * 120.00
Cologne, Ribs Swirled To Right, Sheared Mouth, Pontil, Aqua, 8 3/4 In. .... * 10.00
Cologne, Richard Hudnut, Violet Sec, Toilet Water, Gold On Cork, 23 In. 385.00

Cologne, Ricketts, Bristol On Smooth Base, Octagonal, Olive Green, 7 1/4 In. .... * 140.00
Cologne, Rolled Collared Mouth, Pontil, 12 Sided, Aqua, 4 5/8 In. .... * 32.50
Cologne, Rolled Collared Mouth, Pontil, 12 Sided, Sapphire Blue, 7 5/8 In. .... * 80.00
Cologne, Rolled Mouth, Pontil, Oval, Aqua, 3 3/4 In. .... * 30.00
Cologne, Rolled Mouth, Pontil, Stain, Rectangular, Aqua, 5 3/4 In. .... * 45.00
Cologne, Roped Corners, Square, Smooth Base, 6 3/8 In. .... * 20.00
Cologne, Roped Corners, Tapered, Pontil, Square, Aqua, 7 5/8 In. .... * 40.00
Cologne, Sandwich Glass, 12 Sided, Peacock Blue Green, 5 In. 70.00
Cologne, Sandwich Type, Corseted, Octagonal, Smooth Base, Teal Blue, 4 5/8 In .... * 230.00
Cologne, Sandwich Type, Corseted, Tooled Mouth, Octagonal, Cobalt, 6 In. .... * 130.00
Cologne, Sandwich Type, Flake, 12 Sided, Teal Blue, 4 3/4 In. .... * 50.00
Cologne, Sandwich Type, Flared Mouth, 12 Sided, Smooth Base, Violet, 5 5/8 In .... * 65.00
Cologne, Sandwich Type, Free Blown, Tapering, Pontil, Crack, Blue, 16 In. .... * 75.00
Cologne, Sandwich Type, Long Tapering Neck, Amethyst, 9 3/4 In. .... * 160.00
Cologne, Sandwich Type, Pontil, 12 Sided, Sapphire Blue, 4 1/2 In. .... * 100.00
Cologne, Sandwich Type, Tapered, Pontil, Blue, Opalescent, 10 7/8 In. .... * 85.00
Cologne, Sandwich Type, Tapering Neck, Pontil, Chip, 12 Sided, 8 In. .... * 210.00
Cologne, Sandwich Type, 12 Sided, Stain, Amethyst, 7 1/2 In. .... * 110.00
Cologne, Sandwich, Paneled, Cobalt, 5 5/8 In. 48.00
Cologne, Sandwich, Paneled, Label, Violet Purple, 11 In. 120.00
Cologne, Sandwich, Tapers Inward From Shoulder To Base, Blue, 7 In. 90.00
Cologne, Scroll & Beading, Milk Glass, Opalescent, 9 1/2 In. 31.00
Cologne, Sheared Mouth, Pontil, Oval, Aqua, 3 15/16 In. .... * 45.00
Cologne, Sheared Mouth, Pontil, Square, 8 1/4 In. .... * 7.00
Cologne, Shield Shape, Flared Mouth, Pontil, Aqua, 3 15/16 In. .... * 15.00
Cologne, Silver Overlay, Floral, Emerald Green, 5 In. 110.00
Cologne, Steche Floral, Rectangular, Smooth Base, Deep Amethyst, 4 3/8 In. .... * 60.00
Cologne, Sterling Stopper & Holder, Cobalt, 6 In. 65.00
Cologne, Steuben, Flower Petal Stopper, 4 Sided, Smoky Amber, 5 1/2 In. 75.00
Cologne, Superior Cologne Water, Vertical Ribs, Neck Ring, Aqua, 3/4 Quart .... * 25.00
Cologne, Tapering From Base To Mouth, 12 Sided, Cobalt, 11 1/2 In. .... * 130.00
Cologne, Tapering From Base To Neck, Blue, Opalescent, 11 1/4 In. .... * 100.00
Cologne, Tapering From Base To Neck, 12 Sided, Fiery Opalescent, 7 1/2 In. .... * 160.00
Cologne, Tapering, Crack, Square, 7 3/4 In. .... * 30.00
Cologne, Thumbprint, Tapering From Base To Neck, Square, Amethyst, 5 3/4 In. .... * 150.00
Cologne, Toilet Water, McK G I-7, Tam-O'-Shanter Stopper, Blown, Blue 45.00
Cologne, Toilet Water, Ribs Swirled To Left, Pale Yellow Green, 5 3/4 In. .... * 400.00
Cologne, Toilet Water, Ribs Swirled To Left, Pontil, Cobalt, 5 5/8 In. .... * 175.00
Cologne, Toilet Water, Sandwich Type, Pontil, Flake, Purple, 5 3/4 In. .... * 280.00
Cologne, Toilet Water, Sandwich Type, Vertical Ribs, Cobalt, 6 In. .... * 130.00
Cologne, Toilet Water, Vertical Ribs, Amethyst, 6 In., Pair .... * 150.00
Cologne, Toilet Water, Vertical Ribs, Sapphire Blue, 6 In. .... * 270.00
Cologne, Tooled Collared Mouth, Applied Handles, Smooth Base, 7 In. .... * 20.00
Cologne, Tooled Collared Mouth, 12 Sided, Smooth Base, Deep Violet, 11 In. .... * 95.00
Cologne, Tooled Flared Mouth, Rectangular, Stain, Aqua, 7 In. .... * 70.00
Cologne, Tooled Mouth With Ring, Smooth Base, Blue Green, 4 5/8 In. .... * 55.00
Cologne, Tooled Mouth, Emerald Green, 4 1/4 In. 25.00
Cologne, Tooled Mouth, Pontil, Hexagonal, Cobalt, 3 7/8 In. .... * 190.00
Cologne, Urns & Floral, Beveled Corners, Rectangular, Aqua, 6 1/2 In. .... * 45.00
Cologne, Val St.Lambert, Belgium, Vaseline, 8 X 6 1/2 In. 75.00
Cologne, Val St.Lambert, Etched, Gold Trim, 7 1/2 In. 25.00
Cologne, Vertical Ribs & Spiral Banner Of Stars, Milk Glass, 5 3/4 In. .... * 70.00
Cologne, Vertical Ribs & Spiral Banner Of Stars, Milk Glass, 6 1/2 In. .... * 55.00
Cologne, Vertical Ribs, Beaded, Smooth Base, Milk Glass, 5 3/4 In. .... * 65.00
Cologne, Vertical Ribs, Pontil, Stain, 3 1/4 In. .... * 17.50
Cologne, Vial, Free Blown, Tooled Mouth, Pontil, Aqua, 9 1/2 In. .... * 5.00
Cologne, Vial, Rolled Collared Mouth, Pontil, Light Green, 9 3/4 In. .... * 5.00
Cologne, Vial, Sheared Mouth, Smooth Base, Light Green, 8 1/2 In. .... * 10.00
Cologne, Victorian Girl Portrait Medallion, Gold Trim, Milk Glass, 9 In. 55.00
Cologne, Violin Shape, Rolled Mouth, Pontil, Aqua, 3 1/2 In. .... * 25.00
Cologne, Violin, Flared Mouth, Pontil, Chip, Aqua, 5 7/8 In. .... * 25.00
Cologne, Violin, Pontil, Aqua, 5 3/4 In. .... * 80.00
Cologne, Violin, Rolled Collared Mouth, Aqua, 6 1/2 In. .... * 150.00
Cologne, Wide Beveled Corners, Rectangular, Smooth Base, Amethyst, 4 3/4 In. .... * 55.00
Cologne, 6 Panels, Tooled Mouth, Smooth Base, Violet Blue, 9 In. .... * 220.00

Cologne, 12 Sided, Cork Stopper, Deep Amethyst, 7 1/4 In.	75.00
Cordial, Cambridge, Royal Blue, 12 Ozs.	20.00
Cordial, Cut Glass, Teardrop Stopper, Pinwheel & Crosshatching, 6 1/2 In.	85.00
Cornish Mead, Barrel, Brown, Miniature	7.00
Cornish Mead, Elf, Miniature	7.00
Cornish Mead, King Arthur, Miniature	12.00
Cornish Mead, Lighthouse, Blue, Miniature	8.00
Cornish Mead, Mermaid, No.1, Miniature	8.00
Cornish Mead, Running Light, Miniature	7.00
Cornish Mead, Smuggler On The Barrel, Miniature	7.95
Cornish Mead, Tin Mine, Miniature	8.00
Cornish Mead, Toby, Miniature	8.00
Cosmetic, A.S.Hinds, Portland, Me., Honey & Almond Cream, 2 In.	1.50
Cosmetic, Barbasol, 8 Panels, Screw On Tin Cap, C.1915, 3 1/4 In.	8.50
Cosmetic, C.Damschinsky Liquid Hair Dye, N.Y., BIMAL, Haze, Aqua, 3 1/4 In.	2.75
Cosmetic, Chamberlain's Hand Lotion, 2 1/2 In.	2.50
Cosmetic, Cold Cream, Larkin Co., Prunus Blossoms, 2 Ozs.	17.50
Cosmetic, Cremex Shampooing Vase, Blue, 8 1/2 In. ...... Illus	55.00
Cosmetic, Currier's Cocoanut Cream For The Hair, Aqua, 6 3/4 In.	6.00
Cosmetic, Dr.D.Jayne's American, Hair Dye, Collared Mouth, Aqua, 5 In.	* 50.00

Cosmetic, Cremex Shampooing Vase, Blue, 8 1/2 In.

Cosmetic, Hinds' Honey & Almond Cream,
50 Cents, 5 1/2 In.

Cosmetic, Rogers'
Nursery Hair Lotion,
Aqua, 6 1/2 In.

Cosmetic, Ely's Cream Balm, 4 In.	1.50
Cosmetic, Hagan's Magnolia Balm, Milk Glass, 5 In.	6.50
Cosmetic, Hinds' Honey & Almond Cream, 50 Cents, 5 1/2 In. ...... Illus	2.50
Cosmetic, Hurd's Golden Gloss For The Hair, Rectangular, Aqua, 6 In.	35.00
Cosmetic, Katherion For The Hair, OP, 6 In.	15.00
Cosmetic, Larkin Sachet Powder, Jar, Oz.	2.00
Cosmetic, Macassar Oil For The Hair, London, Flared Lip, Aqua, 3 1/2 In.	16.50
Cosmetic, Masco Tonique For The Hair, 6 1/4 In.	3.50
Cosmetic, Noxema Shaving Cream, Jar, Cobalt Blue, 1/2 Gallon	48.00
Cosmetic, Palmer Baby Powder, Blue Green, 5 1/8 In.	5.00
Cosmetic, Paragon Hair Coloring, Amber, 3 1/2 In.	6.00
Cosmetic, Parker's Hair Balsam, N.Y., Blop Lip With Skirt, Amber, 6 1/2 In.	3.00
Cosmetic, Paul Westphal, Auxiliator For The Hair, N.Y., 8 In.	5.00
Cosmetic, Pomade, Muzzled Bear, Sandwich, Black Amethyst, 3 1/4 In.	165.00
Cosmetic, Pomade, Muzzled Bear, X Bazin, Phila., Sandwich, Opalescent, 4 In.	165.00
Cosmetic, Powder, Sterling Silver Filigree, Cobalt, 2 1/2 In.	25.00
Cosmetic, Rogers' Nursery Hair Lotion, Aqua, 6 1/2 In. ...... Illus	22.00
Cosmetic, Scheffler's Hair Colorine, Best In World, 4 In.	1.50
Cosmetic, Tonic Deluxe, 7 1/2 In. ...... Illus	35.00

Cosmetic, Tonic Deluxe, 7 1/2 In.
(See Page 58)

Cosmetic, Wavenlock, Hair
Tonic, Cobalt Blue, 10 In.

Cosmetic, Vegederma, The Queen Of Hair
Tonics, Cures Dandruff

Cosmetic, Turtle Hair Oil, Figural, Turtle, Glass Head, Amber, 5 In.	75.00
Cosmetic, Vegederma, The Queen Of Hair Tonics, Cures Dandruff *.....Illus*	7.50
Cosmetic, Warner's Log Cabin Rose Cream, Embossed Metal Cap, Aqua, 2 1/2 In	35.00
Cosmetic, Wavenlock, Hair Tonic, Cobalt Blue, 10 In. *.....Illus*	75.00
Cosmetic, Wyeth's Sage & Sulphur Compound, 6 1/2 In. *.....Illus*	7.50
Cosmetic, 7 Sutherland Sisters Hair Grower, N.Y., Aqua *.....Illus*	10.00
Cuervo Barranqueno Tequila, Soccer Ball	17.95
Cure, see Medicine	
Cut Glass, Baccarat, Red Medallions On Stopper & Body, Cut Floral, 7 In.	185.00
Cut Glass, J.Hoare, Monarch, 24-Point Star Bottom, 12 In.	210.00
Cut Glass, Jar, Sachet, Strawberry Diamond, Sterling Top, Unger Bros., 3 In.	25.00
Cut Glass, Oil & Vinegar, Hawkes, 7 1/2 In.	75.00
Cut Glass, Talcum, Star & Diamond, Sterling Top, Unger Bros., 3 1/8 In.	40.00
Cut Glass, Water, Strawberries, 8 X 5 1/2 In.	125.00
Cyrus Noble, Assayer	75.00 To 120.00
Cyrus Noble, Bartender	65.00 To 120.00
Cyrus Noble, Blacksmith	37.50 To 50.00
Cyrus Noble, Burro	40.00 To 110.00
Cyrus Noble, Clipper Ship	20.00
Cyrus Noble, Drummer	30.00 To 40.00
Cyrus Noble, Gambler	35.00 To 50.00
Cyrus Noble, Gambler's Lady	32.95 To 40.00
Cyrus Noble, Gold Panner	375.00 To 400.00
Cyrus Noble, Lilienthal Centennial, 1876	*Color* XXXX.XX
Cyrus Noble, Miner	250.00 To 300.00
Cyrus Noble, Miner's Daughter	35.00 To 50.00
Cyrus Noble, Old Private Stock, C.1898, Amber	*Color* XXXX.XX
Cyrus Noble, Snowshoe Thompson, 1972	*Color* XXXX.XX
Cyrus Noble, Snowshoe Thompson	*Color* 135.00

*Dant figural bottles first were released in 1968 to hold J.W.Dant
alcoholic products. The company has made the Americana series, field
birds, special bottlings, and ceramic bottles.*

Dant, Alamo	5.00

Cosmetic, Wyeth's Sage & Sulphur Compound, 6 1/2 In.
(See Page 59)

Cosmetic, 7 Sutherland Sisters Hair
Grower, N.Y., Aqua
(See Page 59)

Dant, American Legion	8.00
Dant, Boeing 747 .... *Illus*	7.00
Dant, Boston Tea Party	3.00
Dant, Eagle, Black .... *Illus*	6.00
Dant, Eagle, Facing Left	2.50
Dant, Eagle, Facing Right	10.00
Dant, Field Bird, Bob White	8.00
Dant, Field Bird, California Quail	8.00
Dant, Field Bird, Mountain Quail	8.00
Dant, Field Bird, Pheasant	9.00
Dant, Field Birds, Prairie Chicken, Edition No.3 .... *Illus*	8.00
Dant, Field Bird, Ruffed Grouse	8.00
Dant, Field Bird, Woodcock	8.00
Dant, Fort Sill	5.00 To 6.00
Dant, Indy 500	5.00
Dant, Mt.Rushmore	7.95
Dant, Paul Bunyan .... *Color* XXXX.XX	

*Decanters were first used to hold the alcoholic beverages that had been
stored in kegs. At first a necessity, the decanter later was merely an
attractive serving vessel.*

Decanter, see also Beam, Bischoff, Kord, etc.

Decanter, Amelung Type, Blown, Flint, Tapered, Quart	40.00
Decanter, Amelung Type, C.1750, Blown, Faceted Stopper, Engraved, Quart	125.00
Decanter, Amelung Type, Blown, Flint, C.1790, Tapered, Quart	35.00
Decanter, Amelung Type, Blown, Flint, Gilt Trim, Square, 7 In.	40.00
Decanter, Amelung Type, Blown, Flint, Rectangular, Soda Lime, 5 1/4 In.	35.00
Decanter, Amelung Type, Blown, Flint, Tapered, Quart	40.00
Decanter, Amelung, Cut Glass, Honeycomb Neck, Flute Base, Pint	42.00
Decanter, Amethyst, 11 X 7 In.	35.00
Decanter, Art Glass, Enamel Floral, Bulbous, Applied Handles, 12 In.	32.00
Decanter, Baccarat, Block Cut Stopper, Paneled, 9 In.	60.00
Decanter, Baccarat, Bulbous Stopper, Crystal, 13 1/4 In.	20.00
Decanter, Bar, Flint, C.1800, Blown, Neck Rings, Quart	28.00
Decanter, Blown, Amethyst, 8 3/4 In.	20.00
Decanter, Blown, Clear Steeple Stopper & Neck Rings, Cranberry, 23 In.	55.00
Decanter, Blown, Flared Mouth, Pontil, Wear, Olive Green, 8 1/2 In.	* 100.00
Decanter, Blown, Flint, Barrel, Similar To McK G II-27, Pint	120.00

Decanter, Blown, Flint, C.1750, 11 Panels, Base Pattern, 1/2 Pint 40.00
Decanter, Blown, Flint, C.1790, Folded Lip, 1/2 Pint 35.00
Decanter, Blown, Flint, C.1800, Neck Ring, Bar Lip, Quart 30.00
Decanter, Blown, Flint, C.1800, Neck Ring, Flange Lip, Quart 35.00
Decanter, Blown, Flint, C.1800, Neck Ring, Pint 35.00
Decanter, Blown, Flint, C.1800, Neck Ring, Quart .... 30.00 To 32.00
Decanter, Blown, Flint, C.1800, Rough Pontil, 1/2 Pint 35.00
Decanter, Blown, Flint, C.1850, Pressed Mushroom Stopper, 2 Rings, Quart 38.00
Decanter, Blown, Flint, Riverboat, Pillar Mold, 8 Ribs, Neck Ring, Quart 80.00
Decanter, Blown, Flint, 11 Panels, 1/2 Pint 40.00
Decanter, Blown, Flint, 1/2 Pint 35.00
Decanter, Blown, Ground Stopper, Crimped, 9 3/4 In. 25.00
Decanter, Blown, Hollow Stopper, Wheel Cut Grapes, Long Neck, Pint 18.00
Decanter, Blown, Light Olive Amber, 10 1/2 In. .... * 120.00
Decanter, Blown, Light Olive Green, 10 In. .... * 80.00
Decanter, Blown, Olive Amber, 10 3/8 In. .... * 90.00
Decanter, Blown, Olive Green, 5 3/4 In. .... * 85.00
Decanter, Blown, Olive Green, 7 1/4 In. .... * 75.00
Decanter, Blown, Pontil, White Loopings, Olive Amber, 8 In. .... * 270.00
Decanter, Blown, Pontil, White Loopings, Olive Amber, 10 3/8 In. .... * 330.00
Decanter, Blown, Sterling Overlay & Stopper, Amber, 12 In. 75.00
Decanter, Blown, Teardrop Stopper, Applied Crystal Handle, Blue, 12 1/2 In. 75.00
Decanter, Blown, Victorian, Enameled, 13 1/2 In. 35.00
Decanter, Blown, 3 Applied Neck Rings, Ring Type Stopper, 9 1/2 In. 35.00
Decanter, Blown, 3 Mold, Sunburst Stopper, Quart 130.00
Decanter, Bohemian Glass, Castle & Deer, Ruby, 21 In., Pair 250.00
Decanter, Bohemian Glass, Cut & Engraved, Ruby, 15 In., Pair 90.00
Decanter, Bohemian Glass, Faceted Stopper, Castle & Deer, Amber, 12 1/2 In. 150.00
Decanter, Bohemian Glass, Vintage, Blown Stopper, 12 In. 75.00
Decanter, Brandy, Cut Glass, Czechoslovakia, C.1885, 8 In., Pair 88.00
Decanter, Brandy, 3 Mold, Similar To McK G III-2, 10 3/4 In. 155.00
Decanter, Bulbous, White Enamel, Gold Trim, C.1800, Green, 8 3/4 In. 60.00
Decanter, Cambridge, Nautilus, 6 1/2 In. 14.00
Decanter, Captain's, Cut Glass, Hawkes, Zipper Stopper, 7 1/2 In. 375.00
Decanter, Captain's, Cut Glass, Pinwheels, Amethyst Overlay, 12 1/2 In. 70.00
Decanter, Captain's, Cut Glass, Teardrop Stopper, Pinwheel & Star, 6 1/2 In. 300.00
Decanter, Carnival Glass, Grape & Lattice, Marigold, 11 5/8 In. 75.00
Decanter, Cased Glass, White Gold Swirls, Green With Pink, 16 In., Pair 45.00
Decanter, Claret, Bohemian Glass, Enamel Floral, Rigaree Foot, Ruby, 9 In. 110.00

Dant, Eagle, Black
(See Page 60)

Dant, Boeing 747
(See Page 60)

Dant, Field Birds, Prairie
Chicken, Edition No.3
(See Page 60)

Decanter, Claret, Silver Deposit, Gorham Overlay, Apple Green, 8 1/2 In.	250.00
Decanter, Cranberry Glass, Crystal Stopper, Cut To Clear, 15 In.	185.00
Decanter, Cut Designs, Flared Mouth, Pontil, Hexagonal, 10 In.	* 20.00
Decanter, Cut Glass, Ball Stopper, Double Lozenge, 12 In.	115.00
Decanter, Cut Glass, Brilliant Period. Amethyst To Clear, 14 In	135.00
Decanter, Cut Glass, Bull's-Eyes, Topaz To Clear, 12 In.	100.00
Decanter, Cut Glass, Cranberry Stopper, Threading, & Handle, 10 In.	95.00
Decanter, Cut Glass, Deep Cuttings, 12 X 5 In.	135.00
Decanter, Cut Glass, Diamond Stopper, Handle, Hobstar & Diamond, 15 In.	165.00
Decanter, Cut Glass, Edinburgh, Scotland, Faceted Stopper, Cane, 9 1/2 In.	75.00
Decanter, Cut Glass, English, Faceted Stopper, Gadroons, C.1790, 11 1/4 In.	55.00
Decanter, Cut Glass, Etched Banding, Signed W, 10 1/2 In.	28.00
Decanter, Cut Glass, Faceted Neck Ring, Loop Cut Base, 16 1/4 In.	35.00
Decanter, Cut Glass, Faceted Stopper, Castle & Animals, Amber, 12 1/2 In.	138.00
Decanter, Cut Glass, Faceted Stopper, Diamond & Fan, Ruby To Clear, 13 In.	45.00
Decanter, Cut Glass, Faceted Stopper, 24-Point Star Base, 10 In.	95.00
Decanter, Cut Glass, Gooseneck, 12 1/2 In.	125.00
Decanter, Cut Glass, Gorham Sterling Handle & Hinged Lid, Pillars, 10 In.	250.00
Decanter, Cut Glass, Hawkes, Teardrop Stopper, Waffle In Diamond, 12 In.	125.00
Decanter, Cut Glass, Hobstar, Star, Butterfly, & Wild Flower, Footed, 12 In.	125.00
Decanter, Cut Glass, Lapidary Stopper, Crosscut & Strawberry Diamond, 11 In	110.00
Decanter, Cut Glass, Lapidary Stopper, Crosscut Diamond & Fan, 11 In.	110.00
Decanter, Cut Glass, Lapidary Stopper, Fan & Crosscut Diamond, 11 1/2 In.	165.00
Decanter, Cut Glass, Lapidary Stopper, Honeycomb Handle & Neck, Canes, 9 In.	175.00
Decanter, Cut Glass, Middlesex, Faceted Stopper, Matching Handle, 12 In.	325.00
Decanter, Cut Glass, Mushroom Stopper, St.Louis Neck, Pedestal, 11 In.	200.00
Decanter, Cut Glass, Nailhead, 13 1/2 In.	100.00
Decanter, Cut Glass, Paneled Stopper & Neck, Cane, Square Bottom, 7 In.	45.00
Decanter, Cut Glass, St.Louis Neck, Pinwheel, Fan, & Miter, 11 1/2 In.	160.00
Decanter, Cut Glass, Sterling Silver Stopper, Cranberry To Clear, 11 1/2 In	325.00
Decanter, Cut Glass, Sterling Stopper, Hobstar & Cane, 10 In.	110.00
Decanter, Cut Glass, Sunburst, Bulbous Base, 12 In.	225.00
Decanter, Cut Glass, Teardrop Stopper, Creswick, Neck Ring, 13 In.	150.00
Decanter, Cut Glass, Teardrop Stopper, Hobstar, Cane, & Diamond Point, 14 In.	150.00
Decanter, Cut Glass, Vintage, Cranberry To Clear, 16 In., Pair	275.00
Decanter, Cut Glass, Waterford, Mushroom Stopper, 13 In.	75.00
Decanter, Daum Nancy, Cameo Cut, Enamel Swirls, Handled, 10 3/4 In.	425.00
Decanter, F.P.Adams, Boston, Mass., Applied Handle, Ring Lip, Amethyst, 10 In.	16.00
Decanter, Fluted, Rolled Collared Mouth, Pontil, Oval, 7 1/2 In.	* 25.00
Decanter, Free Blown, Fluted, Long Neck, Pontil, Chip, 10 1/2 In.	* 10.00
Decanter, Free Blown, Sheared Mouth, Pontil, Crack, Olive Amber, 10 1/4 In.	* 35.00
Decanter, Ground Stopper, Enamel Floral, Frosted White To Pink, 11 In.	45.00
Decanter, Ground Stopper, 3 Neck Rings, Ribbed Base, 11 In.	25.00
Decanter, Handle, Spout, Embossed, Pontil, Cobalt, 9 In.	22.50
Decanter, Hollow Stopper, White Enamel Flowers, Cranberry, 12 In.	120.00
Decanter, Imitation Cut Pattern, 9 1/2 In.	28.00
Decanter, Juice, Diamond-Quilted, Cut Stopper, Amberina, 12 In.	250.00
Decanter, Mary Gregory, Girl, Crystal Steeple Stopper, Sapphire Blue, 11 In.	105.00
Decanter, McK G I-20, Flint	90.00
Decanter, McK G I-20, 3 Mold, Ribbed Stopper	90.00
Decanter, McK G I-27, Blown, Flint, 3 Mold, Quart	165.00
Decanter, McK G I-29, Blown, 3 Mold, 2 Neck Rings, Quart	65.00 To 100.00
Decanter, McK G I-29, 3 Mold, 2 Triple Neck Rings, Barrel Shape, Quart	* 45.00
Decanter, McK G II-3, Keene Type, Pontil, Crack, Olive Green, Quart	*1500.00
Decanter, McK G II-7, 3 Mold, Barrel Shape, Cruet Lip	120.00
Decanter, McK G II-9, Keene Type, Diamond, Sunburst, Olive Amber, Quart	* 650.00
Decanter, McK G II-9, Keene Type, Pontil, Olive Amber, Quart	* 650.00
Decanter, McK G II-18, 3 Mold, Neck Rigaree, Quart	70.00 To 95.00
Decanter, McK G II-27, Blown, Flint, Barrel Shape, Pint	120.00
Decanter, McK G II-28, Keene Type, Burst Bubble, Yellow Green, Quart	*2000.00
Decanter, McK G II-29, 3 Mold, Quart	95.00
Decanter, McK G III-5, Blown, Flint, 3 Mold, Pint	16.00
Decanter, McK G III-5, Blown, Flint, 3 Mold, 3 Rigaree Rings, Quart	100.00
Decanter, McK G III-14, Blown, Flint, 1/2 Pint	120.00
Decanter, McK G III-15, 3 Mold, Quart	95.00

Decanter, McK G III-16, Keene Type, Diamond, Sunburst, Olive Amber, Pint .... * 400.00
Decanter, McK G III-16, Keene Type, Diamond, Sunburst, Olive Amber, Pint .... * 625.00
Decanter, McK G III-24, Blown, Flint, 3 Mold, Quart .... 90.00 To 95.00
Decanter, McK GIV-7, Blown, Flint, Quart 145.00
Decanter, Merry Christmas & Happy New Year, Drum Shape, Cloudy, 9 In. 110.00
Decanter, Midwestern, Ribs Swirled To Right, Globular, Aqua, 8 5/8 In. .... * 85.00
Decanter, Old Tom Moore Whiskey, 10 In. ....*Illus* 32.00
Decanter, Opaline, French, Ball Stopper, Dimpled, Blue, 8 1/2 In. 20.00
Decanter, Overlay, Gilt Trim, Cranberry Cut To Clear, 13 1/2 In. 50.00
Decanter, Overlay, Teardrop Stopper, Gilt Trim, Cobalt To Clear, 15 In., Pair 350.00
Decanter, Pillar Mold, 10 3/4 In. 155.00

Decanter, Old Tom Moore Whiskey, 10 In.

Decanter, Pressed Glass, Argus, Bakewell Pears, Neck Rings, Flange Lip, Quart 95.00
Decanter, Pressed Glass, Ashburton, Pint 92.00
Decanter, Pressed Glass, Bellflower, Bar Lip, Cut Shoulders, Quart 135.00
Decanter, Pressed Glass, Bellflower, Pint 250.00
Decanter, Pressed Glass, Bellflower, Single Vine, Bar Lip, Frosted, Pint 125.00
Decanter, Pressed Glass, Bellflower, Thumbprint Shoulder, Bar Lip, Quart 135.00
Decanter, Pressed Glass, Beveled Diamond & Star, Ruby Stained, 11 In. 45.00
Decanter, Pressed Glass, Block, Bulbous, Pint 22.00
Decanter, Pressed Glass, Bull's-Eye & Diamond Point, Bar Lip, Quart 97.50
Decanter, Pressed Glass, Bull's-Eye, Bar Lip, Quart 40.00
Decanter, Pressed Glass, Bull's-Eye, Bulbous, Pint 22.00
Decanter, Pressed Glass, Cable, Ground Stopper, Pint 45.00
Decanter, Pressed Glass, Diamond Point, Quart .... 95.00 To 135.00
Decanter, Pressed Glass, Fine Rib, Bar Lip, Quart 58.00
Decanter, Pressed Glass, Flat Diamond & Panel, Quart 85.00
Decanter, Pressed Glass, Flint, Ashburton, Pint 55.00
Decanter, Pressed Glass, Flint, Bigler, Bar, Quart 40.00
Decanter, Pressed Glass, Flint, Broken Column, 10 1/2 In. 75.00
Decanter, Pressed Glass, Flint, Bull's-Eye, Bar Lip, Quart 37.50
Decanter, Pressed Glass, Flint, Diamond Thumbprint, Applied Bar Lip, 11 In. 135.00
Decanter, Pressed Glass, Flint, Diamond Thumbprint, Bar Lip, Quart, 10 1/2 In 135.00
Decanter, Pressed Glass, Flint, Diamond Thumbprint, Bar Lip, 1/2 Pint, 7 In. 70.00
Decanter, Pressed Glass, Flint, Diamond Thumbprint, Bar, Rounded Lip, Pint 125.00
Decanter, Pressed Glass, Flint, Diamond Thumbprint, Pewter Stopper, Quart 125.00
Decanter, Pressed Glass, Flint, Excelsior, Flared Lip, Pint 39.00
Decanter, Pressed Glass, Flint, Flute, Bar Lip, Quart 30.00
Decanter, Pressed Glass, Flint, Gothic On 7 Panels, 10 In. 40.00
Decanter, Pressed Glass, Flint, Honeycomb, 13 In., Pair 120.00
Decanter, Pressed Glass, Flint, Horn Of Plenty, Bar Lip, Quart 85.00
Decanter, Pressed Glass, Flint, Pillar & Bull's-Eye, Bar, Quart 55.00
Decanter, Pressed Glass, Flint, Pillar, Bar Lip, Quart 45.00
Decanter, Pressed Glass, Flint, Tulip & Sawtooth, Applied Handle, Pint 64.00
Decanter, Pressed Glass, Flint, Waffle & Thumbprint, 10 5/8 In. 20.00

Decanter, Pressed Glass, Horn Of Plenty, Quart 110.00
Decanter, Pressed Glass, Horn Of Plenty, Quart .... * 125.00
Decanter, Pressed Glass, Horn Of Plenty, 14 In., Pair 185.00
Decanter, Pressed Glass, Inverted Thumbprint, 10 In. 12.50
Decanter, Pressed Glass, Thumbprint, Bar Lip, Quart 85.00
Decanter, Rubena Verde, Cut Green Stopper, Applied Ruffled Footing, 12 In. 215.00
Decanter, Sandwich Glass, Flint, Diamond Thumbprint, Bar Lip, 10 1/2 In. 135.00
Decanter, Sandwich Glass, Lattice & Oval Panel, Quart 85.00
Decanter, Sandwich Glass, Steeple Stopper, Bull's-Eye & Flute, 12 In., Pair .... * 250.00
Decanter, Ship's, Blown Stopper, Slender Neck, 9 7/8 In. .... * 35.00
Decanter, Silver Deposit, Amethyst, 9 In. .... * 60.00
Decanter, Silver Overlay, Green, 12 In. 135.00
Decanter, Silver Overlay, Leaves, Cobalt, 9 1/4 In. 85.00
Decanter, Silver Overlay, Silver Stopper, 10 1/2 In., Pair 1120.00
Decanter, Silver Overlay, 12 In. 65.00
Decanter, Stiegel Type, Enamel Decoration, C.1780, 6 In. ....Color XXXX.XX
Decanter, Thos.Morre, Old Possum Hollow, Cut Glass, Smoky Brown, Quart 50.00
Decanter, Vertical Ribs, Oval, Stain, Aqua, Quart .... * 40.00
Decanter, Water, H & H, Double Collared Mouth, IP, Aqua, 6 3/8 In. 65.00
Decanter, Waterford, Cut Glass, Silver Label & Chain, "Port, " 9 1/4 In. 70.00
Decanter, Wedgwood, 1969, Zorro, Black Don, 10 1/2 In. 35.00
Decanter, Wine, Carnival Glass, Diamond & Sunburst, Purple 125.00
Decanter, Wine, Clear Bubble Stopper, Clear Reeded Handle, Green, 10 1/4 In. 78.00
Decanter, Wine, Josephine Hutte, Faceted Stopper, Enamel Floral, 13 1/4 In. 75.00
Decanter, Wine, Mary Gregory, Steeple Stopper, Girl, Lime Green, 10 1/4 In. 110.00
Decanter, 2 Applied Rings, Ground Pontil, Cobalt, 6 In. 30.00
Decanter, 3 Mold, Barrel Shape, Pressed Wheel Stopper, Pint 120.00
Decanter, 4 Compartments, Tooled Mouth, 11 In. .... * 20.00
Delft, Polychrome, Bird & Floral, Hand-Painted, 6 In. 9.00
Demijohn, Amber, Gallon 10.00
Demijohn, Applied Collar, Amber, 2 Gallon 8.00
Demijohn, Applied Lip, OP, 5 Gallon 30.00
Demijohn, Aqua, 1/2 Gallon 2.00
Demijohn, Blown, Olive Green, 11 1/4 In. 70.00
Demijohn, Bulbous, Lamp & Shade, Light Olive Amber, 16 1/4 In. .... * 50.00
Demijohn, Bulbous, Pontil, Chip, Yellow Amber, 21 In. .... * 500.00
Demijohn, Bulbous, Pontil, Golden Amber, 11 3/4 In. .... * 425.00
Demijohn, Bulbous, Pontil, Golden Amber, 17 In. .... * 200.00
Demijohn, Bulbous, Pontil, Light Olive Amber, 10 7/8 In. .... * 60.00
Demijohn, Bulbous, Pontil, Light Olive Amber, 11 1/2 In. .... * 90.00
Demijohn, Bulbous, Pontil, Olive Amber, 18 1/4 In. .... * 75.00
Demijohn, Bulbous, Pontil, Olive Amber, 10 In. .... * 210.00
Demijohn, Bulbous, Pontil, Red Amber, 18 In. .... * 150.00
Demijohn, Chip, Flattened Oval, Yellow Green, 9 1/2 In. .... * 25.00
Demijohn, Collared Mouth, Bulbous, Pontil, Stain, Wear, Olive Amber, 9 1/4 In. .... * 55.00
Demijohn, Collared Mouth, Smooth Base, Yellow Green, 12 In. .... * 60.00
Demijohn, Dark Green, 2 Gallon 30.00
Demijohn, Deep Aqua, 32 Ozs. 5.00
Demijohn, Fitted With Lamp & Shade, Olive Amber, 17 1/4 In. .... * 60.00
Demijohn, Flattened Oval, Olive Amber, 19 In. * 130.00
Demijohn, Flattened Oval, Red Amber, 18 In. .... * 140.00
Demijohn, Globular, Collared Mouth, Pontil, Deep Aqua, 12 1/2 In. .... * 80.00
Demijohn, Globular, Pontil, Crack, Seedy Olive Green, 10 1/2 In. .... * 60.00
Demijohn, Globular, Pontil, Dense Amber, 11 1/4 In. .... * 75.00
Demijohn, Green, 3 Gallon 20.00
Demijohn, Honey Amber, 2 Gallon 20.00
Demijohn, Kidney Shape, Bruise, Olive Amber, 18 1/4 In. .... * 80.00
Demijohn, Kidney Shape, Chip, Olive Amber, 17 1/2 In. .... * 210.00
Demijohn, Kidney Shape, Olive Amber, 12 1/4 In. .... * 270.00
Demijohn, Kidney Shape, Pontil, Olive Amber, 10 1/2 In. .... * 230.00
Demijohn, Kidney Shape, Olive Amber, 17 1/4 In. .... * 95.00
Demijohn, Kidney Shape, Olive Amber, 17 1/2 In. .... * 130.00
Demijohn, Lake Dunsmore, OP, 3 In. 25.00
Demijohn, OP, Amber, 2 Gallon 12.00
Demijohn, OP, Green, 13 In. 35.00

Demijohn, Our Little Pet Jug, Crimped, Applied Handle, 2 3/4 In. 12.00
Demijohn, Pontil, Chip, Flattened Oval, Golden Amber, 17 1/4 In. .... * 60.00
Demijohn, Pontil, Crack, Flattened Sides, Olive Amber, 10 1/2 In. .... * 55.00
Demijohn, Pontil, Flattened Oval, Aqua, 18 1/2 In. .... * 60.00
Demijohn, Pontil, Flattened Oval, Deep Olive Amber, 12 In. .... * 50.00
Demijohn, Pontil, Flattened Oval, Yellow Green, 18 1/4 In. .... * 120.00
Demijohn, Pontil, Green, 17 1/2 In. .... * 60.00
Demijohn, Pontil, Olive Amber, 12 3/4 In. .... * 85.00
Demijohn, Pontil, Olive Amber, 16 1/2 In. .... * 190.00
Demijohn, Pontil, Olive Amber, 16 3/4 In. .... * 90.00
Demijohn, Pontil, Olive Amber, 22 1/2 In. .... * 130.00
Demijohn, Rolled Collared Mouth, Globular, Pontil, Olive Amber, 8 1/2 In. .... * 70.00
Demijohn, Sheared Mouth With Ring, Aqua, 14 3/4 In. .... * 40.00
Demijohn, Sheared Mouth With Ring, Crack, Olive Amber, 17 In. .... * 35.00
Demijohn, Sheared Mouth With Ring, Flake, Flattened Oval, Amber, 18 1/4 In. .... * 140.00
Demijohn, Sheared Mouth With Ring, Olive Amber, 16 3/4 In. .... * 160.00
Demijohn, Sheared Mouth With Ring, Olive Green, 15 3/4 In. .... * 80.00
Demijohn, Sheared Mouth With Ring, Oval, Olive Amber, 16 1/2 In. .... * 40.00
Demijohn, Sheared Mouth With Ring, Pontil, Crack, Olive Amber, 10 1/2 In. .... * 100.00
Demijohn, Sheared Mouth With Ring, Pontil, Dark Olive Amber, 12 1/2 In. .... * 120.00
Demijohn, Sheared Mouth With Ring, Pontil, Flattened Oval, Olive, 11 In. .... * 170.00
Demijohn, Sheared Mouth With Ring, Yellow Green, 11 3/4 In. .... * 40.00
Demijohn, Sheared Mouth, Pontil, Flattened Oval, Olive Amber, 11 1/2 In. .... * 65.00
Demijohn, Sloping Collared Mouth, Pontil, Light Olive Amber, 19 In. .... * 65.00
Demijohn, Sloping Collared Mouth, Pontil, Yellow Green, 1/2 Gallon .... * 50.00
Demijohn, Smooth Base, Kidney Shape, Olive Amber, 17 In. .... * 170.00
Demijohn, Smooth Base, Oval, Olive Amber, 17 In. .... * 85.00
Demijohn, Wicker Covered, Aqua, Quart 12.00
Demijohn, 2 On Shoulder, Pontil, Oval, Yellow Green, 1/2 Gallon .... * 50.00
Dickel, Golf Club 16.00
Donohue, Race Car No.66 .... 22.50
Double Springs, Bentley, 1927 .... 29.00 To 30.00
Double Springs, Buick, 1913 .... 22.00 To 34.00
Double Springs, Bull 16.00
Double Springs, Cadillac .... 17.95 To 30.00
Double Springs, Cale Yarborough Kar-Kare, 1973 .... 22.00 To 34.00
Double Springs, Chicago Water Tower .... 18.95 To 19.00
Double Springs, Duffer .... 8.00 To 12.00
Double Springs, Excalibur Phaeton III, 1976 .... 24.95
Double Springs, Georgia Bulldog 11.00
Double Springs, Gold Coyote .... 11.00 To 12.00
Double Springs, Matador 14.00
Double Springs, Mercedes Benz 24.95
Double Springs, Mercer .... 22.00 To 30.00
Double Springs, Model T Ford, 1913 .... 18.95 To 31.00
Double Springs, Mug 4.00
Double Springs, Peasant Boy 7.50
Double Springs, Peasant Girl 7.50
Double Springs, Pierce Arrow 30.00
Double Springs, Red Owl 8.00
Double Springs, Rolls Royce, 1912 .... 22.00 To 34.00
Double Springs, Stanley Steamer 1909, 1971 .... Color 45.00
Double Springs, Stutz Bearcat .... 22.00 To 40.00
Double Springs, Tiger On Football 12.00
Double Springs, Wild Catter 6.50
Downer Glass Works, Flask, Chestnut, Expanded Diamond, Amber, 5 1/2 In. 5.00
Downer Glass Works, Flask, Chestnut, Expanded Diamond, Aqua, 5 1/2 In. 5.00
Downer Glass Works, Flask, Chestnut, Expanded Diamond, Blue, 5 1/2 In. 5.00
Downer Glass Works, Flask, Chestnut, Expanded Diamond, Purple, 5 1/2 In. 5.00
Dresser, Actress, Milk Glass, 11 In. 45.00
Dresser, Gold Decoration, Open Pontil, Cobalt, 6 1/4 In. .... Color XXXX.XX
Dresser, Greentown, No.11, Faceted Stopper, 7 1/2 In. 30.00
Dresser, Hobnail, 7 In., Pair 20.00
Dresser, Mary Gregory, White Enamel Boy, Faceted Stopper, 8 In. 115.00
Dresser, Mary Gregory, White Enamel Girl, Faceted Stopper, 8 In. 115.00

Dresser, **Milk Glass,** Bulbous, Glossy, Gold & Blue Paint, 9 1/2 In. 20.00
Dresser, **Milk Glass,** Leaf, Parkville, 1874, 9 1/2 In. 21.00
Dresser, **Milk Glass,** Painted, 11 In. 47.50
Dresser, **Mouth Lotion & Listerine,** Paneled, Clear Stopper, Rubena, 5 In., Pai 48.00
Dresser, **Painted,** Bulbous, Milk Glass, 8 In., Pair 60.00
Dresser, **Pressed Glass,** Bohemian, Mushroom Stopper, Gold, Footed, Green, 9 In. 125.00
Dresser, **Pressed Glass,** Queen's Necklace, 6 1/2 In. 37.50
Drug, **A.Vogeler & Co.,** Balto., Aqua, 5 1/2 In. 6.00
Drug, **Benton,** Myers & Co., Cleveland, Ohio, Pottery, Gallon 30.00
Drug, **Counter Jar,** 3 Mold, Ground Stopper, Cobalt, 3 1/4 In. Diameter 39.00
Drug, **Day's Pharmacy,** San Rafael, Cal., 5 In. 4.00
Drug, **Doster-Northington Co.,** Birmingham, Ala., Pottery, Gallon 30.00
Drug, **E.S.Leadbeater & Sons,** Alexandria, Va., 1792, Neck Ring, Aqua, 9 1/2 In. 12.50
Drug, **Effervescent Artificial Kissingen Salt,** 5 1/2 In. ....*Illus* 8.00
Drug, **Eye Wash Stopper,** Cobalt, 5 1/2 In. .... * 20.00
Drug, **Hinchman & Alward,** Druggists, Virginia City, Mont., 5 In. 8.00
Drug, **J.F.Hancock,** Manufacturing Pharmacists, Baltimore, 4 In.N ....*Illus* 18.00

Drug, Effervescent
Artificial Kissingen
Salt, 5 1/2 In.

Drug, J.F.Hancock,
Manufacturing Pharmacists,
Baltimore, 4 In.N

Drug, **J.W.Doran,** Juneau, Alaska, 6 In. 20.00
Drug, **Louisburg Dispensary,** N.C., Pint 40.00
Drug, **Marine Hospital Service,** 1798 & 1871, BIMAL, 7 In. 20.00
Drug, **Nelson & Baker,** Detroit, Mich., BIMAL, Amber, 3 Quart 25.00
Drug, **New York Pharmacal Association,** Cobalt, 1/2 Gallon 37.00
Drug, **O'Rourke & Hurley,** Druggists, Little Falls, N.Y., Cobalt, 5 In. 6.00
Drug, **O'Rourke & Hurley,** Little Falls, N.Y., Cobalt, 4 In. 8.50
Drug, **Owl Drug Co.,** Milk Glass, 5 In. 25.00
Drug, **Owl Drug Co.,** 1 Wing, Milk Glass, 4 In. 24.00
Drug, **Owl Drug Co.,** 1 Wing, Milk Glass, 5 In. 28.00
Drug, **Owl Drug Co.,** 3 1/2 In. 3.00
Drug, **Owl,** Amber, 3 1/2 In. 18.00
Drug, **Owl,** Carlton, Alum, 6 In. 8.00
Drug, **Owl,** Citrate, Embossed Owl & Crown, ABM, Emerald, Pint 17.00
Drug, **Owl,** Embossed, Crown Top, Emerald Green, 9 3/4 In. 7.00
Drug, **Parke Davis & Co.,** Det.Palmer, Green, 7 1/2 In. ....*Color* XXXX.XX
Drug, **R.W.Davis Co.,** Chicago, Fluted Neck, Paneled Base, Milk Glass, 11 In. 125.00
Drug, **Reed & Cutler,** Druggists, Boston, OP, 8 1/2 In. 22.00
Drug, **South Carolina Dispensary,** Dug, Aqua, 1/2 Pint 30.00
Drug, **Strong Cobb & Co.,** Cleve., Ohio, Cunningham & Ihmsen, Cobalt, 10 In. 25.00
Drug, **Suire Eckstein & Co.,** Druggist, Cincinnati, Graphite Pontil, 5 In. 11.00
Drug, **U.S.A. Hospital Dept.,** Stain, Blue, 9 In. 45.00
Drug, **U.S.A.Hospital Dept.,** Stain, Olive Yellow, Quart 80.00
Early Times, Alaska Centennial 30.00
Early Times, California Centennial .... 23.00 To 28.00
Early Times, Colorado Centennial 28.00

Early Times, Connecticut Centennial	23.00
Early Times, Delaware Centennial	28.00
Early Times, Florida Centennial	23.00
Early Times, Hawaii Centennial	23.00
Early Times, Indiana Centennial	23.00
Early Times, Iowa Centennial	23.00 To 28.00
Early Times, Kansas Centennial	23.00
Early Times, Missouri Bicentennial	10.00
Early Times, Missouri Centennial	23.00
Early Times, Nevada Centennial	23.00 To 28.00
Early Times, New Jersey Centennial	28.00
Early Times, New Mexico Centennial	23.00
Early Times, North Carolina Centennial	23.00
Early Times, Virginia Centennial	23.00
Early Times, Washington Centennial	23.00 To 28.00
Early Times, Wyoming Centennial	23.00 To 28.00
Error, CN Disinfectang, West Co., 3 1/2 In.	75.00
Error, B.Fosgate's Anodyne Cordial, Backward N, Bruise, Aqua, 4 3/4 In.	* 20.00
Error, Ball Ideal Fruit Jar, Patent July 14, 1988, Quart	7.00
Error, Ball Mason Perffct Jar, Pint	19.00
Error, Ball Perffct Mason, Pint	3.75
Error, California Tooth Wash, Backward S, 4 1/2 In.	30.00
Error, Doctors Fellers & Ireland's, Backward S, Eclectic, Aqua, 4 1/4 In.	* 45.00
Error, Dr.Langley's Bitters, 99 Backwards, Aqua, 3/4 Quart, W-206	* 70.00
Error, Dr.Langley's Root & Herb Bitters, Backwards, Aqua, 8 1/2 In., W-206	32.00
Error, Dr.Langley's Root & Herb Bitters, 99 Backwards, Aqua, Pint, W-206e	* 45.00
Error, Dr.Wilcox's Compound Extract, Backward S, Yellow Green, Quart	* 475.00
Error, Fruit Jar, Glocker Sanitary, Patent 1911, Hrs Pnding, Quart	28.00
Error, Fruit Jar, Mason's Improved, C F J Co On Reverse, Aqua, Quart	6.00
Error, Fruit Jar, Mason's Patent, Misspelled, Tudor Rose, Purple, 1/2 Gallon	50.00
Error, Fruit Jar, Masons Patent Nov.30th, 1858, Whittled, Ice Blue, Quart	14.50
Error, General Lafayette, Backward N, Flask, McK G I-92, Pint	*4400.00
Error, Haserot Conpany Fruit Jar, Cleveland, Mason's Patent, Quart	6.00
Error, Honesdale Glassworks, Ap., Mineral Water, Aqua, 7 1/2 In.	18.00 To 22.00
Error, Keystone Mason, Letter T In Patent Under S In Mason, 1/2 Gallon	* 30.00
Error, Kimball's, Backward S, Jaundice Bitters, Wear, Olive Amber, Pint, W-202	* 170.00
Error, L.Q.C.Wishart's Pine Tree Tar Cordial, Philaa, 1859, Green, 7 1/2 In.	60.00
Error, McK G I-22, Washington & Baltimore, 3 Ss, Flake, Aqua, Quart	* 400.00
Error, McK G I-80, Flask, Lafayette & DeWitt, Backward D, Amber, Pint	* 800.00
Error, McK G I-102, Flask, Calabash, Jeny Lind & Glass Factory, Green	* 775.00
Error, McK G I-103, Flask, Calabash, Jeny Lind, Pontil, Aqua, Quart	* 60.00
Error, McK G I-104, Flask, Calabash, Jeny Lind, Sapphire Blue, Quart	* 950.00
Error, McK G I-104, Flask, Calabash, Jeny Lind, Yellow Green, Quart	*1250.00
Error, McK G I-105, Flask, Calabash, Jeny Lind & Factory, Aqua, Quart	* 190.00
Error, McK G I-107, Flask, Calabash, Jeny Lind, Fislerville, Crack, Green	* 350.00
Error, McK G IV-32, Masonic & Shepards, Backward S, Blue, Pint	* 475.00
Error, Plantation Bourbon, C.A.Richards & Co., Backward N, Amber, 3/4 Quart	* 20.00
Error, Red Top Rye, Top Misspelled, Amber, Pint	15.00
Error, Roche's Embrocation For The H Oping Cough, Octagonal, 5 In.	7.50
Error, Sands's Sarsaparilla, New York, Aqua, 6 1/4 In.	15.00 To 25.00
Error, Sanford's In 39, 2 Mold, Collared Base, Amethyst, 2 1/2 In.	3.25
Error, Saratoga Star Spring, Backward S In Spring, Stoddard, Amber, Quart	42.00
Error, Saratoga, Star, Spring, Mineral Water, Backward S, Amber, Quart	* 20.00
Error, Saratoga, Star, Spring, Mineral Water, Backward S, Emerald Green, Quart	* 75.00
Error, Shaker Digestive Cordiala, J.White, N.Y., Haze, Aqua, 5 3/4 In.	12.50
Error, Shea-Bocoveraz & Co., S.F., Misspelled, Tooled Top, Amber, Fifth	20.00
Error, Solomans & Co., Market Squae, Savannah, Georgia, Aqua, 3 3/4 In.	12.00
Error, Udolpho Wolfe's Schiedam Aromatic Schnapps, Baskward S, Green, Pint	* 35.00
Error, W.N.Walton's, Backwards, 1962, Jamaica Rum, Amber, 12 In.	180.00
Error, Willington Glass Works, Backward N & S, Amber, Quart	* 45.00

*Ezra Brooks fancy bottles were first made in 1964. The Ezra Brooks
Distilling Company is from Frankfort, Kentucky.*

Ezra Brooks, American Legion, Hawaii, 1973, No.3	8.95 To 15.00
Ezra Brooks, American Legion, Miami, 1974, No.4	10.00 To 20.00

Ezra Brooks, American Legion, 1971, No.1 .... 7.95 To 18.00
Ezra Brooks, American Legionnaire, 1972, No.2 .... 18.00
Ezra Brooks, Amvets, Dolphin, 1974 .... 12.00 To 15.00
Ezra Brooks, Antique Cannon, 1969 .... 7.00 To 15.00
Ezra Brooks, Antique Phonograph, 1970 .... 8.95 To 20.00
Ezra Brooks, Arizona Desert Scene, 1969 $ 3.95 To 10.00
Ezra Brooks, Astronaut, Gallon 49.95
Ezra Brooks, Balloon Clown, 1974 .... 12.00 To 18.00
Ezra Brooks, Bare Knuckle Fighter, 1972 * 7.00 T 12.00
Ezra Brooks, Basketball, 1974 .... 3.95 To 20.00
Ezra Brooks, Beaver, 1973 .... 6.00 To 14.00
Ezra Brooks, Betsy Ross, 1975 .... 12.95 To 20.00
Ezra Brooks, Bertha, 1970, Elephant .... 9.95 To 15.00
Ezra Brooks, Big Daddy Lounges, Florida, 1969 .... 3.95 To 11.00
Ezra Brooks, Bird Dog, 1971 .... 10.00 To 13.00
Ezra Brooks, Birthday Cake, Club, No.2, 1972 .... 4.95 To 10.00
Ezra Brooks, Bordertown, 1970 .... 3.95 To 12.00
Ezra Brooks, Bowler, 1973 .... 3.95 To 14.00
Ezra Brooks, Brahma Bull, 1972 .... 9.00 To 15.00
Ezra Brooks, Bucket Of Blood, 1970 .... 4.95 To 8.00

Ezra Brooks, California
Quail, 1970

Ezra Brooks,
Chicago Water Tower,
1969

Ezra Brooks, Bucky Badger, No.1, 1974, Football 20.00
Ezra Brooks, Bucky Badger, No.3, 1975, Hockey 20.00
Ezra Brooks, Bucky Badger, No.2, 1975, Hockey .... 17.00 To 20.00
Ezra Brooks, Bronco Buster, 1974 .... 9.95 To 25.00
Ezra Brooks, Buffalo Hunt, 1971 .... 5.95 To 15.00
Ezra Brooks, Bulldog, 1972 .... 9.95 To 18.00
Ezra Brooks, Cake .... 4.95 To 8.00
Ezra Brooks, California Quail, 1970 ....Illus 10.00
Ezra Brooks, Canadian Honker, 1975 .... 10.00 To 25.00
Ezra Brooks, Casey At The Bat, 1973 .... 14.00
Ezra Brooks, Cb Convoy Radio, 1976 .... 10.00 To 15.00
Ezra Brooks, Ceremonial Indian, 1970 .... 12.00 To 20.00
Ezra Brooks, Charolais, 1973 .... 9.95 To 16.00
Ezra Brooks, Cheyenne Shootout, 1970 .... 4.95 To 20.00
Ezra Brooks, Chicago Fire, 1975 .... 20.00
Ezra Brooks, Chicago Water Tower, 1969 ....Illus 14.00
Ezra Brooks, Christmas Decanter, 1965 .... 10.00
Ezra Brooks, Christmas Decanter, 1966 .... 10.00
Ezra Brooks, Christmas Decanter, 1967 .... 10.00
Ezra Brooks, Cigar Store Indian, 1968 .... 3.95 To 10.00
Ezra Brooks, Clown, 1972 .... 9.95 To 15.00
Ezra Brooks, Clydesdale, Horse, 1974 .... 8.00 To 20.00

Ezra Brooks, **Colt Peacemaker Flask,** Gun Series, 1969 .... 4.95
Ezra Brooks, **Conquistador's Drum & Bugle,** 1972 .... 7.50 To 16.00
Ezra Brooks, **Corvette,** 1957 Classic, 1977 .... 17.00 To 25.00
Ezra Brooks, **Court Jester,** 1972 .... 8.95 To 15.00
Ezra Brooks, **Creighton Blue Jay,** 1976 .... 22.00
Ezra Brooks, **Dakota Cowboy,** 1975 .... 20.00 To 35.00
Ezra Brooks, **Dakota Cowgirl,** 1976 .... 17.00 To 25.00
Ezra Brooks, **Dead Wagon,** 1970 .... 3.95 To 15.00
Ezra Brooks, **Delta Belle,** 1969 .... *Illus* 15.00
Ezra Brooks, **Democratic Convention,** Donkey, 1976, New York ....*Color* 14.95

Ezra Brooks, Delta Belle, 1969

Ezra Brooks, Gamecock,
1970, South Carolina

Ezra Brooks, Gold
Prospector, 1970

Ezra Brooks,
Golden Horseshoe, 1970

Ezra Brooks, **Dirt Bike,** 1973 .... 6.50 To 12.00
Ezra Brooks, **Flintlock Dueling Pistol,** 1968 .... 6.50 To 12.00
Ezra Brooks, **Duesenberg,** 1971 .... 15.00
Ezra Brooks, **Equestrienne,** 1974 .... 8.00 To 20.00
Ezra Brooks, **Ceremonial Indian,** 1970 .... 14.00 To 22.00
Ezra Brooks, **Distillery,** No.1, Club Bottle, 1970 .... 7.50 To 20.00
Ezra Brooks, **Fire Engine,** 1971 .... 12.00
Ezra Brooks, **Fireman,** 1975 .... 20.00
Ezra Brooks, **Fisherman,** 1974 .... 17.00
Ezra Brooks, **Florida Gator,** No.2, 1973 .... 18.00
Ezra Brooks, **Florida Gator,** No.3, 1975 .... 22.00
Ezra Brooks, **Football Player,** 1974 .... 20.00
Ezra Brooks, **Foremost Astronaut,** 1970 .... 2.95 To 12.00
Ezra Brooks, **Foremost Man** .... 12.00 To 14.95
Ezra Brooks, **Fresno Grape,** 1970 .... 5.95 To 15.00
Ezra Brooks, **Gamecock,** 1970, South Carolina ....*Illus* 18.00
Ezra Brooks, **Gold Prospector,** 1970 ....*Illus* 10.00
Ezra Brooks, **Golden Horseshoe,** 1970 ....*Illus* 18.00

Ezra Brooks, Go Big Red, No.1, 1970 .... 22.50 To 28.00
Ezra Brooks, Go Big Red, No.2, 1971 .... 11.95 To 20.00
Ezra Brooks, Go Big Red, No.3, 1972 .... 9.95 To 18.00
Ezra Brooks, Go Tiger Go, 1973 .... 9.50 To 15.00
Ezra Brooks, Gold Eagle, 1971 .... 9.00 To 20.00
Ezra Brooks, Gold Horseshoe, 1970 .... 8.00 To 15.00
Ezra Brooks, Gold Rooster, 1969 .... 40.00 To 60.00
Ezra Brooks, Gold Seal, 1972 .... 8.00 To 15.00
Ezra Brooks, Golden Grizzly Bear, 1968 .... 3.50 To 10.00
Ezra Brooks, Grandfather's Clock, 1970 .... 4.95 To 12.00
Ezra Brooks, Greater Greensboro Open, No.1, 1972, Golf .... 11.95 To 22.00
Ezra Brooks, Greater Greensboro Open, No.2, 1973, Golf .... 30.00 To 50.00
Ezra·Brooks, Greater Greensboro Open, No.3, 1974, Golf 40.00
Ezra Brooks, Greater Greensboro Open, No.4, 1975, Golf .... 45.00 To 60.00

Ezra Brooks, Iowa Statehouse, 1971

Ezra Brooks, Iron Horse Train, 1969

Ezra Brooks, King Of Clubs, 1969
(See Page 71)

Ezra Brooks, Gun Series, Set Of 4, 1969 .... 15.00 To 20.00
Ezra Brooks, Hambletonian, 1971 .... 5.95 To 12.00
Ezra Brooks, Happy Goose, 1975 .... 14.95 To 19.00
Ezra Brooks, Harolds Club Dice, 1968 .... 3.95 To 9.00
Ezra Brooks, Hereford, 1972 .... 9.00 To 15.00
Ezra Brooks, Historical Flask, 1970 .... 4.00
Ezra Brooks, Hollywood Bottle, Cops, 1972 .... 9.00 To 16.00
Ezra Brooks, Hummingbird Kachina, No.2, 1973 .... 35.00 To 40.00
Ezra Brooks, Hunter, 1974 .... 6.50 To 20.00
Ezra Brooks, Idaho Potato, 1973 .... 11.95 To 18.00
Ezra Brooks, Indian Elephant, 1973 .... 7.00 To 15.00
Ezra Brooks, Iowa Statehouse, 1971 .... *Illus*   30.00
Ezra Brooks, Iron Horse Train, 1969 .... *Illus*   10.00

Ezra Brooks, Jack Of Diamonds, 1969 .... 3.50 To 12.00
Ezra Brooks, Japanese Dueling Pistol .... 26.00 To 28.00
Ezra Brooks, Jayhawk, No.2 .... 5.00 To 6.00
Ezra Brooks, Kachina Doll, No.1, 1971 .... 75.00 To 100.00
Ezra Brooks, Kachina Doll, No.2, 1973, Hummingbird .... 35.00 To 40.00
Ezra Brooks, Kachina Doll, No.3, 1975 .... 18.00 To 25.00
Ezra Brooks, Kachina Doll, No.4, 1975, Maiden .... 17.50 To 25.00
Ezra Brooks, Kachina Doll, No.5, 1976 .... 17.50 To 25.00
Ezra Brooks, Kansas Jayhawk, 1969 .... 5.00 To 12.00
Ezra Brooks, Katz Cat, Blue Point, 1969 .... 9.95 To 15.00
Ezra Brooks, Katz Cat, Seal Point, 1969 .... 8.95 To 15.00
Ezra Brooks, Katz Cat, Philharmonic Conductor, 1970 .... 5.00 To 14.00
Ezra Brooks, King Of Clubs, 1969 .... Illus 12.00
Ezra Brooks, Kitten On A Pillow, 1975 .... 10.00 To 18.00
Ezra Brooks, Liberty Bell, 1970 .... 5.00 To 12.00
Ezra Brooks, Lion On Rock, 1971 .... 3.95 To 12.00
Ezra Brooks, Liquor Square, 1972 .... 11.00 To 18.00
Ezra Brooks, Maine Lobster, 1970 .... Illus 32.00
Ezra Brooks, Maine Potato, 1973 .... 7.00 To 20.00

Ezra Brooks, Maine Lobster, 1970

Ezra Brooks, Mr.Foremost, 1969

Ezra Brooks, Oil Gusher, 1969

Ezra Brooks, Man O' War, 1969 .... 7.00 To 20.00
Ezra Brooks, Map, Club Bottle, 1973 .... 9.90 To 20.00
Ezra Brooks, Masonic Fez, 1976 .... 10.00 To 15.00
Ezra Brooks, Max "The Hat" Zimmerman, 1976 .... 17.00 To 25.00
Ezra Brooks, Michigan-Minnesota, 1975 .... 15.00 To 20.00
Ezra Brooks, Military Tank, 1972 .... 12.00 To 17.95
Ezra Brooks, Minnesota Hockey Player, 1975 .... 17.00 To 25.00
Ezra Brooks, Minuteman, 1975 .... 20.00
Ezra Brooks, Missouri Mule, 1972 .... 8.00 To 25.00
Ezra Brooks, Mr.Foremost, 1969 .... Illus 18.00
Ezra Brooks, Oil Gusher, 1969 .... Illus 12.00
Ezra Brooks, Panda, 1972 .... 9.95 To 15.00

Ezra Brooks, Penguin, 1973 .... 6.50 To 14.00
Ezra Brooks, Penny Farthington, 1973 .... 6.9K To 15.00
Ezra Brooks, Phoenix Bird, 1971 .... 24.95 To 40.00
Ezra Brooks, Pirate, 1971 .... 4.50 To 12.00
Ezra Brooks, Pistol .... 6.50 To 8.00
Ezra Brooks, Pistol, Japan, 1968 .... 26.00 To 50.00
Ezra Brooks, Potbellied Stove, 1968 .... 9.50 To 11.50
Ezra Brooks, Princeton Tiger .... 9.50 To 11.50
Ezra Brooks, Quail 7.50
Ezra Brooks, Queen Of Hearts, 1969 .... 3.50 To 12.00
Ezra Brooks, Race Car, Indy, 1970 .... 12.95 To 20.00
Ezra Brooks, Ram, 1973 .... 9.50 To 18.00
Ezra Brooks, Razorback, 1970 .... 5.00 To 15.00
Ezra Brooks, Red Dice .... 3.95 To 5.00
Ezra Brooks, Reno Arch, 1968 .... 2.95 To 12.00
Ezra Brooks, Republican Convention, Elephant, 1976, Kansas City ....Color 14.95
Ezra Brooks, Sailfish, 1971 .... 7.50 To 12.00
Ezra Brooks, Salmon, 1971 .... 24.00 To 40.00
Ezra Brooks, San Francisco Cable Car, Brown, 1968 .... 3.95 To 10.00
Ezra Brooks, San Francisco Cable Car, Gray, 1968 .... 3.95 To 10.00
Ezra Brooks, San Francisco Cable Car, Green, 1968 .... 3.95 To 10.00
Ezra Brooks, Sea Captain, 1971 .... 10.00 To 12.00
Ezra Brooks, Senator, 1972 .... 9.95 To 18.00
Ezra Brooks, Setter, 1974 .... 17.00 To 25.00
Ezra Brooks, Silver Dollar, Black Base, 1970 .... 5.00 To 11.00
Ezra Brooks, Silver Dollar, White Base, 1970 .... 2.95 To 4.95
Ezra Brooks, Silver Saddle, 1973 .... 22.50 To 40.00
Ezra Brooks, Silver Spur, 1971 .... 9.95 To 18.00
Ezra Brooks, Ski Boot, 1972 ....Illus 16.00
Ezra Brooks, Slot Machine, 1971 .... 18.00 To 20.00
Ezra Brooks, Snowmobile, 1972 .... 5.95 To 16.00
Ezra Brooks, South California Trojan, 1974 .... 12.50 To 22.00
Ezra Brooks, South Dakota National Guard, 1976 .... 15.00 To 25.00
Ezra Brooks, Spirit Of '76, 1974 .... 8.00 To 17.00
Ezra Brooks, Sprint Car, 1971 .... 11.95 To 18.00
Ezra Brooks, Stagecoach, 1969 ....Illus 9.00
Ezra Brooks, Stan Laurel Bust .... 17.00 To 25.00
Ezra Brooks, Stonewall Jackson, 1974 .... 21.00 To 35.00
Ezra Brooks, Strongman, 1974 .... 6.50 To 17.00
Ezra Brooks, Sturgeon, 1975 .... 10.00 To 17.00
Ezra Brooks, Tecumseh, 1969 .... 8.00 To 15.00
Ezra Brooks, Telephone, 1971 .... 12.00
Ezra Brooks, Tennis Player, 1973 .... 4.95 To 14.00
Ezra Brooks, Terrapin, 1974, Maryland .... 15.00 To 20.00
Ezra Brooks, Texas Longhorn, Steer, 1971 .... 14.00 To 20.00
Ezra Brooks, Thunderbird, 1956 Type 40, 1977 .... 17.00 To 25.00
Ezra Brooks, Stock Market Ticker Tape, 1970 .... 3.95 To 10.00
Ezra Brooks, Tonopah, 1972 .... 5.95 To 18.00
Ezra Brooks, Totem Pole, No.1, 1972 .... 9.90 To 18.00
Ezra Brooks, Totem Pole, No.2, 1973 .... 7.50 To 20.00
Ezra Brooks, Tractor, 1971 .... 12.00 To 16.00
Ezra Brooks, Train .... 6.00 To 6.50
Ezra Brooks, Trojan Horse, 1974 .... 12.50 To 16.00
Ezra Brooks, Trout & Fly, 1970 .... 6.50 To 12.00
Ezra Brooks, V.F.W., 1973 .... 8.00 To 14.00
Ezra Brooks, V.F.W., No.2, White & Gold, 1975 .... 15.00 To 20.00
Ezra Brooks, Vermont Skier, 1973 .... 13.00 To 15.00
Ezra Brooks, Virginia Cardinal, 1973 .... 9.00 To 20.00
Ezra Brooks, Walgreen Drugs, 1974 .... 14.95 To 25.00
Ezra Brooks, Weirton Steel, 1974 .... 14.00 To 25.00
Ezra Brooks, West Virginia Mountaineer, 1971 .... 70.00 To 110.00
Ezra Brooks, Whale, 1973 .... 8.00 To 22.00
Ezra Brooks, Wheat Shocker, 1971 .... 3.95 To 16.00
Ezra Brooks, White Tail Deer, 1974 .... 14.95
Ezra Brooks, White Turkey, 1971 .... 15.00 To 18.95

Ezra Brooks, Wichita Centennial, 1970 .... *Illus*   18.00
Ezra Brooks, Winston Churchill, 1969 .... 3.95 To 12.00
Ezra Brooks, Zimmerman's Hat, 1968 .... 4.95 To 16.00
     Face Cream, see Cosmetic, Medicine
Famous Firsts, Americana Ship 32.00
Famous Firsts, Balance Scales 32.00
Famous Firsts, Bersaglieri 12.95
Famous Firsts, Centurion 12.95
Famous Firsts, Coffee Grinder 25.00
Famous Firsts, Garibaldi 12.95
Famous Firsts, Indianapolis No.1 .... 18.00
Famous Firsts, Indy Car, No.11 .... 18.00
Famous Firsts, Napoleon 12.95

Ezra Brooks, Ski Boot, 1972
(See Page 72)

Ezra Brooks, Stagecoach, 1969
(See Page 72)

Ezra Brooks, Wichita Centennial, 1970

Famous Firsts, Phonograph 25.00
Famous Firsts, Renault Car 22.00
Famous Firsts, Sewing Machine 25.00
Famous Firsts, Yacht American, 13 In. 30.00
Famous Firsts, Animal Pitcher Bottle 21.00
Famous Firsts, Dino By Ferrari 16.50
Famous Firsts, Gold Racer, No.32 .... 9.95 To 14.00
Famous Firsts, Honda Motorcycle 29.00
Famous Firsts, Johnny Reb Telephone .... 25.00 To 27.50
Famous Firsts, Natchez Mail Packet 32.50
Famous Firsts, San Francisco Cable Car, Fifth 39.50
Famous Firsts, Swiss Chalet Barometer 27.50
Famous Firsts, Telephone Flora 26.00
Famous Firsts, Winnie Mae, Fifth 39.50
Famous Firsts, Winnie Mae, 1/2 Pint 23.50
Famous Firsts, Yankee Doodle Telephone 27.50
Famous Firsts, Yankee Clipper Pitcher 21.00

Figural bottles are specially named by the collectors of bottles. Any
bottle that is of a recognizable shape, such as a human head, or a pretzel, or
a clock, is considered to be a figural. There is no restriction as to date
or material.

Figural, Austrian Woman, Robj, Paris, 11 1/4 In. 60.00
Figural, Baby, Spanish, Milk Glass, 12 In. 35.00
Figural, Baby In Basket, 5 In. ....*Illus* 55.00
Figural, Bank, Bulbous, Pottery, Brown Glaze, 6 1/4 In. .... * 170.00
Figural, Barrel, Metal Faucet, Quart 9.00
Figural, Barrel, Mold Blown, Hoops, 5 In. 12.00
Figural, Barrel, Pottery, Brown Glaze, 2 3/4 In. .... * 80.00
Figural, Barrel, Redware, Mottled Brown Glaze, 4 3/4 In. .... * 120.00
Figural, Barrel, 7 1/2 In. 10.00
Figural, Basket, Aqua, 3 In. .... * 12.50
Figural, Basket, Tooled Collared Mouth, Smooth Base, Aqua, 4 3/8 In. .... * 25.00
Figural, Basket, Tooled Mouth, Smooth Base, Aqua, 4 1/4 In. .... * 25.00
Figural, Bear Around Column, Milk Glass, 11 In. ....*Illus* 360.00
Figural, Bear, A.Z.& Co., N.Y., Pomade, Sandwich Type, Opalescent, 3 3/4 In. .... * 210.00
Figural, Bear, Applied Face, Milky Dark Gray, 11 In. ....*Illus* 275.00
Figural, Bear, Applied Face, Kummel Type, Sheared Mouth, Pontil, Olive Green .... * 675.00
Figural, Bear, Applied Face, Sheared Mouth, Pontil, Dark Teal Blue *1250.00
Figural, Bear, Black Amethyst, 11 In. 125.00
Figural, Bear, F.Knapp, Philada., Tax Stamp, 3 3/4 In. .... * 35.00
Figural, Bear, Kummel Label, Smooth Base, Olive Green, 3/4 Quart .... * 40.00
Figural, Bear, Kummel Type, Applied Nose, Smooth Base, Deep Amber, 10 7/8 In. ...... * 130.00
Figural, Bear, Kummel Type, Black, 11 In. 39.00

Figural, Baby In Basket, 5 In.

Figural, Bear Around Column,
Milk Glass, 11 In.

Figural, Bear,
Applied Face,
Milky Dark Gray, 11 In.

Figural, Bear, Kummel Type, Milk Glass, 10 3/4 In. ....*Illus* 90.00
Figural, Bear, Kummel Type, Milk Glass, 11 1/4 In. .... * 100.00
Figural, Bear, Kummel Type, Pontil, Dense Amethyst, 11 In. .... * 45.00
Figural, Bear, Milk Glass, 11 In. 105.00
Figural, Bear, Muzzled, Pomade, Sandwich, Black Amethyst, 3 1/4 In. 150.00
Figural, Bear, Pomade, Sandwich Glass, Black, 3 3/4 In. 155.00
Figural, Bear, Pomade, Sandwich Type, Chipped, Black Amethyst, 3 3/4 In. .... * 95.00
Figural, Bear, Pottery, Ciasa, Mexico, Beige & Brown, 8 X 6 In. 15.00
Figural, Bear, Sitting, Black Amethyst, 10 3/4 In. 85.00
Figural, Bear, Sitting, Black Amethyst, 11 1/2 In., Pair 50.00
Figural, Bear, Sitting, Milk Glass, Black, 11 In., B-242 .... 110.00 To 175.00
Figural, Bear, Sitting, Milk Glass, 11 In., B-242 .... 95.00 To 175.00
Figural, Beau Peep Products, 6 1/4 In. .... * 17.50
Figural, Bellows, Applied Decorations, Pontil, White Loopings, 13 1/4 In. .... * 120.00
Figural, Bellows, Applied Rigaree, Repaired, Pontil, 14 1/2 In. .... * 40.00
Figural, Bellows, Applied Rigaree, Sheared Mouth & Double Ring, 7 In. .... * 30.00
Figural, Bellows, Nailsea, White Striations, Cranberry, 14 1/2 In. 195.00
Figural, Billy Club, Ground Mouth, Screw Cap, Amber, 10 5/8 In. .... * 35.00

Figural, Boxer Bob
Fitzsimmons, Frosted &
Flesh Color, 15 In.

Figural, Bear,
Kummel Type,
Milk Glass, 10 3/4 In.
(See Page 74)

Figural, Charlie Chaplin,
12 3/4 In.
(See Page 76)

Figural, **Book,** Bennington Battle, C.1849, Flint Enamel, Brown, 1/2 Gallon	350.00
Figural, **Boot,** Geo.S.Colburn, West Gardner, Mass., Buttoned, Aqua, 5 In.	35.00
Figural, **Boot,** Laced On Side, Pottery, Rockingham Glaze, 6 3/4 In.	* 90.00
Figural, **Boot,** Lady's, Saratoga Dressing, Lacing On Side, Chip, Aqua, 4 1/2 In	* 30.00
Figural, **Boot,** Lady's, Smooth Base, 4 In.	* 15.00
Figural, **Boot,** Lady's, Tooled Collared Mouth, Smooth Base, 4 1/2 In.	* 10.00
Figural, **Boot,** Lady's, Tooled Collared Mouth, Smooth Base, 4 3/8 In.	* 40.00
Figural, **Boot,** Lady's, Union Dressing, Lacing On Side, Flake, Aqua, 4 1/2 In.	* 22.50
Figural, **Bottle In Basket,** Milk Glass, 12 In.	100.00
Figural, **Boxer Bob Fitzsimmons,** Frosted & Flesh Color, 15 In. .... *Illus*	510.00
Figural, **Broom,** Crude Neck, Pint	15.00
Figural, **Bulldog,** Head Removes To Reveal Neck, Frosted, 9 In.	90.00
Figural, **Bullfighter,** Painted, 12 In.	5.00
Figural, **Bunch Of Grapes,** Cap Marked Bologna, Purple, 5 In.	27.50
Figural, **Bunker Hill Monument,** 12 In.	75.00
Figural, **Bunker Hill,** Monument, Milk Glass, 8 In.	75.00
Figural, **Bunny Rabbit,** Germany, C.1920, 2 1/2 In.	5.50
Figural, **Bust Of Beecher,** Patent June 9th, 1874, 6 5/8 In.	* 45.00
Figural, **Bust Of Cleveland,** Frosted & Clear, 10 In.	* 85.00
Figural, **Bust Of Columbus,** Milk Glass, 3 In.	150.00
Figural, **Bust Of Columbus,** 13 In.	650.00
Figural, **Bust Of Columbus,** 1892, Clear Pedestal, Milk Glass, 6 In.	125.00
Figural, **Bust Of Czar,** 13 In.	395.00
Figural, **Bust Of Czarina,** 13 In.	395.00
Figural, **Bust Of French General,** 12 In.	22.50
Figural, **Bust Of Garibaldi,** Pontil, Hole, Crack, 10 7/8 In.	* 15.00
Figural, **Bust Of General Grant,** 12 In.	27.50
Figural, **Bust Of George Washington,** Cobalt, 9 1/2 In.	27.50
Figural, **Bust Of Italian General,** 9 1/2 In.	27.50
Figural, **Bust Of Man,** Marked Granger, Tooled Collared Mouth, 6 1/2 In.	* 50.00
Figural, **Bust Of Man,** 1859 M.J.Owens 1953 On Base, Frosted & Clear	* 40.00
Figural, **Bust Of Old Soldier,** 12 In.	25.00
Figural, **Bust Of Paul Kruger,** 12 In.	395.00
Figural, **Bust Of Queen Elizabeth,** 12 In.	27.50
Figural, **Bust Of Washington,** Pottery, 8 1/2 In.	* 70.00
Figural, **Bust Of Woman,** Flake, 6 1/2 In.	* 20.00
Figural, **Cabbage,** Elongated, Ceramic, 9 In.	25.00
Figural, **Cannon,** Phalon & Son On Shield, Smooth Base, 7 3/8 In.	* 140.00
Figural, **Cannon,** Phalon & Son On Shield, Smooth Base, 9 3/4 In.	* 150.00

Figural, Carry Nation, 8 3/4 In.	6.95
Figural, Castle Tower, Bruise, Crack, Triangular, 11 1/2 In.	* 5.00
Figural, Cat, Blue Bow, Ground Lip, 11 In.	20.00
Figural, Cat, Blue Bow, Threaded, Ground Lip, 8 In.	15.50
Figural, Charlie Chaplin, 12 3/4 In. *Illus*	100.00
Figural, Cherub Holding Bottle On Shoulder, Embossed, Stain, BIMAL, 14 In.	15.00
Figural, Chinaman, Tooled Mouth, Smooth Base, 5 1/4 In.	* 35.00
Figural, Chinese Woman, Tooled Flared Mouth, Pontil, 8 3/4 In.	* 120.00
Figural, Cigar, Amber, 5 1/4 In.	23.00
Figural, Cigar, Amber, 5 1/2 In.	10.00
Figural, Cigar, Political Campaign, 1912, Amber, 5 1/2 In.	25.75
Figural, Cigar, Tooled Mouth, Crack, Amber, 5 In.	* 20.00
Figural, Cigar, 7 In.	20.00
Figural, Cigar, 7 1/2 In.	30.00
Figural, Cigars, Ground Mouth, Amber, 5 In.	50.00
Figural, Clam, Ground Mouth, Screw Cap, Chip, Cobalt, 5 1/4 In.	* 120.00
Figural, Clam, Ground Mouth, Screw Cap, 3 3/4 In.	* 15.00
Figural, Clam, Paint, Smooth Base, 5 1/4 In.	* 10.00
Figural, Clam, Tooled Mouth, Smooth Base, 3 1/2 In.	* 15.00
Figural, Clam, 3 In.	30.00 To 52.00
Figural, Clam, 4 In.	20.00 To 25.00
Figural, Clock, Star On Reverse, 6 1/2 In.	42.00
Figural, Clown, French Wine, 2 Piece, Milk Glass, 15 In.	200.00
Figural, Clown, Grapette, Bank	2.50
Figural, Clown, Pharmacy, Screw Cap, 4 1/2 In.	4.50
Figural, Clown, Pharmacy, Screw Cap, 5 In.	4.50
Figural, Clown, Tooled Collared Mouth, Smooth Base, 7 1/2 In.	* 40.00
Figural, Clown On Ball, Head Closure Broken, Frosted & Clear, 12 1/2 In.	* 5.00
Figural, Coachman, Bennington, C.1850, 9 7/8 In. *Illus*	325.00
Figural, Coachman, Bennington, C.1850, 10 3/4 In. *Illus*	500.00
Figural, Coachman, Bennington, Cream Mottling, 10 1/2 In.	425.00
Figural, Coachman, Bennington, Rockingham Glaze, Chip, 10 1/2 In.	* 350.00
Figural, Coachman, Bennington, Signed Norton, 7 1/2 In.	200.00
Figural, Coachman, Bennington, Signed Lyman P Fenton *Illus*	300.00
Figural, Coachman, Rockingham, 9 1/2 In.	75.00
Figural, Coachman, Tall Hat, Bennington, Rockingham Glaze, 10 1/2 In.	* 400.00
Figural, Coachman, Van Dunck's, 8 1/2 In. *Illus*	55.00
Figural, Coffeepot, Ceramic, Dark Brown, 6 In.	25.00
Figural, Colonial Lady, Dresser Perfume With Dabber, Frosted & Blue, 5 In.	25.00
Figural, Colonial Woman Holding Liquor Bottle, Blue & White, 7 In.	60.00

Figural, Coachman, Bennington,
C.1850, 9 7/8 In.

Figural, Coachman, Bennington,
C.1850, 10 3/4 In.

Figural,
Coachman, Bennington,
Signed Lyman P Fenton

Figural, Columbus Monument, Spanish Version, Milk Glass, 10 In. 75.00
Figural, Columbus, 13 In. 650.00
Figural, Corn, Ground Top, Painted, 5 1/2 In. 10.00
Figural, Corncob Pipe, Amber Stem, 10 In. .... *Illus* 35.00
Figural, Crying Baby, Bust, T.P.S.& Co., N.Y., Patent June 2nd, 1874, 6 In. .... * 70.00
Figural, Cucumber, Collared Mouth, Smooth Base, 6 In. .... * 25.00
Figural, Cucumber, Labels, Ground Mouth, Smooth Base, Blue Green, 4 1/2 In. .... * 80.00
Figural, Cucumber, Pottery, Tan, Green, 6 In. 27.50
Figural, Czarina & Czar Of Russia, C.1900, Milk Glass, 10 5/8 In., Pair 300.00
Figural, Dagger, 8 1/2 In. 15.00
Figural, Dog, Florida Manhattan, Strawhat Closure, 3 1/2 In. 15.00
Figural, Dolphin, Tail Up, Green & Black Eyes, Tail Stopper, 14 In. 27.50
Figural, Doughnut, Pottery, Brown Glaze, 7 3/8 In. .... * 25.00
Figural, Draped Female, Crack, Golden Amber, 8 3/4 In. .... * 170.00
Figural, Draped Plump Nude, Marked Depose, C.1880, Frosted & Clear, 13 In. 45.00
Figural, Duck Wearing Cape & Hat, Beak Pours, Ceramic, 12 In. .... *Illus* 20.00
Figural, Duck, Atterbury, Milk Glass, 11 3/4 In. .... * 250.00
Figural, Duck, Swimming, 5 In. 30.00
Figural, Ear Of Corn, Smooth Base, Yellow, 3/4 Quart .... * 170.00
Figural, Ear Of Corn, Smooth Base, 10 3/4 In. .... * 35.00
Figural, Ear Of Corn, Square Collared Mouth, Smooth Base, Yellow, 3/4 Quart .... * 170.00
Figural, Ear Of Corn, Whiskey Giveaway, Milk Glass, 3 In. 10.00
Figural, Eiffel Tower, Bon Sur, White Bakelite Cap, 9 In. 10.00
Figural, Eiffel Tower, French Perfume, 4 In. 3.50
Figural, Eiffel Tower, Gold Screw-On Closure, Hemisphere Issue, 6 1/4 In. 5.00
Figural, Elephant, Grapette, Bank 2.50
Figural, Elephant, Old Sol, Amber, 8 1/2 In. 9.00
Figural, Elephant, Old Sol, Design Patented, Smooth Base, Amber, 10 1/4 In. .... * 15.00
Figural, Falstaff, Bols Label On Cork, Royal Doulton, 3 1/2 In. 60.00
Figural, Fiddle, Stephen Foster Commemorative, Label, ABM, 4 3/4 In. 6.00
Figural, Fish, Amber, 9 3/4 In. 15.00
Figural, Fish, Amber, 10 In. 35.00
Figural, Fish, Amber, 14 In. 12.00

Figural, Corncob Pipe, Amber Stem, 10 In.

Figural, Duck Wearing Cape
& Hat, Beak Pours,
Ceramic, 12 In.

Figural, Coachman,
Van Dunck's, 8 1/2 In.
(See Page 76)

Figural, Fish, Cut Glass, Ground Stopper, 8 1/2 In. 125.00
Figural, Fish, Ground Lip, Green, 8 In. 25.00
Figural, Fish, Ground Lip, Green, 9 In. 30.00
Figural, Fish, Machined Mouth, Smooth Base, Golden Amber, 9 7/8 In. .... * 10.00
Figural, Fish, Paint, Ground Mouth, Screw Cap, 8 3/4 In. .... * 20.00
Figural, Fish, R.Cooper Railway Terminus, Brighton, Lambeth, Chip, Tan, 7 In. .... * 85.00
Figural, Fish, Red Eyes, Ground Lip, 15 In. 27.50
Figural, Fish, Tooled Collared Mouth, Smooth Base, Golden Amber, 3 In. .... * 210.00

Figural, Grant's Tomb, Metal Bust Cover, Milk Glass, 10 In.

Figural, Hand Holding Bottle, Frosted, 10 In.

Figural, Hand
Holding Bottle, 11 In.

Figural, Flintlock Pistol, Bisque, White Glaze Inside, 12 In.	45.00
Figural, Flintlock Pistol, Bisque, 12 In.	45.00
Figural, Foot Warmer, Triangular, Pottery, Rockingham Glaze, 11 In.	* 130.00
Figural, Four Hens On Tree Stump, Chelsea Type, Gold Mounted, 3 In.	150.00
Figural, Fox, Porcelain, 6 In.	35.00
Figural, George Washington, 9 1/2 In.	6.95
Figural, Girl & Boy Climbing Tree, Frosted Figures, OP, 11 1/4 In.	65.00
Figural, Girl With Muffle, Corker, 6 In.	25.00
Figural, Globe, Smooth Base, 2 In.	* 15.00
Figural, Grant's Tomb, Head Missing, Holes, Square, Milk Glass, 8 1/4 In.	* 90.00
Figural, Grant's Tomb, Metal Bust Cover, Milk Glass, 10 In. ......Illus	625.00
Figural, Grapes, Sheared Mouth, Rough, 3 3/8 In.	* 5.00
Figural, Gun, Pottery, Brown Glaze, 11 1/4 In.	* 120.00
Figural, Gun, Silver Painted Handle, 7 In.	* 25.00
Figural, Hand Holding Bottle, Frosted, 10 In. ......Illus	95.00
Figural, Hand Holding Bottle, 11 In. ......Illus	55.00
Figural, Hand With Bottle, 9 1/2 In.	10.00
Figural, Hand, Black Bakelite Cap, Label, Frosted, 4 1/4 In.	5.00
Figural, Hand, Black Bakelite Cap, Label, 5 In.	4.00
Figural, Hand, Labels, Smooth Base, Chip, 5 1/4 In.	* 15.00
Figural, Hand, Palm Down, 5 1/8 In.	26.50
Figural, Hat, Olive Green, 4 In.	100.00
Figural, Heart, John Hart & Co., Smooth Base, Golden Amber, 1/2 Pint	* 210.00
Figural, Hen On Nest, French Bonbon, Milk Glass, 15 In.	200.00
Figural, Hessian Soldier, Smooth Base, 7 1/4 In.	* 20.00
Figural, High Shoe, Side Laced, Bennington, 7 X 6 1/2 In.	100.00
Figural, Horse, Flora Temple, Harness Trot, 1859, Dark Amber, Quart	375.00
Figural, Horseshoe, Embossed Frog On Lily Pad, Miniature	15.00
Figural, Hot Tamale, Austria, Patent Applied For, 8 In.	30.00
Figural, Hot Tamale, Porcelain, Patent Applied For, 6 In.	30.00
Figural, Hound Dog, Screw Top, Cobalt, 3 1/2 In.	4.00
Figural, Hula Girl, Hawaii, Miniature	9.00
Figural, Indian, Standing With Bow, Smooth Base, Frosted, 13 1/4 In.	* 160.00
Figural, see also Bitters, Cologne, Perfume	
Figural, Indian Queen, see Bitters, Brown's Indian Queen	
Figural, Irishmen On Barrel, 12 In.	19.00
Figural, Joan Of Arc, Bonbon, Milk Glass, 17 In.	395.00
Figural, John Bull, Golden Amber, 11 1/2 In. ......Illus	170.00
Figural, John L.Sullivan, 2 Parts, Lavender & Frosted, 14 3/4 In.	* 375.00

Figural, King Kamehameha, Hawaii, Miniature 9.00
Figural, Kneeling Woman, Art Deco, Porcelain, Lavender & Gold, 5 In. 18.00
Figural, Lady In Rocking Chair, Ground Mouth, 5 1/4 In. .... * 70.00
Figural, Lady Wearing Bustle Holding Muff, Smooth Base, 6 1/4 In. .... * 80.00
Figural, Lady's Leg & Shoe, C.1880, 12 In. 32.00
Figural, Lighthouse, 7 1/2 In. .... 5.00 To 10.00
     Figural, Indian Queen, see Bitters, Brown's Celebrated Indian Herb
Figural, Lincoln, Bank, Lincoln Foods, Inc., Mass., C.1930, 8 3/4 In. 20.00
Figural, Lincoln, Bank, Lincoln Foods, Inc., Mass., C.1950, Tin Cap, 8 1/2 In. 25.00
Figural, Locomotive, 11 1/2 In. .... *Illus* 65.00
Figural, Log Cabin With 2 Hillbillies, Ceramic, 6 In. 20.00
Figural, Log Cabin, Smokine, Amber, 7 In. .... *Illus* 250.00
Figural, Log Cabin, Smokine, Stain, Amber 3/4 Quart 160.00
Figural, Log Cabin, 10 1/2 In. .... *Illus* 85.00

Figural, John Bull, Golden Amber, 11 1/2 In.
(See Page 78)

Figural, Locomotive, 11 1/2 In.

Figural, Madonna, Mexican, Amber, 12 In. 15.00
Figural, Madonna, Mexican, Amber, 13 In. 15.00
Figural, Madonna, Mexican, Amethyst, 12 In. 15.00
Figural, Madonna, Mexican, Amethyst, 13 In. 15.00
Figural, Madonna, Mexican, Aqua, 12 In. 15.00
Figural, Madonna, Mexican, Aqua, 13 In. 15.00
Figural, Madonna, Mexican, Cobalt, 12 In. 15.00
Figural, Madonna, Mexican, Cobalt, 13 In. 15.00
Figural, Madonna, Mexican, Green, 12 In. 15.00
Figural, Madonna, Mexican, Green, 13 In. 15.00
Figural, Madonna, Reproduction, Deep Amethyst, 12 1/2 In. .... * 5.00
Figural, Madonna, Tooled Mouth, Smooth Base, Yellow Amber, 14 1/2 In. .... * 30.00
Figural, Madonna, 14 In. 9.00
Figural, Magnifying Glass, Babbitt's Chromo Lens, Metal, Wood, Amber, 10 In. .... * 100.00
Figural, Mailbox, U.S.Mail, Stain, Pint .... *Illus* 80.00
Figural, Man On Barrel, Pottery, Brown Glaze, 9 5/8 In. .... * 30.00
Figural, Man On Barrel, Pottery, Rockingham Glaze, Chip, 8 1/2 In. .... * 60.00
Figural, Man On The Moon, Black Pedestal, Amber, 13 1/2 In. .... *Illus* 375.00
Figural, Man Sitting On Barrel, 'what We Want,' Blue, 6 In. 75.00
Figural, Man Smoking Pipe, Rockingham, 7 5/8 In. 120.00
Figural, Man Wearing Tricorner Hat, Rockingham, 7 3/4 In. 115.00
Figural, Man With Mirror In Stomach, Giggle Soup, 5 1/4 In. 45.00
Figural, Man, Hat Closure, 3 1/4 In. 7.00
Figural, Man, John Bull, Smooth Base, Golden Amber, 11 5/8 In. .... * 190.00
Figural, Man, Old Style Colony Winery, Porcelain, 4/5 .... *Illus* 15.00
Figural, Matador, 1969, 12 In. .... *Color* XXXX.XX
Figural, Mermaid, Pottery, Brown & Green Glaze, 8 1/4 In. .... * 90.00
Figural, Mermaid, Pottery, Rockingham Glaze, 7 In. .... * 45.00

Top left to right: Figural, Log Cabin, Smokine, Amber, 7 In.; Figural, Log Cabin, 10 1/2 In.; Figural, Mailbox, U.S. Mail, Stain, Pint; Figural, Man On The Moon, Black Pedestal, Amber, 13 1/2 In. (*See Page 79*)
Below left: Figural, Man, Old Style Colony Winery, Porcelain, 4/5. (*See Page 79*)

Figural, Mermaid, Pottery, Rockingham Glaze, 7 3/4 In.	* 45.00
Figural, Mermaid, Pottery, Rockingham Glaze, 7 3/4 In.	* 50.00
Figural, Monk, Embossed, Amber, 10 In.	70.00
Figural, Monkey, Cork, 5 In.	20.00
Figural, Monkey, Milk Glass, 3 In.	100.00
Figural, Monument, Figures Ascending, Pontil, Square, 9 3/16 In.	* 50.00
Figural, Monument, Sesquicentennial, 1880, Baltimore Glassworks, Amber	* 350.00
Figural, Moon Mullins, Pottery, 7 In.	*Color* XXXX.XX
Figural, Moses In Bulrushes, Smooth Base, 4 3/4 In.	* 45.00
Figural, Moses, 11 In.	7.95
Figural, Mr.Pickwick, 9 In.	6.95
Figural, Mrs.Butterworth, Lever Bros., Screw Cap, Amber, 10 In.	2.00
Figural, Negro Playing Banjo, High Hat & Tails, Ceramic, 11 1/2 In.	39.00
Figural, Negro Waiter, Black Head, Frosted & Clear, 13 1/2 In. .... *Illus*	140.00
Figural, Negro Waiter, Black-Painted Head, Frosted, 14 1/4 In.	* 150.00
Figural, Nude Child, Germany, Flared Mouth, Smooth Base, 4 3/8 In.	* 35.00
Figural, Nude, Arms Up, Frosted & Draped, France, C.1880, 13 In.	45.00
Figural, Nude, Sabina Glass, 1 In. Satin Base, 5 1/4 In.	27.50
Figural, Old-Fashioned Girl In Corset, 6 1/2 In.	15.00
Figural, Onion, Black Amethyst, 6 1/2 Quart	275.00
Figural, Owl, Amber, 8 In.	30.00
Figural, Owl, Milk Glass, 4 In.	20.00
Figural, Owl, Milk Glass, 5 In.	20.00
Figural, Owl, Mold Blown, Emerald Green, 10 In.	37.50
Figural, Owl, Pint, 9 1/2 In.	25.00
Figural, Oyster, Paint, Ground Mouth, Screw Cap, 6 1/4 In.	* 25.00
Figural, Parrot, Head Stopper, Milk Glass, 8 In.	16.50
Figural, Parrot, Head Stopper, Milk Glass, 10 In.	18.50
Figural, Peasant Woman, Fulham, Stoneware, Salt Glaze, Buff, C.1850, 9 3/4 In.	50.00

Figural, Penguin, Black With White, 5 1/2 In.	5.00
Figural, Penguin, 8 In.	3.50
Figural, Pig In Green Stocking Cap Smoking Pipe, Porcelain, 6 1/4 In.	50.00
Figural, Pig, Anna Pottery, Future Of America, Rye, 15 In. *Illus*	5000.00
Figural, Pig, Beiser & Fischer, N.Y., Amber, 3/4 Quart *Illus*	600.00
Figural, Pig, Drink While It Lasts From This Hog's–, Crack, Chip, 6 3/4 In.	* 85.00
Figural, Pig, Female, Pottery, 6 In.	200.00
Figural, Pig, Fine Old Bourbon In A Hog's–, Pottery, Chips, Brown, 7 3/4 In.	* 900.00
Figural, Pig, Good Ole Bourbon In A Hog's–, Gold Amber	* 270.00
Figural, Pig, Good Ole Rye In A Hog's–, Pottery, Chip, Gray, 8 1/2 In.	*2000.00
Figural, Pig, He Won't Squeal, Something Good In A Hog's–, 4 3/8 In.	* 40.00
Figural, Pig, John Gavlratz, St.Louis, Mo., Pottery, Chip, Brown, 7 5/8 In.	* 950.00
Figural, Pig, Paperweight, Theodore Netter Distilling Co., 6 7/8 In.	* 80.00
Figural, Pig, Pottery, Brown Glaze, 7 In.	* 150.00
Figural, Pig, Pottery, Flake, Brown Glaze, 6 3/4 In.	* 110.00
Figural, Pig, Railroad Lines Inscription, Pottery, Brown Glaze, 7 In.	*1050.00
Figural, Pig, Railroad, Bourbon, Midwestern, C.1880, 7 In. *Illus*	900.00
Figural, Pig, Sheared Mouth, Smooth Base, 6 3/4 In.	* 35.00
Figural, Pig, Sheared Top, Bubbles, 7 In.	45.00

(See Page 80)

Below left to right: Figural, Negro Waiter, Black Head, Frosted & Clear, 13 1/2 In.; Figural, Pig, Anna Pottery, Future Of America, Rye, 15 In.
Bottom row left to right: Figural, Pig, Beiser & Fischer, N.Y., Amber, 3/4 Quart; Figural, Pig, Railroad, Bourbon, Midwestern, C. 1880, 7 In.

Figural, Pig, Something Good In A Hog's & He Won't Squeal, 4 In.	70.00
Figural, Pig, Something Good In A Hog's– & He Won't Squeal, 4 1/4 In.	50.00
Figural, Pig, Something Good In A Hog's–, Christmas & New Year, 4 In.	45.00
Figural, Pig, Stoneware, Glossy Glaze, 6 1/2 In.	* 300.00
Figural, Pineapple, Hawaii, Miniature	9.00
Figural, Pistol, Victorian, Cork, 9 In.	25.00
Figural, Pocketbook, Pottery, Chip, Tan & Cream Glaze, 4 3/4 In.	* 50.00
Figural, Potato, Brown & Silver, Collared Mouth, Smooth Base, 6 1/2 In.	* 20.00
Figural, Potato, Gold Paint, Collared Mouth, Smooth Base, 6 1/4 In.	* 30.00
Figural, Powder Horn, Stephen Green Imperial Pottery, Lambeth, 8 In.	* 40.00
Figural, Pretzel, Porcelain, 6 In.	30.00
Figural, Queen Elizabeth, Bottom Closure, 3 1/2 In.	5.00
Figural, Rachel At The Well, Satin Glass, 12 In.	50.00

Figural, Rebecca At The Well, 8 In.	35.00
Figural, Robert E.Lee Bust, 11 In. .... *Illus*	410.00
Figural, Sandeman, Royal Doulton, Marked A, 10 1/2 In.	40.00
Figural, Sandeman, Royal Doulton, Original Label, 10 In.	45.00 To 52.00
Figural, Santa Claus, Husted, 13 In. .... *Illus*	95.00
Figural, Scallop, Ground Mouth, Screw Cap, 5 In.	* 30.00
Figural, Scallop, Painted, Ground Mouth, Screw Cap, 4 7/8 In.	* 15.00
Figural, Scotsman, Beret Stopper, Ceramic, 17 In.	35.00
Figural, Seated Man With Cane, Rockingham, 8 3/4 In.	115.00
Figural, Senorita, Milk Glass, 13 In.	50.00
Figural, Senorita, 1969, 12 In. .... *Color* XXXX.XX
Figural, Shampoodle, Blue, 8 In.	14.00
Figural, Shoe, BIMAL, 6 In.	12.00
Figural, Shoe, Molded Laces, Rockingham, Dark Glaze, 6 1/2 In.	35.00
Figural, Shoe, Side Buttons, Purpled, 4 1/2 In.	7.50
Figural, Shoe, Toe Showing, Black Amethyst, 3 5/8 In.	* 75.00
Figural, Shoe, Tooled Collared Mouth, Smooth Base, 3 1/4 In.	* 10.00
Figural, Shoe, Tooled Collared Mouth, Smooth Base, 3 1/4 In.	* 40.00
Figural, Shoe, 3 3/8 In.	12.50
Figural, Sitting Pup, MMST, 3 1/2 In.	4.50
Figural, Slipper, Bow, 5 3/4 In.	22.75
Figural, Slipper, Collared Mouth, Pontil, 4 1/2 In.	* 30.00
Figural, Slipper, Label & Tax Stamp, 3 7/8 In.	* 10.00
Figural, Slipper, Label, Pontil, 5 3/8 In.	* 85.00
Figural, Slipper, Pontil, 3 3/8 In.	* 25.00
Figural, Slipper, Tooled Collared Mouth, Smooth Base, 3 1/4 In.	* 10.00
Figural, Slipper, Tooled Collared Mouth, Smooth Base, 4 3/16 In.	* 55.00
Figural, Slipper, Tooled Mouth, Smooth Base, 6 In.	* 100.00
Figural, Soldier With Bagpipes, Robj.Gilt & White, 5 1/2 In., Pair	85.00
Figural, Soldier With Pig's Head, German Letters, Porcelain, 7 1/2 In.	69.50
Figural, South American King, Licores Ranuzzi, Stain, Blue Green, 10 1/2 In.	* 20.00
Figural, Squatting Squaw, Amber, 6 In.	40.00
Figural, Statue Of Liberty Base, Metal Top, Milk Glass, White, 15 In.	395.00
Figural, Statue Of Liberty, Smooth Base, Milk Glass, 15 1/4 In.	* 375.00
Figural, Three Cupids Supporting Globe, Depose, 11 3/4 In.	300.00
Figural, Three Cupids Supporting Globe, 12 In.	27.50
Figural, Toilet, Toilet Water, 2 1/2 In.	3.00
Figural, Toreador, Painted, 12 In. .... *Illus*	10.00
Figural, Tower Of Pisa, 7 1/2 In.	10.00
Figural, Triple Tower & Globes, 13 1/2 In.	65.00

Figural,.
Robert E. Lee, Bust, 11 In.

Figural, Santa Claus,
Husted, 13 In.

Figural, Toreador,
Painted, 12 In.

Figural, Trylon & Perisphere, New York World's Fair, 1939, Milk Glass, 9 In. 30.00
Figural, Turk On A Barrel, Sapphire Blue, 11 3/4 In. ....*Illus* 270.00
Figural, Turtle, Ground Mouth, 5 3/8 In. *2200.00
Figural, Turtle, Repro, Paperweight, Green .... * 5.00
Figural, Turtle, Tooled Mouth, Amber, 5 In. .... * 100.00
Figural, Twisted Antelope Horn, C.1880, 15 In. 26.00
Figural, Victorian Lady, Head Stopper, Milk Glass, 11 In. 19.50
Figural, Violin, Amber, 8 In. 18.00
Figural, Violin, Amber, 9 1/2 In. 10.00
Figural, Violin, Blue, 9 In. 27.50

Figural, Turk On A Barrel,
Sapphire Blue, 11 3/4 In.

Figural,
Whisk Broom, 10 In.

Figural, Violin, Deep Purple, 7 1/2 In. 22.50
Figural, Violin, Green, 9 1/4 In. 6.00
Figural, Violin, Hanging Holder, Cobalt, 12 1/2 In. 10.00
Figural, Violin, Light Blue, 7 1/2 In. 22.50
Figural, Violin, Patent Applied For, Rough, Golden Amber, 6 1/2 In. .... * 110.00
Figural, Violin, Scale On Back, Green, 10 In. 25.00
Figural, Violin, Wooden & String Accesories, Chips, Yellow Amber, Pint .... * 40.00
Figural, Violin, 5 In. 18.00
Figural, Violin, 7 1/2 In. 7.50
Figural, Violin, 11 In. 12.50
Figural, Whisk Broom, Smooth Base, 7 1/2 In. .... * 20.00
Figural, Whisk Broom, 10 In. ....*Illus* 25.00
Figural, Windmill, Occupied Japan, Blue & White, 4 1/2 In. 6.00
Figural, Woman, Old Style Colony Winery, Porcelain, 4/5 ....*Illus* 15.00
Figural, Yam, Pottery, Inside Glaze, 7 3/4 In. .... * 65.00
Figural, Your Health, Uncle Sam, 6 In. 65.00
Figural, Zorro, Royal Doulton ....*Illus* 25.00
Fire Grenade, American Fire Extinguisher Co., Quilted, Chip, 6 1/4 In. .... * 100.00
Fire Grenade, C.& N.W.R.R., Blue Fluid, Iron Brackets, 18 In. 50.00
Fire Grenade, HSN Monogram, Raised Diamonds, Globular, Yellow, Pint .... * 80.00
Fire Grenade, Diamond, Patent June 29th, 1869, 3 Panels, Stain, Aqua, 6 1/8 In .... * 310.00
Fire Grenade, Harden Hand & Star, Vertical Ribs, Chip, Green, Pint .... * 140.00
Fire Grenade, Harden Hand, May 27 84, Vertical Ribs, Bulbous, Amber, 8 1/4 In .... * 190.00
Fire Grenade, Harden Hand, Vertical Ribs, Cornflower Blue, 7 7/8 In. .... * 45.00
Fire Grenade, Harden's, Footed, Blue 25.00
Fire Grenade, Harden's Hand, Fire Extinguisher, Vertical Ribs, Blue, Pint 30.00
Fire Grenade, Harden's Hand, Patent 1871 & 1883, Diamonds, Footed, Blue .... * 20.00
Fire Grenade, Harden's Hand, Patent, Footed, Sapphire Blue, 4 7/8 In. .... * 190.00
Fire Grenade, Harden's Hand, Patented, Footed, Rough, Blue, 5 In. .... * 45.00
Fire Grenade, Harden's Hand, Vertical Ribs, Chips, Sapphire Blue, 6 3/4 In. .... * 15.00
Fire Grenade, Harden's Improved Hand Extinguisher, Bulbous, Cobalt .... * 375.00
Fire Grenade, Harden's Improved, Patent Oct.7, 1884, Bubbles, Amethyst, 5 In. 80.00
Fire Grenade, Harden's Improved, Patent Oct.7th, 1884, Cobalt, 2 3/8 In. .... * 160.00

Fire Grenade, Harden's Hand, Fire Extinguisher, Vertical Ribs, Blue, Pint 30.00
Fire Grenade, Harkness Destroyer, 6 Neck Rings, Globular, Purple Blue, Pint .... * 350.00
Fire Grenade, Harkness Hand, Horizontal Ribs, Bulbous, Cobalt .... * 200.00
Fire Grenade, Hayward Hand, Corrugated, Smooth Base, Aqua, 6 In. .... * 40.00
Fire Grenade, Hayward Hand, N.Y., Vertical Ribs, Crack, Amber, 6 In. .... * 25.00
Fire Grenade, Hayward Hand, Patent, Vertical Ribs, Globular, Cobalt, 6 In. .... * 65.00
Fire Grenade, Hayward's Hand, Patent Aug.8, 1871, Cornflower Blue, 6 1/4 In. .... * 240.00
Fire Grenade, Hayward's Hand, Patent Aug.8, 1871, Flattened, Aqua, 6 3/8 In. .... * 40.00
Fire Grenade, Hayward's Hand, Patent Aug.8th, 1871, Green Yellow, Pint .... * 45.00

Figural, Woman,
Old Style Colony Winery,
Porcelain, 4/5
(See Page 83)

Figural, Your Health,
Uncle Sam, 6 In.
(See Page 83)

Figural, Zorro,
Royal Doulton
(See Page 83)

Fire Grenade, Healy's Hand, Collared Mouth, Stain, Amber, 10 3/4 In. .... * 100.00
Fire Grenade, Korbeline, Hexagonal Pattern, Bulbous, Amber, 7 1/4 In. .... * 100.00
Fire Grenade, Mason Clyde, N.Y., Glass Works, C, 1800, Lion Face, Green, 6 In. 25.00
Fire Grenade, Patent Sept.29th, 1863, Ground Mouth, Bulbous, Aqua, 5 In. 110.00
Fire Grenade, S.F.Hayward, Patent Aug.8, 1871, Ground Mouth, Cobalt, 6 In. .... * 70.00
Fire Grenade, Star Harden Hand Grenade, 8 In. .... Illus   175.00
Fire Grenade, Vertical Ribs, Collared Mouth, Globular, Olive Green, Pint .... * 200.00
    Fitzgerald, see Old Fitzgerald
Flagon, Salt Glaze, Round, Enamel Bouquets, 1769, 6 1/2 In. 1400.00

> Flasks have been made since the 18th century in america. The free blown,
> mold blown, and decorated flasks are all popular with collectors. The
> numbers that appear with some of the entries are those used in the Mc
> Kearin book, American Glass. The numbers used in the entries in the
> form Van R-0 or Mc Kearin G l-0 refer to the books 'Early
> American Bottles & Flasks' by Stephen Van Rensselaer and 'American
> Glass' by George P. and Helen Mc Kearin.

Flask, Anchor Embossed On Bottom, Strap Side, Amber, 7 1/2 In. .... Illus   6.00
Flask, Anchor & Chain, Strap Side, Yellow Amber, 1/2 Pint 200.0
Flask, Anchor & Jno F.Horne, Knoxville, Tenn., Amber, Quart .... * 100.00
Flask, Anchor & Spring Garden Glass Works & Cabin & Tree, Stain, Aqua, Pint 50.00
Flask, Anchor & Spring Garden Glass Works & Cabin, Yellow Green, 1/2 Pint 475.00
Flask, Anchor, Amber, Pint 10.00
Flask, Anchor, Amber, Quart .... * 32.50
Flask, Applied Handle, Amber, 8 In. 35.00
Flask, Applied Handle, Dark Red Amber, 9 1/4 In. 25.00

Flask, Applied Lip, Aqua, 1/2 Pint 3.75
Flask, Applied Metal Vines & Floral, Concave Sides, Silver Cap, Green, 9 In. 75.00
Flask, Aqua, Pint 3.50
Flask, Art Nouveau, Woman & Cigarette, Sterling Silver, Unger Bros., 6 In. 250.00
Flask, Baltimore Glass Works & Anchor & Sheaf Of Wheat, Aqua, Pint 70.00
Flask, Baltimore Glass Works & Eagle & Resurgam, Pontil, Olive Green, Pint .... * 450.00
Flask, Baltimore Glass Works & Eagle & Resurgam, Stain, Amber, Pint .... * 170.00
Flask, Baltimore Glass Works & Eagle & Resurgam, Yellow Amber, Pint .... * 250.00
Flask, Baltimore Glass Works & Sheaf Of Wheat & Fork, Blue Green, Quart .... * 700.00
Flask, Baltimore Glass Works & Sheaf Of Wheat, Fork, & Rake, Amber, Quart .... * 525.00
Flask, Baltimore Glass Works & Sheaf Of Wheat, Olive Yellow, 1/2 Pint .... * 450.00
Flask, Baltimore Glass Works & Sheaf Of Wheat, Pontil, Aqua, 1/2 Pint .... * 80.00
Flask, Baltimore Glass Works & Sheaf Of Wheat, Pontil, Red Amber, Quart .... * 700.00
Flask, Baltimore Glass Works & Sheaf Of Wheat, Wear, Puce, 1/2 Pint .... * 700.00
Flask, Basket Weave, Pint, 7 1/2 In. .... *Illus* 10.00
Flask, Batsto Mansion 1974 & Citizens Committee, 1956, Repro, Amber, Pint .... * 10.00
Flask, Bennington, Rockingham Glaze, C.1850, 6 In. .... *Illus* 225.00
Flask, Bird & L.C.& R. Co., Strap Side, BIMAL, 1/2 Pint 12.50
Flask, Blown, Applied Lip, Green, 5 1/2 In. 70.00
Flask, Blown, Applied Lip, Pale Yellow Green, 5 In. 35.00
Flask, Blown, Double Collared Mouth, Pontil, Ovoid, Amber, Pint .... * 55.00
Flask, Blown, Flattened & Elongated, Pontil, Dark Amber, 8 3/4 In. .... * 30.00
Flask, Blown, Sheared Mouth, Pontil, Aqua, 4 3/4 In. .... * 40.00
Flask, Blown, Tooled Mouth, Pontil, Wear, Red, White, & Blue, Green, 7 In. .... * 250.00
Flask, Book, Bennington, C.1850, 10 3/4 In. .... *Illus* 400.00

Fire Grenade, Star Harden
Hand Grenade, 8 In.
(See Page 84)

Flask, Basket Weave,
Pint, 7 1/2 In.

Flask, Anchor Embossed On Bottom,
Strap Side, Amber, 7 1/2 In.
(See Page 84)

Flask, Book, Bennington, Parted Spirits, C.1850, 8 In. .... *Illus* 250.00
Flask, Book, Bennington, 2 Quart, 7 3/4 In. .... *Illus* 225.00
Flask, Brandy, Hinged Top, Sterling Overlay, Black, Starr & Frost, 4 In. 35.00
Flask, Bristol, C.1800, Silver Mounts, Amethyst, 8 1/2 In. .... *Color* XXXX.XX
Flask, Brown Forham Distillers, Pint 7.50
Flask, C.A.Richard's, Coffin, Aqua, Pint 20.00
Flask, C.Jouard, Strap Side, Union Oval, Amber, Pint, 8 1/4 In. 10.00
Flask, Calabash, Baltimore & Sheaf Of Wheat, Pontil, Blue, Quart *3000.00
Flask, Calabash, Hunter & Dog & Man With Horse & Tree, Aqua, 9 1/4 In. 85.00
Flask, Calabash, Hunter & Fisherman, Double Collar, Pontil, Aqua .... * 65.00
Flask, Calabash, Hunter & Fisherman, IP, Green .... * 450.00
Flask, Calabash, Hunter & Fisherman, IP, Wear, Puce Amber .... * 475.00
Flask, Calabash, Hunter & Fisherman, Pontil, Aqua .... * 65.00
Flask, Calabash, Jenny Lind & Fislervile Glass Works, Repro, Aqua .... * 15.00
Flask, Calabash, Jenny Lind & Fislerville, Repro, Applied Handle, Green .... * 45.00
Flask, Calabash, Jenny Lind & Fislerville, Repro, Ruby & Amber, Quart .... * 40.00
Flask, Calabash, Louis Kossuth & S.Huffsey & Mississippi, Pontil, Aqua .... * 500.00

Flask, Bennington,
Rockingham Glaze, C.1850, 6 In.
(See Page 85)

Flask, Book, Bennington,
Parted Spirits, C.1850, 8 In.
Flask, Book,
Bennington, 2 Quart, 7 3/4 In.
Flask, Book,
Bennington, C.1850, 10 3/4 In.
(See Page 85)

Flask, Calabash, Roosevelt & Eagle & T V A & Dam & 1936, Repro, Aqua, Quart .... * 20.00
Flask, Calabash, Sheaf Of Wheat & Duffy, Pontil, Light Green .... * 200.00
Flask, Calabash, Sheaf Of Wheat & Duffy, Ribbed, Pontil, Aqua .... * 100.00
Flask, Calabash, Sheaf Of Wheat & Tree, Double Collar, Pontil, Green .... * 250.00
Flask, Calabash, Sheaf Of Wheat & Tree, Pontil, Deep Wine Color *1300.00
Flask, Calabash, Sheaf Of Wheat, Rake, & Fork & Star, Broken, Amber .... * 275.00
Flask, Calabash, Soldier, Ribbed Edges, IP, Deep Aqua .... * 210.00
Flask, Calabash, Union & Clasped Hands & Eagle & Banner, Aqua, 9 1/4 In. 50.00
Flask, Calabash, Union & Clasped Hands & Eagle, Yellow Green, Quart .... * 425.00
Flask, Calabash, Union, Clasped Hands, & 13 Stars & Eagle, Amber, Quart .... * 190.00
Flask, Calabash, Union, Clasped Hands, & 13 Stars & Eagle, Aqua, Quart 50.00
Flask, Cedarburst, Amber, 6 In. 4.00
Flask, Champion & Balt.Md., Aqua, Pint, 8 1/4 In. 85.00
Flask, Chas.J.Smith, Strap, BIMAL, Pint 2.00
Flask, Chestnut Type, Flattened, Hobnail, Pontil, Blue Green, 5 3/4 In. .... * 55.00
Flask, Chestnut Type, Flattened, Hobnail, Pontil, Dark Amber, 5 1/2 In. * 95.00
Flask, Chestnut Type, Hobnail, Sheared Mouth, Pontil, 4 In. .... * 100.00
Flask, Chestnut, Aqua, 11 3/8 In. 65.00
Flask, Chestnut, Blown, Applied Mouth, Pontil, Olive Amber, 5 1/2 In. .... * 65.00
Flask, Chestnut, Blown, Applied Mouth, Pontil, Olive Amber, 12 3/4 In. .... * 120.00
Flask, Chestnut, Blown, Applied Rigaree, Pontil, Olive Amber, 4 1/4 In. .... * 110.00
Flask, Chestnut, Blown, Collared Mouth, Pontil, Aqua, 8 3/4 In. .... * 35.00
Flask, Chestnut, Blown, Collared Mouth, Pontil, Aqua, 10 5/8 In. .... * 30.00
Flask, Chestnut, Blown, Collared Mouth, Pontil, Broken, Amber, 2 5/8 In. .... * 25.00
Flask, Chestnut, Blown, Collared Mouth, Pontil, Bruise, Olive Green, 10 1/2 In .... * 50.00
Flask, Chestnut, Blown, Collared Mouth, Pontil, Clear Olive Green, 7 In. .... * 65.00
Flask, Chestnut, Blown, Collared Mouth, Pontil, Crack, Olive Green, 5 In. .... * 30.00
Flask, Chestnut, Blown, Collared Mouth, Pontil, Olive Amber, 4 1/2 In. .... * 20.00
Flask, Chestnut, Blown, Collared Mouth, Pontil, Olive Amber, 5 1/4 In. .... * 90.00
Flask, Chestnut, Blown, Collared Mouth, Pontil, Olive Amber, 5 7/8 In. .... * 70.00
Flask, Chestnut, Blown, Collared Mouth, Pontil, Olive Amber, 6 1/8 In. .... * 80.00
Flask, Chestnut, Blown, Collared Mouth, Pontil, Olive Amber, 7 3/4 In. .... * 70.00
Flask, Chestnut, Blown, Collared Mouth, Pontil, Olive Amber, 8 In. .... * 65.00
Flask, Chestnut, Blown, Collared Mouth, Pontil, Olive Amber, 8 1/2 In. .... * 55.00
Flask, Chestnut, Blown, Collared Mouth, Pontil, Olive Amber, 9 1/4 In. .... * 110.00
Flask, Chestnut, Blown, Collared Mouth, Pontil, Olive Amber, 9 1/2 In. .... * 100.00
Flask, Chestnut, Blown, Collared Mouth, Pontil, Olive Amber, 11 In. .... * 100.00
Flask, Chestnut, Blown, Collared Mouth, Pontil, Olive Amber, 12 1/4 In. .... * 120.00
Flask, Chestnut, Blown, Collared Mouth, Pontil, Olive Amber, 12 1/2 In. .... * 140.00
Flask, Chestnut, Blown, Collared Mouth, Pontil, Olive Green, 3 3/8 In. .... * 220.00
Flask, Chestnut, Blown, Collared Mouth, Pontil, Olive Green, 5 3/4 In. .... * 65.00
Flask, Chestnut, Blown, Collared Mouth, Pontil, Olive Green, 8 5/8 In. .... * 75.00
Flask, Chestnut, Blown, Collared Mouth, Pontil, Stain, Chip, Green, 5 In. .... * 30.00
Flask, Chestnut, Blown, Collared Mouth, Pontil, Stain, Olive Amber, 8 In. .... * 40.00
Flask, Chestnut, Blown, Collared Mouth, Pontil, Stain, Olive Green, 9 1/4 In. .... * 70.00
Flask, Chestnut, Blown, Collared Mouth, Pontil, Stain, Yellow, 3 3/4 In. .... * 40.00
Flask, Chestnut, Blown, Collared Mouth, Pontil, Wear, Olive Green, 9 1/4 In. .... * 60.00
Flask, Chestnut, Blown, Collared Mouth, Pontil, Yellow Green, 5 1/8 In. .... * 65.00
Flask, Chestnut, Blown, Collared Mouth, Pontil, 6 3/4 In. .... * 45.00

Flask, Chestnut, Blown, Collared Mouth, Pontil, Yellow Green, 6 1/2 In. .... * 75.00
Flask, Chestnut, Blown, Collared Mouth, Stain, Olive Green, 7 3/4 In. .... * 55.00
Flask, Chestnut, Blown, Collared, Pontil, Crack, Olive Amber, 10 1/2 In. .... * 25.00
Flask, Chestnut, Blown, Larson, Blown, Pontil, Amethyst, 2 5/8 In. .... * 220.00
Flask, Chestnut, Blown, Mouth Ring, Pontil, Burst Bubble, Green, 5 1/4 In. .... * 65.00
Flask, Chestnut, Blown, Mouth Ring, Pontil, Stain, Red Amber, 6 1/2 In. .... * 65.00
Flask, Chestnut, Blown, Mouth Ring, Pontil, Wear, Olive Amber, 3 1/2 In. .... * 95.00
Flask, Chestnut, Blown, Mouth Ring, Pontil, Wear, Olive Amber, 10 3/4 In. .... * 55.00
Flask, Chestnut, Blown, Mouth Ring, Pontil, Wear, Red Amber, 5 1/2 In. .... * 50.00
Flask, Chestnut, Blown, OP, Deep Aqua, 8 In. 75.00
Flask, Chestnut, Blown, Pontil, Wear, Olive Amber, 3 5/8 In. .... * 250.00
Flask, Chestnut, Blown, Rolled Collared Mouth, Pontil, Aqua, 3 1/2 In. .... * 95.00
Flask, Chestnut, Blown, Sheared Mouth With Ring, Aqua, 16 1/4 In. .... * 40.00
Flask, Chestnut, Blown, Sheared Mouth, Pontil, Aqua, 5 1/4 In. .... * 45.00
Flask, Chestnut, Blown, Sheared Mouth, Pontil, Olive Amber, 6 3/4 In. .... * 30.00
Flask, Chestnut, Blown, Square Mouth, Pontil, Wear, Amber, 6 3/4 In. .... * 60.00
Flask, Chestnut, Bubbles, Olive Yellow, 5 1/4 In. 70.00
Flask, Chestnut, Citron, 5 In. 250.00
Flask, Chestnut, Flattened, Blown, Applied Handle, Dark Amber, 7 In. 65.00
Flask, Chestnut, Flattened, Blown, Pontil, Chip, Olive Green, 4 5/8 In. .... * 25.00
Flask, Chestnut, Flattened, Blown, Square Mouth, Pontil, Aqua, 4 1/2 In. .... * 65.00
Flask, Chestnut, Flattened, Elongated, Diamond & Hexagon, Stain, Green, 7 In. .... * 100.00
Flask, Chestnut, Flattened, Elongated, Ribs Swirled To Right, Aqua, 6 In. .... * 60.00
Flask, Chestnut, Flattened, Elongated, 16 Diamonds, Pontil, Green, 7 3/4 In. .... * 80.00
Flask, Chestnut, Flattened, Elongated, 22 Ribs Swirled To Left, Green, 6 In. .... * 180.00
Flask, Chestnut, Flattened, Larson, Blown, Pontil, Ruby, 2 3/4 In. .... * 140.00
Flask, Chestnut, Flattened, Larson, Ribs Swirled To Right, Amethyst, 5 In. .... * 170.00
Flask, Chestnut, Flattened, Midwestern, Diamond, Ribbed, Wear, Green, 5 In. .... * 250.00
Flask, Chestnut, Flattened, Midwestern, Expanded Diamond, Blue Green, 5 In. .... * 400.00
Flask, Chestnut, Flattened, Midwestern, Ribs Swirled To Left, Amber, 5 In. .... * 140.00
Flask, Chestnut, Flattened, Midwestern, Ribs Swirled To Right, Aqua, 6 1/2 In .... * 85.00
Flask, Chestnut, Flattened, Midwestern, Ribs Swirled To Right, Cobalt, 4 In. .... * 375.00
Flask, Chestnut, Flattened, Midwestern, Vertical Ribs, Pontil, Amber, 5 1/2 In .... * 275.00
Flask, Chestnut, Flattened, Midwestern, Vertical Ribs, Pontil, Amber, 7 3/8 In .... * 300.00
Flask, Chestnut, Flattened, Midwestern, 12 Diamonds, Pontil, Amber, 4 7/8 In .... * 425.00
Flask, Chestnut, Flattened, Midwestern, 24 Ribs Swirled To Left, Amber, 5 In. .... * 350.00
Flask, Chestnut, Flattened, Midwestern, 24 Ribs Swirled To Left, Amber, 5 In. .... * 500.00
Flask, Chestnut, Flattened, Midwestern, 24 Ribs Swirled To Right, Green, 5 In .... * 900.00
Flask, Chestnut, Flattened, Midwestern, 24 Ribs Swirled To Right, Green, 8 In. .... * 175.00
Flask, Chestnut, Flattened, Midwestern, 24 Vertical Ribs, Pontil, Amber, 6 In. .... * 275.00
Flask, Chestnut, Flattened, Midwestern, 24 Vertical Ribs, Stain, Amber, 7 In. .... * 425.00
Flask, Chestnut, Flattened, Midwestern, 30 Ribs Swirled To Right, Aqua, 7 In. .... * 60.00
Flask, Chestnut, Flattened, Nailsea Type, Swirled Ribs, Black, White, 5 In. .... * 160.00
Flask, Chestnut, Flattened, Ribbed, Sheared Mouth, Pontil, Amethyst, 3 1/2 In. .... * 80.00
Flask, Chestnut, Flattened, Ribs Swirled To Right, Sapphire, 5 1/4 In. .... * 175.00
Flask, Chestnut, Flattened, 16 Diamond, Sheared Mouth, Stain, Aqua, 4 1/2 In. .... * 95.00
Flask, Chestnut, Flattened, 20 Ribs Swirled To Left, Flake, Amber, 7 In. .... * 100.00
Flask, Chestnut, Flattened, 24 Ribs Swirled To Right, Pontil, Green, 7 1/4 In .... * 210.00
Flask, Chestnut, Flattened, 24 Vertical Ribs, Pontil, Aqua, 4 1/2 In. .... * 140.00
Flask, Chestnut, Flattened, 24 Vertical Ribs, Pontil, Green, 7 1/2 In. .... * 100.00
Flask, Chestnut, Flattened, 30 Broken Swirl Ribs & 21 Vertical, Aqua, 5 In. 75.00
Flask, Chestnut, Handled, Red Amber, Pint .... 14.00 To 37.00
Flask, Chestnut, Handled, Red Amber, Quart 14.00
Flask, Chestnut, Larson, Diamond Quilted, Pontil, Emerald, 5 1/4 In. .... * 175.00
Flask, Chestnut, Larson, 18 Ribs Swirled To Right, Pontil, Purple, 5 In. .... * 220.00
Flask, Chestnut, Ludlow, OP, Light Green, 6 1/2 In. 60.00
Flask, Chestnut, Midwestern, Expanded 10 Diamond, Pontil, Red Amber, 5 1/4 In .... * 950.00
Flask, Chestnut, Midwestern, Expanded 10 Diamond, Pontil, Red Amber, 5 5/8 In .... * 925.00
Flask, Chestnut, Midwestern, Expanded 10 Diamond, Stain, Yellow, 4 7/8 In. .... * 550.00
Flask, Chestnut, Midwestern, Granddaddy, Broken Swirl, Pontil, Amber, 8 3/4 In *1400.00
Flask, Chestnut, Midwestern, Ribs Swirled To Left, Pontil, Amber, 5 In. .... * 240.00
Flask, Chestnut, Midwestern, Vertical Ribs, Pontil, Amber, 4 5/8 In. .... * 300.00
Flask, Chestnut, Midwestern, 16 Ribs Swirled To Right, Wear, Cobalt, 5 1/4 In .... * 450.00
Flask, Chestnut, Midwestern, 20 Vertical Ribs, Pontil, Aqua, 6 1/2 In. .... * 45.00
Flask, Chestnut, Olive Amber, 5 5/8 In. 55.00

Flask, Chestnut, Olive Amber, 6 3/4 In. 55.00
Flask, Chestnut, Olive Gold, 6 1/2 In. 100.00
Flask, Chestnut, Olive Gold, 7 3/4 In. 100.00
Flask, Chestnut, Olive Gold, 8 1/2 In. 100.00
Flask, Chestnut, Olive Green, 5 In 76.00
Flask, Chestnut, Olive Green, 5 5/8 In. 55.00
Flask, Chestnut, Olive Green, 6 In. 55.00
Flask, Chestnut, Olive Green, 7 1/8 In. 55.00
Flask, Chestnut, Olive Green, 8 1/4 In. 55.00
Flask, Chestnut, Olive Green, 8 3/4 In. 40.00
Flask, Chestnut, OP, Apple Green, 4 In. 48.00
Flask, Chestnut, Stiegel, Daisy In Square, Pontil, Amethyst, 5 1/8 In. *2000.00
Flask, Chestnut, Tooled Collar, OP, Light Apple Green, Quart 50.00
Flask, Chestnut, Tooled Lip, OP, Light Apple Green, Quart 50.00
Flask, Chestnut, 8 Broken Swirl Panels & 8 Panels, 4 1/2 In. 185.00
Flask, Chestnut, 16 Swirled Ribs, Aqua, 6 1/4 In. 65.00
Flask, Chestnut, 18 Ribs Swirled To Left, Flattened, Olive Yellow, 7 In. .... * 110.00
Flask, Chestnut, 18 Swirled Ribs, Green Aqua, 6 1/2 In. 65.00

Flask, Coffin, Dr.L.H.Hallock,
Sebewaing, Mich., Aqua, Pint

Flask, Chestnut, 18 Vertical Ribs, Aqua, 6 In. 80.00
Flask, Chestnut, 24 Swirled Ribs, Amber, 4 3/4 In. 280.00
Flask, Chestnut, 24 Vertical Ribs, Amber, 5 In. 250.00
Flask, Chestnut, 24 Vertical Ribs, Red Amber, 5 1/4 In. 250.00
Flask, Clasped Hands & Eagle With Banner, Aqua, 1/2 Pint 60.00
Flask, Clasped Hands & 13 Stars, Aqua, Pint 53.00
Flask, Cleveland & Stevenson, Campaign, '93, Amber, Pint 275.00
Flask, Cleveland Bust In Panel, Aqua, Pint .... * 120.00
Flask, Cleveland Bust To Left & Hendricks Bust To Right, Collar, Pint .... * 500.00
Flask, Clyde Glass Works, N.Y., Amber, Quart .... * 40.00
Flask, Clyde Glass Works, N.Y., Amber, 1/2 Pint .... * 60.00
Flask, Clyde Glass Works, N.Y., Burst Bubble, Amber, Pint .... * 65.00
Flask, Clyde Glass Works, N.Y., Smooth Base, Aqua, Quart .... * 35.00
Flask, Cobalt, Pint 525.00
Flask, Coffin, A.Weinberg, Tacoma, W.T. In Slug Plate, Scroll, 1/2 Pint 200.00
Flask, Coffin, Dr.L.H.Hallock, Sebewaing, Mich., Aqua, Pint .... Illus 10.00
Flask, Columbus, Man In Barrel & On A Barrel & Cock, Yellow Amber, 1/2 Pint .... * 140.00
Flask, Corn For The World, Light Green, 1/2 Pint 275.00
Flask, Corn Whiskey, Ear Of Corn Shape, Pewter Screw On Cap, 6 1/2 In. 85.00
Flask, Cornucopia & Basket, Olive Green, Pint 65.00
Flask, Cornucopia & Urn, Dark Amber, Pint 65.00
Flask, Cornucopia & Urn, Green, Pint 62.00
Flask, Cornucopia & Urn, Olive Amber, Pint 55.00
Flask, Cornucopia & Urn, Repro, Similar To McK G III-4, Cobalt, Pint .... * 10.00
Flask, Crolius, N.Y., C.1790, Stoneware, Blue Slip Floral & Leaf, 8 In. 1400.00
Flask, Crystal & Silver, Drew & Sons, London, 1918, 6 In. 65.00
Flask, Cunninghams & Ihmsen Glassmakers, Pittsburgh, Mouth Ring, Aqua, Pint .... * 45.00
Flask, Dancing Sailor & Musician, Pontil, Olive Green, 1/2 Pint .... * 775.00

Flask, Diamond Quilted, 1/2 Pint 35.00
Flask, Diamond Quilted, Quart 10.00
Flask, Diamond, Canteen Shape, 6 5/8 In. .... * 30.00
Flask, Dog & Grapes, Cobalt, 1/2 Pint 60.00
Flask, Double Diamond, Shot Glass Stopper, Tooled Mouth, 1/2 Pint .... * 15.00
Flask, Double Dipped Pitkin Type, Dimpled, OP, 1/2 Pint 100.00
Flask, Double Eagle & Banner & C & I, Aqua, 1/2 Pint .... * 45.00
Flask, Double Eagle & Banner & Cunningham & Co., Bruise, Olive Yellow, Pint .... * 200.00
Flask, Double Eagle & Banner & Cunningham & Co., Pittsburgh, Amber, Quart .... * 150.00
Flask, Double Eagle & Banner & Cunningham & Co., Pittsburgh, Aqua, Pint .... * 55.00
Flask, Double Eagle & Banner & Dot, Pontil, Olive Amber, 1/2 Pint .... * 70.00
Flask, Double Eagle & Banner & Geo.A.Berry & Co., Mouth Ring, Aqua, Pint .... * 40.00
Flask, Double Eagle & Banner & Granite Glass Co., Pontil, Olive Amber, Pint .... * 150.00
Flask, Double Eagle & Banner & Louisville, Ky., Glass Works, Aqua, Pint .... * 40.00
Flask, Double Eagle & Banner & Louisville, Ky., Glass Works, Aqua, Quart .... * 70.00
Flask, Double Eagle & Banner & Pittsburgh, Collar, Olive Green, Quart .... * 150.00
Flask, Double Eagle & Banner & Pittsburgh, Collar, Yellow Green, Pint .... * 160.00
Flask, Double Eagle & Banner & Pittsburgh, Pa., Applied Ring, Amber, Pint .... * 65.00
Flask, Double Eagle & Banner & Pittsburgh, Pa., Aqua, 1/2 Pint .... * 50.00
Flask, Double Eagle & Banner & Pittsburgh, Pa., Black Olive Green, Pint .... * 140.00
Flask, Double Eagle & Banner & Pittsburgh, Pa., Dark Olive Green, Quart .... * 140.00
Flask, Double Eagle & Banner & Pittsburgh, Pa., Emerald Green, Pint .... * 160.00
Flask, Double Eagle & Banner & Pittsburgh, Pa., McC & Co., Amber, Pint .... * 60.00
Flask, Double Eagle & Banner & Stoddard, N.H., Pontil, Olive Amber, Pint .... * 110.00
Flask, Double Eagle & Banner & X, Pontil, Olive Green, 1/2 Pint .... * 220.00
Flask, Double Eagle & Banner Above Panel, Aqua, 1/2 Pint .... * 45.00
Flask, Double Eagle & Banner Above Panel, Deep Amber, 1/2 Pint .... * 70.00
Flask, Double Eagle & Banner Above Panel, Sheared Mouth, Amber, 1/2 Pint .... * 55.00
Flask, Double Eagle & Banner Above Panel, Sheared Mouth, Olive Amber, Quart .... * 110.00
Flask, Double Eagle & Banner Above Panel, Yellow Green, Pint .... * 190.00
Flask, Double Eagle & Banner, Aqua, 1/2 Pint .... * 45.00
Flask, Double Eagle & Banner, Burst Bubble, Yellow, Pint .... * 190.00
Flask, Double Eagle & Banner, Chip, Amber, Pint .... * 70.00
Flask, Double Eagle & Banner, Collared Mouth, Light Green, 1/2 Pint 65.00
Flask, Double Eagle & Banner, Collared Mouth, Yellow Green, Pint .... * 250.00
Flask, Double Eagle & Banner, Mouth Ring, Flake, Amethystine, 1/2 Pint .... * 450.00
Flask, Double Eagle & Banner, Sapphire Blue, Pint *1550.00
Flask, Double Eagle & Banner, Stoddard, Pontil, Olive Amber, Pint .... * 80.00
Flask, Double Eagle & Cunningham & Co., Pittsburgh, Aqua, Quart .... 55.00 To 75.00
Flask, Double Eagle & Granite Glassworks, Stoddard, N.H., Amber, Pint 130.00
Flask, Double Eagle & Pittsburgh, Applied Mouth With Ring, Aqua, Pint .... * 50.00
Flask, Double Eagle & Pittsburgh, Aqua, Pint 60.00
Flask, Double Eagle & Pittsburgh, Aqua, Quart 30.00
Flask, Double Eagle & Pittsburgh, Ice Blue, 1/2 Pint · 45.00
Flask, Double Eagle & Pittsburgh, Pa., Aqua, Quart 40.00
Flask, Double Eagle & Pittsburgh, Pa., Chip, Citron, 1/2 Pint .... * 250.00
Flask, Double Eagle & Pittsburgh, Pa., In Cartouche, Green, Pint 170.00
Flask, Double Eagle & Pittsburgh, Pa., Olive Amber, Pint 125.00
Flask, Double Eagle & Pittsburgh, Pa., Pint 59.00
Flask, Double Eagle & Plain Ovals, Yellow Green, Pint, 7 1/2 In. 150.00
Flask, Double Eagle & Stoddard, Amber, 1/2 Pint 65.00
Flask, Double Eagle & Stoddard, N.H. In Oval, Embossed, OP, Amber, Pint 84.00
Flask, Double Eagle & Stoddard, N.H., OP, Amber, Pint 90.00
Flask, Double Eagle & Stoddard, N.H., Granite Glass Co., Amber, Pint 125.00
Flask, Double Eagle & Stoddard, OP, Olive Green, Pint 85.00
Flask, Double Eagle & Zanesville, Ohio, Amber Swirl, Aqua, 1/2 Pint 75.00
Flask, Double Eagle Above Oval Panel, Applied Mouth With Ring, Aqua, Pint 35.00
Flask, Double Eagle Above Panel & Zanesville, Ohio, Pint, Aqua .... * 210.00
Flask, Double Eagle Above Panel, Smooth Base, Aqua, Pint .... * 40.00
Flask, Double Eagle On Wreath, Aqua, 1/2 Pint 60.00
Flask, Double Eagle Over Oval, Aqua, Pint 38.50
Flask, Double Eagle Over Oval, Aqua, 1/2 Pint 34.00
Flask, Double Eagle, Amber, 1/2 Pint .... 50.00 To 68.00
Flask, Double Eagle, Amber, Pint .... 65.00 To 75.00
Flask, Double Eagle, Applied Mouth With Ring, Golden Amber, Quart .... * 90.00

Flask, Double Eagle, Aqua, 1/2 Pint 45.00
Flask, Double Eagle, Aqua, Pint .... 39.00 To 40.00
Flask, Double Eagle, Banner, & Pittsburgh, Pa., Collar, Aqua, 1/2 Pint 60.00
Flask, Double Eagle, Banner, & Pittsburgh, Pa., Mouth Ring, Stain, Aqua, Quart 40.00
Flask, Double Eagle, Banner, & Wreath, Applied Mouth, Aqua, 1/2 Pint 40.00
Flask, Double Eagle, Cloudy, Aqua, Pint 30.00
Flask, Double Eagle, Double Collared Mouth, Aqua, 1/2 Pint 50.00
Flask, Double Eagle, Haze, Aqua, Pint 32.50
Flask, Double Eagle, Olive Amber, Pint 85.00
Flask, Double Eagle, Olive Green, 1/2 Pint 90.00
Flask, Double Eagle, Olive Green, Pint .... 50.00 To 125.00
Flask, Double Eagle, OP, Deep Olive, Pint 85.00
Flask, Double Eagle, OP, Olive Green, 1/2 Pint .... 89.00 To 115.00
Flask, Double Eagle, OP, Olive, 1/2 Pint 80.00
Flask, Double Eagle, OP, Olive, Pint 75.00
Flask, Double Eagle, Pint .... 35.00 To 45.00
Flask, Double Eagle, Pittsburgh Type, Applied Mouth, Aqua, Pint .... * 35.00
Flask, Double Eagle, Pittsburgh Type, Applied Mouth, Aqua, Quart .... * 55.00
Flask, Double Eagle, Pittsburgh Type, Aqua, Pint 25.00
Flask, Double Eagle, Pittsburgh Type, Chips, Blue Green, Pint .... * 40.00
Flask, Double Eagle, Pittsburgh Type, Mouth Ring, Aqua, Pint .... * 40.00
Flask, Double Eagle, Pittsburgh Type, Mouth Ring, Aqua, 1/2 Pint .... * 25.00
Flask, Double Eagle, Pittsburgh Type, Pontil, Crack, Aqua, Quart .... * 50.00
Flask, Double Eagle, Pittsburgh, Green Aqua, Pint 75.00
Flask, Double Eagle, Pottery, Rockingham Glaze, Pint .... * 325.00
Flask, Double Oak & Tree In Panel, Double Collared Mouth, Amber, 1/2 Pint ...... * 60.00
Flask, Double Panel, Vertical Ribs, Sheared Mouth, IP, Aqua, 1/2 Pint .... * 45.00
Flask, Double Scroll, Applied Mouth With Ring, IP, Aqua, Quart 60.00
Flask, Double Scroll, Repro, Similar To McK G IX-11, Amethyst, Pint .... * 25.00
Flask, Double Scroll, Repro, Similar To McK G IX-11, Cobalt, Pint .... * 30.00
Flask, Double Scroll, Sheared Mouth, IP, Stain, Aqua, Pint 35.00
Flask, Double Sheaf Of Wheat Tied With Loop, Aqua, Pint, 7 7/8 In. 80.00
Flask, Double Sheaf Of Wheat, Applied Mouth With Ring, Aqua, Pint 50.00
Flask, Double Sheaf Of Wheat, Applied Mouth With Ring, Stain, Aqua, Pint 55.00
Flask, Double Sheaf Of Wheat, Applied Mouth, Smooth Base, Aqua, Pint 50.00
Flask, Double Sheaf Of Wheat, Aqua, Pint 68.00
Flask, Double Sheaf Of Wheat, Fork, & Rake, Pontil, Crack, Green, 1/2 Pint ...... * 120.00
Flask, Double Success To The Railroad, Dug, Olive Amber, Pint 500.00
Flask, Double Success To The Railroad, Repro, Aqua, Pint .... * 15.00
Flask, Double Success To The Railroad, Repro, Aqua, Pint .... * 20.00
Flask, Double Success To The Railroad, Repro, Olive Green, Pint .... * 40.00
Flask, Double Sunburst, Repro, Similar To McK G VIII-2, Amethyst, Pint .... * 20.00
Flask, Double Sunburst, Repro, Similar To McK G VIII-2, Cobalt, Pint .... * 150.00
Flask, Double Union & Clasped Hands, Aqua, Quart 75.00
Flask, Double Union, Clasped Hands, & 13 Stars, Cornflower Blue, Quart .... * 550.00
Flask, Double Union, Clasped Hands, Shield, & 13 Stars, Yellow, Quart .... * 400.00
Flask, Double Washington, Repro, Blue, Pint .... * 7.50
Flask, Double Washington, Repro, Gray Blue, Pint .... * 20.00
Flask, Eagle & Clasped Hands & 13 Stars, L & W Base, Stain, Yellow, Pint 60.00
Flask, Eagle & Clasped Hands, Aqua, 1/2 Pint 55.00
Flask, Eagle & Clasped Hands, L & W On Base, Aqua, Pint 60.00
Flask, Eagle & Cornucopia & Kensington Glassworks, C.1850, Aqua, 1/2 Pint 275.00
Flask, Eagle & Cornucopia, Repro, Amethyst, 1/2 Pint .... * 20.00
Flask, Eagle & D.Kirkpatrick & Co. & Chattanooga, Chip, Aqua, Pint .... * 260.00
Flask, Eagle & Furled Flag, Repro, Similar To McK G II-54, Green, Pint .... * 15.00
Flask, Eagle & Granite Glass & Eagle & Stoddard, Pontil, Amber, Quart .... * 500.00
Flask, Eagle & Granite Glass Co., Stoddard, N.H., Dark Amber, Pint 10.00
Flask, Eagle & Grapes & Clevenger Bros.Glassworks, Repro, Amber, Quart .... * 15.00
Flask, Eagle & Grapes, Repro, Similar To McK G II-55, Amber, Quart .... * 5.00
Flask, Eagle & Pittsburgh, Pa. In Oval, 1/2 Pint 30.00
Flask, Eagle & Resurgam & Baltimore Glass Works, Collar, Amber, Pint 175.00
Flask, Eagle & Stars & Grapes, Repro, Light Green, Quart .... * 12.50
Flask, Eagle In Raised Panel, Tooled Double Collared Mouth, Quart .... * 22.50
Flask, Eagle To Right & D.Kirkpatrick & Co. & Tennessee, Aqua, Quart *2100.00
Flask, Eagle, Tooled Double Collared Mouth, Smooth Base, Aqua, Quart .... * 40.00

Flask, England, Marked W In Diamond, Screw On Cap, C.1915, Pewter, 6 Ozs. 15.00
Flask, F.Noyes Spirit Merchant, Nottingham, Pottery, Cream & Brown, 1/2 Pint .... * 75.00
Flask, Father Of His Country & Taylor Never Surrenders, Aqua, Pint 35.00
Flask, Feeney & Donahue, Millville, Mass., Strap, BIMAL, Pint 2.00
Flask, Flora Temple & Harness Trot, Applied Handle, Label, Amber, Pint .... * 350.00
Flask, Flora Temple & Harness Trot, Handle & Mouth Ring, Brown Topaz, Pint .... * 350.00
Flask, Flora Temple & Harness Trot, Mouth Ring, Emerald Green, Pint .... * 575.00
Flask, Flora Temple & Harness Trot, Mouth Ring, Smoky Amber, Pint .... * 525.00
Flask, Flora Temple & Harness Trot, Oct.15th, 1858, Chip, Amber, Quart .... * 275.00
Flask, Flora Temple & Harness Trot, Oct.15th, 1858, Chip, Copper, Quart .... * 275.00
Flask, Flora Temple & Harness Trot, Oct.15, 1859, Handle, Copper, Quart .... * 375.00
Flask, Flora Temple & Harness Trot, Oct.15, 1859, Handle, Puce Amber, Quart .... * 350.00
Flask, Flora Temple, Partial Label, Puce, Pint 150.00
Flask, Flora Temple, Sheared Mouth With Ring, Medium Green, Quart *4700.00
Flask, For Pike's Peak & Arsenal Glassworks, Fissure, Yellow Green, Pint .... * 450.00
Flask, For Pike's Peak & Arsenal Glassworks, Flakes, Olive Yellow, Pint .... * 525.00
Flask, For Pike's Peak & Arsenal Glassworks, Flakes, Yellow Green, Pint .... * 380.00
Flask, For Pike's Peak & Eagle & Arsenal Glassworks, Yellow Green, Pint .... * 700.00
Flask, For Pike's Peak & Eagle & Arsenal Glassworks, Yellow, Quart .... * 550.00
Flask, For Pike's Peak & Eagle & Banner, Crack, Aqua, Pint .... * 40.00
Flask, For Pike's Peak & Eagle & Banner, Flake, Aqua, 1/2 Pint .... * 40.00
Flask, For Pike's Peak & Eagle & Banner, Pontil, Emerald Green, Pint *1025.00
Flask, For Pike's Peak & Eagle & C.Ihmsen & Co., Pittsburgh, Aqua, Pint .... * 400.00
Flask, For Pike's Peak & Eagle & Ceredo, Green, Pint, 7 3/4 In. 75.00
Flask, For Pike's Peak & Eagle & Ihmsen & Co., Stain, Aqua, Pint .... * 400.00
Flask, For Pike's Peak & Old Rye & Eagle & Pittsburgh, Aqua, Quart .... * 60.00
Flask, For Pike's Peak & Eagle & Old Rye, Aqua, Quart 55.00
Flask, For Pike's Peak & Eagle, Aqua, Pint 65.00
Flask, For Pike's Peak & Eagle, Pittsburgh, Apple Green, Pint 65.00
Flask, For Pike's Peak & Eagle, Pontil, Deep Aqua, Pint .... * 575.00
Flask, For Pike's Peak & Eagle, Ribbon, & Ceredo, Aqua, 1/2 Pint 75.00
Flask, For Pike's Peak & Eagle, Whittled, Aqua, Pint 50.00
Flask, For Pike's Peak & Hunter Shooting Deer, Aqua, 1/2 Pint 100.00
Flask, For Pike's Peak & Hunter Shooting Deer, Stain, Amber, Pint .... * 575.00
Flask, For Pike's Peak & Hunter Shooting Deer, Yellow Green, Pint .... * 450.00
Flask, For Pike's Peak & Hunter Shooting Deer, Yellow Green, Pint, Vr9g7 .... * 525.00
Flask, For Pike's Peak & Hunter Shooting Deer, Yellow Green, Quart .... * 700.00
Flask, For Pike's Peak & Hunter, Chips, Stain, Ice Blue, Pint *2200.00
Flask, For Pike's Peak & Hunter, Deer, & E.Kauffeld, Amethyst, Quart *1650.00
Flask, For Pike's Peak & Man Shooting Deer, Stain, Aqua, Quart 75.00
Flask, For Pike's Peak & Old Rye & Eagle & Pittsburgh, Aqua, 1/2 Pint .... * 75.00
Flask, For Pike's Peak & Old Rye & Eagle & Pittsburgh, Yellow Olive, Pint .... * 700.00
Flask, For Pike's Peak & Old Rye & Pittsburgh, Stain, Aqua, 1/2 Pint 50.00
Flask, For Pike's Peak & Prospector & Eagle & Banner, Amber, Pint .... * 475.00
Flask, For Pike's Peak & Prospector & Eagle & Banner, Amber, Pint .... * 525.00
Flask, For Pike's Peak & Prospector & Eagle & Banner, Aqua, 1/2 Pint .... * 40.00
Flask, For Pike's Peak & Prospector & Eagle & Banner, Aqua, 1/2 Pint .... * 55.00
Flask, For Pike's Peak & Prospector & Eagle & Banner, Aqua, 1/2 Pint .... * 80.00
Flask, For Pike's Peak & Prospector & Eagle & Banner, Aqua, Pint .... * 80.00
Flask, For Pike's Peak & Prospector & Eagle & Banner, Ring, Aqua, Pint .... * 35.00
Flask, For Pike's Peak & Prospector & Eagle & Banner, Ring, Aqua, Quart .... * 65.00
Flask, For Pike's Peak & Prospector & Eagle & Banner, Stain, Aqua, 1/2 Pt. .... * 45.00
Flask, For Pike's Peak & Prospector & Eagle & Banner, Stain, Aqua, Pint .... * 40.00
Flask, For Pike's Peak & Prospector & Eagle & Banner, Yellow Amber, Quart .... * 675.00
Flask, For Pike's Peak & Prospector & Eagle & Ceredo, Amber, 1/2 Pint .... * 850.00
Flask, For Pike's Peak & Prospector & Eagle & Ceredo, Aqua, Pint .... * 75.00
Flask, For Pike's Peak & Prospector & Eagle & Ceredo, Green, 1/2 Pint .... * 175.00
Flask, For Pike's Peak & Prospector & Eagle & Ceredo, Olive Yellow, Quart .... * 575.00
Flask, For Pike's Peak & Prospector & Eagle & Ceredo, Yellow Green, Quart *1200.00
Flask, For Pike's Peak & Prospector & Eagle, Yellow Green, Quart *1150.00
Flask, For Pike's Peak & Prospector & Hunter Shooting Deer, Amber, Pint .... * 525.00
Flask, For Pike's Peak & Prospector & Hunter Shooting Deer, Aqua, 1/2 Pint .... * 120.00
Flask, For Pike's Peak & Prospector With Derby & Eagle, Aqua, Quart .... * 65.00
Flask, For Pike's Peak & Prospector With Derby & Eagle, Yellow Amber, Pint .... * 330.00
Flask, For Pike's Peak & Prospector With Hat, Pack, & Cane, Aqua, Pint .... * 45.00

Flask, For Pike's Peak & W.McC & Co., Glass Works, Pittsburgh, Aqua, Pint .... * 360.00
Flask, For Pike's Peak, Flake, Aqua, 1/2 Pint .... * 30.00
Flask, For Pike's Peak, Stain, Chip, Aqua, Quart .... * 25.00
Flask, For Pike's Peak, OP, Aqua, 1/2 Pint 195.00
Flask, Franklin & 1888 & Wheaton, Millville, N.J., Repro, Milk Glass, Pint .... * 5.00
Flask, Frederick, Horizontal Rows Of Hobnail, Pontil, Olive Amber, Pint .... * 100.00
Flask, G.W.K.& Co., Z.O., Embossed, Ring Lip, Aqua, 1/2 Pint 14.50
Flask, Gahn, Belt & Co., Baltimore, Maryland, Lip Ring, Flat Oval, 1/2 Pint 5.50
Flask, Gemel, Nailsea Type, Pontil, White & Blue Loopings, 10 In. .... * 55.00
Flask, Geo.W.Robinson, No.75 Main St., W.Virginia, Aqua, Quart .... * 70.00
Flask, Geo, W.Robinson, No.75 Main St., W.V.A., Smooth Base, Aqua, Pint .... * 45.00
Flask, George Washington & Eagle & Stars, 1732-1932, Screw Cap, 8 In. 14.00
Flask, General MacArthur & God Bless America, 1942, Repro, Blue, 1/2 Pint .... * 10.00
Flask, German Silver Top, Leather Around Top, 21 Ozs. 23.50
Flask, Gilbert Bros. & Co., Baltimore, Md., 8 In. 1.00
Flask, Girl On Bicycle & Eagle & A & DHC, Applied Mouth Ring, Aqua, Pint .... * 120.00
Flask, Girl On Bicycle & Not For Joe, Applied Mouth With Ring, Amber, Pint .... * 600.00
Flask, Girl On Bicycle & Not For Joe, Green Aqua, Pint, 7 5/8 In. 65.00
Flask, Girl On Bicycle & Not For Joe, Sapphire Blue, Pint *1600.00
Flask, Grandfather's, 24 Vertical Ribs, Red Amber, 8 In. 1000.00
Flask, Granite Glass Co. & Stoddard, N.H., Burst Bubble, Amber, Quart .... * 250.00
Flask, Granite Glass Co. & Stoddard, N.H., Red Amber, Pint 120.00
Flask, Granite Glass Co. & Stoddard, N.H., Sheared Mouth, Olive Amber, Pint .... * 130.00
Flask, Granite Glass Co. & Stoddard, N.H., Smooth Base, Red Amber, Pint .... * 100.00
Flask, Granite Glass Co., Stoddard, N.H., Sheared Lip, Amber, Pint 149.00
Flask, Granite Glass Works, Amber, Pint 85.00
Flask, Grapes In Panel, Smooth Base, Crack, Amber, Pint .... * 25.00
Flask, Happiness, Comic Couple, Ceramic, 1/2 Pint 12.00
Flask, Henry Chapman & Co., Montreal, Pocket, Ovoid, Screw Cap, 1/2 Pint * 250.00
Flask, Here's Hoping May You Live Long & Prosper, Pint 24.00
Flask, Hobnail, Double Dipped, Pinches Sides, Restored, Blue, 5 1/4 In. .... * 20.00
Flask, Hobnail, Horizontal Rows, Corrugated Edges, Pontil, Green, 1/2 Pint .... * 110.00
Flask, Hobnail, Horizontal Rows, Sheared Mouth, Pontil, Blue Green, Pint .... * 225.00
Flask, Hobnail, Horizontal Rows, Sheared Mouth, Pontil, Cobalt, Pint .... * 350.00
Flask, Historic Batsto Village, 1766-1848, Repro, Aqua, Pint .... * 20.00
Flask, Honest Measure, Miniature 7.00
Flask, Horseman & Hound, Sheared Mouth, Pontil, Deep Puce, Pint *1000.00
Flask, Horseman & Running Dog, Sheared Mouth, Pontil, Aqua, 1/2 Pint .... * 160.00
Flask, Horseman Galloping To Right & Hound, Chip, Puce, Pint .... * 900.00
Flask, Horseman Galloping To Right & Hound, Citron, Pint .... * 375.00
Flask, Horseman Galloping To Right & Hound, Handle, Pontil, Amber, Pint *1800.00
Flask, Horseman In Uniform To Right & Hound, Olive Yellow, Quart .... * 550.00
Flask, Horseman In Uniform To Right & Hound, Pontil, Amber, Quart .... * 425.00
Flask, Horseshoe & Here's To You, Long Life & Prosperity, Pint 20.00
Flask, Hunter & Grapevine, Sheared Mouth, Pontil, Cobalt, 1/2 Pint .... * 280.00
Flask, Hunter & Running Hounds, Double Collared Mouth, Pontil, Citron, Pint .... * 375.00
Flask, Hunter Shooting Rabbit & Dog With Birds, Pontil, Pint .... * 150.00
Flask, Hunter With Rabbit & Wreath, Bruise, Cobalt, Pint .... * 180.00
Flask, Indian & Cunninghams & Eagle & Continental, Yellow Green, Quart .... * 850.00
Flask, Indian Shooting Bird & Dog & Eagle, Chip, Aqua, Quart .... * 200.00
Flask, Isabella Glass Works & Anchor & Glass Factory, Aqua, Quart .... * 80.00
Flask, Isabella Glass Works & Anchor & Glass Factory, Chip, Green, 1/2 Pint .... * 400.00
Flask, Isabella Glass Works & Anchor & Sheaf Of Wheat, Pontil, Aqua, Pint .... * 90.00
Flask, J.C.Childs Co., Strap, BIMAL, Quart 3.50
Flask, J.N.Kline & Cos' Aromatic Cordial, Pocket, Amber 1/2 Pt. .... * 90.00
    Flask, Jenny Lind, see Flask, McK G I-100-McK G I-109,
    Flask, Calabash, Jenny Lind
Flask, John Fitzgerald Kennedy, 1917-1963, Repro, Blue, Quart .... * 10.00
Flask, John McKeon & Co., Strap, BIMAL, 1/2 Pint 2.00
Flask, Jones & Co., Embossed Bear, Straight Sided, Aqua, Pint 7.00
Flask, Keene & Masonic, Similar To McK G IV-7, Amber, Pint 225.00
Flask, Keene, 20 Vertical Ribs, Flat Melon Shape, Pontil, Olive Amber, Pint .... * 275.00
Flask, Keene, 20 Vertical Ribs, Flat Melon Shape, Pontil, Yellow Green, Pint .... * 425.00
Flask, Keene, 20 Vertical Ribs, Flattened Melon, Pontil, Olive Amber, Pint .... * 325.00
Flask, Kent, Ohio, Yellow Green, Pint 775.00

Figural, Moon Mullins, Pottery, 7 In.

Flask, McK G II-68,
New London Glassworks, Pint

Flask, McK G II-61,
Eagle & Liberty & Willington, Quart

Flask, McK G VIII-18,
Sunburst & Coventry, 1/2 Pint

Flask, McK G VIII-16,
Sunburst & Coventry, 1/2 Pint

Flask, McK G VIII-3,
Sunburst & Coventry, Pint

Flask, McK G II-66,
New London Glassworks, Quart

Flask, McK G I-80,
Lafayette & DeWitt Clinton, Pint

Whiskey, Van Schuyver & Co.,
Portland, Oregon, C.1910, Fifth

Cyrus Noble, Lilienthal Centennial, 1876

Cyrus Noble, Old Private Stock, C.1898, Amber

Cyrus Noble, Snowshoe Thomson, 1972

Pickle, Heinz, Canister, C.1890

Food, Cutting Packing Co.,
San Francisco, C.1880, Display Jar

Blown, Jar, Salem Co.,
New Jersey, C.1840, 9 1/2 In.

Pottery, Toth Kiss Samuel, Kesurit,
1880, Green, 12 In.

Pottery, 1877, Green, 9 In.

Figural, Matador,   Figural, Senorita,
1969, 12 In.   1969, 12 In.

Apothecary, Amadou,
Blue, 9 In.

Apothecary, Benzina Rectific,
Ground Pontil, 6 In.

Apothecary, Collod:
Officinale, Ground Pontil,
6 In.

Medicine, Warner's
Diabetes Cure, Amber

Medicine, Warner's
Safe Cure, 7 In.

Medicine, Warner's
Safe Remedy, 7 In.

Medicine, Warner's
Safe Rheumatic Cure

Medicine, Warner's
Safe Rheumatic Remedy
Blob Top

Medicine, Warner's Compound,
Paper Label, Amber

Medicine, Warner's Safe Remedy
For The Kidneys & Liver, Paper Label

Medicine, Warner's Safe Nervine, Paper Label

Medicine, Craig's Kidney
& Liver Cure, Amber

Medicine, Spark's
Kidney & Liver
Cure, Amber

Medicine, Craig's Kidney
& Liver Cure, Dark Amber

Bitters, Tippecanoe,
Stomach

Kontinental Classics, Gandy Dancer

Kontinental Classics, Lumberjack

Flask, **Key,** Smooth Base, Aqua, Pint .... * 40.00
Flask, **L.G.Co. On Bottom,** Red Amber, 1/2 Pint 27.00
Flask, **L.Verner,** Strap, BIMAL, Quart 2.50
Flask, **Lady's Pocket,** English Cameo, Hinged Sterling Top, Citron, 5 1/2 In. 650.00
Flask, **Lady's,** Cut Glass, Sterling Fittings, 3 3/4 In. 65.00
Flask, **Lady's,** Cut Glass, Sterling Lid, Russian, Starred Buttons, 6 In. 165.00
Flask, **Lancaster Glass Works & Full Pint,** Smooth Base, Aqua, Pint .... * 50.00
Flask, **Larson,** Chestnut Type, Expanded Diamond, Pontil, Amethyst, 5 1/4 In. .... * 120.00
Flask, **Larson,** Ribs Swirled To Right, Pontil, Amethyst, 4 3/4 In. .... * 65.00
Flask, **Larson,** Ribs Swirled To Right, Pontil, Amethyst, 5 1/2 In. .... * 110.00
Flask, **Lestoil,** Franklin, Blue .... *Illus* 5.00
Flask, **Lestoil,** General Washington & Eagle, Amber, 8 In. 3.75
Flask, **Lestoil,** Liberty, Green .... *Illus* 5.00
Flask, **Lestoil,** Washington .... *Illus* 5.00

Flask, Lestoil,   Flask, Lestoil,   Flask, Lestoil,
Liberty, Green   Franklin, Blue   Washington

Flask, McK G I-42,
Washington & Captain
Bragg, Aqua, 9 In.
(See Page 94)

Flask, **Louisville,** Ky. Glass Works In Circle, Crack, Ice Blue, Pint .... * 40.00
Flask, **Louisville,** Ky., Glass Works, Strap Sided, Aqua, Quart 44.50
Flask, **M.Carney Lawrence,** Strap Side, Quart 6.00
Flask, **M.F.Biern Magnolia Hotel,** Phila., Pocket, Ovoid, Amber, 1/2 Pint .... * 275.00
Flask, **Man To Left With Bag & Hat Flying Off & Drafted & Eagle,** Aqua, Pint .... * 550.00
Flask, **Mantua Glass Works,** 16 Ribs, Pale Green, 1/2 Pint 65.00
Flask, **Mantua,** Hip, Amethyst, 1/2 Pint 350.00
Flask, **Masonic & Eagle & J P,** Repro, Similar To McK G IV-1, Aqua, Pint .... * 20.00
Flask, **Masonic & Seeing Eye,** Amber, Pint 135.00
Flask, **Masonic,** Olive Green .... *Color* XXXX.XX
Flask, **McK G I-1,** General Washington & Eagle, Pontil, Yellow Green, Pint *1150.00
Flask, **McK G I-2,** General Washington & Eagle, Pontil, Aqua, Pint .... * 550.00
Flask, **McK G I-2,** Washington & Eagle, Green Tint, Aqua, Pint 300.00
Flask, **McK G I-3,** General Washington & Eagle, Flake, Pontil, Aqua, Pint *1550.00
Flask, **McK G I-5,** General Washington & Eagle, C.1850, Light Green, Pint 3250.00
Flask, **McK G I-6,** Washington & Laird S.C. Pitt., Stain, Green, Pint *1650.00
Flask, **McK G I-7,** G.Geo.Washington & Eagle & F.L., Pontil, Aqua, Pint .... * 950.00
Flask, **McK G I-8,** Washington & Eagle & F.L., C.1850, Green, Pint 6500.00
Flask, **McK G I-9,** G.G.Washington & Eagle, Pontil, Green, Pint *2800.00
Flask, **McK G I-10,** G.Washington & Eagle, Pontil, Yellow Amber, Pint *5100.00
Flask, **McK G I-10,** Light Green 375.00
Flask, **McK G I-10,** OP, Aqua To Green 525.00
Flask, **McK G I-11,** Bust Of Washington & Eagle, C.1850, Aquamarine, Pint 700.00
Flask, **McK G I-11,** Washington & Eagle & 13 Stars, Pontil, Aqua, Pint .... * 820.00
Flask, **McK G I-12,** Washington & Eagle, C.1850, Light Green, Pint 3250.00
Flask, **McK G I-13,** Washington & Eagle & B.K., C.1850, Yellow Green, Pint 6000.00
Flask, **McK G I-14,** Aqua 225.00
Flask, **McK G I-14,** Portrait, OP, Olive Green 190.00
Flask, **McK G I-14,** Washington & Eagle 225.00
Flask, **McK G I-14,** Washington & Eagle & T.W.D., 1776, Chip, Green, Pint *1700.00
Flask, **McK G I-16,** Washington & Eagle & T.W.D., Bruise, Stain, Aqua, Pint .... * 120.00
Flask, **McK G I-16,** Washington & Eagle, Aqua 215.00
Flask, **McK G I-17,** Washington & Taylor & Baltimore, Pontil, Copper, Pint *2200.00
Flask, **McK G I-17,** Washington & Taylor & Baltimore, Pontil, Purple, Pint *2050.00
Flask, **McK G I-20,** Columbia & 13 Stars & Eagle & B & W, Aqua, Pint .... * 400.00
Flask, **McK G I-20,** Washington & Fells Point & Balto, Pontil, Green, Pint .... * 850.00

Flask, McK G I-23, Washington & Baltimore Glass, Pontil, Green, Quart *2600.00
Flask, McK G I-24, Washington & Bridgeton & Taylor, Chip, Amber, Pint .... * 825.00
Flask, McK G I-24, Washington & Bridgeton & Taylor, Pontil, Green, Pint .... * 400.00
Flask, McK G I-25, Washington & Bridgetown, Pontil, Green, Quart .... * 250.00
Flask, McK G I-25, Washington & Clay, Aqua, Quart 200.00
Flask, McK G I-26, Washington & Eagle & 12 Stars, Pontil, Green, Quart .... * 750.00
Flask, McK G I-26, Washington, Eagle, & 12 Stars, Aqua, Quart .... * 170.00
Flask, McK G I-28, Albany Glass Works, Aqua, Pint 45.00
Flask, McK G I-28, Washington & Albany & Frigate, Amber, Pint 350.00
Flask, McK G I-28, Washington & Albany Glass Works & Ship, Amber 850.00
Flask, McK G I-28, Washington & Albany Glass Works & Ship, Green, Pint .... * 675.00
Flask, McK G I-28, Washington & Albany & Ship, Burst Bubble, Green, Pint *1650.00
Flask, McK G I-28, Washington & Albany Glass & Ship, Crack, Amber, Pint .... * 750.00
Flask, McK G I-28, Washington, Albany Glass Works, & Ship, Amber, Pint .... * 750.00
Flask, McK G I-30, Washington & Albany Glass, Check, Green, 1/2 Pint .... * 370.00
Flask, McK G I-30, Washington & Albany Glass, Chip, Citron, 1/2 Pint .... * 950.00
Flask, McK G I-31, Washington & Jackson, Amber 170.00
Flask, McK G I-31, Washington & Jackson, Amber, Pint 175.00
Flask, McK G I-31, Washington & Jackson, Olive Amber, Pint .... * 150.00
Flask, McK G I-31, Washington & Jackson, Pontil, Yellow Amber, Pint .... * 170.00
Flask, McK G I-31, Washington & Jackson, Seedy Yellow Amber, Pint .... * 380.00
Flask, McK G I-32, Washington & Jackson, Olive Amber, Pint .... * 150.00
Flask, McK G I-32, Washington & Jackson, Olive Amber, Pint .... * 250.00
Flask, McK G I-32, Washington & Jackson, Sheared Mouth, Aqua, Pint .... * 270.00
Flask, McK G I-33, Washington & Jackson, Wear, Olive Amber, Pint .... * 200.00
Flask, McK G I-34, Washington & Jackson, Olive Amber, 1/2 Pint .... * 275.00
Flask, McK G I-35, Calabash, Washington & Tree, Pontil, Aqua .... * 80.00
Flask, McK G I-35, Calabash, Washington Bust .... * 80.00
Flask, McK G I-36, Calabash, Washington & Tree, Pontil, Stain, Aqua .... * 55.00
Flask, McK G I-36, Calabash, Washington & Tree, Whittled 100.00
Flask, McK G I-36, Calabash, Washington Bust .... * 55.00
Flask, McK G I-37, Washington & Taylor & Dyottville, Amber, Quart .... * 700.00
Flask, McK G I-37, Washington & Taylor & Dyottville, Bruise, Green, Pint .... * 400.00
Flask, McK G I-37, Washington & Taylor & Dyottville, Claret, Quart .... * 900.00
Flask, McK G I-37, Washington & Taylor & Dyottville, Sapphire, Quart .... * 800.00
Flask, McK G I-37, Washington, Taylor & Dyottville, Yellow Green, Quart .... * 375.00
Flask, McK G I-37, Washington & Taylor, Blue Green 175.00
Flask, McK G I-38, Washington & Taylor & Dyottville, Aqua, Pint 40.00
Flask, McK G I-38, Washington & Taylor & Dyottville, Claret, Pint .... * 750.00
Flask, McK G I-38, Washington & Taylor & Dyottville, Cornflower, Pint .... * 850.00
Flask, McK G I-38, Washington & Taylor & Dyottville, Flake, Puce, Pint .... * 700.00
Flask, McK G I-38, Washington & Taylor & Dyottville, Olive Yellow, Pint .... * 550.00
Flask, McK G I-38, Washington & Taylor & Dyottville, Olive Yellow, Pint .... * 575.00
Flask, McK G I-39, Washington & Taylor & Dyottville, Emerald, Quart 450.00
Flask, McK G I-39, Washington & Taylor & Dyottville, Olive Amber, Quart .... * 600.00
Flask, McK G I-39, Washington & Taylor & Dyottville, Yellow, Quart .... * 600.00
Flask, McK G I-39, Washington & Taylor, Dyottsville, C.1850, Green, Quart 450.00
Flask, McK G I-40, Washington & Taylor & Dyottville, Aqua, Pint .... * 60.00
Flask, McK G I-40, Washington & Taylor & Dyottville, Aqua, Pint .... * 600.00
Flask, McK G I-40, Washington & Taylor & Dyottville, Cobalt, Pint *1750.00
Flask, McK G I-40, Washington & Taylor, Double Collar, Aqua, Pint 40.00
Flask, McK G I-40, Washington & Taylor, Double Collar, Stain, Aqua, Pint 45.00
Flask, McK G I-41, Washington & Taylor & Dyottville, Green, 1/2 Pint .... * 120.00
Flask, McK G I-41, Washington, Taylor, Dyottville, Olive Green, 1/2 Pint *1250.00
Flask, McK G I-41, Washington, Taylor, Blue Green 150.00
Flask, McK G I-41, Washington & Taylor, Dyottville, Chip, Aqua, 1/2 Pint .... * 85.00
Flask, McK G I-42, Washington & Captain Bragg, Aqua, 9 In. ....*Illus* 85.00
Flask, McK G I-42, Washington & Taylor & Captain Bragg, Aqua, Quart 55.00
Flask, McK G I-42, Washington & Taylor & Captain Bragg, Aqua, Quart .... * 95.00
Flask, McK G I-42, Washington & Taylor & Captain Bragg, Aqua, Quart .... * 100.00
Flask, McK G I-43, Washington & Taylor, Aqua 75.00
Flask, McK G I-43, Washington & Taylor, Flake, Amethyst, Quart *1900.00
Flask, McK G I-44, Washington & Taylor & Duty, Emerald Green, Pint .... * 650.00
Flask, McK G I-44, Washington & Taylor & Duty, Sapphire Blue, Pint *1550.00
Flask, McK G I-44, Washington & Taylor, Rough, Amber, Pint .... * 800.00

Flask, McK G I-45, Washington & Taylor, Double Collar, Aqua, Quart .... * 150.00
Flask, McK G I-46, Washington & Taylor, Pontil, Aqua, Quart .... * 80.00
Flask, McK G I-47, Washington, Father Of His Country, Steel Blue, Quart *1450.00
Flask, McK G I-47, Washington, Pontil, Green, Quart .... * 225.00
Flask, McK G I-48, Washington, Father Of His Country, Olive Green, Pint .... * 550.00
Flask, McK G I-48, Washington, Pontil, Flake, Citron, Pint .... * 750.00
Flask, McK G I-48, Washington, Pontil, Sea Green, Pint .... * 250.00
Flask, McK G I-49, Washington & Taylor, Aqua, Pint 50.00
Flask, McK G I-49, Washington & Taylor, Pontil, Aqua, Pint .... * 75.00
Flask, McK G I-50, Washington & Taylor, Pontil, Emerald Green, Pint .... * 500.00
Flask, McK G I-51, Washington & Taylor, Burst Bubble, Green, Quart .... * 500.00
Flask, McK G I-51, Washington & Taylor, Cornflower Blue, Quart *1000.00
Flask, McK G I-51, Washington & Taylor, Stain, Deep Sapphire Blue 1300.00
Flask, McK G I-51, Washington & Taylor, Stain, Light Green, Quart 60.00
Flask, McK G I-52, Washington & Taylor, Collared, Sage Green, Pint .... * 475.00
Flask, McK G I-52, Washington & Taylor, Double Collar, Olive Amber, Pint .... * 575.00
Flask, McK G I-52, Washington & Taylor, Double Collar, Sage Green, Pint .... * 475.00
Flask, McK G I-52, Washington & Taylor, Olive Amber, Pint .... * 575.00
Flask, McK G I-53, Washington & Taylor, Sheared Mouth, Green, 1/2 Pint *1350.00
Flask, McK G I-54, Washington & Taylor, Collar, Blue Green, Quart 400.00
Flask, McK G I-54, Washington & Taylor, Deep Blue 2150.00
Flask, McK G I-54, Washington & Taylor, Emerald Green 425.00
Flask, McK G I-54, Washington & Taylor, Green, Quart 120.00
Flask, McK G I-54, Washington & Taylor, Wear, Yellow Amber, Quart .... * 475.00
Flask, McK G I-55, Washington & Taylor, Bruise, Olive Green, Quart .... * 475.00
Flask, McK G I-55, Washington & Taylor, Emerald Green, Quart .... * 600.00
Flask, McK G I-55, Washington & Taylor, Pontil, Blue Green, Quart .... * 150.00
Flask, McK G I-55, Yellow Green 495.00
Flask, McK G I-56, Washington & Taylor, Golden Amber, 1/2 Pint .... * 600.00
Flask, McK G I-56, Washington & Taylor, Ground Mouth, Citron, 1/2 Pint *1100.00
Flask, McK G I-56, Washington & Taylor, Light Golden Amber, 1/2 Pint .... * 600.00
Flask, McK G I-56, Washington & Taylor, Pontil, Green, Pint .... * 350.00
Flask, McK G I-57, Washington & Sheaf Of Wheat, Olive Green, Quart *1400.00
Flask, McK G I-58, Washington & Sheaf Of Rye, Pontil, Aqua, Pint .... * 95.00
Flask, McK G I-59, Washington & Sheaf Of Wheat, Stain, Aqua, 1/2 Pint 50.00
Flask, McK G I-59, Washington & Sheaf Of Wheat & Tools, Aqua, 1/2 Pint 50.00
Flask, McK G I-60, Washington & Lockport Glass, Bruise, Green, Quart *1700.00
Flask, McK G I-61, Double Washington, IP, Blue, Quart *3900.00
Flask, McK G I-61, Double Washington, Pontil, Emerald Green, Quart .... * 850.00
Flask, McK G I-62, John Q.Adams & Eagle & J.T.& Co., Rough, Aqua, Pint *5800.00
Flask, McK G I-64, Jackson & Eagle & 10 Stars, Crack, Aqua, Pint .... * 950.00
Flask, McK G I-65, Jackson & Eagle & J.T.& Co., Pontil, Aqua, Pint *1000.00
Flask, McK G I-66, Jackson & Eagle & J.R.& Laird, Violet, Pint *4700.00
Flask, McK G I-67, Jackson & Eagle & B & M, Bruise, Pint *5400.00
Flask, McK G I-68, Jackson & Floral & Acorns, Pontil, Aqua, Pint *2550.00
Flask, McK G I-68, General Jackson, Facing Left, Green, Pint 2100.00
Flask, McK G I-69, Jackson & Masonic & Knox & McKee, Aqua, Pint .... * 2500.00
Flask, McK G I-71, Major Ringgold, Aqua, Pint .... 125.00 To 149.00
Flask, McK G I-71, Taylor & Major Ringgold, Crack, Lavender Gray, Pint *3000.00
Flask, McK G I-71, Taylor & Major Ringgold, Pontil, Amethystine, Pint *1450.00
Flask, McK G I-72, Taylor & Major Ringgold, Pontil, Aqua, Pint .... * 160.00
Flask, McK G I-73, Taylor & Fells Point & Balto, Pontil, Amethyst, Pint *2450.00
Flask, McK G I-73, Taylor & Fells Point, Bubbly, Aqua, Pint 80.00
Flask, McK G I-74, Taylor & Corn For The World, Pontil, Aqua, Pint .... * 850.00
Flask, McK G I-75, Taylor & Corn For The World, Chip, Olive Green, Pint *2000.00
Flask, McK G I-75, Taylor & Cornstalk, Olive Green 2000.00
Flask, McK G I-76, Taylor & Eagle & 10 Stars, Pontil, Aqua, Pint *2800.00
Flask, McK G I-77, Rough & Ready & Eagle & Masterson, Aquamarine, Quart 2100.00
Flask, McK G I-77, Rough & Ready & Masterson, Pale Green 2500.00
Flask, McK G I-77, Rough & Ready & Masterson, Pontil, Green, Quart *2200.00
Flask, McK G I-77, Taylor & Eagle & Masterson, C.1850, Aqua, Quart 2100.00
Flask, McK G I-78, Taylor & Rob.T Ramsay, Bruise, Aqua, Pint .... * 900.00
Flask, McK G I-79, Grant & Eagle & Banner, Stain, Aqua, Pint .... * 95.00
Flask, McK G I-79, Grant & Wreath & Eagle & Banner, Stain, Aqua, Pint .... * 95.00
Flask, McK G I-79, Grant & Wreath & Eagle, Banner, & Union, Green, Pint .... * 350.00

Flask, McK G I-80, Lafayette & DeWitt Clinton, Pint ....*Color* XXXX.XX
Flask, McK G I-81, Lafayette & DeWitt Clinton, Olive Amber, 1/2 Pint .... * 850.00
Flask, McK G I-82, Lafayette & DeWitt Clinton, Crack, Olive, 1/2 Pint *2800.00
Flask, McK G I-83, Lafayette & Masonic Arch 2300.00
Flask, McK G I-83, Lafayette & Masonic, Pontil, Olive Amber, Pint *2500.00
Flask, McK G I-84, Lafayette & Masonic, Crack, Olive Amber, 1/2 Pint *3000.00
Flask, McK G I-85, Lafayette & Coventry, Potstone, Olive Amber, Pint .... * 550.00
Flask, McK G I-85, Lafayette, Olive Green 835.00
Flask, McK G I-86, Lafayette & Coventry & S & S, Olive Amber, 1/2 Pint .... * 750.00
Flask, McK G I-86, Lafayette & Coventry, Pontil, Aqua, 1/2 Pint *2800.00
Flask, McK G I-86, Lafayette, Amber 525.00
Flask, McK G I-86, Olive Amber 450.00
Flask, McK G I-86, Olive Green 450.00
Flask, McK G I-87, Lafayette & Coventry & S & S, Olive Amber, 1/2 Pint *3800.00
Flask, McK G I-88, Lafayette & Masonic, Pontil, Olive Green, Pint *2000.00
Flask, McK G I-89, Lafayette & Masonic Arch, Olive Amber, 1/2 Pint *2200.00
Flask, McK G I-90, Lafayette & T.W.D. & Kensington, Pontil, Aqua, Pint .... * 450.00
Flask, McK G I-91, Lafayette & Eagle & T.W.D., Stain, Pontil, Aqua, Pint .... * 275.00
Flask, McK G I-93, Lafayette & Masonic & Eagle, Pontil, Blue Green, Pint *2100.00
Flask, McK G I-94, Franklin & Dyott, Amber 1650.00
Flask, McK G I-94, Franklin & T.W.Dyott, M.D., & Kensington, Amber, Pint *1550.00
Flask, McK G I-95, Franklin & T.W.Dyott, M.D., Pontil, Stain, Aqua, Pint .... * 240.00
Flask, McK G I-96, Franklin & Dyottville, OP, Aqua 275.00
Flask, McK G I-96, Franklin & T.W.Dyott, M.D., Green, Quart *1300.00
Flask, McK G I-97, Double Franklin, Aqua, Quart 250.00
Flask, McK G I-97, Double Franklin, Pontil, Golden Amber, Quart *3800.00
Flask, McK G I-98, Franklin & Wheeling Glassworks, Pontil, Green, Pint *4800.00
Flask, McK G I-99, Calabash, Jenny Lind .... * 600.00
Flask, McK G I-99, Calabash, Jenny Lind *1050.00
Flask, McK G I-99, Calabash, Jenny Lind & Huffsey, Pontil, Emerald, Quart *1050.00
Flask, McK G I-99, Calabash, Jenny Lind & S.Huffsey, Yellow Amber, Quart .... * 60.00
Flask, McK G I-99, Calabash, Jenny Lind, Aqua *1000.00
Flask, McK G I-99, Jenny Lind, Blue-Green, 11 In. ....*Illus* 950.00
Flask, McK G I-99, Jenny Lind, Teal Green 350.00
Flask, McK G I-100, Calabash, Jenny Lind & Kossuth, Pontil, Aqua .... * 85.00
Flask, McK G I-101, Calabash, Jenny Lind .... * 70.00
Flask, McK G I-101, Calabash, Jenny Lind & Millfora, Pontil, Aqua, Quart .... * 70.00
Flask, McK G I-102, Calabash, Jenny Lind .... * 775.00
Flask, McK G I-102, Calabash, Jenny Lind & Glass Factory, Green .... * 775.00
Flask, McK G I-103, Calabash, Jenny Lind .... * 60.00
Flask, McK G I-103, Calabash, Jenny Lind, Aquamarine 95.00
Flask, McK G I-104, Calabash, Jenny Lind .... * 950.00
Flask, McK G I-104, Calabash, Jenny Lind *1250.00
Flask, McK G I-104, Calabash, Jenny Lind & Factory, Sapphire Blue, Quart .... * 950.00
Flask, McK G I-104, Calabash, Jenny Lind & Factory, Yellow Green, Quart *1250.00
Flask, McK G I-105, Calabash, Jenny Lind & Factory, Aqua, Quart .... * 190.00
Flask, McK G I-106, Calabash, Jenny Lind *5000.00
Flask, McK G I-106, Calabash, Jenny Lind & Tree, Pontil, Aqua, Quart *5000.00
Flask, McK G I-107, Calabash, Jenny Lind .... * 350.00
Flask, McK G I-107, Calabash, Jenny Lind .... * 410.00
Flask, McK G I-107, Calabash, Jenny Lind & Fislerville, Amber .... * 410.00
Flask, McK G I-107, Calabash, Jenny Lind, OP 55.00
Flask, McK G I-108, Double Jenny Lind & Lyre, Violin, Pontil, Aqua, Pint .... * 900.00
Flask, McK G I-108, Jenny Lind & Lyre, Pint 800.00
Flask, McK G I-109, Double Jenny Lind & Lyre, Violin, Green, Quart *1700.00
Flask, McK G I-110, Calabash, Kossuth & Jenny Lind, OP, Aqua 130.00
Flask, McK G I-110, Double Jenny Lind & Lyre, Violin, Pontil, Aqua, Quart *1250.00
Flask, McK G I-111, Kossuth & Bridgeton & Sailboat, Pontil, Green, Pint .... * 700.00
Flask, McK G I-112, Calabash, Kossuth & S.Huffsey, Blue Green, Quart 550.00
Flask, McK G I-112, Calabash, Kossuth, Mississippi, Aqua 495.00
Flask, McK G I-112, Calabash, Louis Kossuth .... * 900.00
Flask, McK G I-112, Calabash, Louis Kossuth *1550.00
Flask, McK G I-112, Calabash, Louis Kossuth & Mississippi, Dark Amber *1200.00
Flask, McK G I-112, Calabash, Louis Kossuth & Mississippi, Olive Green *1550.00
Flask, McK G I-112, Calabash, Louis Kossuth & S.Huffsey, Blue Green .... * 900.00

Flask, McK G I-112, Kossuth & Frigate Mississippi, Blue Green 800.00
Flask, McK G I-113, Calabash, Kossuth & Tree, Aqua 110.00
Flask, McK G I-113, Calabash, Kossuth & Tree, Olive Yellow .... * 575.00
Flask, McK G I-113, Calabash, Kossuth & Tree, Pontil, Stain, Emerald .... * 400.00
Flask, McK G I-113, Calabash, Louis Kossuth .... * 400.00
Flask, McK G I-114, Byron & Scott, Amber, 1/2 Pint 140.00
Flask, McK G I-115, Wheat Price & Co. & Fairview Works, Green, Pint *2000.00
Flask, McK G I-116, Wheat Price & Co. & Fairview Works, Green, Pint *6250.00
Flask, McK G I-117, Byron & Scott, Olive Amber, 1/2 Pint 155.00
Flask, McK G I-117, Columbia & Kensington & Union Co., Aqua, Pint .... * 675.00
Flask, McK G I-118, Columbia & Kensington & Union, Aventurine, 1/2 Pint *3600.00
Flask, McK G I-119, Columbia & 13 Stars & Eagle, Pontil, Cobalt, Pint .... *
Flask, McK G II-1, Eagle & 10 Stars, Sheared Mouth, Pontil, Aqua, Pint .... * 160.00
Flask, McK G II-2, Eagle & Beaded Oval Panel, Pontil, Yellow Green, Pint .... * 750.00
Flask, McK G II-3, Eagle & 9 Stars, Pontil, Crack, Aqua, Pint .... * 225.00
Flask, McK G II-4, Eagle & Oval Panel & 10 Stars, Pontil, Aqua, Pint .... * 460.00
Flask, McK G II-6, Eagle & 9 Pearls & Cornucopia, Pontil, Aqua, Pint .... * 560.00
Flask, McK G II-7, Eagle & Sunburst, Pontil, Crack, Yellow Green, Pint *2600.00
Flask, McK G II-8, Eagle & Medallion, Pontil, Flake, Olive Yellow, Pint *5600.00
Flask, McK G II-8, Eagle & Medallion, Pontil, Violet Tinge, Pint *6400.00

Flask, McK G I-99, Jenny Lind, Blue-Green, 11 In.
(See Page 96)

Flask, McK G II-9, Double Eagle & Snake, Pontil, Amethystine, Pint .... *
Flask, McK G II-9, Double Eagle, Monongahela, C.1850, Amethyst, Pint 6500.00
Flask, McK G II-10, Eagle & W.Ihmsen's & Argiculture, Pontil, Aqua, Pint *1050.00
Flask, McK G II-11, Eagle & Cornucopia, Pontil, Bruise, Aqua, 1/2 Pint .... * 450.00
Flask, McK G II-11, Washington & Eagle, C.1850, Aquamarine, Pint 700.00
Flask, McK G II-12, Eagle & Cornucopia, Pontil, Chip, Aqua, 1/2 Pint .... * 525.00
Flask, McK G II-14, Eagle & Cornucopia, C.1850, Aquamarine, 1/2 Pint 450.00
Flask, McK G II-14, Eagle & Inverted Cornucopia, C.1850, Aqua, 1/2 Pint 450.00
Flask, McK G II-15, Eagle & Cornucopia, Pontil, Chip, Aqua, 1/2 Pint .... * 425.00
Flask, McK G II-16, Eagle & Cornucopia, Pontil, Flake, Aqua, 1/2 Pint .... * 175.00
Flask, McK G II-17, Eagle & Cornucopia, Monongahela, Aqua, 1/2 Pint 200.00
Flask, McK G II-17, Eagle & Cornucopia, Pa., C.1850, Aqua, 1/2 Pint 200.00
Flask, McK G II-17, Eagle & Cornucopia, Pontil, Aqua, 1/2 Pint .... * 200.00
Flask, McK G II-18, Eagle & Zanesville, Pontil, Red Amber, 1/2 Pint *1300.00
Flask, McK G II-19, Eagle & Flags & Morning Glory, Pontil, Aqua, Pint .... * 825.00
Flask, McK G II-19, Eagle & Morning Glory, Rockingham Glaze, Pint .... * 925.00
Flask, McK G II-21, Eagle & 13 Stars & For Pike's Peak, Aqua, Pint .... * 60.00
Flask, McK G II-21, For Pike's Peak & Eagle, Aqua, Pint 50.00
Flask, McK G II-22, Eagle & Union & Lyre & 14 Stars, Pontil, Aqua, Pint .... * 800.00
Flask, McK G II-23, Eagle & 14 Stars & Floral, Pontil, Aqua, Pint *1175.00
Flask, McK G II-24, Aqua, Pint 165.00
Flask, McK G II-24, Double Eagle & Louisville, Aqua, Pint 125.00
Flask, McK G II-24, Double Eagle, Aqua, Pint 120.00
Flask, McK G II-24, Double Eagle, Blue Aqua 90.00
Flask, McK G II-24, Eagle & 14 Stars, IP, Chip, Golden Amber, Pint .... * 800.00
Flask, McK G II-24, Eagle & 14 Stars, Pontil, Stain, Yellow Green, Pint *1050.00
Flask, McK G II-24, Eagle & 14 Stars, Pontil, Yellow Green, Pint .... * 675.00
Flask, McK G II-24, Eagle & 14 Stars, Sheared Mouth, Blue, Pint *2900.00
Flask, McK G II-24, Eagle & 14 Stars, Sheared Mouth, Honey Amber, Pint .... * 900.00
Flask, McK G II-24, Louisville & Double Eagle, Blue, Pint 1900.00

Flask, McK G II-25, Eagle & Banner & 5 Stars, Pontil, Amber, Quart *1300.00
Flask, McK G II-25, Eagle & Banner & 14 Stars, Pontil, Chip, Aqua, Pint .... * 280.00
Flask, McK G II-26, Double Eagle, C.1850, Emerald Green, Quart 750.00
Flask, McK G II-26, Eagle & Banner & 5 Stars, Ring, Blue Green, Quart .... * 600.00
Flask, McK G II-26, Eagle & Banner & 5 Stars, Chip, Green, Quart .... * 550.00
Flask, McK G II-26, Eagle & Banner & 5 Stars, Yellow Green, Quart *1200.00
Flask, McK G II-26, Eagle & Shield, C.1850, Emerald Green, Quart 750.00
Flask, McK G II-26, Eagle & 5 Stars, Pontil, Yellow Green, Quart .... * 850.00
Flask, McK G II-26, Louisville & Double Eagle, Amber, Quart 925.00
Flask, McK G II-27, Eagle & Farley & Taylor, Pontil, Aqua, 2 1/2 Quart *3250.00
Flask, McK G II-29, Eagle In Panel, Sheared Mouth, Pontil, Aqua, Pint .... * 800.00
Flask, McK G II-30, Eagle On Panel, Ribbed, Pontil, Aqua, 1/2 Pint .... * 250.00
Flask, McK G II-31, Double Eagle & Louisville, Ribbed, Aqua, Quart 165.00
Flask, McK G II-31, Eagle In Panel, Vertical Ribs, Pontil, Emerald, Quart .... * 800.00
Flask, McK G II-32, Double Eagle, Ribbed, Pale Yellow Green, Pint, 8 In. 310.00
Flask, McK G II-32, Eagle On Panel, Ribbed, Pontil, Aqua, Pint .... * 425.00
Flask, McK G II-33, Eagle & 5 Stars & Louisville, Amber, 1/2 Pint *1300.00
Flask, McK G II-33, Eagle & 5 Stars & Louisville, Blue Green, 1/2 Pint .... * 825.00
Flask, McK G II-33, Eagle & 5 Stars & Louisville, Ribbed, Aqua, 1/2 Pint 600.00
Flask, McK G II-35, Eagle & Banner & Louisville, Ribbed, Aqua, Quart .... * 100.00
Flask, McK G II-36, Eagle & Banner & Louisville, Ribbed, Aqua, Pint .... * 110.00
Flask, McK G II-37, Eagle & 13 Stars & Ravenna & Anchor, Amber, Pint .... * 350.00
Flask, McK G II-37, Eagle & 13 Stars & Ravenna & Anchor, Ice Blue, Pint .... * 275.00
Flask, McK G II-38, Eagle & Banner & Dyottville Glass Works, Aqua, Pint .... * 120.00
Flask, McK G II-39, Eagle, Banner & Shield, Smooth Base, Aqua, Pint .... * 50.00
Flask, McK G II-40, Double Eagle & Kensington, Haze, Aqua, Pint 110.00
Flask, McK G II-40, Eagle & Panel, Sheared Mouth, Olive Yellow, Pint .... * 850.00
Flask, McK G II-40, Eagle Above Panel, Pontil, Bruises, Emerald, Pint .... * 550.00
Flask, McK G II-41, Eagle Above Panel & Tree, Pontil, Aqua, Pint .... * 120.00
Flask, McK G II-42, Eagle & T.W.D. & Frigate, Pontil, Aqua, Pint .... * 200.00
Flask, McK G II-43, Eagle & T.W.D. & Cornucopia, Pontil, Aqua, 1/2 Pint .... * 350.00
Flask, McK G II-44, Eagle & T.W.D. & Cornucopia, Pontil, Aqua, 1/2 Pint .... * 220.00
Flask, McK G II-45, Eagle & Cornucopia, Pontil, Aqua, 1/2 Pint .... * 150.00
Flask, McK G II-46, Eagle & Cornucopia, Pontil, Crack, Aqua, 1/2 Pint .... * 85.00
Flask, McK G II-47, Eagle & 3 Stars & Tree, Pontil, Aqua, Quart .... * 475.00
Flask, McK G II-48, Coffin & Hay, Aqua, Quart 200.00
Flask, McK G II-48, Eagle & Coffin & Hay, Pontil, Green, Quart *1850.00
Flask, McK G II-48, Flag & Eagle, Medium Green 775.00
Flask, McK G II-49, Eagle & Coffin & Hay, Pontil, Olive Green, Pint *3500.00
Flask, McK G II-50, Eagle & Coffin & Hay, Pontil, Aqua, 1/2 Pint .... * 425.00
Flask, McK G II-51, Eagle & Coffin & Hay, Pontil, Aqua, Pint *1200.00
Flask, McK G II-51, Eagle & For Our Country, OP, Aqua 125.00
Flask, McK G II-52, Eagle & Flag & For Our Country, Ribbed, Pontil *1300.00
Flask, McK G II-52, Eagle & Flag, Aqua 119.00
Flask, McK G II-53, Eagle & For Our Country, Pontil, Stain, Aqua, Pint .... * 110.00
Flask, McK G II-54, Eagle & For Our Country, Burst Bubble, Aqua, Pint .... * 210.00
Flask, McK G II-55, Eagle & Grapes, Ribbed, Pontil, Wear, Amber, Quart .... * 950.00
Flask, McK G II-56, Eagle & Grapes, Ribbed, Pontil, Green, Pint *1100.00
Flask, McK G II-57, Eagle & J.P.F. & Cornucopia, Pontil, Olive, Pint .... *
Flask, McK G II-58, Eagle & Cornucopia, Pontil, Flake, Olive, 1/2 Pint *4100.00
Flask, McK G II-60, Charter Oak, Olive Amber 1900.00
Flask, McK G II-60, Eagle & Liberty & Oak Tree, Pontil, Amber, 1/2 Pint *1100.00
Flask, McK G II-60, Eagle & Liberty & Oak Tree, Pontil, Green, 1/2 Pint *1700.00
Flask, McK G II-61, Eagle & Liberty & Willington, Quart ....*Color* XXXX.XX
Flask, McK G II-61, Eagle & Willington Glass Co., Amber, Quart 145.00
Flask, McK G II-61, Eagle & Willington Glass Co., Green, Quart 90.00
Flask, McK G II-61, Eagle & Willington Glass Co., Olive Amber, Quart 80.00
Flask, McK G II-61, Eagle & Willington Glass Co., Olive Green, Quart 90.00
Flask, McK G II-61, Eagle & Willington Glass Co., Pontil, Olive Green, Quart ..... * 200.00
Flask, McK G II-61, Eagle & Wreath & Willington, Golden Amber, Quart .... * 125.00
Flask, McK G II-61, Eagle & Wreath & Willington, Olive Amber, Quart .... * 160.00
Flask, McK G II-61, Eagle & Wreath & Willington, Olive Green, Quart .... * 140.00
Flask, McK G II-61, Eagle & Wreath & Willington, Red Amber, Quart .... * 200.00
Flask, McK G II-61, Emerald Green 250.00
Flask, McK G II-62, Blue Green 225.00

Flask, McK G II-62, Eagle & Willington Glass Co., Olive Green, Pint 80.00
Flask, McK G II-62, Eagle & Willington Glass, Bruise, Green, Quart .... * 275.00
Flask, McK G II-62, Eagle & Willington Glass, Flake, Amber, Pint .... * 100.00
Flask, McK G II-62, Eagle & Willington, Rolled Lip, Olive Green 125.00
Flask, McK G II-62, Eagle, Wreath, & Liberty & Willington, Olive Green .... * 120.00
Flask, McK G II-63, Eagle & Liberty & Willington, Olive Amber, 1/2 Pint 85.00
Flask, McK G II-63, Eagle & Willington Glass Co., Olive Amber, Pint 75.00
Flask, McK G II-63, Eagle & Willington Glass, Flakes, Emerald, 1/2 Pint .... * 375.00
Flask, McK G II-63, Eagle & Wreath & Willington, Olive Amber, 1/2 Pint .... * 100.00
Flask, McK G II-63, Eagle & Wreath & Willington, Olive Green, 1/2 Pint .... * 110.00
Flask, McK G II-63, Eagle & Wreath & Willington, Olive Green, 1/2 Pint .... * 125.00
Flask, McK G II-63, Olive Amber 95.00
Flask, McK G II-63, Willington & Eagle, Amber, 1/2 Pint 90.00
Flask, McK G II-64, Eagle & Liberty & Willington, Olive Amber, Pint 80.00
Flask, McK G II-64, Eagle & Willington Glass Co., Olive Green, Pint 85.00
Flask, McK G II-64, Eagle & Willington Glass Co., Olive Green, Quart 90.00
Flask, McK G II-64, Eagle & Willington Glass, Pontil, Olive Green, Pint .... * 150.00
Flask, McK G II-64, Eagle & Wreath & Willington Glass Co., Amber, Pint .... * 110.00
Flask, McK G II-64, Eagle & Wreath & Willington Glass Co., Green, Pint .... * 150.00
Flask, McK G II-65, Eagle & Liberty & Westford Glass, Amber, 1/2 Pint 120.00
Flask, McK G II-65, Eagle & Westford Glass Co., Crack, Amber, 1/2 Pint .... * 10.00
Flask, McK G II-65, Eagle & Westford, Amber, 1/2 Pint 135.00
Flask, McK G II-65, Eagle & Wreath & Westford, Olive Amber, 1/2 Pint .... * 90.00
Flask, McK G II-66, Eagle & New London, Aqua, Pint 270.00
Flask, McK G II-66, Eagle & 7 Stars & New London & Anchor, Green, Quart *1025.00
Flask, McK G II-66, Eagle & 7 Stars & New London, Collar, Aqua, Quart .... * 325.00
Flask, McK G II-66, Eagle & 7 Stars & New London, Collar, Yellow, Quart .... * 500.00
Flask, McK G II-66, New London Glassworks, Pint .... Color XXXX.XX
Flask, McK G II-66, New London Glassworks, Quart .... Color XXXX.XX
Flask, McK G II-67, Eagle & New London & Anchor, Olive Yellow, 1/2 Pint .... * 400.00
Flask, McK G II-67, Eagle & New London, Burst Bubble, Aqua, 1/2 Pint .... * 125.00
Flask, McK G II-67, Eagle & New London, Chip, Blue Green, 1/2 Pint .... * 210.00
Flask, McK G II-67, Eagle & New London, Pontil, Flake, Green, 1/2 Pint .... * 400.00
Flask, McK G II-67, Eagle & 9 Stars & New London Glass, Amber, 1/2 Pint 375.00
Flask, McK G II-67, Eagle & 9 Stars & New London, Olive Amber, 1/2 Pint .... * 660.00
Flask, McK G II-67, Eagle & 9 Stars & New London, Yellow, 1/2 Pint *1150.00
Flask, McK G II-67, New London Glass Works, OP, Aqua 325.00
Flask, McK G II-68, Eagle & New London, Pontil, Green & Yellow, Pint *1700.00
Flask, McK G II-68, Eagle & 7 Stars & New London & Anchor, Amber, Pint .... * 375.00
Flask, McK G II-68, Eagle & 7 Stars & New London & Anchor, Citron, Pint .... * 650.00
Flask, McK G II-68, Eagle & 7 Stars & New London, Copper, Quart .... * 900.00
Flask, McK G II-68, Eagle & 7 Stars & New London, Yellow Olive, Pint .... * 475.00
Flask, McK G II-68, New London Glassworks, Pint .... Color XXXX.XX
Flask, McK G II-69, Eagle & Cornucopia, Pontil, Rough, Amethyst, 1/2 Pint .... * 900.00
Flask, McK G II-69, Eagle & Inverted Cornucopia, Yellow Green, 1/2 Pint *1000.00
Flask, McK G II-70, Eagle, Sheared Mouth, Pontil, Olive Amber, Pint .... * 175.00
Flask, McK G II-71, Double Eagle, Lengthwise, Olive Amber 235.00
Flask, McK G II-71, Eagle On Panel, Pontil, Olive Amber, 1/2 Pint .... * 200.00
Flask, McK G II-72, Cornucopia & Eagle, Olive Amber, Pint 90.00
Flask, McK G II-72, Eagle & Cornucopia, Aqua, Pint 70.00
Flask, McK G II-72, Eagle & Cornucopia, Pontil, Amber & Green, Pint .... * 850.00
Flask, McK G II-73, Eagle & Cornucopia & X, Aqua, Pint .... * 90.00
Flask, McK G II-73, Eagle & Cornucopia & X, Flake, Olive Amber, Pint .... * 70.00
Flask, McK G II-73, Eagle & Cornucopia & X, Olive Amber, Pint .... * 100.00
Flask, McK G II-73, Eagle & Cornucopia & X, Pontil, Olive Amber, Pint *2050.00
Flask, McK G II-73, Eagle & Cornucopia, Pontil, Olive Amber, Pint .... * 75.00
Flask, McK G II-73, Eagle & Cornucopia, Olive Green, Pint 50.00
Flask, McK G II-74, Eagle & Cornucopia & X, Pontil, Aqua, Pint .... * 110.00
Flask, McK G II-74, Eagle & Cornucopia & X, Yellow Green, Pint .... * 575.00
Flask, McK G II-75, Eagle & Cornucopia, Pontil, Olive Amber, Pint *2200.00
Flask, McK G II-76, Concentric Ring & Eagle 5100.00
Flask, McK G II-76, Eagle & Rings, Pontil, Chip, Green, 3/4 Quart *4500.00
Flask, McK G III-1, Cornucopia & Palm, Stain, Crack, Green, 1/2 Pint .... * 725.00
Flask, McK G III-2, Cornucopia, Sheared Mouth, Pontil, Aqua, 1/2 Pint .... * 130.00
Flask, McK G III-2, Cornucopia, Stain, Flake, Aqua, 1/2 Pint .... * 65.00

Flask, McK G III-2, Double Cornucopia, Aqua, 1/2 Pint 100.00
Flask, McK G III-4, Cornucopia & Urn, Olive Amber, Pint 59.00
Flask, McK G III-4, Cornucopia & Urn, OP, Deep Olive Green, Pint 65.00
Flask, McK G III-4, Cornucopia & Urn, Pontil, Aqua, Pint .... * 230.00
Flask, McK G III-4, Cornucopia & Urn, Pontil, Green, Pint .... * 260.00
Flask, McK G III-4, Cornucopia & Urn, Pontil, Olive Amber, Pint .... * 65.00
Flask, McK G III-4, Cornucopia & Urn, Pontil, Olive Green, Pint .... * 50.00
Flask, McKg III-4, Cornucopia & Urn, Sheared Lip, Olive Amber 65.00
Flask, McK G III-4, Cornucopia, Green Yellow, Pint, 6 7/8 In. 105.00
Flask, McK G III-4, Double Cornucopia, Dark Green, Pint 100.00
Flask, McK G III-5, Cornucopia & Urn, Pontil, Crack, Olive Amber, Pint .... * 50.00
Flask, McK G III-6, Cornucopia & Urn, Reproduction, Amber, Pint .... * 40.00
Flask, McK G III-6, Cornucopia & Urn, Sheared Mouth, Amber, Pint .... * 40.00
Flask, McK G III-7, Cornucopia & Urn, OP, Amber 57.00
Flask, McK G III-7, Cornucopia & Urn, Pontil, Flake, Green, 1/2 Pint .... * 250.00
Flask, McK G III-7, Cornucopia & Urn, Pontil, Green Aqua, 1/2 Pint .... * 110.00
Flask, McK G III-7, Cornucopia & Urn, Pontil, Olive Amber, 1/2 Pint .... * 90.00
Flask, McK G III-7, Cornucopia & Urn, Pontil, Olive Green, 1/2 Pint .... * 65.00
Flask, McK G III-7, Cornucopia, Olive Amber, Pint, 5 1/4 In. 85.00
Flask, McK G III-7, Vase & Cornucopia, Olive Green, 1/2 Pint 110.00
Flask, McK G III-8, Cornucopia & Pearl & Urn, Pontil, Yellow, 1/2 Pint .... * 80.00
Flask, McKg III-8, Cornucopia & Urn, Green, 1/2 Pint 130.00
Flask, McK G III-9, Cornucopia & Pearl & Urn, Pontil, Aqua, 1/2 Pint .... * 95.00
Flask, McK G III-10, Cornucopia & Leaf & Urn, Pontil, Amber, 1/2 Pint .... * 95.00
Flask, McK G III-11, Cornucopia & Urn, Collar, Olive Green, 1/2 Pint .... * 130.00
Flask, McK G III-11, Cornucopia & Urn, Pontil, Olive Amber, 1/2 Pint .... * 65.00
Flask, McK G III-12, Cornucopia & Urn, Pontil, Amber, 1/2 Pint .... * 80.00
Flask, McK G III-13, Cornucopia & Urn, Pontil, Blue Green, 1/2 Pint .... * 340.00
Flask, McK G III-13, Cornucopia & Urn, Pontil, Olive Amber, 1/2 Pint .... * 275.00
Flask, McK G III-14, Cornucopia & Urn, Emerald Green, 1/2 Pint .... * 425.00
Flask, McK G III-15, Cornucopia & Urn, Pontil, Aqua, 1/2 Pint .... * 80.00
Flask, McK G III-15, Cornucopia & Urn, Pontil, Yellow Green, 1/2 Pint .... * 375.00
Flask, McK G III-16, Cornucopia & Urn & Lancaster Glass, Ice Blue, Pint .... * 600.00
Flask, McK G III-16, Cornucopia & Urn & Lancaster, Chip, Yellow, Pint .... * 275.00
Flask, McK G III-16, Cornucopia & Urn & Lancaster, Yellow Green, Pint .... * 300.00
Flask, McK G III-16, Wharton's Whiskey & Whitney Glassworks, Amber 295.00
Flask, McK G III-16, 3 Mold, Dark Green .... *Illus* 345.00
Flask, McK G III-17, Cornucopia & Urn, Pontil, Blue Green, Pint .... * 400.00
Flask, McK G III-17, Cornucopia & Urn, Pontil, Emerald Green, Pint .... * 300.00
Flask, McK G III-17, Cornucopia & Urn, Sheared Mouth, Amber, Pint .... * 50.00
Flask, McK G III-17, Cornucopia & Urn, Stain, Pontil, Yellow, Pint .... * 260.00
Flask, McK G IV-1, Justus Perry & Masonic, Blue Green 425.00
Flask, McK G IV-1, Justus Perry, Deep Aqua, Pint 300.00
Flask, McK G IV-1, Masonic & Arch & Eagle & Banner, Blue Green, Pint .... * 275.00
Flask, McK G IV-1, Masonic & Eagle, Blue Green, Pint 325.00
Flask, McK G IV-1, Masonic & Eagle, Pontil, Emerald, Pint .... * 675.00

Flask, McK G III-16, 3 Mold, Dark Green

Flask, McK G IV-1, Masonic & Eagle, Pontil, Olive Amber, Pint .... * 800.00
Flask, McK G IV-1, Scroll, Double 6-Pointed Stars, Amber, Quart .... * 475.00
Flask, McK G IV-2, Masonic & Eagle & H S, Pontil, Crack, Olive, Pint .... * 700.00
Flask, McK G IV-3, Masonic & Eagle & J.K.B., Bruise, Pontil, Pint .... * 850.00
Flask, McK G IV-3, Masonic & Eagle & J.K.B., Chip, Yellow Amber, Pint *3000.00
Flask, McK G IV-3, Masonic & Eagle & J.K.B., Pontil, Yellow Green, Pint *1600.00
Flask, McK G IV-3, Masonic & Eagle & J.K.B., Wear, Yellow Green, Pint *1500.00
Flask, McK G IV-4, Baltimore Monument & Corn For The World, Aqua, Quart 140.00
Flask, McK G IV-4, Baltimore Monument & Ear Of Corn, Apricot, Quart *1000.00
Flask, McK G IV-4, Corn For The World, Aqua, Quart 135.00
Flask, McK G IV-4, Corn For The World, Golden Amber, Quart 350.00
Flask, McK G IV-4, Masonic & Eagle & J.K.B., Chip, Olive Green, Pint *1750.00
Flask, McK G IV-5, Masonic & Eagle & Star, Pontil, Green, Pint .... * 550.00
Flask, McK G IV-7, Masonic & Eagle & Star, Pontil, Emerald Green, Pint .... * 850.00
Flask, McK G IV-8, Masonic & Eagle, Pontil, Aqua, Pint .... * 525.00
Flask, McK G IV-10, Masonic & Eagle, Ribbed, Pontil, Green, Pint .... * 700.00
Flask, McK G IV-11, Masonic & Eagle, Stain, Pontil, Light Green .... * 450.00
Flask, McK G IV-11, Masonic & Eagle, Stain, Pontil, Light Green .... * 450.00
Flask, McK G IV-14, Masonic & Eagle, Pontil, Blue Green, 1/2 Pint .... * 750.00
Flask, McK G IV-16, Masonic & Eagle, Pontil, Clear Green, Pint *3900.00
Flask, McK G IV-16, Masonic & Eagle, Pontil, Olive Green, Pint *2500.00
Flask, McK G IV-17, Masonic & Eagle & Banner & Keene, Olive Green, Pint .... * 160.00
Flask, McK G IV-17, Masonic & Eagle & Keene, Pontil, Olive Green, Pint .... * 130.00
Flask, McK G IV-17, Masonic & Eagle & Keene, Pontil, Olive Green, Pint .... * 160.00
Flask, McK G IV-17, Masonic & Keene 175.00
Flask, McK G IV-17, Masonic & Keene, Amber, Pint 170.00
Flask, McK G IV-17, Masonic & Keene, Light Amber 175.00
Flask, McK G IV-17, Masonic & Keene, Olive Amber, Pint 130.00
Flask, McK G IV-17, Masonic, Olive Green, Pint 165.00
Flask, McK G IV-18, KCCNC & Eagle & Masonic Arch, Amber, Pint 295.00
Flask, McK G IV-19, Masonic & Eagle & KCCNC, Olive Amber, Pint .... * 150.00
Flask, McK G IV-19, Masonic & Eagle & KCCNC, Pontil, Amber, Pint .... * 200.00
Flask, McK G IV-19, Masonic & KCCNC, Amber 185.00
Flask, McK G IV-20, Masonic & Arch & Eagle & Banner, Olive Amber, Pint .... * 200.00
Flask, McK G IV-20, Masonic & Eagle & KCCNC, Pontil, Olive Amber, Pint .... * 250.00
Flask, McK G IV-20, Masonic, Olive Amber, Pint 165.00
Flask, McK G IV-21, Keene & Masonic, Olive Green, Pint 165.00
Flask, McK G IV-21, Masonic & Arch & Eagle & Banner, Amber, Pint .... * 150.00
Flask, McK G IV-21, Masonic & Eagle, Pontil, Olive Amber, Pint .... * 200.00
Flask, McK G IV-22, Masonic & Eagle & 1829, Pontil, Stain, Pint *9000.00
Flask, McK G IV-24, Burst Bubble At Base, Olive Amber 250.00
Flask, McK G IV-24, Masonic & Eagle & Banner, Olive Amber, 1/2 Pint .... * 190.00
Flask, McK G IV-24, Masonic & Eagle, OP, Olive Amber 160.00
Flask, McK G IV-24, Masonic & Eagle, Pontil, Aqua, 1/2 Pint .... * 550.00
Flask, McK G IV-24, Masonic & Keene, Amber, 1/2 Pint 185.00
Flask, McK G IV-26, Masonic & Eagle & NEG, Pontil, Olive, 1/2 Pint .... * 900.00
Flask, McK G IV-27, Masonic & Eagle & N.E.G.Co., Bruise, Green, Pint .... * 200.00
Flask, McK G IV-27, Masonic & Eagle & N.E.G.Co., Olive Amber, Pint *1150.00
Flask, McK G IV-27, Masonic & Eagle & N.E.G., Pontil, Flake, Aqua, Pint *2000.00
Flask, McK G IV-27, Masonic & NEG Co, Aqua 475.00
Flask, McK G IV-28, Masonic & Arch, Pontil, Olive Green, 1/2 Pint *2000.00
Flask, McK G IV-28, Masonic & Arch, Wear, Emerald Green, 1/2 Pint *1050.00
Flask, McK G IV-29, Masonic & Pillars, Pontil, Olive Amber, 1/2 Pint *6000.00
Flask, McK G IV-30, Masonic & Square & Compass, Pontil, Olive, 1/2 Pint *7300.00
Flask, McK G IV-32, Farmer's Tools & Eagle & Zanesville, Amber, Pint .... * 450.00
Flask, McK G IV-32, Masonic & Eagle & Zanesville, Bruise, Amber, Pint .... * 600.00
Flask, McK G IV-32, Shepard & Zanesville, Aqua, 6 5/8 In. 275.00
Flask, McK G IV-34, Masonic & Franklin & Kensington, Pontil, Blue, Pint .... * 500.00
Flask, McK G IV-36, Masonic & Franklin, Pontil, Crack, Green, Pint .... * 160.00
Flask, McK G IV-37, Masonic & Eagle & T.W.D., Pontil, Aqua, Pint .... * 180.00
Flask, McK G IV-38, Masonic, Union, & Clasped Hands & Eagle, Aqua, Quart .... * 80.00
Flask, McK G IV-39, Masonic & Eagle & H & S, Bruise, Flake, Aqua, Quart .... * 65.00
Flask, McK G IV-40, Masonic & Union & H & S, Flake, Amber, Pint .... * 250.00
Flask, McK G IV-40, Masonic, Union, Clasped Hands & H & S, Amber, Pint .... * 250.00
Flask, McK G IV-42, Calabash, Masonic, Pontil, Yellow Green, Quart .... * 400.00
Flask, McK G IV-42, Calabash, Union & Clasped Hands .... * 400.00

Flask, McK G IV-42, Calabash, Union & Clasped Hands, Aqua .... 35.00 To 75.00
Flask, McK G IV-42, Calabash, Union & Eagle & Masonic, Aqua, Quart .... * 55.00
Flask, McK G V-1, Double Success To The Railroad, Aqua, Pint 350.00
Flask, McK G V-1, Double Success To The Railroad, Bruise, Yellow, Pint .... * 900.00
Flask, McK G V-1, Double Success To The Railroad, Pontil, Green, Pint *1300.00
Flask, McK G V-1, Double Success To The Railroad, Sapphire Blue 3900.00
Flask, McK G V-1, Double Success To The Railroad, Sapphire Blue, Pint *2500.00
Flask, McK G V-1, Nick On Edge, Dark Mustard Green 600.00
Flask, McK G V-2, Double Success To The Railroad, Pontil, Olive, Pint *1000.00
Flask, McK G V-3, Double Success To The Railroad, Burst, Amber, Pint .... * 150.00
Flask, McK G V-3, Double Success To The Railroad, Olive Amber, Pint 225.00
Flask, McK G V-3, Double Success To The Railroad, Olive Yellow, Pint .... * 190.00
Flask, McK G V-3, Double Success To The Railroad, Stain, Aqua, Pint .... * 225.00
Flask, McK G V-4, Double Success To The Railroad, Crack, Aqua, Pint .... * 325.00
Flask, McK G V-4, Double Success To The Railroad, Olive Amber, Pint .... * 350.00
Flask, McK G V-4, Success To The Railroad, Aqua, Pint .... 400.00 To 675.00
Flask, McK G V-4, Success To The Railroad, Aquamarine, Pint 125.00
Flask, McK G V-5, Double Success To The Railroad, Green, Pint .... * 400.00
Flask, McK G V-5, Double Success To The Railroad, Olive Green, Pint .... * 175.00
Flask, McK G V-5, Success To The Railroad, Olive Green, Pint 200.00
Flask, McK G V-5, Lowell Railroad, Amber, 1/2 Pint 210.00
Flask, McK G V-5, Success To The Railroad, Olive Green, Pint 180.00
Flask, McK G V-5, Success To The Railroad, OP, Olive Green 230.00
Flask, McK G V-6, Double Success To The Railroad, Bruise, Amber, Pint .... * 230.00
Flask, McK G V-6, Success To The Railroad, Amber, Pint 200.00
Flask, McK G V-7, Double Success To The Railroad, Olive Green, Pint .... * 550.00
Flask, McK G V-8, Success To The Railroad & Eagle, Bubble, Green, Pint 140.00
Flask, McK G V-8, Success To The Railroad & Eagle, Pontil, Olive, Pint .... * 170.00
Flask, McK G V-9, Railway Horse & Cart & Eagle, Bubble, Amber, Pint .... * 120.00
Flask, McK G V-9, Success To The Railroad & Eagle, Olive Amber, Pint .... * 190.00
Flask, McK G V-9, Success To The Railroad, Olive Green 275.00
Flask, McK G V-10, Lowell Railroad & Eagle, Bruise, Amber, 1/i Pint .... * 200.00
Flask, McK G VI-1, Baltimore & Bragg, Pontil, Yellow Green, 1/2 Pint *1000.00
Flask, McK G VI-2, Baltimore & Fells Point, Wear, Yellow Green, 1/2 Pint .... * 650.00
Flask, McK G VI-2, Baltimore Monument & Sailboat, Amethyst, 1/2 Pint *1250.00
Flask, McK G VI-3, Baltimore & Liberty, Pontil, Olive Amber, Pint *2800.00
Flask, McK G VI-4, Baltimore & Corn For The World, Flake, Amber, Quart .... * 525.00
Flask, McK G VI-4, Baltimore Monument & Corn, Cornflower Blue, Quart *1700.00
Flask, McK G VI-4, Baltimore Monument & Corn, Flake, Amber, Quart .... * 525.00
Flask, McK G VI-4, Baltimore Monument & Corn, Olive Yellow, Quart .... * 650.00
Flask, McK G VI-4, Baltimore Monument & Ear Of Corn, Blue Green, Quart *1550.00
Flask, McK G VI-4, Baltimore Monument & Ear Of Corn, Puce, Quart *1150.00
Flask, McK G VI-5, Baltimore & Corn For The World, Wear, Amber, Quart .... * 850.00
Flask, McK G VI-6, Baltimore & Corn For The World, Pontil, Amber, Pint *1050.00
Flask, McK G VI-7, Baltimore & Corn For The World, Wear, Puce, 1/2 Pint *1100.00
Flask, McK G VIII-1, Sunburst Double Dots In Rings, Pontil, Green, Pint *1050.00
Flask, McK G VIII-1, Sunburst, Pontil, Olive To Amber, Pint *4400.00
Flask, McK G VIII-2, Sunburst, Burst Bubble, Green, Pint .... * 600.00
Flask, McK G VIII-2, Sunburst, Corrugated Edges, Light Green, Pint .... * 400.00
Flask, McK G VIII-2, Sunburst, Corrugated Edges, Pint .... * 975.00
Flask, McK G VIII-3, Sunburst & Coventry, Pint .... *Color* XXXX.XX
Flask, McK G VIII-3, Sunburst, Corrugated Edges, Amber, Pint .... * 450.00
Flask, McK G VIII-3, Sunburst, Corrugated Edges, Olive Green, Pint .... * 525.00
Flask, McK G VIII-3, Sunburst, Olive Amber, Pint .... *Illus* 450.00
Flask, McK G VIII-4, Sunburst, Double Matlese Cross, Pontil, Pint *9900.00
Flask, McK G VIII-5, Sunburst, Corrugated, Pontil, Olive Green, Pint .... * 550.00
Flask, McK G VIII-5, Sunburst, Double Rings & Dot, Pontil, Amber, Pint *1100.00
Flask, McK G VIII-6, Sunburst, Double Dots, Pontil, Olive Amber, Pint *2200.00
Flask, McK G VIII-7, Sunburst, Double Depressed Circle, Amber, Pint *1250.00
Flask, McK G VIII-8, P & W & Keen & Sunburst, Olive Green, Pint 425.00
Flask, McK G VIII-8, Sunburst, Keen & P & W, Pontil, Olive Amber, Pint .... * 500.00
Flask, McK G VIII-9, P & W & Keen & Sunburst, Olive Green, 1/2 Pint 525.00
Flask, McK G VIII-9, Sunburst & Keen & P & W, Amber, 1/2 Pint .... * 425.00
Flask, McK G VIII-9, Sunburst & Keen & P & W, Olive Green, 1/2 Pint .... * 325.00
Flask, McK G VIII-9, Sunburst, Keen & P & W, Pontil, Aqua, 1/2 Pint .... * 650.00

Flask, McK G VIII-10, Sunburst & Keen & P & W, Olive Amber, 1/2 Pint .... * 425.00
Flask, McK G VIII-10, Sunburst, Amber 425.00
Flask, McK G VIII-10, Sunburst, Olive Green, 1/2 Pint 500.00
Flask, McK G VIII-11, Double Sunburst, Corrugated Edges, Green, 1/2 Pint *2600.00
Flask, McK G VIII-12, Sunburst, Chip, Olive Green, 1/2 Pint *4500.00
Flask, McK G VIII-12, Sunburst, Crack, Bruise, Sea Green, 1/2 Pint .... * 950.00
Flask, McK G VIII-14, Sunburst, Double Dot, Flake, Yellow Green, 1/2 Pint .... * 650.00
Flask, McK G VIII-14, Sunburst, Double Dot, Flake, Yellow Green, 1/2 Pint *1000.00
Flask, McK G VIII-14, Sunburst, Double Dot, Pontil, Olive Green, 1/2 Pint *1000.00
Flask, McK G VIII-14a, Double Sunburst & Dot, Blue Green, 1/2 Pint *1150.00
Flask, McK G VIII-16, Double Sunburst & Dot In Circle, Green, 1/2 Pint .... * 450.00
Flask, McK G VIII-16, Sunburst & Coventry, 1/2 Pint ....*Color* XXXX.XX
Flask, McK G VIII-16, Sunburst, Light Olive Amber, 1/2 Pint 250.00
Flask, McK G VIII-16, Sunburst, Olive Green .... 270.00 To 450.00
Flask, McK G VIII-16, Sunburst, Pontil, Olive Amber, 1/2 Pint .... * 525.00
Flask, McK G VIII-18, Double Sunburst & Dot, Crack, Amber, 1/2 Pint .... * 120.00
Flask, McK G VIII-18, Sunburst & Coventry, 1/2 Pint ....*Color* XXXX.XX
Flask, McK G VIII-20, Double Sunburst, Dark Amber, Pint .... * 850.00
Flask, McK G VIII-22, Sunburst, Double Design, Pontil, Puce, Pint *3000.00
Flask, McK G VIII-22, Sunburst, Double Design, Pontil, Topaz, Pint *3700.00
Flask, McK G VIII-24, Sunburst, Double Design, Pontil, Amber, 1/2 Pint *1000.00

Flask, McK G VIII-3, Sunburst, Olive Amber, Pint
(See Page 102)

Flask, McK G IX-6,
Scroll, Louisville, Ky.,
Aqua, 8 1/2 In.

Flask, McK G VIII-25, Sunburst, Double Design, Pontil, Puce, 1/2 Pint *2000.00
Flask, McK G VIII-26, Sunburst, Pontil, Olive Green, Pint *3200.00
Flask, McK G VIII-26, Sunburst, Pontil, Rolled Mouth, Pint .... * 350.00
Flask, McK G VIII-26, Sunburst, Pontil, Yellow Green, Pint *6000.00
Flask, McK G VIII-27, Double Sunburst, Corrugated Edges, Aqua, 1/2 Pint .... * 300.00
Flask, McK G VIII-27, Double Sunburst, Olive Green, 1/2 Pint *1950.00
Flask, McK G VIII-27, Sunburst, Faint Green Tint 475.00
Flask, McK G VIII-28, Double Sunburst, Corrugated Edges, Aqua, 1/2 Pint .... * 225.00
Flask, McK G VIII-29, Keen & Sunburst, Rock In Glass, Aqua, Pint 550.00
Flask, McK G VIII-29, Sunburst, Flakes, Yellow Green, 1/2 Pint *1100.00
Flask, McK G VIII-29, Sunburst, Ribbed, Pontil, Blue Green, 1/2 Pint .... * 300.00
Flask, McK G VIII-30, Sunburst, Ribbed, Stain, Pontil, Green, 1/2 Pint .... * 900.00
Flask, McK G IX-1, Double Scroll, Sheared Mouth, IP, Amber, Quart 575.00
Flask, McK G IX-1, Scroll, Double Star, Bruise, Amber, Quart .... * 475.00
Flask, McK G IX-1, Scroll, Double Star, Bruise, Chip, Yellow Green, Quart .... * 275.00
Flask, McK G IX-1, Scroll, Double Star, Stain, Sapphire Blue, Quart .... * 850.00
Flask, McK G IX-1, Scroll, Double Star, Stain, Yellow Green, Quart .... * 400.00
Flask, McK G IX-1, Scroll, IP, Aqua, Quart 60.00
Flask, McK G IX-2, Scroll, Double Star, Chip, Ice Blue, Quart .... * 230.00
Flask, McK G IX-2, Scroll, Double Star, Collar, Yellow Green, Quart .... * 700.00
Flask, McK G IX-2, Scroll, Double Star, Pontil, Cobalt, Quart *2400.00
Flask, McK G IX-2, Scroll, Double Star, Pontil, Yellow, Quart .... * 600.00
Flask, McK G IX-2a, Scroll, Yellow Green 775.00
Flask, McK G IX-4, Scroll, Double Star, Pontil, Copper, Quart .... * 725.00
Flask, McK G IX-6, Scroll, Double Star & Louisville, Aqua, Quart .... * 140.00
Flask, McK G IX-6, Scroll, Louisville, Ky., Aqua, 8 1/2 In. ....*Illus* 155.00
Flask, McK G IX-7, Scroll, Double Star & Louisville Glass, Aqua, Quart .... * 225.00
Flask, McK G IX-8, Scroll, Double Star & Louisville Glass, Aqua, Pint .... * 240.00

Flask, McK G IX-8, Scroll, Louisville, Ky., Glassworks, Aqua, Pint 130.00
Flask, McK G IX-9, Scroll, Double Stars & Louisville, Stain, Green, Pint .... * 330.00
Flask, McK G IX-10, Scroll, Double Star, Pontil, Sapphire Blue, Pint *1700.00
Flask, McK G IX-10, Scroll, Double 8-Pointed Stars, Amber, Pint .... * 375.00
Flask, McK G IX-10, Scroll, Double 8-Pointed Stars, Stain, Amber, Pint .... * 350.00
Flask, McK G IX-10, Scroll, Double 8-Pointed Stars, Yellow Green, Pint .... * 375.00
Flask, McK G IX-11, Scroll, Aqua, Pint .... 48.00 To 90.00
Flask, McK G IX-11, Scroll, Double 8-Pointed Stars, Olive Green, Pint .... * 600.00
Flask, McK G IX-12, Scroll, Double Star, Pontil, Olive Green, Pint .... * 750.00
Flask, McK G IX-12, Scroll, 6 & 8-Pointed Stars, Blue Green, Pint .... * 410.00
Flask, McK G IX-13, Scroll, Double Star, Bruise, Pontil, Olive Amber, Pint .... * 400.00
Flask, McK G IX-13, Scroll, Double 7-Pointed Stars, Yellow Amber, Pint .... * 475.00
Flask, McK G IX-14, Scroll, Double Star, Bruise, Pontil, Amber, Pint .... * 350.00
Flask, McK G IX-14, Scroll, Double Star, Pontil, Yellow Green, Pint .... * 750.00
Flask, McK G IX-16, Scroll, Double Star, Pontil, Olive Amber, Pint .... * 600.00
Flask, McK G IX-16, Scroll, Double Star, Rough, Sapphire Blue, Pint .... * 950.00
Flask, McK G IX-17, Scroll, OP, Lime Green, Pint 125.00
Flask, McK G IX-18, Scroll, Double Star, Pontil, Sapphire Blue, Pint *1450.00
Flask, McK G IX-18, Scroll, Double Star, Pontil, Yellow Green, Pint .... * 600.00
Flask, McK G IX-20, Scroll, Double 6 & 8-Petaled Flowers, Aqua, Pint .... * 110.00
Flask, McK G IX-21, Scroll, Double Star, Pontil, Aqua, Pint .... * 350.00
Flask, McK G IX-22, Scroll, Double Star, Pontil, Aqua, Pint .... * 450.00
Flask, McK G IX-23, Scroll, Double Star & Heart, Crack, Aqua, Pint .... * 325.00
Flask, McK G IX-24, Scroll, Dots & A & Dots, Pontil, Aqua, Pint .... * 400.00
Flask, McK G IX-25, Scroll, Dots & C & Dots, Rough, Blue Green, Pint .... * 310.00
Flask, McK G IX-26, Scroll, Star & S.M'Kee & Star, Pontil, Aqua, Pint .... * 575.00
Flask, McK G IX-29, Scroll, Aqua, 2 Gallon 300.00
Flask, McK G IX-29, Scroll, Double 8-Pointed Stars, Aqua, 1/2 Gallon .... * 375.00
Flask, McK G IX-31, Scroll, Double 6-Pointed Stars, Amber, 1/2 Pint .... * 500.00
Flask, McK G IX-31, Scroll, Double 6-Pointed Stars, Aqua, 1/2 Pint .... * 95.00
Flask, McK G IX-32, Scroll, Star & Fleur-De-Lis, Yellow Green, 1/2 Pint .... * 650.00
Flask, McK G IX-34, Aqua .... * 100.00
Flask, McK G IX-34, Scroll, Aqua 80.00
Flask, McK G IX-34, Scroll, Double Star & Fleur-De-Lis, Amber, 1/2 Pint .... * 425.00
Flask, McK G IX-35, Scroll, Double Star & Fleur-De-Lis, Green, 1/2 Pint .... * 650.00
Flask, McK G IX-35, Scroll, Double Star, Flake, Yellow Green, 1/2 Pint .... * 500.00
Flask, McK G IX-35, Scroll, Double Star, Rough, Yellow Green, 1/2 Pint .... * 425.00
Flask, McK G IX-36, Scroll, Double Star, Flake, Aqua, 1/2 Pint .... * 75.00
Flask, McK G IX-36, Scroll, Uneven Lip, IP, Aqua, 1/2 Pint 45.00
Flask, McK G IX-37, Scroll, Double Star, Pontil, Aqua, 1/i Pint .... * 80.00
Flask, McK G IX-37, Scroll, Double Star, Rough, Olive Green, 1/2 Pint .... * 550.00
Flask, McK G IX-37, Scroll, Star, & Fleur-De-Lis, Yellow Green, 1/2 Pint .... * 550.00
Flask, McK G IX-38, Scroll, Star, BP & B, & Fleur-De-Lis, Aqua, 1/2 Pint .... * 270.00
Flask, McK G IX-39, Scroll, Double Star, Crack, Moonstone, 1/2 Pint .... * 575.00
Flask, McK G IX-39, Scroll, Double Star, Pontil, Blue, 1/2 Pint *7000.00
Flask, McK G IX-39, Scroll, Star & BP & B, Yellow Green, 1/2 Pint *1050.00
Flask, McK G IX-41, Scroll, Anchor & Pearls, Chip, Aqua, 1/2 Pint .... * 225.00
Flask, McK G IX-42, Scroll, Fleur-De-Lis & Jr.& S, Pontil, Aqua, 1/2 Pint .... * 675.00
Flask, McK G IX-43, Scroll, Pearls & Beads & Jr & Son, Pontil, Aqua, Pint .... * 600.00
Flask, McK G IX-44, Scroll, Dots & Fleur-De-Lis, Pontil, Aqua, Pint .... * 550.00
Flask, McK G IX-45, Scroll, Double Fancy Design, Pontil, Green, Pint *1850.00
Flask, McK G IX-46, Scroll, Double Fancy Design, Bruise, Aqua, Quart .... * 900.00
Flask, McK G IX-47, Scroll, R.Knowles & Co., Union, Stain, Aqua, Pint *2000.00
Flask, McK G IX-48, Scroll, M'Carty & Torreyson, Wellsburg, Aqua, Pint *1050.00
Flask, McK G IX-49, Scroll, M'Carty & Torreyson, Violin, Aqua, Quart *1000.00
Flask, McK G X-1, Good Game, OP, Aqua 240.00
Flask, McK G X-1, Stag & Good Game & Willow, Pontil, Aqua, Pint .... * 325.00
Flask, McK G X-2, Stag & Good Game & Willow, Pontil, Aqua, 1/2 Pint .... * 725.00
Flask, McK G X-3, Sheaf & Wheat & Grapes, Pontil, Aqua, 1/2 Pint .... * 200.00
Flask, McK G X-4, Taylor & Captain Bragg, Pontil, Chip, Aqua, Pint .... * 250.00
Flask, McK G X-5, Taylor & Captain Bragg, Pontil, Yellow Olive, Pint *1100.00
Flask, McK G X-6, Taylor & Captain Bragg, Pontil, Copper, 1/2 Pint .... * 975.00
Flask, McK G X-6, Taylor & Captain Bragg, Pontil, Stain, Green, 1/2 Pint .... * 925.00
Flask, McK G X-7, Sailboat & Bridgetown, Pontil, Stain, Aqua, 1/2 Pint .... * 200.00
Flask, McK G X-8, Sailboat & Star & Floral, Pontil, Aqua, 1/2 Pint .... * 170.00

Flask, McK G X-8, Sloop & Star, Blue 2900.00
Flask, McK G X-9, Sailboat & Star, Pontil, Green, 1/2 Pint .... * 275.00
Flask, McK G X-10, Sheaf Or Rye & Liberty, Sheared Mouth, Aqua, Pint .... * 500.00
Flask, McK G X-11, Liberty & Sheaf Of Rye, Pontil, Aqua, 1/2 Pint .... * 375.00
Flask, McK G X-14, Murdock & Cassel & Zanesville, Pontil, Green, Pint *1250.00
Flask, McK G X-15, Summer & Tree & Winter & Tree, Smoky Yellow, Pint *1600.00
Flask, McK G X-15, Summer Tree & Winter Tree, Mouth Ring, Aqua, Pint 60.00
Flask, McK G X-15, Summer, Tree, & Bird & Winter, Tree, & Bird, Wine, Pint .... * 900.00
Flask, McK G X-16, Summer Tree & Winter Tree & Bird, Aqua, 1/2 Pint .... * 100.00
Flask, McK G X-16, Summer Tree & Winter Tree, Stain, Aqua, 1/2 Pint 55.00
Flask, McK G X-17, Double Summer Tree, Pontil, Crack, Blue Green, Pint .... * 95.00
Flask, McK G X-18 .... *Illus* 20.00

Flask, McK G X-18

Flask, McK G X-18, Double Summer Tree, Burst Bubble, Green, Quart .... * 875.00
Flask, McK G X-19, Summer & Winter, Pontil, Bruises, Chips, Citron, Quart .... * 675.00
Flask, McK G X-19, Summer Tree & Winter Tree & Bird, Amber, Quart .... * 610.00
Flask, McK G X-21, American System & Steamboat, Pontil, Aqua, Pint ....*.10,500.00
Flask, McK G X-22, Hard Cider & Barrel & Log Cabin, Pontil, Blue, Pint *5600.00
Flask, McK G X-24, Jared Spencer & Manchester Con., Pontil, Olive, Pint ....*.26,000.00
Flask, McK G X-25, Medallion & Diamond Quilted, Pontil, Olive, Pint ....*.18,500.00
Flask, McK G X-26, Medallion & Diamond Quilted, Pontil, Olive, Pint ....*.16,000.00
Flask, McK G X-27, New Granite Glass Works, Stoddard, Pontil, Amber, Pint *2800.00
Flask, McK G X-28, New Granite Glass Works, Crack, Olive Amber, 1/2 Pint *3700.00
Flask, McK G X-30, Great Western & Hunter & Stag, Collar, Aqua, Pint .... * 525.00
Flask, McK G X-30, Trapper & Buck, C.1850, Aquamarine, Pint 375.00
Flask, Merry Christmas & Happy New Year, Strap Side, 5 In. 24.00
Flask, Midwestern Type, 24 Ribs Swirled To Right, Pontil, 5 5/8 In. .... * 250.00
Flask, Midwestern, Hip, Sapphire Blue, 1/2 Pint 700.00
Flask, Midwestern, Pitkin Type, Ribs Swirled To Left, Flake, Aqua, 6 1/2 In. .... * 70.00
Flask, Midwestern, Ribs Swirled To Left, Canteen Shape, Cobalt, 4 7/8 In. .... * 225.00
Flask, Midwestern, Vertical Ribs, Sheared Lip, OP, Ice Blue, Pint 195.00
Flask, Midwestern, 16 Broken Swirl Ribs, Amethystine, 4 5/8 In. 245.00
Flask, Monroe, Pink Floral, Embossed Scrolls, Stained Blue Green, 6 In. 87.50
Flask, Mounted Soldier, Citron, Quart 200.00
Flask, Nailsea Type, White Ribs, Flattened, Pontil, Olive Amber, 6 1/4 In. .... * 200.00
Flask, Nailsea Type, 18 Ribs, Flattened, Pontil, Red & White Stripes, 7 In. .... * 90.00
Flask, Nailsea, Double, Red & White, 10 In. 220.00
Flask, Nailsea, Reclining, White Loopings & Red Stripes, 7 In. 85.00
Flask, New Jersey Tercentenary, 1664-1964, Repro, Amber, Pint .... * 10.00
Flask, Newburgh Glass Co., Patent Feb.27th, 1866, Ring, Olive Yellow, Pint .... * 175.00
Flask, Not For Joe & Eagle & Lady Riding Bike & A & DHC, Aqua, Pint 95.00
Flask, Oak & Tree, Amber, 1/2 Pint .... * 60.00
Flask, Old Man With Flowing Beard, Wearing Hat, Dark Amber, Pint 15.00
Flask, Olry & Co., Phila., C.1865, Pewter & Leather Encased, Pint 9.95
Flask, Palm Tree & S.C.Dispensary, Double Collar, Bruise, Aqua, 1/2 Pint .... * 55.00
Flask, Palmer & Madigan, Strap, BIMAL, Pint 2.00
Flask, Palmer & Madigan, Strap, BIMAL, Quart 3.50

Flask, Patent June 23, '57 & Oct.21, '57, Pewter Screw Cap, Amber, 7 1/4 In.	16.00
Flask, Patent, Embossed, Stoddard Type, Amber, Pint	25.00
Flask, Peter Owens, Brooklyn, Strap, BIMAL, 1/2 Pint	2.00
Flask, Pewter & Glass, C.1866, 1/4 Pint	18.00
Flask, Pewter & Glass, 1886, Pint	* 25.00
Flask, Pewter & Leather Encased, C.1865, 1/2 Pint	9.95
Flask, Pewter Screw Cap, 3 1/4 In.	5.00
Flask, Picnic, Clock & Cobweb, 1/2 Pint	9.00
Flask, Picnic, Clock With Web, Haze, Pint	20.00
Flask, Picnic, Quilted, 5 1/4 In.	5.00
Flask, Picnic, Spider Web, 2 Pint	8.00
Flask, Pinched Sides, Sheared Mouth, Pontil, Ovoid, Aqua, 4 5/8 In.	* 25.00
Flask, Pitkin Type, Diamond, Collared Mouth, Pontil, 4 1/8 In.	* 70.00
Flask, Pitkin Type, Diamonds, Collared Mouth, Pontil, 4 1/8 In.	* 70.00
Flask, Pitkin Type, Dimpled, OP, 1/2 Pint	100.00
Flask, Pitkin Type, Ribs Swirled To Left, Bruise, Olive Amber, 6 3/4 In.	* 80.00
Flask, Pitkin Type, Ribs Swirled To Left, Pontil, Flake, Yellow, 6 1/2 In.	* 300.00
Flask, Pitkin Type, Ribs Swirled To Left, Pontil, Olive Amber, 5 1/4 In.	* 225.00
Flask, Pitkin Type, Ribs Swirled To Left, Pontil, Olive Amber, 6 1/2 In.	* 200.00
Flask, Pitkin Type, Ribs Swirled To Left, Pontil, Olive Amber, 6 1/2 In.	* 190.00
Flask, Pitkin Type, Ribs Swirled To Right, Olive Amber, 6 3/4 In.	* 375.00
Flask, Pitkin Type, Ribs Swirled To Right, Pontil, Flake, Amethyst, 5 3/4 In.	*4500.00
Flask, Pitkin Type, Ribs Swirled To Right, Pontil, Flecks, Olive Amber, 5 In.	* 240.00
Flask, Pitkin Type, Ribs Swirled To Right, Pontil, Olive Amber, 3 7/8 In.	* 900.00
Flask, Pitkin Type, Ribs Swirled To Right, Pontil, Olive Amber, 5 In.	* 180.00
Flask, Pitkin Type, Ribs Swirled To Right, Pontil, Olive Amber, 5 7/8 In.	* 150.00
Flask, Pitkin Type, Ribs Swirled To Right, Pontil, Olive Green, 6 1/4 In.	* 190.00
Flask, Pitkin Type, Vertical Ribs, Pontil, Flake, 5 In.	* 20.00
Flask, Pitkin Type, Vertical Ribs, Pontil, Olive Amber, 4 3/16 In.	* 400.00
Flask, Pitkin Type, 14 Ribs Swirled To Right, Squat, Yellow Green, 4 3/4 In.	* 300.00
Flask, Pitkin Type, 16 Ribs Swirled To Right, Pontil, Aqua, 6 1/4 In.	* 85.00
Flask, Pitkin Type, 16 Ribs Swirled To Right, Pontil, Yellow Green, 5 1/2 In	* 350.00
Flask, Pitkin Type, 18 Vertical Ribs, Pontil, Wear, Green, 5 1/4 In.	* 210.00
Flask, Pitkin Type, 20 Ribs Swirled To Right, Pontil, Olive Amber, 6 1/2 In.	* 225.00
Flask, Pitkin Type, 24 Ribs Swirled To Right, Pontil, 6 1/2 In.	* 300.00
Flask, Pitkin Type, 28 Vertical Ribs, Pontil, Wear, Pint	* 170.00
Flask, Pitkin Type, 30 Ribs Swirled To Right, Pontil, Olive Yellow, 5 3/4 In	* 425.00
Flask, Pitkin Type, 32 Ribs Swirled To Left, Sheared Mouth, Green, 7 1/2 In.	* 170.00
Flask, Pitkin Type, 32 Ribs Swirled To Left, Stain, Pontil, Olive, 7 1/2 In.	* 230.00
Flask, Pitkin Type, 32 Ribs Swirled To Right, Pontil, Green, 7 In.	* 400.00
Flask, Pitkin Type, 36 Ribs Swirled To Left, Pontil, Amber, 5 3/4 In.	* 475.00
Flask, Pitkin Type, 36 Ribs Swirled To Left, Pontil, Olive Amber, 5 1/8 In.	* 160.00
Flask, Pitkin Type, 36 Ribs Swirled To Left, Pontil, Olive Amber, 5 1/8 In.	* 175.00
Flask, Pitkin Type, 36 Ribs Swirled To Left, Pontil, Olive Amber, 5 1/2 In.	* 250.00
Flask, Pitkin Type, 36 Ribs Swirled To Left, Pontil, Olive Amber, 7 In.	* 250.00
Flask, Pitkin Type, 36 Ribs Swirled To Left, Pontil, Olive Green, 6 3/4 In.	* 300.00
Flask, Pitkin Type, 36 Ribs Swirled To Right, Dark Olive Amber, 5 1/4 In.	* 300.00
Flask, Pitkin Type, 36 Ribs Swirled To Right, Pontil, Green Aqua, 6 In.	* 200.00
Flask, Pitkin Type, 36 Ribs Swirled To Right, Pontil, Olive Amber, 2 1/2 In.	*2100.00
Flask, Pitkin Type, 36 Ribs Swirled To Right, Pontil, Olive Amber, 4 In.	* 350.00
Flask, Pitkin Type, 36 Ribs Swirled To Right, Pontil, Olive Amber, 5 In.	* 160.00
Flask, Pitkin Type, 36 Ribs Swirled To Right, Pontil, Olive Amber, 5 1/2 In.	* 225.00
Flask, Pitkin Type, 36 Ribs Swirled To Right, Pontil, Olive Amber, 6 In.	* 190.00
Flask, Pitkin Type, 36 Ribs Swirled To Right, Pontil, Olive Amber, 6 1/2 In.	* 150.00
Flask, Pitkin Type, 36 Ribs Swirled To Right, Pontil, Olive Amber, 6 1/2 In.	* 250.00
Flask, Pitkin Type, 36 Ribs Swirled To Right, Pontil, Olive Amber, 7 1/4 In.	* 300.00
Flask, Pitkin Type, 36 Ribs Swirled To Right, Pontil, Olive Green, 5 1/2 In.	* 250.00
Flask, Pitkin Type, 36 Vertical Ribs, Pontil, Olive Green, 5 3/4 In.	* 160.00
Flask, Pitkin Type, 42 Ribs Swirled To Right, Pontil, Olive Green, 6 In.	* 350.00
Flask, Pitkin, American Eagle, Amber	Color XXXX.XX
Flask, Pitkin, Amethystine Streaks, Aqua, Gallon, 10 3/4 In.	600.00
Flask, Pitkin, Green	Color XXXX.XX
Flask, Pitkin, Kent, Light Green, 1/2 Pint	365.00
Flask, Pitkin, Light Olive Green, 5 In.	200.00
Flask, Pitkin, Mantua, Blue Green, Pint	350.00

Flask, **Pitkin,** Mantua, Dark Green, Pint 250.00
Flask, **Pitkin,** Midwestern, Light Green, Pint 200.00
Flask, **Pitkin,** Swirled Ribs, Green, 7 1/2 In. .... *Illus* 325.00
Flask, **Pocket,** Gorham Sterling, Fish, Dragonfly, & Flora, C.1883, 4 1/2 In. 75.00
Flask, **Pocket,** Mary Gregory, Silver-Plated Mounts, 5 1/2 In. 123.00
Flask, **Pottery,** Brown Glaze, 6 In. .... * 90.00
Flask, **Powder,** Embossed Birds, Leather Thong, Amber, 6 1/4 In. 19.50
Flask, **Preacher's,** Neck Off-Center, Turning Purple, 1/2 Pint 25.00

Flask, Pitkin, Swirled Ribs, Green, 7 1/2 In.

Flask, **Prospector With Pickax & Map & Gold Mine & 1 Quart,** Aqua, Quart 350.00
Flask, **Pumpkin Seed,** Embossed, Screw Lid, 1/2 Pint 30.00
Flask, **Pumpkin Seed,** Embossed, Screw Lid, Pint 30.00
Flask, **Pumpkin Seed,** English Type, Reef Design Glop Top, Aqua, 1/2 Pint 25.00
Flask, **Pumpkin Seed,** F.Zimmerman, Portland, Oregon, Pint 70.00
Flask, **Pumpkin Seed,** Jas. Bull, Aqua, 5 In. 16.50
Flask, **Pumpkin Seed,** Jas. Bull, 5 1/4 In. 22.50
Flask, **Pumpkin Seed,** Picnic, Huguley's, 1 1/2 Ozs. 25.00
Flask, **Pumpkin Seed,** Picnic, 5-Pointed Star, 3 1/2 In. 7.00
Flask, **Pumpkin Seed,** Quilted, 1/2 Pint 10.00
Flask, **Pumpkin Seed,** Quilted, Pint 10.00
Flask, **Pumpkin Seed,** Quilted, Screw Lid, 1/4 Pint 15.00
Flask, **Pumpkin Seed,** Stiegel Type, C.1750, OP, Aqua, 5 3/4 In. 30.00
Flask, **Pumpkin Seed,** 3 3/8 In. 3.00
Flask, **Pumpkin Seed,** 5 1/2 In. 3.00
Flask, **Pumpkin Seed,** 7 In. 4.50
Flask, **Pyne Smith,** Strap, BIMAL, Pint 2.00
Flask, **Ravenna Glass Co. & Traveler's Companion,** Golden Amber, Pint .... * 425.00
Flask, **Ravenna Glass Co. & Traveler's Companion,** Golden Amber, Quart .... * 275.00
Flask, **Ravenna Glass Company & Eagle & 13 Stars,** Olive Green, Pint .... * 350.00
Flask, **Ravenna Glass Works & Star,** Smooth Base, Aqua, Pint .... * 25.00
Flask, **Ravenna Glass Works,** Smooth Base, Yellow, Pint .... * 325.00
Flask, **Redware,** Black Splotch Decoration, 8 In. 170.00
Flask, **Redware,** Brown Glaze, 8 In. .... * 90.00
Flask, **Redware,** Mottled Brown Glaze, 6 1/2 In. .... * 75.00
Flask, **Redware,** 6 1/2 In. 105.00
Flask, **Ribs Swirled To Right,** Flattened, Elongated, Pontil, Blue Green, 8 In. .... * 45.00
Flask, **Ribs Swirled To Right,** Flattened Ovoid, Pontil, Ruby, 6 In. .... * 190.00
Flask, **Richmond,** Va., Strap Sided, 1/2 Pint 12.00
Flask, **Robert E.Lee & Jefferson Davis,** Repro, Milk Glass, Quart .... * 7.50
Flask, **Rubena,** Diamond-Quilted, Star Cut Diamonds, Sterling Collar, 5 In. 60.00
Flask, **S On Base,** Strap Side, Amber, 1/2 Pint 3.00
Flask, **S On Base,** Strap Side, Amber, Pint 3.00
Flask, **S.C.Dispensary,** Strap Side, Stain, Aqua, 1/2 Pint 15.00
Flask, **Saddle,** Blown, Olive Amber, 11 1/4 In. .... * 45.00
Flask, **Saddle,** Blown, Rope Neck, Flared Lip, Olive Yellow, 9 1/4 In. 19.00
Flask, **Saddle,** Blown, Sheared Mouth, Olive Amber, 10 1/4 In. .... * 35.00

Flask, Saddle, Blown, Smooth Base, Olive Amber, 13 1/2 In. .... * 95.00
Flask, Saddle, Persian Type, Applied Neck String, Blue Green, 9 1/2 In. .... * 15.00
Flask, Saddle, Persian, Aqua, 9 In. ....*Color* XXXX.XX
Flask, Sailor & Chapman & Musician & Balt.Md., Pontil, Aqua, 1/2 Pint .... * 150.00
Flask, Sailor & Chapman & Musician & Balt.Md., Rough, Green, 1/ Pint .... * 550.00
Flask, Sailor Dancing & Musician On Bench, Crack, Amber, 1/2 Pint .... * 350.00
Flask, Sandwich Glass, Swirled, OP, Cobalt, 6 1/4 In. 135.00
Flask, Sheaf Of Wheat & Coffin, Diamond Quilted, DSG Co. Base, Amber, Pint .... * 55.00
Flask, Sheaf Of Wheat & Fork & Traveler's Companion, Olive Amber, Quart .... * 120.00
Flask, Sheaf Of Wheat & Fork & Westford Glass Co., Olive Amber, 1/2 Pint .... * 70.00
Flask, Sheaf Of Wheat & Fork & Westford Glass Co., Red Amber, 1/2 Pint .... * 100.00
Flask, Sheaf Of Wheat & Star & Traveler's Companion, Olive Amber, Quart 70.00
Flask, Sheaf Of Wheat & Tibby Bros., Pitts., Pa., BIMAL, Pint 20.00
Flask, Sheaf Of Wheat & Tools & Mechanics Glass Works, Green, Quart .... * 575.00
Flask, Sheaf Of Wheat & Tools & Traveler's Companion & Star, Amber, Quart 70.00
Flask, Sheaf Of Wheat & Tools & Traveler's Companion, Olive Amber, Quart 90.00
Flask, Sheaf Of Wheat & Tools & Westford Glass Co., Amber Green, Pint 90.00
Flask, Sheaf Of Wheat & Tools & Westford Glass Co., Olive Amber, Pint 80.00
Flask, Sheaf Of Wheat & Tools, & Star, Golden Amber, 1/2 Pint .... * 225.00
Flask, Sheaf Of Wheat & Westford, Olive Green, 1/2 Pint 90.00
Flask, Sheaf Of Wheat & Westford, Red Amber, Pint 90.00
Flask, Sheaf Of Wheat, Aqua, Pint .... * 110.00
Flask, Sheaf Of Wheat, Fork, & Rake & Westford Glass Co., Olive Amber, Pint .... * 60.00
Flask, Sheaf Of Wheat, Fork, & Rake & Westford Glass Co., Olive Amber, Pint .... * 75.00
Flask, Sheaf Of Wheat, Fork, & Rake & Westford Glass Co., Olive Amber, Pint .... * 85.00
Flask, Sheaf Of Wheat, Fork, & Rake & Westford Glass Co., Olive Amber, Pint .... * 85.00
Flask, Sheaf Of Wheat, Fork, & Rake & Westford Glass Co., Red Amber, Pint .... * 95.00
Flask, Sheaf Of Wheat, Fork, & Rake & 5-Pointed Star, Pontil, Amber, Pint .... * 125.00
Flask, Sheaf Of Wheat, Fork, & Rake & 5-Pointed Star, Potstone, Green, Quart .... * 400.00
Flask, Sheaf Of Wheat, Label, Aqua, Pint .... * 140.00
Flask, Soldier & Baltimore & Ballet Dancer & Chapman, Green, Pint .... * 450.00
Flask, Soldier & Baltimore & Ballet Dancer & Chapman, Olive Green, Pint .... * 525.00
Flask, Soldier On Horseback, Yellow, Quart 310.00
Flask, Spring Garden Glass & Anchor & Cabin & Tree, Blue, Pint *3800.00
Flask, Spring Garden Glass Works & Anchor & Cabin & Tree, Amber, Pint .... * 475.00
Flask, Spring Garden Glass Works & Anchor & Cabin & Tree, Citron, Pint .... * 400.00
Flask, Spring Garden Glass Works & Cabin & Tree, Pontil, Aqua, 1/2 Pint .... * 95.00
Flask, Spring Garden Glass Works & Cabin & Tree, Flake, Green, 1/2 Pint .... * 550.00
Flask, Spring Garden Glass Works & Cabin & Tree, Stain, Aqua, 1/2 Pint 45.00
Flask, Staffordshire, Double, Flattened, Man's Portraits, C.1825, 7 5/8 In. 60.00
Flask, Star & Traveler's Companion, Sheared Mouth, IP, Aqua, 1/2 Pint 120.00
Flask, Star & Eye & AD & GRJA, Pontil, Olive Amber, Pint .... * 120.00
Flask, Star & Eye & AD & GRJA, Pontil, Olive Green, Pint .... * 150.00
Flask, Star, Eye, & AD & Star, Arm & GRJA, Collar, Olive Amber, Pint .... * 100.00
Flask, Star, Single Seam, Ground Top, Pewter Lid, Amber, Pint 20.00
Flask, Sterling Silver, Screw-On Hinged Cap, C.A.Vanderbilt, C.1909, 7 In. 95.00
Flask, Stiegel Type, Ovoid, 16 Diamonds, 6 In. 125.00
Flask, Stoddard Type, Amber, 1/2 Pint 18.00
Flask, Stoddard Type, Amber, Pint 18.00
Flask, Stoddard, Granite Glass Works, Open Bubble, Amber, Pint 120.00
Flask, Stoneware, Blue Decoration On Sides, 8 In. 120.00
Flask, Stoneware, Gunmetal Glaze, 8 In. 50.00
Flask, Stoneware, Incised Bird, 7 In. 320.00
Flask, Stoneware, Port Dundas Pottery Co., Glasgow, 1874, Cherries, 7 In. 56.00
Flask, Stoneware, Rhenish Type, Man & Boy, Cobalt Tree Bark, 1/4 Pint 90.00
Flask, Strap Side, Amber, 1/2 Pint 3.00
Flask, Strap Side, Amber, Pint 3.00
Flask, Strap Side, Aqua, 1/2 Pint 4.00
Flask, Strap Side, Aqua, Pint 4.00
Flask, Success To The Railroad, Olive Green ....*Color* XXXX.XX
Flask, Traveler's Companion & Lancaster & Erie Co., Yellow Green, Pint 650.00
Flask, Traveler's Companion & Lancaster, Erie Co., N.Y., Blue Green, Pint .... * 575.00
Flask, Traveler's Companion & Lockport Glass Works, Pontil, Green, Pint *1100.00
Flask, Traveler's Companion & Railroad Guide, Pontil, Green, 1/2 Pint .... * 400.00
Flask, Traveler's Companion & Star, IP, Golden Amber, 1/2 Pint .... * 250.00

Flask, Traveler's Companion, Sheared Mouth, Pontil, Aqua, 1/2 Pint .... * 150.00
Flask, Union & Clasped Hands & Cannon & F A & Co., Stain, Amber, 1/2 Pint .... * 130.00
Flask, Union & Clasped Hands & Cannon, Flag & F A & Co., Aqua, 1/2 Pint 85.00
Flask, Union & Clasped Hands & Eagle & A & Co., Crack, Amber, Pint .... * 15.00
Flask, Union & Clasped Hands & Eagle & A & Co., Yellow Green, Quart .... * 190.00
Flask, Union & Clasped Hands & Eagle & Banner, Flake, Aqua, 1/2 Pint .... * 30.00
Flask, Union & Clasped Hands & Eagle & Banner, Flake, Aqua, Pint .... * 30.00
Flask, Union & Clasped Hands & Eagle & Banner, Chip, Aqua, Quart .... * 40.00
Flask, Union & Clasped Hands & Eagle & C.I.& Sons, Chip, Aqua, Pint 30.00
Flask, Union & Clasped Hands & Eagle & C.I.& Sons, Chip, Dark Amber, Pint .... * 50.00
Flask, Union & Clasped Hands & Eagle & Pittsburgh, Aqua, Quart 55.00
Flask, Union & Clasped Hands & Eagle & Ribbon, Aqua, Pint 95.00
Flask, Union & Clasped Hands & Eagle With Banner, Aqua, Quart 65.00
Flask, Union & Clasped Hands & Eagle With Banner, Aqua, 1/2 Pint 37.00
Flask, Union & Clasped Hands & Eagle, Aqua, 1/2 Pint 35.00
Flask, Union & Clasped Hands & Eagle, Aqua, Pint 35.00
Flask, Union & Clasped Hands & Eagle, Banner, & Waterford, Aqua, Quart .... * 55.00
Flask, Union & Clasped Hands & Eagle, 1/2 Pint 60.00
Flask, Union & Clasped Hands & Eagle, Pint 35.00
Flask, Union & Clasped Hands & F.A.& Co. & Cannon & Flag, Amber, Pint 185.00
Flask, Union & Clasped Hands & F A & Co. & Cannon, Chip, Yellow, Pint .... * 200.00
Flask, Union & Clasped Hands & L F & Co. & Eagle, Chip, Aqua, Quart .... * 75.00
Flask, Union & Clasped Hands & W.Frank & Sons & Cannon & Flag, Blue, Pint 75.00
Flask, Union & Clasped Hands & Waterford & Eagle, IP, Aqua, Quart 75.00
Flask, Union & Clasped Hands & Whitney Glass Works, Amber, Pint 5.00
Flask, Union & Clasped Hands & Wm.Frank & Son, Pittsburgh, Aqua, Pint 175.00
Flask, Union & Clasped Hands & Wm.Frank & Sons & 13 Stars, Amber, Pint .... * 250.00
Flask, Union & Clasped Hands & Wm.Frank & Sons, Crack, Yellow .... * 275.00
Flask, Union & Clasped Hands & 13 Stars, Dove, & Ribbon, Aqua, 1/2 Pint 49.50
Flask, Union & Clasped Hands, Aqua, Quart 65.00
Flask, Union & Clasped Hands, Pint 75.00
Flask, Union & Clasped Hands, Red Amber, 1/2 Pint 75.00
Flask, Union & Clasped Hands, Strap Sided, Bubbles, Amber, Pint 7.00
Flask, Union & Clasped Hands, 1/2 Pint 85.00
Flask, Union & Clasped Hands, 13 Stars, & Masonic & Eagle & H & S, 1/2 Pint .... * 85.00
Flask, Union & Old Rye & A & DHA In Banner & Pittsburgh, Aqua, Pint 100.00
Flask, Union & Old Rye & Eagle & A & D.H.C., Stain, Yellow Green, Quart .... * 150.00
Flask, Union Glass Works, New London, Ct., Chip, Olive Amber, Pint *5200.00
Flask, Union Glass Works, New London, Ct., Crack, Yellow Olive, Pint .... * 750.00
Flask, Union Glass Works, New London, Double Collared Mouth, Aqua, Pint .... * 325.00
Flask, Union Glass Works, New London, Sloping Collared Mouth, Aqua, Pint .... * 200.00
Flask, Union Glass Works, New London, Smooth Base, Yellow Olive, Pint .... * 750.00
Flask, Union, Aqua, Pint 75.00
Flask, Union, Clasped Hands & Eagle & E Wormser & Co., Aqua, Quart .... * 60.00
Flask, Union, Clasped Hands, FA & Co., & 13 Stars & Cannon, Aqua, 1/2 Pint 50.00
Flask, Union, Clasped Hands, & L F & Co. & Eagle & Pittsburgh, Aqua, Pint .... * 45.00
Flask, Union, Clasped Hands, & L.F.& Co. & Eagle & Pittsburgh, Aqua, Quart 75.00
Flask, Union, Clasped Hands, & Old Rye & Eagle & A & D.H.C., Aqua, Pint .... * 50.00
Flask, Union, Clasped Hands, & W.Frank & Sons & Cannon, Aqua, Pint .... * 60.00
Flask, Union, Clasped Hands, & 11 Stars & Eagle & Banner, Amber, 1/2 Pint .... * 65.00
Flask, Union, Clasped Hands, & 13 Stars & Cannon & Flag, Amber, Pint .... * 225.00
Flask, Union, Clasped Hands, & 13 Stars & Eagle & A & Co., Citron, Pint .... * 360.00
Flask, Union, Clasped Hands, & 13 Stars & Eagle & Banner, Amber, 1/2 Pint .... * 55.00
Flask, Union, Clasped Hands, & 13 Stars & Eagle & Banner, Amber, Quart .... * 150.00
Flask, Union, Clasped Hands, & 13 Stars & Eagle & Banner, Aqua, 1/2 Pint .... * 30.00
Flask, Union, Clasped Hands, & 13 Stars & Eagle & Banner, Aqua, Pint .... * 40.00
Flask, Union, Clasped Hands, & 13 Stars & Eagle & Banner, Aqua, Quart .... * 45.00
Flask, Union, Clasped Hands, & 13 Stars & Eagle & Banner, Crack, Aqua, Quart .... * 40.00
Flask, Union, Clasped Hands, & 13 Stars & Eagle & Banner, Stain, Amber, Pint .... * 85.00
Flask, Union, Clasped Hands, & 13 Stars & Eagle & Banner, Stain, Aqua, Pint .... * 45.00
Flask, Union, Clasped Hands, & 13 Stars & Eagle, Mouth Ring, Aqua, Pint 30.00
Flask, Union, Clasped Hands, Waterford, & 13 Stars & Eagle, Citron, Quart 150.00
Flask, Union, Clasped Hands, 13 Stars & A & D.H.C., & Eagle, Citron, Pint .... * 180.00
Flask, Violin, Aqua, Pint 45.00
Flask, Violin, Ice Blue, 1/2 Pint 10.00

Flask, Warranteed, 1/4 Pint 4.00
Flask, Washington & Albany Glass Works & Frigate, Repro, Blue, Pint .... * 10.00
Flask, Washington & Albany Glass Works & Frigate, Reproduction, Green, Pt. .... * 10.00
Flask, Washington & Albany & Frigate, Repro, Crack, Amber, 1/2 Pint .... * 7.50
Flask, Washington & G.Z.Taylor, Pontil, Bubbles, Aqua, Pint 95.00
Flask, Washington & Taylor & Dyottville, Repro, Amethyst, Quart .... * 50.00
Flask, Washington & Taylor, Aqua, Pint 35.00
Flask, Washington & Taylor, Lavender, Quart 2000.00
Flask, Washington & Taylor, Repro, Similar To McK G I-50, Aqua, Pint .... * 7.50
Flask, Westford Glass Co. & Sheaf Of Wheat & Tools, Amber, Pint 120.00
Flask, Westford Glass Co. & Sheaf Of Wheat, Deep Olive Amber, Pint 145.00
Flask, Whiskey, New Hampshire Officer's, Pewter Cap, 1862, 6 In. 50.00
Flask, Whiskey, 1886, Pewter Lip, Cap, & Bottom Half, 6 In. 20.00
Flask, Whitney Glass Works On Bottom, Stain, Yellow Amber, 1/2 Pint 24.00
Flask, Whitney Glass Works, Inside Screw, Amber, Pint .... * 35.00
Flask, Will You Take A Drink & Will A Duck Swim, Chip, Aqua, Pint .... * 175.00
Flask, Will You Take A Drink & Will A Duck Swim, Stain, Aqua, Pint .... * 125.00
Flask, Will You Take A Drink & Will A Duck Swim, Yellow Green, Quart .... * 750.00
Flask, Will You Take A Drink & Will A Duck, Opalescent Neck, Aqua, 1/2 Pint ..... * 150.00
Flask, Wine, Flat Sides, Collar, Improved Pontil, Green, Quart 35.00
Flask, Wine, Jas.Tharps, Washington, D.C., Round Slug Plate, Amber, 1/2 Pint 20.00
   Flask, Zanesville, see also Flask, Zanesville, Chestnut
Flask, Zanesville City Glass Works In Panel, Smooth Base, Amber, Pint .... * 190.00
Flask, Zanesville City Glass Works, Stain, Aqua, Pint 65.00
Flask, Zanesville, Chestnut, 24 Ribs Swirled To Right, Yellow Green, 6 In. 625.00
Flask, Zanesville, Dark Amber, 1/2 Pint 700.00
Flask, Zanesville, Flat, Golden Amber, Pint 1300.00
Flask, Zanesville, Hip, Deep Amber, 1/2 Pint 700.00
Flask, 16 Ribs Swirled To Left, Canteen Shape, Chip, Sapphire, 5 1/4 In. .... * 55.00

Food, Essence Of Cinnamon, Pontil, 4 1/4 In.
(See Page 111)

Food, Heinz Ketchup, Clear, 9 In.
(See Page 111)

Food, Ice Cream Freezer, Consolidated Mfg., 10 In.
(See Page 111)

*Food bottles inculde all of the many grocery store containers, such as
catsup, horseradish, jelly, and other foodstuffs. A few special items, such as
vinegar, are listed under their own headings.*
   Food, Peppersauce, see Peppersauce
Food, A.Moll, Grocers, St.Louis, Mo., Pottery, 1/2 Gallon 30.00
Food, Absolutely Pure Horse Radish, Richard Webber, Glass Lid, Aqua, Quart 12.00
Food, Blueberry, Blob Lip, Dug, Aqua, 12 In. 14.00
Food, Blueberry, Fluted Shoulders, Collared Mouth, Aqua, 11 1/4 In. .... * 35.00

Food, Blueberry, Fluted Shoulders, Crack, Aqua, 11 1/4 In. .... * 35.00
Food, Blueberry, Fluted Shoulders, Double Collar, Amber, 11 1/4 In. .... * 325.00
Food, Blueberry, Fluted Shoulders, Smooth Base, Olive Green, 11 1/4 In. .... * 325.00
Food, C.B.Ellin's Horseradish, New York, Aqua, 5 In. 5.00
   Food, California Perfume Co., see Avon, California Perfume Co.
Food, Capers, Emerald, 8 In. 6.00

Food, Old Style Salad
Mustard, 5 In.
(See Page 112)

Food, Mellin's Infant's, Boston
(See Page 112)

Food, My Own Homemade Tomato Catsup, 6 1/2 In.
(See Page 112)

Food, Capers, Fluted, Emerald Green, 6 1/2 In. 4.50
Food, Capers, Fluted, Emerald Green, 8 In. 5.50
Food, Catsup, 3 Mold, Whittled, Aqua, 10 In. 13.00
Food, Clam Bouillon, Scott & Gilbert Co., San Francisco, 3 3/4 In. 4.00
Food, Confiserie Nationale Candy, Hoboken, N.H., Bulbous, 9 In. 28.00
Food, Cottage Cheese, Pint 1.00
Food, Cutting Packing Co., San Francisco, C.1880, Display Jar ....Color XXXX.XX
Food, Davis O.K. Baking Powder, Embossed, Corker, 4 1/2 In. 2.00
Food, Derby Mustard, Milk Glass, 4 In. 3.00
Food, E.E.Gray & Co., Boston, Mass., Pottery, Gallon 30.00
Food, E.R.Durkee & Co., N.Y., Belt & Gloved Hand, Patent 1877, 8 1/2 In. 5.95
Food, Elliman's Royal Embrocation For Horses Slough, Green, 7 1/2 In. 8.50
Food, Essence Of Cinnamon, Pontil, 4 1/4 In. .... Illus 12.00
Food, F.Brown's Essence Of Jamaica Ginger, Philada., Aqua, 5 1/2 In. 5.00
Food, Flavoring Extracts, 5 1/2 In. 2.25
Food, Franklin Caro Co. Candy, Square, Gallon 30.00
Food, Genuine Sanford's Ginger, Patent 1876, 6 3/4 In. 3.95
Food, Genuine Sanford's Ginger, 1876, Rectangular, Aqua, 7 1/2 In. 3.95
Food, Giessen's Union Mustard, N.Y., Eagle, Smooth Base, 5 In. .... * 45.00
Food, Guth Fruit Tablets, Baltimore, 4 Sided, BIMAL, Aqua, Gallon 40.00
Food, H.J.Heinz Co., Patent, 115, Applied Collar, Urn Shape, Haze, 7 In. 6.50
Food, H.J.Newhauser Mustard, Eagle, N.Y., Pontil, Rolled Mouth, 5 In. .... * 310.00
Food, Hansen's Laboratory Rennet Extract, Little Falls, N.Y., Jug, Gallon 22.00
Food, Heinz Ketchup, Clear, 9 In. .... Illus 8.00
Food, Heinz Ketchup, 8 Sided, Miniature 7.00
Food, Horlick's Malted Milk, BIMAL, Gallon 4.00
Food, Ice Cream Freezer, Consolidated Mfg., 10 In. .... Illus 20.00
Food, Indian Root Beer Extract, BIMAL, Aqua, 4 1/2 In. 4.00
Food, Jar, Barrel, Rolled Mouth, Pontil, 5 1/8 In. .... * 10.00
Food, John Wyeth & Bro., Beef Juice, Stain, Swirled Glass, 3 1/2 In. 2.50
Food, Jumbo Peanut Butter, Embossed Elephant, Lb. 6.00
Food, Jumbo Peanut Butter, 5 1/2 Ozs. 1.75
Food, Kis-Me-Gum, 11 In. 37.50
Food, Knapp's Root Beer Extract, Snappsan, Puritan Man, Green, 4 In. 5.50
Food, Lea & Perrin's Worcestershire Sauce, Aqua, 7 1/4 In. 2.50

Food, Lea & Perrin's Worcestershire Sauce, Glass Stopper, 11 1/4 In. 4.50
Food, London, Beveled Corners, Pontil, Rectangular, Yellow Green, 5 In. .... * 40.00
Food, London, Pontil, Square, Amber Striations, Yellow Green, 5 1/2 In. .... * 220.00
Food, Longfield & Scott, North Of England, Sauce, Aqua, 7 1/4 In. 8.00
Food, M & R Brand Flavors, Acme Flavoring Co., 2 3/4 In. 1.00
Food, Maltese Cross Banana, 8 In. 6.00
Food, Mellin's Infant's, Boston .... Illus 9.50
Food, Murdock Liquid, Boston & London, 12 Sided, Amber, 7 In. 8.00
Food, Mustard, Beveled Corners, OP, Aqua, 5 In. 5.00
Food, Mustard, Folded Lip, OP, 5 In. 10.00
Food, Mustard, London, Pontil, Square, 5 1/2 In. .... * 30.00
Food, My Own Homemade Tomato Catsup, 6 1/2 In. .... Illus 5.00
Food, Ohio Cider, 7th St., Dug, Dark Amber, Quart 20.00
Food, Old Judge Coffee, Embossed, Quart 3.50
Food, Old Style Salad Mustard, 5 In. .... Illus 2.50

Food, Peppermint, A.Graf Distilling Co.

Food, Saratoga Relish, C.1873

Food, Penguin Syrup, Tin Screw Cap, 8 In. 4.50
Food, Pepper Sauce, see Pepper Sauce
Food, Peppermint, A.Graf Distilling Co. .... Illus 5.00
Food, Pickle, see Pickle
Food, Planter's Peanuts, Embossed, Square, 9 In. 40.00
Food, Planter's Peanuts, 5 Pound 24.00
Food, Pure Apple Cider, Balwin, Ga., Pottery, Red, White, & Blue, Gallon 30.00
Food, Pure Honey, Embossed Beehive, 4 Gothic Arches, Lb., 6 3/4 In. 6.00
Food, Pure Ponce Molasses, Dewell, N.H., Stoneware, Cobalt, Quart 30.00
Food, R.J.C., Condiment, 6 Sided, Rolled Lip, OP, Aqua, 6 In. 13.00
Food, Saratoga Relish, C.1873 .... Illus 55.00
Food, Sauce, Free Blown, Ring Lip, Irregular Shoulders, Aqua, 8 3/4 In. 11.50
Food, Soyerssauce, Violin Shape, Collared Mouth, Pontil, Amber, 1/2 Pint .... * 625.00
Food, Sunshine Brand Coffee, Embossed, Quart 3.00
Food, Sylmar Brand Olive Growers, Los Angeles, Cal., 10 In. 4.00
Food, Sylmar Brand, Los Angeles, Olive Growers, 10 1/4 In. 10.00
Food, Towle's Log Cabin Maple Syrup, Packer Lip, 9 1/4 In. 4.50
Food, Union Pacific Tea Co., Embossed Elephant, Coffin Flask, Haze, 1/4 Pint 75.00
Food, Valentine's Meat Juice, Amber, 3 1/4 In. .... 3.00 To 6.00

*Fruit jars made of glass have been used in the United States since the
1850s. Over one thousand different jars have been found with varieties of
closures, embossing, and colors. The date 1858 on many jars refers to a
patent, not the age of the bottle. Be sure to look in this listing under any
name or initial that appears on your jar. If not otherwise indicated the jar
is clear glass, quart size. The numbers used in the entries in the form
T-0 refer to the book 'A Collectors' Manual of Fruit Jars' by
Julian Harrison Toulouse.*

Fruit Jar, A & DH Chambers, Pittsburgh, Union, Wax Sealer, Aqua, Quart 18.00

Fruit Jar, Aqua, 1/2 Gallon, 8 In.

Fruit Jar, A.Stone & Co., Philada., Aqua, 7 In.

Fruit Jar, Atlas E-Z Seal, Pint
(See Page 114)

Fruit Jar, A.Dufour & Co., Barrel, OP, 1/2 Gallon	145.00
Fruit Jar, A.Kline, Aqua, 1/2 Gallon	40.00
Fruit Jar, A.P.Donaghho, Parkersburg, Crockery, Gallon	27.50
Fruit Jar, A.P.Donaghho, Parkersburg, W.Va. In Blue Stencil, Stoneware, 8 In	25.00
Fruit Jar, A.Stone & Co., Philada., Aqua, 7 In. *Illus*	400.00
Fruit Jar, Acme, Pint	1.50 To 5.00
Fruit Jar, Acme, Quart	1.95
Fruit Jar, Acme, Shield, Glass Lid, Wire Bail, Smoky, 1/2 Gallon	10.00
Fruit Jar, Acme, Shield, 6-Pointed Star On Lid, Bicentennial, Quart	4.00
Fruit Jar, Acme, Stars & Stripes In Shield, Glass Lid, Wire Bail, Pint	4.50
Fruit Jar, Acme, Stars & Stripes In Shield, Glass Lid, Wire Bail, Quart	3.50
Fruit Jar, Acme, Stars & Stripes In Shield, Glass Lid, Wire Bail, 1/2 Gallon	7.50
Fruit Jar, Acme, Trademark, Mason's Patent Nov.30th, 1858, Aqua, Quart	65.00
Fruit Jar, Airtight, Pint	20.00
Fruit Jar, Almy, Aqua, Quart	70.00
Fruit Jar, Amazon Swift Seal In Circle, Glass Lid, Wire Bail, Blue, Pint, T-1	8.50
Fruit Jar, Amazon Swift Seal In Circle, Glass Lid, Wire Bail, Blue, Quart	8.50
Fruit Jar, Amazon Swift Seal, 1/2 Gallon	5.00
Fruit Jar, American Porcelain, Midget	95.00
Fruit Jar, American Porcelain, N A G Co., Porcelain Lined, Quart	25.00
Fruit Jar, Anchor Hocking, Bicentennial, 2-Piece Metal Lid, Pint	1.00
Fruit Jar, Anchor Hocking, Bicentennial, 2-Piece Metal Lid, Quart	1.00
Fruit Jar, Aqua, 1/2 Gallon, 8 In. *Illus*	39.00
Fruit Jar, Atlas E-Z Seal, A On Base, Glass Lid, Wire Bail, 1/2 Gallon, T-1	4.00
Fruit Jar, Atlas E-Z Seal, Apple Green, Quart, T-1	16.00
Fruit Jar, Atlas E-Z Seal, Amber, Quart	22.00 To 26.00
Fruit Jar, Atlas E-Z Seal, Aqua, Pint	.60 To .70
Fruit Jar, Atlas E-Z Seal, Aqua, Quart	.60 To .70
Fruit Jar, Atlas E-Z Seal, Blue Lid, Wire Bail, 1/2 Pint	8.50
Fruit Jar, Atlas E-Z Seal, Blue, 1/3 Pint	6.00
Fruit Jar, Atlas E-Z Seal, Cornflower Blue, Quart	18.00
Fruit Jar, Atlas E-Z Seal, Embossed Base, Aqua, 1/2 Pint	6.00
Fruit Jar, Atlas E-Z Seal, Embossed Base, Aqua, Pint	.75
Fruit Jar, Atlas E-Z Seal, Embossed Base, Aqua, Quart	.75
Fruit Jar, Atlas E-Z Seal, Embossed Base, Medium Green, Quart, T-1	6.50
Fruit Jar, Atlas E-Z Seal, Embossed Base, 1/2 Pint, T-1	6.00
Fruit Jar, Atlas E-Z Seal, Embossed Base, Quart, T-1	.75
Fruit Jar, Atlas E-Z Seal, Glass Lid, Wire Bail, Blue, Pint	3.00 To 6.50
Fruit Jar, Atlas E-Z Seal, Glass Lid, Wire Bail, Blue, Quart	2.50

Fruit Jar, Atlas E-Z Seal, Glass Lid, Wire Bail, Blue, 1/2 Gallon 6.00
Fruit Jar, Atlas E-Z Seal, Glass Lid, Wire Bail, 1/2 Pint .... 3.00 To 4.00
Fruit Jar, Atlas E-Z Seal, Glass Lid, Wire Bail, Pint 2.50
Fruit Jar, Atlas E-Z Seal, Glass Lid, Wire Bail, Quart .... 1.00 To 2.00
Fruit Jar, Atlas E-Z Seal, Light Green, 1/2 Pint 5.00
Fruit Jar, Atlas E-Z Seal, Light Green, 1/2 Gallon 3.00
Fruit Jar, Atlas E-Z Seal, Milk Glass Lid, Wire Bail, Amber, Quart 45.00
Fruit Jar, Atlas E-Z Seal, 1/3 Pint 2.00
Fruit Jar, Atlas E-Z Seal, 1/2 Pint .... 1.00 To 2.50
Fruit Jar, Atlas E-Z Seal, Pint .... Illus   4.00
Fruit Jar, Atlas E-Z Seal, Quart .... 1.00 To 2.00
Fruit Jar, Atlas E-Z Seal, 1/2 Gallon 1.00
Fruit Jar, Atlas Good Luck Mason, Glass Lid, Wire Bail, Quart, T-1 .... 3.00
Fruit Jar, Atlas Good Luck Mason, Glass Lid, Wire Bail, 1/2 Gallon, T-1 .... 6.00
Fruit Jar, Atlas Good Luck, Clover Leaf, Glass Lid, Wire Bail, 1/2 Gallon 10.00
Fruit Jar, Atlas Good Luck, 1/2 Pint 7.50
Fruit Jar, Atlas Good Luck, Pint .... 1.50 To 2.50
Fruit Jar, Atlas H Over A Mason, Zinc Lid, 1/2 Pint 3.00
Fruit Jar, Atlas Improved Mason, Quart 1.95
Fruit Jar, Atlas Mason Improved Patent, Aqua, Quart .... 2.50 To 9.00
Fruit Jar, Atlas Mason Improved Patent, Green, Quart 12.00
Fruit Jar, Atlas Mason Improved Patent, Olive Green, Quart 6.00
Fruit Jar, Atlas Mason Improved Patent, Pint 1.95
Fruit Jar, Atlas Mason Improved Patent, Quart 1.95
Fruit Jar, Atlas Mason Improved Patent, Square Shoulders, Aqua, Pint 3.50
Fruit Jar, Atlas Mason Improved Patent, Square Shoulders, Aqua, Quart 3.00
Fruit Jar, Atlas Mason Improved Patent, Zinc Band, Apple Green, Quart 10.00
Fruit Jar, Atlas Mason Improved Patent, Zinc Band, Cornflower Blue, Pint 12.00
Fruit Jar, Atlas Mason Improved Patent, 1/2 Gallon 5.00
Fruit Jar, Atlas Mason Improved, Aqua, Quart 5.00
Fruit Jar, Atlas Mason Improved, Quart 5.00
Fruit Jar, Atlas Mason's Patent Nov.30th, 1858, Apple Green, 1/2 Gallon 12.00
Fruit Jar, Atlas Mason's Patent Nov.30th, 1858, Blue, 1/2 Gallon 5.50
Fruit Jar, Atlas Mason's Patent Nov.30th, 1858, Olive Green, 1/2 Gallon 25.00
Fruit Jar, Atlas Special Mason, Wide Mouth, Blue, Quart 4.00
Fruit Jar, Atlas Special Mason, Wide Mouth, Blue, 1/2 Gallon 6.00
Fruit Jar, Atlas Strong Shoulder Mason, Cornflower Blue, 1/2 Gallon 18.00
Fruit Jar, Atlas Strong Shoulder Mason, Light Olive Green, Quart 10.00
Fruit Jar, Atlas Strong Shoulder Mason, Salesman's Sample, 3 In. 10.00
Fruit Jar, Atlas Wholefruit, Pint .... 1.75 To 3.00
Fruit Jar, Atlas Wholefruit, Quart 1.75
Fruit Jar, Atlas Wholefruit, 1/2 Gallon 1.50
Fruit Jar, Automatic Sealer, Aqua, Quart 90.00
Fruit Jar, B B G M Co., Aqua, Quart 19.50
Fruit Jar, B B G M Co., Monogram, Quart 12.00
Fruit Jar, B B G M Co., Monogram, 1/2 Gallon 15.00
Fruit Jar, B B G M Co., Reproduction, Amber, Quart 20.00
Fruit Jar, B.B.Wilcox, Aqua, Quart 55.00
Fruit Jar, Bagley & Co., Ltd., London, C S & Co On Base, C.1879, Green, Pint 19.50
Fruit Jar, Ball Eclipse, Wide Mouth, Glass Lid, Wire Bail, Pint 1.00
Fruit Jar, Ball Eclipse, Wide Mouth, Glass Lid, Wire Bail, 1/2 Gallon 3.50
Fruit Jar, Ball Eclipse, Wide Mouth, Pint 2.00
Fruit Jar, Ball Eclipse, Wide Mouth, Quart .... 2.00 To 2.50
Fruit Jar, Ball Eclipse, Wide Mouth, 1/2 Gallon 4.00
Fruit Jar, Ball Eclipse, 7-14-08 On Base, Glass Lid, Wire Bail, Pint, T-3 .... 3.50
Fruit Jar, Ball Freezer Jar, Pint 1.50
Fruit Jar, Ball Freezer Jar, Quart 1.00
Fruit Jar, Ball Ideal, Aqua, 1/2 Pint .... 12.50 To 15.00
Fruit Jar, Ball Ideal, Bicentennial Design, Pint 2.00
Fruit Jar, Ball Ideal, Bicentennial Design, Quart 2.00
Fruit Jar, Ball Ideal, Blue, 1/2 Pint .... 8.00 To 14.00
Fruit Jar, Ball Ideal, Blue, Pint .... .70
Fruit Jar, Ball Ideal, Blue, Quart .... .70 To 1.00
Fruit Jar, Ball Ideal, Date, Aqua, Pint, T-3 .... 1.85 To 2.00
Fruit Jar, Ball Ideal, Date, Blue, 1/2 Pint, T-3 .... 9.00

Fruit Jar, **Ball Ideal,** Date, Blue, Pint .... 2.50 To 5.00
Fruit Jar, **Ball Ideal,** Date, Blue, Quart, T-3 .... 1.00 To 2.00
Fruit Jar, **Ball Ideal,** Date, Glass Lid, Aqua, 1/2 Gallon 5.00
Fruit Jar, **Ball Ideal,** Date, Glass Lid, Wire Bail, Aqua, Pint 3.50
Fruit Jar, **Ball Ideal,** Date, Glass Lid, Wire Bail, Aqua, Quart 3.00
Fruit Jar, **Ball Ideal,** Date, Glass Lid, Wire Bail, 1/2 Gallon, T-3 .... 3.50
Fruit Jar, **Ball Ideal,** Date, Quart, T-3 .... 1.00
Fruit Jar, **Ball Ideal,** Glass Lid, Wire Bail, Blue, 1/2 Gallon .... 3.00 To 5.00
Fruit Jar, **Ball Ideal,** Glass Lid, Wire Bail, Pint .... 1.00 To 2.50
Fruit Jar, **Ball Ideal,** Glass Lid, Wire Bail, Quart .... 1.00 To 2.00
Fruit Jar, **Ball Ideal,** Glass Lid, Wire Bail, 1/2 Gallon .... 2.50 To 3.00
Fruit Jar, **Ball Ideal,** 1/3 Pint 2.50
Fruit Jar, **Ball Ideal,** 1/2 Pint .... 1.00 To 2.50
Fruit Jar, **Ball Ideal,** 1/2 Gallon 2.75
Fruit Jar, **Ball Improved Mason,** Aqua, Quart 1.95
Fruit Jar, **Ball Improved Mason,** Patent Nov.30th, 1858, Pint 4.00
Fruit Jar, **Ball Improved Mason,** Patent Nov.30th, 1858, 1/2 Gallon 10.00
Fruit Jar, **Ball Improved Mason,** Quart 4.00
Fruit Jar, **Ball Improved,** Aqua, Quart 1.95
Fruit Jar, **Ball Improved,** Dark Aqua, Quart 3.00
Fruit Jar, **Ball Improved,** Glass Lid, Zinc Ring, Aqua, Quart 2.50
Fruit Jar, **Ball Improved,** Glass Lid, Zinc Ring, Light Green, Quart 2.50
Fruit Jar, **Ball Improved,** Glass Lid, Zinc Ring, Quart 2.50
Fruit Jar, **Ball Improved,** Quart 3.50
Fruit Jar, **Ball Improved,** Zinc Lid, Dark Aqua, Quart 4.00
Fruit Jar, **Ball Improved,** Zinc Lid, Pint 3.00
Fruit Jar, **Ball Imrpoved,** Glass Lid, Zinc Ring, Aqua, Quart 2.50
Fruit Jar, **Ball Imrpoved,** Quart 3.50
Fruit Jar, **Ball Improved,** 1/2 Gallon 5.00
Fruit Jar, **Ball Jar,** Mason's Patent Nov.30th, 1858, Aqua, 1/2 Gallon 6.00
Fruit Jar, **Ball Mason,** Amber Swirls, Emerald Green, Pint 69.00
Fruit Jar, **Ball Mason,** Aqua, Pint 1.50
Fruit Jar, **Ball Mason,** Aqua, Quart 1.00
Fruit Jar, **Ball Mason,** Aqua, 1/2 Gallon 1.50
Fruit Jar, **Ball Mason,** Bubbles, Smooth Lip, Green, Quart 2.50
Fruit Jar, **Ball Mason,** Deep Green, Pint 10.00
Fruit Jar, **Ball Mason,** Lime Green, 1/2 Gallon 9.00
Fruit Jar, **Ball Mason,** Patent Nov.30th, 1858, Aqua, Quart 5.00
Fruit Jar, **Ball Mason,** Patent Nov.30th, 1858, Pint 3.00
Fruit Jar, **Ball Mason,** Patent 1858, Smooth Lip, Aqua, Quart 3.00
Fruit Jar, **Ball Mason,** T05 On Base, Bubbles, Smooth Lip, Blue, Quart 2.50
Fruit Jar, **Ball Mason,** Zinc Cap, Aqua, 1/2 Gallon 2.50
Fruit Jar, **Ball Mason,** Zinc Cap, Dark Aqua, Quart 3.00
Fruit Jar, **Ball Mason's Patent 1858,** Aqua, Quart 5.00
Fruit Jar, **Ball Perfect Mason,** Amber, 1/2 Gallon .... 15.00 To 25.00
Fruit Jar, **Ball Perfect Mason,** Aqua, Pint 1.00
Fruit Jar, **Ball Perfect Mason,** Aqua, 1/2 Gallon 1.50
Fruit Jar, **Ball Perfect Mason,** Block Letters, Aqua, Quart 1.00
Fruit Jar, **Ball Perfect Mason,** Block Letters, Blue, Quart, T-4 .... 5.00
Fruit Jar, **Ball Perfect Mason,** Block Letters, Blue, 1/2 Gallon, T-4 .... 15.00
Fruit Jar, **Ball Perfect Mason,** Block Letters, Green, Pint, T-4 .... 5.00
Fruit Jar, **Ball Perfect Mason,** Blue, 1/2 Pint 13.00
Fruit Jar, **Ball Perfect Mason,** Blue, Pint 1.25
Fruit Jar, **Ball Perfect Mason,** Blue, Quart 1.25
Fruit Jar, **Ball Perfect Mason,** Emerald Green, Pint 9.50
Fruit Jar, **Ball Perfect Mason,** Green, Quart 10.00
Fruit Jar, **Ball Perfect Mason,** Olive Amber, Pint 50.00
Fruit Jar, **Ball Perfect Mason,** Olive Green, Quart 15.00
Fruit Jar, **Ball Perfect Mason,** Salt & Pepper, Zinc Lids, 1933, Pair 12.00
Fruit Jar, **Ball Perfect Mason,** Script, Zinc Lid, Apple Green, 1/2 Gallon 28.00
Fruit Jar, **Ball Perfect Mason,** Script, Zinc Lid, 1/2 Pint 2.50
Fruit Jar, **Ball Perfect Mason,** Zinc Cap, Aqua, 1/2 Gallon 2.00
Fruit Jar, **Ball Perfect Mason,** 1/2 Gallon .... *Illus* 20.00
Fruit Jar, **Ball Sanitary Sure Seal,** Blue, 1/2 Gallon 6.00
Fruit Jar, **Ball Special,** Blue, Pint 2.00

Fruit Jar, Ball Special, Blue, Quart 3.00
Fruit Jar, Ball Standard, Wax Sealer, Bubbles, Green, Quart 5.00
Fruit Jar, Ball Standard, 1/2 Gallon 15.00
Fruit Jar, Ball Sure Seal, Aqua, Quart 1.95
Fruit Jar, Ball Sure Seal, Aqua, 1/2 Gallon 3.95
Fruit Jar, Ball, Amber, 1/2 Gallon 25.00
Fruit Jar, Ball, Aqua, Pint 1.50
Fruit Jar, Ball, Aqua, Quart 1.00

Fruit Jar, Ball Perfect Mason, 1/2 Gallon
(See Page 115)

Fruit Jar, Clarke Co., Cleveland, O.
(See Page 117)

Fruit Jar, Ball, Aqua, 1/2 Gallon 1.50
Fruit Jar, Ball, Buffalo, 1976, Hand Blown, Amber, Quart 20.00
Fruit Jar, Ball, Deep Green, Quart 24.00
Fruit Jar, Ball, Triple L, Zinc Cap, Aqua, 1/2 Gallon, T-1 .... 2.50
Fruit Jar, Ball, Triple L, Zinc Cap, Light Green, 1/2 Gallon, T-1 .... 4.00
Fruit Jar, Ball, Triple L, Olive Amber, Quart, T-1 .... 30.00
Fruit Jar, Ball, Zinc Lid, Light Olive Green, Quart 11.00
Fruit Jar, Ball, 1/3 Pint 3.00
Fruit Jar, Ball, 1/2 Pint 2.00
Fruit Jar, Bamberger's Sure Seal, Aqua, Quart 13.00
Fruit Jar, Banner, Aqua, Pint 3.95
Fruit Jar, Banner, Aqua, Quart 3.95
Fruit Jar, Banner, Pint 5.00
Fruit Jar, Banner, Quart 5.00
Fruit Jar, Beaver, Aqua, 1/2 Gallon 22.00
Fruit Jar, Beaver, Embossed, Glass Lid, Metal Ring, 1/2 Gallon 22.00
Fruit Jar, Beaver, Midget 55.00
Fruit Jar, Beaver, Quart 18.00
Fruit Jar, Beaver, 5 On Base, Ground Mouth, Quart 23.00
Fruit Jar, Beaver, 12 On Base, Ground Lip, Quart 23.00
Fruit Jar, Beehive, Quart 95.00
Fruit Jar, Beehive, 1/2 Gallon 15.00
Fruit Jar, Bernardin, Latchford Marble Glass Co., Embossed, Quart 3.50
Fruit Jar, Best, Aqua, 1/2 Gallon 25.00
Fruit Jar, Bloeser, Aqua, Quart 100.00
Fruit Jar, Blue Ribbon, Glass Lid, 2 Side Clamps, Pint 10.00
Fruit Jar, Blue Ribbon, Glass Lid, 2 Side Clamps, Quart 7.50
Fruit Jar, Boldt Mason Jar, Pint 18.00
Fruit Jar, Boldt Mason, Aqua, Quart 11.00
Fruit Jar, Borden's Condensed Milk Co., Baby, Milk Glass Lid, 1/2 Pint 10.50
Fruit Jar, Boyd Mason, Genuine, Aqua, Quart 3.00
Fruit Jar, Boyd Perfect Mason, Block Letters, Green, Quart, T-3 .... 5.00
Fruit Jar, Boyd Perfect Mason, Blue, 1/2 Gallon 2.50
Fruit Jar, Boyd Mason, Genuine, Green, Pint 4.50
Fruit Jar, Boyd Mason, Genuine, Green, Quart 4.00
Fruit Jar, Boyd Mason, Genuine, Pint 2.00
Fruit Jar, Boyd Mason, Genuine, Zinc Lid, Aqua, Pint 4.50

Fruit Jar, **Boyd Mason,** Genuine, Zinc Lid, Aqua, Quart 4.50
Fruit Jar, **Boyd Mason,** Genuine, Zinc Lid, Aqua, 1/2 Gallon 5.00
Fruit Jar, **Boyd Perfect Mason,** Pint 3.00
Fruit Jar, **Boyd Perfect Mason,** Quart 2.00
Fruit Jar, **Brockway Clear-Vu Mason,** Pint 3.00
Fruit Jar, **Brockway Clear-Vu Mason,** Quart 2.50
Fruit Jar, **Brockway Sur-Grip Mason,** Pint 3.00
Fruit Jar, **Brockway Sur-Grip Mason,** Quart 3.00
Fruit Jar, **Brown & Co.,** Geo.D., Aqua, Quart 50.00
Fruit Jar, **C F J Co.,** Mason's Improved Patent, May 23rd, 1871, Aqua, Quart 10.00
Fruit Jar, **C F J Co.,** Mason's Improved, Aqua, Midget .... 8.00 To 10.00
Fruit Jar, **C F J Co.,** Mason's Improved, Aqua, Quart .... 2.50 To 3.95
Fruit Jar, **C F J Co.,** Mason's Improved, Aqua, 1/2 Gallon 2.00
Fruit Jar, **C F J Co.,** Mason's Improved, Clyde, N.Y., Aqua, Quart 4.00
Fruit Jar, **C F J Co.,** Mason's Improved, Clyde, N.Y., Midget 12.50
Fruit Jar, **C F J Co.,** Mason's Improved, Clyde, N.Y., Pint, T-2 .... 395.00
Fruit Jar, **C F J Co.,** Mason's Improved, Clyde, N.Y., Quart, T-2 .... 4.50
Fruit Jar, **C F J Co.,** Mason's Improved, Clyde, N.Y., Zinc Ring, Aqua, Pint, T-2 .... 5.00
Fruit Jar, **C F J Co.,** Mason's Improved, Cylde, N.Y., Zinc Ring, Aqua, Quart 4.50
Fruit Jar, **C F J Co.,** Mason's Improved, Glass Lid, Aqua, Midget .... 7.00 To 9.00
Fruit Jar, **C F J Co.,** Mason's Improved, Glass Lid, Zinc Ring, 1/2 Gallon 4.50
Fruit Jar, **C F J Co.,** Mason's Improved, Nov.30th, 1858, Quart, T-1 .... 1.95
Fruit Jar, **C F J Co.,** Mason's Improved, Quart .... 1.25 To 2.50
Fruit Jar, **C F J Co.,** Mason's Improved, Trademark, 1/2 Gallon 8.00
Fruit Jar, **C F J Co.,** Mason's Improved, Whittled, Zinc Lid, Midget 8.00
Fruit Jar, **C F J Co.,** Mason's Improved, Zinc Ring, Aqua, 1/2 Gallon 4.50
Fruit Jar, **C F J Co.,** Mason's Patent Nov.30th, 1858, Aqua, Quart, T-1 .... 6.00
Fruit Jar, **C F J Co.,** Mason's Patent Nov.30th, 1858, Aqua, 1/2 Gallon 10.00
Fruit Jar, **C F J Co.,** Mason's Patent Nov.30th, 1858, Blue, Quart 22.00
Fruit Jar, **C F J Co.,** Mason's Patent Nov.30th, 1858, Quart, T-1 .... 4.00
Fruit Jar, **C F J Co.,** Mason's Patent Nov.30th, 1858, Stain, Aqua, Quart 3.00
Fruit Jar, **C F J Co.,** Mason's Patent Nov.30th, 1858, Zinc Lid, Aqua, Midget 14.00
Fruit Jar, **C F J Co.,** Mason's Patent Nov.30th, 1858, 1/2 Gallon, T-1 .... 8.00
Fruit Jar, **C F J Co.,** Mason's Trademark, Cloudy, Aqua, Midget 12.00
Fruit Jar, **C F J Co.,** Mason's Trademark, Midget 15.00
Fruit Jar, **C.F.Spencer,** Lift Top, Quart, T-2 .... 80.00
Fruit Jar, **C.F.Spencer,** Quart 65.00
Fruit Jar, **C G Co.,** Quart .... 6.50 To 7.50
Fruit Jar, **C.S.& Co.,** 189, Wide Mouth, Applied Ring, Apple Green, Pint 14.00
Fruit Jar, **Canton Domestic,** Pint 90.00
Fruit Jar, **Canton Domestic,** Quart .... 25.00 To 55.00
Fruit Jar, **Canton Domestic,** 1/2 Gallon 55.00
Fruit Jar, **Chattanooga Mason,** 1/2 Gallon 6.50
Fruit Jar, **Chef,** Embossed Face, Quart 2.00
Fruit Jar, **Chef,** Quart .... 3.95 To 4.00
Fruit Jar, **Christmas Mason,** Aqua, Pint .... 45.00 To 50.00
Fruit Jar, **Christmas Mason,** Ball On Reverse, Aqua, Pint 50.00
Fruit Jar, **Clark's Peerless In Circle,** Glass Lid, Wire Bail, Aqua, Quart, T-4 .... 11.00
Fruit Jar, **Clark's Peerless,** Aqua, Quart .... 5.95 To 8.50
Fruit Jar, **Clark's Peerless,** Glass Lid, Wire Bail, Cornflower, 1/2 Gallon 18.00
Fruit Jar, **Clark's Peerless,** Pint .... 8.00 To 15.00
Fruit Jar, **Clark's Peerless,** Quart 10.00
Fruit Jar, **Clarke Co.,** Cleveland, O. .... *Illus*   25.00
Fruit Jar, **Clarke,** Aqua, Pint 75.00
Fruit Jar, **Clarke,** Aqua, Quart 45.00
Fruit Jar, **Clarke,** Aqua, 1/2 Gallon 45.00
Fruit Jar, **Clarke,** Cleveland, Grasshopper-Type Clamp, Aqua, Quart 47.00
Fruit Jar, **Clarke,** Cleveland, Grasshopper-Type Clamp, Aqua, 1/2 Gallon 52.00
Fruit Jar, **Clyde Improved Mason,** Pint, T-4 .... 8.00
Fruit Jar, **Clyde Improved Mason,** Quart, T-4 .... 8.00
Fruit Jar, **Clyde,** The, Pint .... 4.00 To 5.50
Fruit Jar, **Clyde,** The, Quart 4.00
Fruit Jar, **Clyde,** The, Script, Glass Lid, Wire Bail, Ground Lip, Pint, T-3 .... 14.00
Fruit Jar, **Clyde,** The, Script, Glass Lid, Wire Bail, Ground Lip, Quart, T-3 .... 12.00
Fruit Jar, **Cohansey Glass MFG 4 On Base,** Aqua, Pint, T-5 .... 42.00

Fruit Jar, Cohansey Jelly, 1877 On Base, Pint, T-5 .... 46.00
Fruit Jar, Cohansey, Aqua, Quart .... 12.00 To 19.00
Fruit Jar, Cohansey, Aqua, 1/2 Gallon 14.00
Fruit Jar, Cohansey, Barrel, Aqua, Quart, T-3 .... 110.00
Fruit Jar, Cohansey, Barrel, Glass Lid, Clamp, Quart, T-3 .... 116.00
Fruit Jar, Cohansey, Embossed Front, 1/2 Pint 50.00
Fruit Jar, Cohansey, Glass Lid, Wire Clamp, Green Aqua, 1/2 Gallon 22.00
Fruit Jar, Cohansey, Jelly Glass Type, Tin Lid, Aqua, Pint 50.00
Fruit Jar, Cohansey, Jelly, Tin Lid, Pint 50.00
Fruit Jar, Cohansey, Pint .... 20.00 To 25.00
Fruit Jar, Cohansey, Quart .... 12.00 To 22.50
Fruit Jar, Cohansey, 1/2 Gallon .... 12.00 To 22.50
Fruit Jar, Cohansey, Wax Sealer, Barrel, Glass Lid, Aqua, Quart, T-5 .... 95.00
Fruit Jar, Cohansey, 1877, Barrel, Metal Lid, Aqua, 1/2 Gallon, T-5 .... 85.00
Fruit Jar, Columbia, Aqua, Quart 20.00
Fruit Jar, Conserve Jar, Aqua, Pint 6.00
Fruit Jar, Conserve Jar, Pint .... 5.00 To 6.00
Fruit Jar, Crown Cordial & Extract, 1/2 Gallon 3.95
Fruit Jar, Crown Mason, Porcelain-Lined Zinc Lid, Pint 3.50
Fruit Jar, Crown Mason, Porcelain-Lined Zinc Lid, Quart 2.50
Fruit Jar, Crown, Aqua, Imperial Quart 4.00
Fruit Jar, Crown, Aqua, Midget 14.95
Fruit Jar, Crown, Aqua, Quart 3.00
Fruit Jar, Crown, Aqua, 1/2 Gallon 4.00
Fruit Jar, Crown, Embossed, Glass Lid, Metal Ring, Aqua, Imperial Pint 5.00
Fruit Jar, Crown, Embossed, Glass Lid, Metal Ring, Aqua, Imperial Quart 5.00
Fruit Jar, Crown, Embossed, Glass Lid, Metal Ring, Aqua, Pint 5.00
Fruit Jar, Crown, Embossed, Glass Lid, Metal Ring, Aqua, Quart 5.00
Fruit Jar, Crown, Ground Mouth, Midget 8.00
Fruit Jar, Crown, Imperial, Midget .... 7.00 To 15.00
Fruit Jar, Crown, Made In Canada, Quart 4.00
Fruit Jar, Crown, Made In Canada, Zinc Screw Band, Quart 2.50
Fruit Jar, Crown, Midget .... 6.00 To 20.00
Fruit Jar, Crystal Jar, Quart 26.00
Fruit Jar, Crystal Jar, 1/2 Gallon .... 24.00 To 32.50
Fruit Jar, Cunningham & Ihmsen, 1/2 Gallon 20.00
Fruit Jar, Curtis & Moore, Boston, Lightning Closure, Aqua, 1/2 Gallon 16.00
Fruit Jar, Dandy, The, Amber, 1/2 Gallon 95.00
Fruit Jar, Dandy, The, Light Golden Amber, Quart 90.00
Fruit Jar, Dandy, The, Pale Straw Color, Quart 125.00
Fruit Jar, Dandy, The, Stain, Amber, 1/2 Gallon 75.00
Fruit Jar, Dandy, The, 1/2 Gallon 81.00
Fruit Jar, Darling Improved, Midget 100.00
Fruit Jar, Darling, The, Monogram, Aqua, Quart 34.00
Fruit Jar, Dexter, 1/2 Gallon 18.00
Fruit Jar, Diamond, Midget 55.00
Fruit Jar, Diamond, Quart 4.00
Fruit Jar, Dictator, D.I.Holcomb 12/14/1869, Tin Lid, Aqua, Quart 52.75
Fruit Jar, Doolittle, Midget 85.00
Fruit Jar, Doolittle, Pint 20.00
Fruit Jar, Double Safety, Aqua, 1/2 Pint 7.00
Fruit Jar, Double Safety, Glass Lid, Wire Bail, Pint 4.00
Fruit Jar, Double Safety, Glass Lid, Wire Bail, 1/2 Gallon 6.00
Fruit Jar, Double Safety, 1/2 Pint 5.75
Fruit Jar, Double Safety, Pint .... 1.00 To 3.00
Fruit Jar, Double Safety, Quart .... 1.00 To 3.00
Fruit Jar, Double Safety, S K O Base, Pint, T-4 .... 4.00 To 5.00
Fruit Jar, Double Safety, S K O Base, Quart, T-4 .... 4.00
Fruit Jar, Double Safety, Script, Bubbles, Glass Lid, Wire Bail, 1/2 Pint 5.50
Fruit Jar, Drey Ever Seal, Glass Lid, Wire Bail, Pint .... 1.00 To 3.00
Fruit Jar, Drey Improved Ever Seal, Glass Lid, Wire Bail, Pint, T-2 .... 3.00
Fruit Jar, Drey Improved Ever Seal, Glass Lid, Wire Bail, Quart, T-2 .... 2.50
Fruit Jar, Drey Perfect Mason, Quart 1.00
Fruit Jar, Drey Square Mason, Carpenter's Square, Quart 2.00
Fruit Jar, Drey Square Mason, Pint 3.00

Fruit Jar, Dur-Seal, Quart 4.00
Fruit Jar, E G Co., Imperial, Aqua, Midget 38.50
Fruit Jar, E G Co., Imperial, Aqua, 1/2 Gallon 17.50
Fruit Jar, E G Co., Imperial, Excelsior, Quebec, 1878, Green, 1/2 Gallon 35.00
Fruit Jar, E G Co., Imperial, Quart 15.00
Fruit Jar, E G Co., Imperial, 1/2 Gallon 25.00
Fruit Jar, E G Co., Aqua, Midget 29.95
Fruit Jar, E G Co., Aqua, Quart 19.95
Fruit Jar, E G Co., Midget 25.00
Fruit Jar, Eagle, Aqua, 1/2 Gallon 75.00
Fruit Jar, Eagle, Whittled, Quart 65.00
Fruit Jar, Economy, Lid & Clip, Pint 3.50
Fruit Jar, Economy, Trademark, June 9 & 23, 1903 On Base, Amethyst, Quart, T-2 .... 7.00
Fruit Jar, Economy Trademark, Kerr Mfg.Co. On Base, Tin Lid, Pint 5.50
Fruit Jar, Economy, Trademark, Kerr Mfg.Co. On Base, Turning Purple, Quart 6.00
Fruit Jar, Economy, Trademark, Kerr, 1903, Sun-Colored Amethyst, 1/2 Gallon 16.00
Fruit Jar, Economy, Trademark, Patent June 9, 1909 On Base, Amethyst, Quart 6.00
Fruit Jar, Economy, Trademark, Portland, Oregon, Amethyst To Clear, Quart, T-1 .... 3.00
Fruit Jar, Electric, Trademark, Aqua, Quart .... 8.50 To 9.75
Fruit Jar, Electric, World Globe, Aqua, Quart 60.00
Fruit Jar, Empire, In Stippled Cross In Frame, Pint, T-2 .... 2.50 To 7.50
Fruit Jar, Empire, In Stippled Cross In Frame, Quart, T-2 .... 7.50
Fruit Jar, Empire, 1/2 Pint 4.50
Fruit Jar, Empire, Pint 4.00
Fruit Jar, Empire, Quart .... 4.00 To 17.00
Fruit Jar, Empire, 1/2 Gallon 8.50
Fruit Jar, Eureka, Quart 6.00
Fruit Jar, Everlasting Improved In Circle, Turning Purple, Quart 10.00
Fruit Jar, Everlasting Improved, Quart 16.00
Fruit Jar, Everlasting Jar, Aqua, Quart 15.00
Fruit Jar, Everlasting Jar, Quart 16.00
Fruit Jar, Excelsior Improved, Whittled, Aqua, Quart .... 38.00 To 58.00
Fruit Jar, F & S, Pint 8.00
Fruit Jar, F A & Co. On Base, IP, Aqua, 1/2 Gallon 125.00
Fruit Jar, F A & Co. On Base, Whittled, Cork Type Top, IP, 1 1/2 Pint 125.00

Fruit Jar, Flaccus
Bros.Steer's Head,
Amber, 6 In.
(See Page 120)

Fruit Jar, Flaccus
Bros.Table Delicacies,
Pint

Fruit Jar, Flaccus Co.,
E.C., Steer's Head,
Green, 6 1/2 In.

Fruit Jar, Flaccus
Co., E.C., Steer
Head, 7 In.
(See Page 120)

Fruit Jar, Faxon Buffalo, Aqua, Quart 14.50
Fruit Jar, FCG Co. 7, SK & Co. On Base, Aqua, 1/2 Gallon 16.00
Fruit Jar, Federal, Quart 85.00
Fruit Jar, Fink & Nasse, St.Louis, Aqua, Quart 56.00
Fruit Jar, Flaccus Bros.Steers Head, Amber, 6 In ....*Illus* 300.00
Fruit Jar, Flaccus Bros.Table Delicacies, Pint ....*Illus* 75.00
Fruit Jar, Flaccus Co., E.C., Steer's Head, Flowers & Berries, Pint 40.00
Fruit Jar, Flaccus Co., E.C., Steer's Head, Green, 6 1/2 In. ....*Illus* 300.00
Fruit Jar, Flaccus Co., E.C., Steer's Head, Pint 40.00
Ftuit Jar, Flaccus Co., E.C., Steer's Head, Simplex Lid, Pint 37.00
Fruit Jar, Flaccus Co., E.C., Steer's Head, Threaded Lid, Honey Amber, Pint 250.00
Fruit Jar, Flaccus Co., E.C., Steer's Head, Threaded Lid, Square, 2/3 Pint 75.00
Fruit Jar, Flaccus Co., E.C., Steer's Head, Threaded Lid, Square, Pint 75.00
Fruit Jar, Flaccus Co., E.C., Steer's Head, 7 In. ....*Illus* 65.00
    Fruit Jar, Foster, see Fruit Jar, Sealfast Foster
Fruit Jar, Franklin-Dexter, Quart .... 25.00 To 32.00
Fruit Jar, Franklin-Dexter, 1/2 Gallon 25.00
Fruit Jar, Franklin, Burst Bubble, Aqua, Quart 29.95
Fruit Jar, Fruit Growers Trade Co., Stain, Aqua, Quart 40.00
Fruit Jar, Fruit-Keeper, Aqua, Pint 32.00
Fruit Jar, Fruit-Keeper, Aqua, Quart 25.00
Fruit Jar, Fruit-Keeper, C G Co, Apple Green, Quart 29.00
Fruit Jar, Fruit-Keeper, C G Co, Stain, Apple Green, 1/2 Gallon 30.00
Fruit Jar, Fruit-Keeper, Monogram, Aqua, Quart 22.00
Fruit Jar, Fruit-Keeper, Pint ....*Illus* 32.00
Fruit Jar, Fruit-Keeper, Quart 25.00
Fruit Jar, G J, Aqua, Quart 23.00
Fruit Jar, G J, 1/2 Gallon 27.00
Fruit Jar, G J, Gilchrist Jar, Aqua, Quart 28.50
Fruit Jar, G W Weston & Co, Saratoga, N.Y., Bruise, Olive Amber, Quart .... * 400.00
Fruit Jar, Gayner, The, Glass Top, Pint ....*Illus* 1.50
Fruit Jar, Gayner, The, Glass Top, Quart .... 4.00 To 5.00
Fruit Jar, Gem Improved, Green, 1/2 Gallon 8.00
Fruit Jar, Gem Improved, Made In Canada, Clear Lid, Olive Green, Quart 20.00
Fruit Jar, Gem Improved, Made In Canada, Olive Green, Quart 24.00
Fruit Jar, Gem Improved, Made In Canada, Pint 2.50
Fruit Jar, Gem, Aqua, Midget 21.00
Fruit Jar, Gem, Aqua, Quart 8.50
Fruit Jar, Gem, Cloudy, Aqua, Midget 17.00
Fruit Jar, Gem, Cross, Aqua, Quart .... 7.50 To 10.00
Fruit Jar, Gem, Cross, Midget 30.00
Fruit Jar, Gem, Cross, 1/2 Gallon 8.00
Fruit Jar, Gem, Midget 20.00
Fruit Jar, Gem, Quart .... 5.00 To 6.00
Fruit Jar, Gem, The, Aqua, Quart 5.95
Fruit Jar, Gem, The, C F J Monogram, Aqua, Midget, T-9 .... 55.00
Fruit Jar, Gem, The, C F J Monogram, Aqua, Quart, T-9 .... 8.95
Fruit Jar, Gem, The, Dated Base, Aqua, Quart 5.00
Fruit Jar, Gem, The, HGW, 1/2 Gallon 12.00
Fruit Jar, Gem, The, Hourglass, Aqua, Quart, T-10 .... 11.75
Fruit Jar, Gem, The, Quart .... 5.95 To 8.50
Fruit Jar, Gem, The, 1 1/2 Quart 12.00
Fruit Jar, Gem, The, 1/2 Gallon .... 5.95 To 10.00
Fruit Jar, Genuine Mason, Arched, Aqua, Pint 7.95
Fruit Jar, Genuine Mason, Blue, Pint 8.50
Fruit Jar, Genuine Mason, Green, Pint 7.75
Fruit Jar, Genuine Mason, Zinc Lid, Aqua, Pint 9.50
Fruit Jar, Gilberds Jar, Star, Pint 150.00
Fruit Jar, Gilberos Improved, Quart 75.00
    Fruit Jar, Gilchrist, see Fruit Jar, G J
Fruit Jar, Glassboro Improved, Quart 12.00
Fruit Jar, Globe, Amber, Pint 65.00
Fruit Jar, Globe, Amber, Quart .... 28.00 To 40.00
Fruit Jar, Globe, Amber, 1/2 Gallon 30.00
Fruit Jar, Globe, Aqua, Pint 18.00

Fruit Jar, **Globe,** Aqua, Quart .... 8.00 To 12.00
Fruit Jar, **Globe,** Aqua, 1/2 Gallon 12.00
Fruit Jar, **Globe,** Glass Lid, Wire Clamp, Aqua, Quart 12.50
Fruit Jar, **Globe,** Haze, Amber, 1/2 Gallon 27.00
Fruit Jar, **Globe,** Light Aqua, Pint 35.00
Fruit Jar, **Globe,** Pint .... 13.00 To 17.00
Fruit Jar, **Globe,** 77 On Base, Wire Holder, Yellow Amber, Quart 35.00

Fruit Jar, Fruit-Keeper, Pint
(See Page 120)

Fruit Jar, Gayner, The, Glass Top, Pint
(See Page 120)

Fruit Jar, **Globe,** 1886, Glass Top, Quart 18.00
Fruit Jar, **Golden State,** Quart 10.00
Fruit Jar, **Golden State,** 1/2 Gallon .... 10.00 To 14.00
Fruit Jar, **Golden Tree Brand Syrup,** New England Maple Syrup Co., 20 Ozs. 14.75
Fruit Jar, **Good Housekeepers,** Cobalt, Quart 18.00
Fruit Jar, **Good Housekeepers Regular Mason,** Pint 2.50
Fruit Jar, **Good Housekeepers Regular Mason,** Quart 1.50
Fruit Jar, **Good Luck,** Pint .... 2.50 To 4.00
Fruit Jar, **Good Luck,** Quart .... 2.50 To 4.00
Fruit Jar, **Green Mountain,** Pint 5.95
Fruit Jar, **Green Mountain,** Quart 5.95
Fruit Jar, **Griffen,** 1 1/2 Quart 110.00
Fruit Jar, **Griffen,** 1/2 Gallon 90.00
Fruit Jar, **H.H.Zigler,** Pottery, Olive Glaze, 8 In. 17.50
Fruit Jar, **Hahne & Co.,** Newark, N.J., Embossed Star Reverse, Aqua, Pint 20.00
Fruit Jar, **Haines's,** Aqua, Quart 70.00
Fruit Jar, **Hamilton,** Quart 35.00
     Fruit Jar, **Hansee's, see Fruit Jar, Home Palace, Hansee's**
Fruit Jar, **Hartell's Air Tight,** 1/2 Gallon 50.00
Fruit Jar, **Hazard & Co.,** Shrewsberry, Quart 12.00
Fruit Jar, **Hazel Atlas E-Z Seal,** Glass Lid, Aqua, Pint 7.50
Fruit Jar, **Hazel Atlas,** Quart 8.00
Fruit Jar, **Hazel HA Preserve Jar,** Aqua, 1/2 Pint 8.00
Fruit Jar, **Hazel HA Preserve Jar,** Quart 4.50
Fruit Jar, **Hazel,** Embossed On Milk Glass Lid, Zinc Band, Amber, Quart 75.00
Fruit Jar, **Hero Cross,** Aqua, Quart 17.00
Fruit Jar, **Hero Cross,** Mason's Improved, Aqua, Quart .... 2.50 To 2.95
Fruit Jar, **Hero Cross,** Mason's Improved, Aqua, 1/2 Gallon 2.95
Fruit Jar, **Hero Cross,** Mason's Improved, Glass Lid, Aqua, Midget 9.00
Fruit Jar, **Hero Cross,** Mason's Improved, Midget 13.00
Fruit Jar, **Hero Cross,** Mason's Improved, Pint 2.75
Fruit Jar, **Hero Cross,** Mason's Improved, Quart .... 1.25 To 2.75
Fruit Jar, **Hero Cross,** Mason's Patent Nov.30th, 1858, Amber, Pint 60.00
Fruit Jar, **Hero Cross,** Mason's Patent Nov.30th, 1858, Amber, Quart 75.00
Fruit Jar, **Hero Cross,** Mason's Patent Nov.30th, 1858, Amber, 1/2 Gallon 65.00
Fruit Jar, **Hero Cross,** Mason's Patent Nov.30th, 1858, Apple Green Midget 150.00

Fruit Jar, Hero Cross, Mason's Patent Nov.30th, 1858, Apple Green, Quart 29.00
Fruit Jar, Hero Cross, Mason's Patent Nov.30th, 1858, Aqua, Quart 2.95
Fruit Jar, Hero Cross, Mason's Patent Nov.30th, 1858, Midget .... 7.50 To 11.00
Fruit Jar, Hero Cross, Mason's Patent Nov.30th, 1858, Quart 5.00
Fruit Jar, Hero Cross, Mason's Patent Nov.30th. 1858. 1/2 Gallon 5.50
Fruit Jar, Hero Cross, Quart 27.00
Fruit Jar, Hero Improved, Aqua, Quart 19.95
Fruit Jar, Hero, The, Cloudy, Quart 19.00
Fruit Jar, Hero, The, Quart 15.00
Fruit Jar, Hero, The, 1/2 Gallon 15.00
Fruit Jar, Hero, The, Gallon 350.00
Fruit Jar, Heroine, The, Aqua, Quart 18.00
Fruit Jar, Heroine, The, Aqua, 1/2 Gallon 25.00
Fruit Jar, Heroine, The, Cunninghams & Ihmsen, Pittsburgh, Aqua, 1/2 Gallon 25.00
Fruit Jar, Heroine, The, Quart 20.00
Fruit Jar, Home Palace, Hansee's, Pint 65.00
Fruit Jar, Home Palace, Hansee's, 1/2 Gallon 50.00
Fruit Jar, Honest Mason Jar, Patent 1858, Pint 15.00
Fruit Jar, Honest Mason, Patent 1858, Quart 12.00
Fruit Jar, Howe Jar, The, Pint 50.00
Fruit Jar, Howe, The, Scranton, Pa., Amethyst, Quart 45.00
Fruit Jar, I G Co., Aqua, Quart 11.00
Fruit Jar, Ideal, The, Midget 58.00
Fruit Jar, Independent, Purple, Quart 25.00
Fruit Jar, Ivanhoe, Pint 1.95
Fruit Jar J & B Fruit Jar, Aqua, Pint .... 32.00 To 40.00
Fruit Jar, J & B Fruit Jar, Pint 32.00
Fruit Jar, J & B Fruit Jar, Quart 40.00
Fruit Jar, J.J.Squire, Pat'd Oct. 1864 & 1865, Damaged, Aqua, Quart .... * 190.00
Fruit Jar, J.M.Clark, Louisville, Ky., Amber, Quart 15.00
Fruit Jar, Jas.Hamilton & Co., Greensboro, Pa. In Shield, Stoneware, 8 In. 40.00
Fruit Jar, Jeanette Home Packer, J.Mason, Quart .... 1.75 To 3.00
Fruit Jar, Johnson & Johnson, Labels, Contents, Amber, 1/2 Pint 15.00
Fruit Jar, Johnson & Johnson, Zinc Band, Cobalt, Quart 115.00
Fruit Jar, K On Base, Aqua, 1/2 Gallon 6.00
Fruit Jar, Kerr Economy, Trademark, Turning Purple, 1/2 Gallon 2.00
Fruit Jar, Kerr Economy, Trademark, Wire Clamp, Green Tinge, Pint 5.50
Fruit Jar, Kerr Glass Top Mason, Pint 2.50
Fruit Jar, Kerr Glass Top Mason, Quart 2.00
Fruit Jar, Kerr Self Sealing Mason, Amber, Quart .... 7.00 To 9.00
Fruit Jar, Kerr Self Sealing Mason, Cobalt Streak, Aqua, Quart 12.00
Fruit Jar, Kerr Self Sealing Mason, Glass Lid, Aqua, 1/2 Pint 2.50
Fruit Jar, Kerr Self Sealing Mason, Instant Coffee, Pint 2.00
Fruit Jar, Kerr Self Sealing Mason, Instant Coffee, Quart 3.00
Fruit Jar, Kerr Self Sealing Mason, Patent Aug.31st, 1915, Pint, T-5 .... 3.00
Fruit Jar, Kerr Self Sealing Mason, Patent Aug.31st, 1915, Quart, T-5 .... 2.50
Fruit Jar, Kerr Self Sealing Mason, Patent Aug.31st, 1915, 1/2 Gallon, T-5 .... 3.00
Fruit Jar, Kerr Self Sealing Mason, Patent, 2-Piece Lid, Quart 3.00
Fruit Jar, Kerr Self Sealing Mason, Zinc Lid, 1/2 Pint 2.00
Fruit Jar, Kerr Self Sealing Mason, 65th Anniversary, Blue Stread, Quart 14.00
Fruit Jar, Kerr Self Sealing Mason, 65th Anniversary, Cobalt Streak, Quart 12.50
Fruit Jar, Kerr Self Sealing Mason, 65th Anniversary, Gold Paint, Quart 22.00
Fruit Jar, Kerr Self Sealing Mason, 65th Anniversary, Green Streak, Quart 10.00
Fruit Jar, Kerr Self Sealing Mason, 65th Anniversary, 1903-1968, Quart 16.00
Fruit Jar, Keystone, Pint 6.00
Fruit Jar, Keystone, Quart 6.00
Fruit Jar, Kilner Jar, The, Pint 10.00
Fruit Jar, King, Head, Pint, T-2 .... 10.00
Fruit Jar, King, On Banner Below Crown, Amber, 1/2 Pint, T-1 .... 15.00
Fruit Jar, King, On Banner Below Crown, Amber, Pint, T-1 .... 10.00
Fruit Jar, King, On Banner Below Crown, Amber, Quart, T-1 .... 10.00
Fruit Jar, Kinsella 1874 True Mason, Quart 6.00
Fruit Jar, Kivlan & Onthank, 1/2 Pint 7.50
Fruit Jar, Kline, A.R., Glass Stopper, Inside Haze, Quart 100.00
Fruit Jar, Kline, A.R., Improved, Aqua, Quart 30.00

Fruit Jar, Knowlton Vacuum, Aqua, Pint .... 13.00 To 22.00
Fruit Jar, Knowlton Vacuum, Star, Aqua, Quart 18.00
Fruit Jar, Knowlton Vacuum, Star, Patent May 1903, Cornflower Blue, Quart 28.00
Fruit Jar, Knowlton Vacuum, Star, 6 Holes In Top, Cornflower, 1/2 Gallon 33.00
Fruit Jar, Knox Mason, K, Metal Band With Tin Insert, 1/2 Pint 5.50

Fruit Jar, Lafayette, Patent
1884 & 1885, Aqua, 10 1/2 In.

Fruit Jar, Lightning, Pint

Fruit Jar, Knox Mason, K, Square, Pint, T-2 .... 3.00
Fruit Jar, Knox Mason, K, Square, Quart, T-2 .... 2.50
Fruit Jar, L G W, Mason's Improved, Pint .... 6.00 To 9.95
Fruit Jar, L G W, Mason's Improved, Quart 6.00
Fruit Jar, Lafayette, Aqua, Quart .... 68.00 To 70.00
Fruit Jar, Lafayette, Aqua, 1/2 Gallon 80.00
Fruit Jar, Lafayette, Patent 1884 & 1885, Aqua, 10 1/2 In. .... *Illus* 70.00
Fruit Jar, Lafayette, Portrait, Bubbles, Green, 7 1/4 In., T-4 .... 45.00
Fruit Jar, Lafayette, Quart 68.00
Fruit Jar, Lamb Mason, Pint 1.00
Fruit Jar, Lamb Mason, Quart 4.00
Fruit Jar, Leader, The, Amber, Quart .... 65.00 To 75.00
Fruit Jar, Leader, The, Aqua, Quart 36.00
Fruit Jar, Leader, The, Bubbles, Honey Amber, Quart 85.00
Fruit Jar, Leader, The, Honey Amber, 1/2 Gallon 95.00
Fruit Jar, Leader, The, Pint 35.00
Fruit Jar, Leotric, Aqua, Pint 3.95
Fruit Jar, Leotric, Aqua, Quart 3.95
Fruit Jar, Leotric, Aqua, 1/2 Gallon 10.95
Fruit Jar, Leotric, In Circle, D C 4 On Base, Green, Quart, T-1 .... 11.50
Fruit Jar, Leotric, Pint 5.00
Fruit Jar, Leotric, Quart .... 3.95 To 5.00
Fruit Jar, Leotric, Salem, J. On Base, Green, Quart 10.50
Fruit Jar, Leotric, 1/2 Gallon 9.95
Fruit Jar, Lightning, Amber, Pint .... 43.00 To 44.00
Fruit Jar, Lightning, Amber, Quart .... 25.00 To 28.00
Fruit Jar, Lightning, Amber, 1/2 Gallon .... 24.00 To 35.00
Fruit Jar, Lightning, Aqua, Pint 2.50
Fruit Jar, Lightning, Aqua, Quart .... 2.50 To 3.95
Fruit Jar, Lightning, Golden Amber, Quart 25.00
Fruit Jar, Lightning, Honey Amber, 1/2 Gallon 28.00
Fruit Jar, Lightning, Pint .... *Illus* 5.00
Fruit Jar, Lightning, Pint .... 2.00 To 6.00
Fruit Jar, Lightning, Quart 2.00
Fruit Jar, Lightning, Trademark, Amber, Quart 22.50
Fruit Jar, Lightning, Trademark, Aqua, Pint 1.00
Fruit Jar, Lightning, Trademark, Aqua, Quart 1.00
Fruit Jar, Lightning, Trademark, Cornflower Blue, Quart 25.00
Fruit Jar, Lightning, Trademark, Glass Lid, Aqua, Quart, T-2 .... 2.75
Fruit Jar, Lightning, Trademark, Glass Lid, Quart 2.75
Fruit Jar, Lightning, Trademark, Ground Top, Aqua, Pint 1.00

Fruit Jar,
Liverpool, 6 1/2 In.

Fruit Jar, Ludlow Patent,
Aqua, 6 In.

Fruit Jar, Mason's Patent
Nov.30th, 1858, Amber,
1/2 Gallon
(See Page 125)

Fruit Jar, Lightning, Trademark, Ground Top, Aqua, Quart	1.00
Fruit Jar, Lightning, Trademark, Pint	.75
Fruit Jar, Lightning, Trademark, Quart	.75
Fruit Jar, Lightning, Trademark, Putnam On Base, Aqua, 1/2 Pint	5.50
Fruit Jar, Lightning, Trademark, Putnam On Base, Blue Aqua, Pint	6.00
Fruit Jar, Lightning, Trademark, Putnam 6 On Base, Aqua, Pint	7.50
Fruit Jar, Lightning, Trademark, Putnam 34 On Base, Apr 25 82, Green, Quart	25.00
Fruit Jar, Lightning, Trademark, Putnam 107 On Base, Bubbles, Blue, Pint	7.50
Fruit Jar, Lightning, Trademark, Putnam 286 On Base, 1/2 Gallon	9.00
Fruit Jar, Lightning, Trademark, Putnam 328 On Base, Amber, Quart	42.00
Fruit Jar, Lightning, Trademark, Putnam 372 On Base, Aqua, 1/2 Gallon	8.00
Fruit Jar, Lightning, Trademark, Putnam 458 On Base, Blue Aqua, Pint	475.00
Fruit Jar, Lightning, Trademark, Putnam 780 On Base, Aqua, Pint	7.50
Fruit Jar, Lightning, Trademark, Putnam 835 On Base, Aqua, Quart	275.00
Fruit Jar, Lightning, Trademark, Wide Mouth, Glass Lid, Wire Bail, Pint	3.00
Fruit Jar, Lightning, Trademark, Wide Mouth, Glass Lid, Wire Bail, Quart	2.50
Fruit Jar, Liverpool, 6 1/2 In. .... *Illus*	30.00
Fruit Jar, Lockport Mason, Aqua, Quart	2.50
Fruit Jar, Lockport Mason, Aqua, 1/2 Gallon	11.00
Fruit Jar, Lockport Mason, Quart	4.00
Fruit Jar, Ludlow Patent, Aqua, 6 In. .... *Illus*	600.00
Fruit Jar, Ludlow's, Aqua, Quart	110.00
Fruit Jar, Ludlow's, Citron Tint, Quart	100.00
Fruit Jar, Lustre, Aqua, Pint	3.95
Fruit Jar, Lustre, Aqua, Quart	3.95
Fruit Jar, Lustre, Pint	4.00
Fruit Jar, Lustre, Quart	5.00
Fruit Jar, Lustre, R.E.Tongue & Bros., Phila., Aqua, Quart, T-4	7.00
Fruit Jar, Lyman, W.W., Crimped Tin Lid, Pint	75.00
Fruit Jar, Lyman, W.W., Quart	40.00
Fruit Jar, Lyon & Bossard's Jar, East Stroudsburg, Pa., Whittled, Aqua, Quart	185.00
Fruit Jar, M G Co., Haze, Aqua, Quart	5.00
Fruit Jar, Macomb, 1899, Pottery, 1/2 Gallon	15.00
Fruit Jar, Magic Fruit Jar, Star, Honey Amber, 1/2 Gallon	300.00 To 400.00
Fruit Jar, Mansfield Improved Mason, Pint	5.00 To 12.50
Fruit Jar, Mansfield Improved Mason, Quart	10.00
Fruit Jar, Manufactured For J.T.Kinney, N.J., Klein Stopper, 1/2 Gallon	80.00
Fruit Jar, Marion, The, Aqua, Quart	8.00
Fruit Jar, Marion, The, Green, Quart	12.00
Fruit Jar, Marion, The, Pint	8.00
Fruit Jar, Mason Jar Of 1872, The, Aqua, Quart, T-2	20.00
Fruit Jar, Mason Jar Of 1872, The, Whitney Glass Works, Stain, Quart, T-1	16.00

Fruit Jar, Mason, Amber, Pint 35.00
Fruit Jar, Mason, Aqua, Pint 3.95
Fruit Jar, Mason, Bank, 1/4 Pint 12.00
Fruit Jar, Mason, Bicentennial, Liberty Bell, Quart 3.00
Fruit Jar, Mason, Block Letters, Amber, Pint .... 30.00 To 40.00
Fruit Jar, Mason, Block Letters, Dark Aqua, Quart 5.00
Fruit Jar, Mason, Block Letters, Smooth Lip, Amber, Pint 45.00
Fruit Jar, Mason, Curved, Deep Green, Pint 24.00
Fruit Jar, Mason, Curved, Deep Green, Quart .... 15.00 To 20.00
Fruit Jar, Mason, Curved, Deep Olive, Quart 50.00
Fruit Jar, Mason, Liberty Bell, 1776-1876, Pint 3.00
Fruit Jar, Mason, Liberty Bell, 1776-1876, Quart 3.00
Fruit Jar, Mason, Quart 4.50
Fruit Jar, Mason, Script, Amethyst To Clear, Quart, T-6 .... 5.00
Fruit Jar, Mason, Shoulder Seal, Zinc Lid, Green, 1/2 Gallon 29.00
Fruit Jar, Mason, Small Block Letters, Dark Aqua, Quart 5.00
Fruit Jar, Mason, The, Aqua, 1/2 Gallon 5.00
Fruit Jar, Mason, The, Quart 5.00
Fruit Jar, Mason, The, 1/2 Gallon 5.00
Fruit Jar, Mason, Zinc Lid, Pint 6.00
    Fruit Jar, Mason's C F J Co., see Fruit Jar, C F J Co.
    Fruit Jar, Mason's Cross, see Fruit Jar, Hero Cross
Fruit Jar, Mason's Fruit Jar, 1/2 Gallon, T-2 .... 5.00
Fruit Jar, Mason's Improved, Aqua, Quart 3.00
Fruit Jar, Mason's Improved, Clyde, N.Y., Pint 9.50
Fruit Jar, Mason's Improved, Clyde, N.Y., Quart 9.50
Fruit Jar, Mason's Improved, Monogram, Pint 10.00
Fruit Jar, Mason's Improved, Stain, Amber, Quart 50.00
Fruit Jar, Mason's Improved, 1/2 Gallon 9.00
Fruit Jar, Mason's Patent Nov.30th, 1858, Amber, 1/2 Gallon .... Illus 55.00
Fruit Jar, Mason's Patent Nov.30th, 1858, Aqua, Midget 10.00
Fruit Jar, Mason's Patent Nov.30th, 1858, Aqua, Quart 3.50
Fruit Jar, Mason's Patent Nov.30th, 1858, Aqua, 1/2 Gallon .... 2.00 To 7.00
Fruit Jar, Mason's Patent Nov.30th, 1858, Ball On Reverse, Aqua, Pint 5.00
Fruit Jar, Mason's Patent Nov.30th, 1858, Blue, 1/2 Gallon 10.00
Fruit Jar, Mason's Patent Nov.30th, 1858, Deep Blue, Quart 1.50
Fruit Jar, Mason's Patent Nov.30th, 1858, Deep Green, Quart 15.00
Fruit Jar, Mason's Patent Nov.30th, 1858, Glass Lid, Yellow, 1/2 Gallon 100.00
Fruit Jar, Mason's Patent Nov.30th, 1858, Green, Pint 5.00
Fruit Jar, Mason's Patent Nov.30th, 1858, Green, Quart 5.00
Fruit Jar, Mason's Patent Nov.30th, 1858, Green, 1/2 Gallon 8.00
Fruit Jar, Mason's Patent Nov.30th, 1858, Midget 12.00
Fruit Jar, Mason's Patent Nov.30th, 1858, Olive Green, Quart 18.00
Fruit Jar, Mason's Patent Nov.30th, 1858, Pint .... 4.50 To 5.00
Fruit Jar, Mason's Patent Nov.30th, 1858, Quart, T-7 .... 1.50 To 10.00
Fruit Jar, Mason's Patent Nov.30th, 1858, Smooth Lip, Deep Aqua, Quart 1.50
Fruit Jar, Mason's Patent Nov.30th, 1858, Snowflake On Back, Amethyst, Quart 39.00
Fruit Jar, Mason's Patent Nov.30th, 1858, Snowflake On Back, Aqua, Midget 110.00
Fruit Jar, Mason's Patent Nov.30th, 1858, Snowflake On Back, Quart 39.00
Fruit Jar, Mason's Patent Nov.30th, 1858, Star Base, Aqua, Midget 23.00
Fruit Jar, Mason's Patent Nov.30th, 1858, Snowflake, Lilac, 1/2 Gallon 55.00
Fruit Jar, Mason's Patent Nov.30th, 1858, Union Shield, 1/2 Gallon 100.00
Fruit Jar, Mason's Patent Nov.30th, 1858, Whittled, Green, Pint 575.00
Fruit Jar, Mason's Patent Nov.30th, 1858, Whittled, Vaseline, Pint 150.00
Fruit Jar, Mason's Patent Nov.30th, 1858, Whittled, Zinc Lid, Midget 8.00
Fruit Jar, Mason's Patent Nov.30th, 1858, With Letter N, Pint 5.00
Fruit Jar, Mason's Patent Nov.30th, 1858, Zinc Lid, Apple Green, 1/2 Gallon 12.00
Fruit Jar, Mason's Patent Nov.30th, 1858, Zinc Lid, Aqua, 1/2 Gallon 8.00
Fruit Jar, Mason's Patent Nov.30th, 1858, Zinc Lid, Cornflower, 1/2 Gallon 12.00
Fruit Jar, Mason's Patent Nov.30th, 1858, 1/2 Gallon .... 4.50 To 5.00
Fruit Jar, Mason's Patent Nov.30th, 1858, 12 In Base, Aqua, Quart 1.00
Fruit Jar, Mason's Patent Nov.30th, 1858, 72 On Base, Aqua, Quart 1.00
Fruit Jar, Mason's Patent Nov.30th, 1858, 183 On Base, Aqua, Quart 1.00
Fruit Jar, Matthias & Henderson, Cloudy, Aqua, Quart 28.00
Fruit Jar, McDonald New Perfect Seal, Blue, Pint .... 2.50 To 12.00

Fruit Jar, McDonald New Perfect Seal, Blue, Quart 2.00
Fruit Jar, McKee & Co., S., Pittsburgh, Pa., Wax Sealer, Aqua, Quart 15.00
Fruit Jar, Millville Atmospheric, Aqua, 1/2 Gallon 35.00
Fruit Jar, Millville Atmospheric, Pint 30.00
Fruit Jar, Millville Atmospheric, Quart .... 25.00 To 27.00
Fruit Jar, Millville Atmospheric, Whitall's Patent 1861, Crack, Aqua, Quart .... * 35.00
Fruit Jar, Millville Atmospheric, Whitehall's, 1861, 1/2 Gallon .... *Illus* 30.00
Fruit Jar, Millville Atmospheric, Whitall's, June 18, 1861, Aqua, Quart 28.00
Fruit Jar, Millville Atmospheric, Whitall's, June 18, 1861, Blue, Quart 30.00
Fruit Jar, Millville Atmospheric, Whittled, Dome Lid, 1/2 Gallon 75.00
Fruit Jar, Millville Atmospheric, 1/2 Pint 50.00
Fruit Jar, Millville Atmospheric, 1/2 Gallon 27.00
Fruit Jar, Millville Improved, Aqua, 1/2 Gallon 65.00
Fruit Jar, Millville Improved, C.W.T. Co. Monogram, Quart 45.00

Fruit Jar, Millville Atmospheric, Whitehall's, 1861, 1/2 Gallon

Fruit Jar, Protector, 7 In.
(See Page 127)

Fruit Jar, Millville, Aqua, 1/2 Pint 46.00
Fruit Jar, Millville, Aqua, Quart .... 16.00 To 22.00
Fruit Jar, Millville, Aqua, 1/2 Gallon 80.00
Fruit Jar, Millville, 1/2 Pint 40.00
Fruit Jar, Millville, Pint 25.00
Fruit Jar, Millville, Quart .... 15.00 To 25.00
Fruit Jar, Millville, Stain, Quart 10.00
Fruit Jar, Millville, 1/2 Gallon .... 18.00 To 28.00
Fruit Jar, Mission Mason, Aqua, Pint 6.00
Fruit Jar, Mission Mason, Aqua, Quart .... 5.00 To 7.00
Fruit Jar, Mission Mason, Aqua, 1/2 Gallon 12.50
Fruit Jar, Mission Mason, Pint .... 5.00 To 10.00
Fruit Jar, Mission Mason, Quart .... 3.00 To 10.00
Fruit Jar, Mission Mason, 1/2 Gallon 7.50
Fruit Jar, Model Mason, Quart 12.00
Fruit Jar, Moore & Co., John M., Patent Dec.3rd, 1861, Aqua, Quart 60.00
Fruit Jar, Moore & Co., John M., Patent Dec.3rd, 1861, 1/2 Gallon 75.00
Fruit Jar, Moore, John M., Fislerville, Whittled, 1/2 Gallon 110.00
Fruit Jar, Mountain Mason, Quart 15.00
Fruit Jar, Nu Seal, Smalley's Trademark, Quart 3.95
Fruit Jar, Ohio Quality Mason, Quart .... 10.00 To 11.00
Fruit Jar, Osotite, Light Aqua, Quart 40.00
Fruit Jar, Lorillard & Co., P., Amber, Pint 8.00
Fruit Jar, Lorillard & Co., P., Amber, Quart 5.00
Fruit Jar, Lorillard & Co., P., Dated Lid, Quart 3.50
Fruit Jar, Lorillard & Co., P., W.Helme Co. On Lid, 1872, Red Amber, Pint 14.25

Fruit Jar, Palace Home Jar, Hansee's, Quart 40.00
Fruit Jar, Patent June 9, 1860, Cincinnati, Ohio, Aqua, 1/2 Gallon 75.00
Fruit Jar, Patent Sept.18, 1860, Aqua, Quart 65.00
Fruit Jar, Patented Oct.19, 1858, Aqua, 1/2 Gallon 60.00
Fruit Jar, Pearl, The, Aqua, Quart 53.00
Fruit Jar, Pearl, The, Quart 40.00
Fruit Jar, Peoria, 1858, Pottery, Quart 12.50
Fruit Jar, Perfect Seal, Pint 2.75
Fruit Jar, Perfect Seal, Quart 2.75
Fruit Jar, Perfection Seal, Mar.29 1887, Wire Clamps, Quart 35.00
Fruit Jar, Pettit, Aqua, Pint 9.00
Fruit Jar, Pettit, Aqua, Quart 4.00
Fruit Jar, Pettit, Pint .... 6.00 To 9.50
Fruit Jar, Pettit, Quart 6.00
Fruit Jar, Pettit, Westville, N.J. On Base, Aqua, Pint, T-1 .... 9.00
Fruit Jar, Pettit, Westville, N.J., Glass Lid, Metal Clamp, Blue, Quart, T-1 .... 12.50
Fruit Jar, Philip Kabis Pottery, Unglazed, Olive, 5 1/2 In. 30.00
Fruit Jar, Porcelain Lined In Arch, Patent Nov.26, '67, Aqua, 1/2 Gallon 27.50
Fruit Jar, Potter & Bodine, Barrel Shape, Aqua, Quart 375.00
    Fruit Jar, Potter & Bodine, see also Fruit Jar, Airtight
Fruit Jar, Premium, Coffeyville, Kansas, Pint .... 22.00 To 22.50
Fruit Jar, Premium, Coffeyville, Kansas, Quart .... 17.00 To 18.00
Fruit Jar, Presto, Glass Top, Quart 1.95
Fruit Jar, Princess, Quart 10.00
Fruit Jar, Protector, Paneled, Aqua, Quart, T-2 .... 25.00
Fruit Jar, Protector, Quart, T-1 .... 40.00
Fruit Jar, Protector, 7 In. .... *Illus*   30.00
Fruit Jar, Puritan, The, Quart .... 125.00 To 200.00
Fruit Jar, Putman, Amber, Pint 41.00

Fruit Jar, Quick Seal, Pint
(See Page 128)

Fruit Jar, Safety Valve,
Patent May 21, 1895, 8 1/4 In.
(See Page 128)

Fruit Jar, Putman, On Base, Amber, Pint .... 35.00 To 41.00
Fruit Jar, Putman, On Base, Amber, Quart 20.00
Fruit Jar, Queen, Pint .... 1.65 To 2.00
Fruit Jar, Queen, Quart 1.50
Fruit Jar, Queen, S K O, Pint .... 1.25 To 1.50
Fruit Jar, Queen, S K O, Quart .... 1.25 To 1.95
Fruit Jar, Queen, The, Circle Of Dates, Aqua, Quart, T-1 .... 38.00
Fruit Jar, Queen, The, Green, 1/2 Gallon 45.00
Fruit Jar, Queen, The, Light Green, 1/2 Gallon 40.00
Fruit Jar, Queen, The, Quart .... 10.00 To 15.00
Fruit Jar, Queen, The, 1/2 Gallon .... 12.00 To 18.00
Fruit Jar, Queen, Trade Mark, Shield & Stars, Square, 1/2 Pint, T-2 .... 12.00
Fruit Jar, Queen, Trade Mark, Wide Mouth Adjustable, Improved, Quart, T-3 .... 6.00
Fruit Jar, Queensland, Green, Quart Plus 80.00

Fruit Jar, Quick Seal, Blue, Pint 1.50
Fruit Jar, Quick Seal, Blue, Quart 1.50
Fruit Jar, Quick Seal, In Circle, Glass Lid, Wire Bail, Aqua, Quart, T-3 .... 3.00
Fruit Jar, Quick Seal, In Circle, 9 On Base, Glass Lid, Wire Bail, Blue, Quart 4.00
Fruit Jar, Quick Seal, Pint .... *Illus* 5.00
Fruit Jar, Quick Seal, Pint .... 1.50 To 2.00
Fruit Jar, Quick Seal, Quart .... 1.50 To 5.00
Fruit Jar, Ranney's Finest Coffee, Zinc Lid, Quart 3.00
Fruit Jar, Rath's, Quart .... 4.00 To 6.00
Fruit Jar, Rau's Improved Groove, Quart 30.00
Fruit Jar, Red Key Mason, Aqua, Pint 4.00
Fruit Jar, Red Key Mason, Aqua, Quart .... 3.50 To 7.00
Fruit Jar, Red Key Mason, Aqua, 1/2 Gallon .... 8.00 To 10.00
Fruit Jar, Red Key Mason, Bubbles, Blue Green, Quart 4.50
Fruit Jar, Red Key Mason, Quart 7.00
Fruit Jar, Reliable Home Canning Mason, Quart 4.00
Fruit Jar, Rickey & Hamilton, Palatine, W.Va., Stoneware, Blue Stencil, 10 In 45.00
Fruit Jar, Robt. Gibson, England & New York, Aqua, Gallon 3.00
Fruit Jar, Root Mason, Aqua, Pint 4.50
Fruit Jar, Root Mason, Aqua, Quart .... 1.85 To 4.00
Fruit Jar, Root Mason, Pint 3.00
Fruit Jar, Root Mason, Smooth Lip, Bubbles, Haze, Aqua, Quart 3.00
Fruit Jar, Root Mason, Zinc Lid, Aqua, Pint 6.00
Fruit Jar, Root Mason, Zinc Lid, Aqua, Quart 3.00
Fruit Jar, Root Mason, Zinc Lid, Aqua, 1/2 Gallon .... 4.00 To 6.50
Fruit Jar, Rose, The, Midget 68.00
Fruit Jar, Rose, The, 1/2 Gallon 35.00
Fruit Jar, Royal Full Measure, Ground Lip, Pint, T-2 .... 8.00
Fruit Jar, Royal On Crown, Amber, Quart, T-3 .... 35.00
Fruit Jar, Royal, A.G.Smalley, Patent April 7th, 1896, 1/2 Gallon, T-1 .... 10.00
Fruit Jar, Royal, Cloudy, 1/2 Gallon 5.75
Fruit Jar, Royal, Quart .... 3.00 To 6.00
Fruit Jar, Royal, Square, Lightning, Blue, 1/2 Gallon, T-6 .... 10.00
Fruit Jar, Royal, Trademark, A.G.Smalley, Patent April, 7th, 1896, Quart, T-1 .... 7.00
Fruit Jar, S G Co, Mason's Patent Nov.30th, 1858, Quart 8.00
Fruit Jar, S G Co, Mason's Patent Nov.30th, 1858, Blue, 1/2 Gallon 18.00
Fruit Jar, S G Co, Mason's Patent Nov.30th, 1858, Haze, Blue, Quart 12.00
Fruit Jar, S G Co, Mason's Patent Nov.30th, 1858, 1/2 Gallon 7.50
Fruit Jar, S G Co, Mason's Patent Nov.30th, 1858, 110 On Base, Aqua, Quart 2.00
Fruit Jar, S G Co, Mason's Patent Nov.30th, 1858, 115 On Base, Aqua, Quart 5.00
Fruit Jar, S With Mason's Patent 1858, Zinc Lid, Light Aqua, Quart 6.50
Fruit Jar, S With Mason's Patent 1858, Aqua, 1/2 Gallon 8.00
Fruit Jar, Safe Seal, Aqua, Pint 4.00
Fruit Jar, Safe Seal, Quart 6.00
Fruit Jar, Safety Seal, Pint 5.00
Fruit Jar, Safety Valve, Burst Bubble, Aqua, 1/2 Pint 11.00
Fruit Jar, Safety Valve, Embossed, Haze Inside, Cornflower Blue, 1/2 Pint 15.00
Fruit Jar, Safety Valve, Greek Key, 1/2 Gallon, T-1 .... 25.00
Fruit Jar, Safety Valve, Patent May 2, 1895, Glass Lid, Bubbles, Quart 15.00
Fruit Jar, Safety Valve, Patent May 21, 1895, Glass Lid, 1/2 Gallon 16.00
Fruit Jar, Safety Valve, Patent May 21, 1895, HG & 5 On Base, Green, Quart 15.00
Fruit Jar, Safety Valve, Patent May 21, 1895, Pint .... 5.50 To 9.00
Fruit Jar, Safety Valve, Patent May 21, 1895, 8 1/4 In. .... *Illus* 40.00
Fruit Jar, Safety Valve, 1/4 Pint 12.00
Fruit Jar, Safety Valve, 1/2 Pint .... 11.00 To 12.50
Fruit Jar, Safety Valve, Quart .... 4.50 To 6.00
Fruit Jar, Safety Valve, 1/2 Gallon 12.00
Fruit Jar, Safety Wide Mouth Mason, Salem Glass Works, N.J., Aqua, Quart 14.00
Fruit Jar, Safety, Amber, Quart 68.00
Fruit Jar, Samco Genuine Mason, Pint 1.50
Fruit Jar, Samco Genuine Mason, Quart .... 1.00 To 1.50
Fruit Jar, Sanford, Patent July, 1900, Glass Lid, Silver Band, Pint 9.00
Fruit Jar, Sanford, Quart 5.00
Fruit Jar, Sanford's On Base, Sun Color, Quart 12.00
Fruit Jar, Sanford's, Sun-Colored Amethyst, Quart 13.00

Fruit Jar, Schaffer, The, Aqua, Quart 160.00
Fruit Jar, Schram Automatic Sealer, Quart 10.00
Fruit Jar, Schram Automatic Sealer, Squat, Pint 5.00
Fruit Jar, Schram, 1/2 Gallon 8.00
Fruit Jar, Sealfast Foster, Glass Lid, Wire Bail, Pint 3.00
Fruit Jar, Sealfast Foster, Glass Lid, Wire Bail, Quart .... 2.50 To 3.00
Fruit Jar, Sealfast Foster, 1/2 Pint 6.00
Fruit Jar, Sealfast Foster, Pint 2.00
Fruit Jar, Sealfast Foster, Quart .... 2.00 To 5.00
Fruit Jar, Sealfast, Pint 1.75
Fruit Jar, Sealfast, Quart 1.75
Fruit Jar, Security Seal, F G Co Monogram, Small Mouth, Glass Lid, Quart 4.00
Fruit Jar, Security Seal, In Triangle, Quart 5.00
Fruit Jar, Selco Surety Seal, Blue, Quart 5.00
Fruit Jar, Silicon, Quart 4.50
Fruit Jar, Simplex, In Diamond, 1/2 Pint 12.00
Fruit Jar, Smalley & Co., Patent April 7th, 1896, Amber, Quart, T-2 .... 36.00
Fruit Jar, Smalley Self Sealer, The, Trademark, Quart 6.95
Fruit Jar, Smalley Self Sealer, The, Wide Mouth, Quart 2.75
Fruit Jar, Smalley, AGS, Amber, Quart, T-1 .... 45.00
Fruit Jar, Smalley, AGS, Quart, T-1 .... 6.00
Fruit Jar, Smalley, Boston & New York, Milk Glass Lid, Amber, Quart 30.00
Fruit Jar, Smalley, Tin Top & Handle, Quart 32.00
Fruit Jar, Standard Mason, Lynchburg, Aqua, Quart 14.95
Fruit Jar, Standard Mason, Lynchburg, Quart 11.50
Fruit Jar, Standard Mason, Pint 5.00
Fruit Jar, Standard, Pint 5.00
Fruit Jar, Standard, Wax Sealer, Aqua, Pint, T-1 .... 55.00
Fruit Jar, Standard, Wax Sealer, W McK & Co Reverse, Aqua, Quart, T-1 .... 21.00
Fruit Jar, Star Glass Co., N.Albany, Inc., Aqua, Quart 25.00
Fruit Jar, Star, Stippled Star, Quart .... 50.00 To 55.00
Fruit Jar, Steer's Head, see Fruit Jar, Flaccus Co.
Fruit Jar, Sterling Mason, Quart 2.50
Fruit Jar, Stoddard, C.1840, Olive, 12 In. ....Color XXXX.XX
Fruit Jar, Stoneware, Tapered Sides, 11 In. 25.00
Fruit Jar, Stoneware, 3 Cobalt Stripes, 7 1/2 In. 40.00
Fruit Jar, Stoneware, 5 Cobalt Stripes, 6 1/2 In. 50.00
Fruit Jar, Sun, Aqua, Pint ....Illus 35.00
Fruit Jar, Sun, Aqua, Quart .... 45.00 To 55.00
Fruit Jar, Sun, Aqua, 1/2 Gallon 40.00
Fruit Jar, Sun, Pint 50.00
Fruit Jar, Sun, Quart .... 35.00 To 50.00
Fruit Jar, Sun, 1/2 Gallon 38.00
Fruit Jar, Sun, Trade Mark, Aqua, Quart ....Illus 48.00
Fruit Jar, Sunshine Brand Coffee, Quart 2.00
Fruit Jar, Superior, AG, Aqua, Quart 9.95

Fruit Jar, Sun,
Aqua, Pint

Fruit Jar, Sun, Trade Mark, Aqua, Quart

Fruit Jar, Swayzee's Double Safety, Pint 15.00
Fruit Jar, Swayzee's Improved Mason, Blue, Quart 2.50
Fruit Jar, Swayzee's Improved Mason, Fleur-De-Lis, Aqua, 1/2 Gallon 6.00
Fruit Jar, Swayzee's Improved Mason, Green, 1/2 Gallon 12.00
Fruit Jar, Swayzee's Improved Mason, Zinc Cap, Aqua, 1/2 Gallon 4.00
Fruit Jar, SWN, Aqua, Quart 45.00
Fruit Jar, T.F., Quart 1.95
Fruit Jar, T.F., 1/2 Gallon 1.95
Fruit Jar, T.F.Reppert, Greensboro, Pa. In Blue Stencil, Stoneware, 10 In. 40.00
Fruit Jar, Telephone Jar, The, Aqua, Quart .... 5.00 To 9.00
Fruit Jar, Telephone, The, Pint 6.00
Fruit Jar, Telephone, The, Quart 6.00
Fruit Jar, Telephone Jar, The, Whitney Glass Works, Glass Lid, Aqua, Quart 12.00
Fruit Jar, Texas Mason, Pint 9.50
Fruit Jar, Texas Mason, Quart 9.50
Fruit Jar, Thompson, Aqua, Quart 85.00

Fruit Jar, Wears, Improved, Pint
(See Page 131)

Fruit Jar, Woodbury Improved, N.J.,
1/2 Gallon, 8 In.
(See Page 131)

Fruit Jar, Tight Seal, Bubbles, Glass Lid, Wire Bail, Blue, Pint 6.00
Fruit Jar, Tight Seal, Glass Lid, Wire Bail, Blue, Quart 4.00
Fruit Jar, Tillyer, Winslow, Ghost Letters, Quart .... 65.00 To 80.00
Fruit Jar, Triomphe, Cross Bow, France, Paper Label, 1/2 Liter 1.50
Fruit Jar, Tropical Canners, 1/2 Gallon 6.00
Fruit Jar, True Fruit, J H S Co, Trademark Registered, 1/2 Gallon, T-1 .... 35.00
Fruit Jar, True Fruit, Quart 2.00
Fruit Jar, Union Arched Block Letters, Wax Sealer, 1/2 Gallon 75.00
Fruit Jar, Union No.4, Haze, Aqua, Quart 110.00
Fruit Jar, Vacuum Seal, New York, Spring Clamp, Quart 3.50
Fruit Jar, Vacuum Seal, 2 Clamps, 1/2 Gallon 9.00
Fruit Jar, Valve Jar, Stain, Aqua, Quart 1200.00
Fruit Jar, Veteran, Aqua, 1/2 Pint 31.00
Fruit Jar, Veteran, Pint 10.00
Fruit Jar, Veteran, Quart .... 10.00 To 12.00
Fruit Jar, Victory, Aqua, Pint, T-1 .... 35.00
Fruit Jar, Victory, In Shield On Lid, Embossed Base, 1/2 Pint, T-3 .... 10.00
Fruit Jar, Victory, Pacific San Francisco Glassworks, Green, Quart, T-2 .... 145.00
Fruit Jar, Victory, 1/2 Pint 8.00
Fruit Jar, Victory, Pint .... 2.95 To 7.00
Fruit Jar, Victory, Quart 6.00
Fruit Jar, Victory, 1864 & 1867, Aqua, Quart 31.00
Fruit Jar, Victory, 1864, Quart, T-1 .... 25.00
Fruit Jar, Wan-Eta Cocoa, Amber, Quart .... 4.00 To 6.95
Fruit Jar, Wan-Eta Cocoa, Boston, Embossed, Aqua, Quart 5.00

Fruit Jar, Wan-Eta Cocoa, Boston, Zinc Lid, Amber, Quart	6.00
Fruit Jar, Wax Sealer, Aqua, Quart	4.00
Fruit Jar, Wax Sealer, Patent 1860, Aqua, 1/2 Gallon	75.00
Fruit Jar, Wax Sealer, Stoneware, Gray, 6 1/4 In.	16.00
Fruit Jar, Wax Sealer, Whittled, Amber, Quart	60.00
Fruit Jar, Wears, Improved, Pint *Illus*	6.50
Fruit Jar, Wears, In Banner, Side Clamps, Pint, T-4	7.00
Fruit Jar, Wears, In Banner, Side Clamps, Quart, T-4	5.00
Fruit Jar, Wears, In Circle, Side Clamps, Quart, T-2	4.00
Fruit Jar, Weideman Boy Brand, Cleveland, Glass Top, Wire Bail, Quart	6.00
Fruit Jar, Weir, As You Like It Horseradish, 1892, Stoneware, Tan, 1/2 Pint	18.00
Fruit Jar, Weir, As You Like It Horseradish, 1892, Stoneware, Tan, Pint	16.00
Fruit Jar, Weir, Gallon	20.00
Fruit Jar, Weir, Pottery, Amber Lid, Quart	9.50
Fruit Jar, Weir, Pottery, Pint	20.00
Fruit Jar, Weir, 1892, Stoneware, Brown Lid, Tan, 1/2 Pint	15.00
Fruit Jar, White Crown, Aqua, Pint	9.00
Fruit Jar, Whitney Mason, Patent 1858, Aqua, Pint, T-1	7.00
Fruit Jar, Whitney Mason, Patent 1858, Embossed In Circle, Aqua, Pint, T-1	8.00
Fruit Jar, Winslow Jar, Aqua, Quart	45.00 To 50.00
Fruit Jar, Winslow Jar, Inside Stain, 1/2 Gallon	30.00
Fruit Jar, Winslow Jar, Wire Clamp, Quart	50.00
Fruit Jar, Woodbury Improved, N.J., 1/2 Gallon, 8 In. *Illus*	25.00
Fruit Jar, Woodbury Improved, WGW Monogram, Aqua, Quart	25.00
Fruit Jar, Woodbury, Aqua, Quart	19.00 To 24.00
Fruit Jar, Woodbury, Quart	25.00 To 27.50
Fruit Jar, Woodbury, WGW Monogram, Aqua, Quart	25.00
Fruit Jar, XX On Base, Wax Sealer, Aqua, Quart	7.00 To 15.00
Galliano, Soldier	9.00

Garnier bottles were first made in 1899 to hold Garnier Liqueurs. The firm was founded in 1859 in France. Figurals have been made through the twentieth century, except for the years of Prohibition and World War II.

Garnier, Apollo	9.95
Garnier, Aztec	12.95
Garnier, Baby Foot Shoe	9.00 To 9.95
Garnier, Berman Vase	12.95
Garnier, Bird	12.95
Garnier, Black Rooster	12.00
Garnier, Blue Pheasant	14.00
Garnier, California Quail	9.00 To 9.95
Garnier, Candlestick, 1955	25.00
Garnier, Cat	12.95
Garnier, Collie Dog	14.00
Garnier, Dog	12.95
Garnier, Drunk On Lamppost	12.95
Garnier, Duck	14.95 To 20.00
Garnier, German Shepherd	14.00
Garnier, Horse Pistol	12.00 To 14.00
Garnier, Indian	9.00 To 12.95
Garnier, Landscape	14.95
Garnier, Napoleon	18.00 To 25.00
Garnier, Oasis	14.95
Garnier, Paris Monument	12.95
Garnier, Parrot	18.50
Garnier, Partridge	18.00
Garnier, Pheasant	14.95
Garnier, Pheasant, Blue	16.00
Garnier, Policeman	9.95
Garnier, Policemen Of The World	9.95
Garnier, Queen Mary Liner	18.95
Garnier, Rooster, Black	14.00
Garnier, Shepherd	14.00
Garnier, Sheriff	9.00 To 9.95
Garnier, Soldier, Red	25.00

Garnier, Train	12.95
Garnier, Trout	12.95
Garnier, White Poodle	12.95
Gemel, Applied Pink & White Enamel Looping, Flattened Ovoid, C.1850, 11 In.	160.00
Gemel, Double, Rockingham, Molded Rose Design, 7 1/4 In.	85.00
Gemel, Engraved Gold Metal Lids, Emerald Green, 5 1/2 In.	35.00
Gilbey, Bell Ringer, Back Bar	40.00

Gin was first made in the 1600s and gin bottles have been made ever since. Gin has always been an inexpensive drink—that is why so many of these bottles were made. Many were of a type called case bottles today.

Gin, Bininger, see Bininger	
Gin, Blown, Collared Mouth, Pontil, Olive Amber, 10 1/4 In.	* 30.00
Gin, Blown, Flared Mouth, Flake, Square, Olive Amber, 9 In.	* 20.00
Gin, Blown, Part Of Mouth Missing, Burst Bubble, Olive Amber, 13 1/4 In.	* 35.00
Gin, Blown, Pontil, Crack, Square, Olive Amber, 18 3/4 In.	* 550.00
Gin, Blown, Rolled Mouth, Pontil, Square, Olive Amber, 19 1/4 In.	* 525.00
Gin, Blown, Rolled Mouth, Pontil, Stain, Square, Olive Amber, 10 In.	* 35.00
Gin, Blown, Rolled Mouth, Tapered, Pontil, Square, Olive Amber, 11 1/2 In.	* 75.00
Gin, Blown, Sheared Mouth, Pontil, Olive Green, 15 1/2 In.	* 525.00
Gin, Blown, Tapered Sides, Pontil, Square, Olive Amber, 14 1/8 In.	* 140.00
Gin, Case, see Case Gin	
Gin, London Jockey, Clubhouse, Collared Mouth, Bruise, Green, 3/4 Quart	* 55.00
Gin, London Jockey, Clubhouse, Collared Mouth, Emerald Green, 3/4 Quart	* 225.00
Gin, London Jockey, Clubhouse, Collared Mouth, Olive Green, 3/4 Quart	* 250.00
Gin, London Jockey, Clubhouse, Collared Mouth, Yellow Amber, 3/4 Quart	* 300.00
Gin, London Jockey, Clubhouse, Collared Mouth, Yellow Green, 3/4 Quart	* 120.00
Gin, London Royal Nectar, Square, Aqua, 10 In.	11.00
Gin, Morley's Buchlin, Square, 12 In.	14.00
Gin, Park & Tilford Dry, Embossed, Glass Stopper, Aqua, Quart	5.00
Gin, Sir Robt. Burnett, Stain, Aqua, Miniature	5.00
Gin, Sloping Collared Mouth, Square, Smooth Base, Olive Amber, 10 3/4 In.	* 15.00
Gin, Star & 8 Dates On Bottom, Olive, 10 1/2 In.	17.50
Gin, Tapered Sides, Square, Deep Amber	15.00
Gin, Tapered Sides, Square, Olive, 11 In.	15.00
Gin, Tipstaff, Stephen Green, Stoneware, 9 In.	140.00
Gin, Very Old, Jug, Handle, Smooth Base, Olive Amber, Quart	* 160.00
Gin, 3 Concentric Rings On Bottom, Olive, 9 In.	12.50
Gin, 3 Mold, Applied Collar, Olive Green, 10 1/2 In.	16.00
Glenmore, Masquers English Vodka, 4/5 _____ Illus	3.00

Glue bottles are often included with information about ink bottles. The numbers in the form C-0 refer to the book Ink Bottles and Inkwells by William E. Covill, Jr.

Glue, A.Richards & Co. Combined & Cement, Pontil, Aqua, 3 1/8 In., C-1750	* 25.00
Glue, Carter's Nickel Mucilage, Aqua, 2 1/2 In.	5.00
Glue, Le Page's Gold Medal, Flared Rolled Lip, Aqua, 2 3/4 In.	4.00
Glue, Le Page's Gold Medal Mucilage, Double Ring, Aqua, 2 3/4 In.	5.00
Glue, Le Page's Mucilage By Russia Cement Co., 3 1/2 In _____ Illus	22.00
Glue, Sanford's Royal Crown Mucilage, 4 In. _____ Illus	12.00
Glue, Sheared Lip, Double Flange Shoulder, Bell Shape, Aqua, 3 1/4 In.	4.00
Glue, Spalding's, Stained, Dug, Aqua, 3 1/4 In.	6.50
Glue, Spalding's, Tubular Pontil, Aqua, 3 1/4 In., C-751	* 30.00
Grant, Drummond, Highlander, 14 In.	14.95 To 15.00
Grant, Lamond, Clanswoman	14.95 To 15.00
Grenadier, Fire Chief	18.00 To 30.95
Grenadier, Fra Junipero Serra	29.00 To 29.50
Grenadier, Lillie Hitchcock Coit, San Francisco	39.95
Grenadier, Loyal Order Of Moose, Porcelain, 13 1/2 In.	5.00 To 19.00
Grenadier, Soldier, Baylor's 3rd, 1969	22.00 To 28.00
Grenadier, Soldier, Black Soldier	17.95
Grenadier, Soldier, Captain, Confederate, 1970	14.00 To 19.00
Grenadier, Soldier, Captain, Union Army, 1970	14.00 To 19.00
Grenadier, Soldier, Connecticut	24.00
Grenadier, Soldier, Continental Marines, 1969	35.00 To 75.00

(See Page 132)

(See Page 134)

Top left to right: Glenmore, Masquers English Vodka, 4/5; Glue, Le Page's Mucilage By Russia Cement Co., 3 1/2 In.; Glue, Sanford's Royal Crown Mucilage, 4 In. *Right:* Hoffman, Mark Donohue's 66 Sunoco McLaren, 1972.

Grenadier, Soldier, Corporal Grenadier, 1970	12.00 To 19.00
Grenadier, Soldier, Eugene, 1969	22.00 To 28.00
Grenadier, Soldier, General Billy Mitchell	26.50 To 30.00
Grenadier, Soldier, General Douglas MacArthur	26.50 To 30.00
Grenadier, Soldier, General George Washington, 1973	19.95 To 29.50
Grenadier, Soldier, General Robert E.Lee	19.95 To 27.50
Grenadier, Soldier, General Ulysses S.Grant, 1975	19.95 To 27.50
Grenadier, Soldier, George S.Custer, 1970	14.00 To 24.00
Grenadier, Soldier, Jeb Stuart, 1970	14.00 To 24.00
Grenadier, Soldier, Joan Of Arc Club Bottle	28.00
Grenadier, Soldier, John Paul Jones	26.50
Grenadier, Soldier, King's African Rifle Corps, 1971	12.00 To 19.00
Grenadier, Soldier, King's African Rifle Corps, Quart	12.00 To 29.00
Grenadier, Soldier, L.C.M.C. Governor Foot Guard	17.95 To 20.00
Grenadier, Soldier, Lannes, 1970	22.00 To 35.00
Grenadier, Soldier, Lassal, 1969	69.95
Grenadier, Soldier, Major Coldstream	12.00 To 19.00
Grenadier, Soldier, Murat, 1970	22.00 To 28.00
Grenadier, Soldier, Napoleon, 1969	89.95
Grenadier, Soldier, Ney, 1969	22.00 To 28.00
Grenadier, Soldier, Officer 3rd Guard, 1971	12.00 To 19.00
Grenadier, Soldier, Official Scots Fusileer, 1971	12.00 To 19.00
Grenadier, Soldier, Pancho Villa	22.00 To 26.00
Grenadier, Soldier, Pancho Villa On Horseback	25.00 To 30.00
Grenadier, Soldier, St.Jeanne D'Arc, 1971	75.00 To 100.00
Grenadier, Soldier, Stonewall Jackson, 1976	35.00 To 40.00
Grenadier, Soldier, Teddy Roosevelt	29.00
Grenadier, Soldier, Washington, Blue Rifles	12.50
Grenadier, Soldier, Wisconsin Iron Brigade, Miniature	12.50
Grenadier, Soldier, 1st Official Guard 17th Dragoon, 1970	12.00 To 19.00
Grenadier, Soldier, 1st Pennsylvania, 1970	65.00
Grenadier, Soldier, 1st Regiment Virginia Volunteers	14.50
Grenadier, Soldier, 2nd Maryland, 1969	69.00
Grenadier, Soldier, 3rd Guards Regiment	12.00 To 14.00
Grenadier, Soldier, 3rd New York, 1969	13.95 To 28.00
Grenadier, Soldier, 18th Continental, 1970	18.00 To 28.00
Grenadier, Soldier, 1821 British Guards	12.00
Grenadier, Soldier, 1821 Officer Grenadier, 1970	19.00

Hamm, Bear No.1, 1972 .... · 10.00
Hamm, Bear No.2, 1973 .... 8.50
Hamm, Bear, Bartender, 1973 .... 5.95 To 8.95
    Hand Lotion, see Cosmetic, Medicine
Heaven Hill, Old Home .... 3.95 To 6.50
Hoffman, A.J.Foyte, No.2 .... 17.50 To 21.95
Hoffman, Alaskan Pipeline 25.00
Hoffman, Bald Eagle 59.90
Hoffman, Bartender, Musical Decanter 29.50
Hoffman, Bear & Cub, Musical Decanter 55.00
Hoffman, Betsy Ross, Musical Decanter .... 47.50 To 65.00
Hoffman, Big Red Machine .... 24.95 To 25.00
Hoffman, Bobcat & Pheasant 55.00
Hoffman, Dancer, Musical Decanter 29.50
Hoffman, Doe & Fawn .... 49.50 To 70.00
Hoffman, Eagle & Fox, Musical Decanter 55.00
Hoffman, Fiddler, Musical Decanter 27.00
Hoffman, Generation Gap, Hippies '76 & Pioneer, 1876, 2 Ozs., Pair 22.95

Hoffman, Mr.Doctor   Hoffman, Mr.Lucky   Hoffman,
Mr.Shoe Cobbler

Hoffman, Harpist 22.00
Hoffman, Lady Godiva 29.95
Hoffman, Mark Donohue's 66 Sunoco McLaren, 1972 .... *Illus* *25.00*
Hoffman, McLaren, No.3, Car 25.00
    Hoffman, Miniature, see Miniature, Hoffman
Hoffman, Mr.Dancer 22.00
Hoffman, Mr.Doctor .... *Illus* *27.00*
Hoffman, Mr.Harpist, Musical Decanter .... 21.95 To 28.95
Hoffman, Mr.Lucky .... *Illus* *29.00*
Hoffman, Mr.Shoe Cobbler .... *Illus* *27.00*
Hoffman, Mrs.Lucky, Musical Decanter .... 22.00 To 27.00
Hoffman, S.T.P., No.20, Racer .... 27.00 To 27.50
Hoffman, Sunoco, No.66, Racer .... 22.00 To 25.00

    Holly City handmade commemorative decanters are produced by
    Wheaton Village Crafts Guild, Millville, N.J.
Holly City, American Freedom Train, Green 30.00
Holly City, American Freedom Train, Honey Amber 30.00
Holly City, Apollo/Soyuz, Dark Amber 50.00
Holly City, Betsy Ross/Flag Day, Amethyst 10.00
Holly City, Christmas, 1971 .... *Color* XXXX.XX
Holly City, Christmas, 1972 .... *Color* XXXX.XX
Holly City, Christmas, 1973 .... *Color* XXXX.XX
Holly City, Christmas, 1974 .... *Color* XXXX.XX
Holly City, Connecticut, Blue 10.00
Holly City, Delaware, Amethyst 10.00
Holly City, George Patton .... *Color* XXXX.XX

Top left to right: Holly City, Georgia, Topaz; Holly City, John F. Kennedy Memorial, Blue; Holly City, Spirit Of '76.
Left: Holly City, 1974, St. Nick, Green

(See Page 136)

Holly City, Georgia, Topaz	*Illus*	10.00
Holly City, Gerald R.Ford 38th President, Amethyst		40.00
Holly City, Graf Zeppelin's 75th Anniversary, Amber		10.00
Holly City, Helen Keller	*Color*	XXXX.XX
Holly City, Israel's 25th Anniversary, Light Amber		15.00
Holly City, Jimmy Carter 39th President, Blue		10.00
Holly City, John F.Kennedy Memorial, Blue	*Illus*	15.00
Holly City, John F.Kennedy Memorial, Cobalt Blue		35.00
Holly City, John Paul Jones	*Color*	XXXX.XX
Holly City, July 4th/Independence Hall, Blue		20.00
Holly City, July 4th/Independence Hall, Honey Amber		20.00
Holly City, Lindbergh's 50th Anniversary, Blue		10.00
Holly City, Maryland, Dark Amethyst		10.00
Holly City, Massachusetts, Green		10.00
Holly City, New Hampshire, Amber		10.00
Holly City, New Jersey, Blue		10.00
Holly City, New York, Light Amber		10.00
Holly City, North Carolina, Green		10.00
Holly City, Paul Revere	*Color*	XXXX.XX
Holly City, Pennsylvania, Green		10.00
Holly City, Rhode Island, Amethyst		10.00
Holly City, Richard M. Nixon 37th President, Amethyst		40.00
Holly City, Samuel Clemens	*Color*	XXXX.XX
Holly City, Sen.Sam Ervin/Sen.Howard Baker, Amber		15.00
Holly City, South Carolina, Blue		10.00
Holly City, Special Apollo XI, Reddish Amber		30.00
Holly City, Spirit Of '76, Blue		20.00
Holly City, Spirit Of '76, Honey Amber	*Illus*	20.00
Holly City, Tall Ships & Wagon Train, Light Blue		40.00
Holly City, The American Circus, Honey Amber		15.00
Holly City, The Jersey Devil, Green		10.00
Holly City, U.S.Marine Corps, Dark Amber		20.00
Holly City, U.S.Navy, Blue		20.00
Holly City, Viking I, Green		15.00

Holly City, Virginia, Blue 10.00
Holly City, Watergate, Amethyst 150.00
Holly City, Watergate, Blue 45.00
Holly City, Watergate, Light Amber 10.00
Holly City, 1976 Democrat Campaign Cabin, Deep Green 20.00
Holly City, 1976 Republican Campaign Cabin, Deep Green 20.00
Holly City, 1973 St.Nick, Topaz 125.00
Holly City, 1974 St.Nick, Green .... Illus 65.00
Holly City, 1975 St.Nick, Blue 35.00
Holly City, 1976 St.Nick, Dark Amber 15.00
Household, Dead Stuck For Bugs, Philadelphia, Pa., Aqua, 8 1/2 In. 25.00
Household, Dr.Hubbard's Vegetable Disinfectant, Boston, Oval, Aqua, 9 1/2 In ... 3.95
Household, E-Z Stove Polish, BIMAL, Miniature 3.00
Household, Geo.Reed Domestic Dyes, Aqua, 4 In. 3.00
Household, Greer's Superior Bluing, Bubbles, BIMAL, Amber, Quart 15.00

Household, Liberty Brand Liquid Blue, 9 In.

Household, Prices Patent Candle Co.,
Aqua, 8 1/2 In.

Ink, Barnes National Ink Combined, 6 In.
(See Page 137)

Household, Howe & Stevens Family Dye Colors, Applied Lip, Aqua, 4 In. 5.00
Household, Liberty Brand Liquid Blue, 9 In. .... Illus 12.50
Household, Lysol, Embossed, BIMAL, Bubbles, Stain, Amber, 4 In. 2.75
Household, Price's Patent Candle Co., Aqua, 8 1/2 In. .... Illus 35.00
Household, Sample Non Equal Furniture Polish, Deep Bros., BIMAL, 3 In. 2.75
    Household, Shoe Polish, see Shoe Polish
Household, Turpentine, W.H.Crandell, Clark & Fox Stoneware, 3 Gallon 975.00
Household, Vapo-Cresline, 5 In. 4.00
Household, Vinci Leather Dressing, Rob't H.Foerderer, Green, 5 1/8 In. 4.00
Household, Water, Frigidaire, Green Satin, 11 In. 15.00
Hudson Bay, Canadian Buffalo & Rubbing Rock .... 12.00 To 18.00
    Hudson Bay, Miniature, see Miniature, Hudson Bay
Hudson Bay, Sailing Ship .... 22.00 To 25.00
I.W.Harper, Bicentennial Barrel 9.95
I.W.Harper, Figural, Porcelain, White, 16 1/2 In. 18.00
I.W.Harper, Green 12.50
I.W.Harper, Man, Blue .... 8.95 To 12.00
I.W.Harper, Man, Gray .... 8.95 To 15.00
I.W.Harper, Man, White 35.00
I.W.Harper, Medal, Pottery, Tan .... Color XXXX.XX
I.W.Harper, Nautical, Ceramic, 1913 .... Color XXXX.XX
I.W.Harper, Pure Old I.W.Harper, Bar, C.1910 .... Color XXXX.XX
I.W.Harper, Wicker Cover, Amber .... Color XXXX.XX

Ink, Brass Cap, 3 In.

Ink, Carter's, Violet, 1899
(See Page 138)

Ink, Carter's, Black Letter, 1906

Ink bottles were first used in the United States in 1819. Early ink
bottles were of ceramic and were often imported. Inks can be identified by
their shape. They were made to be hard to tip over. The numbers used in
entries in the form C-0 or Mc Kearin G I-0 refer to the books
Ink Bottles and Inkwells by William E. Covill, Jr., and
American Glass by George P. and Helen Mc Kearin.

Ink, ABM, Square, Cobalt, 2 1/2 In.		2.50
Ink, Barnes National Ink Combined, 6 In.	Illus	7.00
Ink, Barrel, Patent March 1st, 1870, Tooled Collar, 2 X 2 In., C-671		30.00
Ink, Bell, Aqua, 3 1/4 In.		3.50
Ink, Bertinguiot, Pontil, Olive Amber, 2 3/8 In., C-575		* 120.00
Ink, Billing's, C-232		16.00
Ink, Billing's, Similar To C-856, 2 5/8 In.		20.00
Ink, Bixby, C-590		30.00
Ink, Bixby, Embossed On Base, Aqua, 2 5/8 In.		25.00
Ink, Bixby, Patent March 6, '83, Aqua, 3 3/4 In.		5.00
Ink, Bixby, Patent March 6, '83, Sheared Flared Lip, Aqua, 4 1/4 In.		5.00
Ink, Blown, Sheared Mouth, Pontil, Olive Amber, 2 13/16 In., C-1031		* 300.00
Ink, Boat, 2 Pen Ledges, C-513 & 514		2.50 To 7.50
Ink, Brass Cap, 3 In.	Illus	175.00
Ink, Brockway Machine Bottling Co., Cone, Neck Rings, 3 In.		2.75
Ink, Cabin, Ground Mouth, Smooth Base, 3 1/4 In., C-677		* 350.00
Ink, Cabin, Smooth Base, Hole In Corner, 2 1/2 In., C-680		* 170.00
Ink, Carter, Master, Pottery, Quart		22.00
Ink, Carter's New Carmine Writing Fluid, 1906	Illus	8.00
Ink, Carter's, Black Letter, 1906	Illus	8.00

Ink, Carter's New Carmine Writing Fluid, 1906

Ink, Carter's, Ma & Pa Carter,
Made In Germany, C-1619
(See Page 138)

Ink, **Carter's,** Cathedral, ABM, Cobalt, Pint .... 35.00 To 65.00
Ink, **Carter's,** Cathedral, ABM, Cobalt, Quart .... 35.00 To 50.00
Ink, **Carter's,** Cathedral, Quart 45.00
Ink, **Carter's,** Cone, Aqua, 2 1/2 In. 4.00
Ink, **Carter's,** Cono, Cobalt, 2 1/2 In. 12.00
Ink, **Carter's,** Gothic Arches, Cobalt, 9 3/4 In. 45.00
Ink, **Carter's,** Ma & Pa Carter, Made In Germany, C-1619 .... *Illus* 69.00
Ink, **Carter's,** Master, Collared Mouth With Spout, Green, 5 1/8 In., C-804 .... 70.00
Ink, **Carter's,** Master, Green, 5 1/8 In., C-804 .... * 70.00
Ink, **Carter's,** Master, Stain, Amber, 6 Ozs. 12.50
Ink, **Carter's,** Offset Neck, Square, Similar To C-98, 2 In. 22.50
Ink, **Carter's,** Picture Label, Aqua ....*Color* XXXX.XX
Ink, **Carter's,** Violet, 1899 ....*Illus* 10.00
Ink, **Carter's,** Washington, D.C., Embossed, Quart 12.00
Ink, **Carter's,** 1897, Cone, Aqua, 2 1/2 In. 4.50

Ink, Embossed Bird On Top, Aqua, 2 In.

Ink, H.A.Bartlett & Co., Philadelphia,
Black, Aqua, 2 1/2 In.
(See Page 139)

Ink, **Caw's,** New York, Cube, Aqua, 2 3/4 In. 3.00
Ink, **Caw's,** New York, Paper Label, Cube, Aqua, 2 1/4 In. 3.00
Ink, **Child's,** Redware, 1 3/4 In., Pair 40.00
Ink, **Civil War Traveler's,** Walnut Encased, Spring Action Cap, 2 In. 45.00
Ink, **Cone,** Amber, 2 1/2 In. 4.50
Ink, **Cone,** Honey Amber, 2 1/2 In. 5.50
Ink, **Cone,** Pontil, Aqua, C-12 .... 90.00
Ink, **Cortus,** Embossed, Green, Quart 15.00
Ink, **Cottage,** 2 Pen Ledges, C-509 & 511 .... 2.50 To 7.50
Ink, **Coventry,** C-1198 .... 85.00
Ink, **CPC,** Bell Shape, Thumbprints, Aqua, 2 3/4 In. 12.00
Ink, **CPC,** Bell Shape, Thumbprints, Haze, Aqua, 2 3/4 In. 8.00
Ink, **Cylinder,** Label, Pontil, Amber, 2 1/2 In. 50.00
Ink, **David's Dome,** Green, C-617 .... 65.00
Ink, **David's Non Copying Carmine,** Pouring Spout, Label, Pint 12.00
Ink, **David's Writing Fluid,** Paper Label, Amber ....*Color* XXXX.XX
Ink, **David's Writing Fluid,** Paper Label, Cobalt ....*Color* XXXX.XX
Ink, **David's,** C-1301 .... 30.00
Ink, **De Halsey,** Patente, Domed, Pontil, Olive Amber, 3 1/4 In., C-577 .... * 425.00
Ink, **Denby Pottery,** 7 1/4 In. 16.00
Ink, **Denby,** J.Arnold, London, England, Pottery, Brown, Pint 18.00
Ink, **Diamond & Onyx,** Philadelphia, U.S.A., Ring Lip, Aqua, 5 1/2 In. 25.00
Ink, **Doulton,** Lambeth, Master, Pottery, Dark Brown Glaze, 8 In. 65.00
Ink, **E.Waters,** Troy, N.Y., Master, Petaled Shoulders, Aqua, 5 1/4 In., C-773 .... * 190.00
Ink, **Earthenware,** Dark Brown Splashes, Light Brown, 2 In. 35.00
Ink, **Embossed Bird On Top,** Aqua, 2 In. ....*Illus* 65.00
Ink, **Embossed,** 8 Panels, Milk Glass, 4 In. 125.00
Ink, **English,** House Shape, 2 Troughs, Pen Rest, Green, 2 1/4 In. 7.75
Ink, **English,** 8 Sided, C-565 .... 5.00
Ink, **Express Company Marking,** Newark, N.J., Green ....*Color* XXXX.XX
Ink, **Farley's,** Amber, 1 3/4 In. 250.00

Ink, **Farley's,** Pontil, Octagonal, Olive Amber, 1 3/4 In., C-526 .... * 210.00
Ink, **Farley's,** Tooled Mouth, Pontil, Octagonal, Olive Amber, 3 5/8 In., C-528 .... * 475.00
Ink, **Flint,** 3 Mold, McK G II-18, Olive Amber 135.00
Ink, **Fostoria Safety,** No.486, 2 1/2 In. 6.50
Ink, **Fred D.Allings Mercantile,** 1871, Master, Pour Spout, Teal Green, 5 In. 75.00
Ink, **Free-Blown,** 2 Mold, OP, Olive Green, 4 In. 45.00
Ink, **G.Howarth,** Halifax, C.1850, Pottery, 2 In.Wooden Stand, 7 1/2 In. 160.00
Ink, **Geometric,** OP, McK G II-18d, Olive Amber 80.00
Ink, **Geometric,** McK G II-16, Olive Amber, 2 1/4 In. 82.00
Ink, **Geometric,** McK G II-18, Amber, 2 5/8 In. 130.00
Ink, **Geometric,** McK G III-29, Olive Green, 2 1/4 In. 10.00
Ink, **H.A.Bartlett & Co.,** Philadelphia, Black, Aqua, 2 1/2 In. .... *Illus* 20.00
Ink, **Haley Co.,** Made In U.S.A., BIMAL, Aqua, 10 1/4 In. 13.50
Ink, **Hagan's Superior,** Philadelphia, Aqua ....*Color* XXXX.XX
Ink, **Hard Cider,** Tippecanoe Extract, Collared Mouth, Pontil, 2 In., C-667 .... * 300.00
Ink, **Hard Cider,** Tippecanoe Extract, Collared Mouth, Pontil, 2 In., C-667 .... 300.00
Ink, **Harrison,** Tippecanoe, Cabin, Rolled Mouth, Pontil, 3 1/4 In., C-676 .... *1000.00
Ink, **Harrison's Columbian,** Aqua Pontil, 1 3/4 In. .... *Illus* 85.00
Ink, **Harrison's Columbian,** Bubble, OP, Cobalt, 7 In. 520.00
Ink, **Harrison's Columbian,** Etched, Aqua, 1 3/4 In. 40.00
Ink, **Harrison's Columbian,** Flanged Mouth, Octagonal, Aqua, 2 1/2 In., C-534 .... * 60.00

Ink, Harrison's Columbian, Aqua Pontil, 1 3/4 In.

Ink, J.W.Seaton, Louisville, Ky.,
Aqua, 2 In. *(See Page 140)*

Ink, Levison's Inks, St.Louis, 2 1/2 In.
(See Page 140)

Ink, **Harrison's Columbian,** Master, Crack, Stain, Cobalt, 5 5/8 In., C-764 .... * 140.00
Ink, **Harrison's Columbian,** Master, Octagonal, Aqua, 3 3/4 In., C-536 .... * 85.00
Ink, **Harrison's Columbian,** Master, 12 Sided, Stain, Cobalt, 11 3/16 In., C-763 ....*2200.00
Ink, **Harrison's Columbian,** Patent, Flanged Mouth, Crack, Aqua, 7 1/4 In. .... * 30.00
Ink, **Harrison's Columbian,** Patent, Pontil, Octagonal, Aqua, 2 15/16 In., C-535 ....*Illus* * 40.00
Ink, **Harrison's Columbian,** 12 Sided, Aqua, 7 1/4 In. 175.00
Ink, **Harrison's Columbian,** 8 Sided, Aqua, 1 7/8 In. 70.00
Ink, **Harrison's Columbian,** 8 Sided, Aqua, 2 In. 65.00
Ink, **Harrison's Columbian,** 8 Sided, Aqua, 2 1/2 In. 50.00
Ink, **Harrison's,** Patent, OP, 4 X 2 In. 69.00
Ink, **Higgins' Brick Red Waterproof,** Cork & Plastic Top, Pen, 3 In. 5.50
Ink, **Higgins',** Quill Stopper, Pen Cloth, BIMAL 1 7/8 In. 8.50
Ink, **Hohenthal Brothers & Co.,** Master, Crack, Olive Amber, 8 3/4 In., C-766 .... * 225.00
Ink, **House Shape,** Sunken Base, Rectangular, Light Green, 2 In. 7.25
Ink, **I.C.Hoffman,** Stoneware, Squat, Tan, 7 In. 15.00
Ink, **Igloo,** Sheared Ground Lip, Aqua, 2 In. 8.00
Ink, **J.& I.E.M.,** Igloo, Sheared Ground Lip, Blue Aqua, 1 3/4 In. 15.00
Ink, **J.& I.E.M.,** Offset Neck, Domed, Aqua, 2 1/4 In., C-627 .... * 20.00
Ink, **J.& I.E.M.,** Patent Oct.31, 1865, Offset Neck, Aqua, 2 1/4 In., C-629 .... * 15.00
Ink, **J.& I.E.M.,** Turtle, Sheared Ground Lip, Aqua, 1 5/8 In. 10.00

Ink, J.Bourne & Son, Pottery, Pint	15.00
Ink, J.Bourne & Sons, Pottery, Tan, Pint	5.00
Ink, J.R.Nichols & Co., Boston, Master, Whittled, Lip Ring, Emerald, Pint	12.00
Ink, J.W.Seaton, Louisville, Ky., Aqua, 2 In. ....*Illus*	250.00
Ink, James P.Scott's, Aqua, C-382	65.00
Ink, James P.Scott's, Cabin, Aqua, C-382	50.00
Ink, Job Moses, BIMAL, Aqua, C-503	20.00
Ink, Jone's Empire Black, Umbrella, Rolled Mouth, Pontil, 2 1/4 In.	* 25.00
Ink, Jones' Empire, Master, Collar, 12 Sided, Green, 5 13/16 In., C-769	* 800.00
Ink, Jones' Empire, Master, Collar, 12 Sided, Olive Green, 7 In., C-769	* 650.00
Ink, Jones' Empire, N.Y., Master, 12 Sided, Green, 5 13/16 In., C-769	800.00
Ink, Keller, Detroit, Double Ring Lip, 2 1/16 In.	4.75
Ink, Kurtz Bros., Clearfield, Pa., School Desk, 1 5/8 In.	2.00
Ink, L.Culton, Lambeth, Master, Pottery, Brown, Quart	50.00
Ink, Le Page's Signet, Made In U.S.A., Threaded Top, Rectangular, 2 1/2 In.	.50
Ink, Levison's Inks, St.Louis, 2 1/2 In ....*Illus*	225.00
Ink, Massachusetts Standard, Master, Neck Ring, Amber, Pint, 7 1/2 In.	19.00
Ink, Master, Flared Pour Spout Lip, Bubbles, Puce, 3 In.	35.00
Ink, Master, Whittled, Collared Lip, Seed Bubbles, Blue Aqua, Pint, 8 In.	7.00
Ink, Master, Whittled, Punched Pour Spout, Citron Gold, Quart	5.00
Ink, McK G I-2a, Horizontal Ribs, Pontil, Olive Amber, 2 1/4 In., C-1156	* 375.00
Ink, McK G II-2, Coventry, Blown, 3 Mold, Olive Amber	95.00 To 140.00
Ink, McK G II-2, Geometric Diamond, Olive Green, 2 1/4 In., C-1175	* 90.00
Ink, McK G II-2, Coventry, Geometrics, Olive Green	130.00
Ink, McK G II-16, Three Mold, Geometrics, Olive Amber	65.00 To 70.00
Ink, McK G II-16a, Geometric, Dark Green	95.00
Ink, McK G II-18, Blown, 3 Mold, Olive Amber	140.00
Ink, McK G II-18a, Geometric, Ribbed, Bruise, Amber, 1 3/4 In., C-1184	* 130.00
Ink, McK G II-18b, Geometric, Pontil, Olive Green, 1 7/8 In., C-1185	* 130.00
Ink, McK G II-18e, Geometric, Pontil, Olive Amber, 2 1/4 In., C-1196	* 125.00
Ink, McK G II-18f, Diamonds, Ribbed, Olive Amber, 2 1/2 In., C-1200	* 100.00
Ink, McK G II-29, Diamonds, Ribbed Base, Pontil, Amber, 2 1/4 In., C-1221	* 110.00
Ink, McK G III-29, Keene, Olive Amber	130.00
Ink, Mt.Vernon Glass Co., Dark Olive Green, C-1177	265.00
Ink, N.C.R., C-743	12.00
Ink, Newburg Glass Co., Patent Feb.27, '66, Master, Olive Green, 9 3/4 In.	* 300.00
Ink, Offset Neck, Domed, Aqua, 1 15/16 In.	* 30.00
Ink, Offset Neck, Domed, Smooth Base, Aqua, 1 3/4 In., C-632	* 10.00
Ink, Offset Neck, Pen Ledge, Oval, Aqua, 3 In., C-703	* 20.00
Ink, Offset Neck, Smooth Base, Square, 2 In., C-398	* 22.50
Ink, Omega Watched, Pottery, White & Black Printing, 3 1/2 In.	40.00
Ink, OP, Black Amethyst, C-221	110.00
Ink, OP, Dug, Square, 2 In.	5.00
Ink, OP, Olive Amber, C-221	120.00
Ink, Oval Panel, Bell Shape, Aqua, 2 1/2 In.	10.00
Ink, P.& J.Arnold, London, Master, Denby Pottery, Cone Lip, 1/2 Pint	8.00
Ink, P.& J.Arnold, Pour Lip, Pottery, Quart	11.00
Ink, Panok, BIMAL, 3 In.	15.00
Ink, Paperweight, Funnel-Shaped Top, Cork In Bottom, C-1353	45.00
Ink, Patent Fortschritt P, Brass Cover, Double Pen Rest, 5 1/2 In.	12.00
Ink, Patent March 1st, 1870, Barrel, Free Blown, Smooth Base, 2 In., C-671	* 30.00
Ink, Peerless, Embossed, Dug, Aqua, 3 In.	4.00
Ink, Pennell, C-560	35.00
Ink, Pitkin Type, Ribs Swirled To Left, Flake, Olive Green, 2 1/2 In., C-1125	* 375.00
Ink, Pitkin Type, Ribs Swirled To Left, Olive Amber, 2 1/16 In., C-1135	* 275.00
Ink, Pitkin Type, Ribs Swirled To Left, Pontil, Amber, 2 1/4 In., C-1139	* 325.00
Ink, Pitkin Type, Ribs Swirled To Left, Olive Amber, 2 1/2 In., C-1142	* 300.00
Ink, Pitkin Type, Ribs Swirled To Left, Olive Amber, 2 9/16 In., C-1145	* 300.00
Ink, Pitkin Type, Ribs Swirled To Right, Olive Amber, 2 15/16 In., C-1159	* 350.00
Ink, Pitkin Type, Ribs Swirled To Left, Olive Green, 2 1/4 In., C-1118	* 550.00
Ink, Pitkin Type, Ribs Swirled To Left, Pontil, Olive Amber, 2 In., C-1134	* 275.00
Ink, Pitkin Type, Ribs Swirled To Left, Potstone, Amber, 2 1/4 In., C-1139	* 375.00
Ink, Pitkin Type, Ribs Swirled To Left, Square, Green, 2 1/4 In., C-1120	* 550.00
Ink, Pitkin Type, Ribs Swirled To Right, Crack, Amber, 2 1/4 In., C-1152	* 100.00
Ink, Pitkin Type, 36 Ribs Swirled To Right, Olive Amber, 2 5/8 In., C-1151	* 325.00

Ink, Pontil, Cobalt, C-1064 .... 55.00
Ink, Pontil, Cork Case, Aqua, 1 1/2 In. .... * 30.00
Ink, Pontil, Wooden Case, Aqua, 3 3/8 In., C-1659 .... * 30.00
Ink, Pottery, Pennsylvania, Funnel Type, 10 Panels, Brown, C-1363 .... 40.00
Ink, Pottery, White, 4 In. 4.00
Ink, Pottery, 3 1/2 In. 3.00
Ink, Repro, Geometric, 2 X 1 3/4 In. .... * 25.00
Ink, Repro, Offset Neck, Sheared Mouth, Light Amethyst, 2 1/8 In. .... * 50.00
Ink, S.O.Dunbar, OP, C-520 .... 130.00
Ink, S.O.Dunbar, Taunton, Mass, Master, Collared Lip, Blue Aqua, Quart 12.00

Ink, Stafford's Universal, 8 In.

Ink, Stoddard, Lockport, 12 Sided, OP, Green, 2 1/2 In.

Ink, S.O.Dunbar, Umbrella, OP, Aqua, C-115 .... 85.00
Ink, S.S.Stafford, Cobalt, Quart 22.00
Ink, S.S.Stafford's, Master, Pour Lip, Cobalt, Quart 20.00
Ink, S.S.Stafford's, Pouring Spout, Cobalt, 16 Ozs. 14.00
Ink, Sadler's Bryand & Stralton Business College, Baltimore, Aqua, 2 In. 22.00
Ink, Sanford, No.30, Patent Applied For, Boat Shape, Double Ring, Aqua, 2 In. 12.00
Ink, Sanford, 217, Patent, Boat, Pen Rest, Blue Aqua, 2 In. 14.00
Ink, Sanford's Inks & Library Paste, Aqua, 7 In. 2.50
Ink, Sanford's Inks & Library Paste, Aqua, 9 1/4 In. 2.50
Ink, Sanford's Inks & Library Paste, BIMAL, Amber, 9 1/4 In. 3.50
Ink, Sanford's Inks & Library Paste, BIMAL, Honey Amber, Pint 5.00
Ink, Sanford's, BIMAL, 2 1/2 In. 6.00
Ink, Sanford's, Embossed, Ground Screw Top, Amber, 5 3/4 In. 3.50
Ink, Sanford's, Embossed, Ground Screw Top, Amber, 9 1/2 In. 4.50
Ink, Sanford's, On Bottom, Cone, Aqua, 2 3/4 In. 4.00
Ink, Sanford's, Pouring Spout, Labels, Amber, Pint, 8 1/2 In. .... 14.00 To 24.00
Ink, Sandord's, 276, Sunken Circle, BIMAL, Bubbles, 2 3/4 In. 2.75
Ink, Schoolhouse, Aqua, 2 1/2 In. 6.00
Ink, Schoolhouse, Ring Lip, Aqua, 2 3/8 In. 5.00
Ink, Schoolhouse, 3 In. 4.50
Ink, Stafford's Fountain Pen, Patent May 17, 1892, Traveler's, 5 3/4 In. 13.50
Ink, Stafford's Universal, 8 In. ....Illus 40.00
Ink, Stafford's, BIMAL, Cobalt, Pint 12.00
Ink, Stafford's, Marked Vertically, Tooled Mouth, Green, 3 1/4 In. 10.00
Ink, Stafford's, Master, Pouring Lip, Cobalt, 5 7/8 In. 11.50
Ink, Stafford's, Master, Pouring Lip, Cobalt, 7 1/8 In. 11.50
Ink, Stafford's, Master, 6 In. 16.50
Ink, Stafford's, Pour Spout, Cobalt, Quart 23.00
Ink, Stafford's, Pouring Lip, Blue, 16 Ozs. 9.00
Ink, Stafford's, Pouring Lip, Stain, Cobalt, 6 In. 8.00
Ink, Stafford's, Vertical Embossed, Aqua, 3 In. 5.00
Ink, Stand's, William A.Davis, U.S.Treasury Mucilage, Boston, Aqua, 2 1/2 In. 6.00
Ink, Stoddard, Lockport, 12 Sided, OP, Green, 2 1/2 In. ....Illus 35.00

Ink, Tapestry Paint Co., Chicago, Square Roofed Shoulders, Haze, 2 1/2 In. 7.50
Ink, Thaddeus David's Copying, Paper Label, Green ....Color XXXX.XX
Ink, Traveling, Figural, Man's Brown Leather Shoe, 3 3/4 In. 60.00
Ink, Umbrella, Ring Lip, 8 Sided, Aqua, 3 In. 8.00
Ink, Umbrella, Rolled Lip, 8 Sided, OP, Aqua, 2 1/2 In. 12.00
Ink, Umbrella, Rolled Mouth, Pontil, Chips, Blue Green, 2 1/2 In., C-129 .... * 5.00
Ink, Umbrella, Rolled Mouth, Pontil, Similar To Covil 127, 2 1/2 In. .... * 130.00
Ink, Umbrella, Rolled Mouth, Pontil, Similar To Covil 137, Aqua, 2 1/2 In. .... * 15.00
Ink, Umbrella, Rolled Mouth, Pontil, Similar To Covil 141, Green, 2 1/2 In. .... * 40.00
Ink, Umbrella, Rolled Mouth, Smooth Base, Light Green, 2 1/2 In. 20.00
Ink, Umbrella, Sheared Lip, Haze, Aqua, 2 1/2 In. 9.00
Ink, Umbrella, Sheared Mouth, Similar To Covil 127, Olive Amber, 2 1/2 In. .... * 80.00
Ink, Umbrella, Tooled Mouth, Pontil, Similar To Covil 127, Aqua, 2 3/4 In. .... * 25.00
Ink, Umbrella, 12 Sided, OP, Aqua, 1 3/4 In. 30.00
Ink, Umbrella, 8 Sided, Haze, 2 3/4 In. 6.50
Ink, Underwood, Master, Pour Lip, Cobalt, 30 Ozs. 35.00
Ink, Underwood's, Master, Cobalt, 9 3/4 In. 25.50
Ink, Underwood's, Master, Pinch Spout, 3 Neck Rings, Cobalt, 6 3/4 In. 26.00
Ink, Underwood's, Spout, Cobalt, 6 1/2 In. 40.00

Jack Daniel, Lem Motlow's
Straight Apple Brandy, Pint

Jack Daniel,
Old Time Tennessee
Sour Mash, Pint

Jack Daniel, Old Time, Fifth

Ink, Vertical Ribs, Band Of Diamonds, Pontil, Olive Amber, 2 3/4 In. .... * 120.00
Ink, W.E.Bonney, Master, Barrel, 20 Rings, Pour Spout, Aqua, 5 1/8 In. .... * 150.00
Ink, Walkden's Brilliant Scarlet, Pottery, Tan Glaze, 1 3/4 In. .... * 10.00
Ink, WKG, Whitney Glass Works, Glassboro, N.J., Master, Blue Green, Quart 70.00
Ink, 7 Rings, Collared Mouth, Pontil, Yellow Amber, 2 1/4 In., C-1169 .... * 600.00
Ink, 7 Rings, Flat Collared Mouth, Pontil, Olive Green, 2 7/16 In., C-1170 .... * 500.00
Ink, 12 Sided, Aqua, 3 In. 18.00
Ink, 3W, C-349 .... 18.00
Irish Mist, Soldier 9.00
Jack Daniel, Lem Motlow's Straight Apple Brandy, Pint ....Illus 12.00
Jack Daniel, Old Time, Fifth ....Illus 8.00
Jack Daniel, Old Time Tennessee Sour Mash, Pint ....Illus 5.00
Jack Daniel, Tennessee Centennial Whiskey, Fifth ....Illus 15.00
Jar, B & D, 6 Rings, Rolled Mouth, Pontil, Aqua, 5 1/2 In. .... * 45.00
Jar, Cut Glass, Monarch Pattern, Covered, 6 In. 95.00
Jar, Cut Glass, Strawberry Diamond & Fan, 6 3/4 In. 75.00
Jar, Flanged Lip, Aqua, 9 In. 45.00
Jar, Flanged Lip, Green Yellow, 9 1/2 In. 110.00
Jar, Gold Medal Saleratus, Free Blown, Collar, Pontil, Green, 8 3/8 In. .... * 150.00
Jar, Ointment, McK G I-19, Flint, Blown, 3 Mold, Barrel, Brass Lid 20.00

Jar, Redware, Wide Mouth, 5 In. Diameter Top, 5 3/4 In.	30.00
Jar, Rolled Lip, Square, Olive, 1 1/2 Pint	55.00
Jar, Rolled Collared Mouth, Glass Lid, Pontil, Aqua, 11 1/4 In.	* 75.00
Jar, Rolled Collared Mouth, Pontil, Yellow Green, 10 In.	* 45.00
Jar, Smith Brothers, Covered, Melon Ribbed, Floral Decoration, 4 In.	150.00
Jon-Sol, Hodag, Female & Male, Goto, Japan, 3 1/2 In., Pair	29.90
Jon-Sol, Hodag, Female & Male, Kentucky Whiskey, Empty, 4 3/4 In., Pair	27.90
Jon-Sol, Totem Pole, Towa, Japan, Bisque Finish, Miniature	6.50
Jon-Sol, Wisconsin Baby Robin, Bisque Finish, 4 1/4 In.	9.95
Jon-Sol, Wisconsin Blue Jay, Bisque Finish, 5 In.	9.95
Jon-Sol, Wisconsin Red-Headed Woodpecker, Bisque Finish, 5 In.	9.95
Jug, Grape Design, Amber, Gallon	7.50
Jug, L.Lazarus & Son, Liquid Dealer, Lynchburg, Va., Embossed, Gallon	15.00
Kentucky Gentleman, Confederate Soldier	10.00 To 11.00
Kentucky Gentleman, Gentleman With Cane	15.00
Kentucky Gentleman, Pink Lady	25.00
Kentucky Gentleman, Revolutionary Soldier	10.00
Kentucky Gentleman, Soldier With Stripes	12.00
Kentucky Gentleman, Union Soldier	10.00 To 12.00
Kontinental Classics, Bobby Unser Olsonite Eagle, No.8	Illus 30.00
Kontinental Classics, Billy Vukovich Sugaripe Special, No.2	27.50 To 30.00
Kontinental Classics, Corvette, 1963, Split-Window Coupe	25.00 To 30.00
Kontinental Classics, Gandy Dancer	Color 37.50
Kontinental Classics, Gunsmith	40.00
Kontinental Classics, Lumberjack	Color 37.50
Kontinental Classics, Pioneer Printer/Editor	40.00
Kontinental Classics, Prospector With Burro	40.00
Kontinental Classics, Saddle Maker	40.00
Kontinental Classics, Statue Of Liberty	Color 37.50
Kontinental Classics, Stephen Foster	Color 37.50

Kontinental Klassics, Bobby Unser
Olgonite Eagle, No.8

Jack Daniel, Tennessee
Centennial Whiskey, Fifth
(See Page 142)

Kontinental Klassics,
Stephen Foster

Kord, Dolphin, Miniature	12.00
Koshu, Japanese Mask	20.00
Koshu, Naughty Boy, Frosted, Miniature	3.95
Kummel Bear, see Figural	
Lalique, Atomizer, Nude Females, Gilded Top, Light Amber Base, 5 1/2 In.	125.00
Last Chance Cologne, Western Bar Scene, Wooden Frame, Miniature, 6 Piece	80.00
Laurel & Hardy, Hardy	12.95
Laurel & Hardy, Laurel	12.95
Lewis & Clark, Battle Of Little Big Horn, Set Of 5	175.00
Lewis & Clark, Captain Meriwether Lewis	74.00
Lewis & Clark, Charbonneau	38.00 To 44.00
Lewis & Clark, Kentucky Gentlemen, Set Of 6	58.00
Lewis & Clark, Sacajawea	57.00
Lewis & Clark, York	38.00 To 39.95
Lido, Antique Peddler, Blue Label	21.95

Lionstone, Annie Christmas .... 16.95 To 40.00
Lionstone, Annie Oakley .... 17.95 To 35.00
Lionstone, Bar Scene, Frame & Shelf, Set Of 4 .... 275.00 To 325.00
Lionstone, Bar Scene, 1971, Wooden Frame & Nude Painting, 4 Bottles 350.00
Lionstone, Barber .... *Color XXXX.XX*
Lionstone, Bartender .... 28.95 To 100.00
Lionstone, Baseball Player .... 25.00 To 40.00
Lionstone, Basket Weaver 50.00
Lionstone, Basketball Player .... 25.00 To 40.00
Lionstone, Belly Robber, 4/5 .... *Illus* 50.00
Lionstone, Betsy Ross .... 25.00 To 45.00
Lionstone, Blacksmith .... 30.95 To 52.00
Lionstone, Bluebird, Eastern .... 15.00 To 32.00
Lionstone, Bluebird, Western .... 24.95 To 32.00
Lionstone, Bluebird, Wisconsin .... 17.95 To 34.00
Lionstone, Bluejay, Missouri .... 17.95 To 35.00
Lionstone, Boxers .... 25.00 To 40.00
Lionstone, Buccaneer .... 34.95 To 50.00
Lionstone, Buffalo Bill .... 35.00 To 36.00
Lionstone, Buffalo Hunter .... 32.00 To 35.00
Lionstone, Calamity Jane .... 29.95 To 45.00
Lionstone, Camp Cook .... 17.95 To 42.00
Lionstone, Camp Follower .... 22.50 To 35.00
Lionstone, Cannonade 40.00
Lionstone, Capistrano Swallow, Gold .... 14.95 To 49.00
Lionstone, Capistrano Swallow, Silver .... 49.00 To 69.00
Lionstone, Cardinal, Indiana .... 17.95 To 36.00
Lionstone, Casual Indian .... 9.50 To 31.00
Lionstone, Cavalry Scout .... 9.00 To 21.00
Lionstone, Cherry Valley Club, Gold .... 19.95 To 35.00
Lionstone, Cherry Valley Club, Silver .... 22.50 To 42.00
Lionstone, Chinese Laundryman .... 17.95 To 35.00
Lionstone, Circuit Judge .... 11.95 To 26.00
Lionstone, Cobbler, European Workers Series 40.00
Lionstone, Country Doctor .... 12.95 To 35.00
Lionstone, Cowboy .... 9.00 To 21.00
Lionstone, Cowgirl .... 27.50 To 36.00
Lionstone, Dance Hall Girl .... 30.95 To 70.00
Lionstone, Egg Merchant 50.00
Lionstone, European Workers, Set Of 4 .... 175.00
Lionstone, Flacon .... 21.95 To 35.00
Lionstone, Fire Fighter, No.1, Yellow Hat .... 39.95 To 65.00
Lionstone, Fire Fighter, No.2, With Child .... 28.95 To 55.00
Lionstone, Fire Fighter, No.3, On Pole .... 34.95 To 55.00
Lionstone, Football .... 22.00 To 40.00
Lionstone, Frontiersman, 4/5 .... *Illus* 50.00
Lionstone, Gambel's Quail .... 7.00 To 28.00
Lionstone, Gambler .... 6.95 To 25.00
Lionstone, Gardener 50.00
Lionstone, General George Washington Crossing The Delaware .... 29.95 To 45.00
Lionstone, Gentleman Gambler .... 24.95 To 35.00
Lionstone, Gold Panner .... 59.95 To 125.00
Lionstone, Goldfinch .... 15.00 To 32.00
Lionstone, Golf .... 24.95 To 40.00
Lionstone, Highway Robber .... 7.00 To 37.00
Lionstone, Hockey .... 26.00 To 40.00
Lionstone, Horseshoer, European Workers Series 40.00
Lionstone, Indian Squaw With Papoose 37.50
Lionstone, Jesse James .... 12.95 To 26.00
Lionstone, Johnny Lightning, No.1 .... 24.50 To 50.00
Lionstone, Johnny Lightning, No.2 .... 19.95 To 36.00
Lionstone, Judge Roy Bean .... 14.00 To 41.00
Lionstone, Lonely Luke .... 29.95 To 60.00
Lionstone, Lucky Buck .... 25.00 To 60.00
Lionstone, Madame .... 28.95 To 65.00

Lionstone, Mail Carrier .... 24.95 To 45.00
Lionstone, Meadowlark .... 14.00 To 28.00
Lionstone, Mecklenburg .... 40.00 To 55.00
  Lionstone, Miniature, see Miniature, Lionstone
Lionstone, Mint Bar Scene, With Nude, Set Of 4 .... 500.00
Lionstone, Molly Brown .... 27.50 To 36.00
Lionstone, Molly Pitcher 35.00
Lionstone, Mountain Man .... 17.95 To 50.00
Lionstone, Olsonite Eagle .... 17.50 To 30.00
Lionstone, Oriental Workers, Set Of 6 .... 280.00 To 300.00
Lionstone, Paul Revere .... 26.00 To 45.00
Lionstone, Peregrine Falcon .... 35.00 To 36.00
Lionstone, Perfessor .... 30.95 To 90.00

Lionstone, Frontiersman, 4/5
(See Page 144)

Lionstone, Belly Robber, 4/5
(See Page 144)

Lionstone, Riverboat
Captain, 4/5

Lionstone, Photographer .... *Color* *37.95*
Lionstone, Proud Indian .... 22.00 To 25.00
Lionstone, Railroad Engineer .... 11.95 To 26.00
Lionstone, Renegade Trader .... 27.50 To 35.00
Lionstone, Riverboat Captain, 4/5 .... *Illus* *26.00*
Lionstone, Roadrunner .... 16.95 To 48.00
Lionstone, Roses On Parade .... 17.50 To 90.00
Lionstone, STP Turbo Car .... 14.00 To 21.00
Lionstone, Sahara Golf Invitation 35.00
Lionstone, Saturday Night .... *Color* *35.00*
Lionstone, Screech Owl .... 22.95 To 36.00
Lionstone, Sculptor 50.00
Lionstone, Sheepherder .... 65.00 To 125.00
Lionstone, Sheriff .... 16.00 To 21.00
Lionstone, Shootout At O.K. Corral, Set Of 3 .... 229.95 To 300.00
Lionstone, Silversmith, European Workers Series 40.00
Lionstone, Sodbuster, 4/5 .... *Illus* *26.00*
Lionstone, Sons Of Freedom .... 34.95 To 50.00
Lionstone, Squaw & Papoose .... 34.00 To 35.00
Lionstone, Squawman .... 28.00 To 35.00
Lionstone, Stagecoach Driver, 4/5 .... *Illus* *50.00*
Lionstone, Tea Vendor 50.00
Lionstone, Telegraph Operator .... 14.00 To 35.00

Lionstone,
Sodbuster, 4/5
(See Page 145)

Lionstone, Stagecoach
Driver, 4/5
(See Page 145)

Lionstone, Timekeeper	50.00
Lionstone, Tinker	30.95 To 50.00
Lionstone, Tribal Chief	29.95 To 52.00
Lionstone, Vigilante	14.00 To 24.00
Lionstone, Wells Fargo Man	17.00 To 28.00
Lionstone, Winter At Valley Forge, Bicentennial Series	28.95 To 45.00
Lionstone, Woodhawk	28.95 To 75.00
Lionstone, Woodworker, European Workers Series	40.00
Liqueur, Benedictine, Sheared Mouth, Whittled, Applied String, Olive, Quart	5.00
Liqueur, Cointreau, BIMAL, Amber, Sample	2.00
Liqueur, E.Cusenier Creme De Menthe, Geni Shape, 10 In.	2.50
Liqueur, Sloe Gin, M.J. Weisskopf, Brown, 25/32 Quart	3.50

Luxardo, Apothecary Jar

Luxardo, Calypso Girl

*Luxardo bottles were first used in the 1930s to bottle the italian liqueurs.
The firm was founded in 1821. Most of the Luxardo bottles found today
date after 1943. The dates given are the first year the bottle was made.*

Luxardo, Albicocca, Apricot Brandy	1.60
Luxardo, Amanda, Amaretto Dry	1.70
Luxardo, Amaro Abano	1.60
Luxardo, Apothecary Jar *Illus*	*8.50*
Luxardo, Barrel, Tower Of Fruit	14.00
Luxardo, Buddliu	12.50
Luxardo, Calypso Girl *Illus*	*7.65*
Luxardo, Cannon, Brass Wheels	22.50
Luxardo, Chess Horse, 1970	*Color XXXX.XX*

Luxardo, Clock, Cherry Ardo 7.90
Luxardo, Coffe Carafe 9.85
Luxardo, Creme De Menthe 1.40
Luxardo, Dry Gin 1.15
Luxardo, Fernet 180.00
Luxardo, Ferro China, Iron Tonic Wine .... .90
Luxardo, Figs In Maraschino 8.60
Luxardo, Fish, Quartz, Venetian Murano 40.00
Luxardo, Fruit Basket 14.00
Luxardo, Gondola ....*Illus* 7.50
Luxardo, Kirschwasser 2.90
Luxardo, Lacrime D'Oro, Tears Of Gold 2.95
Luxardo, Maraschino .... 1.35 To 2.55
Luxardo, Marashino, Magnum 5.14
    Luxardo, Miniature, see Miniature, Luxardo
Luxardo, Miss "Belle Epoque, " 1970 ....*Color* XXXX.XX
Luxardo, Mister Luxardo 5.60
Luxardo, Modern Pheasant, 1960 ....*Color* XXXX.XX
Luxardo, Nubian 7.50
Luxardo, Onyx Owl, 1970 ....*Color* XXXX.XX
Luxardo, Owl, Alabaster 34.95
Luxardo, Pelinkovac 1.60
Luxardo, Pineapples In Kirsch 8.60
Luxardo, Pre-War Faenza, 1952 ....*Color* XXXX.XX
Luxardo, Pre-War Medieval Palace, 1952 ....*Color* XXXX.XX
Luxardo, Pre-War Tape Print, 1952 ....*Color* XXXX.XX
Luxardo, Quartz Fish, 1970 ....*Color* XXXX.XX
Luxardo, Sambuca Dei Cesari 1.60
Luxardo, Sangue Morlacco, Cherry Liqueur 1.80
Luxardo, Squirrel ....*Illus* 30.75
Luxardo, Suvaroff Vodka 1.15
Luxardo, Torre Tinta ....*Illus* 7.65
Luxardo, Tower Of Fruit Barrel 14.00
Luxardo, Triplum, Orange Triple Sec 1.90
Luxardo, Vase, Blue & Gold 14.00
Luxardo, Venus De Milo ....*Illus* 9.05
Luxardo, Zodiaco 9.35

Luxardo, Gondola

Luxardo, Squirrel

Luxardo, Venus De Milo

Luxardo, Torre Tinta

McKay, Scotsman .... 7.50 To 9.60
Majolica, Italian, C.1890, Rooster Mark, Floral, Yellow, 3 1/2 In. 20.00
Maloney, Villian .... 4.90 To 4.95
Mary Gregory, Blue, Girl Chasing Butterfly ....*Illus* *195.00*
   MBC, see Miniature, MBC
McCormick, Air Race Pylon, 1972 .... 12.00 To 15.00
McCormick, Air Race, Propeller 15.00
McCormick, Air Race, Reno, 1971 .... 18.00
McCormick, Air Races, Tall .... 9.95 To 12.95
McCormick, Barrel 9.95
McCormick, Bat Masterson .... 19.95 To 25.00
McCormick, Benjamin Franklin .... 24.00 To 28.00
McCormick, Betsy Ross .... 24.00 To 28.00
McCormick, Billy The Kid .... 23.95 To 25.00

Mary Gregory, Blue, Girl Chasing Butterfly

McCormick, Shriner
(See Page 149)

McCormick, Black Bart .... 23.95 To 27.00
McCormick, Bluebird .... 12.50 To 17.00
McCormick, Bookend, Spirit Of 1776, Sons Of Freedom, Pair 100.00
McCormick, Calamity Jane .... 21.00 To 27.00
McCormick, Daniel Boone 21.95
McCormick, Daniel Boone, Frontiersman Series ....*Color XXXX.XX*
McCormick, Davy Crockett 21.95
McCormick, Davy Crockett, Frontiersman Series ....*Color XXXX.XX*
McCormick, Doc Holiday .... 23.95 To 25.00
McCormick, George Washington, Patriot Series .... 24.00 To 25.95
McCormick, Georgia Bulldogs 12.95
McCormick, Georgia Tech Yellow Jackets Football 12.95
McCormick, Gunfighters, Set Of 6 .... 150.00
McCormick, Heritage Whiskey, Philadelphia Gold Bell, 1776-1976 .... 14.00
McCormick, Jeb Stuart .... 27.50 To 33.00
McCormick, Jefferson Davis .... 27.50 To 33.00
McCormick, Jesse James .... 23.95 To 25.00
McCormick, Jim Bowie .... 21.95 To 27.00
McCormick, Jim Bowie, Frontiersman Series ....*Color XXXX.XX*
McCormick, Julia Bulette .... 55.00 To 70.00
McCormick, Jupiter Locomotive .... 10.00 To 27.50
McCormick, Kit Carson 21.95
McCormick, Kit Carson, Frontiersman Series ....*Color XXXX.XX*
McCormick, Mail Car .... 35.00 To 42.50
McCormick, Michigan State Spartan 12.95
McCormick, Michigan Wolverine 12.95
   McCormick, Miniature, see Miniature, McCormick
McCormick, Minnesota Gophers 12.95
McCormick, Mississippe State Bulldog 14.95

McCormick, Missouri Sesquicentennial .... 6.50 To 8.95
McCormick, Ole Miss Rebel 14.95
McCormick, Passenger Car .... 37.50 To 47.50
McCormick, Patrick Henry .... 24.95 To 28.00
McCormick, Paul Revere 29.00
McCormick, Pioneer Theatre, Reno .... 4.95 To 6.50
McCormick, Pirates, Set Of 6 .... 8.95
McCormick, Platte Valley, Jug, Pint 15.00
McCormick, Robert E.Lee .... 27.95 To 33.00
McCormick, Shriner .... Illus   14.95
McCormick, Stonewall Jackson .... 27.50 To 33.00
McCormick, Sun Devil 18.00
McCormick, Tennessee Volunteers 13.95
McCormick, Thomas Jefferson .... 24.00 To 28.00
McCormick, Train Set, 4 Piece 75.00
McCormick, Wild Bill Hickok .... 23.95 To 25.00
McCormick, Wildcat 18.00
McCormick, Wisconsin Badger 13.95
McCormick, Wood Tender .... 19.95 To 37.50
McCormick, Wyatt Earp .... 19.95 To 25.00

Medicine, Abbey's Effervescent Salt, 3 In.

Medicine, Arctic Frostbite Cure, 2 1/2 In.

Medicine bottles held all of the many types of medications used in past centuries. Most of those collected today date from the 1850-1930 period. Bitters, sarsaparilla, poison, and a few other types of medicine are listed under their own headings.

Medicine, A.B.L. Myers, A.M. Rock Rose, New Haven, Collar, Green, Quart .... * 325.00
Medicine, A.F.Whittemore, Essex, Hawe's Healing Extract, Aqua, 3 1/4 In. .... * 40.00
Medicine, A.F.Whittemore, Hawe's Healing Extract, Conn., Aqua, 3 1/4 In. .... * 40.00
Medicine, A.H.Brown, Hair Specialist, Rectangular, Cobalt, 5 1/4 In. 60.00
Medicine, A.J.White Curative Syrup, Rectangular, Aqua, 5 1/8 In. 5.95
Medicine, A.McEckron's R.B.Liniment, N.Y., Pontil, Stain, Oval, Aqua, 6 In. .... * 30.00
Medicine, A.Morse Druggist, Prov., R.I., Flanged Collared Mouth, Aqua, Quart .... * 300.00
Medicine, A.Trask's Magnetic Ointment, OP, Haze, Square, Aqua, 2 1/2 In. 16.00
Medicine, A.Trask's Magnetic Ointment, Square, Haze, Green, 2 3/4 In. 2.50
Medicine, Abbey's Effervescent Salt, 3 In. .... Illus   3.00
Medicine, Abbot Bros. Rheumatic Remedy, Chicago, BIMAL, Amber, 7 1/4 In. 8.00
Medicine, African Hair Restorer, Rectangular, Cobalt, 6 1/2 In. 65.00
Medicine, Alexanders Silameau, Flake, Flat Bell Shape, Blue, 6 1/4 In. .... * 550.00
Medicine, Alexander's Sure Cure For Malaria, Amber, 8 In. 15.00
Medicine, Alkavis Kidney Cure, Label, BIMAL, Amber, 8 In. 8.00
Medicine, Allan's Lung Balsam, Ice Blue, 8 In. 6.50
Medicine, Altenheim Medical Dispensary For Hair, Cincinnati, 8 1/16 In. 4.00
Medicine, Altenheim Medical Dispensary, For The Hair, Lip Ring, 8 1/4 In. 6.50
Medicine, American Eagle Liniment, Hexagonal, 5 In. 20.00
Medicine, American Therapeutic Co., Horseshoe, Pear Shape, Emerald, 7 1/2 In. 7.00
Medicine, Anderson's Dermador, BIMAL, Oval, Aqua, 4 In. 4.00
Medicine, Ara Miraculous, Amber, 5 1/2 In. 3.00
Medicine, Arctic Frostbite Cure, 2 1/2 In. .... Illus   5.00
Medicine, Autenworth, Tooled Top, Blob Seal, Pale Green, 7 1/4 In. 350.00
Medicine, Averill & Fish, Anti-Morbific, Chicago, Square, Amber, 9 1/2 In. 30.00

Medicine, Ayer's Cherry Pectoral, Aqua, 6 In. 14.00
Medicine, Ayer's Cherry Pectoral, Lowell, Mass., Aqua, 7 1/2 In. .... 5.50 To 10.75
Medicine, Ayer's Cherry Pectoral, Lowell, Mass., Pontil, Aqua, 7 1/8 In. .... * 15.00
Medicine, Ayer's Cherry Pectoral, OP, Rectangular, Haze, Aqua, 7 X 2 In. 16.00
Medicine, Ayer's Pills, Lowell, Mass., Aqua, 2 In. 1.50
Medicine, Ayer's Senopos, Canton Mfg.Co., Wide Mouth, BIMAL, Amber, Pint 3.00
Medicine, B.A.Fahnestock Vermifuge, Aqua, 3 1/2 In. 2.00
Medicine, B.P.Co., Pills, BIMAL, Cobalt, 3 In. 5.00
Medicine, B.P.Lyon's Powder, N.Y., Rolled Lip, Dark Amber, 4 1/2 In. 10.00
Medicine, Baker's Great American Specific, R.H.Hurd, Maine, 5 1/2 In. .... * 10.00
Medicine, Baker's Pain Relief, Aqua, 9 In. 7.00
Medicine, Balm Of Thousand Flowers, Petridge & Co., N.Y., Pontil, Aqua, 5 In. .... * 75.00
Medicine, Barker Moore Co., Aqua, 6 In. 2.00
Medicine, Barker's Cod Liver Oil, Whittled, Flask, Aqua, 5 1/4 In. 10.00
Medicine, Barker's Dental Wash, Paper Label, Rectangular, Milk Glass, 7 In. 7.00
Medicine, Barry's Tricophorous For Skin & Hair, Rectangular, Green, 6 In. 8.50
Medicine, Barry's Tricophorous For The Skin & Hair, OP, Aqua, 6 In. 25.00
Medicine, Bartine's Lotion, Whittled, Emerald Green, 6 In. 400.00
Medicine, Blood Food, G.Handyside, Oval, Emerald Green, 6 1/2 In. 80.00
Medicine, Bogle's Hyperion Fluid For The Hair, Whittled, Flask, Aqua, 8 In. 25.00
Medicine, Borinated Tooth Powder, Sample 3.00
Medicine, Brant's Indian Purifying Extract, Flake, Aqua, 1/2 Pint .... * 40.00
Medicine, Brant's Pulmonary Balsam, OP, 7 In. 35.00
Medicine, Brant's Purifying Extract, 10 In. 27.00
Medicine, Brazilian Balm, Aqua, 5 1/2 In. 3.00
Medicine, Bromo Caffeine, Applied Collar, Stain, Cobalt, 3 1/4 In. 1.75
Medicine, Bromo Celery, Amber, 4 In. 3.50
Medicine, Bromo Seltzer, Emerson Drug Co., Baltimore, Md., Cobalt, 2 1/2 In. 10.00
Medicine, Burlington's Vegetable Croup Syrup, Blob Lip, Aqua, 5 1/2 In. 3.50
Medicine, Burton's Family Medicines, Aqua, 9 1/2 In. 10.00
Medicine, By The Kings Royal Patent, R.Turlington Balsam, Aqua, 2 5/8 In. .... * 40.00
Medicine, C.Brinckerhoff's Health Restorative, Price 1 Dollar, Amber, Pint .... * 140.00
Medicine, Caldwell's Syrup Of Pepsin, 4 In. 1.50
Medicine, Caldwell's Syrup Pepsin, Blue, 7 In. 2.00
Medicine, Camm's Spanish Lustral Or Hair Preservative, Aqua, 6 In. 27.00
Medicine, Campbell & Lyon, Umatilla Indian Hogan, Mich., Light Blue, 9 In. 40.00
Medicine, Cardui, The Woman's Tonic, Blue, 9 1/2 In. 3.00
Medicine, Carter's Spanish Mixture, Pontil, Crack, Olive Amber, 3/4 Quart .... * 45.00
Medicine, Castoria, Tip Cap, 5 In. .... .75
Medicine, Celery Compound, Celery Stalks, Cabin, Amber, Pint .... * 50.00
Medicine, Certain Cure For Rheumatism, Aqua, 7 In. 17.00
Medicine, Chamberlain's Colic, Cholera, & Diarrhea Remedy, Aqua, 4 1/2 In. 5.00
Medicine, Chamberlain's Cough Remedy, Blue, 5 3/4 In. 2.50
Medicine, Chamberlain's Pain Balm, Rectangular, BIMAL, Haze, Aqua, 7 In. 2.50
Medicine, Chapman's Cholera Syrup, 4 Salem St., Pontil, Aqua, 6 5/8 In. .... * 160.00
Medicine, Chapman's Genuine No.4 Salem St., Chip, Crack, Olive Amber, Quart .... * 250.00
Medicine, Christie's Magnetic Fluid, Pontil, Rectangular, Aqua, 4 3/4 In. .... * 25.00
Medicine, Citrate Iron & Quinine, Philadelphia, 7 1/2 In. .... *Illus* 12.00
Medicine, Citrate of Magnesia, 8 In. .... *Illus* 8.00
Medicine, Citrate Magnesia, BIMAL, Sun-Colored Amethyst, 12 Ozs. 1.00
Medicine, Clark & Co. Peruvian Syrup, Aqua, 8 1/2 In. 5.00
Medicine, Clark's Rheumatic Elixir, Aqua, 7 1/4 In. 5.50
Medicine, Clarke's Blood Mixture, Stain, Cobalt, 11 In. 25.00
Medicine, Clemens Indian Tonic, Geo.W.House, Crack, Aqua, 5 1/2 In. .... * 250.00
Medicine, Clickener's Sugar Coated Vegetable Purgative Pills, Aqua, 2 In. 32.00
Medicine, Clock's Excelsior Hair Restorer, Stain, Aqua, 7 In. 20.00
Medicine, Cod Liver Oil, Raised Fish, Amber, 7 1/2 In. 5.00
Medicine, Coltsfoot Expectorant Trademark, Rectangular, Stain, Aqua, 6 In. 3.00
Medicine, Connell's Brahminical Moon Plant East Indian, Amber, Pint .... * 50.00
Medicine, Constitutional Catarrh Remedy, Aqua, 7 1/4 In. 5.00
Medicine, Converse Treatment Institute, Mt.Vernon, Ohio, BIMAL, 8 3/4 In. 10.00
Medicine, Cr.S.S.Fitch, OP, Oval, 7 In. 30.00
Medicine, Craig's Kidney & Liver Cure Company, Oval, Amber, 9 1/2 In. 200.00
Medicine, Craig's Kidney & Liver Cure, Amber .... *Color* XXXX.XX
Medicine, Craig's Kidney & Liver Cure, Dark Amber .... *Color* XXXX.XX

Medicine, Cramer's Cure, Dug, Sample 2.50
Medicine, Crescent Polish Co., Van Wert, Ohio, Paper Label, Green, 4 1/2 In. 7.00
Medicine, Criswell's Bromo-Pepsin, Cures Headache, Amber, 2 1/2 In. 7.95
Medicine, Cuticura System Of Curing Constitutional Humors, Aqua, 9 1/4 In. 7.00
Medicine, Cuticura Treatment For Affections Of The Skin, Square, Aqua, 7 In 5.00
Medicine, Cuticura Treatment For Affections Of The Skin, Square, Aqua, 9 In 4.00
Medicine, D.R.Pierce Golden Medical Discovery, Label, BIMAL, 5 1/2 In. 15.00
Medicine, Dadd's Healing, Horses & Cattle, 6 1/2 In. ....*Illus* 7.50
Medicine, Dalbys Carminative, Pontil, Conical, Aqua, 3 3/4 In. .... * 80.00
Medicine, Dana's Cough Syrup, Belfast, Maine, Aqua, 6 1/2 In. 3.00
Medicine, Dandruff Cure, Ring Collar, Rectangular, Amethyst, 7 1/2 In. 9.95

Medicine, Citrate Iron & Quinine,
Philadelphia, 7 1/2 In.

Medicine, Dadd's
Healing, Horses & Cattle,
6 1/2 In.

Medicine, Citrate Of Magnesia, 8 In.
(See Page 150)

Medicine, Darby's Prophylactic Fluid, Phila., BIMAL, Aqua, 7 1/2 In. 4.00
Medicine, Davis Pain Killer, OP, Aqua, 4 1/2 In. 14.00
Medicine, Davis Vegetable Pain Killer, OP, Aqua, 7 In. 28.00
Medicine, Davis Vegetable Pain Killer, OP, Aqua, 9 In. 90.00
Medicine, Davis Vegetable Pain Killer, Pontil, Rectangular, Aqua, 5 In. .... * 10.00
Medicine, Davis' Vegetable Pail Killer, Dug, Haze, Aqua, 4 7/8 In. 15.00
Medicine, Davis' Vegetable Pain Killer, Blob Lip With Skirt, Aqua, 6 In. 3.00
Medicine, Davis' Vegetable Pain Killer, Blob Lip With Skirt, Aqua, 7 In. 4.00
Medicine, De Lacy's Cin-Ko-Na & Iron, Square, Amber, 9 1/2 In. 10.00
Medicine, Doctor Asher Atkinson, City Of New York, Collar, Green, 3/4 Quart .... * 450.00
Medicine, Double Distilled Witch Hazel, Dickinson, 3 Mold, Amber, 11 1/2 In. 7.50
Medicine, Dover's Powder, Pontil, Aqua, 1 7/8 In. .... * 15.00
Medicine, Dr.A.Roger's Liverwort, Tar & Chanchalagua, Flakes, Aqua, 1/2 Pint .... * 75.00
Medicine, Dr.Acker's Tu-Ber Ku Cough Mixture, Selma, Amethyst, 7 1/2 In. 6.00
Medicine, Dr.B.Ober's Compound Extract Of Mountain Ash, Pontil, Aqua, Pint .... * 200.00
Medicine, Dr.Baker's Pain Panacea, Aqua, 5 In. 30.00
Medicine, Dr.Bell's Anti-Pain, Paducah, Ky., Rectangular, 5 In. 5.00
Medicine, Dr.Bell's Pine Tar Honey Compound, 8 1/2 In. 15.00
Medicine, Dr.Browder's Compound Syrup Of Indian Turnip, Aqua, 1/2 Pint .... * 100.00
Medicine, Dr.C.W.Roback's Scandinavian Blood Purifier, Aqua, 8 3/4 In. .... * 60.00
Medicine, Dr.Carey's Marsh Root, Aqua, 7 1/2 In. 5.00
Medicine, Dr.Craig's Vitalized Ozone For Inflamation, Aqua, 4 1/2 In. 20.00
Medicine, Dr.Cumming's Vegetine, Aqua, 9 3/4 In. .... 3.00 To 3.95
Medicine, Dr.Cumming's Vegetine, Oval Flask, Blob Lip, Aqua, 9 3/4 In. 5.00
Medicine, Dr.Cumming's Vegetine, Oval, Aqua, 9 1/2 In. .... * 3.95
Medicine, Dr.Cumming's Vegetine, Oval, Aqua, 9 3/4 In. 3.95
Medicine, Dr.D.Jayne's Alterative, Phila., Oval, Aqua, 7 In. 5.00
Medicine, Dr.D.Jayne's Alterative, Philada., Pontil, Rectangular, Aqua, 6 In. .... * 15.00
Medicine, Dr.D.Jayne's Carminative Balsam, OP, 5 In. 25.00
Medicine, Dr.D.Jayne's Carminative Balsam, Philada., Pontil, Aqua, 5 1/4 In. .... * 30.00
Medicine, Dr.D.Jayne's Expectorant, BIMAL, Rectangular, Aqua, Trial Size 3.00

Medicine, Dr.D.Jayne's Expectorant, Blob Lip, 8 Sided, Aqua, 6 3/4 In. 5.00
Medicine, Dr.D.Jayne's Expectorant, OP, 7 In. 39.00
Medicine, Dr.D.Jayne's Hair Tonic, Philada., Pontil, Oval, Aqua, 4 1/2 In. .... * 70.00
Medicine, Dr.D.Jayne's Indian, Expectorant, Phila., Rectangular, Aqua, 5 In. .... * 70.00
Medicine, Dr.D.Jayne's Liniment Or Counter Irritant, Phila., OP, 6 1/2 In 45.00
Medicine, Dr.D.Jayne's Tonic Vermifuge, Strength Giver, Aqua, 5 1/2 In. 5.00
Medicine, Dr.D.R.Bouvier's Buchu Gin, Stain, Miniature 15.00
Medicine, Dr.Daniel's Veterinary Colic Cure No.2, Cork, 3 1/2 In. 2.50
Medicine, Dr.Daniel's Veterinary Colic Drops, Square, Lavender, 3 1/2 In. 4.25
Medicine, Dr.Fenner's Kidney & Backache Cure, Amber, 10 In. 22.00
Medicine, Dr.Gordak's, Iceland Jelly, Pontil, Rectangular, Aqua, 6 3/4 In. .... * 100.00
Medicine, Dr.Greene's Nervura, Aqua, 9 1/4 In. 4.00
Medicine, Dr.H.Anders & Co., Hauriexhac Fontevitate, Glass Stopper, 9 In. 19.00
Medicine, Dr.H.Kelsey, Lowell, Mass., Oval, Aqua, 6 X 3 In. 20.00
Medicine, Dr.H.W.Jackson Druggist Vegetable Home Syrup, Bruise, Amber, 6 In .... * 300.00
Medicine, Dr.H.W.Jackson Druggist Vegetable Home Syrup, Olive Amber, 4 In. .... * 500.00
Medicine, Dr.Harter's Iron Tonic, BIMAL, Amber, 6 In. 12.50
Medicine, Dr.Hartshorn's Family, Bull's-Eye, BIMAL, 7 In. 12.00
Medicine, Dr.Hayne's Arabian Balsam, Pitting, Amber, Quart 18.00
Medicine, Dr.Hayne's Arabian Balsam, R.I., 12 Sided, Aqua, 4 1/2 In. 3.00

Medicine, Dr.J.Pettit's Canker Balsam, 4 In.

Medicine, Dr.Miles's New Cure For The Heart, 9 In.
(See Page 153)

Medicine, Dr.Shoop's Cough Cure, 7 In.
(See Page 153)

Medicine, Dr.Higgins' Great Antalgica, Pontil, 12 Sided, Aqua, 5 3/4 In. .... * 30.00
Medicine, Dr.Hubbard's Vegetable Disinfectant, Oval, Aqua, 6 1/2 In. 3.95
Medicine, Dr.J.H.McLean's Tar Wine Balm, St.Louis, Cork, Stain, Aqua, 5 In. 4.00
Medicine, Dr.J.P.Miller's Magnetic Balm, Rectangular, Haze, Aqua, 4 3/4 In. 3.00
Medicine, Dr.J.Pettit's Canker Balsam, 4 In. .... *Illus* 8.50
Medicine, Dr.J.V.Wilson's, Norwich, Conn., Pontil, Stain, Aqua, 7 1/4 In. .... * 15.00
Medicine, Dr.J.W.Poland's White Pine Compound, Aqua, 7 In. 5.50
Medicine, Dr.Jaugo's Spanish Ague Remedy, Paper Label, IP, 8 In. 30.00
Medicine, Dr.Job Sweet's Relaxative Ointment, Mass., Aqua, 3 1/4 In. 7.00
Medicine, Dr.Kennedy's Medical Discovery, Mass., Collared, Aqua, 8 3/4 In. 6.00
Medicine, Dr.Kennedy's Medical Discovery, Roxbury, Mass., Aqua, 9 In. 4.50
Medicine, Dr.Kennedy's Prairie Weed, Roxbury, Mass., Aqua, 8 1/2 In. 9.00
Medicine, Dr.Kilman's Female Remedy, Label, Contents, Aqua, 8 1/2 In. 17.00
Medicine, Dr.Kilmer's Cure, Sample, Aqua, 4 1/4 In. 2.95
Medicine, Dr.Kilmer's Indian Cough Cure, Stain, Aqua, 5 3/4 In. 15.00
Medicine, Dr.Kilmer's Kidney, Liver & Bladder Cure, Aqua, 8 In. 5.00
Medicine, Dr.Kilmer's Swamp Root Cure Specific, Aqua, Pint .... * 15.00
Medicine, Dr.Kilmer's Swamp Root Cure, Amethyst, 7 In. 14.95
Medicine, Dr.Kilmer's Swamp Root Cure, London, Sample 9.75

Medicine, Dr.Kilmer's Swamp Root Kidney & Bladder Cure, Aqua, 8 In. 4.45
Medicine, Dr.Kilmer's Swamp Root Kidney & Bladder Cure, 8 1/4 In. 5.45
Medicine, Dr.Kilmer's Swamp Root Kidney & Liver Cure, Sample Size 1.50
Medicine, Dr.Kilmer's Swamp Root Kidney Cure, Sample 5.00
Medicine, Dr.Kilmer's Swamp Root Kidney, Liver & Bladder Cure, Aqua, 7 In. 2.45
Medicine, Dr.Kilmer's Swamp Root Kidney, Liver, & Bladder, Amethyst, 7 In. 14.95
Medicine, Dr.Kilmer's, Square Collar, Sample, Aqua, 3 1/8 In. 2.95
Medicine, Dr.King's New Discovery For Coughs & Colds, Blob Lip, Aqua, 8 In. 5.00
Medicine, Dr.L.E.Keeley's Cure For Drunkenness, Oval, Amethyst, 5 1/2 In. 99.95
Medicine, Dr.Lunt's Ague Killer, 7 In. 50.00
Medicine, Dr.M.M.Fenner's Peoples Remedies, 1872-1898, Amber, 10 1/4 In. 17.50
Medicine, Dr.McMunn's Elixir Of Opium, Crack, Aqua, 4 1/8 In. .... * 12.50
Medicine, Dr.Merriman's Kalliodont For Beautifying The Teeth, Amber, 12 In 10.00
Medicine, Dr.Mile's Restorative Nervine, Aqua, 8 In. 3.50
Medicine, Dr.Mile's Restorative Nervine, Embossed, Cork, 8 3/8 In. 3.00
Medicine, Dr.Miles' New Cure For The Heart, 9 In. ....*Illus* 22.00
Medicine, Dr.Miles' New Heart Cure, Aqua, Sample Size 9.00
Medicine, Dr.Moore's Essence Life, Pontil, Aqua, 3 3/4 In. .... * 25.00
Medicine, Dr.Mowe's Couch Balsam, Lowell, Mass., Applied Lip, Aqua, 4 In. 5.00
Medicine, Dr.Pierce's Extract Of Smart Weed, Paneled, Blob Lip, Aqua, 7 In. 8.00
Medicine, Dr.Pierce's Favorite Prescription, Buffalo, N.Y., Aqua, 8 1/4 In. 4.00
Medicine, Dr.Pierce's Golden Medical Discovert, Rectangular, Green, 8 In. 5.50
Medicine, Dr.Pinkham's Emmenagogue, Pontil, Square, Aqua, 6 In. 40.00
Medicine, Dr.Pinkham's Emmenagogue, Square, Aqua, 6 In. .... 32.75 To 40.00
Medicine, Dr.Porter's, N.Y., OP, Blue Aqua, 5 In. .... 20.00 To 24.00
Medicine, Dr.R.Merwin, Restore To Manly Vigor, Square, Blue Green, 5 1/2 In. 8.00
Medicine, Dr.Roger's Vegi-Medica Syrup, Paneled, Collared Lip, Aqua, 9 In. 7.00
Medicine, Dr.Rose's, Philada., OP, Haze, Aqua, 5 3/4 In. 12.00
Medicine, Dr.S.A.Tuttle, Boston, Mass., Aqua, 6 1/4 In. 3.50
Medicine, Dr.S.A.Weaver's Canker & Salt Rheum Syrup, R.I., Oval, Aqua, Quart .... * 35.00
Medicine, Dr.S.Pitcher's Castoria, Blob Lip, Aqua, 5 3/4 In. 2.00
Medicine, Dr.S.Pitcher's Castoria, Bubbles, C.1880, Aqua, 5 1/4 In. 5.75
Medicine, Dr.S.Pitcher's Castoria, Rectangular, Aqua, 5 3/4 In. 2.95
Medicine, Dr.S.S.Fitch, OP, Rectangular, 5 X 2 In. 18.00
Medicine, Dr.S.S.Fitch, 707 B'Way, N.Y., Whittled, Flask, Aqua, 6 1/2 In. 18.00
Medicine, Dr.S.S.Fitch, 707 B.Way, N.Y., OP, Aqua, 4 1/2 In. 25.00
Medicine, Dr.S.S.Fitch, 707 B.Way, N.Y., Pontil, Rectangular, Aqua, 4 5/8 In. .... * 15.00
Medicine, Dr.S.S.Fitch, 714 Broadway, N.Y., Pontil, Oval, Aqua, 6 3/8 In. .... * 40.00
Medicine, Dr.Sage's Catarrh Remedy, BIMAL, Aqua, 2 1/4 In. 2.50
Medicine, Dr.Sanford's Liver Invigorator, Aqua, 7 1/2 In. 6.00
Medicine, Dr.Seth Arnold's Balsam, Aqua, 4 In. 3.00
Medicine, Dr.Shoop's Cough Cure, 7 In. ....*Illus* 8.00
Medicine, Dr.Shoop's Family, Racine, Wis., Embossed, Cork, Cloudy, 6 3/4 In. 4.50
Medicine, Dr.Sullivan's Sure Solvent, A Reliable Tonic, 7 5/8 In. 3.00
Medicine, Dr.Tebbetts', Physiological Hair, Regenerator, Puce, 1/2 Pint .... * 100.00
Medicine, Dr.Thatcher's Liver & Blood Syrup, Stain, Yellow Amber, 3 3/8 In. 5.00
Medicine, Dr.Thenard Gold Lion Iron Tonic, Stain, Amber, Quart 65.00
Medicine, Dr.Thompson's Eye Water, New London, Applied Collar, Aqua, 1 In. 2.00
Medicine, Dr.Thrall's Compound Extract Of Cohosh Pond Lily, Aqua, 8 In. .... * 260.00
Medicine, Dr.Tobias Venetian Horse Liniment, N.Y., Aqua, 8 In. 6.00
Medicine, Dr.Tobias Venetian Liniment, N.Y., Oval Flask, Aqua, 4 In. 5.00
Medicine, Dr.Tobias, Venetian Liminent, Pontil, Rectangular, Aqua, 1/2 Pint .... * 20.00
Medicine, Dr.Tobias, New York, Venetian Liniment, Aqua, 6 1/4 In. .... * 12.50
Medicine, Dr.Tobias, New York, Venetian Liniment, Oval, Aqua, 4 In. .... * 20.00
Medicine, Dr.Tobias, Venetian Horse Liniment, New York, Aqua, 8 In. .... * 45.00
Medicine, Dr.Townsend's Hay Fever & Asthma Remedy, Embossed, 7 1/2 In. 5.00
Medicine, Dr.Van Wert's Balsam, N.Y., Aqua, 5 In. 2.00
Medicine, Dr.Van Wert's Balsam, Watertown, N.Y., Rectangular, Haze, 6 In. 3.00
    Medicine, Dr.W.B.Caldwell's, see Medicine, Caldwell's Syrup of
    Pepsin, Caldwell's Syrup Pepsin
Medicine, Dr.W.Evan's Teething Syrup, OP, Cloudy, Aqua, 2 1/2 In. 5.00
Medicine, Dr.Ward's Liniment, BIMAL, Aqua, 8 1/2 In. 10.00
Medicine, Dr.Ward's Liniment, BIMAL, AQUA, 5 IN. 7.00
Medicine, Dr.Wheeler's Nerve Vitalizer, Embossed, Cork, 7 3/4 In. 2.50
Medicine, Dr.Whittlesey's Dyspepsia Cure, 8 In. ....*Illus* 15.00

Medicine, Dr.Whittlesey's Dyspepsia Cure, 8 In.
(See Page 153)

Medicine, Dr.Wistar's Wild Cherry Balsam, Phila.

Medicine, Ely's Nasal Cream Balm, Amber, 3 1/2 In.

Medicine, Dr.Williams Pink Pills For Pale People, For Export, 2 In.	4.00
Medicine, Dr.Wistar's Balsam Of Wild Cherry, Dug, Aqua, 4 3/16 In.	2.00
Medicine, Dr.Wistar's Balsam Of Wild Cherry, Octagonal, Aqua, 6 1/4 In.	* 25.00
Medicine, Dr.Wistar's Balsam Of Wild Cherry, Philada., 8 Sided, 6 1/2 In.	5.00
Medicine, Dr.Wistar's Balsam Of Wild Cherry, Philada, Haze, Aqua, 5 In.	10.50
Medicine, Dr.Wistar's Wild Cherry Balsam, Phila. *Illus*	40.00
Medicine, Dr.Wood's Aromatic Spirit, Bellows Falls, Vt., Oval, Aqua, Pint	* 70.00
Medicine, Dr.Young's Healing Antiseptic, Amber, 5 1/2 In.	8.00
Medicine, Drandriff's Vegetable Antidote For Ague, Piqua, Ohio, Aqua, Pint	5.00
Medicine, Dyer's Healing Embrocation, Prov., R.I., Oval, Aqua, 5 1/4 In.	35.00
Medicine, E.S.Reed's Sons Apothecary, Sphinx, N.J., Milk Glass, 4 1/2 In.	* 30.00
Medicine, Electro Chemical Compound Of Blackberry, Olive Amber, 1/2 Pint	* 50.00
Medicine, Ely's Cream Balm, Hay Fever & Catarrh, Cork, Haze, Amber, 2 3/4 In.	3.75
Medicine, Ely's Nasal Cream Balm, Amber, 3 1/2 In. *Illus*	2.50
Medicine, Emitol Tablets, Meier Dental & Surgical Co., Stain, Cobalt, 3 In.	6.00
Medicine, Eno's Fruit Salt Derivative Compound, 8 Sided, Stain, Blue, 7 In.	7.50
Medicine, Eno's Fruit Salt, 8 Sided, Aqua, 2 1/2 In.	8.50
Medicine, Essence Of, Peppermint, By The, Kings Patent, Square, Aqua, 2 7/8 In	* 40.00
Medicine, F.Brown's, Ess Of, Jamaica Ginger, Philada, Aqua, 5 3/4 In.	2.45
Medicine, Farmer's Horse, S.F., Cal., XXX, Aqua, 6 In.	8.00
Medicine, Fellow's Syrup Of Hypophosphites, Oval, Aqua, 8 In.	3.95
Medicine, Fenner's, see Dr.M.M.Fenner's Peoples Remedies	
Medicine, Fenning's Fever Curer, Flat Front, 6 1/2 In.	15.00
Medicine, Fisher's Seaweed Extract, Embossed Manx Shrub, Emerald, 5 In.	46.50
Medicine, Flagg's Good Samaritan Immediate Relief, 5 Sided, Aqua, 3 1/2 In.	34.00
Medicine, Flared Mouth, Tubular Pontil, Olive Amber, 5 In.	* 20.00
Medicine, Foley's Kidney Cure, Sample	4.00
Medicine, Foley's Honey & Tar, Chicago, Blue Aqua, 4 In.	3.00
Medicine, Foley's Kidney & Bladder Remedy, Rectangular, Amber, 9 1/4 In.	5.50
Medicine, Foley's Kidney Cure, BIMAL, Rectangular, Aqua, Sample Size	3.00
Medicine, Foley's Kidney Cure, Chicago, BIMAL, Aqua, 4 1/4 In.	3.75
Medicine, Forest's Juniper Tar, Embossed Witehurst Flask, Cork, 3 1/2 In.	5.00
Medicine, Friedenwald's, see Medicine, Dr.D.R.Bouvier's Buchu	
Gin	
Medicine, G.R.& N. Cure & Magical Pain Extractor, Haze, Aqua, 5 In.	11.00
Medicine, G.W.Merchant Chemist, Lockport, N.Y., Bruise, Emerald, 5 3/4 In.	* 70.00
Medicine, G.W.Merchant Chemist, Lockport, N.Y., Pontil, Emerald, Pint	* 220.00
Medicine, G.W.Merchant Chemist, Lockport, N.Y., Rough, Blue Green, 5 1/2 In.	* 50.00
Medicine, G.W.Stone's Liquid Cathartic, Olive Amber, 3/4 Quart	* 825.00
Medicine, Gardner, Tooled Mouth, Smooth Base, Oval, 4 1/4 In.	* 10.00
Medicine, Gargling Oil, Green, 5 1/2 In.	5.00
Medicine, Gargling Oil, Lockport, N.Y., Aquamarine, 7 1/4 In.	12.50
Medicine, Gargling Oil, Lockport, N.Y., Rectangular, Yellow Green, 5 1/2 In.	* 20.00

Medicine, Gauvin's Syrup For Babies, Aqua, 5 In. 3.00
Medicine, Genuine Essence, OP, 5 X 1 In. 18.00
Medicine, Genuine Essence, Applied Collar, Rectangular, Aqua, 4 1/2 In. 2.00
Medicine, Genuine Essence, Dug, Aqua, 4 1/2 In. 12.50
Medicine, Genuine Essence, Pontil, Rectangular, Aqua, 4 7/8 In. .... * 10.00
Medicine, Genuine, Swaim's Panacea, Philadelphia, Rectangular, Aqua, 7 7/8 In ...... * 450.00
Medicine, Gibson's Tablets, E.C.Rich, New York, Aqua, 12 1/2 In. 15.00
Medicine, Gilbert & Co., Phila., OP, 5 X 1 In. 18.00
 Medicine, Gin, see Gin
Medicine, Glenn & Co., Phila., Ointment, 3 Mold, Brass Lid, 3 3/4 In. 20.00
Medicine, Glover's Imperial Distemper Remedy, Blob Lop, Amber, 5 In. 5.00
Medicine, Glover's Imperial Mange, Amber, 6 1/2 Ozs. 5.00
Medicine, Gold Dandruff Cure, Rectangular, Amethyst, 7 1/2 In. 9.95
Medicine, Golden's Liquid Beef Tonic, Lip Ring, Teal Blue Green, 9 3/4 In. 6.00
Medicine, Greene's Warranted Pulmonary Syrup Of Tar, Aqua, 6 1/2 In. 6.00
Medicine, Griscom's Bone Marrow Liniment, 8 In. 10.00
Medicine, Guinn Pioneer Blood Renewer, Amber, 9 1/2 In. 17.00
Medicine, Guinn's Pioneer Blood Renewer, Macon, Ga., BIMAL, Amber, 9 In. 20.00
 Medicine, H.H.Warner's, see Medicine, Warner's
Medicine, H.Lake's Indian Specific, Pontil, Rectangular, Aqua, 8 In. .... * 320.00
Medicine, H.M.Parchen & Co., Helena, M.T., 4 1/4 In. 12.00
Medicine, Hair's Asthma Cure, Stain, 8 In. 8.00
Medicine, Hale's Honey Of Horehound & Tar, N.Y., Aqua, 8 1/2 In. 4.50
Medicine, Hall's Catarrh Cure, Flared Square Collar, Amethysy, 4 1/2 In. 2.50
Medicine, Hall's Catarrh Cure, 4 1/2 In. .... *Illus* 5.00
Medicine, Hampton's V.Tincture, Mortimer & Mowbray, Balto., Yellow, 6 3/8 In 600.00
Medicine, Harper's Cephalgine For Headache, Washington, D.C., 5 In. 2.00
Medicine, Haviland & Co., New York, Charleston & Augusta, Pontil, Aqua, 6 In. ...... * 50.00
Medicine, Hay's Hair Health, BIMAL, Yellow Amber, 3 In. 3.00
Medicine, Hay's Hair Health, Apr.1, 1912, Rectangular, Amber, 7 In. 6.50
Medicine, Hayner's Cure, Label, White, Gallon 27.50
Medicine, Hayner's Rock & Roll Cure For Coughs & Colds, Blue, White, Pint 65.00
Medicine, Healy & Bigelow Kickapoo Indian Cough Cure, Aqua, 9 1/4 In. 5.50
Medicine, Healy & Bigelow Kickapoo Indian Oil, Aqua, 5 1/2 In. 3.50
Medicine, Healy & Bigelow Kickapoo Indian Oil, BIMAL, Aqua, Trial Size 4.00
Medicine, Healy & Bigelow Kickapoo Indian Oil, BIMAL, 5 1/2 In. 8.50
Medicine, Healy & Bigelow, Indian Sagwa, Rectangular, Aqua, 1/2 Pint .... * 10.00
Medicine, Henry's Magnesia, Calcined, 4 In. .... *Illus* 4.00
Medicine, Herb Juice, Embossed, Cork, Cloudy, 8 1/4 In. 2.00
Medicine, Hick's Capudine For Headaches, Indented Panel, Flask, Amber, 3 In. 4.00
Medicine, Hobensack's Medicated Worm Syrup, Aqua, 4 1/2 In. 4.50
Medicine, Hobensack's Medicated Worm Syrup, Paneled, Aqua, 4 3/4 In. 4.50
Medicine, Howe's Arabian Tonic Blood Purifier, Aqua, 9 1/2 In. .... 18.00 To 22.00
Medicine, Humphrey's Co., Embossed Horse's Head, BIMAL, Square, 1/2 Pint 10.00
Medicine, Humphrey's Homeopathic Veterinary Specific, 6 3/4 In. 8.00
Medicine, Humphrey's Homeopathic Veterinary Specific, Embossed, 2 In. 2.00
Medicine, Hunt's Liniment, G.E.Stanton, N.Y., Pontil, Rectangular, Aqua, 5 In. ...... * 25.00

Medicine, Hall's Catarrh Cure, 4 1/2 In.

Medicine, Henry's Magnesia,
Calcined, 4 In.

Medicine, Hunt's Remedy, Aqua, 7 In.	4.00
Medicine, Hyde's Cough Cure, Willoughby, O., Brown, 5 1/2 In. .... *Illus*	1.00
Medicine, Indian Sagwa, see Medicine, Healy & Bigelow	
Medicine, Indianapolis Cordial, 10 In.	10.00
Medicine, J.B.Wilder & Co., Louisville, Rectangular, Aqua, 6 1/2 X 2 In.	29.50
Medicine, J.E.Combault's Caustic Balsam, Canada & U.S., Green, 2 1/2 In.	6.25
Medicine, J.H.Gaylord Pine Tree Balsam, Stain, Green, 4 3/4 In.	3.00
Medicine, J.R.Reeves Co., Anderson, Ind., Stain, Amethyst, 6 1/2 In.	6.95
Medicine, J.R.Rowand, Philada., Pontil, Hexagonal, Aqua, 4 1/4 In.	* 30.00
Medicine, J.R.Spalding's Rosemary & Castor Oil, Pontil, Oval, Aqua, 5 In.	* 25.00
Medicine, J.Russell Spaulding, Genuine, Boston, Paneled, OP, Dug, Aqua, 8 In.	65.00
Medicine, J.W.Hawkes, M.D., Manchester, N.H., 12 Panels, OP, 6 1/2 In.	22.00
Medicine, J.W.Hunnewell & Co., Universal Cough Remedy, Boston, Aqua, 6 In.	20.00
Medicine, Jacob's Cholera & Dysentery Cordial, 1853, Square, 7 In.	35.00
Medicine, Jacobs & Brown, Hamilton, O., Embossed, Rectangular, Aqua, 5 3/4 In.	50.00
Medicine, Jacobs & Brown, Hamilton, O., Pontil, Rectangular, Aqua, 5 3/4 In.	* 65.00
Medicine, John J.Smith, Louisville, Stain, Blue Aqua, 6 In.	15.00
Medicine, John Wyeth & Bro., Phila., Liquid Extract, Malt, Amber, 9 1/4 In.	24.00
Medicine, John Wyeth & Bro., Philadelphia, Liq.Ect.Malt, Amber, 9 In.	7.00
Medicine, John Wyeth & Bro., Take Next Dose At, Dose Cap, Cobalt, 6 1/2 In.	8.00
Medicine, John Wyeth & Bros., Dose Cap, ABM, Dug, Cobalt, 6 1/4 In.	5.00
Medicine, Johnson's American Anodyne Liniment, Pontil, Aqua, 4 1/2 In.	* 15.00
Medicine, Johnson's American Anodyne Liniment, Whittled, Aqua, 4 1/2 In.	7.00
Medicine, Jones, American Cholacogue, Pontil, Rectangular, Aqua, 1/2 Pint	* 280.00
Medicine, Kara Tonic, Rectangular, Turning Purple, 10 In.	12.00
Medicine, Kelly's Percuro, Pontil, Inside Haze, 6 In.	140.00
Medicine, Kemp's Cough Balsam, Leroy, N.Y., Rectangular, Aqua, 2 5/8 In.	3.50
Medicine, Kendall's Spavin Cure For Human Flesh, 10 Sided, Aqua, 5 1/4 In.	5.00
Medicine, Kendall's Spavin Cure, BIMAL, 5 3/4 In.	4.00
Medicine, Kendall's Spavin Cure, Enosburgh Falls, Vt., Amber, 5 1/2 In.	3.50
Medicine, Kendall's Spavin Cure, Enosburgh Falls, Vt., 12 Sides, Aqua, 6 In.	4.50
Medicine, Kendall's Spavine Cure, 12 Sided, Yellow Amber, 5 1/2 In.	* 20.00
Medicine, Kepler Cod Liver Oil With Malt Extract & Iron, Blue Green, 8 In.	7.00
Medicine, Kerr's System Renovator, Cincinnati, Square, Amber, 8 In.	15.00
Medicine, Kickapoo Oil, see Medicine, Healy & Bigelow	
Medicine, Kilmer's Kidney, Liver, & Bladder Cure, London, Stain, 5 5/8 In.	8.00
Medicine, Kilmer's Swamp Root Cure, BIMAL, Rectangular, Aqua, Sample Size	3.00
Medicine, King's Patent, Turlington, Balsam, 1854, Violin, Aqua, 2 5/8 In.	* 60.00
Medicine, Kodal Dyspepsia Cure, Light Green, 9 1/4 In.	10.00
Medicine, L.Hunnewell Tolu Anodyne, Boston, Mass., Aqua, 4 In.	4.00
Medicine, Lactopeptine, Paper Label, Cobalt, 7 7/8 In.	15.00
Medicine, Lanman & Sevin Ess.Wintergreen, Free Blown, Pontil, 5 1/8 In.	* 25.00
Medicine, Laxative Senna, Green, 7 In.	2.00
Medicine, Lediard's, Morning Call, Collar, Bruise, Square, Green, Quart	* 150.00
Medicine, Liebig's Beef Wine & Iron, Chicago, Green, 3 1/4 In.	8.00
Medicine, Life Plant, BIMAL, Amber, 8 1/2 In.	25.00
Medicine, Lightning Hot Drops, Blue, 5 In.	2.50
Medicine, Liquid Opodeldoc, Flared Mouth, Pontil, Aqua, 4 3/4 In.	* 15.00
Medicine, Liquifruta Cough Cure, Rectangular, Green, 5 1/4 In.	175.00
Medicine, Liquore Purgativo Profre Arena Napoli, Cobalt, 6 3/4 In.	* 10.00
Medicine, Liquozone, Chicago, Amber, 5 3/4 In.	3.00
Medicine, Lord's Opeldoc, Arched Panel, Oval, Aqua, 5 In.	6.95
Medicine, Lord's Opeldoc, Embossed Man & Crutches, Aqua, 5 In.	6.95
Medicine, Louden & Co.'s Alterative, Philada., Pontil, Oval, Aqua, 6 1/2 In.	* 30.00
Medicine, Louden's Indian Expectorant, Oval, 7 1/2 In.	60.00
Medicine, Louis Daudelin Co., Blood Wine, 8 1/2 In.	3.00
Medicine, Lyon Acid Cure Solution, Pottery, Ginger Beer Shape, 5 In.	15.00
Medicine, Lyons Powder, B & P, N.Y., Misshapen, Rolled Lip, Aqua, 4 1/4 In.	12.00
Medicine, Lyons Powder, B.& P.N.Y., Pontil, Apricot Color, 4 3/8 In.	* 80.00
Medicine, M.B.Robert's Vegetable Embrocation, Pontil, Green, 5 In.	* 95.00
Medicine, Macassar Oil, Flared Lip, OP, Aqua, 3 1/2 In.	15.00
Medicine, Magic Mosquito Bite Cure & Insect Exterminator, Aqua, 7 1/2 In.	4.95
Medicine, Magic Mosquito Bite Cure & Insect Exterminator, Aqua, 7 3/4 In.	6.00
Medicine, Malydor Private Physician, Flask, 1/2 Pint	7.00
Medicine, Marvin Cod Liver Oil, 8 1/2 In.	2.00

Kontinental Classics, Statue Of Liberty

Kontinental Classics, Stephen Foster

Luxardo, Chess Horse, 1970.

Luxardo, Miss "Belle Epoque," 1970

Luxardo, Modern Pheasant, 1960

Luxardo, Onyx Owl, 1970

Luxardo, Pre-War Faenza, 1952   Luxardo, Pre-War Tapa Print, 1952

Luxardo, Pre-War Medieval Palace, 1952

Luxardo, Quartz Fish, 1970

Lionstone, Photographer

Lionstone, Saturday Night

Lionstone, Barber

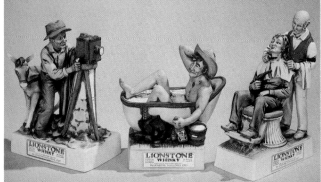

I.W.Harper, Wicker Cover, Amber

I.W.Harper, Medal, Pottery, Tan

I.W.Harper, Pure Old
I.W.Harper, Bar, C.1910

I.W.Harper, Nautical, Ceramic, 1913

Holly City, Christmas,
1971

Holly City, Christmas,
1972

Holly City, George Patton   Holly City, John Paul Jones

Holly City, Christmas,
1973

Holly City, Christmas,
1974

Holly City,
Samuel Clemens

Holly City,
Helen Keller

Holly City,
Paul Revere

McCormick, Kit Carson,
Frontiersman Series

McCormick, Davy Crockett,
Frontiersman Series

McCormick, Daniel Boone,
Frontiersman Series

McCormick, Jim Bowie,
Frontiersman Series

Dant, Paul Bunyan

Double Springs, Stanley Steamer 1909, 1971

Ezra Brooks, Democratic Convention, Donkey, 1976, New York

Ezra Brooks, Republican Convention, Elephant, 1976, Kansas City

Holly City, Spirit Of '76

Medicine, Mathewson's Horse Remedy, 50 Cents, Aqua, 7 In. 25.00
Medicine, Mathis Family Liniment, Toms River, N.J., Aqua, Sample 6.00
Medicine, McElree's Cardui, Aqua, 8 1/2 In. 2.50
Medicine, McElree's Cardui, Green, 7 1/2 In. 2.00
Medicine, McLean's Strengthening Cordial, Aqua, Pint 10.00
Medicine, McLeon's Strengthening Cordial, Aqua, 9 In. 15.00
Medicine, Medical Department, U.S.N., 50CC, Flared Lip, 4 In. 3.00
Medicine, Medical Dept., U.S.N., Embossed, Turning Purple, Pint 7.50
Medicine, Merchant's Celebrated Gargling Oil, Yellow Green, 5 1/2 In. .... * 25.00
Medicine, Merrellhs Hepatine For The Liver, Phila., Aqua, 7 In. 2.00
Medicine, Mette & Kanne Tonic, St.Louis, Mo., Amber, Pint 12.50
Medicine, Mexican Mustang Liniment, IP, Light Blue Green, 7 1/2 In. .... * 20.00
Medicine, Mexican Mustang Liniment, OP, Aqua, 4 In. 125.00
Medicine, Mexican Mustang Liniment, Pontil, Aqua, 4 In. .... * 15.00
Medicine, Mexican Mustang Liniment, Rolled Lip, OP, Aqua, 4 In. 10.00

Medicine, Hyde's Cough Cure, Willoughby, O., Brown, 5 1/2 In.
(See Page 156)

Medicine, Otto's Cure For The
Throat & Lungs, Aqua, 7 In.
(See Page 158)

Medicine, Mexican Mustang Liniment, Rolled Mouth, Pontil, Aqua, 4 In. .... * 20.00
Medicine, Mitchell's Eye Salve, Threaded Mouth, Square, Cobalt, 1 1/2 In. 3.00
Medicine, Mixer's Cancer & Scrofula Syrup, Rectangular, 8 In. 16.00
Medicine, Modoc Indian Oil, 6 1/$\overline{2}$ In. 4.00
Medicine, Monell's Teething Cordial, N.Y., Octagonal, Aqua, 6 In. 2.00
Medicine, Morse's Celebrated Syrup, Prov., R.I., IP, Aqua, 9 1/2 In. 50.00
Medicine, Mother's Friend, Pradfield Recl Co, Rectangular, Aqua, 7 In. 4.75
Medicine, Mounsey's Preston Salts, Rolled Mouth, Pontil, Aqua, 1 3/4 In. .... * 30.00
Medicine, Mounsey's Preston Salts, Sheared Mouth, Pontil, Aqua, 2 In. .... -* 45.00
Medicine, Moxie Nerve Food Co., Lowell, Mass., Aqua, 9 7/8 In. .... * 15.00
Medicine, Moxie Nerve Food, Blob Top, BIMAL, 10 In. 5.00
Medicine, Moxie Nerve Food, Lowell, Mass., Patent, Label, Ice Blue, Quart .... * 50.00
Medicine, Mrs.E.Kidder, Dysentery Cordial, Boston, Aqua, 7 3/4 In. 16.00
Medicine, Mrs.N.M.Gardners Indian Balsam Of Liverwort, Aqua, 5 1/4 In. .... * 95.00
Medicine, Mrs.S.A.Allen's World's Hair Restorer, N.Y., Amber, 7 In. 8.00
Medicine, Mrs.S.A.Allen's, World's Hair Restorer, N.Y., Amber, 1/2 Pint .... * 20.00
Medicine, Mrs.Winslow's Soothing Syrup, Blown, Embossed, Aqua, 5 In. 10.00
Medicine, Mrs.Winslow's Soothing Syrup, Curtis & Perkins, Aqua, 5 In. 5.00
Medicine, Mrs.Winslow's Soothing Syrup, Curtis & Perkins, Aqua, 5 1/2 In. 2.50
Medicine, Mrs.Winslow's Soothing Syrup, Curtis & Perkins, 5 In. .... * 15.00
Medicine, Mrs.Winslow's Soothing Syrup, Dug, OP, Aqua, 5 In. 8.00
Medicine, Mulford's Digestive Malt Extract, Philadelphia, Amber, 8 1/2 In. 5.50
Medicine, Mulford's Laxative Salts Of Fruit, Cobalt, 3 1/2 In. 3.50
Medicine, Munyon's, Paw-Paw, Rectangular, Amber, Pint .... * 5.00
Medicine, Myer's Rock Rose, John F.Henry, N.Y., Rectangular, Aqua, 9 1/4 In. .... * 25.00
Medicine, Myer's, Rock Rose, New Haven, Collared Mouth, Square, Green, Quart .... * 400.00
Medicine, Myer's, Rock Rose, New Haven, Rectangular, IP, Aqua, 9 In. .... * 55.00

Medicine, **N.Jenkins Rheumatism**, Gout & Neuralgia Annihilator, Amber, 9 In. 10.00
Medicine, **National Remedy Co.**, N.Y., Blue, 5 1/4 In. 2.00
Medicine, **Nature's Hair Restorative**, Stain, Aqua, 6 5/8 In. 4.00
Medicine, **No.1 Shaker Syrup**, Canterbury, N.H., Stain, Aqua, 7 1/2 In. 22.00
Medicine, **Nowell's Pec't Oral Honey Of Liverwort**, Pontil, Aqua, 5 In. .... * 40.00
Medicine, **Nubian Tea For The Liver**, Spencer Co., Chattanooga, Ambor, 8 In. 20.00
Medicine, **Omega Oil**, BIMAL, Deep Aqua, 3 In. 3.00
Medicine, **Omega Oil**, BIMAL, Deep Aqua, 6 In. 4.50
Medicine, **One Minute Cough Cure**, 6 3/4 In. 6.00
Medicine, **Orrick's Vermifuge Or Worm Destroyer**, OP, Aqua, 5 1/2 In. .... * 9.50
Medicine, **Osgood's**, India Cholagogue, New York, Rectangular, Aqua, 5 3/8 In. .... * 45.00
Medicine, **Otto's Cure For The Throat & Lungs**, Aqua, 7 In. .... *Illus* 5.00
Medicine, **Owl Drug Co.**, 1 Wing, Cork, Amber, 4 1/2 In. 33.00
Medicine, **Oz.VIII**, Flat Panel, ABM, Lavender, 7 1/2 In. 4.25
Medicine, **Ozomulsion**, BIMAL, Honey Amber, 8 1/2 In. 8.00

Medicine, Paine's Celery Compound, Amber

Medicine, Pettit's American
Cough Cure, Aqua, 7 In.

Medicine, **Ozomulsion**, Tooled Lip, Rectangular, Stain, Amber, 8 3/4 In. 10.00
Medicine, **Padre's Elixir Tonic**, ABM, Stain, Miniature 5.00
Medicine, **Pain Expeller For Rheumatism**, Gout, & Neuralgia, 5 In. 3.50
Medicine, **Paine's Celery Compound**, Amber .... *Illus* 6.00
Medicine, **Paine's Celery Compound**, Amber, 10 In. 15.00
Medicine, **Paine's Celery Compound**, Chas.J.Smith, Strap Flask, 1/2 Pint 1.50
Medicine, **Paine's Celery Compound**, Label, Square, Amber, Pint .... * 2.00
Medicine, **Paine's Celery Compound**, Square, Amber, 9 3/4 In. .... 3.95 To 7.50
Medicine, **Paine's Celery Compound**, 3 Mold, Amber, 10 In. 6.50
Medicine, **Parchen & D'Achevl**, Butte, M.T., 3 1/2 In. 16.00
Medicine, **Parker's Hair Balsam**, N.Y., Rectangular, Amber, 7 In. 2.75
Medicine, **Peptenzyme**, Reed & Carnrick, Cobalt, 9 In. 6.00
Medicine, **Peptenzyme**, Threaded Mouth, Cobalt, 2 1/2 In. 3.00
Medicine, **Pepto Mangan Gude**, Aqua, 11 Ozs. 1.00
Medicine, **Peptogenic Milk Powder**, Fairchild & Foster, Amber, 7 3/4 In. 7.00
Medicine, **Pestireaux's Pills**, Round Bottom, 1 1/2 In. 5.00
Medicine, **Pettit's American Cough Cure**, Aqua, 7 In. .... *Illus* 8.00
Medicine, **Phelp's Arcanum**, Worcester, Mass., Chip, Bruise, Amber, 3/4 Quart .... * 300.00
Medicine, **Phelp's Rheumatic Elixir**, Beveled Corners, 5 1/2 In. 3.00
Medicine, **Phoenix Nerve Beverage**, Boston, Crown Top, Quart 14.00
Medicine, **Pill**, Wide Mouth, Amber, 2 1/2 In. 1.00
Medicine, **Pillow Inhaler Co.**, Philadelphia, Pa., Light Green, 7 1/2 In. 5.00
    Medicine, **Pine Tree Tar Cordial, see Medicine, Wishart's**
Medicine, **Piso Company**, Hazeltine & Co., Tooled Top, Green, 5 1/2 In. 5.50
Medicine, **Piso's Cure For Consumption**, Applied Lip, Stain, Aqua, 6 7/8 In. 9.50
Medicine, **Piso's Cure For Consumption**, Hazeltine & Co., Aqua, 5 1/4 In. 2.25
Medicine, **Piso's Cure For Consumption**, Hazeltine & Co., Emerald, 5 1/4 In. 3.95
Medicine, **Piso's Cure For Consumption**, Hazeltine & Co., Stain, Aqua, 5 In. 1.45

Medicine, Piso's Cure For Consumption, Rectangular, Emerald, 5 1/8 In. 5.00
Medicine, Piso's Cure, The Piso Company, Hazeltine & Co., Emerald, 5 1/4 In. 3.95
Medicine, Polar Star Cough Cure, Rectangular, Aqua, 5 3/4 In. 6.50
Medicine, Polar Star Cough Cure, Rectangular, Sample, Aqua, 3 7/8 In. 4.45
Medicine, Porter's Cure Of Pain, Embossed, Aqua, 6 In. 3.00
Medicine, Porter's Cure Of Pain, Embossed, 4 In. 2.50
Medicine, Preston's Vegetable Purifying Catholicon, N.H., Aqua, 9 1/2 In. 85.00
Medicine, Preston's, Hed-Ake, Cures You, While You Wait, 4 In. 10.95
Medicine, Prof. Dean's King Cactus Oil Barbed Wire Remedy, 9 1/2 In. 60.00
Medicine, Prof.Callan's World Renowned Brazilian Gum, Haze, Aqua, 4 In. 3.50
Medicine, Prof.Dean's King Cactus Oil, Barbed Wire Cure, Pint 60.00
Medicine, Prof.Dean's King Cactus Oil, Barbed Wire Cure, Quart 60.00
Medicine, Prof.I.Hubert's Malvina Lotion, Toledo, Ohio, Amber, 5 In. 3.25
Medicine, Prof.W.H.Peeke's Remedy, N.Y., BIMAL, Square, Amber, 8 In. 17.00
Medicine, Prutonuclein Pill, Ground Lip, Round Bottom, Amber, 2 In. 3.50
Medicine, Psychine For Consumption, 181 Pearl St., N.Y., Blue Aqua, 8 In. 8.00
Medicine, Quaris Cod Liver Oil Jelly, Pontil, Aqua, 5 1/4 In. .... * 120.00
Medicine, R.F.Hemsley Pharmaceutist, Pontil, Oval, Aqua, 4 3/4 In. .... * 110.00
Medicine, R.R.R.Radway & Co., N.Y., Pontil, Rectangular, Aqua, 4 3/4 In. .... * 30.00
Medicine, Radam's Microbe Killer No.1, Pottery, Gallon 35.00
Medicine, Radam's Microbe Killer No.2 In Black, Stoneware, Gallon 30.00
Medicine, Radam's Microbe Killer, Black Print Under Glaze, 11 In. 90.00
Medicine, Ramon's, The Little Doctors, Tin Lid, 8 X 7 1/2 In. 36.00
Medicine, Rawleigh's, 7 3/8 In. 1.00
Medicine, Red Sea Balsam, New Bedford, Mass., 12 Sided, Aqua, 4 1/4 In. 3.00
Medicine, Reed Cutler & Co., Vegetable Pulmonary Balsam, Aqua, 7 1/4 In. 7.00
Medicine, Reed's Gilt Edge Tonic, Square, Amber, 9 In. 15.00
Medicine, Reed's Gilt Edge Tonic, 1878, Square, Amber, 8 3/4 In. .... * 20.00
Medicine, Reliable Old Time Preparation For Home Use, Dr.Fahrney, 9 In. 3.00
Medicine, Renne's Pain Killing Magic Oil, Aqua, 6 In. 4.00
Medicine, Rex For The Blood, Louisville, Ky., Rectangular, Amber, 8 1/2 In. 9.00
Medicine, Rhode's Fever & Ague Cure, Rectangular, Aqua, 8 1/4 In. 30.00
Medicine, Roche's Embrocation For Whooping Cough, Edwards & Son, 5 In. 5.00
Medicine, Roderic Wild Cherry Cough Balsam, L.Verner, Flask, 1/2 Pint 1.25
Medicine, Roderic Wild Cherry Cough Balsam, Octagonal, 5 1/4 In. 3.50
Medicine, Rohrer's Expectoral Wild Cherry Tonic, IP, Amber, 3/4 Quart .... * 150.00
Medicine, Rosewood Dandruff Cure, J.R.Reeves Co., Amethyst, 6 1/2 In. 6.95
Medicine, Rowand's Tonic Mixture, Philada, 6 Sided, 6 In. 25.00
Medicine, Rowland's Macassar Oil For Hair, London, Flared Top, 3 In. 30.00
Medicine, Royal Balmo Embalming Fluid, Portland, Oregon, 8 In. 6.00
Medicine, Rushton's Cod Liver Oil, New York, BIMAL, Aqua, 10 1/2 In. 14.00
Medicine, S.A.Richmond, Md., Samaritan Nervine, C.1882, Flint, 8 X 3 In. 3.00
Medicine, S.B.Kitchel's Liniment, Whittled, Square, Aqua, 8 In. 5.00
Medicine, S.Grover Graham's Dyspepsia Cure, Newburgh, N.Y., Stain, 8 1/4 In. 6.50
Medicine, Samaritan Nervine, S.A.Richmond, Md., C.1882, Flint, 8 In. 3.00
Medicine, Samaritan Nervine, St.Joseph, Mo., C.1886, Flint, 8 In. 3.00
Medicine, Schenck's Seaweed Tonic, BIMAL, Aqua, 9 In. 11.00
Medicine, Schenck's Seaweed Tonic, Haze, 8 1/2 In. 12.00
Medicine, Schenk's Seaweed Tonic, BIMAL, Aqua, 9 In. 11.00
Medicine, Scott's Emulsion, Rectangular, BIMAL, 3 In. 3.00
Medicine, Selden's Wigwam Liniment, N.Y., Oval, Aqua, Quart .... * 240.00
Medicine, Selden's Wigwam Liniment, N.Y., Pontil, Stain, Oval, Aqua, 1/2 Pint .... * 65.00
Medicine, Selden's Wigwam Liniment, N.Y., Stain, Oval, Aqua, 5 7/8 In. .... * 40.00
Medicine, Seymour's, Balsam Of, Wild Cherry, Octagonal, Aqua, 6 5/8 In. .... * 240.00
Medicine, Shaker Syrup No.1, Canterbury, N.H., Pontil, Aqua, 7 1/4 In. .... * 55.00
Medicine, Shiloh For Coughs & Colds, Sample 75.00
Medicine, Silver Pine Healing Oil, BIMAL, Rectangular, Aqua, 8 1/4 In. 4.00
Medicine, Simmon's Squaw Vine Wine Compound, Rectangular, Aqua, 9 In. 8.50
Medicine, Sloan's Ointment, OP, Square, Aqua, 2 1/2 X 1 1/4 In. 13.50
Medicine, Slocum's Coltsfoot Expectorant, Rectangular, Haze, Green, 3 In. 1.50
Medicine, Smith's Green Mountain Renovator Remedy Company, Amber, 8 3/4 In 18.00
Medicine, Smith's Green Mountain Renovator, Rectangular, Olive Amber, Pint .... * 350.00
Medicine, Smith's Green Mountain Renovator, St.Albans, Vt., Amber, 8 5/8 In. .... * 20.00
Medicine, Smith's Throat & Lung Balm, Aqua, 5 3/4 In. 3.00
Medicine, South Carolina Dispensary, Double Ring Lip, Haze, Dug, 9 1/4 In. 14.00

Medicine, Sozodont For Teeth & Breath, Sample Size 2.50
Medicine, Spark's Kidney & Liver Cure, Amber ....*Color* XXXX.XX
Medicine, Spohn's Distemper Cure, Goshen, Ind., Aqua, 5 In. 10.00
Medicine, St.Jacob's Oel, A.Vogler & Co., Baltimore, Aqua, 6 1/2 In. .... * 2.00
Medicine, St.Jakob's Oel, St.Jakob's Oil Ltd., Baltimore, Haze, 6 1/2 In. 2.50
Medicine, Star Of David With J.W.L., Ring Top, Blob Seal, Olive Amber, 7 In. 400.00
Medicine, Steel's Glucolein, San Francisco, Tooled Mouth, Aqua, 5 3/4 In. 40.00
Medicine, Stephen Sweet's Infallible Liniment, BIMAL, 6 In. 8.00
Medicine, Swaim's Panacea, Phila., 12 Panels, Pontil, Olive Green, 3/4 Quart .... * 150.00
Medicine, Swaim's Panacea, St.Louis, Mo., Pint 15.00
Medicine, Swank's Pharmacy, Carpenter & Green Sts., Cobalt, 5 3/16 In. .... * 45.00
Medicine, T.A.Slocum's, For Consumption & Lung Troubles, Aqua, 10 In. 9.00
Medicine, T.L., New York, C.1750, Blob Seal, Ring Top, Pale Green, 6 3/4 In. 300.00
Medicine, Thapcrim's Comforter, Pontil, Rectangular, Aqua, 4 1/2 In. .... * 20.00
Medicine, Tilden & Co., New Lebanon, Label, Square, Electric Blue, 7 1/2 In. .... * 100.00
Medicine, To-Ka Blood Tonic, Mex.Med.Co., Oval, Aqua, 8 1/2 In. 4.95
Medicine, Toms Russian Liniment, Pontil, Square, Aqua, 4 1/2 In. .... * 65.00
Medicine, Tonsilene, Lip Rings, Rectangular, Stain, Green, 5 3/4 In. 2.50
Medicine, Tooled Flared Mouth, 12 Sided, Smooth Base, Amethyst, 4 1/2 In. .... * 60.00
Medicine, Trask's Ointment, 2 3/4 In. 1.75
Medicine, Turlington, Balsam Of Life ....*Illus* 5.00
Medicine, Turlington's Balsam, King's Patent, Violin Shape, Aqua, 2 5/8 In. .... * 35.00
Medicine, Tus Sano Cures, Coughs & Colds, 6 3/4 In. 20.00
Medicine, Twitchell Champlin Neuralgic Anodyne, Aqua, 6 In. 3.00
Medicine, Twitchell Champlin & Co's., Anodyne, Aqua, 6 In. ....*Illus* 6.00
Medicine, Universal Hair Restorer, Rectangular, Cobalt, 6 3/4 In. 60.00
Medicine, Universal Hair Restorer, Rectangular, Cobalt, 7 1/2 In. 65.00
Medicine, University Free, Philadelphia, Hexagonal, Aqua, 5 7/8 In. .... * 110.00
Medicine, Van Arsdale's Myrrholphean For The Hair, Aqua, 8 In. ....*Illus* 20.00
Medicine, Vans Mexican Hair Restorative, Chicago, BIMAL, 9 In. 17.50
Medicine, Vaporizer, Turpo Electric Vaporizer, 3 1/2 In. ....*Illus* 4.50
Medicine, Vaughn's Vegetable Lithontriptic Mixture, Aqua, Pint 25.00
Medicine, Vaughn's, Vegetable Lithontriptic Mixture, Square, Aqua, 3/4 Quart .... * 50.00
Medicine, Vaughn's Vegetable Lithontriptic Mixture, Square, Aqua, 7 1/2 In. 18.00
Medicine, Vaughn's Vegetable Lithontriptic, Aqua, 6 1/2 In. ....*Illus* 40.00
Medicine, Vegetable Pulmonary Balsam, BIMAL, Aqua, 5 In. 3.50
Medicine, Veno's Lightning Cough Cure, Rectangular, Cornflower, 5 1/4 In. 300.00
Medicine, Vermifuge, Pontil, 3 In. ....*Illus* 20.00
      Medicine, W. B. Caldwell's, see Medicine, Caldwell's
Medicine, Warner's Compound, Paper Label, Amber ....*Color* XXXX.XX
Medicine, Warner's Diabetes Cure, Amber ....*Color* XXXX.XX
Medicine, Vick's, Cobalt, 1 In. 5.00
Medicine, Vin-Tone, Food Tonic, Oval, Amber, 8 3/4 In. 14.95
Medicine, W.A.Bergengren Swedish Botanic Compound, Aqua, 8 3/4 In. 15.00
Medicine, W.B.Hurd & Co. Liver Stimulant & Cathartic, Aqua, 9 1/2 In. 6.00
Medicine, W.H.Bull's Herbs & Iron, Amber, 9 1/2 In. 15.00
Medicine, W.T.& Co., Acorn Stopper, Rectangular, Milk Glass, 7 1/2 In. 27.50
Medicine, W.T.& Co., Acorn Stopper, Rectangular, Milk Glass, 8 In. 27.50
Medicine, Wakesfield's Black Berry Balsam, Rectangular, Stain, Green, 5 In. 3.00
Medicine, Warner's Kidney & Liver Cure, Rochester, N.Y., Amber, 9 1/2 In. 10.00
Medicine, Warner's Log Cabin Extract, Amber, 8 In. 65.00
Medicine, Warner's Log Cabin Extract, 8 1/4 In. 80.00
Medicine, Warner's Nervine, Pint 27.00
Medicine, Warner's Safe Cure, Amber, 11 In. 155.00
Medicine, Warner's Safe Cure, Concentrated, Amber, 6 In. 30.00
Medicine, Warner's Safe Cure, D.C., Pint 45.00
Medicine, Warner's Safe Cure, Free Sample 14.00
Medicine, Warner's Safe Cure, Free Sample, Amber, 4 In. 13.50
Medicine, Warner's Safe Cure, London, Amber, 1/2 Pint .... 35.00 To 88.00
Medicine, Warner's Safe Cure, London, Amber, 7 3/8 In. 110.00
Medicine, Warner's Safe Cure, London, Dark Green, 7 1/8 In. 147.00
Medicine, Warner's Safe Cure, London, Dug, Yellow Amber, Pint 90.00
Medicine, Warner's Safe Cure, London, Green, 1/2 Pint .... 88.00 To 160.00
Medicine, Warner's Safe Cure, London, Green, Pint .... 100.00 To 150.00
Medicine, Warner's Safe Cure, London, Honey Amber, 7 In. 120.00

Top: Medicine, Turlington, Balsam Of Life.
Center: Medicine, Twitchell Champlin & Co's, Anodyne, Aqua, 6 In.
Right: Medicine, Van Arsdale's Myrrholphean For The Hair, Aqua, 8 In.
Above: Medicine, Vaporizer, Turpo Electric Vaporizer, 3 1/2 In.
Right: Medicine, Vermifuge, Pontil, 3 In.; Medicine, Vaughn's Vegetable Lithontripic, Aqua, 6 1/2 In.

(See Page 160)

Medicine, Warner's Safe Cure, London, Honey Amber, 9 3/8 In.		95.00
Medicine, Warner's Safe Cure, London, Yellow Amber, 1/2 Pint		75.00
Medicine, Warner's Safe Cure, London, 1/2 Pint		85.00
Medicine, Warner's Safe Cure, Melbourne, Pint	30.00 To	45.00
Medicine, Warner's Safe Cure, Melbourne, Red, 1/2 Pint		90.00
Medicine, Warner's Safe Cure, Rochester, Cure In Slug Plate, 1/2 Pint		25.00
Medicine, Warner's Safe Cure, Rochester, Dug, 1/2 Pint		13.00
Medicine, Warner's Safe Cure, 7 In.	*Color*	XXXX.XX
Medicine, Warner's Safe Diabetes Cure, N.Y., Amber, 9 1/4 In.		40.00
Medicine, Warner's Safe Kidney & Liver Cure, N.Y., Amber, 9 1/2 In.		18.00
Medicine, Warner's Safe Kidney & Liver Cure, Rochester, Amber, Pint		* 15.00
Medicine, Warner's Safe Kidney & Liver Cure, Rochester, Bruise, Amber, Pint		* 55.00
Medicine, Warner's Safe Kidney & Liver Remedy, Dug, Amber, 16 Ozs., 10 In.		15.00
Medicine, Warner's Safe Nervine, London, Amber, 1/2 Pint		55.00

Medicine, Warner's Safe Nervine, London, Olive Green, 1/2 Pint 110.00
Medicine, Warner's Safe Nervine, London, Yellow Amber, 1/2 Pint 100.00
Medicine, Warner's Safe Nervine, Paper Label ....*Color* XXXX.XX
Medicine, Warner's Safe Nervine, Rochester, N.Y., Amber, Pint .... * 25.00
Medicine, Warner's Safe Nervine, Rochester, N.Y., Dark Amber, 1/2 Pint .... * 45.00
Medicine, Warner's Safe Remedies, ABM, Amber, 12 1/2 Ozs. .... 12.00 To 20.00
Medicine, Warner's Safe Remedies, Amber, 7 In. 13.00
Medicine, Warner's Safe Remedies, Blob Top, ABM, Aqua, 12 In. 18.00
Medicine, Warner's Safe Remedies, Rochester, Bruise, Oval, 9 1/4 In. .... * 27.50
Medicine, Warner's Safe Remedies, Rochester, N.Y., Amber, 1/2 Pint 30.00
Medicine, Warner's Safe Remedies, Rochester, N.Y., Amber, 9 1/4 In. 20.00
Medicine, Warner's Safe Remedy For Kidneys & Liver, Label ....*Color* XXXX.XX
Medicine, Warner's Safe Remedy, Brown, 9 1/2 In. ....*Illus* 28.00

Medicine, Warner's Safe Remedy, Brown, 9 1/2 In.

Medicine, Warner's Safe Remedy, 7 In. ....*Color* XXXX.XX
Medicine, Warner's Safe Rheumatic Cure, Applied Rolled Collar, Amber, 9 In. 36.00
Medicine, Warner's Safe Rheumatic Cure ....*Color* XXXX.XX
Medicine, Warner's Safe Rheumatic Cure, Blob Top ....*Color* XXXX.XX
Medicine, Warner's White Wine Of Tar Syrup, Coldwater, Mich., 7 1/4 In. 3.50
Medicine, Weaver's Canker & Salt Rheum Syrup, IP, Aqua, Quart 37.00
Medicine, Wheatley's Compound Syrup, 6 In. 40.00
Medicine, Wheeler's Tissue Phosphates, BIMAL, Square, Aqua, 9 In. 7.50
Medicine, Wheeler's Tissue Phosphates, Aqua, 8 3/4 In. 5.00
Medicine, White's Hair Restorative, OP, Aqua, 6 1/2 In. 85.00
Medicine, Whittemore's Vegetable Syrup For Diarrhea, Aqua, 5 1/8 In. .... * 85.00
Medicine, Wild Cherry Tonic Cordial, Label, Square, Yellow Amber, Pint .... * 15.00
Medicine, William R.Warner & Co., Tono Symbol, 8 In. 15.00
Medicine, Winchester's Kentucky Liniment, OP, Aqua, 4 1/2 In. 49.00
Medicine, Wishart's Pine Tree Cordial, Green, Pint .... 42.00 To 45.00
Medicine, Wishart's Pine Tree Cordial, Green, Quart 45.00
Medicine, Wishart's Pine Tree Cordial, Light Green, Pint 45.00
Medicine, Wishart's Pine Tree Tar Cordial, Amber, 9 3/4 In. 55.00
Medicine, Wishart's Pine Tree Tar Cordial, Blue Green, 3/4 Quart .... * 50.00
Medicine, Wishart's Pine Tree Tar Cordial, Blue Green, 3/4 Quart .... * 60.00
Medicine, Wishart's Pine Tree Tar Cordial, Medium Green, 8 1/2 In. 45.00
Medicine, Wishart's Pine Tree Tar Cordial, Phila., Amber, Pint .... * 35.00
Medicine, Wishart's Pine Tree Tar Cordial, 1859, Chips, Green, Pint .... * 35.00
Medicine, Wishart's Pine Tree Tar Cordial, 1859, Flake, Green, Pint .... * 55.00
Medicine, Wishart's Pine Tree Tar Cordial, 1859, Green, Pint .... * 75.00
Medicine, Wishart's Pine Tree Tar Cordial, 1859, Yellow Green, Pint .... * 90.00
Medicine, Wishart's Pine Tree Tar Cordial, 1859, Yellow Green, 3/4 Quart .... * 95.00
Medicine, Wishart's Pine Tree Tar Cordial, 1859, Yellow Olive, Pint .... * 65.00
Medicine, Wm.R.Warner & Co., Philadelphia, Vertically, Cobalt, 5 1/2 In. 5.00
Medicine, Youatt's Gargling Oil, Aqua, 9 In. 15.00
  Milk Glass, see also Cologne, Cosmetic, Dresser, Drug, Ink, Medicine
Milk Glass, Belle Of Anderson, Pint 120.00
Milk Glass, Belle Of Anderson, Quart 110.00
Milk Glass, New York World's Fair, 1939, Theme Building, 9 In. 8.95

Milk, Bedford Dairy, Brooklyn, N.Y., Quart

Milk, Bottled For The National Dairy Show, 6 In.

Milk, Brookfield, Double Baby Face, Quart

Milk bottles were first used in the 1880s. The characteristic shape and printed or embossed wording identify these bottles for collectors.

Milk, **A.B.Munroe,** East Providence, R.I., 1930, Ribbed, 1/2 Pint	4.00
Milk, **A.G.Smalley,** Boston & New York On Bottom, Turning Color, Pint	5.00
Milk, **A.G.Smalley,** Handle, Quart	18.00
Milk, **A.G.Smalley,** Tin Handle, Quart	28.00
Milk, **Adair,** Gallon	1.95
Milk, **Albany Ice Cream Company,** Embossed, Stain, Quart	4.00
Milk, **Alpine Milk Co.,** Quart	2.00
Milk, **Alta-Crest,** March 28, 1929, Fired-On Blue Letters, Dacro Pint	5.00
Milk, **Ayrshire Dairy,** Great Falls, Montana, Red Pyro, 10 Ozs.	6.00
Milk, **Baby Face,** Embossed, 1/2 Pint	3.00
Milk, **Baby Face,** Embossed, Pint	4.50
Milk, **Baby Face,** Embossed, Quart	4.00
Milk, **Baby Face,** Embossed, Square, 1/2 Pint	2.50
Milk, **Baby Face,** Embossed, Square, Pint	4.00
Milk, **Baby Face,** Embossed, Square, Quart	4.50
Milk, **Baby Face,** Painted, 1/2 Pint	2.50
Milk, **Baby Face,** Painted, Pint	3.50
Milk, **Baby Face,** Painted, Quart	3.50
Milk, **Baby Face,** Painted, Square, 1/2 Pint	2.50
Milk, **Baby Face,** Painted, Square, Pint	3.00
Milk, **Baby Face,** Painted, Square, Quart	3.00
Milk, **Barton's Bee Gardens & Dairy Farm,** Davison, Mich., Embossed, Pint	.75
Milk, **Barton's Bee Gardens & Dairy Farm,** Davison, Mich., Embossed, Quart	.75
Milk, **Bauer Bros.,** Dairy Co., Chicago, Ill., Embossed, Pint	6.00
Milk, **Bedford Dairy,** Brooklyn, N.Y., Quart *Illus*	45.00
Milk, **Bellview Dairy,** Syracuse, N.Y., 1/3 Quart	1.50
Milk, **Bellview Dairy,** Syracuse, N.Y., 1/4 Pint	1.50
Milk, **Big Mac Penitentiary,** McAlester, Oklahoma, Quart	.20
Milk, **Borden's,** Eagle, Pint	3.00
Milk, **Borden's,** Eagle, Quart	3.00
Milk, **Borden's,** Embossed Eagle, 1/2 Pint	5.00
Milk, **Borden's,** 2 In.	2.00
Milk, **Bottled For The National Dairy Show,** 6 In. *Illus*	12.50
Milk, **Brighton Place,** Amber, Quart	35.00
Milk, **Brookfield Dairy,** Hellerstown, Pa., Embossed, Baby Face, 1/2 Pint	3.50
Milk, **Brookfield,** Baby Face, 1/2 Pint	4.50 To 4.60
Milk, **Brookfield,** Double Baby Face, Quart *Illus*	12.00
Milk, **Broughton's Dairy,** Quart	2.00
Milk, **C.S.C.,** Ltd., Canada, Embossed, One Imperial Pint	6.00
Milk, **Canadian,** Bowling Pin Shape, Slug Plate In Center, Imperial Pint	3.00
Milk, **Capitol Dairy Company,** Chicago, Ill., Ribbed, 1928, 1/2 Pint	4.00

Milk, Chestnut Farm Dairy, Washington, D.C., Cow, House, & Tree, Pint	3.00
Milk, Chestnut Farms, Chevy Chase Dairy, Wash., D.C., Ribbed, 1/2 Pint	3.00
Milk, Chevy Chase Dairy, Washington, D.C., 1/2 Pint	.50
Milk, Cheyenne Creamery Company, Ribbed, Turning Purple, Pint	10.00
Milk, Chicago Sterilized Milk Company, 8 In. _................Illus_	100.00
Milk, Clover Dairy, Wilmington, Del., Embossed, 1/2 Pint	4.00
Milk, Cloverland Dairy, Products Co., Inc., New Orleans, Embossed, Pint	6.00
Milk, Cloverland Dairy Products, Co., New Orleans, Embossed, 1/2 Pint	5.00
Milk, Columbia Dairies, S.C., Embossed Rooster, 1/2 Pint	6.00
Milk, Columbia, South Carolina, Embossed Rooster, Pint	3.00
Milk, Conn Dairy, Tin Top, 1/2 Pint	4.25

Milk, Chicago Sterilized
Milk Company, 8 In.

Milk, Hot & Co.,
Potsdam, N.Y.,
Absolutely Pure, 8 1/2 In.
(See Page 165)

Milk, Cop-The-Cream, Embossed, Quart	4.50
Milk, Cop-The-Cream, Embossed, Square, Quart	4.50
Milk, Cop-The-Cream, Painted, Quart	4.00
Milk, Cop-The-Cream, Painted, Square, Quart	4.00
Milk, Cream Top, Embossed, 1/2 Pint	3.50
Milk, Cream Top, Embossed, Pint	3.50
Milk, Cream Top, Embossed, Quart	3.50
Milk, Cream Top, Quart	3.00
Milk, Cream Top, Spoon, Quart	2.50 To 6.50
Milk, Creek View Dairy Farm, Clarington, O., Embossed, Pint	1.50
Milk, Creek View Dairy Farm, Clarington, O., Embossed, Quart	1.50
Milk, Crystal Creamery, Butte, Montana, Black Pyro, 1/2 Pint	4.50
Milk, Curles Neck Dairy, Baby Face, Embossed, Thrift Top, Square, Quart	5.50
Milk, Curles Neck Dairy, Inc., Embossed, Baby Face, Quart	6.00
Milk, Deer Foot Farm, Turnip Shape, Tin Screw Lid, 1/2 Pint	7.00
Milk, Double Baby Face, Embossed, 1/2 Pint	3.00
Milk, Double Baby Face, Embossed, Pint	5.00
Milk, Double Baby Face, Embossed, Quart	5.00
Milk, Double Baby Face, Embossed, Square, 1/2 Pint	3.00
Milk, Double Baby Face, Embossed, Square, Pint	5.50
Milk, Double Baby Face, Embossed, Square, Quart	4.50
Milk, Double Baby Face, Painted, 1/2 Pint	2.50
Milk, Double Baby Face, Painted, Pint	4.00
Milk, Double Baby Face, Painted, Square, 1/2 Pint	2.50
Milk, Double Baby Face, Painted, Quart	4.00 To 5.00
Milk, Double Baby Face, Painted, Square, Pint	3.50
Milk, Double Baby Face, Painted, Square, Quart	4.00
Milk, Driessen Dairy, Appleton, Wis., Slug Plate, 1/2 Pint	3.50
Milk, E.F.Mayer, Embossed, Amber, Quart	28.00 To 45.00
Milk, Edwin P.Hartsock, Du Quoin, Ill., Embossed, Pint	4.00
Milk, Embossed, Amber, Quart	12.00
Milk, Embossed, Dug, Amber, 1/2 Pint	25.00
Milk, Embossed, Dug, Amber, Quart	25.00
Milk, Embossed, Emerald Green, Quart	20.00
Milk, Embossed, 1/4 Pint	1.15 To 2.00
Milk, Embossed, 1/3 Quart	1.50

Milk, Embossed, 1/2 Pint .30 To 2.00
Milk, Embossed, 10 Ozs. 1.00
Milk, Embossed, 12 Ozs. .75
Milk, Embossed, Pint .50 To 2.50
Milk, Embossed, Quart 1.00 To 2.75
Milk, Embossed, Square, Amber, Quart 1.25
Milk, Embossed, Square, 1/4 Pint 1.00
Milk, Embossed, Square, 1/2 Pint 1.00
Milk, Embossed, Square, Pint .50
Milk, Embossed, Square, Quart .75
Milk, Embossed, Tin Closure, 1/4 Pint 8.50
Milk, Embossed, Tin Closure, 1/2 Pint 8.00
Milk, Embossed, Tin Closure, Pint 5.50
Milk, Embossed, Tin Closure, Quart 5.50
Milk, Emmanuel Missionary College, Berrien Springs, Mich., 1/2 Pint 4.00
Milk, English, Painted, Pint 5.00
Milk, Essex Junction, Vt., Embossed, Quart 1.25
Milk, F.B.Fetterly, Oconto Falls, Wis., Pint 4.50
Milk, Fargo, Cream Top, Painted, Square, Quart .75
Milk, Figural, Baby Holding Bottle, Quart 10.00
Milk, Figural, Double Headed Lady, Cream Top, Quart 20.00
Milk, Florida Universal Store Bottle, Ribbed, Embossed 5 Cents, 1/2 Pint 3.50
Milk, Fred Harvey, 1935, Railroad Restaurants & Trains, 10i Pint 5.00
Milk, Friends Farm, Flint, Mich., Embossed & Painted, Quart 1.50
Milk, Gail Borden, Amber, Quart 5.00
Milk, Gascoyne Dairy, Cream Separator, Quart 25.00
Milk, Gascoyne Dairy, Lockport, N.Y., Cream Separator, Quart 35.00
Milk, George Washington, Embossed, Picture, 1/4 Pint 4.00
Milk, George Washington, Embossed Picture, 1/2 Pint 8.50
Milk, Gold Medal Dairy, Huron, S.Dakota, Red Pyro Emblem, 1/2 Pint 5.00
Milk, Golden State Store, 1/2 Gallon 6.00
Milk, Graber Dairy, Golden Guernsey, Quart 2.00
Milk, Green Valley Dairy Rich, Sanford, Florida, Embossed, Pint 3.00
Milk, Gridley Dairy Co., Wisconsin, Amber, Quart 25.00
Milk, H.P.Hood & Son's, Boston, 1929, 24 Ribs, 1/2 Pint 4.50
Milk, H.P.Hood & Son's, Dairy Experts, Mass., 1935, Embossed, 1/2 Pint 4.00
Milk, Hal Pint P-3, Empire On Base, Embossed, Tin Top, 1/2 Pint 5.00
Milk, Hampden Creamery, Embossed Cow's Head, 1/2 Pint 6.00
Milk, Hannibal, Mo. & Palmyra, Mo., Painted, Square, Quart 1.25
Milk, Hartman Farm Dairy Products, Crown Top, Ribbed, Turning Purple, Pint 8.00
Milk, Hawaii, Embossed, 1/2 Pint 5.00
Milk, Hazel's Dairy, Falls Church, Va., Embossed, 1/2 Pint 3.50
Milk, Horlick's, Embossed, Pint 9.50
Milk, Hot & Co., Potsdam, N.Y., Absolutely Pure, 8 1/2 In. *Illus* 55.00
Milk, I.C.United Milk Company, Indiana Harbor, Indiana, 1/2 Pint 3.00
Milk, Independent Dairies, Kansas City, Mo., Embossed, Stain, 1/2 Pint 2.00
Milk, J.A.Ralliff, Warren, Ohio, 1923, Turning Purple, Pint 4.00
Milk, J.D.Watkins & Son, Dairy, Birmingham, Ala., Ribbed, Pint 4.50
Milk, J.H.Moss Dairy, Danville, Va., Pint 4.50
Milk, Jersey Crown Dairy, Hayward, California, Painted, Square, Pint 1.00
Milk, Jersey Crown Dairy, Hayward, California, Painted, Square, 1/2 Pint 1.00
Milk, Jersey Crown Dairy, Hayward, California, Red Paint, Wire Bail, Gallon 4.00
Milk, Jersey Crown Dairy, Hayward, California, Yellow Paint, Square, 1/2 Pint 1.00
Milk, Jersey Crown Dairy, Hayward, California, Yellow Paint, Square, Pint 1.00
Milk, Kingswood Jersey Sterlized, Round Bottom, 8 In. 15.00
Milk, Knoxville Pure Milk Co., Tenn., Blanke Mfg.Co., Stain, Purple, Pint 8.00
Milk, L C Co On Bottom, Embossed Circle On Front, Tin Top, Pint 4.50
Milk, Lake Zurick Dairy, Amber, Quart 15.00
Milk, Lang's Creamery, Inc., Buffalo, N.Y., Green, Quart 75.00
Milk, Liberty Milk Co., Buffalo, N.Y., Statue Of Liberty, Embossed, 1/2 Pint 5.00
Milk, Liberty, Embossed Statue Of Liberty, 1/2 Pint 2.00 To 2.50
Milk, Liberty, Embossed Statue Of Liberty, Pint 2.00 To 2.50
Milk, Liberty, Embossed Statue Of Liberty, Quart 2.00 To 2.50
Milk, Lone Pine Dairy, Hanover, N.J., Scene, Ruby, Quart 3.00
Milk, Maine K9, Seal, Marked One Gill 7.50

Milk, Maine, 48 Seal, 1/2 Pint 4.00
Milk, Martin Country Fresh, Marblehead, Mass., Painted, Square, Quart 3.00
Milk, Massachusetts, Embossed, 1/2 Pint 2.00
Milk, Massachusetts, Embossed, Pint 3.00
Milk, Massachusetts, Embossed, Quart 4.00
Milk, Mayer, Embossed, Amber, Quart 22.00
Milk, McCarthy's Dairy, Las Cruces, N.M., Phone 487 J-1, Embossed, 1/2 Pint 5.00
Milk, McCues Dairy, Long Branch, N.J., Embossed, Pint 4.00
Milk, Mellow Gold, Grade A, Square, 1/2 Pint 4.00
Milk, Mellow Gold, Taste Tells, Kaukauna, Wis., Square, 1/2 Pint 4.00
Milk, Mexican, 1/2 Pint 2.50
Milk, Michigan, Embossed, Quart 4.00
Milk, Michigan, Pyro, Square, Quart 2.00
Milk, Midwest Dairy Products Co., War Bond Slogan, Metal Top, Paint, Quart 25.00
Milk, Miles River Farm, Hamilton, Mass., Crown, Seal, Pint 8.00
Milk, Milk For Health, Inc., Louisville, Ky., Embossed, Square, 1/2 Pint 2.00
Milk, Missouri Pacific Railroad, Embossed, Quart 3.00
Milk, Missouri Pacific Railroad, Embossed, 1/2 Pint 2.00
Milk, Missouri Pacific, Embossed In Red Enamel, 1/2 Pint 3.00
Milk, Missouri Pacific, Embossed, 1/2 Pint 2.00
Milk, Missouri Pacific, Embossed, Quart .... 3.00 To 4.00
Milk, Model Dairy, Canton, N.Y., From TB Tested Cows, Embossed, Quart 5.00
Milk, Montpelier, Vt., Pint 3.00
Milk, Murphy's Dairy, Conn., Pyro Glazed, Green & Orange, 1/2 Gallon 1.00
Milk, Mutual Creamery Company, Salt Lake City, 1922, Maid-O-Clover, 1/2 Pint 7.00
Milk, N.Giard, No.Andover, Mass Seal, Embossed, Quart 3.00
Milk, Nelson Cloverland Creamery, Manistique, Mich., Baby's Face, Quart 1.50
Milk, New Jersey, Embossed, 1/2 Pint .... 1.50 To 2.00
Milk, New Jersey, Embossed, Pint 3.00
Milk, New Jersey, Embossed, Quart .... 1.50 To 4.00
Milk, New York, Embossed, 1/2 Pint 2.00
Milk, New York, Embossed, Pint 3.00
Milk, New York, Embossed, Quart 4.00
Milk, New Vermont Creamery, 1926, Pure Jersey Cream, Ribbed, 1/2 Pint 3.50
Milk, North Dakota, Embossed, Quart 35.00
Milk, North Dakota, Enameled, 1/2 Pint 10.00
Milk, North Shore Dairy, Chicago, Ill., C.1950, Orange Paint, Pint 2.00
Milk, North Shore Dairy, Chicago, Ill., C.1950, Orange Paint, Quart 2.00
Milk, North Shore Dairy, Chicago, Ill., C.1950, Orange Paint, 1/2 Gallon 2.00
Milk, Northfield, Vt., Tin Top, 1/4 Pint 15.00
Milk, Oak Park Dairy, Eau Claire, Wis., Embossed, Ribbed, Dripless, 1/2 Pint 5.00
Milk, Ohio, Embossed, Quart 4.00
Milk, Old Dutch Market Fresh Churned Buttermilk, Embossed, 1/2 Gallon 18.00
Milk, Old Forge Farm, Spring Grove, Pa., Embossed, Quart 25.00
Milk, Osawatomie Dairy, Kansas, Ribbed, Embossed, 1/2 Pint 6.00
Milk, Painted, Amber, 1/2 Pint 2.00
Mil, , Painted, Amber, Quart 2.00
Milk, Painted, 1/4 Pint .... .75
Milk, Painted, 1/2 Pint .... .30 To 1.50
Milk, Painted, 1/3 Quart 1.00
Milk, Painted, Pint .... .25
Milk, Painted, Quart .... .50 To 1.50
Milk, Painted, Square, Amber, Quart 1.00
Milk, Painted, Square, 1/4 Pint .... .30 To .60
Milk, Painted, Square, 1/2 Pint .... .25
Milk, Painted, Square, Pint .... .25
Milk, Painted, Square, Quart .... .25 To 4.50
Milk, Parker Dairy Co., Saginaw, Mich., 1927, Embossed, Ribbed, Pint 4.00
Milk, Pendergast Bros., Dairy, Tucson, Ariz., Orange Pyro, 1/2 Pint 4.50
Milk, Peninsula Dairy, Toothache Cream Top, Quart .... Illus   9.00
Milk, Pennsylvania Dairy, Cream Top, Quart 6.00
Milk, Pennsylvania, Embossed, 1/2 Pint 2.00
Milk, Pennsylvania, Embossed, Pint 3.00
Milk, Pennsylvania, Embossed, Quart 4.00
Milk, People's Dairy, 1934, Amber, Quart .... 30.00 To 40.00

Milk, Pevely & St.Louis Dairy Co., Cream, 4 In.	3.75
Milk, Plains Dairy System, Cheyenne, Wyo., Embossed, Black Pyro, 1/2 Pint	5.00
Milk, Price's Dairy Co., El Paso, Texas - Wash & Return, Ribbed, 1/2 Pint	5.00
Milk, Pure Milk Co., Ohio, Embossed, Amber, Quart	30.00
Milk, Pyro, Cream Top, Pint	3.50
Milk, Pyro, Cream Top, Quart	2.50
Milk, Quality Dairy, Hannibal, Mo., War Slogan, Red Paint, Cream Top, Quart	3.25
Milk, Queen City Dairy Co., Crown Products Brand, 1922-1926, Embossed, Pint	2.50
Milk, Queen City Dairy Co., Crown Products Brand, 1922-1926, Embossed, Quart	2.50
Milk, Ralph P.Meserve, Maple Spring Farm, Saco, Me., 1925, 1/2 Pint	4.50
Milk, Riverside Dairy, Dickerman Farm, Milldale, Conn., Painted, Pint	1.00
Milk, Rocky Mountain Dairy Products, Denver, Colo., Red Pyro, 1/2 Pint	4.00
Milk, Rollin M.Moore, Canton, N.Y., Gill	2.00
Milk, Rosedale Dairy, Silver City, New Mexico, Pyro, Pint	4.00
Milk, Royal Farms Dairy, Cop-The-Cream, 9 In. *Illus*	5.00
Milk, Salem, Ohio, Embossed, 1/2 Pint	1.00
Milk, Salem, Ohio, Embossed, Pint	1.00
Milk, Salem, Ohio, Embossed, Quart	1.00
Milk, Seneca Dairy, Embossed Indian, Pint	9.00
Milk, Smalley, 1/2 Pint	10.00
Milk, Smalley, Pint	10.00
Milk, Smalley, Quart	12.00
Milk, Smalley, 1/2 Gallon	15.00
Milk, Smalley, Tin Top, 1/2 Pint	200.00
Milk, Smalley, Tin Top, Quart	47.00
Milk, Somerset Farms, Mass., Bubbles, 1/2 Pint	6.00
Milk, Sour Cream, Tumbling Run Dairy, Embossed, 1/2 Pint	12.00
Milk, Stockton, California, Quart	3.00
Milk, Sunland Dairy, Ltd., Calexico, El Centro, Cal., 1937, Pint	7.00
Milk, Sunshine Dairy, Embossed Sunset & Trees, 1/2 Pint	5.00
Milk, Superior Dairy, Inc., Martinsburg, W.Va., Neck Ring, Pint	5.00
Milk, Tester, 6 In.	2.50
Milk, Tin Top, 1/2 Pint	4.00
Milk, Thatcher, East, Pint	15.00
Milk, Thatcher, East, Quart	20.00

Milk, Peninsula Dairy, Toothache Cream Top, Quart
(See Page 166)

Milk, Royal Farms Dairy,
Cop-The-Cream, 9 In.

Milk, Thatcher, West, Pint	25.00
Milk, Thatcher, West, Quart	40.00
Milk, Tin Closure, 1/4 Pint	8.00
Milk, Tin Closure, 1/2 Pint	6.00
Milk, Tin Closure, Pint	4.50
Milk, Tin Closure, Quart	5.00
Milk, Turner Centre, Monogram, Tin Top, 1/2 Pint	8.00

Milk, Uncle Sam's Dairy Golden Guernsey, Albany, N.Y., Embossed, 1/2 Pint 2.50
Milk, Uncle Sam's Dairy, Albany, N.Y., Embossed, 1/2 Pint 4.50
Milk, Universal, Store Bottle, Embossed, 1/2 Pint 1.00
Milk, University Of Connecticut, Storrs, Conn., 1/2 Pint 4.00
Milk, Upland Farm, Ipswich, Thatcher Manufacturing, 1916, Crown Top, Quart 8.00
Milk, V.M.& I.C.Co.'s Milk-O, Embossed, Amber, Quart 25.00
Milk, V.M.& I.C.Co.'s Milk-O, Embossed, Amber, 1/2 Pint 25.00
Milk, V.M.& I.C.Co.'s Milk-O, Embossed, Tapered Neck, Amber, 1/2 Pint 10.00
Milk, V.M.& I.C.Co.'s Milk-O, Embossed, Tapered Neck, Amber, Quart 15.00
Milk, V, Buy War Bonds & Stamps, Drink Milk For Health, Quart 25.00
Milk, Vallotton's Milk, Valdosta, Ga., Red Pyro, 1/2 Pint 3.50
Milk, W.E.Hitchcock, Applied Top, 1/2 Gill 2.00
Milk, W.E.Hitchcock, Applied Top, Gill 2.00
Milk, W.I.C.Co., Woodsfield, Embossed, Pint 1.50
Milk, W.I.C.Co., Woodsfield, Embossed, Quart 1.50
Milk, Washington, D.C., Embossed Cow, Tree, & House, Tin Top, Pint 12.00
Milk, Weir Cove Dairy Co., Holidays Cove, W.Va., Embossed, Pint 4.50
Milk, Western Maryland Dairy, Baxter, Embossed, Ribbed, Pint 3.50
Milk, Westleigh Farms, Windsor, Vt., Pint 4.50
Milk, Winston Salem, N.C., 1/2 Pint 3.00
Milk, Windsor Farm Dairy, Amber, Quart 15.00
Milk, Wisconsin, Embossed, 1/2 Pint .... .50 To 2.00
Milk, Wisconsin, Embossed, Pint .... .50 To 2.00
Milk, Wisconsin, Embossed, Quart .... .50 To 2.00
Milk, Wisconsin, Embossed, 1/2 Gallon .... .50 To 2.00
Milk, Wisconsin, Embossed, Gallon .... .50 To 2.00
Milk, Wisconsin, Painted, 1/2 Pint .... .50 To 2.00
Milk, Wisconsin, 1/2 Pint .... .50 To 2.00
Milk, Wisconsin, Painted, Pint .... .50 To 2.00
Milk, Wisconsin, Painted, Quart .... .50 To 2.00
Milk, Wisconsin, Painted, 1/2 Gallon .... .50 To 2.00
Milk, Wisconsin, Painted, Gallon .... .50 To 2.00
Milk, Wisconsin, 1/2 Pint .... .50 To 2.00
Milk, Wisconsin, Pint .... .50 To 2.00
Milk, Wisconsin, Quart .... .50 To 2.00
Milk, Wisconsin, 1/2 Gallon .... .50 To 2.00
Milk, Wisconsin, Gallon .... .50 To 2.00
Milk, Wood Brook Farms, Plainfield, N.J., 1912, Embossed, 1/2 Pint 3.50
Milk, Woodmason's Melrose Dairy, Malvern, Australia, 1/2 Pint 10.00
Milk, Wm.Weckerle & Sons Dairies, Buffalo, N.Y., Scratch, Amber, Quart 38.00
Milk, X SMB M Co 29 & Circle, Embossed, Tin Top, 1/2 Pint 6.00
Milk, Yoder, Va., Dairy, Amber, Quart 6.00

*Mineral water bottles held the fresh natural spring waters favored for
health and taste. Most of the bottles collected today date from the 1850-
1900 period. Many of these bottles have blob tops.*
Mineral Water, Adirondack Spring, Westport, N.Y., Emerald Green, Quart .... * 35.00
Mineral Water, Allovez Spring Co., Green Bay, Wisc., Green, 7 Ozs., 7 1/2 In. 60.00
Mineral Water, Artesian Spring, Ballston Spa, N.Y., Dug, Green, Pint 35.00
Mineral Water, Avon Spring, Aqua, Quart 140.00
Mineral Water, Avon Spring, Smooth Base, Olive Green, Quart .... * 200.00
Mineral Water, Baker's, Louisville, B, IP, Aqua To Emerald, 7 1/4 In. 100.00
Mineral Water, Ballston Spa Lithia, Artesian Spring Co., SA, Green, Pint .... * 30.00
Mineral Water, Ballston Spa, SA, Artesian Spring Co., Emerald Green, Pint .... * 40.00
Mineral Water, Bedford, Stoddard, Amber, Pint 250.00
Mineral Water, Bowden Lithia Spring, Lithia Springs, Ga., Aqua, 1/2 Gallon 20.00
Mineral Water, Buffalo Lithia Spring, Embossed Woman, Aqua, 1/2 Gallon 10.00
Mineral Water, Buffalo Lithia, Aqua, 1/2 Gallon .... *Illus* 10.00
Mineral Water, Buffalo Lithia, Materia Medica, Aqua, 10 1/2 In. .... * 14.75
Mineral Water, Buffalo Lithia, Nature's Materia Medica .... * 5.00
Mineral Water, Buffalo Lithia, Nature's Materia Medica, Aqua, 1/2 Gallon 8.00
Mineral Water, Buffalo Lithia, Nature's Materia Medica, Aqua, 1/2 Gallon .... * 15.00
Mineral Water, Buffalo Spring, Label, Aqua, 1/2 Gallon 10.00
Mineral Water, Carlsbad L.S., Whittled, Olive Green, Quart 5.00
Mineral Water, Champion Spouting Spring, Aqua, Pint 30.00

Mineral Water, Clark & Co., N.Y., Emerald Green, Pint 50.00
Mineral Water, Clark & White, C, Saratoga, Olive Green, Pint 20.00
Mineral Water, Clarke & Co., Bubbly, Olive Green, Pint 45.00
Mineral Water, Clarke & Co., New York, Smooth Base, Olive Green, Pint .... * 45.00
Mineral Water, Clarke & Co., Whittled, Bubbles, Olive Amber, Quart 45.00
Mineral Water, Clarke & White In Arch, Stubby Neck, Bubbly, Quart 30.00
Mineral Water, Clarke & White, C, New York, Black Olive Green, Quart 25.00
Mineral Water, Clarke & White, C, New York, Smooth Base, Olive Green, Quart .... * 20.00
Mineral·Water, Clarke & White, Dark Green, Quart 24.00
Mineral Water, Clarke & White, Emerald, Pint 25.00
Mineral Water, Clarke & White, N.Y., Green, Pint 20.00
Mineral Water, Clarke & White, N.Y., Green, Quart 22.00
Mineral Water, Clarke & White, N.Y., Whittled, Green, 7 3/4 In. 18.00

Mineral Water, Buffalo Lithia, Aqua, 1/2 Gallon
(See Page 168)

Mineral Water, Congress & Empire Spring, Co.,
Green, 7 1/2 In.

Mineral Water, Hathorn
Spring, Saratoga, N.Y.,
Teal Blue, 8 In.
(See Page 170)

Mineral Water, Congress & Empire Co., C, Saratoga, Emerald Green, Pint 15.00
Mineral Water, Congress & Empire Spring Co., C, Emerald Green, Quart .... * 20.00
Mineral Water, Congress & Empire Spring Co., C, Green, Quart 22.00
Mineral Water, Congress & Empire Spring Co., C, Light Olive Green, Quart 30.00
Mineral Water, Congress & Empire Springs Co., C, Saratoga, Olive Green, Pt. .... * 15.00
Mineral Water, Congress & Empire Spring Co., C, Saratoga, N.Y., Citron, Quart .... * 45.00
Mineral Water, Congress & Empire Spring Co., Deep Emerald Green, Pint 12.00
Mineral Water, Congress & Empire Spring Co., E, Amber, Quart 50.00
Mineral Water, Congress & Empire Spring Co., E, Chips, Emerald, Pint .... * 17.50
Mineral Water, Congress & Empire Spring Co., E, Emerald Green, Quart .... * 25.00
Mineral Water, Congress & Empire Spring Co., Emerald Green, Pint 12.00
Mineral Water, Congress & Empire Spring, Co., Green, 7 1/2 In. .... *Illus* 35.00
Mineral Water, Congress & Empire Spring Co., Hotchkiss' Sons, E, Amber, Pint .... * 45.00
Mineral Water, Congress & Empire Spring Co., Hotchkiss', C, Emerald, Pint .... * 30.00
Mineral Water, Congress & Empire Spring Co., Hotchkiss', Yellow Green, Pint .... * 35.00
Mineral Water, Congress & Empire Spring Co., Saratoga, N.Y., Green, 7 3/4 In 32.50
Mineral Water, Congress & Empire Spring Co., Saratoga, N.Y., Olive, 9 3/4 In 22.00
Mineral Water, Congress & Empire Spring, Hotchkiss & Sons, Green, Quart 27.50
Mineral Water, Congress & Empire Spring, Hotchkiss & Sons, Olive, Pint 35.00
Mineral Water, Congress & Empire Spring, Saratoga, N.Y., Teal Blue, Pint 24.00
Mineral Water, Congress & Empire Spring, Saratoga, Whittled, Green, Quart 35.00
Mineral Water, Congress & Empire, Hotchkiss' Sons, Emerald Green, 1/2 Pint 85.00
Mineral Water, Congress & Empire, Hotchkiss' Sons, Olive Green, 1/2 Pint 85.00
Mineral Water, Congress Spring Co., SSNY, Emerald Green, Pint .... * 15.00
Mineral Water, Congress Spring Co., C, Saratoga, N.Y., Emerald Green, Pint .... * 30.00

Mineral Water, Congress, Amber, Pair ....*Color* XXXX.XX
Mineral Water, Crookston Deep Spring Bottling Works, Aqua, 1/2 Gallon 12.00
Mineral Water, D.A.Knowlton, Saratoga, N.Y., Emerald Green, Quart 45.00
Mineral Water, D.A.Knowlton, Saratoga, N.Y., Olive Green, Quart .... * 40.00
Mineral Water, Deep Rock Spring, Oswego, N.Y., Aqua, Pint 5.00
Mineral Water, Empire Spring Co., E, Saratoga, Emerald Green, Quart 20.00
Mineral Water, Empire Spring Co., E, Saratoga, N.Y., Blue Green, Quart 30.00
Mineral Water, Empire Spring Co., E, Saratoga, N.Y., Emerald Green, Pint .... * 25.00
Mineral Water, Empire Spring Co., E, Saratoga, N.Y., Emerald Green, Quart .... * 25.00
Mineral Water, Empire Spring Co., Saratoga, N.Y., Green, Quart 22.00
Mineral Water, Erven Lucas Bols Het Loutsje, Amsterdam, Brown Glaze, 12 In. 9.00
Mineral Water, Excelsior Spring, Green, Quart 25.00
Mineral Water, Excelsior Spring, Saratoga, N.Y., Clear Deep Green .... * 30.00
Mineral Water, Excelsior Spring, Saratoga, N.Y., Green, Pint 35.00
Mineral Water, Excelsior Spring, Saratoga, N.Y., Yellow Green, Quart .... * 40.00
Mineral Water, Excelsior, Saratoga, N.Y., Green, 10 In. 30.00
Mineral Water, Field & Stream Scene, Embossed, Green, 1/2 Gallon 6.50
Mineral Water, Florida, Aqua, 7 In. 3.00
Mineral Water, G.W.Weston & Co., Saratoga, N.Y., Crack, Olive Green, Quart .... * 25.00
Mineral Water, G.W.Weston, Saratoga, N.Y., Black Amethyst, Pint 55.00
Mineral Water, G.W.Weston, Saratoga, N.Y., Olive Green, Pint 30.00
Mineral Water, Gardner & Landor Sharon Sulfur, Pontil, Olive Green, Quart .... * 140.00
Mineral Water, Gettysburg Katalysine, Label, Emerald Green, Quart .... * 60.00
Mineral Water, Gettysburg Katalysine, Yellow Olive, Quart .... * 50.00
Mineral Water, Gettysburg, Green, Quart 26.00
Mineral Water, Geyser Spring, Deep Aqua, Pint 25.00
Mineral Water, Geyser Spring, Saratoga Spouting, Stain, Aqua, Quart .... * 25.00
Mineral Water, Granite State Spring, White Porcelain Stopper, Aqua, Pint 6.00
Mineral Water, Guilford Mineral Spring, Quart 22.00
Mineral Water, Guilford Spring, GMSW, Guilford, Vt., Green, Quart .... * 40.00
Mineral Water, Guilford Spring, Vermont, Green, Quart 35.00
Mineral Water, Guilford, Label, Green, Quart 27.00
Mineral Water, Guilford, Olive Green, Quart 23.00
Mineral Water, Hanbury Smith's Kissingen, Oral, IP, Aqua, 8 In. 80.00
Mineral Water, Hanbury Smith's Seltzers, Applied Lip, Olive Green, 6 1/2 In 18.00
Mineral Water, Hanbury Smith's Vichy, N.Y., Burst Bubble, Blue Green, Pint 20.00
Mineral Water, Hanbury Smith's Vichy, Teal Blue, 1/2 Pint 30.00
Mineral Water, Hanbury Smith's, Potstone, Olive Green, 1/2 Pint .... * 40.00
Mineral Water, Hanbury Smith's, Smooth Base, Olive Amber, Pint .... * 40.00
Mineral Water, Haskin's Spring Co., H.Shutesbury, Mass., Emerald, Quart .... * 95.00
Mineral Water, Hathorn Spring, Olive Amber, Pint 18.00
Mineral Water, Hathorn Spring, Saratoga, Black, Pint .... 17.00 To 20.00
Mineral Water, Hathorn Spring, Saratoga, N.Y., Black Amber, Pint .... * 20.00
Mineral Water, Hathorn Spring, Saratoga, N.Y., Bruise, Wear, Amber, Quart .... * 5.00
Mineral Water, Hathorn Spring, Saratoga, N.Y., Emerald Green .... * 20.00
Mineral Water, Hathorn Spring, Saratoga, N.Y., Emerald Green, Quart .... * 30.00
Mineral Water, Hathorn Spring, Saratoga, N.Y., Teal Blue, 8 In. .... *Illus* 28.00
Mineral Water, Hathorn Spring, Whittled, Emerald, Pint 22.00
Mineral Water, Hathorn Springs, Black Amber, Pint ....*................. 15.00
Mineral Water, Hathorn Springs, Saratoga, N.Y., Bubbles, Emerald, Quart 20.00
Mineral Water, Hathorn Springs, Saratoga, N.Y., Dark Amber, 8 In. 14.00
Mineral Water, Henry Rawls & Co., Albany, Smooth Base, Olive Amber, Quart .... * 160.00
Mineral Water, High Rock Congress Spring Co., Red Amber, 9 1/2 In. 35.00
Mineral Water, High Rock Congress Spring, 1767, C & W, Olive Amber, Pint .... * 85.00
Mineral Water, Hotchkiss, C, Light Olive, Pint 26.00
Mineral Water, Hunyadi Janos, Paper Label, Olive Green, 9 1/4 In. 5.00
Mineral Water, Hygeia, Embossed, Wire Stopper, Ceramic, 1/2 Gallon 17.50
Mineral Water, IVD Valk & Co., Schiedam, Jug, Brown Glaze, 11 1/2 In. 6.00
Mineral Water, John Clarke, N.Y., IP, Green, Pint 175.00
Mineral Water, John Clarke, N.Y., Olive Amber, Quart 60.00
Mineral Water, John Clarke, New York, Pontil, Olive Amber, Quart .... * 60.00
Mineral Water, John Gardner & Son, Sharon Sulfur, Bruise, Green, Pint .... * 60.00
Mineral Water, K.Jiesdorfer, Quelle, Handled Jug, Brown Glaze, 11 1/2 In. 8.00
Mineral Water, Kissingen, Hanbury Smith, IP, Oval, Aqua, 8 In. 75.00
Mineral Water, Kissingen, Hanbury Smith, Smooth Base, Green, Pint .... * 30.00

Mineral Water, Kissingen, Hanbury Smith, Wear, Olive Green, Pint .... * 35.00
Mineral Water, Knowlton, Saratoga, N.Y., Olive Green, Quart 50.00
Mineral Water, Lavator, Saratoga Shape, Embossed, Haze, Emerald, Quart 10.00
Mineral Water, Lexington, 1775, Twin Elm Spring, Gallon 12.50
Mineral Water, Lynch & Clarke, N.Y., Pontil, Chip, Olive Green, Pint .... * 45.00
Mineral Water, Magnetic Spring, Henniker, N.H., Golden Amber, Quart .... * 110.00
Mineral Water, Massena Springs, Saratoga Type, Quart 85.00
Mineral Water, Middletown Healing Springs, Grays & Clark, Amber, Quart .... * 45.00
Mineral Water, Middletown Spring Co., Nature's Remedy, Green, Quart .... * 95.00
Mineral Water, Middletown Springs, Amber, Quart .... 31.00 To 35.00
Mineral Water, Mineral Spring, Embossed, Porcelain Cork, Gallon 5.00
Mineral Water, Minnehaha Natural Spring, Aqua, 13 1/2 In. .... Illus 20.00
Mineral Water, Missisquoi A Springs, Olive Green, Quart .... * 575.00
Mineral Water, Missisquoi A Springs, Smooth Base, Green, Quart .... 35.00 To 40.00
Mineral Water, Missisquoi A Springs, Smooth Base, Olive Yellow, Quart .... * 30.00
Mineral Water, Missisquoi A Springs, Squaw & Papoose, Yellow Green, Quart .... * 350.00
Mineral Water, Morgan's Pure Spring, Defreestville, N.Y., 5 Pint 25.00
Mineral Water, Moses, Figural, Repro, Federal Law Prohibits, Green, 9 3/4 In. .... * 7.50
Mineral Water, Moses, Poland, H.Ricker & Sons, Poland Springs, 11 1/2 In. .... * 25.00
Mineral Water, Oak Orchard Acid Spring, Dark Amber, Quart 48.00
Mineral Water, Oak Orchard Acid Springs, Alabama Genessee Co., Green, Quart 130.00
Mineral Water, Oak Orchard Acid Springs, Flake, Wear, Amber, Quart .... * 45.00
Mineral Water, Oak Orchard Acid Springs, G.W.Merchant, Emerald Green, Quart .... * 40.00
Mineral Water, Oak Orchard Acid Springs, H.W.Bostwick, Blue Green, Quart .... * 45.00
Mineral Water, Oak Orchard Acid Springs, H.W.Bostwick, Stain, Olive, Quart .... * 40.00
Mineral Water, Oak Orchard Acid Springs, Hitchins Factory, Amber, Quart 50.00
Mineral Water, Ober Selters, Nassau, Eagle, Handled Jug, Brown Glaze, 12 In. 7.00
Mineral Water, Ochee Spring, BIMAL, 1/2 Gallon 8.00
Mineral Water, Old Gum Spring, Long Bros., Stoneware, Handle, 1/4 Pint 11.75
Mineral Water, Panacea Spring, Littleton, N.C., Stain, Amber, 1/2 Gallon 39.00
Mineral Water, Patent On Shoulder, Pontil, Olive Amber, Quart .... * 22.50
Mineral Water, Pavilion & United States Spring Co., P, Stain, Olive, Pint .... * 55.00
Mineral Water, Pentucket Spring, G.S.Cushing, Lowell, Blob Top, Aqua, 12 Ozs. 17.00
Mineral Water, Poland Springs, Figure Of Moses, Flake, Aqua, Quart .... * 75.00
Mineral Water, Poland Springs, Figure Of Moses, Flake, Wear, Amber, 11 1/2 In .... * 325.00
Mineral Water, Poland, Figural Moses, Repro, Hiram Richer & Sons, 10 In. .... * 5.00
Mineral Water, Poland, Figural Moses, Repro, 6 In. .... * 10.00
Mineral Water, Pure Water Service Co., Yonkers, N.Y., 5 Pints, 12 In. 15.00
Mineral Water, Quaker Springs, Old Saratoga Springs, Flake, Emerald, Pint .... * 120.00
Mineral Water, Quaker Springs, Saratoga, N.Y., Flake, Emerald, Pint .... * 120.00
Mineral Water, Queen City Pure, Buffalo, N.Y., Porcelain Top, 64 Ozs. 15.00
Mineral Water, Rockbridge Alum Water, Virginia, Square, Olive Green, Gallon .... * 850.00
Mineral Water, Saratoga Red Spring, Crack, Emerald Green, Quart .... * 15.00
Mineral Water, Saratoga Red Spring, Emerald, Quart 42.00
Mineral Water, Saratoga Red Spring, Green, Pint 33.00
Mineral Water, Saratoga Red Spring, Smooth Base, Emerald Green, Pint .... * 30.00
Mineral Water, Saratoga Seltzer, Bruise, Blue Green, Pint .... * 22.50
Mineral Water, Saratoga Seltzer, Deep Blue Green .... * 35.00
Mineral Water, Saratoga Star Spring, Amber, Quart 35.00
Mineral Water, Saratoga Vichy Spouting Spring, V, Chip, Amber, 1/2 Pint .... * 20.00
Mineral Water, Saratoga, A, Spring, Pint 100.00
Mineral Water, Saratoga, Green, Pint 27.00
Mineral Water, Spouting Springs, Pint 22.00
Mineral Water, St.Louis Crystal, 1/2 Gallon 2.95
Mineral Water, St.Regis, Massena Springs, Smooth Base, Emerald Green, Quart .... * 75.00
Mineral Water, Star Spring Co., Saratoga, N.Y., Star, Emerald Green, Pint .... * 60.00
Mineral Water, Star Spring Co.Star, Saratoga, N.Y., Red Amber, Pint .... * 50.00
Mineral Water, Sterling Spring, Blob Top, Amber, Quart 16.00
Mineral Water, Syracuse Springs Excelsior, Smooth Base, Amber, Pint .... * 70.00
Mineral Water, Thompson's, Jug, Gallon 27.50
Mineral Water, Vermont Spring, Saxe & Co., Sheldon, Vt., Olive Green, Quart .... * 20.00
Mineral Water, Vermont Spring, Sheldon, Vt., Green, Quart 35.00
Mineral Water, Veronica Medicinal Spring, Square, Amber, 10 1/2 In. 5.00
Mineral Water, Veronica Spring, Medicinal, Ring Lip, Amber, 10 1/2 In. 5.00
Mineral Water, Veronica, Amber, Quart 5.00

Mineral Water, Minnehaha Natural Spring, Aqua, 13 1/2 In.
(See Page 171)

Mineral Water, White Rock Spring Co.,
Brown, 9 1/2 In.

Mineral Water, Veronica, Natural Medicinal Spring, California, 10 3/4 In.	35.00
Mineral Water, Vichy, Hanbury Smith, N.Y., Smooth Base, Yellow Green, Pint	* 25.00
Mineral Water, Vichy, Hanbury Smith, Stain, Yellow Green, 1/2 Pint	* 45.00
Mineral Water, Vichy, Hanbury Smith, Wear, Emerald Green, 1/2 Pint	* 40.00
Mineral Water, W.K.G., Master, Whitney Glass Works, N.J., Blue Green, Quart	* 70.00
Mineral Water, Washington Lithia Well, Ballston, Spa, N.Y., Aqua, Pint	* 150.00
Mineral Water, Washington Spring Co., Ballston Spa, N.Y., Emerald, Pint	305.00
Mineral Water, Washington Spring, Emerald, Pint	75.00
Mineral Water, Washington Spring, Saratoga, N.Y., Emerald Green, Pint	* 55.00
Mineral Water, Washington Spring, Saratoga, N.Y., Emerald, Pint	70.00
Mineral Water, Watchung Spring, Plainfield, N.J., Arrowhead, Aqua, Gallon	18.00
Mineral Water, Water Well Scene Embossed, Quart	5.00
Mineral Water, White Rock Spring Co., Brown, 9 1/2 In. *Illus*	17.50
Mineral Water, Whitney Glass Works On Base, Green, Quart	23.00
Mineral Water, Witter Springs, BIMAL, Amber, 9 1/2 In.	4.50
Mineral Water, Wm.Betz, Salem, Ohio, IP, Aqua, 7 5/8 In.	132.50
Mineral Water, Wyand Focking, Amsterdam, Handled Jug, Brown Glaze, 12 1/2 In	7.00
Mineral Water, Yonkers Co., N.Y., Slug Plate, Blob, Straw Color, 7 1/4 In.	5.50
Miniature, A-1 Pilsner Beer, Arizona Brewing Company, 4 In.	5.00
Miniature, Alpha Industries, Battle Of The Little Big Horn, Set Of 5	55.00
Miniature, Alta, Jug	5.00
Miniature, Ardo, Gondola & Man	3.95
Miniature, Argentine, Gaucho Boot	7.50
Miniature, Armagnac, Fish Bobbin, The Big Catch	9.95
Miniature, Armagnac, Shotgun Shell, Black	6.95
Miniature, Artistica Artigiana, Horse, Blown Glass	10.00
Miniature, Austrian, Tamale, Giveaway	20.00
Miniature, Ballantine's Scotch Whiskey, C.1930, Pottery Jug, 3 In.	8.00
Miniature, Banker	6.50
Miniature, Bare-Breasted Girl & Drummer & Dancer, Flasher, Italy	19.95
Miniature, Barsottini, Cadillac	9.00
Miniature, Barsottini, Cannon	9.00
Miniature, Barsottini, Egyptian Set, Set Of 4	60.00
Miniature, Barsottini, Italia, 1912	9.00
Miniature, Barsottini, Lanchester	9.00
Miniature, Barsottini, Renault	9.00
Miniature, Barsottini, Snow White & Seven Dwarfs	240.00
Miniature, Beam, Braniff Airlines	1.50
Miniature, Beam, Colonial Liquor	1.50
Miniature, Beam, Crofton Liquor	1.50
Miniature, Beam, Delta Airlines, Atlanta	1.50
Miniature, Beam, Delta Airlines, Chicago	1.50

Miniature, **Beam**, Delta Airlines, Houston 1.50
Miniature, **Beam**, Delta Airlines, Jamaica 1.50
Miniature, **Beam**, Delta Airlines, Los Angeles 1.50
Miniature, **Beam**, Delta Airlines, New Orleans 1.50
Miniature, **Beam**, Delta Airlines, New York 1.50
Miniature, **Beam**, Delta Airlines, San Francisco 1.50
Miniature, **Beam**, Huni, 1975 .... 8.95
Miniature, **Beam**, It's A Boy 1.50
Miniature, **Beam**, It's A Girl 1.50
Miniature, **Beam**, Ponderosa Ranch 2.50
Miniature, **Beam**, Rich's Discount 1.00
Miniature, **Beam**, Rose's Lucky Strike 2.00
Miniature, **Beam**, Sparky's, Virgin Islands 2.00
Miniature, **Beam**, Toni's Classy Inn 2.00
Miniature, **Beer**, Coors, 4 In. .... 5.00 To 7.00
Miniature, **Beneagles**, Barrel 4.00
Miniature, **Beneagles**, Curling Stone 4.00
Miniature, **Beneagles**, Haggis 5.00
Miniature, **Beneagles**, Loch Ness Monster 4.00
Miniature, **Beneagles**, Thistle & Rose Chessman, Bishop 8.50
Miniature, **Beneagles**, Thistle & Rose Chessman, Castle 8.50
Miniature, **Beneagles**, Thistle & Rose Chessman, King 8.50
Miniature, **Beneagles**, Thistle & Rose Chessman, Knight 8.50
Miniature, **Beneagles**, Thistle & Rose Chessman, Pawn 8.50
Miniature, **Beneagles**, Thistle & Rose Chessman, Queen 8.50
Miniature, **Bischoff**, Ashtray 8.25
Miniature, **Bols**, Elephant 6.00
Miniature, **Bols**, Lobster Claw & Creel .... 15.00 To 35.00
Miniature, **Bols**, Owl, Blown Glass 10.95
Miniature, **Bols**, Rhino, Blown Glass 10.95
Miniature, **Borghini**, Black Cat 1.95
Miniature, **Borghini**, Man On Cask 5.95
Miniature, **Borghini**, Nubian Woman 1.95
Miniature, **Borghini**, Nubian Woman, Sitting 2.95
Miniature, **Borghini**, Penguin 6.00
Miniature, **Bresciani**, Ancient Egyptian Urn 5.95
Miniature, **Budweiser Beer**, Salt & Pepper, Pair 6.00
Miniature, **Buton**, Amphora, Apricot Brandy, Silver Metal Trim, 5 In. 9.95
Miniature, **Buton**, Amphora, Cherry Brandy, Silver Metal Trim, 5 In. 9.95
Miniature, **Butterfly**, Brown, Tan, & Red 8.50
Miniature, **Carioca**, Rum, Jug & Lampshade, 2 Handles 17.50
Miniature, **Carioca**, Rum, Ox-Cart 10.00
Miniature, **Cazanove**, Horse 8.00
Miniature, **Cazanove**, Seal 20.00
Miniature, **Certosa**, Fat Monk 8.00
Miniature, **Champagne Lady & Rose**, German 45.00
Miniature, **Chietti**, Sailboat 10.00
Miniature, **Classic Liqueur**, Amaretto 1.00
Miniature, **Classic Liqueur**, Chula 1.00
Miniature, **Classic Liqueur**, Grand Suzette 1.00
Miniature, **Classic Liqueur**, Liquore DiNoee 1.00
Miniature, **Classic Liqueur**, Loch Moor 1.00
Miniature, **Cohodas**, Glass Dog 5.00
Miniature, **Collectors Art**, Afghan Hound, Porcelain, 3 1/2 In. 10.95
Miniature, **Collectors Art**, Bird Dog, Black, Porcelain, 3 1/2 In. 12.95
Miniature, **Collectors Art**, Bird Dog, Brown, Porcelain, 3 1/2 In. 10.95
Miniature, **Collectors Art**, Black Angus Bull, Porcelain, 3 1/2 In. 10.95
Miniature, **Collectors Art**, Brahma Bull 14.99
Miniature, **Collectors Art**, Charolais Bull 14.99
Miniature, **Collectors Art**, Collie, Porcelain, 3 1/2 In. 10.95
Miniature, **Collectors Art**, Dalmation, Porcelain, 3 1/2 In. 10.95
Miniature, **Collectors Art**, Doberman Pinscher, Red, Porcelain 15.95
Miniature, **Collectors Art**, Doberman, Black, Porcelain, 3 1/2 In. 10.95
Miniature, **Collectors Art**, Doberman, Red, Porcelain, 3 1/2 In. 12.95
Miniature, **Collectors Art**, German Shepherd, Black, Porcelain 15.95

Miniature, Collectors Art, Hereford	14.99
Miniature, Collectors Art, Irish Setter, Porcelain, 3 1/2 In.	10.95
Miniature, Collectors Art, Mexican Bull	14.99
Miniature, Collectors Art, Pointer, Black & White, Porcelain	12.95 To 14.99
Miniature, Collectors Art, Polled Hereford, Porcelain, 2 Ozs.	11.95 To 14.99
Miniature, Collectors Art, Poodle, Black, Porcelain	12.95
Miniature, Collectors Art, Poodle, Black, Porcelain, 3 1/2 In.	10.95
Miniature, Collectors Art, Poodle, Silver, Porcelain	12.95
Miniature, Collectors Art, Poodle, Silver, Porcelain, 3 1/2 In.	10.95
Miniature, Collectors Art, Poodle, White, Porcelain, 3 1/2 In.	10.95 To 12.95
Miniature, Collectors Art, Schnauzer, Porcelain, 3 1/2 In.	10.95 To 14.99
Miniature, Collectors Art, Texas Longhorn	14.99
Miniature, Cornish Mead, Barrel, Brown	7.00
Miniature, Cornish Mead, Elf	7.00
Miniature, Cornish Mead, King Arthur	12.00
Miniature, Cornish Mead, Lighthouse, Blue	8.00
Miniature, Cornish Mead, Mermaid, No.1	8.00
Miniature, Cornish Mead, Running Light	7.00
Miniature, Cornish Mead, Smuggler On The Barrel	7.95
Miniature, Cornish Mead, Tin Mine	8.00
Miniature, Cornish Mead, Toby	8.00
Miniature, Courvoisier, Cannon From Mexico	5.00
Miniature, Courvoisier, Cannon, Black Plastic Gun Carriage, 2 1/2 In.	4.50
Miniature, Crigler & Crigler Whiskey	8.00
Miniature, Croizet Cognac, Napoleon	7.00
Miniature, Crown Distilleries Whiskey	7.00
Miniature, Crown Distilleries, Whiskey, Embossed Stopper, Slug Plate, Amber	40.00
Miniature, Cryus Noble, Faro Bank	14.99
Miniature, Cyrus Noble, Assessor	12.99
Miniature, Cyrus Noble, Continental Navy	12.00 To 18.95
Miniature, Cyrus Noble, Faro Bank	14.99 To 15.95
Miniature, Cyrus Noble, Gambler	12.99
Miniature, Cyrus Noble, Gambler With Donkey	25.00
Miniature, Cyrus Noble, Miner	12.99
Miniature, Cyrus Noble, Snowshoe Thompson	10.00 To 14.50
Miniature, Cyrus Noble, Tonopak Tavern	14.99
Miniature, Cyrus Noble, Tun Tavern	12.99 To 18.95
Miniature, Deep Spring, Tennessee Whiskey, Amber	9.00
Miniature, Deep Spring, Tennessee Whiskey, Amber, 4 1/2 In.	10.00
Miniature, Deer, Holland, 1971 _Illus_	4.00
Miniature, Dewar's, Bull, Black	1.95 To 4.95
Miniature, Distillerie Du Matador, Eiffel Tower	18.00
Miniature, Dog On Doghouse & With Insect On Nose, Flasher, Italy	19.95
Miniature, Dog With Bandage On Tail, "It Won't Be Long Now, " German	45.00
Miniature, Dor Argentine, Pig	8.00
Miniature, Dor Argentine, Rabbit	8.00
Miniature, Dr.Bouvier's Buchu Gin	15.00
Miniature, Drinkometer, "The Doctor, Use It Daily, Live Gaily, " German	40.00
Miniature, Drioli, African Dancers, 1970, Set Of 6	35.00
Miniature, Drioli, African Native Musicians, 6 Pieces	90.00
Miniature, Drioli, Bagpiper, 1959	15.00
Miniature, Drioli, Bongo Player	15.00
Miniature, Drioli, Chinaman, Standing	20.00
Miniature, Drioli, Donkey	4.00
Miniature, Drioli, Elephant	4.00
Miniature, Drioli, English Range, 1969, Set Of 6	30.00
Miniature, Drioli, Flute Player	4.00
Miniature, Drioli, Gondola	15.00
Miniature, Drioli, Guitarist	18.00
Miniature, Drioli, Hippies, 1970, Set Of 6	35.00
Miniature, Drioli, Indian Maiden, 3-D	20.00
Miniature, Drioli, Inidan Woman, Flower Decal	15.00
Miniature, Drioli, Jazz Band	175.00
Miniature, Drioli, Man With Bowls	4.00
Miniature, Drioli, Man With Pipe	4.00

Miniature, Drioli, Merchant, Seated, 1970 .... 9.95
Miniature, Drioli, Nubian With Large Bowl 15.00
Miniature, Drioli, Nubian, Hands On Heels 15.00
Miniature, Drioli, Oriental Man 15.00
Miniature, Drioli, Samurai, Green 20.00
Miniature, Drioli, Saxophonist 18.00
Miniature, Drioli, Striped Jug, 1958 .... *Illus* 8.00
Miniature, Drioli, Turkey 4.00
Miniature, Drioli, Vase, 1970, Set Of 3 .... 15.00
Miniature, Drioli, Venus 4.00
Miniature, Drioli, Venus De Milo, 1970 .... 4.00 To 9.95

Miniature, Deer, Holland, 1971
(See Page 174)

Miniature, George
Washington Bust,
Cobalt, 4 In.
(See Page 176)

Miniature, Drioli, Striped Jug, 1958

Miniature, Duca D'Asti, Piazza San Pietro Monument 10.00
Miniature, Duca D'Asti, Roma Arca Di Tito Monument 10.00
Miniature, Duca D'Asti, Roma Fontana Di Trevi Monument 10.00
Miniature, Ducastaing, Fissing Bobbin, Milk Glass 7.50
Miniature, E-Z Stove Polish, BIMAL, Aqua 3.00
Miniature, Eastside Beer, Los Angeles Brewing Coampay, Foil Label, 4 1/4 In 6.00
Miniature, Eastside Beer, Pabst Brewing Company, Foil Label, 4 1/4 In. 6.00
Miniature, Evelt, Light Bulb 5.50
Miniature, Farm Relief, Canadian Gentleman, German, Multicolor 45.00
Miniature, Finlandia, Vodka, Log Shape, Semifrosted 1.95
Miniature, Fire Water, German 45.00
Miniature, Forcoll Argentine 9.00
Miniature, Forcoll Argentine, Binoculars 10.00
Miniature, Forcoll Argentine, Incan Face 8.00
Miniature, Forcoll Argentine, Owl 9.00
Miniature, Forcoll Argentine, Soccer Shoe 8.00
Miniature, Forcoll, Eiffel Tower, 1976 .... 7.50
Miniature, Forcoll, Goose 8.00
Miniature, Forcoll, Owl 8.00
Miniature, Forcoll, Two-Handled Amphora, 1976 .... 7.50
Miniature, Fremont Abbey, Bluejay, Bisque Finish, 2 Ozs., 5 In. 5.95
Miniature, Fremont Abbey, Cardinal, Bisque Finish, 2 Ozs., 5 In. 5.95
Miniature, Fremont Abbey, Duck, Bisque Finish, 2 Ozs., 5 In. 5.95
Miniature, Fremont Abbey, Parakeet, Bisque Finish, 2 Ozs., 5 In. 5.95
Miniature, Fremont Abbey, Pheasant, Bisque Finish, 2 Ozs., 5 In. 5.95
Miniature, Fremont Abbey, Quail, Bisque Finish, 2 Ozs., 5 In. 5.95
Miniature, Funquelen Argentine, Shoe 9.00
Miniature, Gallwey, Irish Soldier .... 7.00 To 9.00

Miniature, Garnier, Animal Set, Set Of 6 .... 25.00
Miniature, Garnier, Baby Trio, 1966, Gold Caps & Metal Stand, Set Of 3 .... 11.95
Miniature, Garnier, Bird Set, Set Of 6 .... 25.00
Miniature, Garnier, Butterfly 6.00
Miniature, Garnier, Butterfly Set, Set Of 6 .... 25.00
Miniature, Garnier, Chess Set, Set Of 6 .... 25.00
Miniature, Garnier, Dog .... 20.00 To 25.00
Miniature, Garnier, Duck 25.00
Miniature, Garnier, Elephant .... 22.00 To 25.00
Miniature, Garnier, Frog 25.00
Miniature, Garnier, Hen With Chicks 25.00
Miniature, Garnier, House Set, Set Of 6 .... 25.00 To 40.00
Miniature, Garnier, Sailor Skittle 25.00
Miniature, Garnier, Dog Set, Set Of 6 .... 25.00
Miniature, George Washington Bust, Cobalt, 4 In. .... *Illus* 5.00
Miniature, Goebel Girl, German 35.00
Miniature, Gold Camel .... 6.50 To 8.95
Miniature, Gold Horseshoe 6.50
Miniature, Gold Sphinx 8.95
Miniature, Grenadier Soldier, Soldiers No.1, Set Of 3 .... 22.00
Miniature, Grenadier Soldier, Soldiers No.2, Miniature, Set Of 3 .... 22.00
Miniature, Grenadier, Mosby's Rangers 12.95
Miniature, Grenadier, Pancho Villa On Horseback 12.45
Miniature, Grenadier, 1st Regiment Virginia Volunteers .... 10.95 To 15.50
Miniature, Grenadier, Set Of Soldiers No.1, Set Of 3 .... 22.00
Miniature, Grenadier, Set Of Soldiers No.2, Set Of 3 .... 22.00
Miniature, Grenadier, Washington Blue Rifles .... 11.95 To 12.95
Miniature, Grenadier, First Regiment Virginia Volunteers .... 12.95 To 14.50
Miniature, Grenadier, 2nd Regiment U.S.Sharpshooters 12.95
Miniature, Grenadier, 2nd Washington Blue Rifles .... 10.95 To 12.50
Miniature, Grenadier, Mosby's Rangers .... 10.95 To 13.50
Miniature, Grenadier, Pancho Villa 12.50
Miniature, Guitar Player & Girl & Boy Dancing, Flasher, Italy 19.95
Miniature, Haas Brothers, Assessor 12.99
Miniature, Haas Brothers, Bartender 12.99
Miniature, Haas Brothers, Miner 12.99
Miniature, Haas Brothers, Old Orient Saloon 13.99
Miniature, Haas Brothers, Tun Tavern 12.99
Miniature, Hammer Brand, Pear, Glass, Germany 3.95
Miniature, Hammer Brand, Strawberry, Glass, Germany 3.95
Miniature, Hance Bros. & White Whiskey, Flask, Amber 7.00
Miniature, Harlequin, No.1 .... 8.00
Miniature, Harlequin, No.2 .... 8.00
Miniature, Have A Ball With Me, German 45.00
Miniature, Heinz Ketchup, 8 Sided 7.00
Miniature, Hippie Band, 1970, Set Of 6 .... 35.00 To 90.00
Miniature, Hoffman, Doctor 12.99
Miniature, Hoffman, Dodge City Frontier Pistol 17.50
Miniature, Hoffman, Ducks, Set Of 8 .... 55.00
Miniature, Hoffman, Generation Gap, Hippies '76 & 1876 Pioneer, 2 Ozs., Pair 22.95
Miniature, Hoffman, German P-80 Pistol 17.50
Miniature, Hoffman, Green Winged Teal, Pair 19.00
Miniature, Hoffman, Harp Player 12.99
Miniature, Hoffman, Leprechaun 12.99
Miniature, Hoffman, Leprechaun Series, Set Of 6 .... 65.00 To 72.00
Miniature, Hoffman, Mr.Shoemaker 12.99
Miniature, Hoffman, Mrs.Shoemaker 12.99
Miniature, Hoffman, Pintailed Duck, Pair 19.00
Miniature, Hoffman, Sandman 12.99
Miniature, Hoffman, Wood Duck, Pair 19.00
Miniature, Hoffman, 1851 Civil War Colt Pistol 17.50
Miniature, Hoffman, 45 Automatic Pistol 17.50
Miniature, Honest Measure Flask 7.00
Miniature, Horseshoe, Embossed Frog On Lily Pad 15.00
Miniature, Hudson Bay, Canadian Buffalo & Rubbing Rock 11.95

Miniature, Hudson Bay, Canadian Nonsuch Ship, 1970	11.95
Miniature, Hula Girl, Hawaii	9.00
Miniature, Inca, Pisco	3.00
Miniature, Irish Mist, Soldier	6.00
Miniature, J.Reiger Whiskey	8.00
Miniature, J.Rieger & Co., Whiskey, Dug	6.00
Miniature, Johnny Pfeiffer Beer, Detroit, Mich., Red, White, & Blue, 6 In.	12.00
Miniature, Jon-Sol, Hodag, Female & Male, Whiskey, Empty, 4 3/4 In., Pair	27.90
Miniature, Jon-Sol, Totem Pole	7.50
Miniature, Jon-Sol, Wisconsin Baby Robin, Bisque Finish, 4 1/4 In.	9.95
Miniature, Jon-Sol, Wisconsin Blue Jay, Bisque Finish, 5 In.	9.95
Miniature, Jon-Sol, Wisconsin Red-Headed Woodpecker, Bisque Finish, 5 In.	9.95
Miniature, Kellerstrass Whiskey	18.00
Miniature, King Kamehameha, Hawaii	9.00
Miniature, Kiss Snookums, German	45.00
Miniature, Kord, Dolphin	12.00
Miniature, Koshu, Naughty Boy, Frosted	3.95
Miniature, Lady Carrying Luggage & Girl Surfing, Flasher, Italy	19.95
Miniature, Larsen Cognac, Invincible Ship, Limoges Porcelain	12.95
Miniature, Larsen, Viking Ship, Limoges	9.00
Miniature, Last Chance Cologne, Western Bar Scene, Wooden Frame, 6 Piece	80.00
Miniature, Last Chance, Banker	6.95
Miniature, Lawson's Whiskey, Dundee, Scotland, Green	5.00
Miniature, Lenin, Old Store Scotch	10.00
Miniature, Lewis & Clark, Expedition, Bisque Finish, Set Of 5	58.00
Miniature, Life Preserver, German	45.00
Miniature, Lincoln, Old Store Scotch	10.00
Miniature, Lindisfarne, Celtic Cross	9.95
Miniature, Lionstone, American Cocker Spaniel	11.95
Miniature, Lionstone, Banker	8.95
Miniature, Lionstone, Bar Scene, Frame, Set Of 6	75.00 To 90.00
Miniature, Lionstone, British Pointer	11.95
Miniature, Lionstone, British Rough Collie	11.95
Miniature, Lionstone, Burmese Girl	8.95
Miniature, Lionstone, Cardinal	30.00
Miniature, Lionstone, Casual Indian	9.00 To 12.95
Miniature, Lionstone, Cavalry Scout	8.95 To 12.95
Miniature, Lionstone, Chlorophonia	12.00
Miniature, Lionstone, Circus Series, Set Of 9	69.95 To 100.00
Miniature, Lionstone, Cowboy	19.00 To 21.00
Miniature, Lionstone, Emerald Toucan	12.00
Miniature, Lionstone, Fancy Birds, Set Of 4	79.95 To 125.00
Miniature, Lionstone, Fat Lady	8.95
Miniature, Lionstone, Fire Eater	8.95
Miniature, Lionstone, Fire Fighter Equipment, 3 Piece Set	35.00 To 39.00
Miniature, Lionstone, French Poodle	11.95
Miniature, Lionstone, German Boxer	11.95
Miniature, Lionstone, German Shepherd	11.95
Miniature, Lionstone, Gentleman Gambler	6.95 To 9.95
Miniature, Lionstone, Giant With Midget	8.95
Miniature, Lionstone, Hummingbird	30.00
Miniature, Lionstone, Lonely Luke	10.95
Miniature, Lionstone, Lucky Buck	10.95
Miniature, Lionstone, Northern Flycatcher	12.00
Miniature, Lionstone, Oriental Woodpecker	30.00
Miniature, Lionstone, Painted Bunting	12.00
Miniature, Lionstone, Perfessor	10.95
Miniature, Lionstone, Proud Indian	8.95 To 9.95
Miniature, Lionstone, Scarlet Macaw	12.00
Miniature, Lionstone, Sheriff	9.00 To 12.95
Miniature, Lionstone, Snake Charmer	8.95
Miniature, Lionstone, Strong Man	8.95
Miniature, Lionstone, Sword Swallower	8.95
Miniature, Lionstone, Tattooed Lady	8.95
Miniature, Lionstone, Western Series, No.2, Set Of 7	75.00

Miniature, Lionstone, Western Series, No.1, Set Of 6	65.00
Miniature, Lionstone, Wild Canary	30.00
Miniature, Lionstone, Yellow Headed Amazon	12.00
Miniature, Liquore De Noce	1.00
Miniature, Lorito, Parrot, C.1930	25.00
Miniature, Luxardo, Baby Amphora	18.00
Miniature, Luxardo, Bear	5.95
Miniature, Luxardo, Bird	25.00
Miniature, Luxardo, Black Cat, 1972	15.00
Miniature, Luxardo, Boar	5.95
Miniature, Luxardo, Buffalo	5.95
Miniature, Luxardo, Burma Ashtray, 1960	8.00
Miniature, Luxardo, Gambia	2.70
Miniature, Luxardo, Gondola	2.70 To 6.00
Miniature, Luxardo, Green Mosaic Ashtray	8.00
Miniature, Luxardo, Hippo	5.90
Miniature, Luxardo, Horseshoe, Giveaway	35.00
Miniature, Luxardo, Lion	5.95
Miniature, Luxardo, Maraschino Luxardo, Straw Pleated	.65
Miniature, Luxardo, Nubian Woman	1.95
Miniature, Luxardo, Paestum	4.00
Miniature, Luxardo, Polar Bear, Porcelain	8.95
Miniature, Luxardo, Rhino	5.95
Miniature, Luxardo, Turkey	25.00
Miniature, Luxardo, Venus	4.00
Miniature, Luxardo, Wild Life Animals, Set Of 6	29.99
Miniature, Luxardo, Wildlife Set, Set Of 6	25.00 To 29.95
Miniature, Mahnattan, Glass Lady	10.00
Miniature, Man Behind Pole & 5 Chorus Girls, Flasher, Italy	19.95
Miniature, Man In Champagne Glass, German	45.00
Miniature, Man In Moon & Couple On Bench, Flasher, Italy	19.95
Miniature, Martin Luther King, Old Store Scotch	10.00
Miniature, Masked Man With Book	8.00
Miniature, MBC, Aladdin Hotel, Las Vegas	8.90
Miniature, MBC, Banker	5.50 To 8.95
Miniature, MBC, Battle Of Concord, Set Of 6	29.95
Miniature, MBC, Butterfly	25.00
Miniature, MBC, Circus Circus Hotel	6.50 To 8.95
Miniature, MBC, Dunes Hotel, Las Vegas	8.95
Miniature, MBC, First National Bank, Blue & Gold	12.50
Miniature, MBC, Foxes, Pair	15.00
Miniature, MBC, Globe	7.95
Miniature, MBC, Gold Horseshoe, Reno	7.00 To 8.95
Miniature, MBC, Gold Rooster, Black Base	6.95
Miniature, MBC, Gold Rooster, White Base	6.95
Miniature, MBC, Hacienda Hotel, Las Vegas	6.50 To 8.95
Miniature, MBC, Hollywood Star	10.00
Miniature, MBC, Gold Horseshoe, Las Vegas	6.95
Miniature, MBC, Gold Horseshoe, Reno	6.95
Miniature, MBC, Kint Tut	8.95
Miniature, MBC, Landmark Hotel, Las Vegas	7.00 To 8.95
Miniature, MBC, Laurel & Hardy Car	19.95
Miniature, MBC, Laurel & Hardy, Pair	15.00 To 35.00
Miniature, MBC, MGM Grand Hotel, Las Vegas	8.95
Miniature, MBC, Peddler, Bisque, 6 In.	8.90
Miniature, MBC, Poodle, Black	7.95
Miniature, MBC, Poodle, White	7.95
Miniature, MBC, Rooster	7.00
Miniature, MBC, Save-Most Man	7.00
Miniature, MBC, Silver Horseshoe, Las Vegas	6.95
Miniature, MBC, Silver Horseshoe, Reno	6.95
Miniature, MBC, Slot Machine	8.95
Miniature, MBC, Song Of Norway Ship	8.95
Miniature, MBC, Sphinx	8.95
Miniature, MBC, Stardust Hotel, Las Vegas	8.95

Miniature, MBC, Stein, Blue 8.95
Miniature, MBC, Stein, Brown 8.95
Miniature, MBC, Stein, Tan 8.95
Miniature, MBC, Tropicana Hotel, Las Vegas 8.95
Miniature, MBC, Wee Bottle Club Globe 8.00
Miniature, , McCormick, Patriot Series, Set Of 8 .... 105.00 To 120.00
Miniature, McGinnis, Baltimore Whiskey 10.00
Miniature, McLech, Cat, Milk Glass 6.50
Miniature, Meier's, Wild Mountain Blackberry Wine, Square Jug, Handle 6.95
Miniature, Merry Christmas, German 45.00
Miniature, Mitchell, Greybeard, 2-Handled Jug, 1941 .... 7.95
Miniature, Mobana, Monkey Holding Banana, Bahamas 3.95
Miniature, Mogen David, American Revolution, Boxed, Set Of 6 .... 24.95
Miniature, Mogen David, Battle Of Concord, Wooden Case, Set Of 6 .... 25.00
Miniature, Mohawk, Jug 6.00
Miniature, Moisette, Seated Monkey With Paw On Mouth 11.95
Miniature, Monarch, Loch Ness Monster 6.00
Miniature, Monkey, German 45.00
Miniature, Monterey, Cerveza 20.00
Miniature, Munchen, Bisque Jug, Flower, Handle, 4 In. 2.95
Miniature, Munchen, Glazed Jug, Flower, Handle, 3 In. 2.95
Miniature, Munchen, Royal Coffee, Ceramic Coffeepot 2.95
Miniature, Murano, Cat 12.00
Miniature, Murano, Dog 12.00
Miniature, Murano, Swan 12.00
Miniature, Muth Beer 10.00
Miniature, Napoleon, Old Store Scotch 10.00
Miniature, Nicholoff, Dancing Bear 45.00
Miniature, Night Cap, Green & White, German 45.00
Miniature, Oertel's Little Brown Jug Ale, Chalkware, 3 In. .... 15.00 To 20.00
Miniature, Okolehao, Hula Girl 9.00
Miniature, Okolehao, King Kamehameha 9.00
Miniature, Okolehao, Pineapple 9.00
Miniature, Old Overholt Straight Rye Whiskey, Flat 30.00
Miniature, Old Scotch, German 40.00
Miniature, Old Store Scotch, Hitler 10.00
Miniature, One Of The Boys, Miniature 45.00
Miniature, P.J.Dowlin Whiskey 7.00
Miniature, Pancho Villa, Gunfighter 12.95
Miniature, Paul Jones Pure Rye, Louisville, Ky., Amber 7.00
Miniature, Paul Jones Whiskey, Cigarette Lighter, Amber 3.00
Miniature, PBR, Bronc Buster 29.95
Miniature, PBR, Camel 8.95
Miniature, PBR, Elmer The Gold Camel 17.95
Miniature, PBR, Laurel & Hardy, Pair .... 1995 To 24.95
Miniature, PBR, Peddlar Man 6.00
Miniature, PBR, Wrangler 29.95
Miniature, Pear, German 35.00
Miniature, Pennsylvania Dutch Woman & Man, Pair 15.00
Miniature, Pig, Something Good In A Hog's – & He Won't Squeal, 4 In. 70.00
Miniature, Pineapple, Hawaii 9.00
Miniature, Platinum Horseshoe 6.50
Miniature, Polar Bear, Argentina, Glazed 14.95
Miniature, Pottery Jug, Mercury By Fuller Morrison, 3 In. .... Illus 10.00
Miniature, Pride Of Kentucky Whiskey, Decanter, Etched, Fluted, Amethyst ... 38.00
Miniature, Quaker Maid Whiskey, Haze, Sun-Colored Amethyst, 4 1/2 In. 10.00
Miniature, Queen's Castle, Barrel O' Scotch, Jug, Handle 2.95
Miniature, Raintree, Clown, No.1, 6 In. 10.95
Miniature, Raintree, Clown, No.2 .... 12.95
Miniature, Robert Burns Bust, White Ceramic, Matte Finish, 4 In. 4.95
Miniature, Roccaccio, Italian Queen 14.95
Miniature, Rocher Freres, Admiral 12.00
Miniature, Rocher Freres, Hindu 12.00
Miniature, Rocher Freres, Sailor 12.00
Miniature, Rocher Freres, Scotch Bagpiper 12.00

Miniature, Pottery Jug, Mercury By Fuller Morrison, 3 In.
(See Page 179)

Miniature, **Rooster,** White & Black	6.50
Miniature, **Rutherford,** Eagle	8.00
Miniature, **Rynbende,** Bermuda Pink Rectory	12.00
Miniature, **Rynbende,** Bulldog	10.00
Miniature, **Rynbende,** Candlestick, Miniature	4.99
Miniature, **Rynbende,** Cruet, Ceramic	4.99
Miniature, **Rybende,** Deer, 1971 .... *Illus*	4.00
Miniature, **Rynbende,** Duck	6.00
Miniature, **Rynbende,** Dutch Woman & Man, Pair	15.00
Miniature, **Rynbende,** English Bulldog, Brown	22.50
Miniature, **Rynbende,** Goose	6.00
Miniature, **Rynbende,** Hare	6.00
Miniature, **Rynbende,** Kangaroo	6.00
Miniature, **Rynbende,** No.44 Delft	6.00
Miniature, **Rynbende,** Oil Lamp, Ceramic	4.99
Miniature, **Rynbende,** Owl	5.50
Miniature, **Rynbende,** Pelican	6.00
Miniature, **Rynbende,** Penguin	6.00
Miniature, **Rynbende,** Sea Lion	6.00
Miniature, **Rynbende,** Shoe, Ceramic	4.99
Miniature, **Rynbende,** Swan	6.00
Miniature, **Rynbende,** White Snowman	11.00
Miniature, **Rynbende,** Windmill, Ceramic	5.99
Miniature, **Sandeman,** Man	35.00
Miniature, **Sarandrea,** Moses	7.50
Miniature, **Sarandrea,** Napoleon	7.50
Miniature, **Sarandrea,** Peasant Man	7.50
Miniature, **Sarandrea,** Peasant Woman	7.50
Miniature, **Sarandrea,** Peasant Woman & Man, Pair	15.00
Miniature, **Sarandrea,** Pieta, White, Italy	9.00
Miniature, **Sarandrea,** Sphinx	7.50
Miniature, **Schlitz Beer,** Salt & Pepper, Pair	6.00
Miniature, **Scotchman Playing Bagpipes,** German	45.00
Miniature, **Security Distilling Co.,** Whiskey, Chicago, Fluted Shoulder	15.00
Miniature, **Shakespeare's Birthplace,** House, Tan & Brown, 2 In.	5.95
Miniature, **Shawhan Distillery Whiskey**	8.00
Miniature, **Ski Country,** Australian Black Swan	12.95
Miniature, **Ski Country,** Baby Robin	12.00
Miniature, **Ski Country,** Baby Snowy Owl	15.00
Miniature, **Ski Country,** Barnum	13.00
Miniature, **Ski Country,** Birth Of Freedom	11.00
Miniature, **Ski Country,** Black Swan	13.00
Miniature, **Ski Country,** Black-Footed Ferret	13.00
Miniature, **Ski Country,** Blue Teal Duck	11.00
Miniature, **Ski Country,** Bonnie	11.00
Miniature, **Ski Country,** Bonnie & Clyde, Pair	24.95

Miniature, Ski Country, Brown Trout	13.00
Miniature, Ski Country, Burro	15.00
Miniature, Ski Country, California Condor	11.95
Miniature, Ski Country, Canadian Goose	18.00
Miniature, Ski Country, Cigar Store Indian	13.00
Miniature, Ski Country, Clown	11.95
Miniature, Ski Country, Clyde Barrow With Machine Gun	11.95
Miniature, Ski Country, Condor	10.00
Miniature, Ski Country, Connecticut Robin	14.00
Miniature, Ski Country, Dove	15.00
Miniature, Ski Country, Elephant	18.00
Miniature, Ski Country, Ferret	13.00
Miniature, Ski Country, Fox On A Log	17.50
Miniature, Ski Country, Grouse	13.00
Miniature, Ski Country, Harpy Eagle	13.95
Miniature, Ski Country, Hawk	15.00
Miniature, Ski Country, Horned Owl	12.50
Miniature, Ski Country, Indian Dancers, Set Of 6	65.00
Miniature, Ski Country, Jenny Lind, Blue	14.00
Miniature, Ski Country, Jenny Lind, Yellow	17.50
Miniature, Ski Country, Kangaroo	11.50
Miniature, Ski Country, Ladies Of Leadville, Blonde & Brunette, Pair	22.50
Miniature, Ski Country, Lion On The Drum	15.00
Miniature, Ski Country, Lipizzan	15.00
Miniature, Ski Country, Majestic Eagle	22.95
Miniature, Ski Country, Mallard Duck	15.00
Miniature, Ski Country, Mountain Eagle	14.95
Miniature, Ski Country, Mountain Goat	11.00
Miniature, Ski Country, Mountain Lion	11.00
Miniature, Ski Country, Mountain Ram	14.95
Miniature, Ski Country, Oregon Caveman	11.95
Miniature, Ski Country, Osprey Hawk	13.50
Miniature, Ski Country, P.T.Barnum	13.00
Miniature, Ski Country, Palomino Stallion	14.00
Miniature, Ski Country, Peace Dove	12.50
Miniature, Ski Country, Peacock	11.00
Miniature, Ski Country, Performing Elephant	15.95
Miniature, Ski Country, Performing Lion	11.95
Miniature, Ski Country, Performing Tiger	12.95
Miniature, Ski Country, Political, Donkey	15.00
Miniature, Ski Country, Political, Elephant	15.00
Miniature, Ski Country, Political, Pair	30.00
Miniature, Ski Country, Prairie Chicken	11.00
Miniature, Ski Country, Raccoon	11.95
Miniature, Ski Country, Ram	15.00
Miniature, Ski Country, Redheaded Duck	11.95
Miniature, Ski Country, Ringmaster	11.95
Miniature, Ski Country, Robin	14.00
Miniature, Ski Country, Sage Grouse	11.95
Miniature, Ski Country, Skier, Blue	10.00
Miniature, Ski Country, Skier, Red	10.00
Miniature, Ski Country, Snowy Owl	22.95
Miniature, Ski Country, Spectacled Owl	12.00
Miniature, Ski Country, Submarine	13.00
Miniature, Ski Country, Swan	12.00
Miniature, Ski Country, Tiger On Ball	15.00
Miniature, Ski Country, Tom Thumb	11.95
Miniature, Ski Country, Trout	11.00
Miniature, Ski Country, Turkey	13.00
Miniature, Ski Country, Wild Turkey	13.00
Miniature, Ski Country, Woodduck	12.95
Miniature, Ski Country, Woodpecker	14.95
Miniature, St.Galmier, Duck	15.00
Miniature, Stag Horns, German	35.00
Miniature, Stardust	6.00

Miniature, Stefanof, Dice, Black Glass	60.00
Miniature, Stein, Blue	8.95
Miniature, Stein, Brown	8.95
Miniature, Stomach Bitters, Kantorowicz, Milk Glass, 5 1/2 In. ....*Illus*	70.00

Miniature, Stomach Bitters, Kantorowicz, Milk Glass, 5 1/2 In.

Miniature, Sun Drug Co., Los Angeles, Whiskey, Embossed, Yellow Amber	60.00
Miniature, Sweet Mash Corn, Jacksonville, Fla., Jug, 3 In.	35.00
Miniature, Tango, German	50.00
Miniature, Taylor & Williams Whiskey	7.00
Miniature, Tenuta, Jim Beam Liquor	1.00
Miniature, Tenuta, Spey Royal Scotch Liquor	1.00
Miniature, Thos. Moore Possom Hollow Whiskey, Pinch, Aluminum Top	6.00
Miniature, Tullamore Dew	1.25
Miniature, Uncle Sam, German	35.00
Miniature, Valenti, Bari Monument	10.00
Miniature, Valenti, Bear	10.00
Miniature, Valenti, Bologna Monument	10.00
Miniature, Valenti, Ferenze Monument	10.00
Miniature, Valenti, Fish	10.00
Miniature, Valenti, Genova Monument	10.00
Miniature, Valenti, Giraffe	10.00
Miniature, Valenti, Leaning Tower Of Pisa	10.00
Miniature, Valenti, Modena Monument	10.00
Miniature, Valenti, Monkey	10.00
Miniature, Valenti, Napoli Monument	10.00
Miniature, Valenti, Penguin	7.50
Miniature, Valenti, Roma Monument	10.00
Miniature, Valenti, Sea Horse	10.00
Miniature, Valenti, White Stallion	10.00
Miniature, Viking Ship	9.50
Miniature, W.L.Perkins Whiskey, St.Paul, Minn., Decanter	8.00
Miniature, Waitress Serving Drinks, German, Multicolor	45.00
Miniature, Wedgwood Flask, Prosit, Serving Maid, Green	65.00
Miniature, Wee Bottle Club, Earth, Brown Land & Blue Sea	8.95
Miniature, Wild Turkey, Battle Of Concord, Wooden Box, Set Of 6	35.00
Miniature, WLS, Bowling Set, Porcelain, Black Ball & 2 White 10 Pins	14.95
Miniature, Woman In Sun Bonnet	8.00
Miniature, Wright & Taylor Whiskey, Stain, Amber	18.00
Miniature, Wyeth & Bro.'s Medicine, Philada., BIMAL, Rectangular	3.00
Miniature, Your Health Fat Man, German, Brown	35.00
Miniature, Your Health Fat Man, German, Multicolor	35.00
Miniature, Your Health, Drinkometer, German, Multicolor	35.00
Miniature, 1st National Bank Of The United States, Blue, Gold Print	11.00
Mobana, Monkey Holding Banana, Bahamas, Miniature	3.95
Mobana, Monkey, Miniature	6.00

Mogen David, American Revolution, Boxed, Miniature, Set Of 6 .... 24.95
Mogen David, Battle Of Concord, Miniature, Set Of 6 .... 25.00
Mogen David, Battle Of Concord, Set Of 6 .... 125.00
Mogen David, Cannon & 5 Man Gun Crew, Miniature, Set Of 6 .... 24.95
Munchen, Bisque Jug, Flower, Handle, 4 In. 2.95
Munchen, Glazed Jug, Flower, Handle, 3 In. 2.95
Munchen, Royal Coffee, Ceramic Coffeepot, Miniature 2.95
Murano, Cat, Miniature 12.00
Murano, Dog, Miniature 12.00
Murano, Swan, Miniature 12.00
National Antique Bottle Jar Exposition, 1976, Amethyst 22.00
National Antique Bottle Jar Exposition, 1976, Aqua 6.00
National Antique Bottle Jar Exposition, 1976, Honey Amber 8.00
National Antique Bottle Jar Exposition, 1976, Light Green 8.00
National Antique Bottle Jar Exposition, 1976, Light Olive Green 10.00
National Antique Bottle Jar Exposition, 1976, Olive Green 12.00
National Antique Bottle Jar Exposition, 1976, Sapphire Blue 12.00
National Antique Bottle Jar Exposition, 1976, Striated, Light Amethyst 16.00
National Antique Bottle Jar Exposition, 1976, Yellow Amber 10.00
National Porcelain, Banker 14.00
New England Glass Co., End-Of-Day, Applied Lip Ring, Olive Green, 10 1/2 In 75.00

Nursing bottles were first used in the second half of the 19th century.
They are easily identified by the unique shape and the measuring units that
are often marked on the sides.

Nursing, Blown, Tooled Mouth, Pontil, Ovoid, 8 3/4 In. .... * 160.00
Nursing, Blown, Tooled Mouth, Pontil, Ovoid, 8 3/4 In. .... * 210.00
Nursing, Blown, Tooled Mouth, Pontil, 8 In. .... * 190.00
Nursing, Bostonian, Flask Type, 6 1/2 In. 10.00
Nursing, Embossed Bear, 5 3/4 In. 3.75
Nursing, Embossed Bulldog, 5 3/4 In. 3.75
Nursing, Embossed Cats, 7 In. .... *Illus* 5.00
Nursing, Embossed Elephant, 5 3/4 In. 3.75
Nursing, Embossed, Happy Baby, 7 In. .... *Illus* 5.00
Nursing, Favorite, Patent 1890, McKinnon & Co., N.Y., Tin Cap, 6 In. .... * 60.00
Nursing, Hazel Atlas, Picture Of Bear, 8 Ozs. 4.00
Nursing, Hygienic Feeder, Semiturtle, 2 Ended, 4 Ozs. 20.00
Nursing, Hygienic Feeder, Semiturtle, 2 Ended, 8 Ozs. 16.00
Nursing, K.H. & 50 Pointed Star, Violin Shape, BIMAL, 2 1/4 In. 5.00
Nursing, Little Papoose, 8 In. .... *Illus* 125.00
Nursing, N.Wood & Sons, Turtle Type, 8 Ozs. 12.00
Nursing, Oriental Nurser, 6 In. 9.00
Nursing, The National Feeding Bottle, 5 1/2 In. .... *Illus* 40.00
Nursing, 16 Vertical Ribs, Aqua, 9 In. 35.00
OBR, Balloon 5.95
OBR, Baltimore Colts 19.95
OBR, Big Red Football Player 10.95
OBR, Black Angus Bull, Fifth 24.95
OBR, Boston Bruins 19.95
OBR, Caboose 14.95
OBR, Covered Wagon 12.95
OBR, Denver Broncos 19.90
OBR, Fifth Avenue Bus 15.00
OBR, General, Locomotive 22.50
OBR, Georgia Tech, White Hats 19.00
OBR, Georgia Tech, Yellow Hats 19.95
OBR, Hockey Player 10.95
OBR, Locomotive, General Sherman 14.95
OBR, Miami Dolphins 19.95
OBR, Minnesota North Stars 19.95
OBR, New York Rangers ....
OBR, Oakland Raiders 19.95
OBR, Philadelphia Eagles 19.95
OBR, Philadelphia Flyers 19.95
OBR, Pierce Arrow 17.00

(See Page 183)

(See Page 183)

(See Page 183)

Top left to right: Nursing, Embossed Cats, 7 In.; Nursing, Embossed, Happy Baby, 7 In.; Nursing, Little Papoose, 8 In.; Oil, Jay B. Rhodes, 7 In.
Left: Nursing, The National Feeding Bottle, 5 1/2 In.

(See Page 183)

OBR, Prairie Wagon	6.95
OBR, River Queen, Gold	22.00
OBR, River Queen, Gray	6.00
OBR, San Francisco 49ers	19.95
OBR, Santa Maria	9.95
OBR, St.Louis Blues	19.95
OBR, St.Louis Cardinals	19.95
OBR, Titanic	75.00
OBR, Train Caboose	17.95
OBR, University Of Georgia	19.95
OBR, University Of Missouri	19.95
OBR, W.C.Fields Bust, No.1	19.95
OBR, W.C.Fields, Bank Dick, No.2	17.95
OBR, Wisconsin Badgers	19.95
Oil, Huile D'Olive, Extra, La Diana, Blob Seal, Black Amethyst, 5 In.	5.00
Oil, Jay B.Rhodes, 7 In. .... *Illus*	*10.00*
Oil, Larkin Co., Machine, Buffalo, Embossed, Corker, 4 3/8 In.	2.50

Oil, Mayor Walnut, Kansas City, Mo., Amber, 5 In.	3.00
Oil, Olive, Free Blown, Sheared Top, OP, 10 1/2 In.	5.00
Oil, Omega, Aqua, 3 1/4 In.	.99
Oil, Omega, Green Trade Mark, Leaf, Amethyst, 4 1/2 In.	1.95
Oil, Omega, Green Trade Mark, BIMAL, Haze, Aqua, 4 5/8 In.	1.20
Oil, Shell-Penn Motor, Quart, 14 1/2 In.	8.00
Oil, Shell, Embossed, Quart, 14 1/2 In.	22.00
Old Crow, Bugatti Royale Decanter	100.00
Old Crow, Chess Set, Rug, 32 Piece	370.00
Old Crow, Chessman, Castle, Dark	12.00
Old Crow, Chessman, King, Dark	15.00
Old Crow, Chessman, King, Light	12.00
Old Crow, Chessman, Knight, Dark	12.00 To 15.00
Old Crow, Chessman, Knight, Light	15.00
Old Crow, Chessman, Pawn, Light	26.50
Old Crow, Chessman, Queen, Dark	15.00
Old Crow, Chessman, Queen, Light	15.00
Old Crow, Crow	15.00
Old Crow, Figurine Red Vest, 1974	9.95 To 19.00
Old Fitzgerald, Blarney, 1970	9.00
Old Fitzgerald, Cabin Still, Deer	5.00
Old Fitzgerald, Cabin Still, Dog	8.00

Old Fitzgerald, Fleur-De-Lis Decanter, 1962

Old Fitzgerald, Rip Van Winkle, 1971

Old Fitzgerald, Tournament Decanter, 1963

Old Fitzgerald, Cabin Still, Ducks Unlimited, 1972	11.00
Old Fitzgerald, Cabin Still, Fish	3.50
Old Fitzgerald, Candlestick, Gold	10.00
Old Fitzgerald, Counties Of Ireland, 1973	10.00
Old Fitzgerald, Fleur-De-Lis Decanter, 1962 *Illus*	20.00
Old Fitzgerald, Hillbilly, Cabin Still, Quart	22.00
Old Fitzgerald, Irish Luck, 1972	12.00
Old Fitzgerald, Irish Patriots, 1971	12.00
Old Fitzgerald, Memphis	16.00
Old Fitzgerald, Nebraska, 1971	20.00
Old Fitzgerald, Rip Van Winkle	10.00
Old Fitzgerald, Rip Van Winkle, 1971 *Illus*	16.00
Old Fitzgerald, Sons Of Erin, 1969	12.00
Old Fitzgerald, Tournament Decanter, 1963 *Illus*	20.00
Old Fitzgerald, Wearin' O' The Green, "God, " 1968	17.00
Old Mr.Boston, Andretti Racing Car, Red, 1972	12.00

Old Mr.Boston, Andretti Racing Car, Yellow, 1973	12.00
Old Mr.Boston, Bookend, Bust, Pair	4.95
Old Mr.Boston, Clown Face	13.00
Old Mr.Boston, Dan Patch	12.00
Old Mr.Boston, Decanter, No.47, 1975, Royal Halburton China	25.00
Old Mr.Boston, F.O.E. Eagle	12.00
Old Mr.Boston, Gold Football, Nebraska	9.95
Old Mr.Boston, Green Bay Packer's Football Player No.15	15.00
Old Mr.Boston, Miss Madison Boat	14.95
Old Mr.Boston, Molly Pitcher	18.00
Old Mr.Boston, Mooseheart	11.00
Old Mr.Boston, Nathan Hale	18.00
Old Mr.Boston, Nebraska, No.1, Gold	14.00
Old Mr.Boston, Paul Bunyan	8.00
Old Mr.Boston, Shriner Camel	20.00
Old Mr.Boston, Venus De Milo	15.00
Old Mr.Tilford, Musical, Gold	15.00
Old Taylor, Castle	3.95
Opium, Chinese, Dug In California, 2 In.	6.00
Pacesetter, Olsonite Eagle No.8	17.50
Pacesetter, Vulkovich Sugarripe	18.00
Pancho Villa, Gunfighter	24.95
Pancho Villa, Padre With Indian Boy	29.95
Paul Lux, Ohio State Football Player, No.7	9.95
Paul Lux, Ship	14.00
PBR, Antique Peddler, Blue Label	29.95
PBR, Antique Trader	15.00
PBR, Bronco Buster	25.00
PBR, Camel	40.00
PBR, Camel, Miniature	8.95
PBR, Elmer The Gold Camel, Miniature	17.95
PBR, Hardy	29.95
PBR, Laurel	29.95
PBR, Laurel & Hardy, Miniature, Pair	24.95
PBR, Wrangler	80.00
PBR, Wrangler, Miniature	29.95
Pepper Sauce, Acorn Design, Fluted Shoulders, Smooth Base, 7 1/2 In.	* 25.00
Pepper Sauce, Aqua, 11 1/2 In.	20.00
Pepper Sauce, Beehive Style, 6 Rings, 5 1/2 In.	16.50
Pepper Sauce, Cathedral Arches, Double Collar, Square, Green, 10 1/8 In.	* 45.00
Pepper Sauce, Cathedral Arches, Horizontal Ribs, Aqua, 7 3/4 In.	* 30.00
Pepper Sauce, Cathedral Arches, Label, Square, Aqua, 9 1/8 In.	* 30.00
Pepper Sauce, Cathedral Arches, Pontil, Square, Aqua, 8 3/4 In.	* 40.00
Pepper Sauce, Cathedral Arches, Pontil, Stain, Hexagonal, Aqua, 8 3/4 In.	* 30.00
Pepper Sauce, Cathedral, Aqua, Open Pontil, 8 3/4 In.	Color XXXX.XX
Pepper Sauce, Cathedral, Blue, 9 In.	Illus 55.00
Pepper Sauce, Cathedral, Bubbles, Aqua, Gallon	50.00
Pepper Sauce, Cathedral, Hexagonal, Glop Top, Aqua, 8 1/2 In.	15.00
Pepper Sauce, Cathedral, 6 Sided, OP, Aqua, 8 1/2 In.	Illus 40.00
Pepper Sauce, Double Collared Mouth, Hexagonal, Smooth Base, Aqua, 9 1/4 In.	* 15.00
Pepper Sauce, E.R.D. & Co., Patent Feb. '74, Hexagonal, Green, 8 In.	* 20.00
Pepper Sauce, E.R.D.& Co., Patent Feb. '77, Ribbed, Blue Green, 8 In.	* 22.50
Pepper Sauce, E.R.D.& Co., Patent Feb.17, 1874, E.R.Durkee, N.Y., Aqua, 8 In.	20.00
Pepper Sauce, E.R.Durkee & Co., N.Y., Patent Feb.17, 1874, Green, 7 7/8 In.	* 45.00
Pepper Sauce, E.R.Durkee & Co., Ribbed, Tapered, Blue Green, 7 3/4 In.	* 20.00
Pepper Sauce, For Family Use, 8 Flutes, Pontil, Aqua, 9 1/4 In.	* 40.00
Pepper Sauce, Fluted, 10 Sided, Round Bottom, Graphite Pontil, 12 In.	16.00
Pepper Sauce, H.E.Swan, Embossed, Flint, Horn Of Plenty, 8 1/2 In.	68.00
Pepper Sauce, H.W.Swan & Co., Tooled Collared Mouth, Square, 8 3/4 In.	* 10.00
Pepper Sauce, Horizontal Ridges, Square, Stain, Aqua, 8 1/4 In.	* 10.00
Pepper Sauce, J.W.Hunnelwell & Co., Boston, 6 Concave Sides, Aqua, 6 1/2 In.	15.00
Pepper Sauce, Ribbed, Hexagonal, Smooth Base, Blue Green, 8 In., Chip	* 15.00
Pepper Sauce, S.& P., Patent, Ridges, Hexagonal, Green, 8 In.	* 50.00
Pepper Sauce, Spiral Ribs, Tapering To Neck, Blue Green, 8 1/2 In., Stain	* 35.00
Pepper Sauce, Vertical Ribs, Tapered Lip With Skirt, 9 3/4 In.	29.50

Pepper Sauce, W.K.L.& Co., Cathedral Arches, Pontil, Square, Aqua, 10 In. .... * 85.00
Pepper Sauce, Wells, Miller & Provost, Fluted, Pontil, Stain, Aqua, 8 1/4 In. .... * 40.00
Pepper Sauce, 4 Sections, Flower Petal-Shaped Bottom, Haze, Aqua, 8 1/2 In. 12.00
Pepper Sauce, 7 Fluted Panels, Collared Mouth, Pontil, Aqua, 7 15/16 In. .... * 35.00
Pepper Sauce, 8 Flutes, 3 Neck Rings, Stain, Chip, Yellow Olive, 8 3/4 In. .... * 300.00
Pepper Sauce, 8 Columns, Paneled Shoulder, Collared Lip, Aqua, 8 1/2 In. 20.00
Pepsi Cola, Clemson University, 12 Ozs. 3.00
Pepsi Cola, Furman, 12 Ozs. 3.00
Pepsi Cola, North Carolina Bicentennial, 16 Ozs. 4.00
Pepsi Cola, North Carolina, 10 Ozs. 5.00
Pepsi Cola, South Carolina Bicentennial, 12 Ozs. 3.00
Pepsi Cola, 75th Anniversary, 12 Ozs. 3.00
Perfume & Snuff, Mordan, Sterling Caps, Ruby Glass, 4 3/4 In. 92.00
   Perfume, see also Cologne, Scent
Perfume.Moser, Crystal Stopper, Gold Floral, Crystal To Emerald, 5 In. 65.00
Perfume, Atomizer, Art Deco, C.1930, Sterling Silver, 3 3/4 In., Pair 42.50
Perfume, Atomizer, DeVilbiss, Rose Cased, 7 1/2 In. 45.00
Perfume, Aurene, No.1455, Melon Ribbed, Gun Metal Iridescent, 5 3/4 In. 250.00
Perfume, Aurene, Signed & Numbered, 4 1/2 In. 375.00
Perfume, Aurene, Signed, No.1414, Blue, 7 3/4 In. 325.00
Perfume, Aurene, Stopper With Dabber, Gunmetal Iridescent, 5 3/4 In. 250.00
Perfume, Babbs Creations Perfume Lady, 5 In. 6.00
Perfume, Baccarat, Amberina Swirl, 6 1/4 In. 38.00

Pepper Sauce, Cathedral, Blue, 9 In.
(See Page 186)

Pepper Sauce, Cathedral, 6 Sided, OP,
Aqua, 8 1/2 In.
(See Page 186)

Perfume, Baccarat, Red Flame Stopper, Chamberstick Shape, 8 In. 18.00
Perfume, Baccarat, Swirl, Blue Decoration, 6 In., Pair 35.00
Perfume, Bird Stopper, Crystal, 6 1/4 In. 10.00
Perfume, Bird, 3 1/2 In. .... *Illus* 30.00
Perfume, Blown Stopper, Ruby Stained, 8 1/2 In., Pair 35.00
Perfume, Blown, Teardrop Stopper, Gold Enamel, Pink Flowers, Blue, 7 1/2 In. 50.00
Perfume, Blue Enamel On Sterling Top, 2 1/4 In. 26.00
Perfume, Bohemian Glass, Lithyalin, 7 1/2 In. 285.00
Perfume, Bohemian Glass, Vintage, Ruby Flashed, 4 1/4 In. 70.00
Perfume, Brass, Mother-Of-Pearl Covered, Screw-On Cap, 2 1/2 In. 12.00
Perfume, Brass, Oriental, Lady With Fan & Flowers, 1 1/2 In. 15.00
Perfume, Bristol, Flowers, 4 1/2 In. 40.00

Perfume, Bird 3 1/2 In.
(See Page 187)

Perfume, Figural, Boy,
Cornucopia, 7 1/2 In.
(See Page 189)

Perfume, Geometric, 3 In.
(See Page 189)

Perfume, Cameo, English, Carved Bamboo Trees, Red, 6 In.	1450.00
Perfume, Cameo, English, Lay Down, Sterling Cap, Water Lily, Blue, 8 1/2 In.	625.00
Perfume, Camphor Glass, Embossed Sitting Nude, Semioval Shape, 4 3/4 In.	30.00
Perfume, Clown's Head, Art Deco, Amber, 3 1/4 In.	38.00
Perfume, Colgate & Co., New York, Perfumers, Rectangular, Amethyst, 2 In.	2.00
Perfume, Colored Geometric Coralene On Transparent Blue, 6 In.	140.00
Perfume, Coralene Seaweed & On Stopper, Blue, 6 In.	135.00
Perfume, Coralene, Colored Coralene Geometrics, Transparent Blue, 6 In.	140.00
Perfume, Crackle, Clear Blown Stopper, Cranberry, 8 In., Pair	78.50
Perfume, Cranberry Glass, Clear Stopper, 3 1/2 In.	48.00
Perfume, Crystal, Swirl Stopper, Swirled, Footed, 10 1/2 In., Pair	35.00
Perfume, Cut Glass, Amber & Clear Stopper, Amber Blocks, 5 In.	58.00
Perfume, Cut Glass, Blue Enamel Sterling Top, Crosshatching, Square, 3 In.	24.00
Perfume, Cut Glass, Brass Top, 6 1/2 In., Pair	63.00
Perfume, Cut Glass, Clear Stopper, Cut Base, Emerald Green, 9 In.	95.00
Perfume, Cut Glass, Cranberry, 4 3/4 In.	64.00
Perfume, Cut Glass, Cut Stopper, 4 1/2 In., Pair	40.00
Perfume, Cut Glass, Enamel Sterling Top, Intaglio Floral, 4 1/2 In.	40.00
Perfume, Cut Glass, Enameled Silver Top, 6 In., Pair	175.00
Perfume, Cut Glass, English, Canes, 7 In.	42.50
Perfume, Cut Glass, Faceted Stopper, Enamel Bird & Floral, Sapphire, 4 In.	65.00
Perfume, Cut Glass, Faceted Stopper, Harvard, 6 In.	25.00
Perfume, Cut Glass, Faceted Stopper, 4 In.	39.50
Perfume, Cut Glass, French Enameled Sterling Stopper, Intaglio, 4 In.	39.00
Perfume, Cut Glass, Gilt Chain & Gilt & Jeweled Top, 3 In.	375.00
Perfume, Cut Glass, Hawkes, Sterling Stopper, 9 1/2 In.	95.00
Perfume, Cut Glass, Hobstar & Prism, 4 1/4 In.	45.00
Perfume, Cut Glass, Lay-Down, Heart Shape, Sterling Screw Top, 3 1/2 In.	28.00
Perfume, Cut Glass, Pagoda Cut In Stopper, 8 1/2 In.	42.00
Perfume, Cut Glass, Quarter Moon Shape, Silver Cap, Graduated, 5 In.	32.00
Perfume, Cut Glass, Silver Gilt Top, 10 1/2 In.	185.00
Perfume, Cut Glass, Square, 5 In.	25.00
Perfume, Cut Glass, Sterling Fittings, China Inlay, Notched Prism, 3 1/4 In.	30.00

Perfume, Cut Glass, Sterling Silver Top, 4 In.	60.00
Perfume, Cut Glass, Sterling Stopper, 3 Rows Panels, 3 1/4 In.	45.00
Perfume, Cut Glass, 24-Point Star Base, 5 3/4 In.	22.00
Perfume, Czechoslovakia, C.1920, Lalique Style, Honey Color, 2 3/4 In.	15.00
Perfume, Daum Nancy, Enamel Cornflowers, Green, Pink, & Frosted, 3 In.	275.00
Perfume, DeVilbiss, Atomizer, Gold & Black Enamel, 7 In., Pair	23.00
Perfume, E.W.Hoyt & Co., Lowell, Mass., 5 1/2 In.	3.00
Perfume, Elysian, Detroit, Emerald Green, 6 1/2 In.	Color XXXX.XX
Perfume, Enclosed In Metal Flowers With Blue Stones, 1 1/4 In.	14.00
Perfume, English Cameo, C.1880, Silver Cap, White Butterfly, Red, 6 1/2 In.	300.00
Perfume, English, Cameo, Lay Down, Blue, Water Lily, Sterling Top, 8 1/2 In.	625.00
Perfume, English Cameo, Silver Top, Carved Floral, Lay Down, Red, 6 1/2 In.	550.00
Perfume, Figural, Boy, Cornucopia, 7 1/2 In.	Illus 50.00
Perfume, Figural, Clown, Head Stopper, Porcelain, 3 In.	15.00
Perfume, Fish Stopper, Relief Vases & Bubbles, 6 1/2 In.	15.00
Perfume, Foote & Jenks Perfumers, Label, Boxed, 3 In.	6.00
Perfume, French Crystal, Copper Wheel Ground, Mythical Figures, 6 In.	60.00
Perfume, French, Gold, Enamel, C.1840, White Cased, Ruby Glass, 6 3/4 In.	75.00
Perfume, French, Opaline, Enameling, Blue, 5 In.	50.00
Perfume, Galle, Cameo, Red To Yellow Flowers, 7 1/2 In.	750.00
Perfume, Galle, Purple To Blue Violets, Frosted Gold, 8 1/4 In.	325.00
Perfume, Geometric, 3 In.	Illus 2.00
Perfume, Gold Leaves & Floral, Multicolor Beading, Ruby Glass, 3 In.	65.00
Perfume, Gold, Lavender, Blue, & Yellow Floral, Cobalt, 5 3/8 In.	48.00
Perfume, Golliwog, Afro Face & Hair, 2 1/2 In.	35.00
Perfume, Golliwog, 5 1/2 In.	Illus 60.00
Perfume, Googlie Face Boy, Germany, C.1920, Milk Glass, 1 3/4 In.	7.50
Perfume, Googlie Face Girl, Germany, C.1920, Milk Glass, 1 3/4 In.	7.50
Perfume, Graja, Art Glass, Blown, Enamel Pink Rose, Brass Stand, 4 1/2 In.	79.00
Perfume, Grossmith's, Thibet, Figural, Oriental Lady, 11 1/2 In.	110.00
Perfume, Ground Top, Metal Screw Cap, Dark Green, 2 In.	12.00
Perfume, Haviland, Limoges, 1895, Garlands & Floral, Gold, Yellow, 5 1/2 In.	45.00
Perfume, Hobnail, Blue, 7 In.	8.00
Perfume, Indian Feather, Twisted, Reliefs, Pigeon's Blood Red, 3 1/2 In.	55.00
Perfume, Jennings Co., Label, 3 In.	2.50
Perfume, Lalique, Beaded, Disc Shape, 5 1/2 In.	65.00
Perfume, Lalique, Black Art Deco Enamel Hobs, Bulbous, Frosted, 5 1/4 In.	115.00
Perfume, Lalique, Black Stain, Beaded Curlicue, Pedestal, 5 1/2 In.	75.00
Perfume, Lalique, Charcoal Branches, Dome Stopper, C.1930, 4 1/2 In.	70.00
Perfume, Lalique, Disc Shape, Cobalt, 3 In.	75.00
Perfume, Lalique, Kissing Doves, Frosted, 4 In.	70.00
Perfume, Le Chic Chic De Vigny, France, Figural, 3 1/2 In.	25.00
Perfume, Lenox, DeVilbiss, Barrel Shape, Turkey Handle, 1 1/2 In.	65.00
Perfume, Long Stopper, Square, Crystal, 5 1/4 In.	15.00
Perfume, Lutz, White Stripes, Green, Blue, & Red, 5 In.	42.50
Perfume, Mary Gregory, Boy, Smoky Amber, 6 In.	84.00
Perfume, Mary Gregory, 3 1/2 In.	25.00
Perfume, Milk Glass, Lightner's Heliotrope, 7 1/2 In.	Illus 55.00
Perfume, Moser Type, Cut Glass, Faceted Stopper, Gold Outlined, Rubena, 6 In.	58.00
Perfume, Moser Type, Gold-Trimmed Clear Ball Stopper, Cobalt, 6 1/4 In.	75.00
Perfume, Moser, Brass Screw Cap, Melon Ribbed, Gold Scrolls, Cranberry, 4 In.	75.00
Perfume, Moser, Crystal Stopper, Enamel Floral, Emerald Green, 5 In.	65.00
Perfume, Moser, Crystal Stopper, Gold Floral, Cranberry, 5 1/2 In.	95.00
Perfume, Moser, Gold Enamel & Blue & White Flowers, Cranberry, 3 In.	65.00
Perfume, Nippon, Blue Maple Leaf Mark, Cobalt & Gold Floral & Scroll, 5 In.	70.00
Perfume, Nippon, Gold Floral Stopper, Gold Panels, Beading, 4 In., Pair	60.00
Perfume, Nippon, Green Maple Leaf Mark, Violets, Gold Lattice, Green, 5 In.	48.00
Perfume, Nippon, Jeweled Stopper, Cottage In Trees Scene, 4 1/2 In.	68.00
Perfume, Nippon, Metro Mark, Roses, Gold Beading, Green, 4 In.	22.00
Perfume, Oriental Lotion, Blue, 7 In.	Illus 27.00
Perfume, Ormolu Screw Cap, Enamel Floral, 4 Lobed, C.1900, Pink, 3 In.	30.00
Perfume, Pairpoint, Bubble Ball Base, 4 Formed Crystal Leaves, 7 1/4 In.	75.00
Perfume, Pairpoint, Controlled Bubbles, 6 1/2 In.	65.00
Perfume, Pairpoint, Delft, Windmill & Sailboats, Blues, 7 1/2 In.	220.00
Perfume, Paperweight, Frosted Stopper, 3 1/2 In.	5.00

Perfume, Porcelain, Hinged Sterling Top, Shield Shape, Floral, White, 3 In.	45.00
Perfume, Porcelain, Sterling Screw-On Top, Floral, White, 2 7/8 In.	65.00
Perfume, Pressed Glass, Daisy Stopper, 8 In.	20.00
Perfume, Purse, Art Glass, Gold, Florals, Chain, Green, 2 In.	40.00
Perfume, Purse, Marked Coralene, Paneled, Domed Top, Emerald Green, 4 In.	15.00
Perfume, Reed's, Embossed Stork & Floral, Crooked Nock, BIMAL, 3 1/4 In.	6.00
Perfume, Rubena, Decorated, 3 Footed, 7 In.	85.00
Perfume, Sabino, Blown-Out, 4 Nude Girls, 6 1/4 In.	42.00
Perfume, Sabino, Frieze Of 5 Women, Blown Out, 6 1/4 In.	42.00
Perfume, Sabino, Pineapple Stopper, Panels Of Nudes, Opalescent, 6 In., Pair	130.00
Perfume, Selick, New York, 2 1/2 In.	3.00
Perfume, Silver Deposit, Art Nouveau, 7 X 4 1/2 In.	17.00
Perfume, Silver Deposit, Bulbous, 4 1/2 X 4 In., Pair	52.00
Perfume, Silver Deposit, Footed, 6 In.	20.00
Perfume, Silver Deposit, Green, 3 1/2 In.	26.00
Perfume, Silver Deposit, Spear Stopper, Scrolls & Geometrics, 8 1/2 In.	42.00
Perfume, Silver Overlay, Bulbous, 4 In.	45.00
Perfume, Silver Overlay, Cranberry, 4 3/4 In.	85.00
Perfume, Soldier With Bagpipes, Robj, France, White Hat Is Stopper, 5 1/2 In	52.00
Perfume, Spray, Ruby & Gold Bands, Tassel, 4 In.	35.00
Perfume, Stars, 4 1/2 In. ....Illus	8.50
Perfume, Sterling Overlay, Minneapolis In Design, 3 1/2 In.	25.00
Perfume, Sterling Silver Deposit, Alvin, 3 1/4 In.	32.50
Perfume, Sterling Silver, Repousse, Dominick & Haff, 5 1/2 In., Pair	375.00
Perfume, Steuben, Aurene, Intaglio Cut, Blue, 10 In.	225.00

(See Page 189)

(See Page 189)

(See Page 189)

Top left to right: Perfume, Golliwog, 5 1/2 In.; Perfume, Milk Glass, Lightner's Heliotrope, 7 1/2 In.; Perfume, Oriental Lotion, Blue, 7 In.
Left: Perfume, Stars, 4 1/2 In.

Perfume, Steuben, Melon, Alabaster Flame Stopper, Green Jade, 5 In. 150.00
Perfume, Steuben, Verre De Soie, Blue Flame Stopper, 4 1/2 In. 125.00
Perfume, Steuben, Verre De Soie, Celeste Blue Short Stopper, 10 In. 125.00
Perfume, Steuben, Verre De Soie, Long Stopper, Green Jade, 10 In. 135.00
Perfume, Steuben, Verre De Soie, Melon Ribbed, Initial K, 6 1/2 In. 80.00
Perfume, Stevens & Williams, Cameo, Cobalt To Cranberry, 7 In. .... * 425.00
Perfume, Stiegel Type, Checkered, 4 3/4 In. 100.00
Perfume, Swirled Feather Stopper, Pigeon's Blood Red, 3 3/4 In. 38.00
Perfume, Taylor's Dummy, Schiaparelli, Figural, Woman, 4 1/2 In. 30.00
Perfume, The Woman I Love, Edward VIII Abdication, Gilt Cap, Dram 7.50
Perfume, Tiffany Glass, Pedestal, Gold Iridescent, 8 In. 575.00
Perfume, Tiffany Silver, Engraved HAHB, 3 1/2 In. 50.00
Perfume, Tiffany, C.1892, Zigzags, Silver Mounts, Amber & Blue, 7 1/4 In. 1100.00
Perfume, Tiffany, Pedestaled, Gold Iridescent, 8 In. 575.00
Perfume, Train Engine, 3 3/4 In. 8.50
Perfume, Val St.Lambert, Etched, Gold Trim, 5 3/4 In. 20.00
Perfume, Val St.Lambert, Pointed Panel & Sawtooth, Topaz, 4 In. 27.00
Perfume, Webb, Butterfly, Citron & White, 8 1/2 In. 550.00
Perfume, Webb, Cameo, Silver Cap, Blue With White, 4 In. 425.00
Perfume, Webb, Cameo, Silver Cap, Citron With White, 4 In. 375.00
Perfume, Webb, Hinged Sterling Lid, Carved Blue & White Daisies, 3 In. 350.00
Perfume, Webb, Lay Down, Cameo, White Floral Carving, Raisin Color, 5 In. 450.00
Perfume, Webb, Lay Down, Silver Screw Cap, Gold Floral, Brown Shading, 7 In. 150.00
Perfume, Webb, Silver Repousse Top, White To Cranberry Lilies, 4 1/4 In. 395.00
Perfume, White, Pink, & Yellow Daisies, Cobalt, 3 1/2 In., Pair 100.00
Perfume, 5 In. .... Illus   60.00

Perfume, 5 In.

Pickle, Cathedral Arches,
Deep Aqua, 11 1/2 In.

Pickle, Atmore's, Cathedral Arches, Square, Lime Green, 11 1/4 In. .... * 225.00
Pickle, Cathedral Arches, Applied Rolled Lip, Deep Aqua, 11 X 3 1/2 In. 60.00
Pickle, Cathedral Arches, Applied Rolled Lip, IP, Aqua, 11 1/2 X 3 1/2 In. 135.00
Pickle, Cathedral Arches, Applied Rolled Mouth, Hexagonal, Aqua, 13 In. 30.00
Pickle, Cathedral Arches, Aqua, 7 1/2 In. 10.00
Pickle, Cathedral Arches, Aqua, 15 In. 30.00
Pickle, Cathedral Arches, Chip, Square, Aqua, 1/2 Gallon .... * 50.00
Pickle, Cathedral Arches, Collared Mouth, Crack, Square, Green, 8 In. .... * 150.00
Pickle, Cathedral Arches, Collared Mouth, Flake, Square, Emerald, Quart .... * 675.00
Pickle, Cathedral Arches, Collared Mouth, Pontil, Square, Aqua, 13 3/4 In. .... * 350.00
Pickle, Cathedral Arches, Collared Mouth, Pontil, Square, Green, Gallon .... * 825.00
Pickle, Cathedral Arches, Collared Mouth, Pontil, Square, Green, 11 3/8 In. .... * 160.00
Pickle, Cathedral Arches, Collared Mouth, Square, Aqua, 1/2 Gallon .... * 95.00
Pickle, Cathedral Arches, Cracks, Square, Green, 7 3/8 In. .... * 70.00
Pickle, Cathedral Arches, Deep Aqua, 11 1/2 In. .... Illus   250.00

Pickle, **Cathedral Arches,** Deep Aqua, 12 In. ....*Color* XXXX.XX
Pickle, **Cathedral Arches,** EHVB, N.Y., Diamonds, Hexagonal, Aqua, 11 3/4 In. .... * 150.00
Pickle, **Cathedral Arches,** Label, Square, Green, 13 1/2 In. .... * 70.00
Pickle, **Cathedral Arches,** Pontil, Flake, Square, Olive Amber, 3/4 Quart *1550.00
Pickle, **Cathedral Arches,** Pontil, Octagonal, Aqua, 9 1/8 In. .... * 260.00
Pickle, **Cathedral Arches,** Pontil, Square, Olive Amber, 1/2 Gallon *3500.00
Pickle, **Cathedral Arches,** Pontil, Stain, Square, Aqua, 8 1/2 In. .... * 15.00
Pickle, **Cathedral Arches,** Repro, Square, Green, 14 In. .... * 55.00
Pickle, **Cathedral Arches,** Rolled Collared Mouth, Square, Aqua, 11 3/4 In. 85.00
Pickle, **Cathedral Arches,** Rolled Collared Mouth, Square, Green, Pint .... * 260.00
Pickle, **Cathedral Arches,** Rolled Collared Mouth, Square, Green, 11 1/2 In. .... * 160.00
Pickle, **Cathedral Arches,** Smooth Base, Square, Aqua, 7 1/4 In. .... * 45.00
Pickle, **Cathedral Arches,** Smooth Base, Square, Green, 13 3/4 In. .... * 340.00
Pickle, **Cathedral Arches,** Smooth Base, Square, Stain, Aqua, 7 1/4 In. .... * 10.00
Pickle, **Cathedral Arches,** Smooth Base, Square, Yellow Green, Quart .... * 600.00
Pickle, **Cathedral Arches,** Square, Aqua, 7 1/8 In. .... * 80.00
Pickle, **Cathedral Arches,** Square, Aqua, 9 In. 12.00
Pickle, **Cathedral Arches,** Square, Aqua, 11 3/4 In. .... * 70.00
Pickle, **Cathedral Arches,** Square, Bright Green, 14 In. ....*Illus* 250.00
Pickle, **Cathedral Arches,** Square, Green, 3/4 Quart .... * 250.00
Pickle, **Cathedral Arches,** Square, Green, 11 3/4 In. .... * 150.00

Pickle, Cathedral Arches, Square,
Bright Green, 14 In.

Pickle, H.J.Heinz Co., Gherkins
(See Page 193)

Pickle, **Cathedral Arches,** Tooled Mouth, Pontil, Crack, Square, Amber, Gallon *1500.00
Pickle, **Cathedral Arches,** 4 Sided, Applied Lip, Aqua, 11 3/4 In. 75.00
Pickle, **Collared Mouth,** Pontil, Oval, Bright Green, 11 3/4 In. .... * 40.00
Pickle, **Cranberry Glass,** Thumbprint, Silver Lid, 4 1/2 In. 85.00
Pickle, **Diamond On 3 Panels,** Fluted Neck, Bulbous, Aqua, 5 3/4 In. .... * 30.00
Pickle, **E.B.Hyssong,** Cassville, Salt Glaze, Blue Cucumbers, 9 1/2 In. 55.00
Pickle, **EHVB NY,** Cathedral Arches, Pontil, Hexagonal, 7 7/8 In. .... * 70.00
Pickle, **Fancy Designs,** Bulged Neck, Smooth Base, Square, Aqua, 5 3/4 In. .... * 20.00
Pickle, **Fluted Neck,** Collared Mouth, Smooth Base, Aqua, 8 3/4 In. .... * 15.00
Pickle, **Flutes,** Stoddard Type, Pontil, Square, Aqua, 5 3/4 In. .... * 40.00
Pickle, **Goofus Glass,** Amber, 15 1/2 In. 45.00
Pickle, **Goofus Glass,** Amethyst Floral & Scroll, Ground Mouth, 9 3/4 In. 12.00
Pickle, **Goofus Glass,** Cabbage Rose, Painted, Ground Mouth, 12 1/2 In. 20.00
Pickle, **Goofus Glass,** Cabbage Rose, Squatty, 5 3/4 In. 12.00

Pickle, Goofus Glass, Embossed Floral, Ground Mouth, Aqua, 9 3/4 In. 5.00
Pickle, Goofus Glass, Floral, Leaf, & Butterfly, Ground Mouth, 12 1/4 In. 15.00
Pickle, Goofus Glass, Sunflower & Pebble, Bulbous, Ground Mouth, 10 1/2 In. 15.00
Pickle, Goofus Glass, Urn Shape, Grape & Leaf, Ground Mouth, 12 1/4 In. 17.50
Pickle, H.J.Heinz Co., Gherkins ....*Illus* 25.00
Pickle, Heinz, Canister, C.1890 ....*Color* XXXX.XX
Pickle, Henry Glazier, Pottery, Cobalt Cucumbers, 8 In. 60.00
Pickle, J.S.Birden & Co., Hartford, Rolled Lip, Bubbles, Aqua, 8 In. 15.00
Pickle, Loetz, Threading, Silver Lid, Rim, & Handle, Blue & Purple, 7 In. 165.00
Pickle, Ovals With Leaves, 4 Sided, Applied Lip, Aqua, 10 3/4 In. 65.00
Pickle, Plain Panels, Embossed Wreath Of Leaves, Whittled, Aqua, 11 In. 65.00
Pickle, Pressed Glass, Statue Of Liberty, 12 In. 125.00
Pickle, Relish, Paneled Corners, Tapered Shoulders, Dug, Aqua, 6 1/2 In. 14.50
Pickle, Rolled Collared Mouth, Pontil, Hexagonal, Aqua, 13 In. .... * 100.00
Pickle, Roth Manufacturing Co., Milwaukee, Cabin Shape, Aqua, 9 1/2 In. 37.00
Pickle, S J G, Cathedral, Collared Mouth, Pontil, Square, Aqua, 9 1/8 In. .... * 180.00
Pickle, Shaker Pickles, E.D.Pettengil Co., Me., 1871, Cathedral, 7 3/4 In. 95.00
Pickle, Skilton Foote & Co., Bunker Hill, BIMAL, Dug, Aqua, 5 1/4 In. 5.00
Pickle, Skilton Foote & Co., Bunker Hill, BIMAL, Haze, Aqua, 2 1/2 In. 2.00
Pickle, Skilton Foote & Co.'s Bunker Hill, Lighthouse, Amber, 11 1/2 In. .... * 360.00
Pickle, Skilton Foote & Co.'s Bunker Hill, Lighthouse, Yellow Green, Pint .... * 300.00
Pickle, Square Plain Panels, Fingerlike Panels On Shoulder, Aqua, 11 1/2 In 95.00
Pickle, Stoddard Type, Fluted, Collared Mouth, Square, Olive Amber, 3/4 Quart .... * 130.00
Pickle, V.C.& Co., Neck Ring, Applied Collar, Haze, Deep Purple, 9 In. 4.50
Pickle, W.M.& P.N.Y., Stoddard Type, Fluted, Stain, Pontil, Square, Aqua, 8 In. .... * 65.00
Pickle, Wells, Miller & Provost, Fluted, Pontil, Bruise, Aqua, 10 7/8 In. .... * 55.00

Poison, Amber, 9 In.

Poison, Blue, 4 1/2 In.

Poison, Cobalt Blue, Hobs, 3 1/2 In.
(See Page 194)

*Poison bottles were usually made with raised designs so the user could feel
the danger in the dark. The most interesting poison bottles were made from
the 1870s to the 1930s.*

Poison, Amber, 3 1/2 In. 6.00
Poison, Amber, 8 1/4 In. 34.00
Poison, Amber, 9 In. ....*Illus* 45.00
Poison, Blue, 4 1/2 In. ....*Illus* 32.00
Poison, Caustic Potash, Barker's Drug Store, Gloucester, Cobalt, 3 3/4 In. 6.50
Poison, Caustic Potash, Barker's Drug Store, Gloucester, Cobalt, 4 1/2 In. 6.50
Poison, Caustic Potash, Barker's Drug Store, Gloucester, Cobalt, 5 3/4 In. 6.50

Poison, Caustic Potash, Barker's Drug Store, Gloucester, Cobalt, 6 1/4 In.	6.50
Poison, Caustic Potash, Paper Label, Flared Lip, Cobalt, 5 1/2 In.	6.00
Poison, Cobalt Blue, Hobs, 3 1/2 In. *Illus*	25.00
Poison, Cobalt Blue, 3 1/2 In. *Illus*	15.00
Poison, Cobalt, 11 In.	17.50
Poison, Cobalt, 13 In.	22.50
Poison, Cobalt, 16 Ozs.	60.00 To 110.00
Poison, Coffin, Amber, 5 In.	85.00
Poison, Coffin, Cobalt, 3 1/2 In.	20.00
Poison, Coffin, Coffin-Shaped Tablet Inside, Cobalt, 7 1/2 In.	100.00
Poison, Embossed On Both Front Panels, 3 Sided, Amber, Pint	15.00
Poison, Horizontal Rows Of Hobnail, Flask, Sheared Mouth, Amethyst, Pint	* 150.00
Poison, Jno Wyeth, Hobnail, Rectangular, 2 7/8 In.	5.50
Poison, Kilner Makers, Embossed, Fluted Sides, Cobalt, 10 In.	19.00
Poison, Norwich, I.G.A. *Illus*	65.00
Poison, Owl Drug Co., Haze, 5 In.	26.00
Poison, Owl Drug Co., 2 Wings, Label, Cobalt, 6 1/2 In.	50.00
Poison, Owl Drug, Tricorner, Cobalt, 3 In.	22.00
Poison, Owl, Tricornered, Cobalt, 2 3/4 In.	24.00
Poison, PP In Circle, BIMAL, Cobalt, 3 In.	9.00
Poison, PP In Circle, BIMAL, Cobalt, 2 1/2 In.	10.00
Poison, Sharpe & Dohme, Diamonds, Sheared Ring Collar, Amber, 3 In.	5.25
Poison, Sharpe & Dohme, Philadelphia, Tricornered, Cobalt, 3 1/4 In.	7.00
Poison, Skeleton In Shroud, Embossed, Ceramic, 6 In.	95.00
Poison, Skull & Crossbones Poison Tinct. Iodine, Light Amber, 3 1/4 In.	4.25
Poison, Skull Shape, Ground Mouth, Smooth Base, 4 In.	* 100.00
Poison, Triangular, Round Back, Amber, 3 1/2 In.	4.50
Poison, Trilet's, Cobalt, 3 1/2 In.	6.00
Poison, Vapo Cresoline Co., Patent June 18, '95, Eng. '94, Aqua, 4 In.	1.25
Poison, Wyeth, Embossed Vertically, Barrel, ABM, Cobalt, 2 In.	5.00
Poison, 1/2 Post, Olive Amber, 4 1/2 In.	200.00
Porcelain, Arita, Japanese, C.1850, Wisteria, Blue & White, 8 3/4 In.	30.00
Porcelain, Chinese Export, Floral & Leaf Neck, White, 12 1/2 In., Pair	225.00
Porcelain, Water, Japanese, C.1850, Dutch Ship & Man, 10 1/4 In.	350.00
Pottery, Carpenter & Son, Glazed, Olive Brown, Pint	11.00
Pottery, Finger Handle, 11 In.	5.00
Pottery, Grumman's Bottling, Norwalk, Conn., Porcelain Stopper, Gray, 24 Ozs.	8.00
Pottery, Herman Carl, Troy, N.Y., 9 In. *Illus*	45.00
Pottery, Jug, Embossed Eagle On Front, Handled, Brown, 9 In.	100.00
Pottery, Jug, Lund Blade Bros., Great Bend, Kansas, Brown & White, Quart	20.00
Pottery, Jug, The Triaca Co., Baltimore, Md., Brown & White, 1/2 Gallon	16.00
Pottery, Jug, 6 In. *Illus*	5.00
Pottery, Korean, C.1790, Red Pine Branches Underglaze, White, 8 1/4 In.	275.00
Pottery, Long Neck, Light Gray Glaze, 9 In.	15.00
Pottery, Old Homestead Ginger Beer, 7 In. *Illus*	15.00
Pottery, Old Jug-Lager Krug Bier, 11 In. *Illus*	17.50
Pottery, Platte Valley Straight Corn Whiskey, 5 1/2 In. *Illus*	7.50
Pottery, Thomas, Huntingdon, Pa., Dark Brown Glaze, 10 In.	7.50
Pottery, Toth Kiss Samuel, Kesurlt, 1880, Green, 12 In. *Color* XXXX.XX	
Pottery, 1877, Green, 9 In. *Color* XXXX.XX	
Rebel Yell, Soldier On Horse	12.95
Rum, Squat, Black Amethyst, Quart	12.50
Sandeman, Capeman, Wedgwood	7.00 To 10.00
Sandeman, Zorro, Royal Doulton	40.00 To 47.50
Sandwich Glass, see Cologne, Toilet Water, Cologne, Sandwich Glass	
Sandwich, Smooth Base, Amethyst, 3 3/8 In.	* 20.00
Sarsaparilla, A.H.Bull, Extract Of, Hartford, Conn., Aqua, 6 7/8 In.	* 30.00
Sarsaparilla, Allen's, Stain, Flakes, Aqua, 8 1/2 In.	* 10.00
Sarsaparilla, Ayer's Compound Extract Of, Lowell, Mass., Aqua, 8 1/2 In.	3.50
Sarsaparilla, Ayer's, OP, Aqua, 7 3/4 In.	50.00
Sarsaparilla, Ayer's, Aqua, 8 1/4 In.	4.00
Sarsaparilla, Ayer's, Compound Extract, Lowell, Mass., U.S.A., Aqua, Pint	* 5.00
Sarsaparilla, Bristol's, Extract Of, Buffalo, Aqua, 5 3/4 In.	* 60.00
Sarsaparilla, Bristol's Genuine, Blob, 10 1/2 In.	16.00
Sarsaparilla, Bristol's, Genuine, New York, Smooth Base, Aqua, Quart	* 22.50

Top left to right: Poison, Cobalt Blue, 3 1/2 In.; Poison, Norwich, I.G.A.; Pottery, Herman Carl, Troy, N.Y., 9 In.; Pottery, Jug, 6 In. *(See Page 194)*

Sarsaparilla, Brown's, Aqua, 9 In. 8.50
Sarsaparilla, Brown's, Dug, 9 1/4 In. 8.00
Sarsaparilla, Brown's, For The Kidneys, Liver, & Blood, Aqua, Pint .... * 10.00
Sarsaparilla, Bush's Smilex, Tubular Pontil, Aqua, Quart .... * 270.00
Sarsaparilla, Dalton's, & Nerve Tonic, Belfast, Maine, 9 In. .... * 7.50
Sarsaparilla, Dana's, Belfast, Maine, Rectangular, Aqua, Pint .... * 12.50
Sarsaparilla, Daniel Bernhard, 1 & 11 Sarsfield St., Boston, Blob Lip, Quart 8.50

Pottery, Old Homestead Ginger Beer, 7 In.
(See Page 194)

Pottery, Old Jug-Lager Krug Bier, 11 In.
(See Page 194)

Pottery, Platte Valley Straight Corn Whiskey, 5 1/2 In.
(See Page 194)

Sarsaparilla, Dr.A.S.Hopkins, Compound Extract, Rectangular, Aqua, Pint .... * 15.00
Sarsaparilla, Dr.Cronk's, Blob Top, Crockery, Glazed, 9 1/2 In. 40.00
Sarsaparilla, Dr.Denison's, Collared Mouth, Pontil, Oval, Green, 7 1/2 In. .... * 270.00
Sarsaparilla, Dr.F.A.Wood's, Dug, Stain, Aqua, 9 In. 8.75
Sarsaparilla, Dr.Greene's, Rectangular, Smooth Base, Aqua, Pint .... * 15.00
Sarsaparilla, Dr.Guysotts Yellow Dock &, Bruise, Aqua, 9 1/2 In. .... * 10.00
Sarsaparilla, Dr.Guysott's Yellow Dock &, Collared Mouth, Aqua, Quart .... * 375.00
Sarsaparilla, Dr.Townsend's, Albany, N.Y., IP, Green, Quart .... * 100.00
Sarsaparilla, Dr.Townsend's, Albany, N.Y., Square, Emerald Green, 3/4 Quart .... * 140.00
Sarsaparilla, Dr.Townsend's, Burst Bubble, Square, Olive Amber, 3/4 Quart .... * 85.00
Sarsaparilla, Dr.Townsend's, Collared Mouth, Pontil, Olive Amber, Quart .... * 120.00
Sarsaparilla, Dr.Townsend's, New York, Square, Emerald Green, 3/4 Quart .... * 60.00
Sarsaparilla, Dr.Townsend's, Pontil, Square, Apricot Color, Quart *1600.00
Sarsaparilla, Dr.Woodworth, Birmingham, Rectangular, Aqua, Quart .... * 110.00
Sarsaparilla, Dr.Wynkoop's Katharismic Honduras, Crack, Sapphire, Quart *1650.00
Sarsaparilla, Hood's, BIMAL, 8 1/2 In. 4.00
Sarsaparilla, Hood's, Apothecaries, Aqua, 9 In. 3.00
Sarsaparilla, Hood's, Dug, Aqua, 9 In. 4.00
Sarsaparilla, Hood's, Lowell, Ma., Rectangular, Aqua, 9 In. .... * 3.95
Sarsaparilla, I.D.Bull's, Extract Of, Hartford, Conn., Aqua, 6 7/8 In. .... * 240.00
Sarsaparilla, J.V.Babcock, Gold Medal, Smooth Base, Amber, Pint .... * 30.00
Sarsaparilla, John Bull Extract Of, Louisville, Ky., Aqua, 8 3/4 In. 100.00
Sarsaparilla, Kelley & Co., Portland, Me., Pontil, Oval, Aqua, 7 3/4 In. .... * 270.00
Sarsaparilla, Log Cabin, 9 In. 70.00
Sarsaparilla, Old Doctor Townsend, Aqua, 10 1/2 In. .... Illus   65.00

Sarsaparilla, Old Doctor Townsend, Aqua, 10 1/2 In.

Sarsaparilla, Old Dr.J.Townsend's, New York, Yellow Green, 3/4 Quart .... * 50.00
Sarsaparilla, Rush's & Iron, A.H.Flanders, Pontil, Rectangular, Aqua, Pint .... * 20.00
Sarsaparilla, Sand's, N.Y., Pontil, Rectangular, Aqua, 6 1/8 In. .... * 40.00
    Scent, see also Cologne, Toilet Water
Scent, Applied Rigaree, Sheared Mouth, Pontil, Chip, 3 1/8 In. .... * 30.00
Scent, Beveled, Ground Mouth, Screw Top, Rectangular, Cobalt, 4 1/4 In. .... * 25.00
Scent, Corset, Beveled Edges, Rectangular, Blue & White Opaque, 2 1/2 In. .... * 60.00
Scent, Cut Design, Blue Overlay, Sheared Mouth, Oval, 3 In. .... * 60.00
Scent, Cut Designs, Rectangular, Smooth Base, Yellow Amber, 2 3/8 In. .... * 10.00
Scent, Cut Paneled Sides, Hexagonal, Ground Base, Emerald Green, 3 3/4 In. .... * 30.00
Scent, Daum Nancy, 1900, Spider Webs, Fuchsias, Frosted Amber, 5 3/4 In. 140.00
Scent, Double Corseted, Hexagonal, Smooth Base, Smoky Amethystine, 2 1/2 In. ...... * 90.00
Scent, E.C., Etched, Cut Designs, Flattened & Elongated, 5 1/8 In. .... * 35.00
Scent, Flattened, Sheared Mouth, White & Gold Trim, 3 1/2 In. .... * 100.00
Scent, Gold Adventurine & White Stripes, Red Lines, Blue Black, 1 5/8 In. 10.00
Scent, Grapes & Leaves, Flattened & Elongated, Smooth Base, 2 1/4 In. .... * 5.00
Scent, L.M.C., 1819, White Stripes Swirled To Left, Beaded, Flat Oval, 2 In. .... * 250.00
Scent, Moser, Gold Warrior Band, Amethyst, 4 In. 88.00
Scent, Peace-Plenty In Depressed Sunburst, Pontil, Sapphire, 3 1/4 In. .... * 450.00
Scent, Red & White Swirled Stripes, Flattened, 3 3/8 In. .... * 65.00

Scent, Ribs Swirled To Right, Bulged Neck, Flattened & Elongated, 3 1/4 In. .... * 17.50
Scent, Ribs Swirled To Right, Chips, Flattened & Elongated, Cobalt, 3 1/4 In .... * 50.00
Scent, Ribs Swirled To Right, Flattened & Elongated, Amethyst, 3 1/4 In. .... * 60.00
Scent, Ribs Swirled To Right, Flattened & Elongated, Yellow Olive, 2 5/8 In .... * 80.00
Scent, Ribs Swirled To Right, Flattened, Elongated, Emerald Green, 3 1/4 In. .... * 55.00
Scent, Ribs Swirled To Right, Flattened, Elongated, Smoky Amethyst, 3 1/8 In .... * 40.00
Scent, Ribs Swirled To Right, Pontil, Flattened, Elongated, Cobalt, 2 7/8 In. .... * 55.00
Scent, Ribs Swirled To Right, Pontil, Flattened & Elongated, 3 In. .... * 15.00
Scent, Ribs Swirled To Right, Pontil, Flattened & Elongated, 3 1/4 In. .... * 10.00
Scent, Ribs Swirled To Right, Pontil, Flattened, Cobalt, 2 In. .... * 80.00
Scent, Ribs Swirled To Right, Pontil, Flattened & Elongated, Cobalt, 3 In. .... * 50.00
Scent, Sandwich Type, Beveled Corners, Flakes, Rectangular, Cobalt, 2 1/2 In. .... * 45.00
Scent, Sandwich Type, Beveled Corners, Oval, Cobalt, 3 1/8 In. .... * 35.00
Scent, Sandwich Type, Beveled Corners, Rectangular, Amethyst, 2 1/4 In. .... * 30.00
Scent, Sandwich Type, Beveled Corners, Rectangular, Amethyst, 3 3/16 In. .... * 40.00
Scent, Sandwich Type, Beveled Corners, Rectangular, Light Green, 3 1/4 In. .... * 35.00
Scent, Sandwich Type, Beveled Corners, Rectangular, Milk Glass, 2 1/2 In. .... * 25.00
Scent, Sandwich Type, Beveled Corners, Rectangular, Milk Glass, 2 1/4 In. .... * 20.00
Scent, Sandwich Type, Beveled Corners, Rectangular, Opalescent, 2 1/2 In. .... * 30.00
Scent, Sandwich Type, Beveled Edges, Rectangular, Blue Opaque, 2 1/2 In. .... * 100.00
Scent, Sandwich Type, Corseted, Ground Mouth, Screw Cap, 2 1/2 In. .... * 30.00
Scent, Sandwich Type, Ground Mouth, Screw Cap, Square, Vaseline, 2 1/2 In. .... * 55.00
Scent, Sandwich Type, Label, Beveled Corners, Rectangular, Cobalt, 2 3/8 In. .... * 90.00
Scent, Sandwich Type, Wide Beveled Corners, Rectangular, Amethyst, 2 1/4 In. .... * 35.00
Scent, Sandwich Type, Wide Beveled Corners, Rectangular, Green, 2 1/4 In. .... * 30.00
Scent, Sandwich Type, Wide Beveled Corners, Rectangular, Teal Blue, 2 1/2 In .... * 45.00
Scent, Sandwich Type, Wide Beveled Corners, Rectangular, 3 1/4 In. .... * 15.00
Scent, Sandwich Type, 3 Horizontal Ribs, Oval, Opalescent, 2 In. .... * 40.00
Scent, Sandwich Type, 3 Ribs, Sheared Mouth, Oval, Amethyst, 2 In. .... * 45.00
Scent, Sandwich, Flint, Pewter Cap, McK 241-28, Blue 40.00
Scent, Sandwich, Flint, Pewter Cap, McK 241-28, Opalescent 32.00
Scent, Sandwich, 2 Mold, Geometrics, Ribbed, Emerald Green, 3 5/16 In. 95.00
Scent, Seahorse, Applied Rigaree, Pontil, Blue Stripes, 3 In. .... * 80.00
Scent, Seahorse, Applied Rigaree, Pontil, Cornflower Blue, 2 1/2 In. .... * 150.00
Scent, Seahorse, Applied Rigaree, Pontil, Flake, 2 7/8 In. .... * 30.00
Scent, Seahorse, Applied Rigaree, Pontil, White Stripes, 3 In. .... * 50.00
Scent, Seahorse, Applied Rigaree, Pontil, 2 5/8 In. .... * 22.50
Scent, Seahorse, Applied Rigaree, Ribs Swirled To Right, 3 1/8 In. .... * 35.00
Scent, Seahorse, Applied Rigaree, Sheared Base, White Stripes, 2 3/4 In. 10.00
Scent, Seahorse, Applied Rigaree, Sheared Mouth, Pontil, 2 1/2 In. .... * 45.00
Scent, Seahorse, Applied Rigaree, Sheared Mouth, Pontil, 2 3/4 In. .... * 10.00
Scent, Seahorse, Applied Rigaree, Sheared Mouth, Pontil, 3 1/4 In. .... * 40.00
Scent, Seahorse, Applied Rigaree, Sheared Mouth, 2 7/8 In. .... * 30.00
Scent, Seahorse, Applied Rigaree, White Stripes, 2 1/8 In. .... * 95.00
Scent, Seahorse, Applied Rigaree, White Stripes, 2 3/4 In. .... * 130.00
Scent, Seahorse, Applied Rigaree, White Swirl, 2 5/8 In. .... * 30.00
Scent, Sheared Mouth, Pontil, Flattened, Blue & White Stripes, 3 1/2 In. .... * 20.00
Scent, Staffordshire, Pear Shape, Gilt Metal Stopper, C.1770, 3 5/8 In. 250.00
Scent, Staffordshire, Pear Shape, Scenes, Silver Mounts, C.1765, 3 1/2 In. 325.00
Scent, Staffordshire, Strawberries & Plums Form, Gilt Metal, C.1770, 3 In. 375.00
Scent, Stellar Designs, Corrugated Edges, Flattened Oval, Green, 2 In. .... * 70.00
Scent, Sunburst, Beaded Edges, Flattened & Elongated, 2 5/8 In. .... * 50.00
Scent, Sunburst, Beaded Edges, Shield Shape, Blue, 2 5/8 In. .... * 130.00
Scent, Sunburst, Beaded Edges, Shield Shape, Cobalt, 3 In. .... * 180.00
Scent, Sunburst, Corrugated Edges, Flattened, 1 3/4 In. .... * 15.00
Scent, Sunburst, Flattened, Smooth Base, Light Blue, 1 1/2 In. .... * 110.00
Scent, Sunburst, Sheared Mouth, Shield Shape, 2 3/4 In. .... * 35.00
Scent, Sunburst, Shield Shape, Emerald Green, 3 In. .... * 90.00
Scent, Sunflower, Shaded Amethyst, 2 5/8 In. .... * 275.00
Scent, Vertical Ribs, Chip, Crack, Flattened & Elongated, Citron, 3/4 In. .... * 5.00
Scent, Vertical Ribs, Flattened & Elongated, Citron, 2 7/8 In. .... * 100.00
Scent, Vertical Ribs, Flattened & Elongated, Cobalt, 2 3/4 In. .... * 55.00
Scent, Vertical Ribs, Flattened & Elongated, Cobalt, 3 1/16 In. .... * 65.00
Scent, Vertical Ribs, Flattened & Elongated, Emerald Green, 3 In. .... * 50.00
Scent, Vertical Ribs, Flattened & Elongated, Smooth Base, Teal Green, 3 In. .... * 40.00

Scent, Vertical Ribs, Pontil, Stain, Flattened & Elongated, Citron, 2 7/8 In. .... * 100.00
Scent, Violin, Ground Mouth, Screw Cap, Smooth Base, Amethyst, 2 1/2 In. .... * 30.00
Scent, Webb, Cameo, White Lilies Cut To Cranberry, Silver Top, 4 1/4 In. 395.00
Scent, White Stripes, Applied Rigaree On Edges, Flattened, 2 5/16 In. .... * 35.00
Scent, Wide Beveled Corners, Rectangular, Deep Sapphire Blue, 2 1/2 In. .... * 50.00
Schlitz, Gold Globe 9.95
Seal, Ambrosial B.M.& E.A.W.& Co., Applied Handle, Amber, 3/4 Quart .... * 125.00
Seal, Amsterdam, Pinched Sides, Square Gin Shape, Yellow Green, 1/2 Pint .... * 45.00
Seal, ASCR, Collared Mouth With Ring, Pontil, Olive Amber, 10 1/2 In. .... * 60.00
Seal, B.F.& Co., N.Y., Ribs Swirled To Left, Applied Handle, Amber, 10 In. .... * 475.00
Seal, Bust Of Man & 1716, Sheared Mouth, Pontil, Crack, Olive Green, 8 1/8 In *1200.00
Seal, Chestnut Grove Whiskey, Applied Handle, Spout, Amber, 3/4 Quart .... * 150.00
Seal, Chestnut Grove Whiskey, Handle, Pontil, Amber, 3/4 Quart .... * 70.00
Seal, Chestnut Grove Whiskey, Handle, Whitney Glass, Crack, Amber, Quart .... * 220.00
Seal, Cognac, W.& Co., Applied Handle, Amber, Pint .... * 200.00
Seal, Con Stantie Wyn, Pontil, Bruise, Crack, Olive Green, 9 In. .... * 60.00
Seal, D.McL, 1834, Applied Rigaree, Pontil, Olive Amber, 10 1/4 In. .... * 500.00
Seal, Danl Jones, 1760, Sheared Mouth With Ring, Broken, Olive Green, 9 In. .... * 850.00
Seal, Dl.Wells, 1764, Sheared Mouth, Pontil, Ovoid, Olive Amber, 11 In. .... * 450.00
Seal, Doneraile House, Patent, Bristol, 3 Mold, IP, Black Amethyst, Quart 260.00
Seal, Dr.Cutler, Pontil, Bruise, Dark Olive Amber, 6 1/2 In. .... * 270.00
Seal, Dr.Girard's Ginger Brandy, Handle, Pontil, Crack, Amber, 3/4 Quart .... * 325.00
Seal, G, Sloping Collared Mouth With Ring, Pontil, Olive Amber, 9 1/4 In. .... * 110.00
Seal, G.W.Huntington, Collared Mouth, IP, Chip, Blue Green, 11 3/4 In. .... * 200.00
Seal, Green Hill, Collared Mouth, Pontil, Bruise, Olive Amber, 7 3/4 In. .... * 70.00
Seal, H.Ellis, 1780, Sheared Mouth With Ring, Flake, Olive Amber, 9 3/4 In. .... * 425.00
Seal, I Alsop, 1763, Sheared Mouth With Ring, Pontil, Olive Amber, 10 3/4 In. *1000.00
Seal, I.F., 1882, H.Ricketts Glassworks, Bristol, Pontil, Olive Green, 9 In. .... * 95.00
Seal, I.W.1695, Sheared Mouth With Ring, Pontil, Chips, Olive Green, 6 In. *1950.00
Seal, J p C McG, 1820, Applied Rigaree, Bruise, Olive Amber, 10 1/4 In. .... * 250.00
Seal, J Head, 1825, Imperial Patent, Ricketts Glassworks, Olive Green, 11 In. .... * 200.00
Seal, J.T.Bickford & Bartlett, Boston, Applied Handle, Chip, Amber, 3/4 Quart .... * 75.00
Seal, J Whitwll Kendal, 1805, Collared Mouth, Pontil, Olive Amber, 11 In. .... * 200.00
Seal, James Oakes Bury, Dark Brown, 10 In. .... *Illus* 800.00

Seal, James Oakes Bury, Dark Brown, 10 In.

Seal, Jas.Hole, 1823, Collared Mouth, Pontil, Olive Amber, 11 1/2 In. .... * 325.00
Seal, Jas.Oakes Bury, 1795, Collared Mouth, Pontil, Olive Green, 10 1/4 In. .... * 310.00
Seal, Jno.Collins, 1736, Pontil, Chips, Rectangular, Olive Green, 10 3/8 In. .... * 650.00
Seal, Jno.Furse, 1823, H.Ricketts Glassworks, Bristol, Olive Amber, 10 1/2 In .... * 210.00
Seal, Jno.Jackson, 1751, Pontil, Chips, Rectangular, Olive Green, 9 In. .... * 525.00
Seal, John Andrew, 1822, Collared Mouth, Pontil, Olive Green, 10 3/4 In. .... * 200.00
Seal, John Pugh, 1794, Collared Mouth, Pontil, Chip, Olive Amber, 11 1/4 In. .... * 280.00
Seal, John Winn, Jr., Ricketts & Co., Bristol, Pontil, Olive Amber, 9 In. .... * 70.00

Seal, Jona Mason, Boston, Collared Mouth With Ring, Olive Amber, 12 1/4 In. .... * 400.00
Seal, Jos.Risdon, 1818, Collared Mouth, Pontil, Olive Amber, 9 3/8 In. .... * 220.00
Seal, Leeds, 1827, Sloping Collared Mouth, Pontil, Olive Amber, 10 3/4 In. .... * 180.00
Seal, LinColl, Sloping Collared Mouth, Pontil, Olive Green, 8 1/4 In. .... * 160.00
Seal, Madeira, 1810, Collared Mouth, Pontil, Olive Amber, 10 3/4 In. .... * 150.00
Seal, N D, 1790, Sheared Mouth With Ring, Pontil, Crack, Olive Amber, 11 In. .... * 260.00
Seal, P.Bastard, 1725, Amber, 8 1/2 In. ....Color XXXX.XX
Seal, P.Bastard, 1730, Amber, 8 1/2 In. ....Color XXXX.XX
Seal, Paul Richards, 1741, Sheared Mouth With Ring, Chips, Olive Amber, 9 In. .... * 950.00
Seal, Pure Cognac, Handle, Pontil, Bell Shape, 8 7/8 In. .... * 600.00
Seal, R Green, 1765, Pontil, Potstone, Crack, Dark Olive Amber, 9 In. .... * 250.00
Seal, RB, Square, & Compass, Pontil, Olive Amber, 7 1/8 In. .... * 400.00
Seal, R.Greene, 1728, Sheared Mouth, Pontil, Olive Green, 6 5/8 In. .... * 675.00
Seal, R.Lenox, Sloping Collared Mouth, Pontil, Olive Amber .... * 100.00
Seal, R Patterson, Sloping Collared Mouth, Pontil, Olive Amber, 10 7/8 In. .... * 55.00
Seal, R.P.A., 1779, Sheared Mouth With Ring, Pontil, Stain, Olive Amber, 11 In .... * 425.00
Seal, Rev.D J.B.Melhursh, Patent, Ricketts & Co., Bristol, Olive Amber, 11 In .... * 190.00
Seal, S B, Chestnut Flask, Blown, Pontil, Olive Amber, 6 1/2 In. .... * 425.00
Seal, S.H.Fay, Sloping Collared Mouth, Pontil, Dark Olive Amber, 15 1/2 In. .... * 220.00
Seal, S.M.& Co., N.Y., Handle, Pontil, Bell Shape, Yellow Amber, Pint .... * 175.00
Seal, S M & Co., N.Y., Handle, Pontil, Crack, Bell Shape, Amber, 3/4 Quart .... * 150.00
Seal, Sherry, Sloping Collared Mouth, Pontil, Olive Amber, 12 1/4 In. .... * 90.00
Seal, Sir W.Strickland Bart Boynton, Pontil, Olive Amber, 11 In. .... * 65.00
Seal, Sir Will Strickland Bart, 1809, Blown, OP, Black Amethyst, Quart 675.00
Seal, Sir Will.Strickland Bart. 1809, Collar, Pontil, Olive Amber, 9 3/8 In. .... * 280.00
Seal, Sir Wm.Strickland B R 1809, Sheared Mouth, Pontil, Olive Amber, 10 In. .... * 190.00
Seal, T.Biddell Evershott, 1720, Sheared Mouth, Pontil, Olive Amber, 6 1/4 In .... * 700.00
Seal, T.Durfey, 1772, Pontil, Dark Olive Amber, 8 1/4 In. .... * 600.00
Seal, Thos, H.Jacobs & Co., Pontil, Stain, Chip, Blue Green, 11 3/4 In. .... * 60.00
Seal, W.Lemchard, 1771, Bristol, OP, Black Amethyst, Pint 800.00
Seal, W.M., 1733, Collared Mouth With Ring, Pontil, Olive Green, 9 1/4 In. .... * 550.00
Seal, Whit Beare At The Bridge Foot & TDC, Broken, Olive Green, 8 3/4 In. *2000.00
Seal, William Pomeroy, Northhill, Ricketts & Co., Pontil, Olive Green, 10 In. .... * 65.00
Seal, Wime P.C.Brooks, 1820, Mouth Ring, Pontil, Olive Green, 9 5/8 In. .... * 140.00
  Seltzer, see also Mineral Water
Shoe Polish, A.A.Cooley, Hartford, Con., Sheared Mouth, Pontil, 4 5/8 In. .... * 110.00
Shoe Polish, Day & Martin Real Japan Blacking, Pottery, 7 1/4 In. 10.00
Shoe Polish, Free Blown, Sheared Mouth, 5 In. .... * 55.00
Shoe Polish, Geo.H.Reed & Sons, Boston, Blacking, Aqua, 4 3/4 In. 4.00
Shoe Polish, Gilt Edge Dressing, Patent 1890, Aqua, 4 In. 4.95
Shoe Polish, Ink For Boot & Shoemakers, Pontil, Olive Amber, 7 1/4 In. .... * 70.00
Shoe Polish, Reakirt's, Japan, Sponge Varnish, Pontil, Olive Amber, 4 3/4 In. .... * 500.00
Shoe Polish, Sheared Mouth, Pontil, Olive Amber, 4 In. .... * 55.00
Shoe Polish, Sheared Mouth, Pontil, Square, Olive Amber, 5 In. .... * 35.00
Shoe Polish, Sheared Mouth, Square, Olive Amber, 4 1/2 In. .... * 50.00
Shoe Polish, Sheared Mouth, Square, Olive Amber, 4 3/8 In. .... * 30.00
Shoe Polish, Sheared Mouth, Square, Olive Amber, 5 In. .... * 75.00
Shoe Polish, Square, Light Green, 4 3/4 In. .... * 35.00
Sicilian Gold, Quart 9.50
Sicilian Gold, Soldier 8.00
Silver Plate, Screw-On Cap, Floral & Beading, Wilcox Co., 5 1/4 In. 18.00
Ski Country, Baby Robin 29.00
Ski Country, Barnum 35.00
Ski Country, Bear 27.00
Ski Country, Bighorn Ram 60.00
Ski Country, Birth Of Freedom 29.95
Ski Country, Black Labrador Retriever 26.95
Ski Country, Black Swan 26.00
Ski Country, Black Swan, Miniature 14.00
Ski Country, Blue Teal Duck 27.50
Ski Country, Bonnie 25.00
Ski Country, Brown Bear 29.00
Ski Country, Burro 24.95
Ski Country, California Condor 21.95
Ski Country, Canada Goose 25.00

Ski Country, Caveman	21.00
Ski Country, Chief On Horse, No.1	35.00
Ski Country, Chief On Horse, No.2	35.00
Ski Country, Cigar Store Indian	26.50
Ski Country, Circus Elephant	35.00
Ski Country, Circus Horse	35.00
Ski Country, Circus Lion	27.00
Ski Country, Clown	30.00
Ski Country, Colorado Bear	24.95
Ski Country, Condor	14.95
Ski Country, Cow	22.95
Ski Country, Dove	21.00
Ski Country, Duck	24.95
Ski Country, Eagle, Gallon	225.00
Ski Country, Fox	32.00
Ski Country, Gila Woodpecker	60.00
Ski Country, Golden Eagle	35.00
Ski Country, Goose	24.95
Ski Country, Great Spirit	35.50
Ski Country, Grouse	29.00
Ski Country, Harpy Eagle	40.00
Ski Country, Holstein	20.00
Ski Country, Horned Owl	30.00
Ski Country, Horned Owl, Gallon	200.00
Ski Country, Indian Chief, No.1	35.50
Ski Country, Indian Chief, No.2	35.50
Ski Country, Indian Dancers	180.00
Ski Country, Indian Dancers, Set Of 6	155.00
Ski Country, Jenny Lind, Blue	30.00
Ski Country, Jenny Lind, Yellow	48.00
Ski Country, Kangaroo	21.00
Ski Country, Koala Bear	15.00
Ski Country, Ladies Of Leadville, Pair	35.00
Ski Country, Lippizan Horse, 4/5	34.95
Ski Country, Loala	20.00
Ski Country, Majestic Eagle	73.95
Ski Country, Majestic Eagle, Gallon	225.00
Ski Country, Mallard Duck	30.00
Ski Country, Mountain Goat	26.50
Ski Country, Mountain Goat, Gallon	155.00
Ski Country, Mountain Lion	23.00
Ski Country, Oregon Caveman	14.95
Ski Country, Ornate Hawk	37.00
Ski Country, Osprey	38.00
Ski Country, P.T.Barnum	30.00
Ski Country, Palomino Horse	35.00
Ski Country, Peace Dove	29.95
Ski Country, Peacock	30.00
Ski Country, Political, Donkey	24.00
Ski Country, Political, Elephant	24.00
Ski Country, Prairie Chicken	25.00
Ski Country, Raccoon	25.00
Ski Country, Ram	39.95
Ski Country, Red Headed Duck	28.00
Ski Country, Red Headed Duck, Miniature	12.50
Ski Country, Red Shouldered Hawk	24.95
Ski Country, Red Skier	14.00
Ski Country, Ring Master	29.95
Ski Country, Skier, Blue	9.95
Ski Country, Skier, Red	9.00 To 15.00
Ski Country, Snowy Owl	60.00
Ski Country, Spectacled Owl	24.95
Ski Country, Swan	25.00
Ski Country, Tom Thumb	31.95
Ski Country, Trout	26.50

Ski Country, Turkey	28.00
Ski Country, White Dove	27.95
Ski Country, White Stallion	35.00
Ski Country, Wood Duck	30.00
Ski Country, Wooden Indian	26.00
Ski Country, Woodpecker	50.00
Smelling Salts, Sterling Filigree Casing & Ball Top, 6 1/4 In.	40.00
Smelling Salts, Sterling Top, Zipper, Pierced, Inside Stopper, 4 In.	25.00

Snuff bottles have been made since the eighteenth century. Glass, metal, ceramic, ivory, and precious stones were all used to make plain or elaborate snuff holders.

Snuff, Amber, 4 1/2 In.	2.00
Snuff, Beveled Corners, Rectangular, Aqua, 7 1/2 In.	* 70.00
Snuff, Carved Ivory, Overcut & Undercut Oriental Figures, 2 1/2 In.	55.00
Snuff, Chinese Export, C.1850, Rose Floral, Ivory Spoon, White, 3 In.	75.00
Snuff, Cinnabar, Chinese, Carved Floral, Spoon, 3 102 In.	75.00
Snuff, Cloisonne, Chinese, Pandas In Bamboo, Pear Shape, 3 1/4 In.	145.00
Snuff, Cinnabar, Chinese, Carved Floral, Spoon, 3 1/2 In.	75.00
Snuff, Dip Mold, Sheared Mouth With Ring, IP, Stain, Olive Amber, 5 1/2 In.	45.00
Snuff, Doct. Marshall's, Aqua, 3 1/2 In.	4.00
Snuff, Doct Marshall's, Pontil, Rectangular, Aqua, 3 1/4 In.	* 30.00
Snuff, E.Roome, Troy, N.Y., Beveled Corners, Crack, Olive Amber, 4 1/2 In.	* 60.00
Snuff, Figural Horseshoe, Metal Cap, Threaded Ground Top, Amber, 4 7/8 In.	12.00
Snuff, First Quality MacCaboy, Pontil, Olive Amber, 4 1/2 In.	* 80.00
Snuff, Free Blown, Collared Mouth, Pontil, Crack, Olive Amber, 4 5/8 In.	* 20.00
Snuff, Free Blown, Collared Mouth, Pontil, Rectangular, Olive Amber, 5 1/4 In	* 70.00
Snuff, Free Blown, Collared Mouth, Pontil, Rectangular, Olive Amber, 6 3/8 In	* 90.00
Snuff, Free Blown, Collared Mouth, Pontil, Wear, Crack, Olive Green, 8 In.	* 40.00
Snuff, Free Blown, Flared Mouth, Pontil, Square, Olive Amber, 8 1/2 In.	* 110.00
Snuff, Free Blown, Octagonal, Olive Amber, 4 1/4 In.	* 80.00
Snuff, Free Blown, Olive Amber, 5 3/4 In.	* 140.00
Snuff, Free Blown, Olive Amber, 6 5/16 In.	* 130.00
Snuff, Free Blown, Pontil, Crack, Globular, Olive Amber, 5 3/4 In.	* 190.00
Snuff, Free Blown, Pontil, Olive Amber, 5 1/2 In.	* 100.00
Snuff, Free Blown, Rolled Collared Mouth, Pontil, Olive Amber, 4 1/2 In.	* 40.00
Snuff, Free Blown, Rolled Collared Mouth, Pontil, Olive Amber, 4 1/2 In.	* 70.00
Snuff, Free Blown, Rolled Mouth, Tubular Pontil, Wear, Olive Amber, 4 7/8 In.	* 110.00
Snuff, Free Blown, Sheared Mouth, Bruise, Wear, Olive Amber, 6 1/8 In.	* 140.00
Snuff, Free Blown, Sheared Mouth, Pontil, Chip, Olive Amber, 6 1/2 In.	* 55.00
Snuff, Free Blown, Sheared Mouth, Pontil, Crack, Olive Amber, 3 1/2 In.	* 40.00
Snuff, Free Blown, Sheared Mouth, Pontil, Crack, Rectangular, 4 7/8 In.	* 15.00
Snuff, Free Blown, Sheared Mouth, Pontil, Rectangular, Olive Amber, 4 3/4 In.	* 50.00
Snuff, Free Blown, Sheared Mouth, Pontil, Rectangular, Yellow Green, 5 1/2 In	* 50.00
Snuff, Free Blown, Sheared Mouth, Pontil, Square, Olive Amber, 6 1/8 In.	* 140.00
Snuff, Free Blown, Sheared Mouth, Pontil, Square, Olive Green, 4 1/8 In.	* 60.00
Snuff, Free Blown, Sheared Mouth, Pontil, Stain, Chip, Green, 5 5/8 In.	* 55.00
Snuff, Free Blown, Sheared Mouth With Ring, Wear, Olive Amber, 7 In.	* 80.00
Snuff, Free Blown, Square, Amber, 4 3/4 In.	* 75.00
Snuff, Free Blown, Square, Olive Amber, 4 3/4 In.	* 35.00
Snuff, Free Blown, Square, Olive Amber, 5 1/4 In.	* 85.00
Snuff, Free Blown, Square, Olive Amber, 5 3/8 In.	* 20.00
Snuff, Free Blown, Square, Seedy Olive Amber, 6 In.	* 95.00
Snuff, Helmes' Railroad Mills, 2-Piece Lid, Amber, Quart	14.00
Snuff, Ivory, Carved Dragons, Artist Signed, 3 X 2 In.	89.00
Snuff, Ivory, Carved Figures & Trees, 3 In.	200.00
Snuff, Ivory, Carved, Spoon In Lid, 3 In.	55.00
Snuff, Ivory, Double Gourd Shape, 3 In.	90.00
Snuff, Ivory, 3 1/2 X 2 In.	60.00
Snuff, J.J.Mapes, 461 Front St., N.Y., Flared Mouth, Pontil, Olive Amber, 4 In	* 275.00
Snuff, Jade, Jade Top, Green, 2 1/2 In.	125.00
Snuff, Jade, Rectangular, 2 1/2 In.	27.50
Snuff, Malachite, Banded, Carved Bonsai Tree, 2 1/4 In.	140.00
Snuff, Malachite, Bosanji Growing Into Side, 2 1/4 In.	125.00
Snuff, Peter & George Lorillard, N.Y., Stoneware, Paper Label, 13 1/2 In.	40.00

Snuff, S.S.Fitch, Flared Lip, OP, 2 3/4 In.	38.00
Snuff, Sheared Lip, Rectangular, Amber, 2 In.	2.00
Snuff, Stoddard, Bubbles, Push-Up Pontil, Dark Amber, 4 3/4 In.	60.00
Snuff, Stoddard, Wide Mouth, Amber, 5 1/2 In.	55.00
Snuff, Thomas Hoyt, 258 Front Street, N.Y., Stoneware, 11 In.	15.00
Snuff, True Cephalick, King's Patent, Flared Mouth, Pontil, Blue Green, 3 In.	* 120.00
Snuff, Whitwell's, OP, Aqua, 2 3/4 In.	35.00

Soda, Cedar Point Pleasure Resort Co., Hutchinson, 7 1/2 In.

Soda, Cedar Point Pleasure Resort, Hutchinson, Aqua, 5 1/2 In.

Soda bottles held soda pop or Coca-Cola or other carbonated drinks. Many soda bottles had a characteristic blob top. Hutchinson stoppers and coddball stoppers were also used.

Soda, see also Mineral Water, Pottery

Soda, A.F.Dietz, Altamont, N.Y., Hutchinson, Registered, Stain, Quart	15.00
Soda, A.Yoerger & Bro., Alton, Ill., Reproduction, Octagonal, Aqua, 1/2 Pint	* 5.00
Soda, B.L.Winn, Dyottville Glassworks, IP, Chips, Wear, Green, 1/2 Pint	* 35.00
Soda, Blount Springs Natural Sulfur Water, Stain, Sapphire Blue, 1/2 Pint	* 35.00
Soda, Blue Ridge, St.Louis, Mo., 24 Fluid Ozs., Quart	8.00
Soda, Bougton & Chase, Rochester, N.Y., IP, Octagonal, Sapphire Blue, Pint	* 950.00
Soda, Bridgeton Glass Works, N.J., Smooth Base, Bruise, 1/2 Pint	* 10.00
Soda, Brownstout, M.T.Crawford, Hartford, Ct., Wear, Chip, Blue Green, Pint	* 40.00
Soda, Burkhardt, Embossed, 7 Ozs.	.25
Soda, C.Burkhardt, Philada., Teal Green, 7 In.	30.00
Soda, Canada Dry Ginger Ale, Carnival Glass, Red Gold, 9 1/2 In.	10.00
Soda, Carpenter & Son Ginger Beer, Olive Brown Glaze, Pint	10.00
Soda, Cedar Point Pleasure Resort Co., Hutchinson, 7 1/2 In. .... *Illus*	70.00
Soda, Cedar Point Pleasure Resort, Hutchinson, Aqua, 5 1/2 In. .... *Illus*	30.00
Soda, Chadsey & Bro., N.Y., IP, Wear, Cobalt, 1/2 Pint	* 70.00
Soda, Cheer Up, 7 Ozs.	1.50
Soda, Clapp, Collared Mouth, Bruise, Amber, 1/0 Pint	* 50.00
Soda, Comstock Cove & Co., Boston, Collared Lip With Ring, Blue Green, 7 In.	7.00
Soda, Congress Water, Amber, Pair .... *Color* XXXX.XX
Soda, Dr.Pepper, 51st Anniversary, Temple, Texas, No Deposit, Quart	10.00
Soda, Dr.Pepper, 7 Ozs.	1.50
Soda, Dyottville Glass Works, A.W.Rapp, IP, Flakes, Wear, Cobalt, 1/2 Pint	* 120.00
Soda, Dyottville Glass Works, Mouth Ring, Yellow Green, 1/2 Pint	30.00
Soda, Dyottville Glass Works, Philada., IP, Green, 1/2 Pint	* 40.00
Soda, Dyottville Glass Works, Philada., IP, Green, 7 1/2 In.	30.00
Soda, Dyottville Glass Works, Stain, Light Green, 1/2 Pint	* 25.00
Soda, E.J.Garrison, Paterson, N.J., Hutchinson, Aqua, 5 In.	5.00
Soda, E.S.& H.Hart, Superior, Union Glass Works, Bruise, Cobalt, 1/2 Pint	* 95.00
Soda, Eagle & Arrows, Collared Mouth, IP, Flake, Yellow Green, 1/2 Pint	* 60.00
Soda, Eagle, Shield, & Flags, Collared Mouth, Wear, Yellow Green, 1/2 Pint	* 120.00
Soda, Embossed Soda Water, Rolled Lip, Squatty Teardrop, Aqua, 7 1/2 In.	40.00
Soda, F.Sherwood, Union Glass Works, Blob Mouth, Stain, Teal Blue, 1/2 Pint	* 170.00
Soda, Fanta, Filled & Capped, 3 1/2 In.	1.00

Soda, **G.Stockder,** Cannon City, Colorado, Embossed, Aqua, 9 In. 7.00
Soda, **G.V.Demott,** Smooth Base, Medium Green, 1/2 Pint .... * 40.00
Soda, **Gardner & Brown,** Round Bottom, Crack, Yellow Green, 9 In. .... * 60.00
Soda, **Geo.Simonds,** Hartford, Ct., IP, Bright Green, 1/2 Pint .... * 70.00
Soda, **Geyser Spring,** Saratoga Springs, Spouting, Stain, Aqua, Pint .... * 15.00
Soda, **Gilbert Bottling Works,** Minn., Hutchinson, Aqua, Quart 15.00
Soda, **Ginger Ale,** Cantrell & Cochrane's, Round Bottom, Green, 9 3/4 In. 5.50
Soda, **Grapette,** Painted Label, Cetro, Frosty, 6 Ozs. 2.00
Soda, **Grapette,** 1909, 1 Cent Deposit, 6 Ozs. 1.50
Soda, **Grapette,** 1946, 6 Ozs. 1.00
Soda, **Grapette,** 1947, 6 Ozs., 7 In. 1.00
Soda, **Grapette,** 6 Ozs., 30 In Wooden Case 40.00
Soda, **Gwinn Bottling Works,** Mich., Hutchinson, Quart 9.00
Soda, **H.C.Breimeyer,** St.Louis, Mo., Blop, Aqua, Quart 7.00
Soda, **H.Jones & Co.,** Ltd., IXL, Hobart & Sydney, Sun-Colored Amethyst, Pint .... * 40.00
Soda, **Haddock & Sons,** Round Bottom, Pontil, Olive Amber, 6 3/4 In. .... * 220.00
Soda, **Haggerty's Glassworks,** N.Y., Green, 1/2 Pint .... * 55.00
Soda, **Hamilton Glass Works,** N.Y., IP, Burst Bubble, Green, 1/2 Pint .... * 45.00
Soda, **Hava Drink,** 12 Ozs. 1.50
Soda, **Henry Gardner,** Trade Mark, West Bromwich, Yellow Green, 1/2 Pint .... * 25.00
Soda, **Hep,** 1941, Painted Label, Green, 7 Ozs. 2.00
Soda, **Hippo,** Nov.2, 1926, 13 Ozs. 5.00
Soda, **Hiram Wheaton & Sons,** Mass., 1926, Crown Top, Green, 8 Ozs., 8 In. 3.75
Soda, **Hugh Goodwin,** Aromatic Ginger Ale, Brooklyn, Octagonal, Aqua, 7 7/8 In. .. * 17.50
Soda, **Hutchinson,** Quart 9.00
Soda, **I.W.Harvey & Co.,** H.Norwich, Conn., Smooth Base, Aqua, 1/2 Pint .... * 30.00
Soda, **J.& A.Dearborn,** Union Glassworks, IP, Bruise, Flake, Blue, 1/2 Pint .... * 110.00
Soda, **J.& J.W.Harvey,** Norwich, Conn., H, IP, Medium Green, 1/2 Pint .... * 130.00
Soda, **J.Boardman & Co.,** New York, Graphite Pontil, Cobalt, 7 1/2 In. 100.00
Soda, **J.Deane,** 164 Broadway, IP, Chip, Green, 1/2 Pint .... * 35.00
Soda, **J.Kennedy,** Pittsburgh, IP, Wear, Blue Aqua, 8 In. 45.00
Soda, **J.T.Brown Chemist,** Double, Stain, Bruise, Torpedo, Blue Green, 1/2 Pint ...... * 170.00
Soda, **J.Tweedle Jr.'s Celebrated Soda Or Mineral,** Stain, Green, 1/2 Pint .... * 90.00
Soda, **J.W.Harris' Soda Water,** New Haven, Conn., Octagonal, Cobalt, 1/2 Pint .... * 120.00
Soda, **Joseph Weber,** Philada., Clover & Cannon, Stain, Aqua, 1/2 Pint .... * 30.00
Soda, **Jumbo Beverage,** Embossed Elephant, 60 Ozs., 13 1/2 In. 7.50
Soda, **K.A.Rouna & Co.,** Ishpeming, Mich., Hutchinson, Quart 9.00
Soda, **Keller & Veltn,** Louisville, 7 1/4 In. .... *Illus*
Soda, **L.Gahre,** Bridgeton, N.J., Stubby, Green, 6 1/2 In. 7.00
Soda, **Lancaster Glass Works,** N.Y., IP, Sapphire Blue, 1/2 Pint .... * 90.00
Soda, **Lancaster X Glass Works,** N.Y., XX, IP, Sapphire Blue, 1/2 Pint .... * 75.00
Soda, **Lemonette,** 1947, 6 Ozs., 7 In. 1.00
Soda, **Luke Beard,** Collared Mouth, Pin Shape, Green, 1/4 Pint .... * 100.00
Soda, **Luke Beard,** Howard St., Boston, Mouth Ring, Deep Green, 1/2 Pint .... * 50.00
Soda, **Mayer & Bernstein,** Albany, N.Y., Hutchinson, Registered, Dug, Aqua, Quart 17.00
Soda, **McNiells,** Elkin, N.C., 6 Ozs. 2.50
Soda, **Mew Langton Co.,** Newport, Squat, Emerald Green, 6 In. 19.50
Soda, **Michigan,** Hutchinson, Quart 8.25
Soda, **Milton Aereated Water Works,** Codd, Aqua, 8 In. .... *Illus* 8.00
Soda, **Mineral Water,** Honesdale Glassworks, Pa., Bright Green, 1/2 Pint .... * 40.00
Soda, **Moxie,** Aqua, Quart 1.50
Soda, **Moxie,** Label, 26 Ozs. 3.00
Soda, **National Bottling Co.,** St.Louis, Mo., 23 Fluid Ozs. 3.00
Soda, **Nehi,** 9 Ozs. 1.50
Soda, **Nicholes & Nippins,** Gravitating Stopper, Patent 1864, Aqua, 1/2 Pint 10.00
Soda, **Nu Grape,** 6 Ozs. 1.50
Soda, **Nu Icy,** March 9, 1920, 1/2 Pint 7.50
Soda, **Orange Crush,** Embossed, Amber, 7 Ozs. 7.50
Soda, **Orangette,** 1947, 6 Ozs., 7 In. 1.00
Soda, **Pentucket Spring Mineral Water,** G.S.Cushing, Lowell, Green, 1/2 Pint .... * 40.00
Soda, **Pepsi Cola,** Anderson College, S.C., 10 Ozs. 2.75
Soda, **Pepsi Cola,** Fountain Syrup, 10 In. .... *Illus* 12.50
Soda, **Pepsi Cola,** Long Island City, 10 In. .... *Illus* 5.00
Soda, **Pepsi Cola,** North Carolina Bicentennial, 10 Ozs. 5.00
Soda, **Pepsi Cola,** North Carolina Bicentennial, 12 Ozs. 3.00

Left to right: Soda, Keller & Veltn, Louisville, 7 1/4 In.; Soda, Milton Aerated Water Works, Codd, Aqua, 8 In.

(See Page 203)

(See Page 203)

Left to right: Soda, Pepsi Cola, Fountain Syrup, 10 In.; Soda, Pepsi Cola, Long Island City, 10 In.

Soda, **Pepsi Cola**, North Carolina Bicentennial, 16 Ozs.	4.00
Soda, **Pepsi Cola**, South Carolina Bicentennial, Clemson University, 12 Ozs.	3.00
Soda, **Pepsi Cola**, South Carolina Bicentennial, Furman, 12 Ozs.	3.00
Soda, **Pepsi Cola**, Virginia Bicentennial, 16 Ozs.	4.00
Soda, **Philadelphia XXX,** Honesdale Glassworks, Wear, Green, 1/2 Pint	* 70.00
Soda, **Premium,** Mineral Waters, IP, Octagonal, Green, 1/2 Pint	* 90.00
Soda, **Priest Natural Soda,** Priest, Mineral Water, Aqua, 1/2 Pint	* 25.00
Soda, **R.Dillon,** Utica, N.Y., Blob Top, Emerald Green, Quart	40.00
Soda, **Registered E.Lyon & Sons,** 25th Jan. 1859, Olive Green, 1/2 Pint	* 30.00
Soda, **Richelicu Root Beer,** Turn Mold, Kickup, Green, 12 In.	4.50
Soda, **Round Bottom,** Fluted, Crack, Olive Amber, 1/2 Pint	* 55.00
Soda, **Round Bottom,** Pontil, Stain, Olive Amber, 1/2 Pint	* 55.00
Soda, **Round Bottom,** Tooled Applied Lip, Aqua, 7 1/4 In.	2.00
Soda, **Round Bottom,** Tooled Applied Lip, Aqua, 9 3/4 In.	2.50
Soda, **Round Bottom,** Tooled Applied Lip, Stain, Aqua, 9 1/2 In.	2.00
Soda, **Royal Crown Cola,** 1936, 12 Ozs.	1.50
Soda, **Royal Crown,** 10 Ozs.	1.50
Soda, **Royal,** St.Louis, Mo., 22 Fluid Ozs.	2.00
Soda, **Seitz & Bro,** Easton, Pa., S, IP, Bruise, Sapphire Blue, 1/2 Pint	* 50.00
Soda, **Seven Up,** U.C.L.A., John Wooden Commemorative, 16 Ozs.	3.50
Soda, **Silver Seal,** American Soda Water Co., St.Louis, Mo., Quart	9.00
Soda, **Squirt,** Swirled, 7 Ozs.	1.00
Soda, **St.Louis,** Mo., ABM, 23 Ozs.	4.00
Soda, **St.Louis,** Mo., 7 Circular Ribs, Pint, 7 Fluid Ozs.	12.00
Soda, **Standard Bottling Co.,** Pawtucket, R.I., U.S.Flag, Blue Aqua, 8 In.	8.00
Soda, **Star Bottling Works,** St.Paul, Minn., Hutchinson, Aqua, 8 Ozs.	10.00
Soda, **Superior Mineral Waters,** Union Glassworks, Flakes, Green, 1/2 Pint	* 45.00
Soda, **T.H.Kelly,** Steubenville, Ohio, Blob, Dug, Aqua, Quart	6.00
Soda, **T.W.Gillett,** New Haven, IP, Octagonal, Sapphire Blue, 1/2 Pint	* 165.00
Soda, **T.W.Gillette,** New Haven, IP, Octagonal, Blue, 1/2 Pint	* 170.00
Soda, **Taylor Never Surrenders,** Union Glass, Crack, Piece Out, Blue, 1/2 Pint	* 40.00

Soda, Tip-Top Bottling Co., St.Louis, Mo., Quart 5.00
Soda, Tweedle's Celebrated Soda Or Mineral, N.Y., Sapphire Blue, 1/2 Pint .... * 175.00
Soda, Union Glass Works, New London, Ct., Bruise, Aqua, 1/2 Pint .... * 200.00
Soda, Union Glass Works, New London, Ct., Bruise, Chips, Green, 1/2 Pint .... * 210.00
Soda, Union Glass Works, New London, Ct., Chip, Aqua, 1/2 Pint .... * 10.00
Soda, Union Glass Works, Philada, IP, Chip, Teal Green, 1/2 Pint .... * 65.00
Soda, Union Glassworks, Superior Mineral Water, Chip, Cobalt, 1/2 Pint .... * 130.00
Soda, Vess Cola, 5 1/2 In. 2.75
Soda, VP Valley Park, Mo., 24 Ozs. 3.00
Soda, W.Eagle's Superior Soda Or Mineral Waters, Green, 1/2 Pint .... * 30.00
Soda, W.H.Hutchinson & Son, Chicago, Aqua Blue, 2 Gallon 65.00
Soda, Wm.A.Kearney, Shamokin, Pa., Hutchinson, Amber, Quart 50.00
Soda, Wm.W.Lappeus, Premium, Soda Or, 10 Sided, Sapphire Blue, 1/2 Pint .... * 230.00
South Jersey Art Glass, North American Log Cabin 15.00
South Jersey Art Glass, North American Log Cabin 15.00
Southern Comfort, Robert E.Lee 295.00
Spice, U.S.Navy, Pepper, Pontil, Octagonal, Aqua, 5 3/8 In. .... * 50.00
Spirit, see also Seal
Spirit, Bell Shape, Dark Olive Green, 8 5/8 In. .... * 300.00
Spirit, Beveled Corners, Rectangular, Dark Olive Amber, 8 In. .... * 70.00
Spirit, Captain's, Squat, Dark Olive Amber, 8 In.   .... * 200.00
Spirit, Daum Nancy, Sterling Top, Purple Floral, Green & Yellow Leaf, 5 In. 325.00
Spirit, Seal Marked Class Of 1846, Dyottville Glass Works, Amber, 11 1/4 In .... * 310.00
Spirit, Seal Marked J.W. 1824, Bulbous, Dark Olive Amber, 10 1/8 In. .... * 250.00
Stiegel Type, Blown, Enameled, Pewter Top, Pint 75.00
Stiegel Type, Blown, Polychrome Enamel Design, 4 1/2 In. 60.00
Stiegel Type, Enamel Decoration, C.1780, 6 In. ....Color XXXX.XX
Stiegel Type, Flint, Half Post, Enameled, C.1750, 7 In. 215.00
Stoneware, see also Pottery
Stoneware, J.Crellin, 45 Williams St., N.Y., 6 In. 50.00
Stoneware, Ribbed, 7 In. 10.00
Stoneware, William Webber, Grafton, Wix., Blue Shoulder Ring, 8 In. 35.00
Stoneware, Wm.Edwards & Co., Cleveland, Ohio, Threaded Stopper, 11 1/4 In. 50.00
Three Mold, Embossed Rutherford & Kay, Black Amethyst, Quart 15.00
Toilet, Blown, Flint, 3 Mold, Blue, 1/2 Pint 175.00
Toilet, Blown, Flint, 3 Mold, Tam-O'-Shanter Stopper, Deep Blue, 1/2 Pint 170.00
Toilet, Flint, Blown, 12 Panels, Similar To McK G I-7, 6 In. 38.00
Toilet, McK G I-7, Flint, Tam-O'-Shanter Stopper, 1/2 Pint 45.00
Tonic, Dr.Jones' Red Clover, Amber, 10 In. ....Illus 35.00

(See Page 206)

(See Page 206)

Left to right: Tonic, Dr. Jones' Red Clover, Amber, 10 In.; Vinegar, H. J. Heinz Co., Barrel, Sampling, C. 1890; Vinegar, White House, 8 1/2 In.

Tonic, Sim's Elixir Of Pyrophosphate Of Iron, Antwerp, N.Y., 7 X 3 X 2 In.	5.00
Vinegar, Champion's, Cathedral, 3 Tier, Stain, Aqua, 15 In.	20.00
Vinegar, H.J.Heinz Co., Barrel, Sampling, C.1890 .... Illus	125.00
Vinegar, Maple Sap & Boiled Cider Vinegar, C.I.Co., N.H., Cobalt, Quart	* 260.00
Vinegar, Rimmol's Toilet, Lead Foil Over Cork, Case Shape, Aqua, 4 3/4 In.	6.00
Vinegar, White House, Apple Shape, Quart	16.00
Vinegar, White House, Apple Shape, 1/2 Gallon	16.00
Vinegar, White House, Corker, 1/2 Gallon	10.00
Vinegar, White House, Onion Decanter, Green, Quart	15.00
Vinegar, White House 8 1/2 In. .... Illus	5.00
Water, Blue & Gold Decorated, Pontil, 11 1/2 In.	65.00
Water, Canton, Blue & White, 10 In.	360.00
Water, Canton, Blue & White, 8 1/2 In.	295.00
Water, Mineral, see Mineral Water	
Water, Moses, see Mineral Water, Moses	
Water, Teardrop Shape, Applied Rope At Neck, Flared Lip, Teal Blue, 9 1/2 In	19.00
Wendon Corporation, Double Eagle Decanter, 9 In.	20.50

Wheaton Commemorative, Andrew Johnson, 1808-1875

Wheaton Commemorative, Apollo 14, Aqua

Wheaton Company was established in 1888. The firm made hand-blown and pressed glassware. In 1938 automatic equipment was added and many molded glass items were made. Wheaton Commemorative made all types of containers for pharmaceuticals and cosmetics, and foods, as well as gift shop antique-style bottles. Wheaton Commemorative bottles since Christmas, 1975, are handmade by Wheaton Village Crafts Guild, Millville, N.J.

Wheaton Commemorative, Abraham Lincoln, Topaz	7.50
Wheaton Commemorative, Alexander Graham Bell, Amber	6.00
Wheaton Commemorative, Andrew Jackson, Green	6.00
Wheaton Commemorative, Andrew Johnson, Ruby	7.00
Wheaton Commemorative, Andrew Johnson, 1808-1875 .... Illus	7.00
Wheaton Commemorative, Apollo 11	25.00
Wheaton Commemorative, Apollo 12	225.00
Wheaton Commemorative, Apollo 12, Red & Flint	425.00
Wheaton Commemorative, Apollo 13	10.00
Wheaton Commemorative, Apollo 13, Flint Reverse Side	375.00
Wheaton Commemorative, Apollo 14, Aqua .... Illus	6.00
Wheaton Commemorative, Apollo 14, Flint	275.00
Wheaton Commemorative, Apollo 15	10.00
Wheaton Commemorative, Apollo 17 .... Illus	20.00
Wheaton Commemorative, Apollo 17, Gold Stopper	7.00

Wheaton Commemorative, Ben Franklin	7.00
Wheaton Commemorative, Betsy Ross, Light Flint	450.00
Wheaton Commemorative, Betsy Ross, Red & Flint	350.00
Wheaton Commemorative, Betsy Ross, Ruby	6.00
Wheaton Commemorative, Betsy Ross, 1969, Ruby *Illus*	*6.00*
Wheaton Commemorative, Billy Graham, Green	6.00
Wheaton Commemorative, Charles Evans Hughes, Blue	6.00
Wheaton Commemorative, Charles Lindbergh, Blue	6.00
Wheaton Commemorative, Christmas, 1971, Flint	950.00
Wheaton Commemorative, Christmas, 1971, Frosted	15.00
Wheaton Commemorative, Christmas, 1972	50.00
Wheaton Commemorative, Christmas, 1973	7.00
Wheaton Commemorative, Christmas, 1973, Brown	500.00
Wheaton Commemorative, Christmas, 1973, Light Topaz	750.00
Wheaton Commemorative, Christmas, 1974, Green	7.00
Wheaton Commemorative, Christmas, 1975, Blue	10.00
Wheaton Commemorative, Christmas, 1976, Amber	10.00

Wheaton Commemorative, Apollo 17
(See Page 206)

Wheaton Commemorative, Betsy Ross,
1969, Ruby

Wheaton Commemorative, General George Smith Patton, Jr.

Wheaton Commemorative, Clark Gable	5.00
Wheaton Commemorative, Douglas MacArthur, Amethyst	6.00
Wheaton Commemorative, Dwight D.Eisenhower	9.00
Wheaton Commemorative, First National Bank, Flint	375.00
Wheaton Commemorative, Franklin D.Roosevelt	15.00
Wheaton Commemorative, General George Smith Patton, Jr. *Illus*	*7.00*
Wheaton Commemorative, General Patton, Aqua	6.00
Wheaton Commemorative, General Patton, Light Green	375.00
Wheaton Commemorative, George Washington	7.00
Wheaton Commemorative, George Washington, Flint, Frosted	6.00
Wheaton Commemorative, Gerald R.Ford	7.00
Wheaton Commemorative, Gerald Rudolph Ford *Illus*	*7.00*
Wheaton Commemorative, Harry S.Truman, Ruby	6.00
Wheaton Commemorative, Harry S.Truman, 1884-1972 *Illus*	*6.00*

(See Page 207)

(See Page 207)

Top left to right: Wheaton Commemorative, Gerald Rudolph Ford; Wheaton Commemorative, Harry S. Truman, 1884–1972; Wheaton Commemorative, Herbert C. Hoover, 1972, Aqua.
Left: Wheaton Commemorative, Mark Twain, Samuel L. Clemens, 1835–1910.

Wheaton Commemorative, Helen Keller	7.00
Wheaton Commemorative, Herbert C.Hoover	7.00
Wheaton Commemorative, Herbert C. Hoover, 1972, Aqua ....*Illus*	*6.00*
Wheaton Commemorative, Humphrey Bogart, Green	6.00
Wheaton Commemorative, James Madison, Blue	10.00
Wheaton Commemorative, James Monroe	10.00
Wheaton Commemorative, Jean Harlow, Topaz	6.00
Wheaton Commemorative, John Adams, Green	7.00
Wheaton Commemorative, John F.Kennedy, Blue	38.00
Wheaton Commemorative, John Paul Jones	7.00
Wheaton Commemorative, John Paul Jones, Flint	235.00
Wheaton Commemorative, July 4th	10.00
Wheaton Commemorative, Lyndon B.Johnson	7.00
Wheaton Commemorative, Mark Twain, Amethyst	6.00
Wheaton Commemorative, Mark Twain, Samuel L.Clemens, 1835-1910 ....*Illus*	*7.00*
Wheaton Commemorative, McGovern & Eagleton, 1972, Topaz	15.00
Wheaton Commemorative, McGovern & Shriver, 1972	10.00
Wheaton Commemorative, Minton	10.00
Wheaton Commemorative, Mother's Day, 1976, Flint, Frosted	10.00
Wheaton Commemorative, Nixon & Agnew, 1968	10.00
Wheaton Commemorative, Nixon & Agnew, 1972	7.00
Wheaton Commemorative, Paul Revere	7.00
Wheaton Commemorative, Paul Revere Cabin	7.00
Wheaton Commemorative, Paul Revere, Blue	6.00
Wheaton Commemorative, Pope Paul VI	7.00
Wheaton Commemorative, President Eisenhower, Amethyst	8.00
Wheaton Commemorative, President Eisenhower, Flint	800.00
Wheaton Commemorative, President Eisenhower, Light Amethyst	425.00
Wheaton Commemorative, President F.D.Roosevelt, Flint	775.00
Wheaton Commemorative, President Jefferson, Red & Flint	350.00
Wheaton Commemorative, President Truman, Brown	500.00
Wheaton Commemorative, President Washington, Face On Both Sides, Frosted	800.00

Wheaton Commemorative, President Washington, Flint	50.00
Wheaton Commemorative, President Wilson, Flint	475.00
Wheaton Commemorative, President Wilson, Wrong Neck, Short	600.00
Wheaton Commemorative, Rev.Martin Luther King	10.00
Wheaton Commemorative, Richard Nixon, Aqua	7.00
Wheaton Commemorative, Robert E.Lee, Green	6.00
Wheaton Commemorative, Robert Kennedy, Green	10.00
Wheaton Commemorative, Sheriff's Association	10.00
Wheaton Commemorative, Skylab I, Blue	6.00
Wheaton Commemorative, Southern 500	15.00
Wheaton Commemorative, Spirit Of '76	10.00
Wheaton Commemorative, St.John, Amethyst	12.50
Wheaton Commemorative, St.Luke, Blue	12.50
Wheaton Commemorative, St.Mark, Green	12.50
Wheaton Commemorative, St.Matthew, Gold	12.50

Wheaton Commemorative, Ulysses S.Grant, Topaz

Wheaton Commemorative,
Will Rogers, 1969, Topaz

Wheaton Commemorative, Theodore Roosevelt, Blue	6.00
Wheaton Commemorative, Thomas Edison, Blue	6.00
Wheaton Commemorative, Thomas Jefferson	10.00
Wheaton Commemorative, Ulysses S.Grant, Topaz	6.00
Wheaton, Commemorative, Ulysses S.Grant, Topaz *Illus*	6.00
Wheaton Commemorative, Vietnam, First Run	10.00
Wheaton Commemorative, Vietnam, Second Run	15.00
Wheaton Commemorative, W.C.Fields	15.00
Wheaton Commemorative, Will Rogers	7.00
Wheaton Commemorative, Will Rogers, Flint	190.00
Wheaton Commemorative, Will Rogers, Topaz	6.00
Wheaton Commemorative, Will Rogers, 1969, Topaz *Illus*	7.00
Wheaton Commemorative, William McKinley, Aqua	7.00
Wheaton Commemorative, Woodrow Wilson, Blue	6.00

Whiskey bottles came in assorted sizes and shapes through the years. Any container for whiskey is included in this category.
   Whiskey, see also Ballantine, Beam, Bininger, Dant, Ezra Brooks,
   Whiskey, Bininger, see Bininger

Whiskey, A.McGinnis Co., Balto., Md., 4 In.	7.50
Whiskey, Alexander & Patterson Finest Quality, Barrel, Oval, 11 1/2 In.	65.00
Whiskey, Ambassador Scotch, Fish Shape, 8 In.	27.50
Whiskey, Ambassador Scotch, Flask, ABM, Green, Pint	5.00
Whiskey, Arak Of Lebanon, Red Felt Covering, 13 In.	5.00
Whiskey, B & B Fine Old, Flask, 1/2 Pint	2.00
Whiskey, Banjo, 11 In.	5.00

Whiskey, Barrel, 14 Rings, Smooth Base, Citron, 3/4 Quart .... * 30.00
Whiskey, Barrel, 20 Rings, Square Collared Mouth, IP, Chip, Amber, 3/4 Quart .... * 35.00
Whiskey, Basket Weave, Jug, Handle, Oval, Smooth Base, Green, 3/4 Quart .... * 25.00
Whiskey, Beech Hill Distilling Co., Cincinnati, O., Quart .... *Illus* 15.00
Whiskey, Beiser & Fischer, N.Y., Plg, Deep Amber, 3/4 Quart Illus. 475.00
Whiskey, Belle Of Anderson, Label, Milk Glass, Pint 80.00
Whiskey, Belle Of Anderson, Label, Milk Glass, Quart 65.00
Whiskey, Belle Of Anderson, Milk Glass, 7 In. 105.00
Whiskey, Belle Of Anderson, Old Fashion, Sour Mash, Milk Glass, 6 7/8 In. .... * 85.00
Whiskey, Belsinger & Co., Clover, Savh, Ga., Sun-Colored Amethyst, Quart 6.50
Whiskey, Ben Franklin Pure Rye, Chicago, Amethyst, Quart 75.00
Whiskey, Bennett & Carrol, Pittsburg, Barrel, 20 Rings, Chip, Amber, 3/4 Quart .... * 120.00
Whiskey, Bernheim Bros. & Uri, Louisville, Ky., Blob Seal, Amber, Quart 45.00
Whiskey, Bernheim Bros. & Uri, Louisville, Ky., Embossed Seal, Amber, Quart 34.00
Whiskey, Berry's Diamond Wedding, Barrel, Embossed, Quart 15.00
Whiskey, Beveled Corners, Crack, Rectangular, Olive Amber, 8 In. .... * 70.00
Whiskey, Blake's, Barrel, Quart 1.50
Whiskey, Bonnie Bros., Louisville, Ky., 9 3/4 In. .... *Illus* 10.00
Whiskey, Brooklyn Glass Works, Patent, Chip, Wear, Yellow Olive, 3/4 Quart .... * 35.00
Whiskey, Buchanan Distillery, Handmade Sour Mash, Cannon, Amber, 9 In. *2500.00
Whiskey, Bulloch, Lade & Co., Ltd., Finest Old Scotch, Decanter, Quart 38.00
Whiskey, Bushwick Glass Works, Patent, Collared Mouth, Amber, 3/4 Quart .... * 40.00
Whiskey, C.Keopper, Indianapolis, Ind., Drum Shape, Porcelain, Footed, Quart 30.00
Whiskey, Caperr's, N.C., Cobalt Quart 187.00
Whiskey, Carstairs' White Seal, Embossed 1788, Amber, 1/2 Pint 12.00
Whiskey, Cascade, Label, Quart 10.00
Whiskey, Casper Co., Winston Salem, N.C., Beehive Jug, Gallon 40.00
Whiskey, Casper's, Honest North Carolina People, Stain, Cobalt, Quart .... * 160.00
Whiskey, Cedar Brook, Label, Quart 10.00
Whiskey, Chestnut Grove, Applied Seal, Handled, OP, Amber, Quart 175.00
Whiskey, Chestnut Grove, Flattened Jug, Applied Handle, Golden Amber, Pint .... * 60.00
Whiskey, Chestnut Grove, G.Wharton, Bell Shape, Golden Amber, 9 3/8 In. .... * 375.00
Whiskey, Chinese, Blue Green, Pint 6.00
Whiskey, Clayton Moor's, Wellington Hotel, Shoofly, Aqua, Pint 8.00
Whiskey, Club House, M.Shaughnossy, St.Louis, Cloudy, Amber, 1/2 Pint 10.00
Whiskey, Club House, M.Shaughnossy, St.Louis, Pint 5.00
Whiskey, Clyde Glass Works, Clyde, N.Y., Pint .... * 25.00
Whiskey, Collared Lip With Ring, Bulging Neck, Olive Yellow, 4 3/4 In. 5.50
Whiskey, Columbian Pure Jamaica Ginger Cordial, 10 In. .... *Illus* 35.00
Whiskey, Compliments Of Ben Johnson, Nelson County, Ky., 1/4 Pint 22.50
Whiskey, Compliments Of Jos.Fein Grocery Co., New Albany, Ind., 1/4 Pint 18.50
Whiskey, Constitutional Beverage, W.Olmsted & Co., Yellow Amber, 3/4 Quart .... * 175.00
Whiskey, Coon Hollow Bourbon, ABM, Pint 3.00
Whiskey, Coon Hollow, Label, Quart 10.00
Whiskey, Corseted, Handle, Pontil, Bell Shape, Amber, 3/4 Quart .... * 100.00
Whiskey, Corseted, Handle, Pontil, Crack, Bell Shape, Amber, 3/4 Quart .... * 80.00
Whiskey, Cottage Brand, Cabin, Shingled Roof, Light Green, Pint .... * 190.00
Whiskey, Crigler & Crigler Distillers, Covington, Ky., 10 In. .... *Illus* 5.00
Whiskey, Crigler & Crigler, Miniature 8.00
Whiskey, Crock, Blue Writing, Miniature 25.00
Whiskey, Crown Distilleries Co., 3 1/2 In. 3.50
Whiskey, Crown Distilleries, Miniature 7.00
Whiskey, Crown Distillers, Embossed Stopper, Slug Plate, Amber, Miniature 40.00
Whiskey, Cruiskeen Lawn Irish, Ceramic Jug, Decoration, 7 In. 25.00
Whiskey, Cuckoo, Haze, Quart 16.50
Whiskey, Cunninghams & Ihmsen, Pittsburgh, Pa., Label, Amber, Quart .... * 70.00
Whiskey, Cut Glass, Hobstar, Diamond, & Fan, 11 In. 110.00
Whiskey, Cut Glass, Middlesex, Rayed Base, 8 In. 300.00
Whiskey, Cyrus Noble, Lilienthal Centennial, 1876 .... *Color* XXXX.XX
Whiskey, Cyrus Noble, Old Private Stock, C.1898 .... *Color* XXXX.XX
Whiskey, Cyrus Noble, Snowshoe Thompson, 1972 .... *Color* XXXX.XX
Whiskey, D.P.Roberts Liquor Dealer, Belle Fourche, S.D., Salt Glaze, Gallon 22.50
Whiskey, D.P.Roberts, Bellefourche, S.D., Jug, Brown Glazed, Pint 55.00
Whiskey, D.Pariser, 417 Broadway, N.Y., Amber, 1/2 Gallon 100.00
Whiskey, Dallemand & Co., Chicago, Amber, Quart 30.00

(See Page 210)

(See Page 210)

(See Page 210)

(See Page 210)

Top left to right: Whiskey, Beech Hill Distilling Co., Cincinnati, O., Quart; Whiskey, Bonnie Bros., Louisville, Ky., 9 3/4 In.; Whiskey, Columbian Pure Jamaica Ginger Cordial, 10 In.
Left: Whiskey, Crigler & Crigler Distillers, Covington, Ky., 10 In.

Whiskey, **Davey Crockett,** Tooled Top, BIMAL, Amber, Fifth	25.00
Whiskey, **Deacon Scotland Yard,** Dark Olive Green, Pint	* 17.50
Whiskey, **Deep Spring Tennessee,** Haze, Amber, 4 1/2 In.	10.00
Whiskey, **Detrick Distilling Co.,** Dayton, O., If You Try Me Once–, 1/2 Pint	17.75
Whiskey, **Dewar's,** Black Bull, Miniature	4.95
Whiskey, **Dewar's Perth,** Doulton, 1895, Salt Glaze, Hunt Scene, Brown, 7 1/2 In	75.00
Whiskey, **Dewar's Scotch,** Miniature	7.00
Whiskey, **Dewar's Scotch,** Royal Doulton, George The Guard, Noke, 10 In.	85.00
Whiskey, **Dr.S.F.Stowe's Ambrosial Nectar,** Patent 1866, Amber, 10 In.	* 30.00
Whiskey, **Duffy Crescent Saloon,** Louisville, Pig, Rooster & Moon, 7 5/8 In.	* 525.00
Whiskey, **Duffy's Malt,** ABM, Quart	25.00
Whiskey, **Dunbar & Co.,** Cordial Schnapps, Schiedam, Olive Amber, 3/4 Quart	* 30.00
Whiskey, **Dunbar & Co.,** Wormwood Cordial, Boston, Stain, Aqua, 3/4 Quart	* 150.00
Whiskey, **Durkin,** Spokane, Quart	30.00
Whiskey, **Dyottville Glassworks,** Phila., Patent, IP, Olive Amber, Quart	* 30.00
Whiskey, **Dyottville Glassworks,** Phila., Smooth Base, Citron	* 45.00
Whiskey, **Dyottville Glassworks,** Phila., Smooth Base, Olive Yellow, Quart	* 15.00
Whiskey, **Dyottville Glassworks,** Phila., Stain, Wear, Citron, Quart	* 12.50
Whiskey, **E & B Bevan,** Pittston, Pa., Valley, Octagonal, Flake, Amber, 3/4 Quart	*1150.00
Whiskey, **E.G.Booz,** Old Cabin, 1840, Amber *Color*	XXXX.XX
Whiskey, **E.G.Booz,** Old Mr.Boston, Bourbon, 1959, 8 1/2 In. *Illus*	17.00
Whiskey, **E.G.Booz's Old C Abon,** Reproduction, Cabin, Amber, Pint	* 50.00
Whiskey, **E.G.Booz's Old Cabin,** Reproduction, Cabin, Blue, 3/4 Quart	* 10.00
Whiskey, **E.G.Booz's Old Cabin,** 1840 On Roof, McK G VII-3, Amber, Quart	* 750.00
Whiskey, **E.G.Booz's Old Cabin,** 1840 On Roof, McK G VII-4, Amber, Quart	* 900.00

Whiskey, E.G.Booz, Old
Mr.Boston, Bourbon,
1959, 8 1/2 ln.
(See Page 211)

Whiskey, E. G. Booz's,
Cabin, McK G VII-4
Amber, 3/4 Quart

Whiskey, E.G.Booz's Old Cabin, 1840, McK G VII-4 Flask, Amber, Pint	625.00
Whiskey, E.G.Booz's, Cabin, McK G VII-4, Amber, 3/4 Quart .....*Illus*	575.00
Whiskey, Eagle Rye, Flask, Strap Sided, Light Amber, Pint	10.00
Whiskey, Elk's Pride Rye, 6 ln. .....*Illus*	20.00
Whiskey, Ellenville Glass Works On Base, Olive Green, 3/4 Quart	* 30.00
Whiskey, Elliott & Burke Fine, Memphis, Jug, Sloped Shoulders, 2 Gallon	39.00
Whiskey, Embossed KZ, Applied Lip, Squat, Deep Amber, Quart	14.00
Whiskey, Ernst L.Arp, Kiel, Aqua, 14 1/2 ln. .....*Illus*	20.00
Whiskey, Extra Superior, Black, 10 ln. .....*Illus*	45.00
Whiskey, F.Chevalier Co., Old Castle, Inside Threads, Fifth	25.00
Whiskey, F.Chevalier Co., Old Castle, Inside Threads, Quart	35.00
Whiskey, F.Chevalier Co., San Francisco, Glsss Stopper, Amber, 1/2 Pint	18.00
Whiskey, F.Chevalier, Merchants, San Francisco, Amber, Quart	35.00
Whiskey, F.Chevalier, San Francisco, Amber, Pint	6.00
Whiskey, F.P.Adams & Co., Boston, Flattened Jug, Handle, Oval, Pint	* 20.00
Whiskey, F.Zimmerman & Co., Mail Order House, Portland, Ore., Amber, Quart	40.00
Whiskey, Farmville, Va., Dispensary, Pint	30.00
Whiskey, Farmville, Va., Dispensary, 1/2 Pint	25.00
Whiskey, Ferdinand Westheimer & Sons, Cin., O., 1/2 Pint	7.00
Whiskey, Fine Old Eagle, Bourbon, Strap-Sided Flask, Amber, Pint	10.00
Whiskey, Fine Old Wheat, Flattened Jug, Handle, Puce Amber, 3/4 Quart	* 110.00
Whiskey, Fire Water, Patent May 30, 1916, 7 1/2 ln.	15.00
Whiskey, Flattened Ewer, Handle, Sheared Mouth, Yellow Green, 3/4 Quart	* 65.00
Whiskey, Fleming's Export Pure Rye, Lady's Leg, Medicinal Purposes, Quart	20.00
Whiskey, For Limousine, Cut Glass, Russian Cut, Sterling Silver Top, 10 ln.	70.00
Whiskey, Forest Lawn, J.V.H., Carafe, Flanged Mouth, Olive Green, 3/4 Quart	* 180.00
Whiskey, Fort Trumbull Glass Co. On Base, Smooth Base, Amber, 3/4 Quart	* 450.00
Whiskey, Four Aces, Pint	3.00
Whiskey, Four Roses, ABM, Stain, Amber, Miniature	5.00
Whiskey, Four Roses, Louisville, Embossed, Amber, Quart	5.00
Whiskey, Free Blown, Handle, Collared Mouth, Pontil, Puce, 1/2 Pint	* 140.00
Whiskey, Free Blown, Handle, Pontil, Flake, Amber, 1/2 Pint	* 30.00
Whiskey, Fulton, Aqua, Gallon	10.50
Whiskey, Fulton, Embossed, ABM, Gallon	15.00
Whiskey, G.O.Blake's Rye & Bourbon, Adams, Taylor & Co., Barrel, Quart	13.00
Whiskey, G.O.Taylor, Trade Mark, 3 Mold, Glop Top, Amber, 11 1/4 ln.	3.50
Whiskey, Gardner's Aphrodisiac Marked With Epoxy, Amber, 3/4 Quart	* 15.00
Whiskey, Gentry, Slote & Co., N.Y., Horse, IP, Oval, Olive Amber, 3/4 Quart	* 300.00
Whiskey, Geo.F.Hewett Co., Private Stock Rye, 3 Mold, 12 ln.	4.00
Whiskey, Gincocktail, S.M.& Co., N.Y., Ribbed, Pontil, Amber, Quart	* 600.00
Whiskey, Goldberg, Bowen & Co., Shoofly, Pint	21.00
Whiskey, Golden Treasure, Barrel, 12 Rings, Collared Mouth, Aqua, 4 7/8 ln.	* 110.00
Whiskey, Golden Treasure, Barrel, 12 Rings, Ground Mouth, Aqua, 3 3/8 ln.	* 50.00
Whiskey, Golden Wedding, Carnival Glass, Marigold, Pint	15.00
Whiskey, Golden Wedding, Carnival Glass, Quart	16.00
Whiskey, Golden Wedding, Carnival Glass, 1/2 Pint	5.00
Whiskey, Golden Wedding, Embossed, Pharmacy Label, 1924, Pint	6.00

Whiskey, Golden Wedding, Label, Pint 7.50
Whiskey, Golden Wedding, Screw Cap, Carnival, 1/10 Pint 16.00
Whiskey, Golden Wedding, 1924, Embossed, Pharmacy Label, Pint 6.00
Whiskey, Good Old Bourbon In A Hog's–, Pig, 6 3/4 In. 50.00
Whiskey, Good Old Rye In A Hog's–, Pig, Embossed, Pottery, 7 In. 350.00
Whiskey, Grant's, Drummond, Bisque, 14 In. 15.00
Whiskey, Grant's, Lamond, Bisque, 14 In. 15.00
Whiskey, Green Mountain, Embossed Man, BIMAL, Quart 9.00
Whiskey, Green River, Gold Embossed Negro & Horse On Leather Cover, Pint 30.00
Whiskey, Green River, Labels & Stamps, Amber, 1/2 Pint 25.00
Whiskey, Griffith Hyatt P Co., Handle, Pontil, Flake, Amber, 3/4 Quart .... * 525.00
Whiskey, Grommes & Ulrich National Club Bourbon, Chicago, Jug, Quart 24.50
Whiskey, Guckenheimer, Pittsburgh, Quart 8.00
Whiskey, H.A.Graef's Son Canteen, N.Y., Canteen Shape, Yellow Olive, Pint ...... * 300.00
Whiskey, H.F.& B.N.Y. On Shield, Melon Shape, Wine Color, 3/4 Quart .... * 140.00
Whiskey, H.G.& B.N.Y., Melon Shape, Collared Mouth, Wine Color, 3/4 Quart ...... * 310.00
Whiskey, H.Guggenheimer & Bro., Cincinnati, O., Lady's Leg, Ribbed, Quart 15.00
Whiskey, H.Rosenthal & Sons, Cincinnati, O., 13 In. .... Illus   10.00
Whiskey, Hamburg Company, Fine, Arkansas, Coffin Flack, Latticework, 1/2 Pint 55.00
Whiskey, Hance Bros. & White, Flask, Amber, Miniature 7.00

(See Page 214)

(See Page 212)

(See Page 212)

Top left to right: Whiskey's Elk's Pride Rye, 6 In.; Whiskey, Ernst L. Arp, Kiel, Aqua, 14 1/2 In.; Whiskey, H. Rosenthal & Sons, Cincinnati, O., 13 In.; Whiskey, Heather Dew, Pottery.
Left: Whiskey, Extra Superior, Black, 10 In.

(See Page 212)

Whiskey, Hance Brothers & White, Phila., Oval Flask, Amber, 3 3/4 In. 5.00
Whiskey, Handle, Chip, Flattened Oval, Amber, Quart .... * 15.00
Whiskey, Handle, Collared Mouth, Pontil, Olive Amber, Pint .... * 240.00
Whiskey, Handle, Pontil, Bulbous, Puce, 8 3/4 In. .... * 120.00
Whiskey, Handle, Pontil, Flattened Oval, Broken, Amber, Pint .... * 40.00
Whiskey, Handle, Pontil, Flattened Oval, Cobalt, 3/4 Quart .... * 700.00
Whiskey, Handle, Pontil, Flattened Oval, Yellow Amber, 3/4 Quart .... * 40.00
Whiskey, Handle, Sheared Mouth With Ring, Pontil, Oval, Copper, 3/4 Quart .... * 70.00
Whiskey, Handmade Sour Mash, 7 Years Old, Pumpkinseed, Cloudy, 4 1/2 In. 19.00
Whiskey, Hanlen Brothers, Harrisburg, Pa., Christmas, Handled, Crockery, Pint 35.00

Whiskey, Hawkin's Rye, Aqua, Quart	20.00
Whiskey, Hayner Distilling Co., Springfield, Ohio, Stoneware, 2 Gallon	38.00
Whiskey, Hayner's Distilling, Dayton & St.Louis, Mo., Quart	22.00
Whiskey, Hayner's Four Cities, Quart	4.00
Whiskey, Hayner's, Troy, Ohio, Nov.30, 1897, Quart	22.00
Whiskey, Hayner's, 1897, Turning Purple, Quart	9.50
Whiskey, Heather Dew, Pottery *Illus*	25.00
Whiskey, Heidelberg Brannt Wein, Bininger & Co., Yellow Olive, 3/4 Quart	* 100.00
Whiskey, Here's To Louisville 1909, 1/4 Pint	18.50
Whiskey, Hesperidina, M.S.Bagley, Barrel, 14 Rings, Yellow Amber, 3/4 Quart	* 40.00
Whiskey, Highland, Doulton, Lambeth, White Viking Ship, Beige, 7 In.	78.00
Whiskey, Hoffschlaeger Co., Ltd., Honolulu, Amber, Fifth	125.00
Whiskey, Holtz & Freystedt Co., N.Y., Jug, Handle, Amber, 3/4 Quart	* 27.50
Whiskey, Hotel Worth Bar, Ft.Worth, Texas, Bootlegger's Flask, Amber, Pint	100.00
Whiskey, Hoty Brothers, Pumpkin Seed, Strap Sided, Lip Ring, 1/2 Pint	15.00
Whiskey, House Of Lords, Square, Aqua, 5th	15.00
Whiskey, Hudson's XXXX Rye, Rectangular, Amber, 1/2 Pint, 5 1/2 In.	20.00
Whiskey, Huguley's, Miniature	15.00
Whiskey, Huguley's, Old Amor Rye, 1894, Boston, Pumpkinseed, 3 In.	12.00
Whiskey, Huguley's, Paper Label, Pumpkin Seed Flask, 3 In.	6.50
Whiskey, I.Goldberg, Amber, 10 In.	35.00
Whiskey, I.Trager Co., Cincinnati, Amber, Quart	2.00
Whiskey, Indian Queen, H.Pharazyn, Right Secured, Yellow Amber, Quart	* 950.00
Whiskey, Indian Queen, Mohawk Pure Rye, Patent 1868, Yellow Amber, 3/4 Quart	* 850.00
Whiskey, J.C.Schnell's Sour Mash Kiln Dried Grain, Crockery, Quart	34.50
Whiskey, J.F.Cutler, BIMAL, Quart	7.00
Whiskey, J.F.Cutter Extra Old Bourbon, C.1871, Glop Top, Amber, Fifth	75.00
Whiskey, J.F.Cutter Extra Old Bourbon, C.1874, Flask, Glop Top, Pint	200.00
Whiskey, J.F.T.& Co., Philad., Handle, Ribbed, Crack, Amber, 3/4 Quart	* 100.00
Whiskey, J.Grossman's Sons, New Orleans, Order Your Whiskey, Amber, Quart	40.00
Whiskey, J.H.Cutter Old Bourbon, C.1871, Martin & Co., Glop Top, Amber, Fifth	175.00
Whiskey, J.H.Cutter Old Bourbon, C.1873, Martin & Co., Flask, Amber, Pint	600.00
Whiskey, J.H.Cutter Old Bourbon, C.1873, Martin & Co., Glop Top, Fifth	200.00
Whiskey, J.H.Cutter Old Bourbon, C.1874, Glob Top, Amber, Fifth	150.00
Whiskey, J.H.Cutter Old Bourbon, C.1877, Glop Top, Amber, Fifth	150.00
Whiskey, J.H.Cutter Old Bourbon, C.1877, Hotaling, Glop Top, Amber, Fifth	350.00
Whiskey, J.H.Cutter Old Bourbon, C.1877, Hotaling, Yellow Green, Fifth	250.00
Whiskey, J.H.Cutter Old Bourbon, C.1880, Bird, Glop Top, Green Amber, Fifth	100.00
Whiskey, J.H.Cutter Old Bourbon, C.1880, Bird, Glop Top, Yellow Amber, Fifth	100.00
Whiskey, J.H.Cutter Old Bourbon, C.1880, Hotaling, A No.1, Amber, Fifth	70.00
Whiskey, J.H.Cutter Old Bourbon, C.1880, Moorman, Hotaling, Flask, Pint	200.00
Whiskey, J.H.Cutter Old Bourbon, C.1882, Hotaling, A No.1, Amber, Fifth	60.00
Whiskey, J.H.Cutter Old Bourbon, C.1883, Hotaling, Coffin Flask, Amber, Pint	200.00
Whiskey, J.H.Cutter Old Bourbon, C.1883, O.K., Glop Top, Fifth	75.00
Whiskey, J.H.Cutter Old Bourbon, C.1884, Hotaling, Coffin Flask, Pint	175.00
Whiskey, J.H.Cutter Old Bourbon, C.1885, A No.1, Glop Top, Amber, Fifth	200.00
Whiskey, J.H.Cutter Old Bourbon, C.1888, Hotaling, A No.1, Amber, Fifth	30.00
Whiskey, J.H.Cutter, A No.1, C.P.Moorman, Applied Top, Amber, Fifth	40.00
Whiskey, J.H.Cutter, No.1, Old Bourbon, Bubbles, Honey Amber, Fifth	25.00
Whiskey, J.K, Perking Co., Owensboro, Ky., Pottery, Gallon	30.00
Whiskey, J.Reiger, Miniature	8.00
Whiskey, J.Rieger & Co., Dug, Miniature	6.00
Whiskey, J.Rieger & Co., Kansas City, Embossed, Purple, Quart	16.00
Whiskey, J.Rieger & Co., Kansas City, Mo., Pink, Quart	35.00
Whiskey, J.T.Gayen, Altona, Cannon On Barrel, Amber, 3/4 Quart	*1050.00
Whiskey, Jackman, Carnival Glass, Marigold, 1/2 Pint	4.95
Whiskey, Jackman, Embossed, Carnival Glass, Pint	9.50
Whiskey, Jackman, 1/2 Pint	12.50
Whiskey, James Maguire Celebrated Montezuma Rye, Metal, Copper Insert, Pint	40.00
Whiskey, Jas.Durkin, Spokane, Wash., Amber, Quart	40.00
Whiskey, Jesse Moore Old Bourbon & Rye, Amber, Quart	35.00
Whiskey, Jesse Moore Old Bourbon, S.F., Tooled Top, BIMAL, Amber, Fifth	15.00
Whiskey, Jesse Moore, Moore Hunt & Co., S.F., 4 Mold, Whittled, Amber, Fifth	100.00
Whiskey, Jno.Greenhow, Wm.S Burg, 1770, Reproduction, Octagonal, Green, 8 In.	* 35.00
Whiskey, John & James Buchanan's Black Label, Sunken Pontil, Amber, Quart	60.00

Whiskey, John F.Callahan, BIMAL, Quart 6.00
Whiskey, John Hollowed, 37 & 39 Adams St., Chicago, 8 Sided, Quart, 11 1/4 In 12.50
Whiskey, John McGlinn & Co., Philada, Amber, Quart 22.00
Whiskey, John W.Stout & Co., X, New York, Collared Mouth, Aqua, 1/2 Pint .... * 15.00
Whiskey, Jonas F.Brown, Minneapolis, Prescription Lip, Strap Side, 6 1/2 In. 3.75
Whiskey, Jones & Banks, Glass Screw Stopper, Square, Amber, 3/4 Quart .... * 65.00
Whiskey, Jos.& Pepper & Co., Distillers, Lexington, Ky., Amber, Quart 9.00
Whiskey, Jos, A.Magnus & Co., Amber, Pint 10.00
Whiskey, JSP Monogram, Malt, Labels, Blue Green, Pint .... * 10.00
Whiskey, JSP Monogram, Malt, Smooth Base, Teal Blue, 1/2 Pint .... * 22.50
Whiskey, Jug, Handle, Collared Mouth, IP, Bulbous, Red Amber, 3/4 Quart .... * 110.00
Whiskey, Jug, Handle, Collared Mouth, IP, Bulbous, Wine Color, Pint .... * 70.00
Whiskey, Jug, Handle, Flattened Oval, Applied Mouth, Red Amber, 1/2 Pint .... * 30.00
Whiskey, Jug, Handle, Flattened Oval, Smooth Base, Red Amber, 1/2 Pint .... * 20.00
Whiskey, Jug, Handle, Pour Spout, Stain, Yellow Amber, 3/4 Quart .... * 100.00
Whiskey, Jug, Handled, Pushed-Up Base, Dark Red Amber, Pint 12.50
Whiskey, Julius Kessler, BIMAL, Quart 2.00
Whiskey, Keller Strauss, St.Louis, Mo., Quart 32.00
Whiskey, Kennel Club, S.F., Tooled Top, Amber, Fifth 30.00
Whiskey, Kroger's, Handled Crock, Gallon 35.00
Whiskey, Ky.G.W., Bruises, Amber, 3/4 Quart .... * 20.00
Whiskey, L.C.Edwards, Non-Refillable, Patent April 28, 1903, Amber, Quart .... * 65.00
Whiskey, Lancaster Glass, Barrel, 20 Rings, Burst Bubble, Amber, 3/4 Quart .... * 160.00
Whiskey, Lawson's, Dundee, Scotland, Green, Miniature 5.00
Whiskey, Lexington Club Pure Rye, For Family Trade, 3 Mold, Lip Ring, Quart 5.50
Whiskey, Licking Valley, Covington, Ky., Not In The Trust Union Made, Quart 15.00
Whiskey, Lighthouse, Amber, 10 1/4 In. 5.00
Whiskey, Lilienthal & Co., S.F., Flask, Amber, Pint 111.00
Whiskey, Littlemore, BIMAL, 1/2 Pint 4.00
Whiskey, Louis Hunter Pure Rye, 1870, Jaffe & Co., Seattle, Amber, Fifth 15.00
Whiskey, Louis Weber, Louisville, W.McC1lly & Co., On Base, Amber, Quart .... * 80.00
Whiskey, Lovejoy & Co., Honolulu, T.H. Monogram, Amber, Fifth 75.00
Whiskey, Lowenstein & Co., Old Harvest Corn, Flask, Dug, 1/2 Pint 2.00
Whiskey, Lowenstein & Co., Old Harvest Corn, Flask, 1/2 Pint 3.00
Whiskey, Lyon Bros. Makers On Base, Olive Green, 3/4 Quart .... * 15.00
Whiskey, M.Salzman Co., Honey Amber, 12 In. ....Color XXXX.XX
Whiskey, M.Salzman Co., One Full Quart, Amber, 11 1/2 In. ....Illus 16.00
Whiskey, Macy & Jenkins, New York, On Base, Jug, Handle, Amber, 3/4 Quart .... * 40.00
Whiskey, Magnus & Dragon, Flask, Amber, Pint 5.00
Whiskey, Maryland Jockey Club, Horse & Jockey, Gallon 575.00
Whiskey, McCormick Straight Corn, Jug, 1/2 Pint 15.00
Whiskey, McGinnis, Baltimore, Miniature 10.00
Whiskey, McLeod-Hatze Co., Honey Amber, 12 In. ....Color XXXX.XX
Whiskey, McLeod-Hatze Co., San Francisco, Amber, 12 In. 21.00
Whiskey, Medicinal Purposes Only, 1932, Pint 30.00
Whiskey, Meredith's Diamond Club Pure Rye, Ohio, Porcelain, White, Quart .... * 75.00
Whiskey, Meredith's Diamond Club Rye, Medicinal, K.T.K., White, 7 1/2 In. 25.00
Whiskey, Meredith's Diamond Club Rye, Medicinal, K.T.K., White, 7 3/4 In. 30.00
Whiskey, Meredith's Diamond Club Pure Rye, Green Letters, Porcelain, Quart 50.00
Whiskey, Merry Christmas & Happy New Year, Pottery, 10 In. 25.00
Whiskey, Miller's Extra Old Bourbon, C.1878, Glop Top, Amber, Fifth 1000.00
Whiskey, Milton J.Hardy Old Bourbon, Louisville, Ky., Amber, Quart 50.00
Whiskey, Mist Of The Morning, Barnett, Barrel, 13 Rings, Yellow, 3/4 Quart 200.00
Whiskey, Mist Of The Morning, Barnett, Barrel, 14 Rings, Amber, 3/4 Quart .... * 225.00
Whiskey, Mohawk Pure Rye, Indian Queen, Amber, 12 1/4 In. ....Illus 975.00
Whiskey, Monks' Old Bourbon, Medicinal Purposes, Olive Amber, 3/4 Quart .... * 190.00
Whiskey, Monogram, Applied Top, Squat, BIMAL, Amber, Fifth 20.00
Whiskey, Moore Trimble & Co., Jug, Handle, Amber, 3/4 Quart .... * 140.00
Whiskey, Moose Bottle, Loyal Order Of Moose Commemorative, Ceramic, 14 In. 14.95
Whiskey, Mt.Vernon Pure Rye, Amber, Pint 16.00
Whiskey, Mt.Vernon Pure Rye, Stain, Amber, Miniature 8.00
Whiskey, Munson Franklin, N.J., Aqua, Quart 6.00
Whiskey, Muri, Louisville, BIMAL, Amber, 3 3/4 In. 6.00
Whiskey, Myers & Co. Pure Fulton, Covington, Ky., Jug, Aqua, 9 X 7 In. 10.00
Whiskey, Myers & Co., Distillers, Pure Fulton Straight, Covington, Gallon 13.00

(See Page 215)

Left to right: Whiskey, M. Salzman Co., One Full Quart Whiskey, Mohawk Pure Rye, Indian Queen, Amber, 12 1/4 In.; Whiskey, Old Ashton, Back Bar, 8 1/2 In.

(See Page 215)

Whiskey, **Myers & Co.,** Pure Fulton, Covington, Ky., Aqua, Gallon	28.00
Whiskey, **Nelson Co.,** Kentucky, Miniature	12.00
Whiskey, **O'Donnel's Brand Irish,** Handled, Crockery, Quart	24.50
Whiskey, **O'Keefe's Malt,** Pottery, Quart	19.00
Whiskey, **O'Keefe's,** Oswego, N.Y., Pottery, Quart	45.00
Whiskey, **Oak Valley Distilling Co.,** San Francisco, 9 1/2 In.	30.00
Whiskey, **Old Ashton,** Back Bar, 8 1/2 In. *Illus*	15.00
Whiskey, **Old Charter,** Bar, Enameled, Haze, Fifth	25.00
Whiskey, **Old Club House,** Label, Handle, Amber, 3/4 Quart	* 17.50
Whiskey, **Old Continental In Acorn,** Black Letters, White Glaze, 1/4 Pint	20.00
Whiskey, **Old Continental,** 1776, Soldier, Collared Mouth, Yellow Amber, Quart	*1300.00
Whiskey, **Old Crow,** Decanter, Royal Doulton, 12 3/4 In.	50.00
Whiskey, **Old Harvest Corn,** Flask, 1/2 Pint	2.00
Whiskey, **Old Hermitage,** Quart	10.00
Whiskey, **Old Joe Gideon,** Embossed, Stain, Amber, 1/2 Pint	4.50
Whiskey, **Old Joe Gideon,** Flask, Amber, Pint	10.00
Whiskey, **Old Kentucky Bourbon,** Handle, Chips, Amber, 3/4 Quart	* 55.00
Whiskey, **Old Kentucky Distillers,** Quart	16.00
Whiskey, **Old Mill,** Whitlock & Co., Handle, Pontil, Amber, 3/4 Quart	* 475.00
Whiskey, **Old Monongahela Rye,** Sheaf Of Grain, Olive Amber, Quart	45.00
Whiskey, **Old Overholt Straight Rye,** Flat, Miniature	30.00
Whiskey, **Old Quaker,** Embossed, Corker, Quart	3.00
Whiskey, **Old Rye,** Pittsburgh, Union Flask, Aqua, Quart	60.00
Whiskey, **Old Sacon,** Enameled, Decanter Shape, Fluted Neck, 8 1/4 In.	25.00
Whiskey, **Old Taylor,** E.H.Taylor & Sons, Frankfort, Paper Label, Quart	4.00
Whiskey, **Old Taylor,** Label, Seals, Pint	35.00
Whiskey, **Old Times,** Grand Prize, 1893-1904, Turning Purple, 1/2 Gallon	50.00
Whiskey, **Old Valley,** Cook & Bernheimer Co., Gold Lion, Amber, 25 1/2 In.	* 225.00
Whiskey, **Old Velvet,** Back Bar, Faceted Stopper, 9 3/4 In. *Illus*	20.00
Whiskey, **Old Wheat,** S.M.& Co., Pontil, Globular, Amber, 1/2 Gallon	* 425.00
Whiskey, **Oldner's Superior Old Rye,** Jug, Handle, Crack, Amber, 1/2 Gallon	*2300.00
Whiskey, **Oldner's Superior Old Rye,** Miner's, Jug, Copper Amber, 1/2 Gallon	*2300.00
Whiskey, **Otto F.Felix,** Gloversville, N.Y., Pottery, Gallon	30.00
Whiskey, **P.Claudius & Co.,** San Francisco, Inside Screw, Amber, Fifth	28.00
Whiskey, **P.J.Dowlin,** Miniature	7.00
Whiskey, **Painted Coat Of Arms,** Collared Mouth, Pontil, Olive Amber, 13 In.	* 65.00
Whiskey, **Parker Rye,** Decanter, Sample, 3 In.	20.00
Whiskey, **Patent,** Dyottville Glass Works, Phila., 3 Mold, Olive Amber, Quart	10.00
Whiskey, **Paul Jones Bourbon,** Squat, Seal, Amber, Quart	20.00
Whiskey, **Paul Jones Four Roses,** ABM, Quart	5.00

Whiskey, Paul Jones Pure Rye, Amber, 4 1/2 In.	9.00
Whiskey, Paul Jones Pure Rye, Squat, Seal, Amber, Quart	20.00
Whiskey, Paul Jones Rye, Seal, Turn Mold, Label, Red Amber, Quart	22.00
Whiskey, Paul Jones Type, Pontil, Amber, Pint	50.00
Whiskey, Paul Jones, Amber, 4 1/4 In.	8.00
Whiskey, Paul Jones, Blob Seal, Amber, Quart	6.00
Whiskey, Paul Jones, Embossed Ships, Amber, 1/2 Pint	6.00
Whiskey, Paul Jones, Embossed Ships, Amber, Pint	6.00
Whiskey, Paul Jones, Louisville, Ky., Collared Lip, Blob Seal, Amber, Quart	9.00
Whiskey, Paul Jones, Louisville, Ky., Label, Collared Lip, Red Amber, Quart	13.00
Whiskey, Paul Jones, Sample, Amber	5.00
Whiskey, Paul Jones, Squat, Seal, Amber, Quart	20.00
Whiskey, Paul Jones, Turn Mold, Applied Seal, Amber, Gallon	35.00
Whiskey, Pennsylvania Club Pure Rye, K.T.K., Pink, Quart	75.00
Whiskey, Perrine's Apple Ginger On 1 Panel, Cabin, Amber, 3/4 Quart	* 100.00
Whiskey, Perrine's Apple Ginger On 2 Panels, Cabin, Amber, 3/4 Quart	* 95.00
Whiskey, Perrine's, Apple, Ginger, Phila., Cabin, Stain, Amber, 3/4 Quart	50.00
Whiskey, Perry & Walter, Tuscaloosa, Ala., Jug, Incised, Chocolate, Gallon	37.00
Whiskey, Pett's Bald Eagle, Oval Flask, Blob Lip, Haze, 1/2 Pint	4.50
Whiskey, Phoenix Glass Works, Philada., Patent, Pontil, Yellow Green, Pint	* 100.00
Whiskey, Phoenix Old Bourbon, Calif., Coffin Flask, Haze, Amber, 1/2 Pint	105.00
Whiskey, Pontil, Chip, Ovoid, Olive Amber, 7 3/8 In.	* 225.00
Whiskey, Pontil, Chip, Wear, Squat, Olive Green, 4 7/8 In.	* 150.00
Whiskey, Pontil, Crack, Globular, Olive Green, 7 1/4 In.	* 220.00
Whiskey, Pontil, Dark Olive Amber, 7 1/8 In.	* 100.00
Whiskey, Pontil, Flake, Squat, Olive Green, 7 1/4 In.	* 65.00
Whiskey, Pontil, Globular, Dark Olive Amber, 5 1/4 In.	*1050.00
Whiskey, Pontil, Octagonal, Dark Olive Amber, 9 3/4 In.	* 250.00
Whiskey, Pontil, Ovoid, Dark Olive Amber, 6 7/8 In.	* 340.00
Whiskey, Pontil, Ovoid, Dark Olive Amber, 7 7/8 In.	* 175.00
Whiskey, Pontil, Square, Dark Olive Amber, 8 7/8 In.	* 360.00
Whiskey, Pontil, Squat, Dark Olive Amber, 5 3/4 In.	* 430.00
Whiskey, Pontil, Squat, Dark Olive Amber, 5 7/8 In.	* 340.00
Whiskey, Pontil, Squat, Dark Olive Amber, 7 3/4 In.	* 70.00
Whiskey, Pontil, Squat, Dark Olive Amber, 7 3/4 In.	* 240.00
Whiskey, Pontil, Squat, Dark Olive Amber, 9 1/4 In.	* 175.00
Whiskey, Pontil, Squat, Olive Green, 7 3/8 In.	* 150.00
Whiskey, Pontil, Stain, Globular, Dark Olive Amber, 8 In.	* 800.00
Whiskey, Pontil, Stain, Squat, Olive Green, 6 5/8 In.	* 200.00
Whiskey, Pontil, Wear, Globular, Dark Olive Green, 6 1/2 In.	* 675.00
Whiskey, Pontil, Wear, Globular, Dark Olive Amber, 8 In.	* 425.00
Whiskey, Pontil, Wear, Squat, Olive Amber, 5 3/8 In.	* 130.00
Whiskey, Pride Of Kentucky Old Bourbon, Livingston & Co., 1/5 Gallon	600.00
Whiskey, Pride Of Kentucky, Decanter, Etched, Fluted, Amethyst, Miniature	38.00
Whiskey, Protection Pure Rye, Chicago, Embossed Dog & Barrel, Quart	65.00
Whiskey, Pure Corn, Camel, Pig, Camark Pottery, 9 In.	45.00
Whiskey, Pure Malt, Bourbon Co., Oval Jug, Handle, Amber, Pint	* 250.00
Whiskey, Pure Old Rye, Pig, Black Stenciling, 2-Toned Glaze, 8 1/2 In.	100.00
Whiskey, Quaker Maid, Amber, 1/2 Pint	22.00
Whiskey, Quaker Maid, Haze, Sun-Colored Amethyst, 4 1/2 In.	10.00
Whiskey, Quirye, Dr.Koch Berlin, Dog's Head, Milk Glass, 3/4 Quart	* 130.00
Whiskey, R & S, Rolehing & Schultz, Inc., Cabin, Bruises, Amber, 3/4 Quart	* 70.00
Whiskey, R & S, Rolehing & Schultz, Inc., Chicago, Cabin, Bruises, 3/4 Quart	* 70.00
Whiskey, R.B.Cutter's Pure Bourbon, Jug, Handle, IP, Deep Puce, Quart	* 250.00
Whiskey, R.M.Hughes & Co., Vinegar, Louisville, Ky., 1/4 Pint	15.00
Whiskey, Raines Sandwich, Figural Sandwich, Pottery, 5 In.	75.00
Whiskey, Raleigh, N.C., Dispensary, Strap Side, 1/2 Pint	42.00
Whiskey, Rheinstrom Bros., Cincinnati, Flakes, Globular, Green, 1/2 Pint	* 25.00
Whiskey, Rheinstrom Bros., Curacao, Gold Decoration, Amber, 4 3/4 In.	* 30.00
Whiskey, Rheinstrom Bros., Curacao, Gold Decoration, Yellow, 10 3/4 In.	* 5.00
Whiskey, Rheinstrom Bros., Gold Decoration, Yellow Green, 10 1/2 In.	* 17.50
Whiskey, Ribs Swirled To Right, Handle, Pontil, Stain, Amber, 3/4 Quart	* 275.00
Whiskey, Ribs Swirled To Right, Pontil, Bell Shape, Amber, 3/4 Quart	* 15.00
Whiskey, Rieger & Co., Kansas City, BIMAL, Quart	4.00
Whiskey, Robinson's Scotch Maid Perfume, 1921, Miniature, Wooden Box, 3	10.00

Whiskey, Rochester Glass Works, Wear, Amber, Pint .... * 10.00
Whiskey, Rose Valley, Louisville, Ky., Glass Label, Stain, Gallon 395.00
Whiskey, Roth & Co., S.F., Inside Screw, Fluted Shoulder, Amber, Fifth 20.00
Whiskey, Roth & Co., S.F., Inside Screw, Tooled Top, Aqua, Fifth 20.00
Whiskey, Roth & Co., San Francisco, Inside Screw Cap, Amber, Quart 35.00
Whiskey, S S W & Co, Flattened Chestnut, Handle, Pontil, Amber, 3/4 Quart .... * 200.00
Whiskey, S.C.Boehm, New York, Shield, BIMAL, Quart 3.50
Whiskey, S.M.& Co., N.Y., Double Collar, Pontil, Bell Shape, Amber, 15 1/4 In. .... * 975.00
Whiskey, S.Rosenthal & Co., N.Y., Embossed, Amber, 1/2 Gallon 100.00
Whiskey, S.Rosenthal, N.Y., 6 Panels, Amber, 1/2 Gallon 60.00
Whiskey, S.Wolf & Sons Fine, Flared Mouth, Flattened Oval, 10 In. .... * 60.00
Whiskey, Salzman & Siegleman Pure Old Rye, Crockery Jug, Brown, White, Quart 25.00
Whiskey, Schweyer's Chicago Club, Quart 15.00
Whiskey, Security Distilling Co., Chicago, Fluted Shoulder, Miniature 15.00
Whiskey, Shawhan Distillery, Miniature 8.00
Whiskey, Sheared Mouth With Ring, Applied Handle, Pontil, Olive Amber, 6 In. *1600.00
Whiskey, Sheared Mouth With Ring, Pontil, Globular, Olive Green, 5 7/8 In. .... * 600.00
Whiskey, Sheared Mouth With Ring, Pontil, Squat, Olive Green, 6 1/4 In. .... * 325.00
Whiskey, Sheared Mouth With Ring, Pontil, Wear, Globular, Olive Green, 9 In. .... * 775.00
Whiskey, Sheared Mouth With Ring, Tapered, Pontil, Wear, Olive Green, 11 In. .... * 190.00
Whiskey, Sheared Mouth, Pontil, Ovoid, Amber, 7 1/2 In. .... * 170.00
Whiskey, Sherman Rye, Hildebrandt, Posner & Co., C.1900, Amber, Quart 20.00
Whiskey, Shoofly, Taylor Pure Rye, Amber, Pint 20.00
Whiskey, Shore Distilling Co., Elk City, Okla., Shoulder Jug, 1/2 Gallon 45.00
Whiskey, Shoteau House, Ft.Benton, Montana, Sterling Overlay, Pint 75.00
Whiskey, Silver Dollar Rye, Embossed Silver Dollars, Paper Label, Pint 12.00
Whiskey, Smith's Fine Old Monongahela Rye, Flask Shape, Ring, Puce, Pint .... * 50.00
Whiskey, Smokine, Alfred Andresen & Co., Cabin, Tooled Mouth, Amber, Pint .... * 160.00
Whiskey, Smokine, Alfred Andresen & Co., Cabin, Tooled Mouth, Amber, Quart .... * 225.00
Whiskey, Sorage's Old Virginia Mountain, 1906, Pint 6.50
Whiskey, Sour Mash 1867, Amber, 10 In. ....*Illus* 95.00
Whiskey, Sour Mash, 1867, Chapin & Gore, Barrel, Yellow Amber, 3/4 Quart .... * 80.00
Whiskey, Sour Mash, 1867, Chapin & Gore, Barrel, 8 Rings, Amber, 3/4 Quart .... * 55.00
Whiskey, South Carolina Dispensary, Monogramed, Pint 20.00
Whiskey, South Carolina Dispensary, Monogramed, Quart 27.00
Whiskey, South Carolina Dispensary, Palm Tree, Pint 32.00
Whiskey, South Carolina Dispensary, Palm Tree, Strap Side, Aqua, Pint 75.00
Whiskey, South Carolina Dispensary, Palm Tree, 1/2 Pint 14.00
Whiskey, Souvenir, 1953 Presidential Inauguration, 12 In. ....*Illus* 12.50
Whiskey, Special & Highland Whisky, Royal Doulton, 1884, Brown, 7 In. 50.00
Whiskey, Spruance & Stanley, S.F., Embossed Horseshoe, Amber, Fifth 65.00
Whiskey, Star, W.B.Crowell, Jr., Handle, Bell Shape, Crack, Amber, 3/4 Quart .... * 125.00
Whiskey, Star, W.B.Crowell, Jr., Handle, Chip, Bell Shape, Amber, 3/4 Quart .... * 250.00
Whiskey, Stout Dyer & Wicks, X, New York, Bulbous, Aqua, Pint .... * 25.00
Whiskey, Strauss Bros. Co., Chicago, Olive Green, 12 1/4 In. ....*Illus* 15.00
Whiskey, Sun Drug Co., Los Angeles, Embossed, Yellow Amber, Miniature 60.00
Whiskey, Sweet Mash Corn, Atlantic Distilling Co., Jacksonville, Fla., 3 In. 25.00
Whiskey, T.J.Dunbar & Co., Cordial Schnapps, Schiedam, Green, 7 3/4 In. 40.00
Whiskey, Tapered Neck, Pontil, Olive Amber, 9 1/4 In. .... * 95.00
Whiskey, Tapered Neck, Pontil, Stain, Globular, Olive Green, 8 3/4 In. *1100.00
Whiskey, Tapered Skirted Lip, Refired Pontil, Dug, Black Amethyst, Quart 25.00
Whiskey, Taylor & Williams, Miniature 7.00
Whiskey, Taylor, Strap Sided, Label, Amber, Pint 10.00
Whiskey, Teakettle Old Bourbon, C.1875, Blob Top, Amber, Fifth 225.00
Whiskey, Teddy's Pet, Turtle Shape, Sample 18.00
Whiskey, That's The Stuff, Barrel, 20 Rings, Pontil, Yellow Amber, 3/4 Quart .... * 700.00
Whiskey, The Old Bushmill Distillery Co., 10 In. ....*Illus* 25.00
Whiskey, Thomas, Spruance Stanley & Co., Flask, Amber, Pint 125.00
Whiskey, Thos. Moore Possom Hollow, Pinch, Aluminum Salt Top, Miniature 6.00
Whiskey, Turner Brothers, N.Y., Barrel, 20 Rings, Golden Amber, 3/4 Quart .... * 75.00
Whiskey, Turner Brothers, N.Y., Barrel, 20 Rings, Red Amber, 3/4 Quart .... * 125.00
Whiskey, Turner Brothers, N.Y., Barrel, 20 Rings, Yellow Green, 3/4 Quart .... * 325.00
Whiskey, Turner Locker Co.'s Coon Club, Cincinnati, Pottery, Quart 85.00
Whiskey, U.S.Mail Box Rye, Patent 1891, Mailbox Shape, Pint .... * 160.00
Whiskey, U.S.Mail Box Rye, Rheinstrom Bros., 6 1/2 In. ....*Illus* 150.00

(See Page 216) *(See Page 218)*

(See Page 218)

Top left to right: Whiskey, Old Velvet, Back Bar, Faceted Stopper, 9 3/4 In.; Whiskey, Sour Mash 1867, Amber, 10 In.; Whiskey, Souvenir, 1953 Presidential Inauguration, 12 In.; Whiskey, U.S. Mail Box Rye, Rheinstrom Bros., 6 1/2 In.; Whiskey, Strauss Bros. Co., Chicago, Olive Green, 12 1/4 In.

Bottom left to right: Whiskey, The Old Bushmill Distillery Co., 10 In.; Whiskey, V. E. Shields & Co., Cincinnati, O., 12 In.; Wine, Victor Borothy, Embossed, Blob Top, Dark Amber, 7 3/4 In.

(See Page 218)

(See Page 220)

Whiskey, **Udolpho Wolfe's,** Schiedam, Aromatic Schnapps, Olive Amber, Pint	* 35.00
Whiskey, **Udolpho Wolfe's,** Schiedam, Aromatic Schnapps, Wear, Olive, 3/4 Quart	* 15.00
Whiskey, **Union Glass Co.,** New London On Base, Light Green, 3/4 Quart .... *Illus*	* 300.00
Whiskey, **V.E.Shields & Co.,** Cincinnati, O., Amber, 12 In. .... *Illus*	17.50
Whiskey, **Van Schuyver & Co.,** Portland, Oregon, C.1910, Fifth .... *Color*	XXXX.XX
Whiskey, **Victor Borothy,** Blob Top, 7 3/4 In. .... *Color*	XXXX.XX
Whiskey, **Vidvard & Sheehan,** Flattened Jug, Handle, Yellow Green, 3/4 Quart	* 850.00
Whiskey, **Virden's Campfire,** Embossed Vertically, Square, Fifth	10.00
Whiskey, **W McC & Co.,** Pitts. On Base, Golden Amber, 3/4 Quart	* 25.00
Whiskey, **W.C.Peacock & Co.,** Honolulu, Amber, Fifth	75.00
Whiskey, **W.H.Jones,** Bear On Shield, BIMAL, Quart	3.50
Whiskey, **W.J.Van Schuyver,** Portland, Inside Screw, Tooled Top, Amber, Fifth	25.00
Whiskey, **W.L.Perkins,** St.Paul, Minn., Decanter, Miniature	8.00
Whiskey, **W.Olmsted & Co.,** Constitutional Beverage, Yellow Amber, 3/4 Quart	* 175.00
Whiskey, **W.Wolf,** Pittsburgh, Barrel, 14 Rings, Cornflower Blue, 3/4 Quart	*2600.00
Whiskey, **Wake Up,** Collared Mouth, Triangular, Olive Green, 3/4 Quart	* 500.00
Whiskey, **Walker's Kilmarnock,** 5 In.	3.50
Whiskey, **Weeks & Gilson,** So.Stoddard, N.H., On Base, Olive Amber, Quart	* 150.00
Whiskey, **Weeks & Potter,** Boston, 3 Mold, Collar Ring, Whittled, 11 1/2 In.	19.00
Whiskey, **Wharton's,** 1850, Chestnut Grove, Flask, Amber, 1/2 Pint	* 175.00
Whiskey, **Wharton's,** 1850, Chestnut Grove, Flat Oval Flask, Amber, 1/4 Pint	* 175.00
Whiskey, **Wharton's,** 1850, Chestnut Grove, Pocket Flask, Sapphire, 1/4 Pint	* 200.00

Whiskey, Wharton's, 1850, Chestnut Grove, Whitney Glass, Jug, Amber, 3/4 Quart .... * 275.00
Whiskey, Wheeling, Va., Old Rye, Deep Aqua, Pint .... * 425.00
Whiskey, Whitlock & Co., N.Y., Aqua Rigaree On Beveled Corners, Amber, Quart .... * 875.00
Whiskey, Whitney Glass Works On Base, Inside Screw Thread, Amber, 3/4 Quart .... * 15.00
Whiskey, Whitney Glass Works, Glassboro, N.J., Ewer, Handle, Amber, 3/4 Quart .... * 100.00
Whiskey, Whitney Glass Works, N.J., Embossed, Seed Bubbles, Green, Quart 20.00
Whiskey, Whitney Glass Works, Glassboro, N.J., On Base, Ewer, Amber, Quart .... * 250.00
Whiskey, Willington Glass Works On Base, Amber, 3/4 Quart .... * 40.00
Whiskey, Wm.Edward's Honest Pure Rye, Inside Screw, Pottery, Quart 95.00
Whiskey, Wm.H.Spears & Co., Old Pioneer, Embossed Bear, S.F., Fifth 95.00
Whiskey, Wolter Bros., Front St., S.F., Tooled Top, Amber, Fifth 50.00
Whiskey, Wright & Taylor, Louisville, Ky., Embossed, Amber, Quart 9.00
Whiskey, Wright & Taylor, Stain, Amber, Miniature 18.00
Whiskey, 1854 Keystone Malt, Philada., Stain, Oval, Amber, Quart 22.00
Whiskey, 1879 Old Jug, Freiberg Bros., Cincinnati, O., Crock, 10 1/2 In. 54.00
Whiskey, 6 Monks Below Fancy Arches, Amber, Quart .... * 75.00
Wild Turkey, Back Bar Piece, No.3 .... 75.00
Wild Turkey, Battle Of Concord, Wooden Box, Miniature, Set Of 6 .... 35.00
Wild Turkey, Charleston Centennial 45.00
Wild Turkey, Mack Truck 15.00
Wild Turkey, No.1 .... 115.00
Wild Turkey, No.2, 5th 60.00
Wild Turkey, No.3 .... 20.00
Wild Turkey, No.4 .... 20.00
Wild Turkey, No.5 .... 18.00
Wild Turkey, No.6 .... 21.00
Williamsburg, Castle 4.50
Windsor, Guardsman, 1776-1976 .... 14.00
Wine, Baxter's Old Navajo Brand, Pottery Jug, 2 Tone, 3 In. 20.00
Wine, Champagne, Long Neck, Bulbous, BIMAL, Emerald Green, 10 In. 3.00
Wine, Chile M.R., Blob Seal, Green, Pint 3.00
Wine, Cushman & Co., Albany, N.Y. In Cobalt Script, 10 1/2 In. 40.00
Wine, Dutch, C.1740, Green, 8 1/4 In. ....Color XXXX.XX
Wine, Dutch, C.1740, Green, 10 In. ....Color XXXX.XX
Wine, English, C.1840, Octagonal, Amber, 7 1/4 In. ....Color XXXX.XX
Wine, Free Blown, C.1790, Applied Seal, Sheared Lip, Black Amethyst, Pint 50.00
Wine, Glob Top, BIMAL, Black Amethyst, 14 In. 4.00
Wine, Herman Bernhardt, Buffalo, N.Y., Shoulder Jug, Gallon 40.00
Wine, Hock, BIMAL, 25 1/2 In. 30.00
Wine, Hock, IP, Blue, 14 In. 28.00
Wine, Hock, Amber, 11 3/4 In. 1.00
Wine, Hock, Red Amber, 12 In. 2.00
Wine, Hock, Teal Blue, 14 1/2 In. 5.00
Wine, J.Beaupre, St.Sauveur, Quebec, Stoneware, Floral, 14 In. 35.00
Wine, J.P.Magullion & Co.Family Store, Boston, Strap-Sided Flask, Pint 7.00
Wine, Mary Gregory, Boy, Clear Bubble Stopper, Bulbous, Cranberry, 8 3/4 In. 135.00
Wine, Meder & Zoom, Holland, Clay, 12 In. 6.50
Wine, Murray & Co., Holyoke, Hock Wines, Cloudy, Sun-Colored Amethyst, 14 In. 2.00
Wine, Palomino Sherry, Spain, Paper Label, Quart 2.00
Wine, Porcelain, Gold-Trimmed Lid, Enamel Floral, Cream Color, 12 In. 30.00
Wine, Port-O, Inc., 6 In. 1.50
Wine, Rice, Bubbles, Green, 9 In. 8.50
Wine, Riesling Extra, Hull Brand, California, Blob Top, Amber, Fifth 12.00
Wine, Rosenblatt Pure, Lady's Leg, Amber, 11 In. 7.00
Wine, S.C.Worman, Philadelphia, Twist Neck, BIMAL, 10 In. 9.00
Wine, Sample & Co., Successors To G.B.Lowerre, N.Y., Stain, Amber, 11 1/2 In. 8.50
Wine, Sol Rath, 1014 Mt.Vernon Ave., Columbus, Ohio, Pint 12.00
Wine, Speer's, Samburg Port, Used In Churches, Yellow Green, 3/4 Quart .... * 35.00
Wine, Steuben Co., Chicago, Cloudy, Rectangular, 7 5/16 In. 2.00
Wine, T & WB, French Wine Store, Oval, Aqua, Pint 6.00
Wine, Tester, Spin Mold, Sheared Re-Fired Lip, Green, 8 1/2 In. 12.00
Wine, Victor Borothy, Embossed, Blob Top, Dark Amber, 7 3/4 In. ....Illus 70.00
Wine, 3 Mold, Double Ring Lip, Whittled, OP, Olive Green, 11 In. 13.75
Zanesville, 24 Swirled Ribs, Globular, Amber, 9 In. 475.00
Zanesville, 24 Swirled Ribs, Globular, Aqua, 7 1/2 In. 250.00